THE LAW AND PRACTICE OF INTERNATIONAL BANKING

BANKING LAW
VOLUME 2

by

G. A. PENN, LL.B., LL.M.
Assistant Director, The Centre for Commercial Law Studies,
Queen Mary College, University of London;
Editor, Journal of International Banking Law;
Chief Examiner in the Practice and Law of International Banking,
Chartered Institute of Bankers

A. M. SHEA, B.A., LL.B., D.Phil., *Barrister and Solicitor (N.Z.)*
Head of Centre for Legal Studies, City University, London;
Deputy Editor, Journal of International Banking Law;
Chief Examiner in the Law Relating to Banking,
Chartered Institute of Bankers;
Cameron Markby Senior Research Fellow in Banking Law,
The Centre for Commercial Law Studies, Queen Mary College, University of London

A. ARORA, LL.B., Ph.D., *Barrister*
Lecturer in Law, University of Liverpool

LONDON
SWEET & MAXWELL
1987

Published in 1987 by
Sweet & Maxwell Ltd.
now of South Quay Plaza,
183 Marsh Wall, London.
Printed in Scotland

Second Impression 1989
Third Impression 1990

British Library Cataloguing in Publication Data

Penn, G. A.
    Banking law
    Vol. 2; The law and practice of
    international banking
    1. Banks and banking, International——
    Law and Legislation
    I. Title   II. Shea, A.M.   III. Arora, A.
    IV. The law and practice of international
    banking
    342.6′8215   K1066

    ISBN 0–421–39010–7
    ISBN 0–421–36070–4 Pbk

Preface

The idea for a two volume work in banking law, the first of which deals with domestic banking law and the second dealing with international banking law, arose out of a series of meetings between Graham Penn and Don Fiddes, a former Director of Studies at the Chartered Institute of Bankers, who were both concerned about the absence of an up-to-date text which covered the entire spectrum of banking law. It soon became clear that such a project would require the specialist knowledge of more than one individual, hence Tony Shea and Anu Arora were invited to "join the team" of authors.

This new work was originally conceived as being intended for degree and post-graduate students and for practitioners who regularly find themselves engaged in this complex area of law. The emphasis in both volumes is directed firmly towards the law in practice, and it is hoped that those who concern themselves with banking law, in its broadest sense, will find some of the answers to the often difficult questions which arise. Where the material fails to provide an answer we hope it will at least lead to other sources, and thus assist in solving practical banking law problems, hence the heavy referencing which is to be found throughout both volumes.

The original conception became slightly altered during production in order that the two volumes would cover the Chartered Institute of Bankers' examinations in both Law Relating to Banking and Practice and Law of International Banking. This slight change in emphasis has led to the omission of some material but the addition of other new chapters, namely, the sizeable chapters on Securities and Insolvency, and the expansion of the original material dealing with Agency, Partnerships and Corporate Customers.

Anybody who writes a book of this sort could not possibly start without the benefit of the learning of others. We have relied heavily upon a number or articles (many of which are acknowledged in the footnotes), and upon the publications listed in the Table of Abbreviations. Special mention must be made, however, of Philip Wood's excellent book, *Law and Practice of International Finance* and of the *Encyclopaedia of Banking Law* which provides the most comprehensive coverage of English Banking Law presently available.

In addition to published material we have placed considerable reliance on the knowledge and practical expertise of many lawyers and bankers, who have made helpful suggestions during the preparation of this work. Unfortuantely, the individuals themselves are too numerous to mention. The authors would, however, wish to acknowledge the very considerable assistance given by the following people:

David Lewis of the Reserve bank of Australia (Volume 1, Chapter 1 on the Regulation of Banks); Maurice Allen of Clifford Chance (Volume 2, Chapter 8 on Transferability of Loans and Loan Participations); Stephen Edlmann of Linklaters and Paines (Volume 2, Chapter 10 on Notes and Commercial Paper); Armel Cates, Robert Palache and Phillip Palmer of Clifford Chance (Volume 2, Chapter 11 on Swaps and Related Instruments); Andrew McKnight of Cameron Markby (Volume 2, Chapter 16 on Legal Opinions). These experts are not, of course, responsible for any errors or omissions, which remain those of the authors alone.

The authors would also like to express their indebtedness to National Westminster Bank PLC for permission to reproduce their standard form documentation in Volume 2, Chapter 12 and for supplying copies.

The law is stated as at May 31, 1987.

London   G. A. Penn
May 31, 1987   A. M. Shea
                                                                     A. Arora

To the late Don Fiddes
who is greatly missed

Table of Abbreviations

Books

Cheshire and North	*Cheshire and North's Private International Law* (Butterworths, 10th ed., 1979)
Delaume	Delaume, *Transnational Contracts* (U.S.A., 1978)
Dicey and Morris	Dicey and Morris, *The Conflict of Laws* (Sweet & Maxwell, 10th ed., 1980)
Donaldson and Donaldson	Donaldson and Donaldson, *The Medium Term Loan Market* (Macmillan, 1982)
Encyclopaedia	*Encyclopaedia of Banking Law*, eds. Cresswell, Blaire, Hill, Wood (Butterworths, 1982)
Finn	Finn, *Fiduciary Obligations* (Law Book Company, 1977)
Gabriel	Gabriel, *Legal Aspects of Syndicated Loans* (Butterworths, 1986)
Goode	Goode, *Legal Problems of Credit and Security* (Sweet & Maxwell/CCLS, 1982)
Gruson	Gruson and Reisner, *Sovereign Lending Managing Legal Risk* (Longwood Publishing Group, 1984)
Kalderen and Siddiqi	Kalderen and Siddiqi, *Sovereign Borrowers* (Butterworths, 1984)
Macdonald	Macdonald, *International Syndicated Loans* (Euromoney Publications, 1983)
Mann	Mann, *The Legal Aspects of Money* (O.U.P., 4th ed., 1982)
Morris	Morris, *The Conflict of Laws* (Sweet & Maxwell, 3rd ed., 1984)
Rendell	Rendell (ed.), *International Financial Law* (Euromoney Publications, 2nd ed., 1983)
Suratgar	Suratgar (ed.), *Default and Rescheduling* (Euromoney Publications, 1984)
Wood	Wood, *The Law and Practice of International Finance* (Sweet & Maxwell, 1980)

Journals

I.F.L.R.   *International Financial Law Review* (Euromoney Publications)

J.I.B.L.   *Journal of International Banking Law* (ESC Publishers Ltd.)

Contents

3. Sovereign Risk

4. Exchange Controls

5. Witholding Taxes

6. International Term Loan Agreements

10. Euronotes and Commercial Paper

11. Swaps and Related Instruments

12. Contract Guarantees and Standby Letters of Credit

13. Commercial letters of Credit

18. Specimen Euro-Commercial Paper Dealer Agreement

Table of Cases

Table of Statutes

International Conventions

1. Governing Law

Introduction

Many of the legal problems associated with international banking trans- **1.01**
actions arise because such transactions inevitably impinge upon the laws of
more than one country. At the very least two systems of law will be applicable, (assuming the transaction is truly international) and in many transactions considerably more than two. For example, a syndicated loan
agreement[1] may impinge upon the laws of at least a dozen different countries, depending upon the geographical make-up of the bank syndicate.
Even in a simple two party loan agreement a number of different legal systems may become involved, for example, because an independent currency
is used, or the loan is guaranteed by a third party based in an independent
country.

Whenever a court is seized of a case which contains a foreign element,
principles of private international law, or conflict of laws, come into operation. It has been said[2] that the objects of private international law are; first,
to ascertain whether a court has jurisdiction to determine the case before it;
secondly, to identify which system of law the court will apply to the facts of
the case before it; and thirdly, to determine whether the court will recognise
or enforce a judgment obtained in a foreign court. It will be the purpose of
the first two chapters of this book to consider these objects and in particular
their impact upon international banking transactions.

It is of the utmost importance that the legal aspects of any international
banking transaction be made as predictable as possible. This question of
predictability does not normally pose a significant problem in purely domestic banking transactions, since the rights and obligations of the various
parties will normally be determined by the local system of law under which
they contract. This will not necessarily be the case in international banking
and it will therefore be crucial to structure the transaction documentation
within a competent legal framework. The most effective way in which this
can be achieved is by selecting both the system of law which governs the
substantive aspects of the transaction, and the courts which will have jurisdiction to resolve any disputes that may arise.

CHOICE OF LAW

It has already been stressed that the parties entering into an international **1.02**
banking transaction will expect their rights and obligations to be as well
defined and predictable as possible. One of the most effective means of
achieving this goal of predictability is by incorporating an express choice of

---

[1] For a more detailed discussion of syndication techniques see Chap. 3 below. See also,
Gabriel, and McDonald.
[2] See Cheshire and North, p. 3.

1

law clause within the terms of the contract documentation which, hopefully, will be recognised as the proper law.

North describes the "proper law of the contract" as a "convenient and succinct expression to describe the law that governs many of the matters affecting a contract. It has been defined as that law which the English or other court is to apply in determining the obligations under the contract."[3]

The typical clause which is used to identify the proper law is normally the shortest in the entire contract[4] and a common example would read . . . "This agreement shall be governed, construed and interpreted in accordance with the laws of England."

The law chosen should obviously relate to a specific legal system and where, as in the United States, a federal system operates, the district, *e.g.* the state of New York, should be referred to.

Factors influencing choice of law

1.03 There are many factors[5] which might influence the parties in their selection of a governing law. Some, like patriotism, tradition, familiarity and convenience, are non-legal, yet would be at least as important as legal considerations such as: the competence of the chosen legal system to adjudicate upon and enforce the contract; the stability of the legal system so chosen; and the perceived independence and sophistication of both the legal system itself and the personnel who adjudicate.[6] It may also be important in some contracts to "insulate" the agreement, so far as possible, from both political interference and changes of law in the borrower's own jurisdiction. In order to achieve this insulation the parties may be forced to select a completely independent system of law. Alternatively the parties may prefer to select the system of law which is most closely connected with the contract and in some contracts an express choice may fail if the law chosen is not so connected.[7]

Whatever factors the parties themselves perceive as significant, one cannot over emphasise the importance of both English and New York law with regard to the choices which are ultimately made. Both London and New York enjoy pre-eminence as centres of international banking and both have a well-developed and extensive body of commercial jurisprudence which is well attuned to modern international banking business. The courts in both jurisdictions are widely regarded as impartial, are presided over by judges who are experienced in international commercial disputes and are capable of determining cases of great import and complexity. All these are significant factors which often persuade parties to stipulate that either English or New York law shall govern their contractual relationships, even where the par-

---

[3] *Ibid.* at p. 209.
[4] See clause 28 in the specimen agreement, Chap. 17 below.
[5] For a fuller discussion of such factors see Wood, p. 3.
[6] *Ibid.*
[7] See paras. 1.07 and 1.10 below.

ties or the proposed banking transaction may not have a close link with either jurisdiction.[8]

However, there will be little point in selecting a system of law to govern an international banking contract if the choice fails to be recognised by the courts in the country where proceedings are ultimately brought.

Will an express choice of law be recognised?

It is obviously impossible to consider the attitudes of all courts throughout **1.04** the world to this important question of party autonomy with regard to choice of law. Our attention in this work will concentrate upon the position under English rules of private international law together with some comparative references to New York law.[9]

THE ATTITUDE OF THE COURTS IN ENGLAND

England appears to be the first country to have acknowledged the intention **1.05** of the parties as the principal determinant of the proper law of a contract. Case law supporting party autonomy can be traced as far back as 1865 when in *P & O Steam Navigation Co.* v. *Shand*[10] the Privy Council abandoned the previously preferred law of the place of contracting. Later that same year in *Lloyd* v. *Guibert*[11] Willes J., stressed, " . . . it is necessary to consider by what general law the parties intended that the transaction should be governed, or rather to what general law it is just to presume that they have submitted themselves in the matter."

This approach has, generally speaking, been followed in subsequent cases[12] and to date there are no reported cases where an English court has refused to give effect to an express choice of law made by the parties. However, although prima facie one cannot deny that under English law parties are free to stipulate in their contract the system of law which is to apply, closer examination of the relevant case law reveals some interesting limitations which have been placed on this supposed freedom.

---

[8] Other important factors which promote the use of English and New York law include: language, which can pose a very serious practical difficulty due to the fact that legal concepts are often difficult to translate concisely; location of the Eurocurrency markets, (which is without doubt one of the most important factors behind the dominance of English and New York law in Eurocurrency contracts). London and New York were the original Eurocurrency market locations and, therefore, those involved in these markets became familiar with the relevant English and New York legal principles. This has continued notwithstanding the growth of new markets, principally in the Far East.

[9] For a brief discussion of the approach taken in other jurisdictions see Wood, Chap. 1.

[10] (1865) 3 Moo.P.C.N.S. 272.

[11] (1865) L.R. 1 Q.B. 115.

[12] See, for example, *James Miller and Partners Ltd.* v. *Whitworth Street Estates* [1970] A.C.583 and *R.* v. *International Trustee for the protection of Bondholders A.G.* [1937] A.C. 500 where Lord Atkin, p. 529, remarked: "Their (the parties') intention will be ascertained by the intention expressed in the contract if any, which will be conclusive."

LIMITATIONS ON PARTY AUTONOMY

1.06   The leading case on party autonomy under English law is *Vita Food Products Inc.* v. *Unus Shipping Co.*[13] in which Lord Wright, giving the leading opinion of the Privy Council said: " . . . where there is an express statement by the parties of their intention to select the law of the contract, it is difficult to see what qualifications are possible provided the intention expressed is *bona fide* and legal and provided there is no reason for avoiding the choice on the ground of public policy."[14]

The decision of the Privy Council in this case has been the subject of considerable criticism,[15] much of which has centred on the qualifications expressed by Lord Wright.[16] Lord Wright's first limitation, that the choice must be bona fide and legal, has been particularly difficult to clarify. A choice will undoubtedly be mala fide if it is made with a morally impeachable or anomalous and unreasonable intention. This would presumably cover a choice which is made deliberately to avoid some mandatory rule of law which would have applied to the contract if the "objectively connected" proper law had been chosen.[17] However, other cases may be less clear. For example, would an "eccentric" or "capricious" choice be struck down? Would an attempt to evade any mandatory provision of the foreign law be enough, or must the provision in question be a fundamental one? The answers to such questions are far from settled, due to the fact that the term "bona fide" has been given a variety of meanings depending on the subject matter at issue.[18]

Turning to the second limb of Lord Wright's limitation, namely that the choice must be legal, here again the position is, to say the least, confusing. Lord Wright failed to indicate by what law the legality of the express choice was to be determined. North[19] presumes that, as with the general problems of creation of contractual obligations, this is to be decided by the proper law "objectively ascertained" but one can suggest a number of credible alternatives.[20] At least one commentator suggests that it cannot fall to be determined by the proper law since . . . "the question is whether the selection of the proper law itself is in fact legal."[21]

1.07   A further consideration is whether the chosen law must be connected in some way with the contract. In the *Vita Food* case Lord Wright addressed this question and concluded . . . "Connection with English law is not as a

---

[13] [1939] A.C. 277.
[14] p. 290.
[15] See, for example, Morris and Cheshire (1949) 56 L.Q.R. 320: Morris (1950) 3 I.L.Q. 60.
[16] An interesting discussion can be found in Cheshire and North, p. 200 *et seq.*
[17] A striking example of this limitation can be seen in the Australian case of *Golden Acres Ltd.* v. *Queensland Estates Pty.Ltd.* [1969] Qd.L.R. 378 where the court struck down an express choice of Hong Kong law in a contract otherwise connected with Queensland. Some commentators, however, suggest that this case supports the existence of a further limitation, that of evasion; See Gabriel, p. 11.
[18] An interesting discussion on the meaning of "bona fide" can be found in Gabriel, p. 9.
[19] Above, n. 14, p. 201.
[20] For example, the *lex loci contractus*, the *lex loci solutionis* or the *lex fori*.
[21] See Gabriel, p. 11.

matter of principle essential."[22] Nevertheless, he still found it necessary to identify connections with English law, albeit rather tenuous ones, because "the underwriters are likely to be English" and "parties may reasonably desire that the familiar principles of English commercial law should apply."[23] An alternative view was taken by Upjohn J. in *Re Helbert Wagg & Co.Ltd.*[24] when he remarked that the court " . . . will not necessarily regard 'the parties' express choice of law 'as being the governing consideration where a system of law is chosen which has no real or substantial connection with the contract looked at as a whole.' "[25]

Where the lack of connection is evidence of evasive intent, there is little doubt that such a choice would be struck down by an English court, but in almost every other case it is submitted that lack of connection would not be fatal.[26]

ALTERNATIVE CHOICE OF LAW CLAUSES

In some situations the parties will be unable to reach agreement on the **1.08** choice of governing law. This frequently arises when one party, as a matter of policy or because of some provision under its own mandatory law is constitutionally prohibited from submitting to an external governing law clause.[27] Various solutions, other than expressing no choice of law in the agreement, have been attempted to deal with this problem, but all would seem to be of dubious validity. The two most common are the alternative choice of law clause and the frozen choice of law clause.

A typical alternative choice of law clause would read as follows:

> "This Agreement shall be governed by English law, provided that in any suit action or proceeding with respect to this agreement brought by any party to the contract in the courts of the Republic of . . . . , this Agreement shall be governed in accordance with the law of the Republic of . . . ."

The proponents of this type of clause argue that such a clause circumvents the difficulties outlined above, yet still enables the parties to apply English law should proceedings be brought in any country other than the one to which the prohibition applies. It is submitted, however, that such clauses

---

[22] Above, n. 13, p. 290, see also *Miller and Partners Ltd.* v. *Whitworth Street Estates Ltd.* [1970] A.C. 583, where Lord Reid remarked, at p. 603: . . . "Parties are entitled to agree what is to be the proper law of their contract . . . there have been from time to time suggestions that parties ought not to be so entitled, but in my view there is no doubt that they are entitled to make such an agreement, and I see no good reason why, subject it may be to some limitations, that they should not be so entitled."

[23] *Ibid.*

[24] [1956] Ch. 323. See also, *The Fehmarn* [1958] 1 W.L.R. 159; affirming [1957] 1 W.L.R. 815.

[25] *Ibid.*, p. 341. See also, *Boissevain* v. *Weil* [1949] 1 K.B. 482 where Denning L.J. said " . . . I do not believe that the parties are free to stipulate by what law the validity of their contract is to be determined." *Cf.* Lord Denning M.R. in *Tzortzis* v. *Monark Line A.B.* [1968] 1 W.L.R. 406, p. 411, where he suggested that the express clause would be "conclusive in the absence of some public policy to the contrary."

[26] At least one learned commentator suggests, however, that the position is much less certain, see Dicey and Morris, p. 755 *et seq.*

[27] This problem is particularly acute in the case of some South American countries which have adopted the Calvo doctrine, see Chap. 3 below.

would not be effective under English rules of private international law since a contract must have a proper law from the outset and cannot be determined retrospectively " . . . by reference to an event (*i.e.* the bringing of proceedings) which was uncertain in the future at the time when obligations under the contract had already been undertaken."[28] The contract cannot float in the absence of law until the proper law is determined by one of the parties taking an appropriate course of action.[29]

On a more practical note, it is difficult to imagine a clause which would bring greater uncertainty to the contract, since there would always be a possibility of proceedings being brought in at least two jurisdictions, one where the prohibition applies and another where it does not. In such a case, since different laws could be applied to the same question, it is quite likely that different conclusions could be reached by the respective courts.

A distinction must be made however between contracts which incorporate an alternative choice of law clause and those which prescribe that different clauses of the contract shall be governed by different systems of law. The former approach, as we have seen, will not be effective, whereas a line of English cases has upheld the validity of contracts which adopt the latter approach.[30] Much will obviously depend on the circumstances of each case. If, however, on the construction of the particular contract in issue it is clear that the parties intended different parts of their contract to be governed by different laws, their intention will be upheld.[31]

FREEZING THE PROPER LAW

1.09 Where the parties are unable to agree on the incorporation of an external governing law the bank (for it is normally the borrower who is impeded by the prohibitions described above) may try to achieve the goals of predictability and stability by "freezing" the borrower's local law at the date of the contract, *viz.*

> "This agreement shall be governed by the laws of the Republic of . . . . . as in effect on the date hereof."

Such a clause is usually reinforced by an event of default in the contract whereby any change in the relevant law enables the bank to terminate the contract and accelerate the outstanding facility.[32]

The difficulty with such a clause is that even if it is a valid choice of the proper law any subsequent change in the chosen law will unquestionably bind the parties, since it is well settled that the proper law is a living law and must be applied when the contract is to be performed, not when the con-

---

[28] Per Megaw L.J. in *Armar Shipping Co.Ltd.* v. *Caisse Algerienne D'Assurance Et De Reassurance* [1980] 2 Lloyd's Rep. 450, p. 455.

[29] *Ibid.* See also, *Black Clawson International Ltd.* v. *Papierwerke Waldhof-Aschaffenburg A.G.* [1981] 2 Lloyd's Rep. 446; *Astro Venturoso Compania Naviera* v. *Hellenic Shipyards S.A.* [1983] 1 Lloyd's Rep. 12. For an excellent article on floating choice of law clauses, see Briggs "The Validity of 'floating' choice of law and jurisdiction clauses" [1986] 4 L.M.C.L.Q. 508.

[30] The most recent case to uphold the validity of such contracts is *Fosikringsak-tieselskapet Vesta* v. *Butcher and others* [1986] 2 All E.R. 488. See also, *Hamlyn & Co.* v. *Talisker Distillery* [1894] A.C. 202, p. 207; *Re Helbert Wagg & Co.Ltd.* n. 24, p. 135; *Citadel Insurance Co.* v. *Atlantic Union Insurance Co. S.A.* [1982] 2 Lloyd's Rep. 543.

[31] See Dicey and Morris, p. 749.

[32] Events of default are considered in greater detail in Chap. 9, below.

tract was made.[33] Such a clause may, however, be deemed not a choice of law but rather an incorporation of law, in which case the contract will be without an express choice of governing law, and subsequent changes in local law, whilst not affecting the incorporation of law clause, may nevertheless negate the effect of any acceleration provisions. In either case the use of such freezing clauses places the bank in a position of uncertainty.

The approach to party autonomy in New York

The approach of the New York courts to the question of party autonomy has been somewhat different.[34] In that jurisdiction the courts, while in broad terms recognising party autonomy, have limited the concept by requiring some "reasonable relationship" between the transaction and the jurisdiction whose law was chosen.[35] Some New York cases have subjected contracts to the more unpredictable "grouping of contacts" theory, even where the agreement in question contained an express choice of law clause.[36] Under this approach the court applied the substantive law of the jurisdiction which had the most significant contacts with the matter in dispute. It should be pointed out, however, that this approach has not been applied in any commercial case where an express choice has been made, and at least one commentator[37] has suggested that the theory no longer has any force with regard to such contracts. Nevertheless, there was always a danger that the "grouping of contacts" approach may be applied in a commercial case.

1.10

This danger has now been effectively removed where the parties make an express choice of New York law in their agreement, by Title 14 of the New York General Obligations Law, which became effective on July 19, 1984.

Section 5–1401 of the General Obligations Law gives greater freedom to contracting parties by enabling them to select New York law as the governing law of their agreement, regardless of the contract's relation or lack of relation to New York. The legislation rejects the *Haag* v. *Barnes*[38] approach and should put an end to much of the uncertainty which previously existed on account of the "reasonable relationship" test. That requirement had always lacked any convincing justification, and had the effect of restricting New York's development as a leading centre of international banking and commerce.

---

[33] *Re Chesterman's Trusts* [1923] 2 Ch. 466, 478; *Kahler* v. *Midland Bank* [1950] A.C. 24; *Re Helbert Wagg & Co.Ltd.*, above, n. 24.

[34] For a fuller discussion of the New York approach see Gruson "Controlling Choice of Law" in *Sovereign Lending: Managing Legal Risk*, (Euromoney Publications Ltd., 1984) Chap. 5; Prebble, "Choice of Law to Determine the Validity and Effect of Contracts: A comparison of English and American Approaches to the Conflict of Laws" 58 Cornell L.Rev. 433 (1973) See also Wood, Chap. 1.

[35] See, for example, *A. S. Rampell, Inc.* v. *Hyster Co.*, 3 NY 2d 165 NYS 2d 475. 144 NE 2d 371 (1957); *Gambar Enterprises, Inc.* v. *Kelly Serv.Inc.*, 69 AD 2d 297, 303, 418 NYS 2d 818, 822 (1979); *Credit Francais International S.A.* v. *Sociedad Financiera de Comerco S.A.* 490 NYS 2d 670 (1985).

[36] See, for example, *Auten* v. *Auten* 308 NY 155, 124 NE 2d 99 (1954); *Haag* v. *Barnes* 9, NY 2d 554, 1765 NE 2d 441 NYS 2d 65 (1961).

[37] See Gruson, above, n. 34, p. 339.

[38] Above, n. 36.

1.11   The new legislation has some important exceptions, however, and will not apply to any contract, agreement or undertaking:

(i) involving less than U.S. $250,000 in the aggregate,

(ii) for labour or personal services,

(iii) relating to any transaction for personal, family or household services, or

(iv) to the extent otherwise expressly provided in the limited conflict of laws provisions (s. 1–105(2)) of the New York Uniform Commercial Code.

The legislation is clearly orientated towards large commercial transactions, or a series of commercial transactions which are large in the aggregate, and consumer contracts will not fall within its purview. One of the main factors behind the exemptions was the fear that New York courts would become inundated with minor consumer disputes, having no connection with New York.[39]

The most striking limitation of the new legislation, however, is that it only applies in cases where a New York court is asked to apply an express choice of New York law. Any contract which does not contain a New York governing law clause (*e.g.* one which expressly chooses another system of law) will continue to fall foul of those unpredictable party autonomy limitations outlined above.

Proper law where no express choice is made

1.12   The importance of incorporating, whenever possible, an express governing law clause, cannot be over emphasised, and it must be said that in practice few international banking transactions fail to provide for an express proper law. As we have seen, however, it may be impossible for the parties to agree on such a clause, or their choice may be held invalid in subsequent proceedings. It is therefore appropriate to consider how the English courts would ascertain the proper law in the absence of a valid express choice.

A. IS THERE AN IMPLIED CHOICE?

1.13   If there is no express choice, then the English courts endeavour to find an implied choice which can be inferred from the terms and nature of the contract and from the general circumstances of the case.[40]

An obvious difficulty with this test is that it begs the question, "How, and in what circumstances, can an intention be inferred?" The court will only have regard to the terms and nature of the contract, not to extraneous circumstances. Furthermore, "the only certain guide is to be found in applying sound ideas of business, convenience, and sense to the language of the contract itself, with a view to discovering from it the true intention of the parties."[41]

Unfortunately, experience has shown that "sound ideas of business,

---

[39] The New York Usury Laws were also a significant factor behind the monetary levels imposed by the legislation.

[40] Dicey and Morris, Rule 146 Sub-Rule 2, p. 735. See also, *Compagnie d'Armement Maritime S.A.* v. *Compagnie Tunisienne de Navigation S.A.* [1971] A.C. 572, p. 595.

[41] *Jacobs* v. *Credit Lyonnais* (1884) 12 Q.B.D. 589, *per* Bowen L.J., p. 601.

etc.," may be difficult to apply in practice. In *Tzortzis* v. *Monark Line A.B*[42] a contract was both made and was to be performed in Sweden. The subject matter of the contract concerned the sale of a ship by Swedish sellers to Greek buyers with no connection whatsoever with England apart from a single clause in the contract providing for arbitration in London. There was no express governing law clause within the terms of the contract. Notwithstanding the absence of any significant connection with England, the Court of Appeal held that English law was the proper law of the contract. Salmon L.J. felt that the arbitration clause "raises an irresistible inference which overrides all other factors."[43] It is submitted, however, that this is overstating the significance of an arbitration clause, and more recent decisions appear to indicate that such a clause is simply one of many factors which the court will take into account.[44]

In so far as international banking contracts are concerned it will be particularly difficult to find an implied choice, since many of the factors, such as language, terminology and currency, which might otherwise indicate an implied choice, are commonly used to comply with standard market practices which have developed over many years, and not because of any preference by the parties.

B. THE CLOSEST AND MOST REAL CONNECTION

Where the parties have not made an express choice and the court is unable to **1.14** infer an implied choice, the contract will be governed by the system of law with which the transaction has its closest and most real connection.[45]

There are many connecting factors which the court will consider in determining which system of law has the closest and most real connection, including: the place where the contract is to be performed[46]; the choice of forum; the language and terminology used in the contract[47] (though this may not be so compelling where the language used is standard market practice)[48]; the currency in which payment is to be made,[49] although again this would not be a dominant factor if the currency in question is frequently used in the market.[50] Other factors may be perceived as important[51] and obviously much will depend on the circumstances of each case. Having

[42] [1968] 1 W.L.R. 406.
[43] *Ibid.*, p. 413. See also, *Kwik Hoo Tong Handel Maatschappij NV* v. *James Finlay & Co.Ltd.* [1927] A.C. 604.
[44] See *Compagnie Tunisienne de Navigation SA.* v. *Compagnie d'Armement Maritime S.A.* above, n. 40 where Lord Wilberforce said, p. 584 . . . "An arbitration clause must be treated as an indication, to be considered together with the rest of the contract and the relevant surrounding facts."
[45] Dicey and Morris, Rule 146 Sub-Rule 3, p. 742.
[46] Place of performance was thought to be the decisive factor in *The Assunzione* [1954] P. 150; [1954] 2 W.L.R. 234.
[47] *The Industrie* [1894] P. 58; *James Miller and Partners Ltd.* v. *Whitworth Street Estates (Manchester) Ltd.* [1970] A.C. 583; *The Adriatic* [1931] P. 241; *The Njegos* [1936] P. 90.
[48] See *Re Helbert Wagg & Co.Ltd.* above, n. 24 where the use of English language was not found to be a compelling factor.
[49] See *The Industrie* above, n. 47; *R.* v. *International Trustee for the Protection of Bondholders A.G.* above, n. 12; *Sayers* v. *International Drilling Co. NV* [1971] 1 W.L.R. 1176.
[50] This would clearly be the case in contracts denominated by the U.S. dollar.
[51] The following factors may be important in certain international banking contracts: the place of contracting; the situs of the lending office (in the case of a loan contract): the place of business of the borrower and the situs of the lending market.

identified the factors which are connected to the transaction, the court then weighs them, qualitatively rather than quantitatively, the aim being to ascertain "how a just and reasonable person would have regarded the problem."[52]

1.15   It is obviously difficult to draw a clear distinction between the second test, that of implied intention, and the closest and most reasonably related test. The factors which the court might consider appear to be identical for both tests. This does not mean, however, that the tests themselves are identical. There is a fundamental difference in approach for, as one commentator points out, referring to the implied intention test,

> "in the latter case, the court would not have before it the systems of law but the contract document and the conduct of the parties and even customs and usage. All these only go to throw further light on the contractual document so as to make clear the implied intention: it is thus derived from the contract document and only from within it. This is the actual difference between the two tests."[53]

Whilst it could be argued that this is a technical difference, not one of substance, the distinction has, nevertheless, been approved in more recent cases, all of which have endorsed the three tier approach.[54]

Conclusion

1.16   The importance of an express choice of law clause in international banking transactions cannot be over-emphasised. However, where the agreement fails to incorporate such a clause, a party seeking to bring predictability to the contract would be well advised to localise the agreement, as far as possible, in the country of the desired law. This in itself will not be as effective as an express choice, and much will depend on how the courts interpret the contacts in issue. Nevertheless it may bring some degree of predictability to a contract which otherwise would have none.

WHAT DOES THE PROPER LAW ACTUALLY GOVERN?

1.17   Having identified the importance of controlling, whenever possible, the determination of the proper law, it next falls to consider what the proper law actually governs. This is an extremely complex question for, as we shall find, although the proper law governs the substantive aspects of the transaction, there will always be some important aspects which are not so governed and which, therefore, cannot be changed by agreement of the parties.

An extensive treatise examining this question is not proposed,[55] and it must be emphasised that an international banking transaction, and its docu-

---

[52] *The Assunzione* above, n. 46, *per* Singleton L.J., p. 176.

[53] See Gabriel, p. 22.

[54] See *James Miller and Partners Ltd.* v. *Whitworth Street Estates (Manchester) Ltd.* above, n. 47; *Compagnie d'Armement Maritime Sa.* v. *Compagnie Tunisienne de Navigation Sa.* above, n. 40; *Coast Lines Ltd.* v. *Hudig and Veder Chartering NV* [1972] 2 Q.B. 34. [1972] 2 W.L.R. 280.

[55] This topic is given excellent coverage by Wood; See Chap. 2 *passim*.

mentation, will always function under more than one legal system. It will be crucial, therefore, for the parties to the transaction to obtain advice from local lawyers situated in jurisdictions whose legal system impacts upon the transaction. Local lawyers will give valuable assistance in structuring the transaction so as to effect binding legal obligations in the jurisdiction in question, and their involvement is essential in many international banking contracts.[56]

Those matters governed by the proper law

A. ESSENTIAL VALIDITY

The essential validity of the contract or of any particular term used in the contract is governed by the proper law.[57] Validity in this sense refers to matters in the contract itself and not preliminary issues such as power and authority of the parties to enter into legally binding obligations. Similarly, the construction and interpretation of contractual terms will be governed by the proper law. That is to say, the meaning of the words used in the contract.[58] Once the meaning of the words has been deduced it falls to be determined what the legal effect of such words will be. Again, this question is governed by the proper law. The parties are free, therefore, to select the system of law which will interpret the often technical expressions used in an international banking contract. This is most important, since although it will basically be a question of fact in each case, a question of law will also arise if the parties use technical expressions which have different meanings in different legal systems. Many of the expressions used in international banking transactions fall into this category,[59] and it is imperative that they be interpreted in a manner consistent with the parties' intentions.

1.18

B. DISCHARGE

As a general rule the question of whether a contract has been discharged also falls to be determined by the proper law,[60] and therefore, a purported discharge which is not effective under such law (but is perhaps under an alternative system of law) will not be a valid discharge. Thus, the question of whether there has been an effective discharge either by performance, frustration, bankruptcy or subsequent legislation will be determined by the proper law.[61] This is an issue which has become particularly relevant in recent years due to the proliferation of moratorium legislation which seeks

1.19

---

[56] See Chap. 16. For a further discussion on the use and importance of local lawyers see Wood, Chap. 18 *passim*. See also the legal opinions appended to the specimen agreement, Chap. 17 below.

[57] *P. & O. Steam Navigation Co.* v. *Shand* (1865) 3 Moo.P.C.N.S. 272. *Sayers* v. *International Drilling Co.* [1971] 1 W.L.R. 1176.

[58] *Chatenay* v. *Brazilian Submarine Telegraph Co.* [1891] 1 Q.B. 79.

[59] The term "negative pledge" is a good example of a technical expression which may be interpreted differently in competing jurisdictions, see Chap. 6, below.

[60] *Ralli* v. *Dennisform* (1851) 6 Exch. 483; *Perry* v. *Equitable Life Assurance Co.* (1929) 45 T.L.R. 468: *R.* v. *International Trustee for the Protection of Bondholders A.G*, above, n. 12; *Kahler* v. *Midland Bank* [1950] 2 All E.R. 621; *Re Helbert Wagg & Co. Ltd.* above, n. 24.

[61] See Morris, p. 296, and the case cited therein.

to extinguish contractual obligations.[62] The practical consequence of such legislation appears to be that, although it may not be an effective discharge under the proper law, it may in effect operate in precisely the same way, since the obligations become impossible to enforce in the local jurisdiction which imposed the moratorium legislation.[63]

C. ILLEGALITY

1.20   The question of whether the contract or a contractual term is illegal is another matter which is not governed by the proper law.[64] The following principles can be extracted from case law: A contract which is illegal by its proper law cannot be enforced in England.[65] A contract which is contrary to English public policy cannot be enforced in England.[66] A contract which is contrary to an English statute which is intended to apply to the transaction will also be illegal. This will cover contracts which contravene English exchange control laws[67] and English securities laws. A contract which is illegal in the place of performance (the *lex loci solutionis*) cannot be enforced in England if English law is the proper law.[68]

A distinction must be made, however, between contracts which are illegal from the outset and those where the illegality arises at a later stage.[69] The effect of any subsequent illegality will fall to be determined by the proper law, whereas initial illegality will (under the proper law) normally render the contract void unless the relevant legal provision provides otherwise.[70]

Those matters not governed by the proper law

1.21   The proper law, although governing many important matters, is not of universal application. Procedural questions are governed by the law of the place where proceedings are brought (the *lex fori*). This will include such matters as whether the courts have jurisdiction to hear the dispute; laws of evidence,[71] including questions as to the admissibility of evidence[72]; and the procedures to be followed during the trial. The evidential provisions of the *lex fori* may be particularly important with regard to documents subject to a stamp duty or other tax. If England were the *lex fori* such documents would

---

[62] See, for example; *Re Helbert Wagg & Co.Ltd.*, above, n. 24; *National Bank of Greece and Athens SA v. Metliss* [1958] A.C. 509; *Adams v. National Bank of Greece SA* [1961] A.C. 255.

[63] *Ibid.*

[64] See Morris, p. 288 *et seq.* and Wood, p. 42 *et seq.*

[65] *Kahler v. Midland Bank* above, n. 60; *Zivnostenska Banka National Corporation v. Frankman* [1950] A.C. 57.

[66] *Vita Food Products Inc. v. Unus Shipping Co.* above, n. 13. But as Morris points out at p. 289, the modern tendency is to place a narrow interpretation on public policy.

[67] *Boissevain v. Weil* [1950] A.C. 327.

[68] *Ralli Brothers v. Compania Naviera Sota y Aznar* [1920] 2 K.B. 287; *R. v. International Trustee for the Protection of Bondholders A.G.* above n. 12.

[69] See Wood, p. 43.

[70] *Ibid.*

[71] This would include the question of whether a witness is competent to give evidence and the burden of proof which has to be satisfied in the cause of action.

[72] *Yates v. Thompson* (1835) 3 Cl. & F. 544: *Bain v. Whitehaven and Furness Ry.* (1850) 3 H.L.Cas. 1.

not be admissible in evidence if the tax or duty had not been paid. Other jurisdictions may well have similar requirements.

The availability of pre-judgment attachment orders (like the Mareva injunction for example) would also be determined by the *lex fori* as would the availability of legal remedies to enforce any claim,[73] and the execution thereof. The question of whether either party enjoys immunity will also fall to be determined by the *lex fori*.[74] This is obviously an issue of considerable importance in some contracts and local legal advice should once again be sought in appropriate cases.

A. STATUS AND CAPACITY

As Wood points out,[75] the various types of institutions that might contract **1.22** under an international banking transaction are myriad. Corporations, partnerships, states, trusts and supra-national organisations all have recognised status and powers under English law. However, it is most unlikely that they would have identical status and power under the laws of a foreign jurisdiction. It is also unlikely that all foreign institutions would fit comfortably into English domestic law categories. It is therefore most important for the contracting parties to appreciate which system of law will govern their status and power, since such law will determine, to a large extent, whether and in what circumstances, those parties are capable of entering into a legally binding commitment.

As a general rule, these questions are determined by the law of the institution's domicile (the *lex domicili*)[76] and by the institution's constitutional documents. There are, however, a number of important exceptions to this general principle.[77]

B. FORMAL VALIDITY

A final matter worthy of mention is that of formal validity. There is little **1.23** modern authority on what law governs the formal validity of a contract, although it is generally recognised to be sufficient to comply with the formalities prescribed by the proper law.[78] Alternatively a contract will be formally valid if it satisfies the formalities prescribed by the laws of the place where the contract is made (the *lex loci contractus*), even if it does not meet those of the proper law.

THE CURRENCY OF CONTRACTUAL DAMAGES

Damages for breach of an international banking contract will fall to be **1.24** determined under the proper law of the contract. Where the proper law is English law the principles applicable are those laid down by Lord Wilber-

---

[73] See Wood, p. 30. See also *Phrantzes* v. *Argenti* [1960] 2 Q.B. 19.
[74] This will of course be particularly important where one of the parties is either a state or state entity. See Chap. 3 below.
[75] See Wood, pp. 31–42.
[76] In the case of a corporation, the *lex domicili* is the country where it is incorporated. The issue of domicile is considered in greater detail in Chap. 2 below.
[77] Wood, above n. 75.
[78] *Van Grutten* v. *Digby* (1862) 31 Beav. 561; see also *Re Bankes* [1902] 2 Ch. 333.

force in *The Folias*,[79] which require that prima facie any judgment in respect of a breach of contract should be given in the currency designated in the contract either expressly or impliedly to be the money of account. In many cases this will be the same as the money of payment, but where they are different it is the money of account that should be selected.[80] Where the parties' intention cannot be deduced from the contract, damages should be given in the currency in which the loss was suffered by the plaintiff, or more accurately, the currency which the defendant knew or could reasonably have contemplated, at the time of the contract, would be the currency in which the plaintiff would suffer his loss.[81] This is most likely to be the currency in which the plaintiff conducts his business rather than the currency in which the loss first arose.

Public international law

1.25 As an alternative to choosing a domestic system of law as the governing law of the contract, the parties may consider the selection of international or "trans-national" law.[82] This proposal begs the question, however, as to whether there is an international law of contract which can be used to determine the rights and obligations of parties contracting under an international banking agreement. The orthodox answer is "no", because international law is concerned only with legal relations between states, and not between states and private persons. Indeed, generally speaking, individuals (including banks and corporate bodies) have no standing in international law to bring claims against states, and must rely on their governments to bring such claim on their behalf. Experience has shown that the governments of lender countries have been reluctant to bring these claims, principally for political reasons, and they cannot be relied upon to enforce rights under an international loan agreement.[83]

Since individuals have no standing in international law, it would obviously be totally inappropriate to select international law as the governing law in a contract where neither party was a state. Even in cases where one of the contracting parties is a state, it is submitted that international law is presently incapable of satisfying the paramount requirement which the parties perceive as being a pre-requisite of any governing law, namely, predictability of result. This view is reinforced by one of the most significance cases (*The Serbian Loans* case) on international loan agreements which came before the Permanent Court of International Justice, and which held that a

---

[79] [1979] A.C. 685. See also *The Food Corporation of India* v. *Carras (Hellas) Ltd. (The Diane)* [1980] 2 Lloyd's Rep. 577; *Jean Kraut A.G.* v. *Albany Fabrics* [1977] Q.B. 182.

[80] *George Veflings Rederi A.S.* v. *President of India* [1978] 1 W.L.R. 982.

[81] *The Folias*, above, n. 79; see also Knott, "Foreign Currency Judgments in Tort: An Illustration of the Wealth—Time Continuum" (1980) 43 M.L.R. 18.

[82] See, generally, Wood, pp. 19–22; Mann, "The Law Governing State Contracts" XXI B.Y.B.I.L. 11 (1944), "Reflections on a commercial Law of Nations XXIII B.Y.B.I.L. 20 (1957), "The Proper Law of Contracts Concluded by International Persons" XXXV B.Y.B.I.L. 34 (1959); Delaume, "The Proper Law of Loans Concluded by International Persons: A statement and a Forecast" 56 Am.J. of Int.L.63 (1962).

[83] See Riesenfeld, "The Powers of the Executive to Govern the Rights of Creditors in the event of Defaults of Foreign Governments" (1982) Uni. of Ill.L.R. 322.

loan from a private lender to a foreign sovereign necessarily had to have the municipal law of some country as its proper law.[84]

It has been suggested by at least one commentator[85] that international law has undergone significant changes since *The Serbian Loans* case[86] and, notwithstanding significant practical and theoretical problems, there is now no reason why international law cannot be selected to govern certain international loan agreements.[87] It is submitted that such a position has not been reached. Few, if any, lenders would agree that international law is sufficiently developed to confer predictability upon international banking contracts, and it is debatable whether any court or tribunal possesses the necessary degree of sophistication to apply "recognised principles of international law" to a dispute arising under such contracts. These fears have been echoed by a number of commentators who recognise the familiar concern that international law is: "too rudimentary to supply all the answers to complex financial schemes,"[88] and would adversely affect the marketability of international banking instruments. Of perhaps more significance is the fact that lenders have a natural disinclination to deviate in any way from established patterns of business.[89]

There can be little doubt that familiarity with the present status quo **1.26** regarding governing law will continue to prejudice the "internationalisation" of banking contracts in relation to the adoption of international law. It is unlikely that this status quo will change in the foreseeable future unless a majority of states determine that they will abide by and enforce recognised principles of international law. A recent decision of the Court of Appeal[90] suggests that the attitude in England might be moving in favour of accepting principles of public international law to govern contractual relations. The case also clarifies the principle that contracts governed by public international law can be enforced by the English Courts wihout offending public policy. Perhaps the position is not quite as pessimistic as previously suggested.

---

[84] See *The Serbian Loans* case, P.C.I. J.Ser. A 13–24 No. 14 (1929), at p. 41; see also Borchard, *State Insolvency and Foreign Bondholders*—Vol. 1. (1951), p. 15.

[85] Pearce, "The 'Internationalisation' of Sovereign Loan Agreements" [1986] J.I.B.L.

[86] Above, n. 84.

[87] Note, however, the qualifications which attach to such a selection, above.

[88] Delume, *op.cit.*, p. 87.

[89] See generally, Chap. 3 below.

[90] See *Deutsche Schachtbau- und Tiefbohrgesellschaft GmbH* v. *Government of the State of R'As all-Khaimah and Another*, *The Times*, April 27, 1987.

2. Jurisdiction

Introduction

2.01 Notwithstanding the parties' choice of an express governing law, it does not necessarily follow that the courts of the chosen governing law shall have, or shall have exclusively, jurisdiction to hear any dispute which may arise between the parties or to enforce the terms of any judgment. The question of which courts have jurisdiction for the adjudication of disputes and enforcement of judgments is as important as the choice of law issue and, therefore, it is common for international banking agreements to contain an express forum selection clause[1] which invariably encompasses the courts of the country whose law has been chosen to govern the agreement.

However, it is important to appreciate that choice of law and jurisdiction are entirely separate issues and they are uniformly treated as such. Whether or not the courts of a particular legal system have jurisdiction is a matter for the *lex fori* to decide in accordance with its own substantive rules of private international law. These substantive rules obviously vary from country to country and it is impossible to consider them all. The purpose of this chapter, therefore, will be to concentrate upon the substantive rules of English private international law with some reference to alternative approaches in other jurisdictions.[2]

The position in England has undergone fundamental change since the remaining provisions of the Civil Jurisdiction and Judgments Act 1982 came into operation,[3] and henceforth, two régimes will apply to the assumed jurisdiction of the English courts. This chapter will initially consider the traditional bases of jurisdiction before examining the impact of recent legislative changes.

---

[1] See, for example, clause 29(2) in the specimen agreement, Chap. 17 below.

[2] For a fuller discussion of the substantive rules of other jurisdictions, see: Wood, Chap. 3; Gruson, "Forum-selection clauses in international and interstate commercial agreements," 1982 U.Ill.L.Rev. 133; Kahn-Freund, "Jurisdiction Agreements: Some Reflections," 26 I.C.L.Q. 825 (1977); Wesser, "Bases of Judicial Jurisdiction in the Common Market Countries," 10 American Journal of Comparative Law 323 (1961); De Winter, "Excessive Jurisdiction in Private International Law" 17 I.C.L.Q. 706 (1968).

[3] The Act became fully effective on January 1, 1987.

ORIGINAL JURISDICTION OF THE ENGLISH COURTS IN RESPECT OF ACTIONS *IN PERSONAM* WHERE THE DEFENDANT IS NOT "DOMICILED" IN THE UNITED KINGDOM OR IN ANY OTHER STATE WHICH IS NOT PARTY TO THE 1968 CONVENTION[3a]

An action *in personam* is simply an action between parties designed to settle **2.02** rights and obligations as between them. Such an action will cover almost every claim which can be brought in an international banking dispute, including: claims for breach of contract or for tort; claims for specific performance of contractual obligations or for an injunction preventing a possible breach of contract.

The traditional bases of jurisdiction

The traditional bases of jurisdiction will be considered under the following **2.03** headings:

    A. submission;
    B. presence;
    C. extended/discretionary jurisdiction.

A. Express submission

The English courts will have jurisdiction over a contractual dispute if the **2.04** defendant voluntarily submits to the jurisdiction of the English courts. However, it must also be possible to serve process on the defendant within the jurisdiction. Leave of the court is required to serve process abroad. Submission will not be deemed voluntary, however, if the defendant appears before the court solely to contest the jurisdiction of the court.[4] Submission may be effected in a variety of ways,[5] but in international banking agreements it is common to provide for express submission within the terms of the contract. A typical example of a non-exclusive jurisdiction clause[6] would read as follows:

> The borrower hereby irrevocably submits to the non-exclusive jurisdiction of the English Courts in relation to any claim or dispute arising

---

[3a] The Brussels Convention on jurisdiction and the enforcement of judgments in civil and commercial matters of 1968, which was brought into effect in the United Kingdom by the Civil Jurisdiction and Judgments Act 1982. Throughout this chapter the term "contracting states" will be used to describe those states which are party to the 1968 Convention (see n. 62 below).

[4] *Re Dulles' Settlement (No. 2)* [1951] Ch. 842. See also R.S.C., Ord. 12, r. 8(1).

[5] One of the parties may commence an action as plaintiff and this, in general terms, would give a court jurisdiction to entertain a counterclaim by the defendant in some related matter. This would not, however, extend to bringing proceedings on an independent ground: see *South African Republic* v. *Compagnie Franco-Belge du Chemin de Fer du Nord* [1897] 2 Ch. 487; *High Commissioner for India* v. *Ghosh* [1960] 1 Q.B. 134.

[6] The distinction between exclusive and non-exclusive jurisdiction clauses will be considered later in this chapter, below para. 2.18.

hereunder and hereby (but without prejudice to any other effective method of service) appoints and designates..............of..............as its authorised agent for service of proceedings.[7]

FACTORS INFLUENCING CHOICE OF FORUM

2.05   In selecting a particular forum the parties (particularly the lending bank) will be influenced by factors similar to those which favour the choice of a particular governing law.[8] The parties will obviously want to ensure that any suit will be heard by an unbiased experienced judiciary capable of dealing with complex commercial disputes. The relationship between the chosen forum and the governing law will also be most important, since many of the objectives behind the express choice of law will fail if the only courts empowered to hear a dispute either refuse to recognise the choice of law or only recognise it insofar as it is consistent with local law.[9] As we have already seen, the ability to insulate the agreement against adverse changes of law in the borrower's country is of paramount importance to lending banks.[10]

Practical financial considerations will also be influential. The lending bank, for example, would wish to ensure, so far as possible, that any judgment eventually obtained could be effectively enforced. Of particular interest, therefore, would be the location of the borrowers assets[11] and the availability of a summary procedure whereby the borrower's assets can be secured against removal to another jurisdiction. The advance of modern technology has greatly eased the burden of moving assets cross-border, and the availability of remedies akin to pre-trial attachment is now crucially important. In England the Mareva injunction[12] provides such a remedy, although it is discretionary and only granted on the balance of convenience.[13] The purpose of the Mareva injunction is to prevent a defendant rendering a judgment against him nugatory, by removing or dissipating his assets abroad. It does not, however, improve the position of the plaintiff as against other creditors of the defendant. Before granting a Mareva injunction the court will usually require to be satisfied that:

(1) the person seeking the injunction has a good arguable case[14];
(2) the defendant appears to have assets within the jurisdiction[15] and there

---

[7] Where the borrower is a sovereign state or state entity, the jurisdiction clause will usually contain an express waiver of immunity and consent to enforcement: see clause 29(2) of the specimen agreement. The significance of such a clause is considered in Chapter 3.

[8] Above, Chap. 1.

[9] See Wood, p. 59.

[10] Above, Chap. 1.

[11] If no suitable forum is available in which the defendant has assets, the plaintiff would be advised to use a forum whose judgment will be recognised and enforced in a jurisdiction where the defendant's assets lie.

[12] The Mareva injunction is so-named after the injunction granted in *Mareva Compania Naviera S.A.* v. *International Bulkcarriers S.A.* [1975] 2 Lloyds Rep. 509. See Rose, "The Mareva Injunction—Attachment *in personam*" [1981] L.M.C.L.Q. 1, 177; Powles, "Viva Mareva!" [1980] J.B.L. 218.

[13] It is now granted by virtue of s.37(3) of the Supreme Court Act 1981.

[14] *Rasu Maritima S.A.* v. *Pertamina* [1978] Q.B. 644, p. 661.

[15] *Third Chandris Shipping Corp.* v. *Unimarine S.A.* [1979] Q.B. 645.

is a real danger that those assets will be removed from the jurisdiction or otherwise dissipated[16] if the injunction is not granted;

(3) the claim at issue must be one over which the court has jurisdiction[17];

(4) there is a real risk that the defendant will be unable or unwilling to satisfy the claim if the injunction is not granted[18]; and

(5) there is a balance of convenience in favour of granting the injunction.[19]

2.06 The emergence of the Mareva injunction has undoubtedly been one of the most significant commercial law developments in England in the past decade. The scope of this new form of injunctive relief is frequently extended by the English judiciary[20] and it has become an indispensable weapon in the banker's armoury, significantly improving the chances of recovery.

It is particularly useful against a defendant residing abroad who possesses assets within the jurisdiction, providing, of course, that effective service can be issued against such a defendant.

Aside from purely financial considerations, the respective parties will also be interested in choosing a forum which is geographically convenient, and where evidence can be fully deployed without unnecessary inconvenience and expense. Language can also be an important factor, particularly if proceedings are ultimately brought in one language and the often voluminous documentation evidencing the agreement between the parties is in another. In such a situation the cost and delay of obtaining a translation may be significant, and there is always a risk that the translation may not accurately reflect the complex legal concepts encapsulated in the original language.

It is usual for the parties and their advisors to give active consideration to these and other factors before entering into any binding agreement. The bargaining position of the parties will obviously be crucial in determining the ultimate choice of forum, and the importance of such choice, providing it is effective, cannot be over-emphasised.

APPOINTING AN AGENT FOR SERVICE

2.07 It has already been stressed that a submission to English jurisdiction clause will only be effective if it is possible to serve process on the defendant.[21] Unless process can be served within the jurisdiction leave of the court is required, and therefore, in order to avoid the unpredictability of an application for service out of the jurisdiction, it is common for one of the parties (normally the borrower) to appoint an agent for service within the English jurisdiction, providing of course English courts are selected as the forum. If

---

[16] It will be enough to show that there is a real risk of the assets being dissipated within the jurisdiction: see *Rasu Maritima S.A.* v. *Pertamina* above, n. 14.

[17] *The Siskina* v. *Distos Compania Naviera S.A.* [1979] A.C. 210.

[18] *Etablissement Esefka International Anstalt* v. *Central Bank of Nigeria* [1979] 1 Lloyd's Rep. 445.

[19] Guidelines for the grant of a Mareva injunction are contained in *Z Ltd.* v. *A-Z and AA-LL* [1982] Q.B. 558.

[20] See, for example, *The Niedersachsen* [1983] 2 Lloyd's Rep. 600, 602; *Orwell Steel (Erection and Fabrication) Limited* v. *Asphalt and Tarmac (U.K.) Ltd.* [1984] 1 W.L.R. 1097; *Hill Samuel & Co.* v. *Littaur (No. 2)* (1985) 129 S.J. 433.

[21] Above.

such an agent is present in England the borrower is deemed to submit to the jurisdiction, and service may be effected upon the agent as of right.[22] If the agent himself is also abroad at the appropriate time, then leave of the court must be obtained for service out of the jurisdiction.[23] It is most important, therefore, carefully to select an agent who will be present within the jurisdiction. Various bodies specialise in this type of appointment and it is common to insist within the submission to jurisdiction clause that the agent be maintained by the borrower.[24] Agents who may themselves be able to claim diplomatic immunity should obviously be avoided, and where such appointments are inevitable a future claim of diplomatic immunity should be guarded against by an appropriate waiver within the documentation.

B. Presence

2.08 A defendant present in England can, generally speaking, always be served with legal process, unless he is domiciled in the E.E.C.,[25] and it is the service of process within the jurisdiction which effectively provides the basis of jurisdiction.

Insofar as individuals are concerned, any physical presence in England, however short, is enough.[26] Presence is also accepted as a basis of jurisdiction in most common law countries, and has been taken to absurd lengths in the United States.[27]

In the case of a partnership, process can be served on any individual member of the partnership who is present in England at the time of service. Alternatively, process may be served at the partnership's principal place of business in England upon the person in control of the partnership business.[28] Similarly, with regard to corporations the crucial factor is presence in England, but this begs the question "when is a corporation present in England?" A company registered in England under the Companies Act 1985 is regarded as present in England and process can be served on the registered office of the company. If the company is registered abroad, the position is less straightforward, although such a company, if it establishes a place of business in England, is obliged to file with the registrar of companies the name(s) and address(es) of the person(s) resident in England and authorised to accept process on its behalf.[29] Service upon such a person will

---

[22] *Tharsis Sulphur Co.* v. *Société des Métaux* (1889) 58 L.J.Q.B. 435; *Montgomery, Jones & Co.* v. *Liebenthal & Co.* [1898] 1 Q.B. 487, R.S.C. Ord. 10, r. 3(1).

[23] R.S.C. Ord. 11, r. 1(1). This issue is considered in greater detail later in this chapter, below.

[24] It will obviously be dangerous for the lender to rely on the borrower maintaining his agent, and there is no substitute for an appropriate agent being appointed at the outset.

[25] For the position with regard to defendants "domiciled" in the E.E.C. see 2.12 *et seq.* below.

[26] *Maharanee of Baroda* v. *Wildenstein* [1972] 2 Q.B. 283. The actual decision in this case would now be different because of the defendants domicile in the E.E.C.

[27] See *Grace* v. *MacArthur* 170 F. Supp. 442 (E.D. Ark. 1959) cited in Wood, p. 62.

[28] See Morris p. 65. It matters not that all the partners are abroad (Ord. 81, r. 3) or that they are all foreigners (*Worcester City and County Banking Co.* v. *Firbank, Panling & Co.* [1894] 1 Q.B. 784).

[29] Companies Act 1985, s.691(i)(b). See also *N.V. Slavenburg's Bank* v. *Intercontinental Natural Resources Ltd.* [1980] 1 All E.R. 955.

be sufficient, even though at the relevant time the company no longer carries on business in England.[30]

A corporation will also be "present" in England if it does business within **2.09** the English jurisdiction. A corporation will only be 'doing business' however, if it has appointed an agent in England with authority to enter into transactions binding upon the company. If, on the other hand, the agent merely acts as a conduit transmitting offers abroad for acceptance, then the company will not be 'doing business' in England.[31] Furthermore, the agent must carry on business at some fixed place in England for a definite period of time (although this requirement is not an onerous one).[32]

The presence of assets within the jurisdiction is deemed sufficient by some countries' substantive rules of private international law,[33] but this would not be sufficient to ground *in personam* jurisdiction in England. Nor would presence of a local subsidiary be sufficient unless it could be argued that the subsidiary was doing business on behalf of its parent in England, as the parent's agent. New York courts, on the other hand, have been prepared to accept jurisdiction over an overseas parent company by treating a local subsidiary as if it were a branch,[34] and have exercised jurisdiction over a foreign subsidiary on the basis of jurisdiction over the parent.[35] Wood, however, emphasises that jurisdiction will only be exercised 'if the parent controls the internal affairs of the subsidiary so that the formal separateness is not maintained.'[36]

C. Extended/discretionary jurisdiction of the English courts

In circumstances where the defendant is not present in England and does not **2.10** submit to the jurisdiction, the court may exercise its discretionary power under Order 11, rule 1(1) of the Rules of the Supreme Court and permit service out of the jurisdiction. However, it must be emphasised that the jurisdiction of the court under Order 11, rule 1(1) is discretionary and will only be exercised in appropriate cases,[37] with extreme caution and full regard in every case to all the circumstances.[38] In exercising its discretion, the court will resolve any doubts concerning the construction of the order in favour

---

[30] *Sabatier* v. *Trading Co.* [1927] 1 Ch. 495.
[31] *Okura & Co. Ltd.* v. *Forsbacka Jernverks Aktiebolag* [1914] 1 K.B. 715; *Vogel* v. *R and A Kohnstamm Ltd.* [1973] Q.B. 133.
[32] See *Dunlop Pneumatic Tyre Co. Ltd.* v. *Actien Gesellschaft für Motor & C., Cudell & Co.* [1902] 1 K.B. 342, where a presence of nine days at a stand in the Crystal Palace cycle show was deemed sufficient.
[33] Germany and Austria are two examples of where 'asset presence' would be sufficient: see Wood, p. 65.
[34] *Taca International Airlines* v. *Rolls Royce of England*, 15 N.Y. 2d 97, 204 N.E. 2d 329 (1965), cited in Wood, p. 63.
[35] *Public Administrator* v. *Royal Bank of Canada* 19 N.Y. 2d 378, 224 N.E. 2d 877 (1967), cited in Wood, p. 64.
[36] *Ibid.*
[37] *Johnson* v. *Taylor Brothers & Co. Ltd.* [1920] A.C. 144.
[38] *Cardova Land Co. Ltd.* v. *Victor Brothers Inc.* [1966] 1 W.L.R. 793; *The Siskina* [1977] 3 W.L.R. 818.

of the defendant,[39] and since applications are made *ex parte*, full and fair disclosure of all relevant facts will be required.[40] The court will also consider whether England is the *forum conveniens*[41] and where it is not, leave will normally be refused.[42]

Insofar as international banking transactions are concerned[43] the court may grant leave in any one of the following cases:

(i) Where relief is sought against a person domiciled within the jurisdiction.[44]

The definition of 'domicile' throughout Order 11, rule 1 is now determined in accordance with sections 41–46 of The Civil Jurisdiction and Judgments Act 1982.[45]

(ii) Where an action is brought on a contract which was made in England or by or through an agent trading or residing in England; or where the contract is by its terms or implication governed by English law; or where the contract contains a term that the English High Court shall have jurisdiction with regard to any action upon the contract.[46]

This particular sub-head is most important in international banking contracts providing, of course, the relevant requirements are satisfied. It will be sufficient if the contract was substantially made in England[47] and as a general rule a contract is made where acceptance is communicated to the offeror, unless acceptance is made by post or telegram, in which case it will be made where acceptance is posted.[48]

The significance of English law being incorporated as the proper law[49] of the contract is once again highlighted by this sub-clause and may, of itself, persuade the court to exercise its discretion and permit service of process abroad.[50]

2.11   (iii) Where an action is brought in respect of a breach of contract committed in England.[51]

It is not necessary under this sub-head for the contract to have been made in England but the breach, by express or implied repudiation or simply by failure to perform, must have occurred in England (for example, by non-repayment in England).[52]

---

[39] *The Hagen* [1908] P. 189; *The Siskina*, above n. 38.

[40] *Bloomfield* v. *Serenyi*, [1945] 2 All E.R. 646.

[41] The doctrine of *forum non conveniens* is considered in greater detail later in this chapter, see para. 2.30 below.

[42] *Mauroux* v. *Sociedade Comercial Abel Pereira da Fonseca S.A.R.L.* [1972] 1 W.L.R. 962; *Kroch* v. *Rossell* [1937] 1 All E.R. 725; *Cordova Land Co. Ltd.* v. *Victor Brothers Inc.* [1966] 1 W.L.R. 793, above, n. 37.

[43] For a fuller discussion of all the sub-heads of Ord. 11, r. 1(1) see Morris, p. 69.

[44] Ord. 11, r. 1(1)(*a*).

[45] Below, para. 2.12.

[46] Ord. 11, r. 1(1)(*d*).

[47] *B.P. Exploration Co. (Libya) Ltd.* v. *Hunt* [1976] 1 W.L.R. 788.

[48] *Cowen* v. *O'Connor* (1888) 20 Q.B.D. 640; *Benaim & Co.* v. *Debono* [1924] A.C. 514.

[49] Above, Chap. 1.

[50] Where the only ground for applying for leave to serve process outside the jurisdiction of the English courts is that the subject of the action is governed by English law, the burden placed on the plaintiff will be a particularly heavy one; see *Spiliada Maritime Corporation* v. *Cansulex Ltd.* [1986] 3 All E.R. 843.

[51] Ord. 11, r. 1(1)(*c*), see Morris pp. 72 *et seq.*

[52] *Ibid.*

(iv) Where an action is founded on a tort and the damage was sustained or resulted from an act committed in England.[53]

This sub-head will be particularly relevant where the tort of negligent misrepresentation is committed by one of the parties.[54] Such a misrepresentation will be deemed to be committed where the misrepresentation is received and acted upon.[55]

(v) Where an action is brought against a person duly served in England and a person abroad is a necessary or proper party to such proceedings.[56]

Whenever the English courts assume jurisdiction by exercise of their discretionary power, the defendant is in the same position as a defendant within the jurisdiction.

JURISDICTION WHERE THE DEFENDANT IS "DOMICILED" IN A "CONTRACTING STATE" UNDER THE 1968 CONVENTION[57]

The Civil Jurisdiction and Judgments Act 1982 (C.J.J.A.)[58] which became **2.12** fully operative on January 1, 1987 gives effect in the United Kingdom to the Brussels Convention on Jurisdiction and Enforcement of Judgments in Civil and Commercial Matters of September 27, 1968.

The scope of the Convention is very wide[59] covering the whole range of civil and commercial matters; its main aims are:

> "to reduce the possibility of forum shopping i.e. the multiplicity of jurisdictions in which the plaintiff, according to his choice, may commence proceedings; and to make judgments to which it applies enforceable in all Member States of the EEC."[60]

A major consequence of the legislative changes brought about by the C.J.J.A. is that two separate and distinct régimes will now apply to the assumed jurisdiction of the English courts. Providing the court has jurisdiction over a defendant "domiciled"[61] in another Convention country,[62] service on the defendant out of the jurisdiction may be effected without leave of the court.[63] If the defendant is domiciled in a non-Convention country

---

[53] Ord. 11, r. 1(1)(*f*).
[54] Below, see also Chap. 7, below.
[55] *Ibid.* See also *Diamond* v. *Bank of London and Montreal Ltd.* [1979] Q.B. 333; *Cordoba Shipping Co. Ltd.* v. *National State Bank, Elizabeth New Jersey*, [1984] 2 Lloyd's Rep. 91.
[56] Ord. 11, r. 1(1)(*c*). See Morris, pp. 70 *et seq.*
[57] See n. 3a above.
[58] See generally Kaye, *Civil Jurisdiction and Enforcement of Foreign Judgments* (1987); Collins, *The Civil Jurisdiction and Judgments Act 1982* (1983); Hartley, *Civil Jurisdiction and Judgments* (1984).
[59] The Convention does not, however, apply to bankruptcy, proceedings relating to the winding up of insolvent companies, judicial arrangements, compositions and analogous proceedings, or to arbitration.
[60] See Schmitthoff's *Export Trade* (8th ed., 1986) p. 624.
[61] Below, para. 2.13.
[62] Convention countries at the time of writing include: Denmark, Germany (Federal Republic), France, Italy, Ireland, Luxembourg, the Netherlands and the United Kingdom.
[63] Provided all the requirements of Ord. 11, r. 1(2) are satisfied.

leave of the court authorising service abroad will still be required under Order 11, rule 1(1).[64]

Meaning of "domicile"

2.13   The term domicile is given a new definition for the purpose of the Convention under section 41 of the C.J.J.A.[65] and an individual is domiciled in the United Kingdom if he is resident in and has a substantial connection with the United Kingdom.[66] This definition does not require the individual to be habitually resident in the United Kingdom, yet it obviously requires more than a mere transient presence.

DOMICILE OF A COMPANY

2.14   The domicile of a company or other legal person or association shall be regarded, for the purpose of the C.J.J.A., as the country in which the company has its "seat,"[67] and a company shall be regarded as having its seat in the United Kingdom if:

(a) it was incorporated or formed under the law of a part of the United Kingdom and has its registered office or some other official address in the United Kingdom; or

(b) its central management and control is exercised in the United Kingdom.[68]

Bases of jurisdiction under the Convention where no jurisdiction clause is included in the agreement

2.15   Whenever possible, an international banking agreement should contain an express jurisdiction clause which, as we will see later in this chapter, affords the greatest degree of predictability to the question of jurisdiction. In the event that such a clause is not incorporated within the terms of the agreement, the Convention provides a general basis of jurisdiction, which applies when the defendant is domiciled in a Contracting State (which is the forum state), and also 'special' bases of jurisdiction when the defendant is not domiciled in a Contracting State (the forum state), yet is domiciled in another

---

[64] Above, para. 2.10.

[65] Surprisingly, the Convention itself made no attempt to define domicile even though it is the primary basis of jurisdiction.

[66] C.J.J.A., s.41(2).

[67] C.J.J.A., s.42(1); see also s.42(5) which provides for those cases where it is necessary to determine the 'place' of the seat.

[68] C.J.J.A., s.42(3). Furthermore, s.42(6) provides that a corporation has its seat in a state other than the United Kingdom if (a) it was incorporated or formed under the law of that state and has its registered office or some other official address there, or (b) its central management and control is exercised in that state. However, because each Contracting State is left to determine the meaning of 'seat' under s.42(7), a corporation will not have its seat in another Contracting State (for the purpose of s.42(6)) if the courts of that state would not regard it as having its seat there.

Contracting State. We will now turn to consider these bases of jurisdiction before examining express jurisdiction clauses under the Convention.

A. General jurisdiction

The general rules for jurisdiction are to be found in Articles 2–4 which pro-   **2.16**
vide that individuals or corporations domiciled in a Contracting State should, whatever their nationality, be sued in the courts of that State.[69] The intention of Article 2 is to prevent the plaintiff from engaging in forum shopping among Contracting States. This general intention is reinforced by Article 3 which prohibits Contracting States from using certain "exorbitant" bases of jurisdiction against persons domiciled in a Contracting State.[70]

B. Special jurisdiction

The special rules for jurisdiction are to be found in Articles 5 and 6 and will   **2.17**
only apply in circumstances where the defendant is being sued in a Contracting State in which he is not domiciled. If the defendant is being sued in the Contracting State in which he is domiciled the courts in that State will not require special jurisdiction since jurisdiction will be derived by virtue of his domicile there under Article 2. The Convention will obviously have no application if the defendant is not domiciled in a Contracting State[71] and in such circumstances jurisdiction will depend on the traditional bases of jurisdiction.[72] The special bases of jurisdiction which are relevant to international banking transactions[73] include:

I. CONTRACT[74]

In matters relating to a contract, the courts of the place of performance of the obligation in question will have jurisdiction.[75] In determining the place of performance the court will apply its own rules of private international law.[76] However, if the parties agree on the place of performance such place will be recognised provided it is not a sham.[77] Many international banking contracts entail several obligations and in such cases it will be the place of performance of the specific obligation upon which the action is founded which determines jurisdiction under the Convention.[78]

---

[69] Art. 2.
[70] See Morris, p. 81.
[71] *Ibid.*
[72] See para. 2.2 *et seq.* above.
[73] Art. 5 provides the full list of circumstances in which the courts of a Contracting State may exercise jurisdiction. See Morris, pp. 82 *et seq.*
[74] Art. 5(1).
[75] This base of jurisdiction has given rise to great difficulty in interpretation. See Morris *ibid.*
[76] Case 12/76 *Industrie Tessili Italiana Como* v. *Dunlop A.G.* [1976] E.C.R. 1473.
[77] Case 54/79 *Zelger* v. *Salinitri* [1980] E.C.R. 89.
[78] Case 266/85 *Shenavai* v. *Kreischer, The Times,* January 16, 1987.

2. TORT[79]

In matters relating to tort, delict or quasi-delict, the courts for the place where the harmful event occurred will have jurisdiction. This basis of jurisdiction may be particularly important where misrepresentation is alleged by the plaintiff[80] and would vest jurisdiction in the courts of either the place where the misrepresentation was uttered or where the damage was suffered,[81] providing, of course, that this was in a Contracting State.

3. BRANCHES AND AGENCIES[82]

As regards a dispute arising out of the operation of a branch, agency or other establishment, the courts for the place in which the branch, agency or other establishment is situated will have jurisdiction. The control exercised by the parent body will be taken into account in determining whether the establishment vests jurisdiction in the local courts, as will a period of location within the jurisdiction which implies some degree of permanence.[83]

C. Exclusive jurisdiction

2.18 There are certain circumstances in which the courts of a particular Contracting State will have exclusive jurisdiction regardless of domicile. The cases in which exclusive jurisdiction will be vested in a court are to be found in Article 16 and those relevant to international banking transactions include:

1. IMMOVABLE PROPERTY[84]

In proceedings relating to rights in immovable property, the courts of the Contracting State in which the property is situated have exclusive jurisdiction.[85]

2. CORPORATIONS[86]

In proceedings relating to the validity of a corporate constitution, the nullity or dissolution of companies or associations, the courts of the Contracting State in which the company or association has its seat[87] will have exclusive jurisdiction. This will not, however, include proceedings relating to the winding-up of insolvent companies since such proceedings are outside the scope of the Convention.[88]

---

[79] Art. 5(3).
[80] For a fuller discussion of the circumstances in which misrepresentation may be alleged, see Chap. 7 below.
[81] Case 21/76 Bier v. Mines de Potasse d'Alsace [1976] E.C.R. 1735.
[82] Art. 5(5).
[83] Case 14/76 De Bloos v. Bouyer [1976] E.C.R. 1497; Case 139/80 Blanckaert & Willems v. Trost [1981] E.C.R. 819.
[84] Art. 16(1).
[85] For a discussion of private international law rules in relation to immovable property see below, Chap. 14.
[86] Art. 16(2).
[87] Above, n. 67.
[88] Above, n. 59.

Jurisdiction clauses

Article 17 of the Convention sets out the circumstances in which a contrac- **2.19**
tual agreement on jurisdiction will be effective to confer exclusive jurisdiction on the courts of a Contracting State, and provides as follows:

> "If the parties, one or more of whom is domiciled in a Contracting
> State, have agreed that a court or the courts of a Contracting State are
> to have jurisdiction to settle any disputes which have arisen or which
> may arise in connection with a particular legal relationship, that court
> or those courts shall have exclusive jurisdiction. Such an agreement
> conferring jurisdiction shall be either in writing or evidenced in writing
> or, in international trade or commerce, in a form which accords with
> practices in that trade or commerce of which the parties are or ought to
> have been aware. Where such an agreement is concluded by parties,
> none of whom is domiciled in a Contracting State, the courts of other
> Contracting States shall have no jurisdiction over their disputes unless
> the court or courts chosen have declined jurisdiction."[89]

Article 17 will only be relevant, therefore, if the parties can agree upon
the court or courts of a Contracting State which are to be vested with exclusive jurisdiction. Furthermore, in order to be formally valid such clauses
must be either: **2.20**
   (i) in writing, or
   (ii) evidenced in writing, or
   (iii) in international trade or commerce, in a form which accords with
practices in that trade or commerce of which the parties are or ought to have
been aware.

If one or more of the parties to an international banking agreement is
domiciled in a Contracting State, an express jurisdiction clause should,
whenever possible, be included within the terms of the agreement for
reasons which have already been discussed. Before considering the precise
wording which such a clause may take, there are a number of issues arising
out of Article 17 which are worthy of mention.

Although Article 17 speaks of a court or courts of a Contracting State
having exclusive jurisdiction, it also applies if the courts of more than one
Contracting State are contemplated within the terms of the parties' contract.[90] In other words, "exclusive jurisdiction" under Article 17 does not
mean "sole jurisdiction." Where a jurisdiction clause is effective under
Article 17, the choice of a particular court or courts cannot be overridden by
other courts in a Contracting State. Furthermore, even when the relevant
agreement is concluded by parties none of whom is domiciled in a Contracting State, courts in another Contracting State shall have no jurisdiction
unless the chosen court has declined jurisdiction.[91] Without more one may
assume, therefore, that the question of domicile is not important. This is not

---

[89] Art. 17(1). However, the version of Art. 17 contained in the C.J.J.A. (Sched. 4) omits the
requirement as to writing where the defendant is domiciled in the United Kingdom. For a
detailed discussion of Art. 17, see Kaye, *Civil Jurisdiction and Enforcement of Foreign Judgments*
loc. cit., n. 58 above, at pp. 1031–1115.
[90] See case 23/78 *Meeth* v. *Glacetal* [1978] E.C.R. 2133.
[91] See Hartley, *loc. cit.*, n. 58 above, at p. 73.

in fact the case and the subtle difference relates to the obligation placed on the chosen court(s). Where the parties are all domiciled outside the Contracting States, the chosen court is not obliged to take jurisdiction, and will determine such matter in accordance with its own law. It is, therefore, national law and not the Convention which deprives all other courts from taking jurisdiction. The Convention only covers cases where the chosen court is a court of a Contracting State. However, it would appear that where the parties choose a court in a non-Contracting State, the Convention does not prevent a court in a Contracting State from declining jurisdiction, although this will again be a matter for national law.[92]

THE WORDING OF THE CLAUSE

2.21 Since the Convention only applies to Contracting States, it is likely that jurisdiction clauses in international banking agreements, where at least one of the parties is domiciled in a Convention country, will be drafted in such a way so as to select the courts of a Contracting State (thereby impliedly excluding the courts of other Contracting States) and will, additionally, select the courts of a non-Contracting State. The jurisdiction of the courts of the non-Contracting State will undoubtedly be non-exclusive, thereby permitting the lender to bring proceedings in a number of different jurisdictions, should this prove necessary.

An example of such a clause may be drafted as follows:

> (i) For the benefit of the Agent Bank, each Manager and each Bank, all the parties irrevocably agree that the courts of England are to have jurisdiction to settle any disputes which may arise out of or in connection with this Agreement and that accordingly any suit, action or proceedings arising out of or in connection with this Agreement may be brought in such courts.
>
> (ii) Without prejudice to sub-clause (i), The Borrower further irrevocably agrees that any suit, action or proceedings arising out of or in connection with this Agreement may be brought in the courts of the State of New York or of the United States for the Southern District of New York or in the courts of [the jurisdiction of the Borrower if such jurisdiction is not a Contracting State] and submits to the non-exclusive jurisdiction of each such court.
>
> (iii) The Borrower irrevocably waives any objection which it may have now or hereafter to the laying of any suit, action or proceedings in any such court as is referred to in this Clause and any claim that any suit, action or proceedings have been brought in an inconvenient forum and further irrevocably agrees that a judgment in any suit, action or proceedings brought in any court as is referred to in this Clause shall be conclusive and binding upon the Borrower and may be enforced in the courts of any other jurisdiction.
>
> (iv) Nothing contained in this Clause shall limit the right of any Bank to take suit, action or proceedings against the Borrower in any court of competent jurisdiction, nor shall the taking of any suit, action or proceedings in one or more jurisdictions preclude the taking of any suit,

---

[92] *Ibid.*, p. 74.

action or proceedings in any other jurisdiction whether concurrently or not.

As this example indicates, a clause incorporated into an agreement which, **2.22** it is hoped, will take advantage of the Convention, will have to be drafted very widely in order to cover the lending bank(s) against every eventuality. It will not be necessary, however, to stipulate that the English courts, referred to in sub-clause (1), have either exclusive or non-exclusive jurisdiction because in relation to Contracting States they impliedly have exclusive jurisdiction. In addition to those clauses outlined in the example, an effective provision for appointment of an agent for service should also be included (to cover actions brought outside Contracting States).

It is permissible, where the exclusive jurisdiction clause has been incorporated for the benefit of one of the parties, for that party to waive the benefit of the clause by bringing proceedings in another court which (but for the exclusive jurisdiction clause) would have jurisdiction under the Convention.

Contracting States cannot require additional formalities to those required under Article 17 and national laws which attempt to impose additional formalities shall have no effect.[93]

The question of benefit

The wording of the specimen clause commences . . . "For the benefit . . . " in order to take advantage of Article 17, the final words of which provide that . . . "If an agreement conferring jurisdiction was concluded for the benefit of only one of the parties, that party shall retain the right to bring proceedings in any other court which has jurisdiction by virtue of this Convention."

The meaning of "benefit" under Article 17 is not entirely clear; however, it will be useful for a lender to bring itself within the terms of the Article (by incorporating suitable wording along the lines found in the example above) since it will then be permitted to bring proceedings in the courts of Contracting States other than those stipulated in the jurisdiction clause.

Submission before the courts of a Contracting State

Article 18 provides that, in addition to jurisdiction derived from other pro- **2.23** visions of the Convention a court of a Contracting State shall have jurisdiction if the defendant appears before the court, but there is no submission where the appearance is solely to contest the jurisdiction.[94] Article 18 will not apply where another court has exclusive jurisdiction under Article 16,[95] nor in circumstances where the parties have expressly provided for jurisdiction in accordance with Article 17.[96]

---

[93] See case 150/80 *Elefanten Schuh* v. *Jacqmain* [1981] E.C.R. 1671.
[94] For a fuller discussion of the scope of Art. 18 see Collins, *loc. cit.*, n. 58 above, at pp. 91–94.
[95] Above, para. 2.18.
[96] See para. 2.19 *et seq.* above.

LEGAL RESTRICTIONS ON JURISDICTION[97]

2.24   There are several grounds upon which an English court's supposed jurisdiction may be called into question and situations where proceedings in such courts may be stayed or struck out. Similarly, an English court may, in certain circumstances, restrain by injunction the institution or continuation of proceedings in a foreign court. This inherent jurisdiction is, however, discretionary and has been sparingly used.[98] It will only be exercised when it is necessary to prevent an injustice.

A. Lis alibi pendens

2.25   One of the most common situations in which an English court may be called upon to exercise its discretion is where simultaneous actions are pending in England and in a foreign jurisdiction between the same parties and involving the same or similar issues (*lis alibi pendens*). As we have seen [99] the typical non-exclusive jurisdiction clause[1] included in most international banking agreements is liberally drafted and will make it possible for proceedings to be commenced contemporaneously in two or more different jurisdictions.[2] Where one of the jurisdictions is England the court may stay the English proceedings, stay the foreign proceedings or require the plaintiff to elect which proceedings he will pursue.[3] However, it has already been stressed that the court exercises its discretion with great caution[4] and insofar as a plea of *lis alibi pendens* is concerned the traditional approach was to refuse a stay of proceedings unless the defendant could show that allowing both actions to continue would be oppressive, unjust or vexatious.[5]

More recently, however, the courts have moved away from this approach by giving the words 'oppressive' and 'vexatious' a more liberal interpretation. It has been said that judicial chauvinism has given way to judicial comity.[6] This new approach was summed up by Lord Diplock in *MacShannon v. Rockware Glass Ltd.*[7] in the following terms:

> "The real test of stay or no stay depends upon what the court in its discretion considers that justice demands. I prefer this test to the test of whether a plaintiff has behaved 'vexatiously' or 'oppressively' on a so-called liberal interpretation of these words. I do not, with respect, believe that it is possible to interpret them liberally without emasculat-

---

[97] See generally, Morris, Chap. 8; Cheshire and North, pp. 112 *et seq.*; Wood, pp. 66 *et seq.*; Morris and North, Chap. 6.

[98] *Logan v. Bank of Scotland (No. 2)* [1906] 1 K.B. 141; *Sealey v. Callan* [1953] P. 135; *Settlement Corporation v. Hochschild* [1966] Chap. 10.

[99] See para. 2.21 above.

[1] See clause 29(2) in the specimen agreement.

[2] the courts of most developed legal systems, including England, will usually accept jurisdiction on the basis of a non-exclusive jurisdiction clause, see Delaume, Chap. 6.

[3] *The Christiansborg* (1885) 10 P.D. 141, pp. 152–153.

[4] Above. See also *Cohen v. Rothfield* [1919] 1 K.B. 410 413; *Settlement Corporation v. Hochschild* [1966] Ch. 10, 15; *Ionian Bank Ltd. v. Couvreur* [1969] 1 W.L.R. 781.

[5] *St. Pierre v. South American Stores (Gath and Chaves), Ltd.* [1936] 1 K.B. 382, 389.

[6] *The Abidin Daver* [1984] 2 W.L.R. 196, 203, cited in Morris, p. 94.

[7] [1978] A.C. 795.

ing them and completely destroying their true meaning . . . in order to justify a stay two conditions must be satisfied, one positive, the other negative:

(a) the defendant must satisfy the court that there is another forum to whose jurisdiction he is amenable in which justice can be done between the parties at substantially less inconvenience or expense and

(b) the stay must not deprive the plaintiff of a legitimate personal or juridical advantage which would be available to him if he invoked the jurisdiction of the English court."[8]

In deciding whether to exercise its discretion the court must weigh the advantage to the plaintiff against the disadvantage to the defendant.[9] All relevant factors in each particular case will be considered including the availability of witnesses,[10] the convenience to both the parties themselves and the witnesses,[11] and the fact that the plaintiff will probably recover a higher award of damages and legal costs in the foreign proceedings.[12] However, the advantage must be a real one and the plaintiff's own belief, however genuine, will not be enough. It must be shown objectively and on the balance of probability to exist.[13]

B. Where the Brussels Convention applies

The Brussels Convention on Jurisdiction and Enforcement of Judgments permits alternative bases of jurisdiction in certain circumstances[14] and there is obviously a risk that proceedings will be brought on the same issue, between the same parties in the courts of at least two Member States. Such a possibility is dealt with by Article 21 of the Convention, which provides that the courts of the jurisdiction in which the second or subsequent sets of proceedings are brought shall decline jurisdiction in favour of the court which was first seized of the motion.   **2.26**

C. Exclusive jurisdiction clauses

Banks obviously prefer non-exclusive jurisdiction clauses, since such a clause enables them to select the most appropriate forum in which to bring proceedings. Borrowers, on the other hand, recognise that unless the forum is exclusive they may be exposed to a multiplicity of suits in various jurisdictions, any one of which may be hostile to the interests of the borrower.   **2.27**

As we have already seen,[15] English courts may stay proceedings in England or restrain by injunction the institution or continuation of proceedings abroad depending upon the circumstances of the case. Insofar as exclusive jurisdiction clauses are concerned, a distinction must be made between

---

[8] *Ibid.*, p. 819.
[9] *The Atlantic Star* [1974] A.C. 436, pp. 468–469.
[10] *MacShannon* v. *Rockware Glass Ltd.*, above, n. 97, p. 812.
[11] *Ibid.*
[12] *Castanho* v. *Brown and Root (UK) Ltd.* [1981] A.C. 557.
[13] Above, n. 97, p. 812.
[14] Above, paras. 2.15 *et seq.*
[15] Above. See also the discussion of *forum non conveniens'* below, para. 2.30.

those clauses to which Article 17 of the Brussels Convention on Jurisdiction and Enforcement of Judgments applies (which have already been discussed)[16] and those which are not affected by the Convention, which we will now consider.

Generally speaking, where a contract provides for a foreign court to have exclusive jurisdiction, an English court will stay proceedings brought in England in breach of such a clause.[17] However, the plaintiff will be allowed to proceed if he can prove that it is just and proper for the English proceedings to continue.[18] The onus is on the plaintiff, not the defendant, as in *lis alibi pendens*,[19] and the plaintiff's case must be a strong one, showing more than a balance of convenience.[20] In exercising its discretion the court will take into account all the circumstances of the particular case including:

2.28   "(a) In what country the evidence on the issues of fact is situated, or more readily available, and the effect of that on the relative convenience and expense of trial as between the English and foreign courts.

(b) Whether the law of the foreign court applies and, if so, whether it differs from English law in any material respects.

(c) With what country either party is connected, and how closely.

(d) Whether the defendants genuinely desire trial in the foreign country or are only seeking procedural advantages.

(e) Whether the plaintiffs would be prejudiced by having to sue in the foreign court because they would:

(i) be deprived of security for their claim;

(ii) be unable to enforce any judgment obtained;

(iii) be faced with a time-bar not applicable in England; or

(iv) for political, racial, religious or other reasons be unlikely to get a fair trial."[21]

If the plaintiff seeks leave to serve process outside the jurisdiction, under Order 11, rule 1,[22] in disregard of an exclusive foreign jurisdiction clause the burden placed upon him will be even greater. An English court will be very reluctant to permit service in such circumstances.[23] Whether the clause effectively provides for "exclusive" jurisdiction will be determined by the proper law of the contract of which the clause forms part.[24]

---

[16] See para. 2.19 above.

[17] *Law* v. *Garrett* (1878) 8 Ch. D. 26; *Austrian Lloyd S.S. Co.* v. *Gresham Life Insurance Society Ltd.* [1903] 1 K.B. 249; *Kirchner & Co.* v. *Gruban* [1909] 1 Ch. 413; *The Cap Blanco* [1913] p. 130; *The Eleftheria* [1970] P. 94; *Trendtex Trading Corporation* v. *Credit Suisse* [1982] A.C. 679; *The Morviken* [1983] 1 Lloyd's Rep. 1; *The Atlantic Song* [1983] 2 Lloyd's Rep. 394; *The Sennar (No. 2)* [1984] 2 Lloyd's Rep. 142.

[18] *The Athenée* (1922) 11 Ll. L. R. 6; *The Fehmarn* [1958] 1 W.L.R. 159; *Evans Marshall & Co. Ltd.* v. *Bertola S.A.* [1973] 1 W.L.R. 349; *The Adolf Warski* [1976] 2 Lloyd's Rep. 241; *Carvalho* v. *Hull Blyth (Augola) Ltd.* [1979] 1 W.L.R. 228; *Trendtex Trading Corporation* v. *Credit Suisse*, above; *The Pia Vesta* [1984] 1 Lloyd's Rep. 169.

[19] Above.

[20] *The Eleftheria*, above n. 6, p. 100.

[21] *Ibid.*

[22] R.S.C., above, n. 42.

[23] See para. 2.10 above; also, *Evans Marshall & Co. Ltd.* v. *Bertola S.A.* above, n. 18, pp. 360–362.

[24] *Ibid.* at p. 361; *the Sindh* [1975] 1 Lloyd's Rep. 372; *The Makefjell* [1976] 2 Lloyd's Rep. 29.

D. Floating jurisdiction clauses[25]

Floating jurisdiction clauses, which permit one of the parties to select the   **2.29**
country whose courts will have exclusive jurisdiction, are becoming
increasingly common in international contracts. Such clauses may find
more favour with borrowers since the choice ultimately made (by the
lender) is commonly selected from one of a number of jurisdictions specified in the clause from the outset and once selected such courts will have
exclusive jurisdiction.
The clause may be expressed in the following terms:

> The Borrower irrevocably agrees that any suit, action or proceedings
> arising out of or in connection with this Agreement shall, at the option
> of the Lender to be declared by him, be brought . . .
> (1) before the English courts such courts possessing exclusive jurisdic-
> tion; or
> (2) before the courts of the State of New York such courts possessing
> exclusive jurisdiction; or
> (3) before the courts of..............(the borrower's jurisdiction) such
> courts possessing exclusive jurisdiction.

Providing the borrower is able to influence the choice of alternative jurisdictions which are included in the clause, he should feel reasonably at ease that
proceedings will not be instituted in a hostile country. Furthermore,
because the courts ultimately chosen will possess exclusive jurisdiction he
will not be exposed to a multiplicity of suits in different jurisdictions. The
validity of floating choice of forum clauses will be determined by the proper
law of the contract[26] and if English law is the proper law, such a choice of
forum clause will be deemed valid and may be given effect.[27]
   Floating choice of forum clauses do however pose significant problems
with regard to predictability of result, since they are often accompanied by
floating choice of law clauses which may[28] be struck down as invalid,
thereby leaving the parties with a totally inappropriate legal document.[29]

E. Forum non conveniens[30]

The final category under which an English court may restrict jurisdiction by   **2.30**
ordering a stay relates to the doctrine of *forum non conveniens*, whereby an
action will be stayed if some other forum is more "appropriate," in the
sense that it is more suitable to meet the ends of justice. It was debatable,
however, until very recently whether a general doctrine of *forum non conve-*

---

[25] See generally on this subject, Briggs "The Validity of "floating" choice of law and jurisdiction clauses" [1986] 4 L.M.C.L.Q.
[26] Above, n. 13.
[27] See Briggs, *loc. cit.*, n. 25 above, pp. 515–517, and the cases cited therein.
[28] It is submitted that such clauses would be struck down under English law. See Brigs above,
pp. 513–515.
[29] See Chap. 1 above.
[30] See generally on this topic, Briggs "The staying of actions on the ground of 'forum non conveniens' in England today" [1984] 2 L.M.C.L.Q. 227; Briggs, " 'Forum non conveniens'—
an update" [1985] 3 L.M.C.L.Q. 360.

niens existed in England and even if it did it could not be compared in either scope or vitality to the doctrine which is applied under New York law.[31] Indeed, as recently as 1978 Lord Salmon said: "this doctrine has never been part of the law of England. And in my opinion, it is now far too late for it to be made so save by Act of Parliament."[32] Lord Diplock in the same case went even further when he said,[33] "It would not be consonant with the traditional way in which judicial precedent has played its part in the development of the common law of England, to attempt to incorporate holus-bolus from some other system of law, . . . doctrines, or legal concepts that have hitherto been unrecognised in English common law.[34] Nevertheless, a stay was granted in *MacShannon*, the House of Lords rejecting the traditional criteria of "oppressive" and "vexatious"[35] in favour of the more flexible test of "What justice in the particular case demands," and "If the distinction between this restatement[36] of the English law and the Scottish doctrine of *forum non conveniens* might on examination prove to be a fine one, I cannot think that it is any worse for that."[37]

This inherent jurisdiction of the English court to stay, strike out or prevent by injunction the commencement or continuation of proceedings,[38] whenever it is necessary to prevent injustice, was affirmed by the House of Lords in *The Abidin Daver*[39] and this case now forms the basis of the English approach.[40] This new approach was summarised by Lord Goff in *Spiliada Maritime Corporation* v. *Cansulex Ltd.*[41] in the following terms:

(i) The basic principle was that a stay would only be granted on the ground of *forum non conveniens* where the court was satisfied that there was some other available forum having competent jurisdiction, which was the appropriate forum for the trial, that is, in which the case could be tried more suitably for the interests of all the parties and the ends of justice.

(ii) In general, the burden of proof rested on the defendant to persuade the court to exercise its discretion to grant a stay, although in respect of such matters raised to persuade the court to exercise its discretion the burden would lie on the party asserting it.

Furthermore, if the court was satisfied that there was another available forum which was prima facie the appropriate forum the burden would then shift to the plaintiff to show that there were special circumstances by which justice required that the trial should nevertheless take place in England.

(iii) The burden resting on the defendant was not just to show that England was not the natural or appropriate forum for the trial but to establish

---

[31] See Gruson, "Forum—selection clauses in international and interstate commercial agreements" [1982] U. Ill. L. Rev. 133, pp. 176–179.

[32] *MacShannon* v. *Rockware Glass Ltd.* above, n. 97, p. 817.

[33] *Ibid.*, at p. 823.

[34] *Ibid.*, at p. 811.

[35] See para. 2.25 above.

[36] As to the full text of this restatement see para. 2.25 above.

[37] *Per* Lord Diplock, above no. 97, p. 812. Lord Fraser in the same case said that the two tests "differ more in theoretical approach than in practical substance", p. 822.

[38] Either within the jurisdiction or abroad.

[39] [1984] A.C. 398.

[40] See, however, the conclusions reached by Briggs *loc. cit.*, n. 28 above.

[41] *Spiliada Maritime Corporation* v. *Cansulex Ltd.* [1986] 3 All E.R. 843; see also *Muduroglu Ltd.* v. *T. C. Ziraat Bankasi* [1986] 3 W.L.R. 606.

that there was another available forum which was clearly or distinctly more appropriate than the English forum.

In that way proper regard was paid to the fact that jurisdiction had been founded in England as of right. There was the further advantage that, on a subject where comity was of importance, it appeared that there would be a broad consensus among major common law jurisdictions.

(iv) Since the question was whether there existed some other forum which was clearly more appropriate for the trial of the action, the court would look first to see what factors existed which pointed in the direction of another forum.

It was desirable to adopt the expression of Lord Keith in *The Abidin Daver*[42] when he referred to the "natural forum" as being "that with which the action had the most real and substantial connection."

So it was for connecting factors in that sense that the court had first to look; and those would include not only factors affecting convenience or expense (such as availability of witnesses), but also other factors such as the law governing the relevant transaction and the places where the parties respectively resided or carried on business.

(v) If the court concluded at that stage that there was no other available forum which was clearly more appropriate for the trial of the action, it would ordinarily refuse a stay.

(vi) If, however, the court concluded at that stage that there was some other available forum which prima facie was clearly more appropriate for the trial of the action, it would ordinarily grant a stay unless there were circumstances by reason of which justice required that a stay should nevertheless not be granted.

THE SEARCH WILL BE FOR THE "NATURAL" FORUM

It would appear that in future cases the search will be for the "natural forum" and the court should consider all the circumstances (beyond simply looking at connecting factors with other jurisdictions) including the fact that the plaintiff would not obtain justice in the foreign jurisdiction. Every case will henceforth turn on its own peculiar facts. As a general rule, however, the decision of the trial judge on the issue of *forum non conveniens* should not be disturbed.[42a]

Arbitration[43]

Arbitration, as opposed to litigation, is often preferred in international trade   **2.31**
transactions[44] but it is seldom considered appropriate for disputes arising out of international loan agreements. One major exception to this general rule can be made, however, in relation to contracts (including loan agreements) with a sovereign state or state entity. Some sovereign governments

---

[42] n. 39 above at p. 415.
[42a] *Ibid.*
[43] See generally Redfern and Hunter, *Law and Practice of International Commercial Arbitration* (1986).
[44] See Chap. 12 below.

cannot, because of constitutional prohibitions,[45] or will not, submit to the jurisdiction of a foreign court. In such cases the lending bank may prefer to submit disputes to arbitration rather than risk bringing proceedings in the sovereign government's local courts, a course of action which is unlikely to meet with any success.[46] Sovereign governments often prefer arbitration, since it is considered that such proceedings do not compromise sovereign dignity in the same way that litigation most certainly would. Furthermore, arbitration permits the parties to select a truly neutral international body, which will, if so requested, keep all proceedings confidential.[47] However, notwithstanding the obvious appeal of arbitration in the cases already mentioned, it is not without its disadvantages, and it is debatable whether it has any place in the majority of international banking transactions.[48]

ARBITRATION OR LITIGATION?

2.32 The comparative advantages and disadvantages of arbitration as opposed to litigation have been comprehensively dealt with by others and will not be fully treated here.[49] Consideration will be restricted to those principles which are particularly significant in international banking transactions.

a. Privacy of Proceedings

2.33 Arbitration is a private process and this, as we have seen,[50] is an advantage in the eyes of those who do not wish details of any proceedings to be disclosed in open court. It can however operate as a disadvantage to banks who may rely, to a certain extent, on the adverse publicity resulting from the publication of a court judgment.

b. Expert Adjudication

2.34 Arbitration offers the parties the opportunity to choose their own judge who may be experienced in the disciplines required to understand the salient facts or law which will arise in a case of dispute. This will be particularly important in many international trade and construction contracts[51] where technical and factual matters are at issue and where arbitration will save the parties both time and money, as well as offering them the prospect of a sensible award.

However, in the majority of banking transactions, disputes do not arise out of technical questions of fact, but rather out of questions of law arising out of the documentation. As we have already seen, providing the parties take appropriate measures within the documentation, they should be able to

---

[45] See Chap. 1 above.

[46] See generally, Chap. 3 below.

[47] See generally, Crawford and Johnson, "Arbitrating with foreign states and their instrumentalities" (1986) I.F.L.R. (April) pp. 11–15.

[48] See generally, Wood pp. 71–73.

[49] See Kerr "*International Arbitration v. Litigation*" (1980) J.B.L. 164; Redfern, "Arbitration: Myth and Reality" (1976) 4. Int'l Bus. Lawyer 450; Yahiel and Cranston, "Arbitration and Dispute Resolution in the International Construction Industry" (1985) 2 Int'l. Construction L.Rev. 231.

[50] See para. 2.31 above.

[51] See generally, Chap. 12 below on the use of arbitration in international trade contracts.

provide for a competent, predictable court to adjudicate upon any legal dispute that may arise.[52]

c. Flexibility and Speed

It is argued[53] that arbitration is more flexible and adaptable and as a result **2.35** quicker than litigation. It is submitted that this is an over-simplification since certain types of international arbitration can take far longer, cost more and be more formal than court proceedings. In many sovereign loan defaults, for example, a lender would probably have time to obtain judgment and commence enforcement proceedings long before arbitration had even commenced.

d. Enforcement

One major weakness of arbitration is the limited power of enforcement **2.36** which the arbitral tribunal may exercise. As a consequence it will often be necessary to institute additional enforcement proceedings in order to implement any award which the tribunal makes.[54] In addition the power to obtain evidence and insist upon the attendance of witnesses will normally be less effective than that of a court.[55]

e. Compromise

It has been suggested[56] that arbitrators are more inclined to make compro- **2.37** mise awards rather than determine the matter one way or the other in accordance with strict principles of municipal law. This approach may be quite acceptable in certain construction or sale of goods contracts, but in a loan agreement where the borrower has simply failed to repay there can ordinarily be no question of compromise. Indeed, the reaction of most bankers is to say: "the borrower has failed to repay: what is there to arbitrate about?"

f. Will the Award be Final?

The effectiveness of any arbitral award will be greatly influenced by the type **2.38** of award which is rendered by the tribunal. A distinction can be made in this respect between final awards and all other forms of award. It will be the parties themselves who agree whether any award will be binding, and under The Arbitration Act 1979, s.3, the parties can agree in advance to exclude certain of the High Court's powers to review. While finality may be important in certain international trade contracts,[57] however, commercial lenders regard access to appeal as essential.[58] Conversely, it is difficult to see what benefit either party can obtain from anything other than a final award,

---

[52] See para. 2.21 above.
[53] See Kerr, loc. cit., n. 36.
[54] This may now be less of a disadvantage since the 1958 International Convention on the Recognition and Enforcement of Foreign Arbitral Awards has now been ratified by many countries, including the United Kingdom and the United States.
[55] However, see Redfern and Hunter, loc. cit, n. 30, pp. 198–201, where it is suggested that the tribunal's powers should be sufficient for it to carry out its task properly and effectively.
[56] Wood, p. 73.
[57] See generally, Chap. 12 below.
[58] Wood, p. 72.

since such interim awards are unlikely to be recognised by the losing party.[59]

ARBITRATION CLAUSES

2.39   There can never be arbitration without the agreement of the parties, and it is common for such agreement to be expressed in the form of an arbitration clause which is included within the terms of the contract.
A typical example would read as follows:

> If any dispute difference or question shall at any time hereafter arise between the parties in respect of or in connection with this agreement, the same shall be referred to the arbitration of a person to be agreed upon by the parties, or failing agreement to be nominated by the London Court of International Arbitration in accordance with and subject to the provisions of the Arbitration Acts 1950 to 1979 or any statutory modification thereof for the time being in force. The parties further agree that all awards shall be binding upon them and waive all rights of appeal or recourse to any court, except such rights as cannot be waived by the law of the place of the arbitration.

Choosing the arbitral body will obviously be important and a number of prominent institutions are available.[60] Many of these institutions enjoy the confidence of most international businessmen and over the years have developed comprehensive rules under which they operate. It cannot be denied that these bodies have greatly increased the appeal of arbitration as a mode of dispute settlement, but it is nevertheless debatable whether such procedures are appropriate for the majority of international banking transactions.

ENFORCEMENT OF FOREIGN JUDGMENTS

2.40   It will obviously be of little practical advantage for a plaintiff to obtain a judgment or award in any court or tribunal if such judgment or award remains ultimately unsatisfied. It may transpire, for example, that a judgment obtained in France cannot be satisfied since all the defendant's assets are to be found in England. In such a situation it falls to be determined whether the English courts will recognise and, if necessary, enforce the French judgment. Alternatively, it may be necessary for the plaintiff to bring a fresh action in England involving a re-hearing on the merits of the case.

The rules applicable to the enforcement of a foreign judgment are the private international law rules of the jurisdiction whose courts are being asked to enforce the judgment, not those of the jurisdiction which granted the

---

[59] But see Redfern and Hunter, *loc. cit.*, n. 30, p. 284, where the value of interim awards is considered.

[60] Examples of such institutions include: The International Centre for Settlement of Investment Disputes (ICSID); UNCITRAL, which does not itself provide arbitration facilities but has made a number of significant contributions in the unification of international arbitration law; the ICC Court of Arbitration; the London Court of International Arbitration; see generally Schmitthoff's *Export Trade*, (8th ed., 1986) pp. 595–609.

judgment. These rules obviously vary from jurisdiction to jurisdiction, and an extensive treatise is neither desirable nor realistically possible. Discussion will, therefore, concentrate first upon the English rules[61] of private international law and, secondly, the comprehensive system of enforcement within the European Community.[62]

Where judgment is obtained in a jurisdiction which is not party to the 1968 Convention

DISTINCTION BETWEEN RECOGNITION AND ENFORCEMENT

Before considering the English rules it is necessary first to distinguish recognition from enforcement. A judgment may be recognised by a court without being enforced, but if a court enforces a foreign judgment it must have first recognised that judgment. Recognition on its own is a defensive process which acts as a shield to block fresh proceedings being commenced in a foreign jurisdiction when judgment has already been obtained elsewhere. Providing the foreign judgment is recognised, the court hearing the fresh proceedings may well dispose of them as *res judicata*. By contrast, where a court is asked to enforce a foreign judgment the requirement is a much more positive once since if enforcement is granted the court will apply all the legal sanctions within its power in order to ensure that the foreign judgment is given effect. **2.41**

NEW PROCEEDINGS OR ENFORCEMENT OF THE FOREIGN JUDGMENT

A judgment creditor cannot enforce the foreign judgment directly in England, but must first bring an action in England on the foreign judgment. Rather than do this he may prefer to bring fresh proceedings in England, in which case the action will be heard again on its merits, a course of action which runs the risk of the court reaching a different conclusion. A new action cannot be commenced, however, if the plaintiff lost the original action or if the foreign judgment has already been satisfied. **2.42**

A. Enforcement at common law

The common law doctrine follows the basic principle that a foreign judgment cannot be enforced in England without the institution of fresh proceedings. The plaintiff can, however, apply for summary judgment in such proceedings under Order 14 of the Rules of the Supreme Court, on the basis **2.43**

---

[61] For a detailed examination of the English rules see Dicey and Morris, Chap. 33; Cheshire and North, Chap. 9; Morris, Chap. 9.
[62] For a discussion of the rules applicable in a number of jurisdictions see Wood, pp. 76–83.

that the defendant has no arguable defence to the claim.[63] This procedure, if successful, will bring a speedy conclusion to enforcement proceedings.

B. Enforcement under statute

2.44   The common law doctrine is subject to a number of important statutory exceptions arising under the Administration of Justice Act 1920, the Foreign Judgments (Reciprocal Enforcement) Act 1933 and the State Immunity Act 1978. Of these the first two are the most important, and the significance of the State Immunity Act will be considered in Chapter 3.

Both the Administration of Justice Act and the Foreign Judgments (Reciprocal Enforcement) Act provide for direct enforcement in England by means of registration of the foreign judgment. The Administration of Justice Act provides for the reciprocal enforcement by registration of judgments obtained from the courts of Commonwealth countries. Registration of such judgments is, however, not a right, and the court in exercising its discretion will consider all the circumstances of the case and determine whether it is just and convenient that the judgment be enforced in England.[64] Registration will not be allowed if the original court lacked jurisdiction to hear the case[65] or if the defendant did not appear in the original proceedings, was not served with process or if it is shown that the judgment was obtained by fraud and the original cause of action would have been contrary to English public policy and therefore could not have been brought in England. A judgment which is effectively registered under the Act will be treated as if it had been obtained in the country in which it is registered.[66]

The Foreign Judgments (Reciprocal Enforcement) Act is intended to replace the system set up under the 1920 Act and facilitates the direct enforcement by registration of foreign judgments obtained in certain Commonwealth and non-Commonwealth countries.[67] The Act provides that registration is available as of right,[68] subject only to the following requirements: that the foreign court acted with jurisdiction[69]; that the defendant received notice of the foreign proceedings; that the judgment was not obtained by fraud; that the judgment is not contrary to public policy in England; and providing the subject matter of the judgment has not previously been the subject of a final and conclusive judgment by another court having jurisdiction over the matter. The effect of registration is identical to that under the 1920 Act, namely, that the foreign judgment has the same

---

[63] *Grant* v. *Easton* (1883) 13 Q.B.D. 302.

[64] See s.9(1), Administration of Justice Act 1920 (A.J.A.).

[65] As to the meaning of jurisdiction for the purpose of the Administration of Justice Act 1920, see Cheshire and North, p. 667.

[66] See s.9(3), (*a*)(*b*), A.J.A.

[67] At the time of writing the Act extended the Administration of Justice Act 1920 to cover the following Commonwealth countries: India, Pakistan, the Australian Capital Territory, Guernsey, Jersey, the Isle of Man, Tonga and Suriname. In addition, the Act extends to the following non-Commonwealth countries: Austria, Belgium, The Federal Republic of Germany, France, Israel, Italy, the Netherlands and Norway.

[68] See s.2, A.J.A.

[69] The actual bases of jurisdiction differ depending upon whether the judgment given related to an action *in personam*. See Cheshire and North pp. 670–675.

force and effect as if it had been given by the court in which it has been registered.

Requirements for recognition and enforcement

There are a number of important requirements which must be satisfied **2.45** before an English court will recognise or enforce a foreign judgment, whether at common law or under the two statutes mentioned above. Some of the requirements, like jurisdiction, have been briefly touched upon, but for the sake of completeness the most important requirements will now be considered.

I. JURISDICTION OF THE FOREIGN COURT[70]

The most fundamental requirement is that the foreign court which gave the **2.46** original judgment must have been a court of competent jurisdiction according to English legal principles of law. In the case of a corporation, the relevant test is whether the corporation carries on business in the foreign country at some definite and more or less permanent place.[71] The presence of a representative in the foreign jurisdiction will not be enough, even if that person is a director who contracts on behalf of the corporation.[72] The Foreign Judgments (Reciprocal Enforcement) Act 1933 is even more restrictive and requires the corporation to have its place of business, and carry on business, in the foreign country.[73] The safest course of action will obviously be to include an effective clause within the documentation evidencing the original contract whereby the defendant submits to the jurisdiction of the foreign court. This would clearly be sufficient in England, and most other jurisdictions.[74] Alternatively, the requirement will be satisfied if the defendant appeared in the foreign proceedings to contest the case or to launch a counterclaim against the plaintiff.[75]

As a general rule the foreign court must have possessed original jurisdiction and the requirement will not be satisfied if jurisdiction was based on "long-arm" or extended rules such as nationality, location of assets within the jurisdiction, or those arising under provisions similar to those found in Order 11 of the Rules of the Supreme Court.[76]

2. FRAUD

The foreign judgment will not be recognised if it was obtained by fraud,[77] **2.47** and this defence has been confirmed in both the Administration of Justice Act[78] and the Foreign Judgments (Reciprocal Enforcements) Act.[79] Fraud,

---

[70] See Morris, pp. 110–117; Cheshire and North, pp. 633–649.
[71] *Littaner Glove Corporation* v. *F. W. Millington Ltd.* (1928). 44 T.L.R. 746; *Sfeir & Co.* v. *National Insurance Co. of New Zealand Ltd.* [1964] 1 Lloyd's Rep. 330.
[72] *Ibid.*
[73] s.4(2)(a)(iv), Foreign Judgments (Reciprocal Enforcement) Act 1933 (F.J.E.).
[74] See Wood, above, n. 48.
[75] The foreign court will not be seized of jurisdiction however if the defendant appeared solely to contest the jurisdiction of the court.
[76] See para. 2.10 above.
[77] *Ochsenbein* v. *Papelier* (1873) L.R. 8 Ch.App. 695.
[78] s.9(2)(d), A.J.A.
[79] s.4(1)(a)(iv), F.J.E.

however, will usually be difficult to prove, and in most cases it will be necessary to reopen the whole case[80] in order to establish that the foreign court has been deceived.

3. PUBLIC POLICY

2.48   The judgment will not be recognised in England if its recognition would be contrary to English principles of public policy.[81] This common law defence was confirmed in both the Administration of Justice Act[82] and the Foreign Judgments (Reciprocal Enforcements) Act.[83] The English courts have, however, limited the scope of public policy as a defence by taking a very narrow view of its application. As a consequence there are very few reported cases in which such a plea has been successful and of these the majority have related to matrimonial rather than commercial matters.[84]

4. CONTRARY TO NATURAL JUSTICE

2.49   A foreign judgment which has been obtained in contravention of the rules of natural justice cannot be enforced in England and this "notion of fair trial" appears to be a pre-requisite for enforcement in most jurisdictions.[85] We have already seen that fraud will generally be a bar to enforcement, but in cases falling short of fraud it is extremely difficult to define the scope of this defence. The merits of the case will obviously be irrelevant, even though the foreign judgment may be manifestly wrong.[86] It would seem that the defence is based upon the principle that the defendant must be given an opportunity to present his side of the case.[87] Therefore this defence may well be satisfied in cases where the defendant has not been given sufficient notice of the hearing to prepare his case, or where the foreign court has refused him the right to plead, but even in such apparently obvious cases the court may still refuse the defence.[88]

5. FOREIGN TAX LAWS

2.50   It is generally recognised that the courts of one country will not recognise or enforce the revenue laws of another country. This principle is followed by the English courts[89] which scrutinise every case in order to ascertain whether the claim is being brought to collect the debts of a foreign country.[90] They will reject both direct and indirect enforcement of such taxes.[91] It has even been suggested that proceedings in England by a foreign

---

[80] *Abouloff* v. *Oppenheimer* (1882) 10 Q.B.D. 295.
[81] *Dalmia Dairy Industries* v. *National Bank of Pakistan* [1978] 2 Lloyd's Rep. 233.
[82] s.9(2)(f), A.J.A.
[83] s.4(1)(a)(v), F.J.E.
[84] *e.g. Re Macartney* [1921] 1 Ch. 522.
[85] See Wood, pp. 79–80.
[86] *Robinson* v. *Fenner* [1913] 3 K.B. 835.
[87] *Jacobson* v. *Frachon* (1928), 138 L.T.
[88] *Ibid.* See also *Scarpetta* v. *Lowenfeld* (1911). 27 T.L.R. 509; *Robinson* v. *Fenner*, above n. 84.
[89] This principle can be traced back as far as the sixteenth century in England; see *Holman* v. *Johnson* (1775) 1 Cowp. 341.
[90] *Buchanan and Macharg* v. *McVey* [1954] I.R. 89; approved by the House of Lords in *Government of India* v. *Taylor* [1955] A.C. 491.
[91] *Rossano* v. *Manufacturers' Life Insurance Co.* [1963] 2 Q.B. 352.

government for direct enforcement of that government's currency control regulations would be contrary to the principle of non-enforcement of foreign revenue laws.[92]

6. ENFORCEMENT MUST RELATE TO A MONEY JUDGMENT

As a general rule, enforcement will only be available in respect of money judgments and not, for example, in respect of an injunction to prevent the defendant from breaching a covenant[93] in an international loan agreement.   **2.51**

Where judgment is obtained from a court within a Contracting State under the 1968 Convention

The jurisdictional provisions of the Brussels Convention on Jurisdiction and Enforcement of Judgments were discussed earlier in this chapter.[94] and here our attention will focus on those provisions of the Convention relating to recognition and enforcement of judgments. These provisions are remarkably liberal and are designed "to allow judgments given in one Contracting State to run freely throughout the Community."[95] The provisions are not limited to money judgments[96] but extend to any form of judgment or order, including injunctions and orders for specific performance which fall within the scope of the Convention.[97]   **2.52**

This is obviously a significant departure from the traditional principles of recognition and enforcement under common law and statute and will be particularly important where the enforcement of non-monetary obligations under an international banking agreement fall to be considered. Another significant departure under the Convention is that (subject to certain limitations described below) the court in which enforcement is sought has no power to investigate the jurisdiction of the foreign court which originally gave judgment,[98] nor (subject to what is said below in para. 2.56) review the merits of the judgment.[99] It will be for the original court to determine whether or not it has jurisdiction and once determined its decision cannot be called into question.

THE DEFENDANT NEED NOT BE DOMICILED IN THE E.E.C.

An important principle to bear in mind is that the enforcement provisions of the Convention apply to all judgments falling within its scope, whether or not such judgments are against persons domiciled or ordinarily resident in a Contracting State. As we have already seen[1] most of the jurisdictional bases under the Convention relate only to persons "domiciled" in a Contracting   **2.53**

---

[92] *Re Lord Cable* [1977] 1 W.L.R. 7, p. 13; but *cf. Kahler v. Midland Bank Limited* [1950] A.C. 24, p. 46.
[93] On breach of covenants generally, see Chap. 6 below.
[94] See para. 2.12 above.
[95] Morris, p. 130.
[96] *Ibid.*
[97] Art. 1. As to the interpretation of what is covered, see Art. 25.
[98] Art. 28.
[99] Art. 29.
[1] See paras. 2.12 and 2.13 above.

State. This restriction does not apply to the enforcement of judgments and, therefore, if an exorbitant or extended basis of jurisdiction is utilised by the courts of a Contracting State[2] against a defendant domiciled outside the E.E.C. a judgment against such a defendant will be enforced throughout the E.E.C.[3]

Recognition

2.54 The fundamental provision relating to recognition can be found in Article 26 of the Convention which provides: 'A judgment given in a Contracting State shall be recognised in the other Contracting States without any special procedure being required.' A request for recognition or enforcement must be supported by an authenticated copy of the judgment and in cases where the judgment has been given in default it must be established that the party in default was served with process.[4] Likewise, a party applying for enforcement must establish, according to the law of the State in which judgment was given, that the judgment is enforceable and has been effectively served upon the defendant.[5]

ENFORCEMENT BY REGISTRATION

2.55 Enforcement in the United Kingdom is by way of registration[6] in the High Court[7] and because the application for registration is made *ex parte*[8] the defendant is not informed of the proceedings and has no right to be heard. This latter requirement enables the plaintiff to preserve the element of surprise and, hopefully, prevents the defendant's assets from being spirited out of the jurisdiction before an attachment order can be made. However, once enforcement has been authorised the defendant is promptly notified[9] and may apply to the High Court to set aside the registration.[10]

GROUNDS FOR REFUSAL

2.56 The grounds on which recognition or enforcement may be refused are set out under Articles 27 and 28. Article 27 provides that a judgment shall not be recognised:

1. if such recognition is contrary to public policy in the State in which recognition is sought;

2. where it was given in default of appearance, if the defendant was not duly served with the document which instituted the proceedings or with an

---

[2] *e.g.* jurisdiction in France based on nationality or in England based on temporary presence.
[3] It would be rather more correct to state that enforcement would be permissible in any other Contracting State.
[4] Art. 46.
[5] Art. 47.
[6] s.4, Civil Jurisdiction and Judgments Act 1982 (C.J.J.A.); see also Art. 31(2) of the Brussels Convention.
[7] s.4(1), (C.J.J.A.).
[8] Art. 34(1).
[9] Art. 35.
[10] Thereafter the defendant has one more right of appeal, but only on a point of law; Arts. 36 and 37.

equivalent document in sufficient time to enable him to arrange for his defence;

3. if the judgment is irreconcilable with a judgment given in a dispute between the same parties in the State in which recognition is sought;

4. if the court of the State in which the judgment was given, in order to arrive at its judgment, has decided a preliminary question concerning the status or legal capacity of natural persons, rights in property arising out of a matrimonial relationship, wills or succession in a way that conflicts with a rule of private international law of the State in which the recognition is sought, unless the same result would have been reached by the application of the rules of private international law of that State;

5. if the judgment is irreconcilable with an earlier judgment given in a non-Contracting State involving the same cause of action and between the same parties, provided that this latter judgment fulfils the conditions necessary for its recognition in the State addressed.

There is no specific provision in the Convention for refusal based upon the ground that the original judgment was obtained by fraud. Under civil law systems this ground is subsumed within the head of public policy and it would appear that in dealing with the Convention English courts will follow civil law jurisprudence in this respect.[11]

Conclusion

Insofar as international banking transactions are concerned, lenders will obviously be well advised to investigate the position relating to recognition and enforcement in the borrower's own jurisdiction and in those jurisdictions where the borrower's assets are situated. These questions should be addressed before any agreement is executed, and the advice of local lawyers will normally be required to confirm the position. As we have seen, the rules can be very complex, but providing appropriate precautions are taken it should be possible for a lending bank to take advantage of the relevant provisions relating to recognition and enforcement of foreign judgments. **2.57**

[11] See Morris p. 132.

3. Sovereign Risk[1]

3.01 Sovereign risk is one aspect of Country Risk, which refers to the assessment of the risk of default by a borrower in a particular country. Country Risk has regard to a large number of risk factors, including war, occupation by foreign powers, civil war, insurrection, revolution, riots, disorders, take-overs by extremist governments, politically motivated default, renegotiation or rescheduling, unilateral changes in debt servicing terms by governmental borrowers, state take-overs of the borrowing enterprise, natural disasters, depression or recession, mismanagement of the economy, credit squeezes, rises in production costs, falls in export earnings, balance of payments problems and exchange controls imposed by reason of suddenly occurring events such as increases in the cost of energy imports, overextension in external borrowings, and devaluation or depreciation of the currency (to name a few).

Our concern in this work is with the legal aspects of sovereign risk, and it must be appreciated that these affect not only sovereign borrowers, (which includes state controlled entities) but also private borrowers who may be affected by sovereign actions such as expropriation of property, or the imposition of exchange controls. We shall use the term "state" to include both the state and entities inseparable from the state, such as departments of the central government. We shall consider the matter under the following headings:

A. Changes in the law of the state in question with particular attention being paid to:
   (a) Expropriation (either confiscations or moratoria)
   (b) Exchange controls (although this is dealt with in a different chapter.)[2]
B. Sovereign immunity
C. Recognition of states
D. State succession

A. CHANGES IN THE LAW OF THE STATE IN QUESTION

3.02 Whether the borrower is a state or private borrower, the loan contract may be effected by changes in the law of the borrower's state. Those changes may be introduced by a state borrower to protect itself, or by the state to protect private borrowers (moratoria, reductions of interest rates, cancellation of maintenance of value clauses), or by the state to afflict private borrowers or lenders (withholding taxes, confiscation, expropriation, etc.). In earlier chapters of this work, we have observed the rules governing the

---

[1] See generally, Wood. Chap. 4; Gruson and Reisner (ed.) chaps. 7–9; Kalderan and Siddigi (ed.) pp. 144–155. For an excellent exposition of country risk from risk analysis viewpoint, see Calverley, *Country Risk Analysis* (ed. 1985).
[2] Below, Chap. 4.

proper law applicable to the contract, and we have seen that the proper law governs most aspects of the contract, and in particular, matters relating to performance, breach, and discharge.[3] If, therefore, a state attempts to change its laws so as to excuse itself from breach, or to change the terms of its obligations, or to discharge its obligations entirely, then whether this is effective is a matter for the proper law of the contract. If the proper law of the contract is the law of the state in question, then a change in the law is effective. These propositions are illustrated by *R. v. International Trustee*[4] where a change in the proper law (New York) was held to be effective to abrogate certain "gold clauses" in a British bond issue. Similarly, in *Re Helbert Wagg & Co. Ltd.*[5] where the agreement was governed by German law, a change in that proper law requiring repayment to be made in German currency to a German custodian was effective to override the contractual provisions for repayment in sterling in London. It is for this reason that lenders should attempt to insulate themselves from changes in the law of the borrower's state by either expressly choosing some other law, or by arranging matters so that there is an implied choice of another law, or so that objectively some other law applies.[6]

If, however, the proper law is not that of the state in question (which we shall refer to as the defaulting state, whether the state itself, or a resident or national, is the borrower) then the general rule is that changes in its law have no legal effect on the loan agreement (though different problems concerning legal immunity from suit, or the practicalities of enforcement, may then arise). This proposition is illustrated by the two Bank of Greece cases[7] (where the Greek government failed to remove the liability of certain bank debtors whose agreements were governed by English law).

There are, however, exceptions to the general rule that the proper law **3.03** determines the effect of changes in law of the borrower or lender's state: the most important of these exceptions are as follows:

1. Regardless of the proper law, an English court will enforce a mandatory domestic law of the U.K.[8]

2. If English law is the proper law, an English court will recognise and defer to laws imposed in the place of performance.[9] (If English law is not the proper law, the proper law would probably be applied).

3. If there is a knowing and conspiratorial attempt to evade the laws of a foreign and friendly country, public policy may prevent the recognition of the agreement.[10] (This would not apply to laws subsequent to the agreement, or to inadvertent contraventions).

4. Where property is concerned, English proper law defers to the law of the state in which the property is situated, and may recognise an expropria-

---

[3] Above.
[4] [1937] All E.R. 167, discussed above, Chap. 1.
[5] [1956] 1 Ch. 323, discussed above, Chap. 1.
[6] For a further discussion of how the lender may attempt to insulate the loan agreement, see Chap. 1, above.
[7] *National Bank of Greece v. Metliss* [1958] A.C. 509; *Adams v. National Bank of Greece* [1961] A.C. 255 already discussed in Chap. 1, and further considered below.
[8] *Boissevain v. Weil* [1950] A.C. 327.
[9] *Ralli Bros v. Companie Naviera Sota y Aznar* [1920] 2 K.B. 287. See also *Kahler v. Midland Bank Ltd.* [1950] A.C. 24, and *Zivonstenska Banka v. Frankman* [1950] A.C. 57.
[10] See, *e.g. Regazzoni v. K. C. Sethia* [1958] A.C. 301.

tion of property. There may be a departure from this exception, inasmuch as certain penal, tax-gathering, or morally repugnant actions or laws may not be recognised even in that case.[11]

5. Certain procedural remedies, involving the co-operation of foreign courts, may be refused by an English court.

6. If a state effectively abolishes a legal entity, or takes measures which otherwise affect its capacity to be sued, this may be effective, these being matters for the law of the domicile or place of incorporation of the borrower.

7. Statutes of limitation may have some effect (imposing time limits after which debts may not be enforced).

8. Exchange Controls may be recognised by an English court.

The first three of these have been largely considered elsewhere, and in this chapter we shall consider the last four of these, in turn, leaving Exchange Controls for Chapter 4 in this volume.

Expropriations

3.04   If the expropriation is of the loan agreement itself (as where a moratorium is declared) the question of whether the change is effective will be determined by the proper law.

If the moratorium is of property, the question generally depends on where the property is situated. Most nations recognise the futility of attempting to insist upon legal rights over property which is within the territory of another state, when that state denies the existence of those rights. One can distinguish between property inside the state at the time of expropriation, property outside the state at the time of expropriation, and property originally inside the state at the time of expropriation which is afterwards removed. The first and last of these are subject to the same principles.

A. PROPERTY INSIDE THE STATE, WHETHER OR NOT SUBSEQUENTLY REMOVED

3.05   The general rule is that English law recognises an expropriation of property within the territory of a state at the time of the expropriation. In *Luther* v. *Sagor*[12] the court recognised the nationalisation by the Russian government of timber situated in Russia. In *Princess Paley Olga* v. *Weisz*[13] the expropriation of personal property (paintings) was recognised. In both of these cases the action was brought unsuccessfully against a person claiming to have acquired title subsequent to the expropriation, who had afterwards taken the property out of the state in question. A more recent decision is *Williams & Humbert Ltd.* v. *W. & H. Trade Marks (Jersey) Ltd.*[14] (the "*Rumasa* case")

[11] Below, paras. 3.04 *et seq.*
[12] [1921] 3 K.B. 532.
[13] [1929] 1 K.B. 718.
[14] [1985] 2 All E.R. 619.

where a Spanish company controlled shares in other companies, including (i) an English company (*W & H*) which held licenses from a Jersey company, and (ii) a Dutch company. The Spanish government expropriated shares in the Spanish company, thus obtaining control over the companies which it controlled. The Jersey company then terminated the licenses which it had given to company *W & H*, claiming to be entitled to do so by its contract. In this action, the question arose whether the plaintiff company (*W & H*) could sue, and also whether the Dutch company was now owned by the Spanish government (as owner of the shares in the parent Spanish company). The defendants (the Jersey company and others) argued that the English court should not recognise the expropriations of the shares in the Spanish company, as this was an attempt to enforce in England an expropriatory law. The House of Lords upheld the decisions of the lower courts, confirming the effectiveness of the expropriations, and the ownership by the Spanish government of the shares in the Spanish company. It made no difference that ownership of Spanish property (the shares) produced effects outside of Spain (these effects being ownership of the Dutch company and the right to sue for breach of contract as owner of *W & H*, the English company). Compulsory acquisition, held the court, was universally recognised and practised, and an English court would recognise the foreign acquisition law in respect of title to property under the control of that state, and it would also recognise the consequences of that change of title. It would not consider the merits of compulsory acquisition.

B. EXPROPRIATION OF PROPERTY NOT IN THE JURISDICTION OF THE EXPROPRIATING STATE

The general rule here is that the expropriation is ineffective. In *Banco de Vizcaya* v. *Don Alfonso de Borbon y Austria*[15] a London bank held bonds and other securities (deposited by the King of Spain) to the order of the bank's Madrid branch. The King ordered the London branch to hold to the order of the Bank of Vizcaya. He was then declared a traitor by the new Spanish government, and his property was expropriated, and Spanish banks were ordered to deliver up property to the Spanish government. The Bank of Vizcaya then requested the London branch to surrender the property, and this action arose. The court held that the King was entitled to the property, as, being outside Spain, it was not subject to Spanish jurisdiction. The expropriatory laws of Spain were local to Spain, affecting only property situated there. Similarly, in *Bank Voor Handel en Sheepvart NV* v. *Slatford*[16] a requisition by the Dutch government of gold held in London was not recognised.

A particular problem arises with "ambulatory" property, such as ships and aircraft. While this is subject to some doubt, the rule may be that such property (say, a ship) cannot be expropriated if at the time it is in an English port,[17] but that an expropriation occurring while the ship is on the high seas

3.06

---

[15] [1935] 1 K.B. 140.
[16] [1953] 1 Q.B. 248.
[17] *Govt. of Republic of Spain* v. *National Bank of Scotland Ltd.* [1939] S.C. 413.

and where its port of registry is in the expropriating country, will be recognised.[18] This distinction seems unsatisfactory, especially given that many ships are registered in places with which their owners have no real connection, and the better rule may be that expropriations should not be recognised except for property within the control of the expropriating state.

3.07   A further problem arises in those cases where a state attempts to expropriate a debt or chose in action. In the *Rumasa* case,[19] the property expropriated was a chose in action: *i.e.* the rights attaching to shares in a Spanish registered company. It seems undoubtedly correct that such a chose should be held to be situated in Spain. The question arises, however, as to the location of debts not so clearly situated. The English view seems to be that the debt is "situated" in the place where it is required to be paid. That place may be specified, but otherwise it would be where the debtor is resident. In *Ralli Bros.* v *Compania Naviera Sota y Aznar*[20] a contract was governed by English law, but provided for payment in Spain. A change in Spanish law affected the amount payable, and the English court would enforce only the amount so limited, as that owing in the place of performance. English law thus defers to the law of the place of payment of a debt. Similarly, in *International Corporation Ltd.* v. *Besser Manufacturing Co. Ltd.*[21] the place of payment of a commission was England, and when non-payment occurred, it was held that the place of breach was in the place where payment should have been made (that being so, an English court had the discretionary jurisdiction available under R.S.C. Ord. 11). In a recent American case (*Allied Bank International* v. *Banco Credito Agricola de Cartago*)[22] the *situs* of a debt was also held to be the place of payment. In this important case, three Costa Rican banks were wholly owned by the Government of Costa Rica, and were subject to Central Bank direction. They issued promissory notes to Allied Bank, payable in New York. In 1981 the Central Bank of Costa Rica suspended all external debt payments and the government made it illegal to pay these without the consent of the Central Bank. Allied Bank sued in New York, and an appeal court held that the property being outside Costa Rica, it was not subject to the "Act of State" doctrine (which resembles the English rule on expropriations, and which will be considered in greater detail later in this chapter).[23] Similarly, in *Braka* v. *Bancomer SNC*,[24] U.S. dollar certificates of deposit issued by Bancomer were held to be situated where Bancomer was—in Mexico. When Bancomer was nationalised by the Mexican government, and afterwards was prohibited from paying in U.S. dollars (it could pay only in Pesos at an artificial exchange rate) Braka sued, but again the Act of state doctrine applied. It is thought that the result would have been the same had similar facts arisen in England. The "*situs*" of

---

[18] *The Jupiter* [1924] P. 236.
[19] Above, para. 3.05.
[20] [1920] 2 K.B. 287.
[21] [1950] 1 K.B. 488.
[22] 566 F.Supp. 1440 (SDNY 1983), aff'd on other grounds 733 F.2d. 23(2d. Cir. 1984), w'drawn, reserved on rehearing 757 F.2d. 516 (2d. Cir. 1984), petition for certioriari filed July 26 1985, No. 85–146, petition dismissed September 23, 1985. See Penn, "Legal issues arising from the Costa Rica debts Cases," [1985] J.B.L. 347.
[23] Below, para. 3.15.
[24] 589, F.Supp. 1465 (SDNY) aff'd 762 F.2d. 222 (2nd. Cir. 1985).

the debt is the place of performance—payment—and where English law is the proper law, it defers to the law of the place of performance.

3.08

The cases just mentioned, however, are all cases where the contract provided for payment in a particular place. If it does not do so, then the *situs* of the debt is the place where the debt (a chose in action) may be recovered by legal action: that is either the place where the debtor is resident[25] or (more likely in a Eurocurrency loan) where according to the contract, repayment can be demanded. If the debtor has more than one residence, then, supposing that there is no express or implied agreement as to the place of payment, the appropriate place is that place at which the money would be expected to be paid in the ordinary course of business.[26]

This gives rise to a difficult problem, since payment in a given currency may perhaps (by usage, and possibly by law) be able to be demanded only in the "home" jurisdiction of that currency. Thus, payment in sterling may perhaps only be demanded in the U.K. and payment in U.S. dollars can only be demanded in the U.S. Suppose that debts payable in place *A* are payable in the currency of country *B*. In this case "payment" in country *A* may really mean only the crediting of an account there, and a powerful argument may be that the true place of performance—the place of payment of the debt—is (expressly, or impliedly) place *B*, in which case an expropriation in place *B* might be effective.[27] At the time of writing, the question is unresolved by judicial decision, though it may shortly be resolved by the case of *Libyan Arab Foreign Bank*, discussed shortly. Despite the logical attractions of the proposition just mentioned—that "payment" must be in the country of the currency—it may be that the courts will not be disposed to accept it. It might be, instead, that the courts will feel that more acceptable results would be reached if the place of "payment" and the situs of the debt were regarded as being in that place where, if either actual cash payment or the crediting of an account does not occur, the effect would be that there would be a breach of contract. In other words, place of "payment" may possibly be treated as equivalent to place of "performance," so that if there is payment there or the crediting of an account, the contract is performed and there is no breach. If a contract requires that an account in country *A* be credited, then certainly a breach of contract occurs in country *A*, if the account is not credited. This is the case whether the currency to be credited is that of country *A* or of country *B*. An additional reason for this conclusion may be that it seems clear that (if one considers Eurodollar accounts kept in London, for example) there are some quantities of dollars kept in London, so that in some cases at least, payment in dollars is feasible. There has also, it seems, been a substantial U.S. Dollar Clearing Scheme in operation in London since 1975, involving many millions of dollars each day "for the presentation and settlement of retail U.S. dollar cheques and similar items drawn on bank branches in the U.K.[28] The extent of this practice is as yet unclear. It seems that balances may be traded between

---

[25] *Jabbour* v. *Custodian of Absentee's Property of State of Israel* [1954] 1 All E.R. 145.
[26] *Ibid.*, 151–152.
[27] See Goode [1987] 3 J.I.B.L., Mann, *The Legal Aspect of Money* (4th ed., 1982) 193–195.
[28] Evidence given by the Chief Inspector of the Banker's Clearing House in *Libyan Arab Foreign Bank* v. *Bankers Trust Co.* (the decision in this case was unreported at the time of writing).

banks, but it seems hardly conceivable that accounts are not credited and debited accordingly in the U.S.

3.09   Generally, however, loans are made payable in a particular place in the currency of that place, so that in the context of term loans, and other contractual agreements of that nature, the problem may rarely arise in practice. This point should be particularly noticed. To this extent, the problem here mentioned will not commonly arise.

The whole matter is presently the subject of litigation in England, expected to come to trial in June 1987. The litigation arises from an action brought by the Libyan Arab Foreign Bank (LAFB) against Bankers Trust Co. The plaintiffs had a deposit account denominated in U.S. dollars at the London Branch of the defendant bank, which was an American bank with their head office in New York and a branch in London. In 1986 the President of the United States made two executive orders which purported to block bank accounts in the U.S. or held by American banks abroad, if those accounts were owned or controlled by the Central Bank of Libya. It seemed that the defendant banks would be committing criminal offences under U.S. law if they were to act in disregard of those executive orders. In April 1986 the account was in credit to the extent of about $131 million, and the plaintiffs demanded payment in London either in cash or by negotiable banker's draft in U.S. dollars payable to LAFB or their order. The defendant did not pay, and a writ was issued. At first instance, summary judgment was given for the plaintiff, on the ground that the defendants had no real defence. But the Court of Appeal allowed the appeal, and ordered that the issues be tried. The main legal questions involved were (a) whether the executive orders were any defence (it was accepted that they gave a defence only if American law was the proper law or if compliance with the demand for payment required some act within the U.S. which would be illegal by American law), and (b) whether demands for payment or transfer of funds in Eurodollar accounts were, as a matter of practice, executed only in the U.S. after clearing there through CHIPS[29] and if so, whether that practice applied to all U.S. dollar dominated accounts in this country, and in either case, whether the practice gave rise to any legal rule concerning the method by which the defendants' obligations to the plaintiffs should be discharged. The trial judge based himself throughout on the premise that a bank account is located solely at the branch where it is kept, and that a demand for payment, including in particular payment in cash, must be made to, and executed by, that branch. On the appeal from his judgment, the Court of Appeal noted that "this premise may well beg the question" since the authorities which had discussed the matter were concerned with accounts denominating in sterling, or whatever was the local currency of legal tender. It did not follow that the same principles necessarily apply to banking operations in relation to accounts denominated in a foreign currency and "it is clear that they do not apply to Eurodollar accounts which are properly so called, at any rate as a matter of banking practices which may well have the effect of usages with legal consequences." The Court of Appeal, therefore, left the question open for future determination.

---

[29] Clearing House Inter Bank Payments System.

A further complication may be added to the arguments already considered. It may be[30] that an expropriation has a different effect than a temporary moratorium or "freezing" of the debt payment. The former is clearly regarded as a matter for the *lex situs*, since it concerns the forced transfer of a proprietory right. But the latter does not involve the transfer of proprietory rights, and amounts merely to a breach of contract, which is a question for the proper law. This argument has much force, although in the *Allied Bank* case already referred to,[30a] the American court decided the case—which was a "freezing" case—on the basis of the *"situs"* of the debt. However, first, the case involved payment in New York in U.S. dollars, and secondly, it may be that the case is distinguishable on the grounds that the American "act of State" doctrine (discussed below) differs from the English position. In *Braka* v. *Bancomer SNC*,[31] payment was in Mexico in U.S. dollars. The case involved neither an expropriation nor a "freezing" but a change in the currency of payment (a breach of contract) and the change was effective. The decision was again based on the *situs* of the debt. The case resembles the *Ralli Bros.* case,[32] where Spain made an effective alteration to the amount of payment (though that involved payment in Spain in pesetas). English law was the proper law, and deferred to the place of payment and of the currency.[33]

3.10

It is thought that there are different problems involved, which require to be more clearly differentiated. Since debts are treated as property, then when an expropriation is in question, as with other property one must determine the *situs* of the property in order to determine the effect of an expropriation. But it may be that a different solution applies to a freezing order if there is a branch of the defendant debtor bank in the U.K. A freezing order does not involve a change of owner, but is merely a bar upon payment.

3.11

First, it may be that country B attempts to freeze a debt owed to a lender, and payable in country B in the currency of country B. In that case, if the law of the contract is that of country B, the order is effective. If the law of the contract is English law (England not being country B) then the order is effective, in the sense that the *Ralli Bros.* case[34] indicates that under a contract governed by English law, an English court will not require a person to do an act which is illegal in the place where that act is to be performed. Conversely, no English attachment (freezing) order would be given by the courts in these circumstances, since the order would have extraterritorial effect.

Secondly, it may be that country B attempts to freeze a debt owed to a lender, and payable in country B in the currency of country A. If the governing law of the contract is that of country B, the order is effective. If the contract is governed by English law then it would seem that the order is still effective, in the sense that an English court would not, in the face of the freezing order, require the bank in country B, where the account is credited,

---

[30] As is argued by Goode, *loc. cit.*, above, n. 27.
[30a] Above, para. 3.07.
[31] Above, para. 3.07.
[32] Above, para. 3.07.
[33] The *situs* of the debt is discussed also by Cashel [1986] 1 J.I.B.L. 30, at pp. 37–40.
[34] Above, para. 3.07.

to arrange any transfer or form of payment for the account holder, even if that bank had an English branch which could be the subject of an order. The English court would not order the performance in country B of acts illegal in that country.

Thirdly, it may be that country B attempts to freeze a debt owed to a lender and payable in country A in the currency of country A. In this case, the order will be ignored by an English court unless the contract is governed by the law of country B.

3.12   Fourthly, it may be that country B attempts to freeze a debt owed to a lender and payable in country A in the currency of country B. Again, if the contract is governed by the law of country B, this is effective. But if it is not so governed, the question for an English court, under the *Ralli Bros.* principle, must simply be "are any acts to be performed in country B by any person which under the law of country B are illegal?" If so, the English court will not require those acts to be done. That is to say, the "situs" of the debt is irrelevant, as is the question of "place of payment." The only question which is relevant is whether acts have to be done in country B which are illegal. Whether those acts amount to "payment" or "performance" is neither here nor there. It follows that the correct solution to the problem posed by the *Libyan Bank* case is, in our view, to determine simply whether any acts had to be done in the U.S. which were illegal by U.S. law. It is not necessary to determine whether the U.S. is, or is not, the place of payment. What seems certain is that the U.K. is the place of "performance" of the contract, since the contractual obligation was to take whatever steps were necessary (including, it may be, the performance of acts in the U.S.) so as to secure the crediting of an account in the U.K. In determining if the bank holding the deposit was in breach, the question (it is submitted) is not, "what was the place of payment," but (if this is different) "what was the place of performance." And clearly, the final place of performance is the U.K. since that is where the account had to be credited. But it is not an answer to the question posed in the *Libyan Bank* case to say that the U.K. is the place of performance, since it may still be that in order to secure performance (crediting of a U.K. account) in England, acts have to be done in the U.S. (credit transfers there) which are illegal under English law, and which English law will not insist upon, under the principle in the *Ralli Bros.* case. In other words, one must distinguish between the final contractual performance (*i.e.* the result which is specified under the contract) and the acts of performance needed to bring about that result. Some acts of performance may need to be done in the U.S. in order to bring about the final contractual performance in the U.K. The "place of performance" may involve both the U.S. and the U.K.

It ought to be observed that it is an unresolved matter whether the *Ralli Bros* principle[34a] applies only where English law is the proper law, or whether it applies in any case where an illegal act must be done in a place of "performance." If, say, the contract is governed by the law of C, and country B (place of performance) makes an act illegal, it may be that an English court, England not being country C, would enforce the contract.

Finally, it may be remarked that an English court certainly could attach

[34a] Above, para. 3.07.

(freeze) an account held in England but denominated in a foreign currency. The order nisi requires the bank not to pay except as directed by the court, and there is no reason why such an order should not be made. It may be that an order absolute, directing the bank to pay some third party, may involve complications if a contrary order, affecting a branch of that bank in the country of the currency concerned, was to be made in that country.

Summary

So far as one can say with any certainly, the position, overall, would seem **3.13** to be as follows:

(i) Expropriations of tangible property situated in a state are subject to the laws of the state, while property situated outside the state is unaffected by changes in the law of that state.

(ii) Expropriations of debts are governed by the law of the place where the debt is situated, and if payment is in the currency of the place of payment, the *situs* of the debt is the place of payment,

(iii) but if an account in one place is to be credited in the currency of another place, it is an unresolved question whether the *situs* of the debt is the place at which the account is to be credited, or the country of the currency, and it may well be the latter place.

(iv) If a freezing order is made (a temporary moratorium), or there is an alteration in the amount of the debt, or a change in the currency of payment, this may be a matter of breach, which is primarily a matter for the proper law, and the *"situs"* of the debt may be irrelevant (though the *Allied Bank*, and *Bancomer* cases[34b] suggest otherwise). But English law, if the proper law, still defers to the place of performance, and where the currency of payment is the same as that of the place of final performance, English law defers to that. If, however, the currency is not that of the place of payment, then it seems probable (if English law governs the contract) that the question for a court ought to be whether any acts leading to the final performance of the contractual obligation have to be carried out in the country which has imposed the moratorium (in which case English courts would recognise the efficacy of the freezing order).

Exceptions to the general rule

There are exceptions to the general rule that expropriations of property are **3.14** recognised where the property is within the control of the expropriating state. These exceptions exist where the provision in question is morally repugnant, or where an attempt is made in England to enforce a foreign revenue or penal provision. An example of a morally repugnant provision occurred in *Frankfurther* v. *W. L. Exner Ltd.*[35] where a Nazi decree expelled the Jewish plaintiff from the operation of a business in Austria. The English

---

[34b] Above, para. 3.07.
[35] [1947] 1 Ch. 629.

court considered both the purpose of the decree and its terms, and refused to recognise it. The courts in the *Rumasa* case[36] agreed that such legislation, affecting human rights, would not be given effect here.

That English courts will not enforce foreign revenue provisions is shown by *Peter Buchanan Ltd. & Macharg* v. *McVey*[37] where McVey removed himself and all assets of a company from Scotland to Northern Ireland, so as to avoid tax. The tax being unpaid, the Revenue attempted to have the company wound up, and the liquidator sued McVey in Northern Ireland, in order to recover the money owing on the assets, etc. The court refused to permit the action, on the ground that the only creditor was the Revenue, and that this was a disguised attempt by the Revenue to enforce the Scottish revenue debts. The only purpose of this action was to enforce the revenue debts, even though the company under its new controller, the liquidator, otherwise had a perfectly valid cause of action against McVey. The decision may be distinguished from the *Rumasa* case,[37a] where the new controller of the company (the Spanish government) merely wished to enforce a broken contract, and was not enforcing revenue or penal provisions. The *Rumasa* case recognised the principle in question, but the House of Lords pointed out that the proceedings were not an attempt to enforce Spanish law, but to enforce the English law of contract. It was not an attempt indirectly to enforce here penal Spanish expropriatory laws, because first it was doubtful that those laws were "penal," and secondly, the argument ignored the separate legal personality of the company and its shareholders, and thirdly (as previously discussed) English courts generally recognised expropriations by states of property within their jurisdictions. The defendants attacked the motives of the Spanish legislation, and alleged oppression, questioning good faith. No English judge could properly entertain such an attack on a friendly state.[38]

It seems clear, therefore, that the circumstances must be similar to those in either *McVey's* case (no other creditors than the Revenue), or those in *Frankfurther's* case (morally repugnant law), failing which expropriations will generally be recognised. The decision of a court in Aden (governed by English common law) that a nationalisation decree should not be recognised because it contravened international law[39] would seem insupportable.[40]

3.15   Mention has already been made of the United States "Act of State Doctrine."[41] This resembles the United Kingdom doctrines discussed, but has significant differences. Essentially, the doctrine states that the U.S. courts will not review or question any act of state done by a state and having effect within its own jurisdiction. "Every sovereign State is bound to respect the independence of every other sovereign State and the courts of one country

---

[36] Above, para. 3.05.

[37] [1956] A.C. 516.

[37a] Above, para. 3.05.

[38] See also *Settebello Ltd.* v. *Banco Totta & Acores*, below para. 3.17, where reference was made to the principle of "comity" in a similar kind of case.

[39] Not providing for compensation.

[40] *The Mary Rose* [1953] 1 W.L.R. 246.

[41] For an illuminating discussion, see Cashel [1986] 1 J.I.B.L. 30. See also Carstan, *Banking on the Act of State* (ed. 1985).

will not sit in judgment on the acts of the government of another done within its own territory." (*Underhill* v. *Hernandez*).[42] For example, in *Bernstein* v. *Van Heyghan Freres* S.A.[43] the plaintiff was forced by the Nazis in Germany to sign over his property to a Nazi nominee. The property in question was a ship, and when the ship was sunk, the plaintiff made a claim upon the insurance policy covering such loss. The U.S. court refused to consider the question of duress, because what had been done was an official act of another state. This may be contrasted with the U.K. attitude, as shown by the *Frankfurther* case.[44] It must be observed that the doctrine does not apply if a state expropriates property outside its own borders, although even there, the U.S. courts will recognise such an expropriation if directed to do so by the U.S. government. In the *Allied Bank case*,[45] the lower court in New York at first applied the Act of State doctrine to justify the acts of Costa Rica, but that was reversed on appeal, since the debts were held to be located outside Costa Rica, while in *Bancomer* case the doctrine applied, since the debts were located in Mexico. It is obvious that U.S. decisions based on the Act of State doctrine are not entirely appropriate precedents for English decisions, which (at least in "freezing" or change of terms cases) are more concerned with the application of Conflicts principles, and with the proper law of the contract. The English rules concerning the deprivation of property within the state do, however, resemble the U.S. doctrine.

There are two main exceptions to the Act of State doctrine. First, there is an exception referred to in the *Bernstein case*,[46] which may be described as the "Bernstein exception." This allows the U.S. courts to question foreign legislation or state acts if the U.S. government informs the courts that the application of the doctrine will not advance U.S. foreign policy. The second exception is known as the "Hickenlooper amendment" and is to the effect that the U.S. courts adjudicate where a foreign state expropriates property in violation of international law. International law requires broadly that (i) the expropriation should be for a public purpose, and (ii) that it is accompanied by prompt, adequate and effective compensation. The case of *The Mary Rose*, criticised above, and decided in Aden, would have been an apt application of the U.S. of State doctrine, but seems insupportable in English law. The extent of the international law exception is debatable, and in *Banco Nacional de Cuba* v. *Sabbatino*[47] the doctrine was held applicable even though a confiscation of property violated customary international law. It is possible that there is a third exception: the case of *Alfred Dunhill of London Inc* v. *Republic of Cuba*[48] gives some indication that the doctrine might not be applied where a commercial activity was involved (in line with the general distinction between "State" and "commercial" activities). But this avenue was not explored in the *Bancomer* or *Allied Bank* cases.[49]

3.16

---

[42] 168 U.S. 250 (1897). This is taken to be the "classic" statement of the doctrine.
[43] 163 F. 2d. 246 (1947).
[44] Above, para. 3.14.
[45] Above, para. 3.07.
[46] Above, para. 3.15.
[47] 376 U.S. 378, 425 (1964).
[48] 425 U.S. 682 (1976).
[49] Or in *Callejo* v. *Bancomer* SA 764 F. 2d. 1101, 1125 (5th. Cir. 1985).

Availability of procedural remedies

3.17   In *Settebello Ltd.* v. *Banco Totta & Acores*[50] a Portuguese company had a contract with an external customer. The Portuguese government issued a decree which enabled companies to suspend for two years any right which their customers had to cancel any contracts exceeding one billion Escudos in value. The plaintiffs claimed that this decree should not be enforced because it was discriminatory (like the morally repugnant cases already referred to). In order to show this, they required evidence from Portugal, and they applied to an English court for a procedural order (Letters of Request) which would ask the Portuguese judicial authorities to help the plaintiffs acquire such evidence. It is hardly strange that the English Court of Appeal declined to ask the Portuguese judiciary to assist in producing evidence designed to show that the laws of Portugal were discriminatory and unjust, and should not be enforced in England. No such procedural remedy would be given, and in this sense the court gave effect to the act of a friendly state. The court indicated that it might have done otherwise had the Portuguese decree failed to reach civilised standards, or was abhorrent on its nature. If, of course, the contract had been governed by English law, then the contract having merely been broken by the Portuguese company, the plaintiffs could have sued in England, since the Portuguese decree would have given no defence. The contracts being governed by Portuguese law, the Change in the law was effective, unless "morally repugnant" as already described.

Changes made to the capacity of an organisation to be sued

3.18   A familiar example of the problem occurs in the U.K. when a receiver acting under a floating charge, or a liquidator, takes control of an insolvent company, sets up a new company, transfers the assets of the old company to the new in return for shares in the new, and then sells the new, debt free, company at a reasonable price. Since we accept this kind of thing domestically, it should not be remarkable that it or something like it is also effective internationally, to divest a borrower of either his assets or his liabilities.

If, therefore, a state wishes to rid its domestic borrower of onerous debts, it may transfer all of the assets of the borrower to another company (such an expropriation being recognised by U.K. courts) and then either wind up the borrower or allow its creditors to proceed against it in fruitless insolvency proceedings. Merely instructing the borrower not to pay will be insufficient, for non-payment is a breach, governed by the proper law. Alternatively, the state can cause the merger of the original borrower with another company, causing the legal existence of the original borrower to cease. Unless the obligations of the original borrower are transferred to the new entity, there would remain no one to be sued.

Inept examples of a state's attempt to achieve something along these lines occurred in the *Bank of Greece* cases. In *National Bank of Greece* v. *Metliss*[51]

---

[50] [1985] 1 W.L.R. 1050. See Penn, *The Principle of International Comity—A Developing Threat to International Commerce* (1984) 14 C.L.B. 2.

[51] [1958] A.C. 509.

bank A issued bonds guaranteed by bank B, and made certain other borrowings. Both banks were Greek banks. In 1949 the Greek government imposed a moratorium suspending payments under the bonds, and also relieving the guarantors of liability to pay. In 1953 the government made a decree (a) dissolving B bank, (b) amalgamating it with another bank to form the National Bank, and (c) providing that the National Bank succeeded to B's rights and liabilities. In this action, bondholders sued the National Bank on the guarantee. It is well established that the capacity of a corporation is governed by the law of the place of incorporation, and the House of Lords so held. Looking at Greek law, therefore, the result was that the National Bank could be sued, because the decree provided that it succeeded to the liabilities of B. As to whether B was liable, in view of the 1949 moratorium, the House of Lords held, of course, that this matter went to the discharge of obligations, and the discharge of obligations depended on the proper law of the contract, which was English. Under English law, B remained liable, and under Greek law the National Bank succeeded to B's liabilities.

The Greek government then issued another decree, retrospectively relieving the National Bank from its obligations under the guarantee. This came before the House of Lords in *Adams* v. *National Bank of Greece*[52] and again the House decided that this amounted to a discharge of an existing obligation, was governed by English law, and that the change in Greek law was ineffective.

If the decree of 1953 had not transferred B's liabilities to the National Bank, the latter could not have been liable. The Greek government could have transferred all of B's liabilities except for the liability under the guarantee, and that also would have been effective. But having transferred the liability, its removal was a question of discharge, which was governed by English law.

In many cases, the old company (the original borrower) will be wound **3.19** up or will have no assets. If, however, it has assets and remains in existence, the question arises as to how an English court would regard a decree or law simply saying that "X no longer has the capacity to be sued." This might be regarded by English law as a valid change in X's capacity, and if that is the case English law holds that questions of capacity (to sue, or to be sued, etc.) are governed by the law of the place of incorporation of a company. If so regarded, the foreign decree would effectively prevent the company from being sued. Alternatively, an English court might regard such a decree not as affecting capacity, but as an attempt to discharge X's liability. If that is the case, the question of discharge would be governed by the proper law, and would be ineffective if the law of the foreign state is not the proper law.[53] Which approach, therefore, is to be adopted? It would seem from *dicta* in the *Metliss* case that there is a difference between cases where all of X's liabilities are transferred (the question then being regarded as one of capacity, with the result then depending on the law of incorporation) and cases where particular liabilities are transferred (the question being regarded as one of discharge, with the result depending on the proper law). In *Re*

---

[52] [1961] A.C. 255.
[53] See Wood, p. 34.

United Railways of Havana and Regla Warehouses[54] the transfer by a state (Cuba) of particular liabilities of a company (for hire payments) was held to be be a question of discharge, governed by the proper law (of Pennsylvania). If, therefore, the original borrower is left with any capacity to remain liable for old debts or to incur new debts, it would seem to be a question of discharge, governed by the proper law. If all capacity is removed, it is a question of capacity, governed by the law of the state of incorporation.

Statutes of limitation

3.20   A state may also pass a law providing that debts remain actionable only for a certain period (for example, in England, on a simple debt, debts are actionable for six years unless acknowledged in writing thereafter).[55] English courts regard limitations of this sort as procedural matters: and procedural matters (as we have already seen)[56] are governed (under English Conflicts rules) by the *lex fori*. If, therefore, the action is brought in England, the six year period would be applicable, notwithstanding contrary provisions under the foreign law. Having established the six year period in this way, however, English courts distinguish (within that period) between foreign rules which (i) bar the debt entirely, and (ii) merely remove the remedy. This depends on the phrasing of the foreign law: thus, "no debt shall be actionable" removes the remedy, while "no debt shall exist" removes the debt. Having made the distinction the result is that if the debt is barred, this is a question of discharge, governed by the proper law, and if the remedy is removed, it is a question for the lex fori. If state X imposes a limitation on actions, by barring the debt, then if the law of X is the proper law (but not otherwise) it is effective. If state $X's$ limitation bars the remedy, then regardless of whether the law of X is the proper law, an English court would allow six years.[57]

Exchange controls

3.21   Exchange controls are a fact of life, inasmuch as a borrower may be affected by controls imposed by his state, so that regardless of foreign legal rules or judgments, he simply cannot pay the money. One cannot sue him in his own country, and if he has no assets elsewhere, actions elsewhere may be pointless. The legal problem raised, however, is whether the imposition of exchange controls is any defence to an English action. Regarding the matter simply as a change in the laws of the state, the answer *prima facie* is that if the law of that state is the proper law of the contract, the exchange controls are effective. Otherwise, they are not.[58] We have observed a number of excep-

---

[54] [1961] A.C. 1007.

[55] Limitation Act 1980.

[56] Above, Chap. 1.

[57] See *M'Elroy* v. *M'Allister* 1949 S.C. 110, and the U.S. Conflicts Restatement, sections 142–143.

[58] See *Re Helbert Wagg & Co. Ltd.* [1956] Ch. 323 (German law proper law, exchange control legislation effective); *Kleinwort Sons & Co. Ltd.* v. *Ungarische Baumwolle Industrie AG* 2 K.B. 678 (Hungarian controls ineffective where English law was the proper law).

tions to this general rule, so that if, for example, the exchange control is English, we would enforce it. If there is a knowing attempt to evade the foreign rule, it may not be recognised, on the ground of public policy. If the foreign exchange law is the law of the place of performance, and if English law is the proper law, then the principle of the *Ralli Bros.* case may cause English law to defer to the place of performance.[59] The major exception, however, is that the proper law will not govern the case if there is a "Fund Agreement." In considering this it is essential to recall that there is no need to be concerned with a fund agreement if the proper law is the law of the state applying the exchange contract, or if the other exceptions apply. Fund agreements are considered in Chapter 4 of this volume, in the context of a general discussion of exchange controls.

For the time being, we shall only say that it is obvious that exchange controls are of considerable significance in international loan agreements. The most obvious protection is that the loan agreement provides for payment not in the borrower's country, B, but in currency A in the country of currency A where that country is unlikely to impose exchange controls (*e.g.* dollars, in New York). Under the (English) restrictive approach to Fund Agreements, it will be seen that regulations of the borrower's country affecting such an agreement would not be enforced by English courts (assuming a proper law choice, etc.) Even so, the reality is that foreign legal remedies may prove fruitless if a borrower's state prohibits repayment. Loan documentation therefore deals with the problem in a variety of clauses, discussed in Chapter 9 below. Obviously it will be one factor in making the loan, that a country is judged likely to impose exchange controls. This is one of the numerous factors involved in the difficult task of assessing "country risk."

B. SOVEREIGN IMMUNITY[60]

Under this topic we consider actions and remedies available in country *A* against the sovereign of country *B*. If one is bringing an action in country *A* against the sovereign of that same state, different considerations apply. For example, an action in the U.K. against the Crown is governed largely by the Crown Proceedings Act 1947, and an action against the governments of British Crown colonies (like Hong Kong) can be brought only under the archaic declaratory procedure known as a "petition of right." **3.22**

In the days when sovereigns were mainly individual persons, they were seen as being above ordinary trade, and were widely exempted from ordinary trade laws. Today, with the decline in personal monarchy, and the considerable growth in the extent to which governments are involved in trade, the immunity given to "sovereigns" is greatly reduced. The modern idea of immunity is generally described as "restrictive," and a distinction is drawn between governmental acts (*acta imperii*) and commercial acts (*acta gestionis*). Generally, in most commercial jurisdictions, the state has immunity in relation to governmental acts, and not in relation to commercial acts. However,

---

[59] Above, para. 3.07.
[60] See Wood, Chap. 4., Gruson and Reisner, ed. *Sovereign Lending: Managing Legal Risk* (1984).

there are numerous differences of approach. Some jurisdictions differentiate "commercial" from "governmental" by reference to the purpose of a transaction (a loan agreement for arms purchases may be governmental) while others look to the nature of the transaction (a loan agreement is commercial). Some jurisdictions allow declaratory judgments, but no legal remedies if the state fails to comply. Some allow seizure of commercial but not governmental assets. Some restrict pretrial remedies (such as injunctions). Some extend the range of actions and remedies if the state consents, and others will not.

We shall consider primarily the position in the United Kingdom, followed by some reference to the position in the United States.

1. The United Kingdom

3.23 The law here is primarily regulated by the State Immunity Act 1978. Nevertheless, it is necessary to consider the common law where (a) the transaction was entered into before November 22, 1978, or (b) where the Act does not apply to the transaction.

A. THE COMMON LAW

3.24 The older common law rules provided for a rigid system of nearly absolute immunity, under which a state could be sued only if it waived its rights and voluntarily accepted the jurisdiction of an English court. But in the fairly recent past, this position changed, to one where the State has no immunity from suit (it probably has in relation to remedies) for commercial transactions. The culmination of this process occurred in *I Congresso del Partido*[61] in which Cuban State enterprises contracted to deliver sugar to a Chilean company, delivery to be aboard Cuban ships owned by Cuban State-controlled companies. After the violent fall of the Chilean government, Cuba broke off diplomatic relations with Chile and decided to end commercial dealings, and accordingly sold the sugar elsewhere. Following arbitration in the U.K., the matter went to the House of Lords, which applied the restrictive theory already referred to. Considering the nature of the transaction (not its purpose) this was a commercial sale of sugar. The Cuban government, therefore, had no immunity from suit. Clearly, the only connection in this case with the U.K. was the arbitration clause which brought the parties to London. The issue of a necessary connection was not raised, and some would say that the U.K. courts should not interfere in foreign disputes with which we have no connection. Lord Denning M. R. has said that a U.K. court should adjudicate on the liability of a state only if the commercial transaction has a close connection, either by the presence of the parties or by the nature of the dispute.[62]

As to enforcement, the rules are less clear. Possibly a distinction will now be made between commercial and state assets (though the old rule was that all assets were immune). Where the court has jurisdiction (as by sub-

---

[61] [1983] 1 A.C. 244; see also *Planmount v. Republic of Zaire* [1908] 2 Lloyd's Rep. 393.
[62] *Rahimtoola v. Nizam of Hyderabad* [1958] A.C. 379, *Thai-Europe Tapioca Service Ltd.* v. *Gvt. of Pakistan* [1975] 3 All E.R. 961.

mission), ordinary procedural rules apply, so that the state can be required to provide security for costs and must make discovery of documents (but clearly cannot be fined or imprisoned for contempt if it declines to obey).

The common law of immunity did not apply to entities separate from the state. These will be considered in due course.

B. STATE IMMUNITY ACT 1978

The Act is the result of a European (not E.E.C.) Convention on State **3.25** Immunity, and it has effect for transactions entered after November 22, 1978. It will be seen that it is necessary to distinguish between the state itself, constituent territories of a federal state, separate entities (not part of the government of its executive organs), and central banks. It is also necessary to distinguish between jurisdiction and enforcement. The Act does not affect any diplomatic immunities given by the Diplomatic Privileges Act 1964 or the Consular Relations Act 1968 (by which, for example, diplomatic premises are given immunity).

States

"State" is defined by section 14(1) as the state itself, its sovereign or head of **3.26** state, the government of the state, and any government department. The Secretary of State may certify whether a territory is a state, or a person its head, and so on.

A. IMMUNITY FROM JURISDICTION

The general rule, stated in section 1, is that the state is immune from the jur- **3.27** isdiction of U.K. courts, except as provided in the Act. The immunity is automatic, and need not be claimed. The exceptions are all important, but it should be noted that the mere fact that immunity is removed does not mean that an English court has jurisdiction, where the case is unconnected with the U.K. There are two steps: (1) Is the state immune? If the answer is in the affirmative, no action may proceed. If the answer is in the negative, one asks the second question, which must be asked whoever one is suing, in any ordinary action: (2) Has the U.K. court jurisdiction? This depends on matters examined elsewhere,[63] and depends on such matters as submission, presence, or the effect of R.S.C., Ord. 11. (In the case of submission, this would simultaneously remove immunity and give the court jurisdiction). This being said, the exceptions, where the state is not immune, are as follows:

(1) Submission to jurisdiction (section 2(1)). Submission may occur at the time of the action, or in a prior contract. Merely agreeing to English proper law is insufficient. Submission can be given by the state's ambassador in the U.K. Submission (a) removes immunity, and (b) under ordinary principles, applicable to any defendant, gives the U.K. court jurisdiction.

(ii) Commercial transactions (section 3). A state is not immune as regards proceedings relating to a "commercial transaction into by the State."

It will, however, be immune even for commercial transactions if (i) the

---

[63] See generally, Chap. 2 above.

other party is also a state, or (ii) if the parties have agreed otherwise in writing: here the contract might exclude the Act entirely (in which case the common law would apply, and the state may not be immune) or it might expressly say in writing that the state is immune (in which case neither the Act, nor the common law, would apply). It is thought that an agreement that other courts have jurisdiction would amount to a contrary agreement. The third exception relates to certain Admiralty matters where a claim relates to a ship or its cargo, etc., and where the matter is governed by the Brussels Convention of 1926.

3.28   "Commercial transaction" means (a) a contract for the supply of goods or services, (b) a loan, financial transaction or guarantees or indemnities in respect of these, (c) any other transaction not involving the exercise of sovereign authority. It follows from the definition that except for the third of these it is (as at common law) the nature, not the purpose of a transaction which counts, and that the reason for breach (financial expediency, or state policy) is immaterial.

(iii) Contracts to be performed in the U.K. Whatever the nature of the transaction, a state is not immune if the contract is to be performed here wholly or partly (as by payment of money). There are certain exceptions (if both parties are states, or if otherwise agreed, and certain other cases). However, most banking transactions will be covered by the commercial transaction exception already mentioned.

(iv) Other exceptions, which are of less importance to bankers in view of the commercial transaction exception, concern written agreements for arbitrations in the U.K.,[64] ships used for commercial purposes,[65] contracts of employment,[66] death or personal injury or damage to or loss of tangible property, caused by an act or omission in the U.K.,[67] any interest of the state in, or its possession or use of, immoveable property in the U.K. or any obligation of the state arising out of its interest in, or possession or use of such property,[68] and the membership of a state (in certain circumstances) of a corporation, unincorporated body, or partnership.[69]

If any of these exceptions applies, the state is not immune from jurisdiction. Enforcement is another matter.

B. IMMUNITY FROM ENFORCEMENT

3.29   The de-immunisation in relation to jurisdiction is very clear, for a commercial transaction. But having obtained judgment (*i.e.* a declaration of liability, or judgment for damages or a sum of money) it may not be possible for the plaintiff to avail himself of all the ordinary legal remedies, against a state or others. The Act proceeds by first excluding[70] all the available remedies (injunctions, specific performance, orders for the recovery of land and other property, all proceedings against the state property to enforce judgments or arbitration awards, and any actions *in rem* or orders for the arrest,

---

[64] s.9.
[65] s.10.
[66] s.4.
[67] s.5.
[68] s.6.
[69] s.8.
[70] s.13(2).

detention or sale of the property) and then goes on to provide for exceptions from immunity. The exceptions are as follows:

(i) If the state gives written consent at the time, or in the contract, or by treaty, and such consent may be partial (*e.g.* exempting military assets).[71]

(ii) Process (orders against property, rather than personal orders like injunctions or specific performance) may be issued if property is used or intended to be used for commercial purposes. One could obtain a distress warrant, or a garnishee order, or an order charging land, etc.

But personal orders, like injunctions (including *Mareva* injunctions)[72] and specific performance are never available (because the penalty for non-compliance is punishment for contempt of court, involving arrest, and fine and imprisonment of the offender).

The difficulty with seizing property under the second exception above is that the most likely target will be funds in a bank account, and it may be difficult to prove the purpose of funds. Apart from that, section 13(5) allows the ambassador to certify that the property is not for commercial purposes, and this is prima facie proof for the matter unless the contrary is proved. Furthermore, in the notorious case of *Alcom Ltd.* v. *Republic of Columbia*[73] the House of Lords held that it was insufficient for a creditor to show that some of the funds in an account were for commercial purposes. If any was used for immunised purposes, the whole fund was immunised, and the creditor must show that the entire fund is intended for commercial purposes. The case involved an embassy bank account, however, and the judgment leaves it uncertain whether this principle applies only to embassy accounts, or to any fund. If the latter, the creditor's task is practically impossible.

Furthermore, if the state is a contracting state under the European Convention on State Immunity enforcement is impossible except in the case of an arbitration agreement or where the state has de-immunised itself under the Convention. But all Convention states have agreed to give effect to judgments against them in any other Convention state. In January 1987, the following countries had signed or ratified the Convention: Austria, Belgium, Cyprus, Germany, Luxembourg, Netherlands, Switzerland and the U.K.

State entities

Not all state owned or controlled entities can be treated as part of the state. **3.30** Many are "separate entities." A separate entity is[74] "distinct from the executive organs of the government of the State and capable of suing or being sued." It is vital to comprehend the definition, because the immunity given to entities which are separate from the state is less significant, both as to jurisdiction and as to enforcement, than that given to a state. The questions of capacity to sue or be sued would fall to be determined by the law of the state in question. What must be shown, apart from that, is that it is not a

---

[71] s.13(3).
[72] For a fuller discussion of the importance of Mareva injunctions, see Chap. 2, above.
[73] [1984] A.C. 580.
[74] s.14(1).

department of state, but is distinct from the government's executive organs. The following cases give some guide to the distinction:

The New Brunswick Development Corpn., a body resembling the English Board of Trade, promoting industrial development, and carrying out the policy of the Government, was not a separate entity, but inseparable from the Government, and immune.[75]

The Central Bank of Nigeria, created by legislation, but which exercised an independent function and which was not under government control and exercising governmental functions, was a separate entity.[76]

A Polish state enterprise, set up and controlled by the State, but which (subject to a general state control) generally ran its own commercial activities, and was expected to make a profit, was a separate entity.[77] This is an important finding in relation to socialist states, where many, and perhaps all enterprises, may be state owned. Commercial enterprises will, nevertheless, ordinarily be separate entities. This does not entail that they will always be liable, for on principles already examined, the state may (for example) abolish the entity, or expropriate its property. The latter occurred in *Empresa Exportada de Azucar* v. *Industria Azucarera Nacional SA*[78] where the Cuban government, wishing to sever contacts with Chile, (a) ordered ships at sea carrying sugar to Chile to turn back, and (b) ordered the transfer of sugar in Chile out of the control of the State enterprise in question. The ships at sea were liable, having broken their contracts under transactions not governed by Cuban law, but the enterprises were not liable for not delivering the sugar in Cuba, for that property had been expropriated by the State, and on principles already discussed,[79] the expropriation was recognised by English courts. There being no property to export, through no fault of their own, the contract was effectively frustrated. (Had the Cuban government merely made it illegal to export, this would not have happened, for under the proper law the illegality was irrelevant, and the enterprise would have been liable.)[80]

A. IMMUNITY FROM JURISDICTION

3.31 Generally, and certainly for commercial contracts, the separate entity is not immune from jurisdiction.[81] It is immune only if the state itself would have been immune (a non-commercial transaction) and the entity is exercising sovereign authority (the breach is an act of state, not a commercial default). In the words of section 14(2) of the Act, the entity is immune if, and only if "(a) the proceedings relate to anything done by it in the exercising of sovereign authority; and (b) the circumstances are such that a state . . . would have been so immune." Since the state would not be immune from jurisdiction given a commercial transaction, (unless the contract so stated) then for

---

[75] *Mellenger* v. *New Brunswick Development Corpn.* [1971] 2 All E.R. 593.
[76] *Trendtex Trading Corpn.* v. *Bank of Nigeria* [1977] Q.B. 529.
[77] *Czarnikow Ltd.* v. *Rolimpex* [1979] A.C. 351.
[78] [1983] 2 Lloyds Rep. 171.
[79] Above, para. 3.05.
[80] Above, Chap. 1.
[81] s.14(2).

present purposes (concerning commercial transactions) a separate entity will never be immune. Even if it were immune, it can submit to jurisdiction, just as a state can.

B. IMMUNITY FROM ENFORCEMENT

Although it is not stated in the Act, the rule as to enforcement must be **3.32** (since no immunity is expressly given) that that if, as will be the normal case, the entity is not immune from jurisdiction, it is subject to normal enforcement, including injunctions and specific performance, and remedies to recover land, etc. It is stated that if the entity is not subject to jurisdiction, but submits to it, enforcement is on the same basis as for states, in which case, for example, injunctions would not be available.[82]

Central banks

Central banks are clearly ordinarily entities separate from the state. But the **3.33** *Nigerian Central Bank* case referred to above was decided on events before the 1978 Act. After the Act, if a central bank is a separate entity it has the same immunity from enforcement (not from jurisdiction) as a state[83] (otherwise, it was felt, such banks would be deterred from maintaining foreign reserves in the U.K.). The central bank's property is not to be regarded as being for commercial purposes. The result is that the bank is liable only if it consents to enforcement. However, if the property is not that of the bank, but that of the state (if, perhaps, it is held in a separate account) then it may be available if for commercial purposes.

Problems with central banks may arise particularly where the bank is requested to give a guarantee of some kind in respect of the debts or liabilities of the state, or of a separate entity. It is essential that when it gives the guarantee, the central bank should be de-immunised by the insertion of an appropriate clause in the guarantee. Such clauses are considered shortly.[83a] Without the insertion of such de-immunising clauses, it is necessary to rely upon the extent to which the central bank (and its home state) consider it important to maintain the reputation of the central bank, for even if one may obtain judgment against the bank, the remedies will be illusory, and to that extent, the guarantee is legally worthless.

Constituent territories of federal states

Many states are federations: such as the United States of America, Canada, **3.34** Australia, and Austria. The constituent territories are treated as separate entities, and have lesser immunity, though an Order in Council may be made treating given territories as states. (This has been done with Austria).

---

[82] s.14(3).
[83] s.14(4).
[83a] Below, para. 3.39.

Dependent territories and dominions

3.35 The dominions (members of the Commonwealth, like New Zealand or Australia) are clearly states, with state immunity. Colonies, like Hong Kong, do not have immunity within the Act, but it may be extended to them by Order in Council. But it may be that the only method of proceeding against such colonies is by way of the "petition of right" if that procedure survives.[84] The Act may be extended by Order in Council to dependent territories such as the Channel Islands or the Isle of Man.

Procedure

3.36 Discovery (the process of obtaining sight of documents possessed by the defendant) is available against states, central banks, or separate entities, but if a state or central bank fails to comply, there is no remedy. Service of writs is possible through the Foreign and Commonwealth Office, and is effective when received by the Ministry of Foreign Affairs for the state in question. But if this requires service outside of the jurisdiction, then R.S.C. Ord. 11 applies[85] and the discretionary approval of the court must be sought. The Act permits[86] an alternative method of service, and it will be recalled that approval is almost automatically given if an agent within the U.K. is appointed, and the state may appoint its ambassador for the purpose. Agreeing to service on an appointed agent is, therefore, very desirable. Additionally, if the diplomatic-channel method of service is not used, a two-months period of grace which is otherwise allowed to a state before it is required to reply to the writ ("enter an appearance") and before default judgments may be given against it (*i.e.* a judgment automatically given in some cases if it does not appear to defend itself), will not apply.[87]

2. The immunity legislation in the U.S.A.[88]

3.37 In the U.S.A., matters are governed by the Foreign Sovereign Immunities Act 1976. We have room here only for a summary of its provisions. It is based upon principles very similar to those in the U.K., but with these differences:

(a) The definition of foreign states includes political subdivisions or agencies or instrumentalities of the state. Whereas in the U.K. a constituent territory of a federal state would be treated as a separate entity with limited immunity, in the U.S.A. it is treated as a state with full immunity.

(b) The definition of instrumentalities and agencies includes corporations owned by a state. In the U.K. these would be treated often as separate entities, but in the U.S.A. they are treated as part of the state, with full immunity. Corporations in socialist states will, therefore, enjoy considerably more immunity (unless they agree otherwise) than in the U.K.

---

[84] See Encylopedia, F(2525).
[85] Discussed above.
[86] s.12(6).
[87] s.12(2–5).
[88] Encyclopedia, F(2601) *et seq*; Wood, p. 105 *et seq*.

(c) In the U.K. whether the court has jurisdiction depends on such matters as presence, submission, or the court's discretion under Order 11. If jurisdiction is established in the normal way, it may be that it is then removed by the effect of our Act. But in the U.S.A., the relevant statute gives jurisdiction, where there is no immunity. That is, if a state is not immune, the courts automatically have jurisdiction. There is merely a single question, whereas in the U.K. there are two questions: (i) has the court a general jurisdiction? (this has nothing to do with immunity, and would be asked of any foreign defendant), and (ii) if the court would have this "ordinary" jurisdiction, is this removed by the fact that the defendant is a state?

(d) In the U.S.A., immunity from jurisdiction is not given if (i) it is expressly or impliedly waived, or (ii) the litigation is based upon some commercial activities which have some connection with the U.S.A. "Commercial activity" means either a regular course of commercial conduct or a particular commercial transaction or act. A sufficient "connection" with the U.S.A. is established by a commercial activity carried on in it, or by an act performed in the U.S.A. in connection with a commercial activity elsewhere, or by an act outside the U.S.A. in connection with a commercial activity elsewhere where the act causes a direct effect in the U.S.A. Presumable borrowings from a U.S. or U.S. resident bank are sufficient, and presumably a default outside the U.S. which affected a U.S. bondholder would amount to a "direct effect" in the U.S.A. In *Carey v. National Oil Corpn.*[89] the Libyan National Oil Co. had a contract to supply oil to a Bahamian subsidiary of a New York corporation. The refined products of the oil would be used in the U.S.A. The benefit of the contract was assigned to a New York resident. On default in the supply of oil, a New York court held that the commercial activity had an insufficient connection with the U.S.A.: it was not carried on in the U.S.A., there was no "act" in the U.S.A., and the loss of products in the U.S.A. was an indirect effect. Again, in *National American Corpn.* v. *Federal Republic of Nigeria*[90] a letter of credit was opened for a New York beneficiary. The issuing bank used a New York bank to advise and pay. A breach of the terms of the latter was held to have occurred in the U.S.A., and the courts had jurisdiction. It is thought likely that wherever there is a payment obligation to be performed in New York, failure to do so will be a breach, even if the account holder is not resident in the U.S.A. This must surely be a "direct effect" in the U.S.A. The discussion above of the *situs* of a debt is relevant. If New York law was chosen as the proper law of the contract, this in itself is an insufficient "connection," and the state would be immune (and of course the court has no jurisdiction). In the U.K., the choice of English law would give the court discretionary jurisdiction under Ord. 11 (this is more or less automatic, if an agent is appointed) and if the activity is commercial, the state would not be immune.

(e) Under the U.K. Act, a borrower can contract out, and will be completely immune. This is not possible in the U.S.A., so that an action brought in that jurisdiction may be very advantageous if some connection can be established.   **3.38**

[89] 453 F Supp 1079 (SDNY 1978) affd 592 F 2d. 673 [1979].
[90] 448 F Supp 622 (SDNY 1978).

(f) In the U.K., declaratory or garnishee proceedings are possible for commercially intended property of a state. Injunctions are not possible. Wider enforcement is available for non-central bank separate entities. In the U.S.A. the position is as follows:

(i) enforcement by execution against property is available for property used for a commercial activity "in" the U.S.A., but only if (a) immunity is waived, expressly or impliedly, or (b) the property is used for the commercial activity upon which the claim is based, or (c) the execution relates to a judgment establishing rights in property which has been taken in violation of international law. This is a very much more restricted approach than in the U.K. It would seem that without a waiver, a bank account (containing funds related to the breach) could not be attached if the state simply defaulted. These limitations do not exist for agencies and instrumentalities, so that the property of a state-owned corporation would be available to creditors, if the entity is engaged in a commercial activity in the U.S.A.

(ii) Prejudgment attachments (like the U.K. *Mareva* injunction) are not available unless the property is used for commercial activity in the U.S.A., and immunity is expressly waived.

(iii) injunctions and specific performance are available.

There is, perhaps, much to be said for the U.K. approach.

Forms of clause waiving immunity

3.39 It will be appreciated that in drafting an appropriate clause, the aim is threefold:

(i) to secure "ordinary jurisdiction";
(ii) to secure waiver of immunity, if any, from jurisdiction;
(iii) to secure the widest possible range of remedies, with a state, or central bank, which has some immunity from enforcement.

The securing of "ordinary jurisdiction" (which one needs to secure in order to sue any debtor, whether sovereign or not) is dealt with in Chapter 2, in this volume, and all that we shall say here is that it may be achieved by a submission to the jurisdiction of the English courts. In order to avoid the need to serve writs outside the country, the practice is to appoint an agent inside the country or countries concerned to receive service.[91] The same applies to actions to be brought in the U.S.A.

The securing of a waiver of immunity overlaps with the securing of ordinary jurisdiction, inasmuch as sovereign immunity (to enforcement or to jurisdiction) may be removed by submission to the jurisdiction. Thus, at the same time a state submits to jurisdiction, it waives its immunity. A waiver of immunity, as we have observed, is effective both in the U.K. and in the U.S.A., in relation to both immunity from jurisdiction and enforcement. The specimen agreement provided in this work[92] requires the borrower to agree that if legal action or proceedings (note the wide definition of "action" and "proceedings," for the avoidance of doubt) is brought:

---

[91] See the speciman clause, 29(2), Chap. 17, below.
[92] Clause 29(1), Chap. 17, below.

(i) against it or its assets;

(ii) in relation to the loan agreement and matters arising from it;

(iii) the borrower shall not claim for itself or its assets and irrevocably waives any immunity which it has now come to have (thus consenting to jurisdiction and enforcement);

(iv) and (so as to make the matter of enforcement abundantly clear) consents generally to the giving of any relief or the sum of any process, including the making, enforcement or execution against any property whatsoever or any order or judgment which the court may make. This last provision allows "relief," including interlocutory actions, such as *Mareva* injunctions, and also allows "process" such as actions against property.

The specimen clause[93] would be effective both in the U.K. and in the U.S.A.

C. RECOGNITION OF STATES

1. General U.K. position

The problem normally arises from *coups d'état*, where by unconstitutional **3.40** means governments are overthrown. In some cases, for a time which may possibly be prolonged, there may be two rival governments. A change in government without a change in the Head of State calls for no new recognition. One need consider only those cases in which the whole regime, including its Head of State, is overthrown.

It is essential to appreciate that (unlike questions of immunity) recognition is not a legal matter for judges to decide, but a political matter, for the government of the U.K. to decide. It has long been the practice of the courts[94] to accept as conclusive a certificate from the Foreign Office stating whether or not a government is recognised. But since April 25, 1980, the U.K. government has ceased to recognise governments, and now recognises only states. The Foreign Office no longer issues certificates. This does not imply that recognition of governments is no longer important, nor that if has ceased to be a political matter. Rather, because it is sometimes an embarrassing political matter to be called upon to recognise (or not to recognise) a government, the U.K. government has extracted itself from the difficulty by refusing to do so. The courts must now by some unkown means infer the political question of recognition from the U.K. government's dealings with the new régime. The means by which this is to be done remain obscure, but presumably the most relevant feature is whether or not the U.K. government meet with, deals with, or enters contracts with the new régime. It is uncertain whether the U.K. courts should consider the matters traditionally considered by the U.K. Foreign Office (occupation of territory, size of population controlled, whether control effective and whether ability to conduct international relations). These seem to be factors relevant to the making of a political decision, whereas the question the U.K. courts must ask themselves is the factual question of whether the U.K.

---

[93] See clause 29, Chap. 17, below.
[94] Since *Taylor* v. *Barclay* (1828) 2 Sim 213.

government has (on the basis of such considerations, but others also, such as, say, hostility to the policies of the foreign régime) made a political decision to recognise. The question for the courts is not "do the facts justify recognition" but "has the U.K. government recognised?" Presumably, however, the U.K. government would not recognise without standard criteria (territory, population and control) so that these facts may remain relevant for consideration by the courts, while being insufficient in themselves.

2. De facto and de jure recognition: dual recognition

3.41 A distinction used to be drawn between recognition of a new régime on a provisional basis (de facto) and recognition of an older more politically established régime (de jure). The distinction may be important in the context of "dual recognition": formerly, one régime might be recognised as *de facto* and one as *de jure* and the law-making power was "divided up" amongst the two governments in the areas which they most influenced (normally, the *de jure* government for international claims, but the *de facto* one for internal matters).[95] It would seem that the U.K. government may still have dealings with new governments upon this basis, and if so, the U.K. courts should recognise that (unexpressed) political decision.

3. Can an unrecognised government sue in England?

3.42 The answer was, and presumably still is, in the negative.[96]

4. Can an unrecognised government be sued in England?

3.43 Again, the answer is in the negative. An unrecognised government can neither sue, nor be sued.

5. Are any legislative, judicial or executive acts of the unrecognised government recognised in England?

3.44 The answer seems to be that acts having legal consequences (legislation, contracts, expropriation of property, divorce decrees) will not ordinarily be recognised,[97] but that "private acts, or acts of everyday occurrence, or perfunctory acts of administration" may be recognised "in the interests of justice and common sense, where no consideration of public policy to the contrary has to prevail."[98] This proposition extends even to laws, "at any

---

[95] See, *e.g. Bank of Ethiopia* v. *National Bank of Egypt & Liouri* [1937] Ch. 513; *Haile Selassie* v. *Cable & Wireless (No. 2)* [1939] 1 Ch. 182, rev'd. 194.
[96] *Berne City* v. *Bank of England* (1804) 9 Ves. 347; *Jones* v. *Garcia del Rio* (1823) Turn. & R. 297.
[97] *Luther* v. *Sagor & Co.* [1921] 1 K.B. 456, rev'd. [1921] 3 K.B. 532; *Adams* v. *Adams* [1971] P. 188; *Taylor* v. *Barclay* (1828) 2 Sim 213; *Eastern Carrying Insurance Co.* v. *National Benefit of Life and Property Insurance* (1919) 35 TLR 292.
[98] *Carl Zeiss Stiftung* v. *Rayner and Keeler Ltd. (No. 2)* [1967] 1 A.C. 853, 954.

rate, in regard to the laws which regulate the day to day affairs of the people."[99]

It should be noted that once a government is recognised, this confers **3.45** retroactive legitimacy on its previous acts, legislation, etc., (unless, in the days when the Foreign Office issued a certificate, the certificate stated an effective date).[1] But recognition of a *de facto* government as *de jure* did not invalidate previous acts of the previous *de jure* government.[2]

6. Liability of one régime for debts of another: state continuity

A change of government (including change of Head of State) does not affect **3.46** the continuance of the state, which remains bound by its obligations.[3] This principle treats a government rather like an agent who contracts debts for his principle, the state, and is very widely accepted, throughout the world. Some socialist states, have, for example, (without necessarily conceding any relationship to the previous, pre-revolutionary, state) recently agreed to honour bonds issued by the previous, pre-revolutionary, state.

7. General position in the U.S.A.

In the U.S.A. the position is like that in the U.K., inasmuch as the U.S. **3.47** courts defer to suggestions of the executive in recognising new régimes.

As to recognising legislative, judicial or executive acts, the U.S. cases are contradictory, and it is possible that (as may well be the case in the U.K.) the judges gave effect to what they perceived at the time to be the policy of the U.S. government.[4]

D. STATE SUCCESSION

We have considered the effect of changes of government (including Head of **3.48** State). We now consider briefly the effect of such matters as the partition of a state, the unification of previously separate states, and the succession of a part of state. In each case the original debtor state has lost some or all of its sovereignty to a successor state. There is both a question of recognition of a new government, and one of the existence or liability of the new state. We have observed the principle that the state remains liable despite changes in governments. The problem here, however, involves changes in the state itself. There is, in effect, no U.K. law on the question of the liability of the

---

[99] *Per* Lord Denning MR, in *Hesperides Hotels Ltd.* v. *Aegean Turkish Holidays Ltd.* [1978] Q.B. 205, 218.

[1] *Luther* v. *Sagor*, above, and the Ethiopian cases, above.

[2] *Gdynia Ameryka Linie* v. *Buguslawski* [1953] A.C. 11.

[3] *Republic of Peru* v. *Dreyfus & Co.* (1888) 38 Ch.D. 348; *Republic of Peru* v. *Peruvian Guano Co.* (1887) 36 Ch.D. 489.

[4] Contrast *Salimoff & Co.* v. *Standard Oil Co. of New York* 262 NY 220 (1933) (soviet expropriatory decree recognised); *The Maret 145 F 2d. 431 (1944) (Soviet nationalisation decree not recognised.); Upright* v. *Mercury Business Machines Co. Inc.* 213 NYS 417 (1961) (assignment of bill, by company created by de facto government, recognised).

successor state. It may be that U.K. courts will have regard to the principles of international law, or it may be that in future the matter will come to be regulated by international treaty. We have no space here further to consider this matter.

4. Exchange Controls[1]

Obviously, it will be one factor in making the loan, that a country is judged **4.01** likely to impose exchange controls. This is one of the numerous factors involved in the difficult judgment of "country risk." Exchange controls may be relevant first, by reason of the conflicts rules which are applied in English law when it considers the effect of a change in the laws of a foreign State. We have seen[2] that generally, the answer depends on whether or not the contract is governed by the law of the State which imposes the exchange controls. But even if not governed by the law of that State, such controls must be regarded as a fact of life, inasmuch as a borrower may be affected by controls imposed by his State, so that, regardless of foreign legal rules or judgments, he simply cannot pay the money. One cannot sue him in his own country, and if he has no assets elsewhere, actions elsewhere may be pointless. The legal problem raised, however, is whether the imposition of exchange controls is any defence to an English action, when the contract is not governed by the law of the foreign State, but is governed, say, by English law. Even where English law was the proper law, we have seen a number of exceptions to the rule that the proper law determines the question.[3] The major exception, however, is that the proper law will not govern the case if there is a "Fund Agreement." In considering this it is essential to recall that there is no need to be concerned with a Fund Agreement if the proper law is the law of the State applying the exchange contract, or if the other exceptions apply.

References to a "Fund Agreement" are references to the Articles of Agreement of the International Monetary Fund, signed in 1944, at Bretton Woods. This agreement has been incorporated into the municipal law of the U.K. and of the U.S.A., and of many other countries. In the U.K., it is now governed by the International Monetary Fund Act 1979.

The important Article is VIII 2(b), which provides as follows: **4.02**

> "Exchange contracts which involve the currency of any member and which are contrary to the exchange control regulations of that member maintained or imposed consistently with this Agreement shall be unenforceable in the territories of any member."

Practically every phrase of this Article contains legal difficulties. We shall consider "exchange contracts," "contracts . . . shall be unenforceable," "involve the currency," "exchange control regulations," "consistently."[4] Our concern is primarily with the approach to the construction of the treaty

---

[1] See generally, Wood, Chap. 5; *Encyclopedia of Banking Law*, para. 1503 *et seq.*; Bentley, *A World Guide to Exchange Control Regulations* 1986/87 (1986, Euromoney).

[2] Above, Chap. 1, esp. paras. 1.17 *et seq.*

[3] Above, Chap. 1, esp. paras. 1.21 *et seq.*

[4] For an excellent discussion, upon which the authors have drawn heavily, see *Encyclopedia*, F(1503) *et seq.*

taken by English courts, though we shall mention the attitudes of other courts. In construing treaties, an English court will have regard to the underlying policy of the treaty, and will not apply technical rules applicable (say) to Acts of Parliament. If at all possible, they will attempt to harmonise their interpretations with those of foreign courts, particularly if there is already a consistent corpus of foreign law on the subject. But where there are differing decisions, they will interpret the text in a normal, non-technical, fashion, having regard to the policy of the treaty.[5]

"EXCHANGE CONTRACTS"

4.03   English courts take a fairly restrictive view of this phrase, interpreting it to mean a contract to exchange the currency of one country into the currency of another. A foreign currency loan in which there is no term to repay in a given currency would not be an exchange contract, because there is no "contract to exchange." But any agreement with a currency conversion clause is affected. In *Wilson, Smithett & Cope Ltd.* v. *Terruzzi*[6] an Italian resident dealt in contracts on the London Metal Exchange, and had an obligation to pay sterling to English metal dealers. Italian exchange controls affected his ability to pay, and the question arose whether his obligation to pay in sterling made the contract an exchange contract. The court held that it did not: there was no obligation to convert Italian currency into English currency.

But the courts are prepared to look beyond the appearance of a transaction, and in particular are prepared to consider other related agreements to determine whether, taken together, there is an exchange contract. In *United City Merchants (Investments) Ltd.* v. *Royal Bank of Canada*[7] in order to enable a Peruvian importer to take money abroad, an English exporter agreed with the Peruvian importer to increase artificially the price of the goods sold, on terms that the amount of the increase would be paid by the English bank to a Miami dollar account in the name of the Peruvian company. Payment to the English exporter was first to be made by a bank in England acting as confirming bank under a letter of credit (issued by a Peruvian bank). The House of Lords held that this was an exchange contract, because the contract between exporter and importer imposed an obligation to swap money paid under the letter of credit (Peruvian currency) for a foreign currency (U.S. dollars). The defendant bank, therefore, was not bound to pay under the credit, even though on the face of it, the credit provided for payment against documents, and itself contained no contract to exchange currencies, and despite the well-established principle that credits are transactions quite separate and autonomous from the underlying contract.[8] Taking the contract and the credit together, it was a disguised exchange contract.[9] Simi-

---

[5] *Stag Line* v. *Foscolo, Margo & Co.* [1932] A.C. 328; *James Buchanan* v. *Babco* [1978] A.C. 141.
[6] [1976] Q.B. 683, (aff'd) 703.
[7] [1983] 1 A.C. 168; [1982] 2 All E.R. 720.
[8] See Chap. 13 below.
[9] The court did allow the part of the contract that did not offend against the exchange controls to be enforced.

larly, in *Mansouri* v. *Singh*[9a] a person desiring to take money out of Iran bought airline tickets there, and brought them to England, where (relying on a term in the contract to refund them in sterling) he asked for a sterling refund. Because of the term, this was held to be an exchange contract, and the seller could raise Iranian exchange controls as a defence.

The restrictive view taken by English courts (contract to exchange currencies) is probably shared by the U.S. courts[10] and has been applied in Belgium.[11] It may be contrasted with a much less restrictive view taken in West Germany,[12] Luxembourg,[13] and France.[14] In those jurisdictions, the phrase "exchange contract" is interpreted to include any agreement which would affect (even indirectly) exchange resources of the State in question. That is, not a "contract to exchange currencies" but a "contract which affects the exchange resources of a country." This wide view obviously encompasses most agreements, including all term loans or bond agreements. In order to repay, the borrower (if required to repay in foreign currency) will have to sell domestic currency to pay for the foreign currency, or (even if allowed to repay in his own currency) is subject to a claim (legal action) abroad (*e.g.* if he defaults) and this might affect exchange resources. The extent of the proposition is shown by a French case[15] in which a contract occurring in France, for a sale of shares in a French company, for French francs, between a Dutch resident seller and a German resident buyer, was held to be an unenforceable exchange contract because of Dutch exchange control regulations (the Netherlands had an interest in the repatriation of foreign currency obtained from the sale of the shares). Given a choice, the lender should obviously bring his action in countries like the U.K., where the restrictive view holds sway.

4.04

"INVOLVE THE CURRENCY OF ANY MEMBER"

It will be recalled that an exchange contract is a "contract to exchange" currency. Accordingly, it would seem that this phrase means (in the U.K.) "Involve an exchange of the actual currency of the member whose exchange controls are considered." But where the wider view of "exchange contract" is taken, and "exchange contract" means "contract affecting the currency of any member," the phrase means "involves an exchange or affects in any direct or indirect way the currency or exchange resources of the member . . . "[16] Suppose that a bank in country *A* makes a loan to a borrower in country *B*, of currency of country *C*, and this is prohibited by regulations of country *B*. It would seem that on the restrictive view (in the U.K.) this is not covered by the Article, but on the wider view (as in France) it would be,

4.05

[9a] [1986] N.L.J. Rep. 260, C.A.

[10] *Banco do Brasil SA* v. *AC Israel Commodity Co.* 12 NY 2d. 371, 190 NE 2d. 235, 239 NYS 2d. 872 (1st Dep't 1963), cert. denied 376 US 906 (1964).

[11] *Emek* v. *Bossers & Mouthaan* I.L.R. (1955) 722.

[12] *Lessinger* v. *Mirau* 22 I.L.R. (1955) 725.

[13] *Societe Filature et Tissage X Jourdain* v. *Epous Heynen-Bintner* 22 I.L.R. (1955) 727.

[14] *De Boer, Widow Moojen* v. *von Reichert* 89 J. Droit Int'l 718, Cour d'appel, Paris 1962.

[15] The *de Boer* case, previous note.

[16] See the *de Boer* case, above.

because it affects the exchange resources of *B*, even though not directly a contract to exchange *B's* actual currency.

"CONTRACTS . . . SHALL BE UNENFORCEABLE"

In *United City Merchants (Investments) Ltd.* v. *Royal Bank of Canada*[17] it was explained that the significance of the word "unenforceable" is that the contract is neither illegal (in any criminal sense) nor void. It exists, but cannot be enforced by legal action. No legal remedies are available. Continental courts have in contrast held that the contract is entirely void and a nullity.[18] Since (in the U.K.) the contract exists, then if at any subsequent time exchange controls were removed, the contract could be enforced normally. Additionally, non-judicial remedies (such as the right to combine accounts) may be available. Even a contractual set-off clause may be enforceable by the lender, since where he exercises his right to set-off, he needs no assistance from the court, and if sued for the deposit in question, he relies on the contractual set-off clause as a defence, and does not ask the court's aid in assisting him towards a remedy.

4.06   The Article refers only to "contracts," and actions based on property rights may be unaffected, provided that the property right is not created by the contract rendered unenforceable.[19] Similarly, actions in tort may be unaffected. It may be that an action to enforce a judgment is unaffected, so that a lender who is able to sue in one jurisdiction (which takes a restrictive approach to the Article) can enforce his judgment in another jurisdiction (where the wider approach is taken).[20] A most important question is whether the lender can recover sums already paid by claiming in quasi-contract. Overseas decisions have held not, and it is thought that the same would apply in the United Kingdom. A quasi-contractual claim depends on an implied contract, and such a contract can be implied only after the original contract has been rescinded. It would seem likely that the lender could rescind, on the ground of failure of the condition implied in nearly all contracts, that the other party must be ready, willing and able to perform. But, having rescinded, it is unlikely that an English court would imply a promise to repay, for this implied contract would be to do something prohibited by the exchange control regulations in question. Similarly, the remedy of tracing would be unavailable, that requiring a fiduciary relationship (not ordinarily existing between lender and borrower).

If the term which is affected by the Article is a minor part of the contract, and can be severed from the rest, leaving a comprehensible and workable contract, severance is possible.[21] But this would not assist with a contract on a bond or loan, where the repayment obligation is the major part of the contract.

The Article does not allow direct enforcement by one State in another State. If, say, property is transferred contrary to the regulations, it cannot be recovered. Contracts are merely made unenforceable.

---

[17] Above, n. 7.
[18] *Clearing Dollars* case, Hamburg Provincial Court, 22 I.L.R. (1955) 730; the *de Boer* case above.
[19] *Kahler* v. *Midland Bank Ltd.* [1950] A.C. 24.
[20] Encyclopedia, F(1605), referring to German and Dutch decisions.
[21] *Sharif* v. *Azad* [1967] 1 Q.B. 605, and the *United City Merchants* case, above, n. 7.

"EXCHANGE CONTROL REGULATIONS"

The Article presumably covers both regulations controlling capital transfers **4.07** (the capital of loans, for example) and current transactions (interest on loans, for example).

Countries may impose a wide range of restrictions: including, for example, tariffs, trade restrictions, price controls, trading with the enemy regulations, legal tender regulations, and so on. Which, if any of these, are "exchange control regulations"? The test must be whether the regulation is aimed at preserving a country's exchange resources, in which case none of the above would be within the Article. In *Loeffler-Behrens* v. *Beermann*[22] Brazilian legal tender regulations were held by a German court (on advice from the fund) to be excluded. The Brazilian law prohibited contracts to be performed in Brazil from stipulating that payment had to be in a currency other than Brazilian. Even a law requiring the acceptance of payment in Brazilian currency would not be an exchange control law, since in itself it does not prevent the person paid from exchanging the currency received.

Wood argues[23] that to be an exchange control regulation it must be (i) a direct control, on (ii) the financial aspects of a transaction, (iii) controlling the movement of currency, property or services, so as (iv) to protect the exchange resources of a country.

"CONSISTENTLY WITH THIS AGREEMENT"

Under Article VIII 2(a) restrictions on current transactions are not allowed **4.08** unless there is a scarcity of a member's currency, or the Fund approves (which it might do tacitly or subsequently). If a restriction is otherwise imposed, it is inconsistent with the agreement, and a foreign court could ignore it. The Fund will advise, where there is doubt. "Current transactions" include payments due in connection with foreign trade, and interest on loans. Under Article VI,3, members are free to make restrictions on capital transfers, so that the problem of whether such restrictions are "consistent" with the Agreement does not arise.

Overriding Public Policy?

In a Dutch case, a court has held that it might ignore regulations which affront Dutch public policy.[24] But that approach is not available directly to an English court, for the Article is by virtue of the International Monetary Fund Act 1979 part of English domestic law, and the Article states that the agreement is unenforceable. Similarly, U.S. courts have rejected this argument.[25] However, as to current account controls, it may be possible that regulations which are discriminatory or oppressive are not aimed at protecting scarce resources, and are not "consistent" with the Fund Agreement.

---

[22] 1964–5 IPRspr No. 194.

[23] *Op. cit.*, 139.

[24] *Indonesian Corpn. PT Escomptobank* v. *NV Assurantie Maatschappij de Netherlanden Van 1945*, 40 I.L.R. (1964) 7.

[25] *Perutz* v. *Bohemian Discount Bank in liquidation* 279 App. Div. 386, 110 NYS 2d. 446 (1952), rev'd 304 NY 533, 110 NE 2d. 6(1953).

Imposition of exchange controls

4.09 In the U.K., exchange controls were abolished in 1979, but the legal framework under which they were, and could again, be established, was not abolished until 1987.[26] This abolition makes it difficult to reimpose exchange controls, because the need for legislative action would inevitably lead to an immediate and probably very dramatic flight of capital from the country. Like many other countries, the U.K. has accepted the provisions of Article VIII, sections 2, 3 and 4 of the International Monetary Fund (IMF) Agreement. Section 2 of that Article involves an undertaking by members not to impose restrictions on the making of payment or transfers for current international transactions, without the approval of the IMF. We have particularly examined section 2(b) by which members undertake not to enforce contracts which involve the currency of any member, and which are contrary to the exchange control regulations of that member imposed consistently with the Fund Agreement. Under section 3, members agree not to indulge in discriminatory currency practices. Under section 4, they undertake to buy back balances of their currencies held by another member, if these have been acquired recently as a result of current transactions, or if their conversion is required in order to make payments for current transactions. If a member has accepted all of these obligations, the currency of that member is said to be "convertible."

Types of exchange controls

4.10 Many different types of controls may be imposed to protect the currency of a State. Some controls are "direct investment controls" that is, controls on direct investments ("inward" investments by non-residents). For example, foreign investments may have to be registered, or the remittance of profits and dividends to non-residents may be restricted, absolutely, partially, or in relation to currencies, or there may be restrictions on the payment of royalty and service payments to non-residents, or there may be restrictions on the repatriation of capital invested by non-residents in the State. The failure to register, where this is required, may itself prevent remittance of profits, or capital repatriation, etc. Some failures may, in some States, be remediable (possibly within a limited time) but in other cases it may be irremediable, in which case the investor would (if appropriate saving provisions were not in the agreement) be locked in to the transaction where the borrower is restricted in his ability to repay.

In the U.K., for example, there are none of these direct investment controls, although under the Taxes Act 1970, s.482, the prior consent of the Treasury is needed if a company wishes to transfer its "fiscal residence" (the centre of its management and control) abroad, or wishes to cease to be resident, or wishes to transfer part of its trade or business abroad, or allow non-resident companies which it controls to issue shares or debentures to any person, or transfers to a person shares in a non-resident company over

---

[26] The Exchange Control Act 1947 was abolished.

which it has control. These are not, in principle, exchange controls, being intended for fiscal reasons (to stop avoidance of tax by the migration of companies to places outside the U.K.), but they may have effects similar to exchange controls. The extent to which the U.K. legislation contravenes the U.K.'s E.E.C. Treaty obligations is to be tested, the matter having been referred in February 1987 by an English court to the European Court for investigation.[27] However, in the context of this work, exchange controls on direct investments are not as significant as those which we now consider.

A second type of exchange control may be described as "borrowing regulations," which concern the effect of those regulations concerning a resident borrower (and non-resident lender). One may also distinguish "lending regulations," which concern the effect of those regulations concerning a resident lender (and non-resident borrower).[28] In relation to borrowing, some countries may control not only foreign borrowings, but also domestic borrowings if the borrower has non-resident shareholders. In some cases, if a resident subsidiary borrows from a non-resident parent, the transaction may be treated as a direct investment, subject to controls already mentioned, or to special rules. In the case of lending regulations, some rules may treat domestic loans to non-resident unrelated companies as an outward investment. In the U.K., there are no borrowing or lending regulations of the type under consideration.

4.11

A third type of exchange control relevant to this discussion are controls upon currency. For example, some regulations may prevent persons from entering into arrangements to provide forward exchange cover. This is permitted in the U.K., if the party providing the cover is a bank. Another type of currency regulation may control the holding of a State's currency or of foreign currency, by either residents or non-residents. In the U.K., there are no restrictions on currency (nor are gold bullion and gold coin subject to exchange control in the U.K.).

In the U.S.A., by way of comparison, there are no requirements for the registration of investments (but only some reporting requirements under the International Investment Survey Act 1976, and some other statutes). There are no regulations limiting the remittance of profits, dividends, interest or other income. There may be reporting requirements for royalty and service payments. There are no restrictions on the repatriation of capital, and no specific borrowing or lending regulations. There are no forward cover regulations. In relation to bank deposits, however, there are reporting requirements, whereby withdrawals, deposits and exchanges of U.S. currency exceeding U.S. $10,000 must be reported to the U.S. Treasury Department. Additionally, U.S. or foreign currency, or other monetary instruments including bearer bonds exceeding U.S. $10,000 in aggregate which are physically transported in or out of the U.S.A., must be reported to the U.S. Customs (though not transfers by draft, wire or other written order). But banks, whether foreign or domestic, need not comply with this deposit regulation.

---

[27] *R. v. H.M. Treasury, ex p. Daily Mail and General Trust PLC, Financial Times*, February 25, 1987.

[28] These useful distinctions are made in Bentley, *A World Guide to Exchange Control Regulations 1986/87* (1986, Euromoney).

4.12   The U.S. government has powers under the Trading with the Enemy Act and the International Emergency Economic Powers Act (IEEPA) to freeze assets of foreign governments and nationals, if the property is subject to U.S. jurisdiction (including foreign-owned bank balances in the U.S., or balances in foreign branches of U.S. banks). These powers have been used, and the Trading with the Enemy Act applies to transactions in relation to nationals of Cuba, North Korea, Cambodia and Vietnam. Under the IEEPA sanctions have been imposed against trading with Libya, Nicaragua and Iran. There are specific regulations affecting Cuban assets.

Loan documentation and exchange controls

4.13   It is obvious from the foregoing that exchange controls are of considerable significance in international loan agreements, though the restrictive approach taken by U.K. courts to the meaning of "Fund Agreements" limits their scope where the law of the State imposing the controls does not govern the contract.

SPECIFYING PLACE AND CURRENCY OF PAYMENT

4.14   The most obvious protection that a lender may take is that the loan agreement provides for payment in currency A in the country of currency A where that country is unlikely to impose exchange controls (*e.g.* dollars, in New York). Under the restrictive approach, regulations affecting this are not observed by English courts (assuming a proper law choice, etc.). Even so, the reality is that foreign legal remedies may prove fruitless if a borrower's State prohibits repayment. Loan documentation deals with the problem in a variety of clauses.

CONSENTS, AND CONDITIONS PRECEDENT

4.15   In many cases, exchange controls may be lifted or waived if some local authority, such as a Central Bank, or Treasury, consents. Some countries may give consents in advance, and some only after the executed loan agreement is filed with the relevant authority (or, maybe, only after a drawdown). Some countries will not authorise anything but scheduled payments or principal and interest, or perhaps also commitment commissions. They may not give advance approval to accelerated amounts (in a case of prepayment, or perhaps on default). Generally speaking, any international loan agreement will make provision for whatever consents may be obtained. First, it will be a condition precedent of a loan agreement that consent has been obtained, for borrowing, repayment, commission, additional payments, etc. Bonds will advertise the exchange control position. Where consents cannot be obtained in advance, the borrower or lender may approach the relevant authority for an indication of the likely result of an application, and some "comfort" may be obtained from this. But in this case, or in cases where (for example) advance approval for accelerated amounts is required, the lender must essentially make a judgment of the commercial risks involved, having regard to the economic and political situation in the borrower's country.

In the specimen loan agreement in this volume,[29] Clause 12 contains conditions precedent, but these are particularly applicable to a sovereign borrower. Para. (a) refers to the law of the State in question authorising the borrowing of loans in foreign currencies, and para. (c) contains a declaration that the borrowings fall within the monetary limits for foreign currency borrowings authorised by law. In the case of a non-sovereign borrower, the agreement would simply say (where consent can be obtained in advance) that it is a condition precedent that consent has been obtained.

CURRENCY TRANSFER AGREEMENTS

If consent can be given by a central body, such as a Central Bank, that body **4.16** may be required to give a "currency transfer agreement" whereby it undertakes to sell the borrower sufficient currency to repay, to ensure that it is made available, and to allow him to remit it abroad. Such an agreement is a contract, rendering the Central Bank liable for default.

In the case of a transaction with a sovereign, or with a public entity, it is also usual to attempt to acquire a currency transfer agreement from the Central Bank of the State, in place of the exchange control consents which apply in case of a private borrower. The Central Bank agrees to (a) obtain and (b) to sell sufficient foreign currency to the borrower to enable it to meet its obligations, and also agrees(c) to allow the borrower to remit this abroad. The agreement should be governed by the same law as the main loan agreement, and should contain similar terms as to jurisdiction, etc., if negotiable. The Central Bank, under U.K. law, is not immune from jurisdiction (it is a separate entity) but its assets have special immunity, unless it consents to execution against those assets. While it is subject to declaratory actions, therefore, stating its liability in damages for breach of any such agreement, it may (without consent to execution) be impossible to enforce the judgment. An additional problem is that such a currency transfer agreement seems (within Article VIII 2(b) of the Fund Agreement), to be "a contract involving the currency of a member" and, therefore, to be subject (even under a contract governed otherwise by U.K. law) to exchange controls imposed by the State. The Central Bank, therefore, could be relieved of any liability under its agreement by a change in the law of the State.

WARRANTIES, COVENANTS AND EVENTS OF DEFAULT

All loan agreements (but not bond issues) will additionally contain an **4.17** express warranty that all necessary exchange controls have been obtained, or will be obtained as they become necessary, and it should be an event of default if any exchange control consent is or becomes necessary and is unobtainable for any cause, or is revoked, or refused, or materially varied. In other words, the warranties are made "evergreen" and if at any time consents are varied or revoked, it will entitle the lender to accelerate (though he still may not be repaid, if the exchange controls prevent the borrower from doing so). In the specimen model loan agreement, in this work, represen-

---

[29] See Chap. 17 below.

tations concern powers and authority,[30] legal validity,[31] no conflict with laws relating to the borrower,[32] consents,[33] and other matters. All of these clauses might relate to exchange controls, and the consent clause certainly would where consent is obtainable in advance. In the case of a private borrower, exchange controls might be specifically mentioned.

The illegality clause, to which reference has already been made,[34] will also give some protection by allowing the lender to call for a prepayment if the law of his own country (including exchange controls) affects his ability to continue with the agreement. This would be unnecessary if the law of the lender's State governed the contract, but otherwise the lender would be in breach under the proper law if he did not continue with a loan prohibited by his own State.

Legal opinions should be obtained, and these will state whether exchange controls are imposed and whether consents are needed, etc. The obtaining of a satisfactory legal opinion is a condition precedent.[35]

Currency indemnity clauses, considered already,[36] dealing with local rules permitting payment to be made, or judgments to be given in the borrower's currency, may have some effect. These require the borrower to indemnify the lender for any conversion losses. The borrower's obligation under such clauses, however, may also be affected by exchange control regulations.

[30] See clause 13(1)(a) in the specimen agreement, Chap. 17 below.
[31] 13(1)(b).
[32] 13(1)(c).
[33] 13(1)(e).
[34] See Chap. 17 below.
[35] Specimen, clause 12(1)(h-j), Chap. 17 below.
[36] See Chap. 17 below.

5. Withholding Taxes[1]

A withholding tax is, as the name suggests, a tax which is collected by **5.01** deduction by the debtor from the sum of money which he is to pay to the creditor. Generally, of course, the tax is levied upon income (interest) but it may be levied upon capital gains, as where bonds are issued at a deep discount and a low or zero rate of interest. The debtor withholds the tax and pays the balance to the creditor, passing on the tax collected to the Revenue authorities. From the Revenue's point of view this is administratively simpler, and it prevents evasion of tax liabilities and the difficult problem of investigating and enforcing the liabilities of foreigners. It is, of course, a principle common to the law of the U.K. and other States that a country will not enforce the tax laws of other States. The only effective remedy which Revenue authorities of "other states" have, therefore, is to collect taxes in advance. Sometimes, if the legislation so allows, the creditor who has been subjected to a withholding tax may reclaim any excess from the Revenue, over that which he should have paid.

In some cases, the difficulty of withholding taxes is reduced by double tax treaties. Otherwise, clauses may be inserted in the contract to attempt to deal with the problem, or avoidance schemes may be adopted. The position is also affected by the applicable law of the contract.

A. Applicable law

If a borrower deducts taxes, and a lender sues in the borrower's country, **5.02** obviously the courts of that country will enforce the laws of that country, regardless of the proper law of the contract. The tax law will be regarded as a mandatory law, overriding any other choice of law. If, however, the lender sues outside the borrower's country, the matter will depend upon the choice of law, and the attitude of the forum to foreign tax laws. We have just remarked that English courts will not enforce foreign tax laws. This is well established, and assistance will not be given either directly or indirectly.[2] But if a borrower deducts taxes from his payment, the question is (probably) not whether the foreign tax law is to be enforced, but whether by paying the reduced sum, the borrower has been discharged from his liability under the contract. The court is not being asked to enforce the foreign revenue law, but to determine the effect of the borrower's reduced payment on his liability. If, therefore, the forum is England, the question of whether the borrower is discharged from his debt liability by paying the reduced sum is treated by English courts as a question for the proper law. If the contract is governed by the law of the borrower's State, then the borrower will be discharged. If it is governed by some other law, the question depends upon that other law. If English law governs, the principle is that changes in

[1] See Wood, Chap. 12; *Encyclopedia*, paras. F(1667) *et seq.*
[2] *Re Visser* [1928] Ch. 877; *Rossano* v. *Manufacturer's Life Insurance Co. Ltd.* [1963] 2 Q.B. 352.

the foreign law do not affect the liability of the borrower, who is not discharged from the debt by payment of a reduced sum. Thus, in *Indian and General Investment Trust Ltd.* v. *Borax Consolidated Ltd.*[3] a U.S. issuer was held not to be entitled to withhold tax on bonds governed by English law.

Assuming that the borrower has assets in the U.K. or in some other jurisdiction with equivalent rules, therefore, it is sufficient in principle that the contract is not governed by the law of the borrower's country. However, to avoid the need for legal action, and certainly in any case where recourse might have to be had to litigation in some third country or especially in the borrower's own State, other measures may be necessary.

B. Avoidance schemes

5.03 While English law does not enforce foreign tax laws, it does not enforce agreements which are designed to evade the revenue laws of a foreign and friendly State.[4] To this extent, then, foreign tax laws are recognised, and "enforced" in the sense that evasive contracts will not be given effect. But "evasion" is a process which generally involves breaking the foreign law, and disguising the fact, and is to be distinguished from "avoidance." The latter involves stepping around the provisions of the law in question: finding loopholes or exemptions. Avoidance is perfectly possible, although of course, the laws of the State in question may be so drafted that avoidance is not possible, or even that schemes entered into with a view to avoiding liability are illegal simply because the attempt is made. (Just such a rule seems to be appearing in the U.K.)[5]

One common scheme of avoidance is for the borrower to use a foreign financing subsidiary (a "borrowing vehicle") which is established in a country (a "tax haven") which allows payments of interest to be made free of tax deductions. Bonds, for example, may be issued in that country, and are guaranteed by the parent. The subsidiary lends on to the parent or group members. This may also have the effect of reducing (say) prospectus requirements, on the ground that the securities are issued abroad. But the scheme will work only if (in addition to the tax haven imposing no withholding tax) the ultimate recipient of the funds (say, the parent) can repay the on-lending to its subsidiary (or pay under its guarantee) without deduction of tax. It is necessary, therefore, not just to find a tax haven, but to find one which has a double tax treaty with the parent's country, so that the parent's country either does not tax interest or limits the amount of the tax it imposes. Additionally, the choice of tax haven may be determined by whether they impose stamp duties, exchange controls, or other legal impediments. They may, for example, require a spread between the rates of borrowing and the on-lending rates, and tax the difference as profits.

5.04 Such schemes cannot work if the recipient's country will not allow the parent to deduct the interest paid to its own vehicle, when its tax liability in its own jurisdiction is computed. A further common difficulty which may be met is that legislators may be concerned to prevent avoidance of general

---

[3] [1920] 1 K.B. 539.
[4] *Re Emery's Investment Trusts* [1959] Ch. 410.
[5] See *Furniss* v. *Dawson* [1984] S.T.C. 153; *W. T. Ramsay Ltd.* v. *IRC* [1982] A.C. 300.

taxes upon profits. Thus, a recipient (in a high tax area) might borrow from its own subsidiary in a low tax area, and agree to pay large amounts of interest, thus enabling the recipient to set the interest expenses against the recipient's general tax liabilities, and the vehicle to pay reduced tax upon that interest. Effectively, the profits are transferred to a low tax area. To avoid this, either the tax haven or the recipient's jurisdiction may impose debt-equity ratios upon the vehicle (which shows that it is truly an independent company), or there may be provisions restricting interest rates payable to reasonable market rates, or both of these.

A second method of avoidance, which might be used with term loans, rather than bonds, is to lend money to an intermediary bank which lends on to the borrower, in cases where the intermediary's jurisdiction allows corporations in that country to pay interest without deduction to banks in that country, and where the intermediary bank may then pay interest to foreign banks without deduction of tax. There are provisions to protect the intermediary from credit risks (so that, *e.g.*, it is obliged to repay the lender only if it receives money from the borrower). There is the additional risk of insolvency of the intermediary, or its non-payment, and there are problems inasmuch as there is no direct contractual relation between the true lender and the borrower, in case of the latter's default.[6]

Double tax treaties

Double tax treaties are treaties between States intended to ensure that a lender is not subject twice to taxation upon the same income. If the borrower's country imposed a withholding tax upon interest, the interest might be further taxed in the lender's own jurisdiction, as profits. States may, therefore, enter into treaties, which have the effect that double taxation is limited. These may have the effect that the lender's country will take account of the foreign taxation, thus limiting the tax payable to the higher rate in the two countries. Alternatively, one country may agree not to tax if tax has been levied in the other country. It may be provided that tax is levied in the country in which interest arises, and not in the other State, but a more generally found provision is that tax may be levied in the country in which the payee of the interest is resident, while the State in which the interest arises may not tax above a specified amount (say, 10 per cent.). The treaty may provide that the limitation on the tax does not apply if the interest payable exceeds a commercial rate (*i.e.* where a high rate is agreed between parent, say, and subsidiary, as part of an avoidance scheme). Further, the limitation on interest may not apply if the payee has a permanent business establishment in the State where the interest arises. The reason for that is that the State may then provide that interest payable to the payee counts as profits earned by that business establishment, and tax it as profit (rather than imposing a withholding tax). In that case, there is often a separate provision in the treaty relating to profits, to avoid double taxation of those. A distinction may be drawn between representative offices (not entering contracts or carrying on business) and others which count as "permanent business establishments."

5.05

---

[6] See Chap. 8, below, concerning transfer and participation in loans.

Contractual provisions

5.06   It is normal to include in a term loan or bond issue clauses which provide specific protection against withholding taxes (and other taxes). A specimen clause is given in the model term loan agreement, Chap. 17 below, in clause 10(2). We have seen that whether laws in the borrower's country affect the validity of these clauses is a question (in English law) for the proper law, while the borrower's State will treat its own laws as mandatory. The general effect of the protective clauses is that (a) the payments are to be made without deduction of tax, but (b) if the borrower is compelled to deduct tax he shall pay promptly and will *either* indemnify the lenders for any deductions *or* pay them additional sums to make sure that they receive the original amounts (the difference between the two things is discussed shortly). Additionally, the borrower may be made to compensate the lender for taxes imposed upon the lender itself (if, say, a charge is imposed on gross interest received). A bond issue would not attempt to render the issuer liable for all taxes imposed upon the bondholder, because (say) he might be a resident of the issuer's country, and liable to tax on interest, etc., which the issuer should not be required to repay. Bond issues generally limit the tax protection to taxes imposed by the issuer's country, because of the unpredictability of the ultimate bondholders. Term loans (especially Euro-currency ones where the bank's funding costs are of extreme importance) generally provide for the effect of tax wherever it occurs: in the borrower's jurisdiction, the lender's jurisdiction, or maybe in the jurisdiction where funds are transferred from, or to.

There are two types of provision in a typical loan clause.[6a] One of these is a "tax indemnity" clause, where the borrower agrees that it will pay all the taxes concerned, for its own account. But it may be that the laws of the borrower's country do not allow him to pay free of taxes in this way. If, therefore, the indemnity clause does not work, so that the bank would not on that basis receive the full amount, the other provision is a "grossing" up provision, providing for the borrower to pay additional sums so as to put the lender back in the position in which he would have been had there been no withholding tax or other tax liability. Some countries, however, may outlaw even grossing up clauses.

5.07   The grossing up clause may, at first sight, seem to achieve exactly the same result as the indemnity clause, since the lender receives the original sum agreed, without deduction. But they are not the same, and the indemnity (if it works) is preferable, and the grossing up clause is expressed to operate only if the indemnity clause does not operate effectively. The difference between the two depends upon complications of the "tax credit" system. Tax credits are a form of relief against tax given by a State in recognition that a person has already been taxed elsewhere, so as to avoid double taxation. Generally the system used is a "credit" system (as opposed to an "exemption" system) and under the credit system the lender deducts the tax already paid, in one of two ways, depending upon the State. First, if his total income is $£X$, and tax on that is $£Y$, but he has already paid $£Z$, he

---

[6a] Both provisions commonly appear in the same clause of a eurocurrency loan agreement. See, for example, clause 10(2) in the specimen agreement, Chap. 17 below.

may set £Z off against £Y, and pay the difference, if any. Alternatively, if the part of his income which has been taxed abroad is £A, and the tax there was £B, and if he were taxed in his own country upon that income he would be taxed in the amount of £C, he may set £C off against £B. In other words, in the former case the deduction may be set off against all the taxpayer's income, while in the second case, the deduction is restricted to that part of the State's own tax which is attributable to the income already taxed abroad. In the first case, the result is that the lender pays at the rate in his own country, but in the second case the result is that he pays at the higher of the rates in the two countries. The exemption system simply takes the view that if the income earned abroad has already been taxed, it should not be taxed again, so that income is disregarded when the taxpayer is taxed in his own country. Here, the lender pays at the rate applicable in the borrower's country, whether higher or lower than in his own.

Under the (usual) tax credit system, the effect of the indemnity clause is that the borrower pays tax on his own account, and the lender is seen by the Revenue authorities as receiving only the original sum agreed. The effect of the grossing up clause, however, is that the lender is seen as receiving the whole of the original sum (tax deducted) plus the additional amounts, and it is these combined sums which are deemed to be his income. He may then have a tax credit, but that sum (based upon the size of the deduction from the original amount) has to be set off against the combined sums, so that effectively he has a higher liability. Take a sum of £100 with deduction at 25 *per cent.*, with an indemnity, where the lender's home tax rate is 30 *per cent.* The lender receives £100, is liable to £30 tax and sets off £25, paying £5. But if the sum is grossed up, instead, he is deemed to receive £100 + £33 (because if the borrower pays £25 tax is deducted on that, which he must make up again, and further tax is deducted on the amount made up, and so on). His home tax on £133 is £39.9 against which he sets £25, paying £14.9. If it can be negotiated, there is no legal reason in his own country why he should not provide for his own additional tax liability to be made up by the borrower.

The availability of tax credits may, however, be a reason for the lender to lend without a grossing up clause on account of withholding taxes. The lender knows that through his own tax system he will (effectively) receive the money back, and all he may require is, perhaps, additional interest to compensate for the delays in his own Revenue's systems, before he receives the tax credit. **5.08**

In case there is a grossing up clause, which is applied, but the lender then receives a tax credit so that his position is better than what it would have been, it may be agreed that the additional benefit will be returned to the borrower. Banks generally are unwilling to agree to such a provision, because of the difficulties in calculation of the benefit, and so on.

If a new tax arises, with the result that grossing up or indemnity clauses come into effect, then the borrower (unless a sovereign, which would be responsible for the laws) may insist upon the right to be permitted to prepay the loan, in full, perhaps with a small compensatory premium. No such term appears in the model loan agreement in this volume, since that involves a loan to a State borrower, which is responsible for any changes in its own laws.

Clause 11 of the specimen term loan agreement[7] contains contractual provisions aimed at dealing with the situation where the law of a lending bank's country (or the place where its branch is situated) changes. This model, which relates to a syndicated loan, deals with changes affecting any of the bank participants, or an Agent bank. If any change of law (or directive, even if it does not amount to a legal change) causes a bank or the agent to become subject to a tax on the principal or interest, or changes the basis of taxation, or imposes such requirements as a liquidity ratio, so that the costs to the bank increase by a material extent, or the amount of principal or interest is reduced by a material extent, and so on, the borrower may be notified and must then compensate the bank for such increased cost, reduction, payment etc. The borrower may then prepay that bank, on giving notice.[8]

[7] See Chap. 17 below.
[8] The issue of pre-payment is considered in greater detail in Chap. 6 below.

6. International Term Loan Agreements

Introduction

The aim of this chapter will be to provide a general overview of international **6.01** term loan agreements, with particular reference to eurocurrency term loans.[1] Many of the aspects commonly associated with such loans are dealt with elsewhere in this work and here we will consider the remaining topics, many of which are of considerable importance in both a legal and practical sense.

Eurocurrency loan agreements are quite different from domestic loans in both structure and scope and in order to fully appreciate the nature of such agreements it will be necessary to consider in some detail the wording of the various clauses commonly found within the loan contract. However, it should be pointed out at this introductory stage, that the practice and law in this area of international banking undergoes constant change and the clauses referred to throughout this chapter are merely illustrative. They should not be considered as "standard" or model clauses. There is no such thing as a standard international term loan agreement. The documentation evidencing every agreement should be tailored to meet the specific needs of the contracting parties.

Many different considerations affect the parties' decision to lend or borrow under a medium term loan agreement. Some of these considerations give rise to common interests, and others to legitimate differences of interest which pre-contract negotiations must resolve. Those drafting the loan documentation must, therefore, fully appreciate the nature and purpose of each particular loan agreement and the interests of the parties who contract under it.

THE NATURE AND MECHANICS OF EUROCURRENCY MEDIUM TERM LOAN AGREEMENTS[2]

This chapter will concentrate upon medium term loan agreements, that is to **6.02** say, loans which have a term of between one and 15 years. Banks occasionally lend for more than 15 years but only in very special circumstances and

---

[1] In order to appreciate fully the legal issues which arise under medium term loan agreements in the eurocurrency market it is necessary to understand the basic concepts and background of the eurocurrency market and in particular the funding mechanism employed in the market; see generally, Clendenning, *The Euro-dollar Market* (1970); Quinn, *The New Euro-markets* (1975); Little, *Eurodollars: The Money Market Gypsies* (1975); Davis, *The Euro-Bank* (1976); Einzig and Quinn, *The Eurodollar system* (6th ed. 1977); Lutz, *The Eurocurrency System*, Banca Nazionale del Lavoro Review No. 110 (Sep., 1974) Vol. 27, pp. 183–200; Donaldson & Donaldson, *The Medium-Term Loan Market* (1982); McDonald, *Syndicated Loans* (1982).

[2] See generally Donaldson & Donaldson *loc. cit.*, n. 1; Calhoun, "Eurodollar Loan Agreements: An Introduction and Discussion of Some Special Problems" 32 Business Lawyer (July 1977) p. 1785.

in so far as eurocurrency loans are concerned most facilities fall within a three to seven year term with very few loans exceeding 10 years.

Governments as well as corporate entities borrow substantially in the eurocurrency markets and many favour the medium term loan facility. One of the main reasons for the continuing popularity of this instrument lies in its inherent flexibility as a lending medium. Medium term loan agreements can be advanced in all shapes and sizes, providing for drawdown to be made immediately, (the "bullet" drawdown), or within a short period of the loan being executed, or in accordance with a fixed amortisation schedule. Alternatively, the loan agreement may provide the borrower with a longer period in which to drawdown the facility and may afford considerable flexibility as to both timing and number of drawdowns which may be made. The most flexible form is the revolving facility which allows the borrower repeatedly to drawdown the loan, or a portion thereof, and to repay any drawn amount either at the borrower's discretion or in accordance with a pre-determined schedule.[3]

The flexibility of these instruments extends to the interest rate mechanisms under which they may operate.[4] The interest rate may be fixed for the entire term of the loan, or occasionally for a shorter period in excess of one year. It is common however for eurocurrency loans to incorporate a floating interest rate mechanism, such rate being tied to a short term market indicator. The market indicator used in most eurocurrency loans is LIBOR[5] (London Interbank Offered Rate) being the rate at which the lending bank is able, in accordance with its normal practices, to acquire the relevant currency from the eurocurrency markets in order to fund the loan.

6.03   The rate at which banks in the market offer to lend the currency in question will obviously vary and some loan agreements specify the names of banks[6] from which interest rate quotations must be obtained. LIBOR therefore reflects the cost of funding the loan from the lender's standpoint, this being a fundamental feature of euromarket lending. A margin is added to LIBOR and it is this margin which compensates the lending bank for the risks and costs incurred.[7] The margin also provides the bank with its operating profit on the loan facility.

Due to the fact that the eurocurrency markets are unregulated, they are considered vulnerable to external events and it is, therefore, common to incorporate specific clauses within the loan documentation to protect the banks against possible future funding difficulties. The clause used is often referred to as the eurodollar or eurocurrency disaster clause[8] and provides that if the euromarkets are disturbed so as to affect the availability of funds or the determination of LIBOR the parties shall negotiate in good faith to

---

[3] These facilities will obviously only be available to the borrower during the commitment period, see clause 4 in the specimen agreement Chap. 17 below.

[4] See clause 8 in the specimen agreement Chap. 17 below.

[5] For an interesting discussion of the concept of LIBOR and other market indicators used in the London interbank market see McDonald *loc. cit.*, n. 1 above, pp. 85–89.

[6] These banks are normally described as "reference" banks.

[7] The margin over LIBOR must compensate the lending bank for all costs, unlike the position under the U.S. Prime Rate where some costs are covered within the market indicator.

[8] See Gooch, "Eurodollar disaster clauses" (1983) I.F.L.Rev. June, 9; Karat, *The Eurodollar disaster clause and corporate restructuring* (1983) I.F.L.Rev. September, 15.

agree new terms upon which the loan will operate.[9] If the parties fail to incorporate an alternative interest rate it is unlikely that an English court would imply one [10] in the event of future market disturbance. In such a case, the court would most probably find an implied term that the original interest rate, applicable before the market disturbance, would continue to apply.[11] This may have serious consequences for the lending bank depending upon how the prevailing market rates have moved since the last occasion when the interest rate was determined.

Additional flexibility is provided by the multicurrency options which can be incorporated within the terms of the agreement. Lenders in the eurocurrency loan market are able to offer borrowers a multicurrency option under which the borrower is permitted, subject to certain qualifications, to drawdown in any currency and in some cases convert at a later date to a different currency. The LIBOR rate attaching to such loans will obviously be the rate applicable to the currency chosen by the borrower. **6.04**

The alternative structures, interest rate mechanisms and currency options outlined above can be combined in a variety of ways, and most lenders are willing to consider any practical combination to meet a specific need. In addition, the loan may be secured or unsecured,[12] guaranteed or unguaranteed,[13] syndicated or unsyndicated[14] or evidenced by notes or not so evidenced.[15] Whatever form the final loan takes, there are certain fundamental legal issues which will undoubtedly arise, many of which have yet to be fully worked out.

Some problems caused by the flexible structures

Where the loan is advanced in the form of a revolving facility there is always a risk that a borrower may later exceed its own borrowing limits as it continues to repay and drawdown under the terms of the agreement. Similarly, the lending bank may experience difficulties with future funding because of lending limits which are imposed in respect of individual borrowers or for all borrowers within a geographical area. These lending limits are normally imposed by local regulatory authorities, and they are becoming increasingly common at the time when failure by both lenders and borrowers in the eurocurrency markets is an everyday fact of life. Furthermore, banks which provide a facility imposing future obligations upon the bank, for example, the obligation to make funds available under a revolving loan or to convert currency under a multicurrency option, may find that their ability to assign **6.05**

---

[9] See clause 9 in the specimen agreement; Chap. 17 below. A similar mechanism is incorporated into most floating rate loans to provide for unforeseen increases in costs or any erosion of the lending bank's margin.

[10] See *King* v. *King* (1980) 41 P. & C.R. 311.

[11] *Ibid.*

[12] As to the legal issues arising from those loans over which security has been taken; see Chap. 14 below.

[13] See Chap. 25 below.

[14] See Chap. 7 below.

[15] See Chap. 10 below.

the loan at some later date is prohibited since many jurisdictions, including England prohibit the assignment of continuing obligations.[16]

One final problem posed by the revolving facility is that any security taken over such loans may be discharged as the loan "revolves," under the rule in *Clayton's case*.[17]

The structure of a eurocurrency loan agreement

6.06   The structure of a eurocurrency loan agreement is based upon a very simple contract whereby the lender promises to advance a certain sum over a certain period of time to the borrower and the borrower promises to pay the loan with interest. Unfortunately, the legal difficulties and problems which are likely to arise if anything goes wrong in this simple contract are many and complex, and, therefore, a large number of additional provisions are normally included in order to protect the parties's respective interests.

As we have already seen, the very fact that the transaction is cross-border will bring into play principles of private international law[18] with all its associated legal complications, and where the borrower is a sovereign state or state entity additional legal complications must be addressed.[19]

Negotiations between lender and borrower may take many weeks and the loan documentation must correctly reflect provisions which have been agreed. In addition to setting out the terms of the loan, the documentation should also

> "provide the ground rules procedures and mechanisms for the fulfilment, performance and enforcement of the different provisions of the contract. It should, as far as possible, anticipate and assess the various legal difficulties and problems that may arise and provide suitably for meeting or surmounting the difficulties and for finding solutions to, or steering clear of, the problems"[20]

We will now consider how the loan documentation may be structured to achieve its desired purpose.

The "drawdown" period

WHAT IF THE LENDER FAILS TO LEND OR THE BORROWER FAILS TO BORROW WITHIN THE "DRAWDOWN" PERIOD?

6.07   There are a number of reasons why the lending bank may, after executing the contract, decide not to make the funds available. The bank may fall into liquidation or erroneously believe that the borrower has failed to satisfy certain conditions precedent[20a] to the loan. Whatever the reason, an English court is unlikely to compel the bank to lend, even though it is contractually

---

[16] For a fuller discussion of the legal problems associated with assignment, see Chap. 8 below.
[17] *Devaynes* v. *Noble*; *Clayton's Case* (1916) 1 Mer. 529.
[18] See Chap. 1 above.
[19] See Chap. 3 above.
[20] K. Venkatachari in Kalderén and Siddiqui (ed.) p. 77.
[20a] Conditions precedent are considered in greater detail at paras. 6.23 *et seq.* below.

bound to do so, since specific performance is not normally available to enforce a lender's commitment to provide funds.[21]

The borrower's remedy in such a case would, therefore, lie in an action for damages. Damages for breach of contract are designed to give the borrower, as nearly as possible, what he would have received had the lending bank performed its obligations under the loan agreement. However, not all loss suffered by the borrower is recoverable, for there must be a sufficient connection between the bank's breach and the borrower's loss. In other words the loss must not be too remote.[22] The loss must arise naturally from the breach itself[23] or have been reasonably foreseeable by the parties, at the time they entered into the contract, as the probable result of the breach.[24]

The possible heads of damage would include[25]:

(a) General damages, particularly where the borrower can only obtain a replacement facility upon more onerous terms.[26]

(b) Damages for consequential or incidental loss including expenses incurred by the borrower in procuring an identical loan elsewhere[27] and any increase in the interest rate applied to the new loan.[28]

FAILURE BY THE BORROWER TO DRAWDOWN THE FACILITY

Eurocurrency loan agreements do not normally commit the borrower to drawdown the facility, but instead confer an option to borrow.[29] The borrower is normally required to give notice of its intention to borrow[30] and is only bound once such notice has been given. If the borrower fails to drawdown the loan after irrevocably committing itself, it is unlikely that specific performance will be available as a remedy to the lender.[31] However, damages may be available in certain circumstances,[32] although it is unlikely that the lender would be able to claim pre-contractual expenses, including administrative costs and legal fees, unless a clause had been included in the agreement providing that such expenses became payable upon execution of the loan. Such clauses are relatively common in eurocurrency loan agreements, as are those which cover the payment of certain fees,[33] notwith-

6.08

---

[21] See *South African Territories* v. *Wallington* [1898] A.C. 309, 314 H.L.; *Rogers* v. *Challis* (1859) 27 Bear 175; *Sichel* v. *Mosenthal* (1862), 30 Bear 371; *cf. Loan Investment Corpn. of Australasia* v. *Bonner* [1970] N.Z.L.R. 724, P.C.

[22] See *The Heron II* [1969] A.C. 350.

[23] *Hadley* v. *Baxendale* (1854) 9 Exch. 341.

[24] *Ibid.* see also, *Victoria Laundry (Windsor) Ltd.* v. *Newman Industries Ltd.* (1949) 2 K.B. 528; *Koufos* v. *Czarnikow Ltd.; The Heron II* [1969] 1 A.C. 350; *Parsons (Livestock) Ltd.* v. *Uttley Ingham & Co. Ltd.* [1978] Q.B. 791; *Wadsworth* v. *Lydall* [1981] 1 W.L.R. 598.

[25] For a detailed discussion of the various heads of damage which may be recoverable by the borrower, see Gabriel, pp. 35–40.

[26] *South African Territories Case* above, n. 21; see also *Manchester and Oldham Bank Ltd.* v. *W. A. Cook & Co.* (1883) 49 L.T. 674, 678.

[27] *Prehn* v. *Royal Bank of Liverpool* (1870) L.R. 5 Exch. 92.

[28] *South African Territories case*, above, n. 21.

[29] See clause 4 in the specimen agreement, Chap. 17 below.

[30] *Ibid.*

[31] *Rogers* v. *Challis* (1859) 27 Bear. 175.

[32] For a fuller discussion of the circumstances in which damages may be available, see Gabriel, pp. 41–43.

[33] The fees which may be payable are considered later in this chapter below paras. 6.11 *et seq.*

standing the fact that the loan is never drawndown.[34] In so far as damages for breach of contract are concerned it is likely, bearing in mind the funding mechanism employed in the eurocurrency markets, that the lender would be able to recover general damages, providing the conditions outlined above in relation to damages for the lender's breach are satisfied.[35] The lender will obviously be under a duty to mitigate its loss, in other words it must take all reasonable steps to minimise its loss by, for example, employing the undrawn funds elsewhere.[36]

Restrictions on the use or purpose of the loan

6.09   Generally speaking, eurocurrency loan agreements do not impose restrictions on the manner in which the funds are to be used, although restrictions are common in rescheduling and project finance agreements.[37] Sovereign borrowers would, no doubt, consider such restrictions an unwelcome interference in domestic affairs, and in practical terms it will obviously be extremely difficult for a lender effectively to police any restriction which is imposed on the use of funds. This difficulty is reflected in the wording of clauses which do attempt to impose restrictions, *viz*:

> ". . . without prejudice to the foregoing [restriction] none of the Agents, the Managers and the Banks shall be bound to enquire as to the applications by the Borrower of the proceeds of the loan, nor shall any of them be responsible for, or for the consequences of, such application."

Notwithstanding the enormous practical difficulty in restricting the use of funds, there are a number of legal considerations which may be of fundamental importance to the lender. In the most extreme case the borrower may utilise the loan proceeds for an illegal purpose, thus rendering the loan contract void under English law if both lender and borrower are aware of all the circumstances.

Even if the lender is unaware of the illegal purpose at the time the loan is executed, it must prevent any further drawdown once it becomes aware of the illegal purpose, lest it be implicated in the illegality and lose its right to enforce the loan.[38] The lender may also be at risk where the loan has been advanced to a sovereign state or state entity[39] and the loan is not commercial in nature. In such a situation the borrower will prima facie be entitled to

---

[34] See clause 4(5) in the specimen agreement, Chap. 17 below.

[35] That is to say the loss must not be too remote, must arise naturally from the borrower's breach and must have been reasonably foreseeable by the parties at the time they entered into the contract, see para. 6.07 above.

[36] See, *Compania Financiera Soleador SA* v. *Hamoor Tanker Corpn. Inc., The Borag* [1981] 1 All ER 856, [1981] 1 W.L.R. 274 where the issue was the recoverability of interest charges paid on a loan taken out by the plaintiff as a consequence of the defendant's breach of contract. Templeman L.J. said (at p. 864) " . . . in the present case if the interest charges were unreasonable, they were too remote: they were not caused by the breach: they were not part of a reasonable form of mitigation: all these matters hang together."

[37] As to the way in which the clause may be worded, see clause 3 in the specimen agreement, Chap. 17 below.

[38] See Chap. 2 above.

[39] See Chap. 3 above.

immunity under English law, thereby preventing the bank from enforcing the loan unless appropriate measures have been included within the terms of the loan documentation.[40]

Where the loan is granted in favour of a corporate borrower it may be **6.10** important to determine whether the borrower intends to use the proceeds for an *ultra vires* purpose.[41] Under English law all persons who deal with a company are deemed to have knowledge of the contents of the Company Memorandum and Articles of Association, and contracts which are *ultra vires* the objects are a nullity and unenforceable.[42] However, providing the company has power to borrow, the lender is entitled to assume that the money will be expended on objects competent to the company.[43] This principle will obviously not apply in circumstances where the lender knows that the loan is to be used for an *ultra vires* purpose, and in such a case the loan will be void and unenforceable.[44]

Other restrictions may be imposed by the local laws of the borrower's own jurisdiction. Some, for example, place restrictions on loans which finance acquisitions and mergers. In every case, therefore, it will be important to obtain the advice of local counsel on issues similar to those highlighted above,[44a] and also to incorporate protective provisions within the loan documentation which enable the lender to bring effective enforcement proceedings should this prove necessary.[45]

Fees

There are a number of different fees which may be payable by the borrower **6.11** in a eurocurrency loan agreement, although most of these are only levied if the loan is being syndicated.[46] Single lender medium term loans have traditionally not levied fees, although they are becoming slightly more common as an important source of profit due to a significant erosion of margins in recent years within the eurocurrency loan market. Borrowers are often prepared to pay more in undisclosed front-end fees rather than higher spreads (which may imply a poorer credit rating). As we have already seen,[47] some of these fees may be payable even though the borrower does not drawdown the facility and may, therefore, operate as a significant disincentive against the borrower seeking alternative funding once it has become committed under the original facility.

The following are examples[48] of the fees which may be payable.

---

[40] *Ibid.* See also, clause 29 in the specimen agreement, Chap. 17 below.
[41] For a detailed discussion of this topic, see Vol. 1 Chap. 16.
[42] *Anglo-Overseas Agencies* v. *Green* [1961] 1 Q.B. 1; [1960] 3 All E.R. 244.
[43] *Re David Payne & Co. Ltd.* [1904] 2 Ch. 608; *cf. Thompson* v. *J. Burke Co., (Caterers), Ltd.* (1975) S.L.T. 67.
[44] *Re Introductions Ltd.* v. *National Provincial Bank* [1970] Ch. 199 [1969] 1 All E.R. 887.
[44a] The importance of obtaining legal opinions is considered in greater detail in Chap. 16 below.
[45] See Chap. 2 above.
[46] See Chap. 7 below.
[47] Above, para. 6.08.
[48] For a fuller discussion of the fees which may be payable, see Donaldson and Donaldson, Chap. 4.

A. COMMITMENT FEES[49]

6.12   In most eurocurrency loan agreements the lender will be committed to make the funds available as soon as the loan is executed,[50] even though the borrower may not drawdown the facility immediately. In such cases the burden of risk rests heavily on the lender which may, as a consequence, require the borrower to pay a commitment fee, on the undrawn portion of the committed facility, to compensate the bank for the risk it bears.[51] The fee payable is usually expressed as a percentage of the undrawn facility on a day to day basis.[52] Fees of less than 1 per cent are normally expressed in terms of basis points, and market practice recognises each basis point as referring to one-hundredth of 1 per cent.

B. FRONT-END FEES

6.13   A variety of front-end fees may be payable by the borrower depending upon the type of facility being advanced. These fees are normally payable once and for all shortly after the loan has been executed, and relate to the entire facility, regardless of whether it is fully drawn, cancelled or pre-paid. Front-end fees are particularly valuable to the lender where there is a risk of early cancellation or pre-payment, and they are commonly found in syndicated loan agreements where they are normally paid to each participating bank in proportion to the exposure being taken.

Front-end fees can be broken down into different categories, *viz.*:

C. PRAECIPIUM OR LEAD MANAGEMENT FEE[53]

6.14   A lead management fee will only apply in major loans which have a group of managers. The fee is paid in recognition of the work done by the lead manager in obtaining the mandate, organising the management group and leading the negotiation process. The documentation normally provides that management fees are payable by the borrower regardless of whether drawdown actually takes place.

D. MANAGEMENT FEE

6.15   Some large loans provide for a management fee in addition to the lead management fee. Where such a fee is levied it is normally divided equally between the management group, and is payable regardless of drawdown.

---

[49] See clause 20(*i*) in the specimen agreement Chap. 17 below.

[50] In some agreements the commitment fee may run from a date earlier than the date the agreement is executed, for example, in circumstances where a commitment letter is accepted by the prospective borrower before formal execution of the loan. Alternatively, some agreements provide that the commitment fee will run from a specified date after the agreement has been executed.

[51] When margins in the market are particularly tight a commitment fee may be levied on the entire facility, regardless of usage. In such cases it is normally referred to as a "facility fee" rather than a commitment fee.

[52] See clause 20(1) in the specimen agreement, Chap. 17 below.

[53] See clause 20(2)(*a*) in the specimen agreement, Chap. 17 below.

E. UNDERWRITING FEE

When the loan is being underwritten, normally by the managers, an **6.16** underwriting fee may be levied, as a percentage of the sum being under-written.

F. PARTICIPATION FEE

Again, this fee, when levied, will be expressed as a percentage of each **6.17** bank's participation in the loan agreement. This fee is normally paid by the manager(s) out of the overall management fee, but in some cases, for example, where the borrower has a poor credit rating, it may be levied in addition to the management fee.

Front end fees compensate the lending bank(s) in two ways; first, the pro-portionate value of the fee levied will be greater if the loan is cancelled or pre-paid by the borrower and will therefore, to a certain extent, offset such cancellation. Secondly, the fact that such fees are levied, notwithstanding drawdown, may dissuade some borrowers from exploiting the market advantages of pre-payment and may thus strengthen the negotiating pos-ition of the original lenders.

There is little doubt that front-end fees have assumed a more practical sig-nificance in recent years because of the substantial erosion of margins on eurocurrency loans. Many banks now view the fee package as an important source of profit as well as a compensatory mechanism.

Other fees which may be payable

G. AGENCY FEES[54]

Agency fees are levied on most loans which provide for the appointment of **6.18** one or more agent banks.[55] The fee is normally paid annually in recognition of the administrative duties carried out by the agent(s). The fee may be expressed as a percentage of the entire facility, or as a pre-agreed fixed sum, and the actual amount levied will normally reflect the value and complexity of the loan.

H. LEGAL FEES[56]

Medium term loan agreements obviously vary in complexity, and this is **6.19** reflected in the level of legal fees. While legal fees are rarely large in percent-age terms, they nevertheless tend to be a major expense, and the lender(s) should always provide for an express clause within the loan agreement whereby the borrower agrees to indemnify the lender(s) in respect of such fees. Rather than make specific reference to legal fees, some loans incorpor-ate an all-embracing expenses clause, which requires the borrower to reim-burse the lender(s) for all expenses incurred in connection with the loan.[57]

[54] See clause 20(2)(c) in the specimen agreement, Chap. 17 below.
[55] The role of the agent bank is considered in more detail in Chap. 7 below.
[56] See clause 21 in the specimen agreement, Chap. 17 below.
[57] *Ibid.*

I. STAMP TAXES[58]

6.20   In ascertaining which country's stamp laws will apply to the loan agreement much will depend on the nationality of the borrower and the law of the place where the loan is executed. The amount, if any, of stamp tax or duty payable will vary widely from one jurisdiction to another, and it is sometimes possible to avoid these taxes by executing the agreement in a jurisdiction which does not apply stamp taxes. In so far as English law is concerned if the loan is executed and retained outside the United Kingdom, it is not stampable until it is brought into the United Kingdom. However, if court proceedings are commenced in the United Kingdom by the lender, the loan agreement would have to be brought into the United Kingdom and stamp duty would then have to be paid. If the loan is not stamped within 30 days of the agreement being executed or entry into the United Kingdom, it cannot be adduced as evidence in court proceedings, and late stamping will therefore be necessary before proceedings on the loan can be commenced. Heavy penalties are imposed upon documents which require late stamping, such penalties increasing in accordance with the delay in stamping.

Because different jurisdictions adopt a variety of stamp duty requirements, it is common for the lender(s) to insist that the loan documentation include a provision whereby the borrower agrees to indemnify the lender(s) against every eventuality covering . . .

> "all stamp, registration and similar taxes or charges imposed by law or by any governmental authority which may be payable or determined to be payable in connection with the execution, delivery, performance or enforcement of this Agreement"[59]

The importance of controlling the jurisdiction in which the loan is executed

6.21   The importance of ascertaining, and controlling, the jurisdiction in which the loan is executed has been highlighted in earlier chapters.[60] In some cases the place of execution will be self evident as the loan will be signed by all relevant parties in one place. Other cases, however, may be less clear, particularly where the agreement is signed by one party, say the borrower, in one jurisdiction and then posted for signature by the lender in another jurisdiction. Under English law, such an agreement would be deemed executed in the jurisdiction where it is accepted, and where a postal method of acceptance is adopted this would be the place where acceptance is posted by the

---

[58] See clause 22 in the specimen agreement Chap. 17 below.

[59] *Ibid.*

[60] See Chaps. 1 and 2 above. In the absence of an express choice of law the place of execution will be an important factor in determining the proper law of the loan agreement. Local execution of the loan may also, in certain cases, confer jurisdiction on the local courts, see Chap. 2. Other important considerations which may be influenced by the place of execution include: the applicability of stamp taxes and similar duties, above para. 6.20. See also *Adams* v. *Lindsell* (1818) 1 B. & Ald. 681; *Hanthorn* v. *Fraser* (1892) 2 Ch. 27; on the applicability of local formal requirements relating to the loan agreement and the applicability of local taxation requirements.

offeree.[61] Under English rules of private international law, if there is a conflict on the question of execution, the issue would fall to be determined by the proper law of the contract.[62]

RESTRICTIONS IMPOSED UPON THE BORROWER WITHIN THE TERMS OF THE LOAN DOCUMENTATION

The lender taking the credit analysis decision in a eurocurrency term loan   **6.22**
agreement usually bases his decision upon a series of assumptions and *caveats*. As Clark and Taylor point out[63]: " . . . The main thrust of these may be paraphrased by the banks' statement that 'we assume that you are able to repay us and that, if you don't we can force you to repay us. If we are wrong, we want to get out of the transaction.' "

These assumptions and *caveats* are effectively given contractual force by the incorporation of certain restrictive clauses within the terms of the loan agreement known as conditions precedent, representations and warranties, covenants and events of default. The restrictive clauses, when taken together, fulfil three specific functions: first, they help to provide the lender with detailed information concerning the borrower; secondly, they provide for certain contractual remedies within the framework of the loan agreement; and thirdly, they give the lender the benefit of certain remedies available under the general law.

A. Conditions precedent[64]

Most eurocurrency term loan agreements expressly provide that the loan   **6.23**
will not become operative until certain conditions have been met. Even after the loan has become operative the borrower is normally required to satisfy further conditions prior to any subsequent drawdown. These conditions are known respectively as conditions precedent and conditions subsequent.

THE LEGAL AND PRACTICAL SIGNIFICANCE OF CONDITIONS PRECEDENT

The purpose of the conditions precedent is to suspend the lender's commit-   **6.24**
ment until the security, if any, is perfected and satisfactory evidence has been received that all pertinent legal matters concerning both the borrower and guarantor, if any, are in order. They also seek to permit the lender(s) to withdraw from the agreement at any time before the "conditions" have been met. In so far as English law is concerned, whether the conditions pre-

---

[61] *Entores Ltd.* v. *Miles Far East Corporation* [1955] 2 Q.B. 327; *Brinkibon Ltd.* v. *Stahog Stahl und Stahlwarenhandelsgesellschaft mbH.* [1982] 2 All E.R. 293.
[62] See Chap. 1 above.
[63] Clark and Taylor, *Representations and conditions precedent in eurocurrency loan agreements* Int'l Fin.L.Rev. (July, 1982) p. 28.
[64] See clause 12 in the specimen agreement, Chap. 17 below.

cedent achieve this purpose will depend upon whether they are conditions precedent to the actual formation of the loan contract. If they are, the lender will be free to withdraw from the agreement at any time before the borrower meets the conditions.[65]

The precise working of the clause will obviously be crucial in determining whether or not the lender is free to withdraw. As Gabriel points out, the wording of the conditions precedent in many agreements places the emphasis upon the borrower's right to borrow,[66] and the conditions precedent operate only upon the lender's obligation to lend once the agreement has been executed. In such a situation " . . . any withdrawal from its commitment to lend, even before the borrower has begun to satisfy any condition, would result in the lender breaching the contract and thus exposing itself to a suit at the instance of the borrower."[67] The danger in such a situation is that difficulties may arise after the loan has been executed, but before the conditions precedent have been satisfied, and these difficulties are not caught by other restrictive clauses. In such a case the lender would be unable to withdraw without breaching the contract.[68] There is English authority which suggests that in such a case the lender cannot withdraw whilst the event (condition) can still be met.[69] It may be important, therefore, in appropriate cases, for the agreement to expressly provide that a formally binding contract will not exist until the conditions precedent have been satisfied by the borrower,[70] otherwise it will not be clear (at least under English law) whether failure by the borrower to bring about the conditions precedent permits the lender to withdraw from the agreement, or merely suspends that agreement.[71]

CONDITIONS PRECEDENT COMMONLY FOUND IN EUROCURRENCY LOAN AGREEMENTS

6.25 The conditions precedent drafted into the loan agreement will vary accordingly to the particular circumstances of all parties who contract under the agreement. There are no standard conditions precedent in eurocurrency loans. Where the borrower is incorporated it is usual for the lender to

---

[65] *Pym* v. *Campbell* (1856) 6 E & B 370; see also, Gabriel, pp. 43–49; Clark and Taylor, *loc. cit.*, n. 63.

[66] *Ibid.*, p. 44.

[67] *Ibid.*

[68] *Ibid.*

[69] *Smith* v. *Butler* [1900] 1 Q.B. 694; *cf. Felixstowe Dock and Railway Co.* v. *British Transport Docks Board* [1976] 2 Lloyd's Rep. 656; *Alan Estates Ltd.* v. *W. G. Stores Ltd.* [1981] 3 W.L.R. 892.

[70] Such a clause may operate upon the borrower's option contract whereby the borrower must give notice before he borrows and thereafter his commitment is binding. See Gabriel, p. 46.

[71] It would seem that there are three possibilities under English law depending upon the precise wording of the clause: (i) each party may be free to withdraw until the event occurs; (ii) The loan agreement may not be binding until the event occurs, but so long as the event can still occur, the parties cannot withdraw; see the cases cited in n. 69 above; (iii) the loan agreement may not be binding until the event occurs, but in the meantime neither party must do anything to prevent the occurrence of the event; see *Mackay* v. *Dick* (1881) 6 App. Cas. 251; it may be the case that one of the parties is bound to do his best to bring about the event, although he will not be liable if he fails to do so, see *Re Anglo-Russian Merchant Traders* [1917] 2 K.B. 679.

require copies of all relevant constitutional documentation. If the company was incorporated in England such documents would include the Memorandum and Articles of Association. In addition, copies of corporate authorisations, such as board resolutions and, where relevant, shareholders' sanctions would also be required. The lender also usually requires satisfactory evidence that any necessary guarantees or other security devices have been perfected, and that any governmental and/or exchange control[72] consents have been obtained. Where the borrower is a sovereign state or state controlled entity a variety of declarations and authorisations from both the state's government and its central bank will also be required.[73]

An additional, and very important, condition precedent is the requirement to furnish legal options, addressed to the lender, and drawn up by lawyers in the jurisdiction of the borrower and of the guarantor, where relevant.[74] The legal opinions should address the legal implications of the loan documentation by examining the impact of the representations and warranties[75] made by the borrower and any guarantor. However, it must be appreciated that legal opinions do not amount to a guarantee that the transaction is a valid and binding agreement. The lawyer's duty is only to exercise reasonable care and skill in furnishing the opinion, which can never amount to guarantee that the transaction is valid and binding, since his opinion will only relate to the laws of his own jurisdiction and will not cover any other legal system which impacts upon the loan agreement.[76]

CONDITIONS SUBSEQUENT[77]

6.26 It is common practice when drafting eurocurrency loans to specify certain "standard" conditions which must be satisfied at or before each subsequent drawdown.[78] These include the condition that the representations and warranties made by the borrower at the time the loan was executed continue to be true, and that no event of default[79] has occurred and is continuing or will result from the drawdown.[80]

The aim of the conditions subsequent is to suspend any subsequent drawdown, unless the borrower's position, both financially and otherwise, is consistent with that as "represented" in the agreement when the loan was originally executed.

It can be clearly seen that the conditions, both precedent and subsequent, described above are included for the benefit of the lending bank(s), and,

---

[72] See Chap. 4 above.

[73] See clause 12(i)(a)-(g) in the specimen agreement, Chap. 17 below. For a fuller discussion of the various declarations and authorisations which may be requested, see Chap. 3 above.

[74] It is also common for a legal opinion to be drawn up by the lawyers who draft the agreement and where the loan is syndicated a legal opinion is usually required from lawyers acting on behalf of the Agent bank(s). On the importance of legal opinions generally, see Chap. 16 below.

[75] The significance of the representations and warranties is considered in para. 6.27 below.

[76] For a fuller discussion on the topic of legal opinions, see Chap. 16 below.

[77] See clause 12(2) in the specimen agreement, Chap. 17 below.

[78] Conditions subsequent are sometimes referred to as continuing conditions precedent or conditions to each loan.

[79] On events of default generally, see Chap. 9 below.

[80] See clause 16 in the specimen agreement, Chap. 17 below.

therefore, can be waived by such bank(s) as if they were never included in the first place.[81]

B. Representations and warranties[82]

6.27   A golden rule in every form of bank lending, be it purely domestic or international, is "know your borrower." This rule is obviously difficult to satisfy in eurocurrency lending, since the close relationship which normally exists between bank and borrower, in domestic lending, is rarely evident in eurocurrency loans. Nevertheless, there are certain fundamental facts about the borrower of which a lending bank must always assure itself, before granting any loan facility. It is principally in order to ascertain these fundamental facts that representations and warranties are incorporated within the loan documentation. In strict legal parlance representations are statements made, and warranties are undertakings given, by the borrower on the basis of which the lender makes the credit available.

Representations and warranties commonly fall into two categories: (1) Those clauses giving various assurances as to the legal validity of the obligations into which the borrower is entering; (2) Clauses relating to the financial condition of the borrower.

REPRESENTATIONS AND WARRANTIES COMMONLY FOUND N EUROCURRENCY TERM LOANS

6.28   The representations and warranties clause usually commences with a number of statements concerning the valid existence and authorisation of the borrower, and include: that the borrower is validly existing under the relevant foreign law[83] and has power to borrow or enter into other obligations, such as the giving of a guarantee, required under the agreement. When considering the capacity of the borrower it is usual to incorporate a statement that the borrower will not be in contravention of any relevant laws or regulations,[84] such as exchange controls or capital controls. There may also be a statement that any necessary government or regulatory approvals have been obtained,[85] a statement that the loan is valid and constitutes a binding obligation upon the borrower, enforceable in accordance with its terms[86]; a statement that no litigation, arbitration or other proceedings are, to the best of the borrower's knowledge, threatened against the borrower which might adversely affect the ability of the borrower to perform its obligations under the loan agreement[87]; a statement that the bor-

---

[81] *Bennett* v. *Fowler* (1840) 2 Bear 302; *Hawksley* v. *Outram* [1892] 3 Ch. 359; *Morrell* v. *Studd and Millington* [1913] 2 Ch. 648. For an excellent discussion of the legal rules relating to waiver, see the Encyclopaedia, para. F 3631 *et seq.*

[82] See clause 13 in the specimen agreement.

[83] See *Lazard Bros & Co.* v. *Midland Bank Ltd.* [1933] A.C. 289; *National Bank of Greece and Athens SA* v. *Metliss* [1958] A.C. 509. See also, the discussion of the English private international law rules relating to the existence of a foreign corporation above, Chap. 1, para. 1.22.

[84] See clause 13(1)(*c*) in the specimen agreement, Chap. 17 below.

[85] See clause 13(1)(*e*) in the specimen agreement, Chap. 17 below.

[86] See clause 13(1)(*b*) in the specimen agreement, Chap. 17 below.

[87] See clause 13(1)(*f*) in the specimen agreement, Chap. 17 below.

rower is not in breach of any of its other obligations which might materially affect its ability to perform its obligations under the loan agreement[88]; a statement that no default has occured[89]; a statement that the recent audited accounts of the borrower reflect a true and fair view of the borrower's financial condition and the borrower has no other material liabilities which are not disclosed in the accounts.[90] It is also common to incorporate an all-embracing material adverse change clause which may read as follows:

> "There has been no material adverse change since . . . . in the financial condition of the Borrower or in the Borrower's ability to perform its obligations under this Agreement."

The difficulty with this clause is that it begs the question: what is **6.29** material? It could be argued that this question is answered by applying an objective test, and English authority certainly appears to support such a notion,[91] in which case the clause will operate in a most unpredicatable manner. The lender should try to avoid such unpredictability, whenever possible, by incorporating either a materiality test[92] or by making the test subjective, *viz*.: "material in the opinion of the lender."

Where the borrower is a sovereign state or state controlled entity it is also common to include a statement that the borrower is subject to civil and commercial law with regard to its obligations under the agreement[93]; a statement that the borrowing constitutes a commercial, rather than a governmental act and that the borrower does not enjoy immunity from set-off, suit or execution in respect of its obligations under the agreement, and finally, a statement that the borrower is a member of the International Monetary Fund.[94]

EVERGREEN REPRESENTATIONS AND WARRANTIES[95]

In many cases, the representations and warranties given by the borrower are **6.30** isolated statements reflecting the circumstances at the time the loan agreement is executed. This, to a certain extent, contradicts the position as perceived by the lending bank, which normally assumes that the matters

---

[88] See clause 13(1)(*g*) in the specimen agreement, Chap. 17 below. The word material obviously begs the question "what is material" and wherever possible a materiality test should be included. See Chap. 9 below.

[89] See clause 13(1)(*d*) in the specimen agreement, Chap. 17 below.

[90] Where the borrower is required on a regular basis to supply financial statements which are not audited, the borrower should be required to present such statements in accordance with generally accepted principles of good accounting practice. This particular warranty will obviously only be as good as the raw financial information which is supplied to the lender.

[91] *Docker* v. *Hyams* [1969] 1 Lloyd's Rep. 333; *affd.* [1969] 3 All E.R. 808, C.A. See also, Gabriel, pp. 58–60.

[92] The significance of the words "material adverse change" is considered in greater detail in relation to Events of Default, see Chap. 9 below.

[93] See clause 13(1)(*i*) in the specimen agreement, Chap. 17 below. The significance of these statements is considered in Chap. 4 above.

[94] See clause 13(1)(*l*) in the specimen agreement, Chap. 17 below. Membership of the International Monetary Fund is perceived as being particularly important in rescheduling agreements, see Chap. 9 below.

[95] See clause 13(2) in the specimen agreement, Chap. 17 below.

represented will remain so throughout the full term of the loan agreement. This particular problem can be resolved in a number of ways. First, the borrower may covenant to maintain the status quo as reflected by the representations and warranties, although in practical terms such a covenant will be virtually impossible to satisfy, since many of the matters covered by the representations and warranties are likely to be beyond the borrower's control. An alternative approach to the problem is to include an appropriate event of default clause linked to the representations and warranties. Such a clause is commonly adopted, notwithstanding that most borrowers, particularly sovereign states, resent the imputation inherent in its inclusion. An additional solution is obtained by including a rather artificial clause[96] within the loan agreement, which provides that the representations and warranties shall survive the execution of the agreement and remain true throughout the full term of the loan. Many loans also provide that the representations and warranties shall be deemed to be repeated at various times, usually before any subsequent drawdown, during the life of the loan.[97]

THE PURPOSE AND SIGNIFICANCE OF THE REPRESENTATIONS AND WARRANTIES

6.31   There are several purposes which the representations and warranties seek to address; they endeavour to provide remedies for misrepresentation in the event of an inaccuracy; they may operate as an estoppel against the borrower[98]; they may enable the lender to cancel the commitment and accelerate the loan if they are linked to an event of default.[99] On a more practical note, they provide a checklist which serves an investigative function for the lender.

Whether they achieve their desired purpose will depend to a large extent on how they are legally construed. There is a significant difference under English law between a representation and a warranty. A representation is a statement of fact,[1] not of opinion, or of law, which is made before the loan agreement has been executed, and in reliance upon the truth of which the lender enters into the loan agreement. It is not, however, an integral part of the contract.[2] A warranty on the other hand is a term of the contract itself. This distinction is of the utmost importance, since the availability of various common law remedies will be determined, to a large extent, by ascertaining whether the statement is a term of the contract. The key to discovering whether a statement is such a term lies in the intention of the parties and such intention is ascertained by applying an objective test.[3]

Appropriate drafting techniques can, however, avoid problems which arise out of the distinction between representations and warranties by

---

[96] This clause is commonly referred to as the "evergreen clause."

[97] See clause 13(2) in the specimen agreement, Chap. 17 below.

[98] *Balkis Consolidated Co.* v. *Tomkinson* [1893] A.C. 396.

[99] *Cherry* v. *Colonial Bank of Australasia* (1896) L.R. 3 P.C. 24; *Mackenzie* v. *Royal Bank of Canada* [1934] A.C. 468.

[1] *Leaf* v. *International Galleries* [1950] 1 All E.R. 693.

[2] *Behn* v. *Burness* (1863) 3 B & S 751.

[3] See *Oscar Chess Ltd.* v. *Williams* [1957] 1 W.L.R. 370: *Dick Bentley Productions Ltd.* v. *Howard Smith (Motors) Ltd.* [1965] 1 W.L.R. 623.

expressly making all statements warranties and, therefore, terms of the contract. Such an approach is common in eurocurrency loan agreements where the borrower "represents and warrants" in respect of every clause in the appropriate section of the documentation.[4] The fact that all statements are made warranties is unfortunately, not the end of the matter, since under English law there is an important distinction between warranties and conditions in so far as the available remedies are concerned. Strictly speaking, a warranty is a contractual term which affects some relatively minor aspect of the contract and, therefore, breach only entitles the innocent party to sue for damages.[5] In general, there is no right to terminate the agreement for breach of warranty. A condition, however, is a term which affects an important aspect of the contract, and breach entitles the innocent party not only to claim damages but also to terminate the contract for the future. Recent cases recognise an important group of intermediate terms which are neither conditions or warranties, breach of which justifies discharge it it amounts to a serious failure in performance.[6]

The distinction between conditions and warranties has in some cases been **6.32** based on the intention of the parties as expressed in the contract, but more recent cases suggest that the use of the words "condition" or "warranty" will not be conclusive.[7] Where no intention is expressed, the distinction may be based upon the seriousness of the failure to perform the contractual term at issue.[8] In other words, where the term broken is so important that it would be unreasonable to expect the innocent party to fulfil its obligations under the contract, it seems likely that the term will be construed as a condition.[9]

The distinction between conditions and warranties under English law has become overlaid with technicalities, and their classification is at the very least unpredictable[10]; it will, therefore, be most important for the lender to avoid any future classification problems by expressly incorporating various remedies within the terms of the loan agreement which cover the eventuality of the representations and warranties being untrue. This is achieved in most eurocurrency loans by linking the representations and warranties to an event of default *viz.* . . .

> "It shall be an event of default in the event that any representation and warranty or warranty of the Borrower or the Guarantor in this Agreement or any other document delivered in connection with this Agreement proves to have been incorrect, incomplete or misleading . . . "[11]

Such a clause clearly indicates that the parties perceive the representations and warranties as fundamental to the contract, giving rise to the right to

---

[4] See clause 13 in the specimen agreement, Chap. 17 below.
[5] *Hong Kong Fir Shipping Co. Ltd.* v. *Kawasaki Kisen Kaisha Ltd.* [1962] 2 Q.B. 26 [1962] 2 All E.R. 474.
[6] *Bunge Corpn.* v. *Tradex SA* [1981] 2 All E.R. 513. *Tradex International SA* v. *Goldschmidt SA* [1977] 2 Lloyd's Rep. 604 *cf. Wallis* v. *Pratt* [1911] A.C. 394.
[7] See, for example, *Schiler A.G.* v. *Wickman Machine Tool Sales Ltd.* [1974] A.C. 235.
[8] *Bunge Corpn.* v. *Tradex SA*, above n. 6.
[9] *Ibid.*
[10] See Reynolds (1963), 79 L.Q.R. 534; Lord Devlin, [1966] Camb. L.R. 192.
[11] See also clause 16(*c*) in the specimen agreement, Chap. 17 below.

cancel the facility and accelerate in appropriate cases.[12] In such a case the representations and warranties would be classified as conditions rather than warranties.[13]

C. Covenants[14]

6.33 Eurocurrency loan agreements invariably contain certain undertakings with which the borrower is required to comply throughout the life of the loan. Such undertakings are generally referred to as "covenants."

The scope and purpose of the covenants which are used by those who draft the loan agreement tend to be as wide as the variety of lenders and borrowers who participate in the eurocurrency market.[15] Their primary objective, when taken together, is to ensure the continued soundness of the credit facility being advanced and to give the lender(s) certain inside information on, and limited control over, the business of the borrower.

The most important covenant made by the borrower is, of course, the borrower's promise to repay the loan either on a particular date or by a series of instalments.[16] This promise to repay is reinforced by additional covenants, the scope of which will be a matter of detailed negotiation between the lender and borrower. Negotiation of the covenants often proves a difficult exercise, since the parties often have such sharply contrasting interests. The borrower will obviously endeavour to retain for itself the greatest possible freedom with regard to the management of its business, whereas the lender will endeavour to impose suitable restrictions over the borrower's operations in order to safeguard its lending. A balance must clearly be struck and much will depend upon the relative bargaining strengths of the parties. The covenants ultimately agreed upon, as with all clauses in the loan agreement, should be specifically tailored. It is, nevertheless, possible to consider certain "fundamental" covenants which are commonly seen in eurocurrency loans.

1. The financial covenants

6.34 The financial covenants are designed to protect the lender's position should the borrower's credit-worthiness begin to deteriorate. They require a flow of financial information from the borrower to the lender which enables the

---

[12] The right to cancel and accelerate the facility is normally the most basic remedy afforded to the lender within the terms of the loan agreement, see clause 16(i) and (ii) in the specimen agreement, Chap. 17 below. In addition, the lender would, of course, be able to sue for the breach of condition.

[13] There may be a problem, however, where the event of default is worded in such a way that it must be "continuing" before default can be declared or where a grace period must elapse before declaration of any default, See Gabriel, p. 56.

[14] See clause 14 in the specimen agreement, Chap. 17 below. See generally on this topic, Wood, Chap. 6; Gabriel, Chap. 5; Kalderén & Siddiqi (ed.) p. 156 *et seq.*; Rendell, pp. 15–16; Clark and Taylor, "Conditions precedent and covenants in Eurocurrency loan agreements" Int'l Fin. L.Rev. (August, 1982) p. 28.

[15] As to the primary functions of the covenants, see Wood, pp. 145–146.

[16] The promise to repay is often contained in a separate clause independent from the other covenants; see clause 5 in the specimen agreement, Chap. 17 below, where the repayment is by means of seven, six-monthly instalments with the final payment on a specified date.

lender to monitor the borrower's financial health, providing, of course, the lender is in a position to check compliance. Ratio covenants,[17] which define certain acceptable requirements in relation to the borrower's financial condition, are commonly employed in this monitoring process. Such covenants may define the acceptable financial condition of the borrower with reference to the value of its net assets, after deduction of net liabilities, the ratio between such assets and liabilities indicating the threshold above which the borrower "covenants" to maintain its position.

An alternative approach is for the borrower to "covenant" that it will maintain a minimum figure for net assets after the deduction of liabilities, commonly defined as the minimum net worth threshold. Similarly the borrower may be required to maintain a certain "ratio" as between current liabilities and current assets or to maintain working capital above a predetermined figure.

Whatever form the ratio covenants take, the specific wording must always be clearly defined within the terms of the loan agreement.[18] Most borrowers can easily arrange their financing and accounting procedures in such a way as to significantly change the value of "working capital," "liquid assets," "minimum net worth," etc., as defined in everyday commercial life. The lender, therefore, must ensure that these and other key phrases are carefully defined in order to prevent accidental or deliberate avoidance of the financial covenants by the borrower.[19]

Compliance with the ratio covenants, provided they are appropriately drafted, should indicate that the borrower's business is being conducted in a prudent fashion, whilst breach of such covenants may be an indication of future financial difficulties, thereby operating as an early warning device. It must be appreciated, however, that financial covenants will only be as good as the raw financial information supplied by the borrower. Accounting standards vary enormously from one country to another and it should never be assumed that the high standards applied in the lender's home jurisdiction will be similar to those applied in the borrower's jurisdiction.

The financial covenants are given "teeth" by linking them to an event of default clause,[20] which is intended to enable the lender to demand repayment as early as possible whilst there is still some prospect of the borrower being able to meet the demand.

HOW EFFECTIVE ARE RATIO COVENANTS?

Where realistic parameters and clear definitions are selected for the ratio covenants there can be no doubt that a significant degree of protection is afforded to the lender. However, their shortcomings must not be overlooked. The financial information required by the covenants will often take many months to prepare, and, therefore, it will be long after the event before any contravention is brought to the lender's notice. It has already been stressed that accounting standards vary from country to country, and

6.35

---

[17] For an excellent discussion of ratio covenants, see Donaldson & Donaldson, Chap. 7.

[18] Eurocurrency loan agreements normally commence with a detailed list of definitions; see clause 1 in the specimen agreement, Chap. 17 below.

[19] See Donaldson & Donaldson, pp. 110–113.

[20] For a fuller discussion of how the events of default clause operates, see Chap. 9 below.

although the lender can partially overcome this by selecting appropriate auditors who will prepare the information, it must be appreciated that the ratio covenants will only be as good as the financial information supplied.

2. Material adverse change clause

6.36 The main alternative to ratio covenants[21] is a continuing material adverse change clause,[22] which will typically provides that it shall be an event of default . . .

> "if there is any material adverse change in the financial condition of the borrower which in the reasonable opinion of the bank may impair the ability of the borrower to perform its obligations under this Agreement.[23]

The legal difficulties posed by such a clause will be considered later,[24] and suffice it to say, at present, that even when the clause incorporates a "materiality" test its language will invariably pose difficulties of proof, due to its discretionary nature. There can, therefore, be little doubt that where the financial condition of the borrower is at issue, well drafted financial covenants are far more suitable than an all-embracing event of default clause. Well-defined covenants establish specific criteria, breach of which may be clearly identified by the lender, while at the same time guiding the borrower as to what must be done in order to avoid an event of default.

3. The negative pledge[25]

6.37 The majority of eurocurrency loan agreements are unsecured, and, therefore, most lenders feel it is vital, whenever possible, to fetter the borrower's ability to create or maintain secured indebtedness. In the event of the lender failing to control the borrower in this way, it may ultimately transpire that the borrower's unencumbered assets are unable to satisfy the lender's unsecured claim.[26]

The mechanism adopted in most eurocurrency loans to achieve this degree of control is the negative pledge clause,[27] which typically provides that the borrower shall not create or permit to subsist any security, usually

---

[21] It should be pointed out that in most loan agreements both ratio covenants and a material adverse change clause are included.

[22] See clause 16(*h*) in the specimen agreement, Chap. 17 below.

[23] This clause is only one example of many variations which may be used in an agreement. For further examples, see Wood, p. 168.

[24] See Chap. 9, para. 9.22 below.

[25] See generally, Wood, pp. 146–152; Gabriel, pp. 82–97; Kalderén & Siddiqi, pp. 156–175; Boardman & Crosthwait, "Wither the Negative Pledge" [1986] 3 J.I.B.L. 162.

[26] This problem will be particularly acute in the event of the borrower becoming insolvent. In such a situation other creditors, holding security, will have priority over the lender's unsecured claim.

[27] See clause 15 in the specimen agreement, Chap. 17 below.

specified as " . . . any mortgage, charge, pledge, lien or other encumbrance; over its assets or revenues unless the loan covered by the negative pledge is 'equally and rateably' secured."[28]

WHAT DOES THE NEGATIVE PLEDGE COVER?

It will be noticed that the wording in the example given is very broad[29] and without more would probably place too heavy a restriction on the borrower's business. It is common, however, to word the negative pledge very restrictively and then list a number of exceptions to its operation.[30]   **6.38**

The most common relaxation relates to encumbrances granted to third party creditors which are "equally and rateably secured."[31] The precise meaning of this phrase is unclear, but it would appear to cover the situation where security is granted to a third party, the proviso being that such security must also be used to secure the original lender's position on the eurocurrency loan equally and rateably[32] with the third party creditors. An alternative view is that where security is granted to a third party an equivalent security is to be granted in favour of the original lender. Much will obviously depend upon the precise wording of the clause, a typical example of which might read as follows:

> The Borrower will not create or permit to subsist any mortgage, charge, lien, pledge or other security interest on or over any of its present or future assets unless all the Borrower's obligations under this Agreement either:
> (a) share (to the satisfaction of the lender) the security afforded by such mortgage, charge, lien, pledge, or other security interest, equally and rateably with the loan, debt, guarantee or other obligation secured thereby,or
> (b) receive (to the satisfaction of the lender) the benefit of either a mortgage, charge, lien, pledge or other security interest, on other assets or revenues of the Borrower which the lender judges to be equivalent to that granted to such loan, debt, guarantee or other obligation.

---

[28] Lenders sometimes attempt to incorporate an automatic security negative pledge, which provides that if the borrower grants a third party security such security will automatically secure the present loan equally and rateably. See Wood, p. 150, and the cases cited therein. It is most doubtful, however, whether a security interest could be perfected by means of a simple automatic security clause, although this would be an issue to be determined by the law of the borrower's country or the country where the relevant asset is located (the *lex situs*). This important issue is considered in greater detail later in this chapter.

[29] For a detailed discussion of how broadly the clause may be drafted, see Kalderén and Siddiqi, above, n. 25. The intention is usually to cover all the borrower's assets, both present and future, which could be used to satisfy any potential claim by the lender.

[30] Encumbrances existing before the execution of the loan would have to be either discharged by the borrower or excepted by the lender if the words "shall not permit to subsist" are included in the negative pledge clause.

[31] Wood, p. 151.

[32] In practical terms it will be difficult to prescribe what is equal and rateable security. How can a mortgage over fixed assets be compared with a floating charge over receivables or a banker's lien? In such cases it is unlikely that the lender will reach agreement with the borrower on the meaning of equal and rateable security, and consequently, the lender would not be disposed to the creation of any third party security.

6.39   Notwithstanding the above, there shall be disregarded for the purpose of this clause:

  (i) Liens which arose or may arise by operation of law . . . ;
  (ii) any mortgage, charge, lien, pledge or other security interest not exceeding £ . . . . . . or . . . per cent. of [the] Borrower's tangible net worth;
  (iii) any mortgage, charge, lien, pledge or other security granted with the written consent of the lender.
  (iv) any mortgage, charge, lien, pledge or other security to secure indebtedness not being external indebtedness. [33]

The exemptions outlined in the above clause are only examples and their precise scope will be a matter for detailed negotiation between the parties. The clause must not be too restrictive so as to effectively preclude the borrower from entering into normal commercial arrangements, and the ill-considered clause may actually force the borrower into taking undesirable financial measures to raise funds, such as selling valuable assets which might otherwise be pledged. It is obviously in the lender's interest to keep the borrower's financial condition as healthy as possible and this should be borne in mind when the wording of the negative pledge is being negotiated. [34]

TO WHOM SHOULD THE NEGATIVE PLEDGE EXTEND?

6.40   Another important issue is whether the negative pledge should only cover security created by the borrower or whether it should encompass security created by related entities of the borrower. Where the borrower is a sovereign state the clause may be drafted so as to extend over governmental agencies and instrumentalities, although most states would strongly resist any attempt to bring either central banks or state-owned enterprises within its parameters. [35] Similarly, in the case of a corporate borrower the clause may extend over its subsidiaries, even though the lender will not, at least under English law, have a direct right of recourse against the assets of such subsidiaries, but only against the value of the borrower's interest in them. [36]

THE LEGAL NATURE OF THE NEGATIVE PLEDGE

6.41   It has already been stressed that the primary purpose of the negative pledge is to prevent third party creditors being preferred to the original lender which advances the eurocurrency loan. The intention in the majority of loan

---

[33] Other common exemptions include: encumbrances existing before the date of the present loan agreement and encumbrances existing over assets which the borrower acquires at a later date, for example, where the borrower purchases land, after he executes the loan, which is subject to an existing mortgage or charge. For a more definitive list of exemptions which may be included, see Kalderén & Siddiqi, pp. 174–175.

[34] Special exemptions are particularly common when the borrower is a sovereign state or state controlled entity, see, for example, clauses 15(2) (i), (ii) and (iii) in the specimen agreement, Chap. 17 below.

[35] See clause 15(2) in the specimen agreement, Chap. 17 below.

[36] Such value being, in practical terms, the value left over after the creditors of the subsidiaries have been satisfied.

agreements is to provide a mechanism whereby the borrower is required to consult the lender should it wish to create any secured indebtedness to third party creditors. In the event of the borrower failing to consult, the creation of such indebtedness will trigger an event of default in the original loan. It is submitted that the clause will rarely provide any other remedy to the original lender, such as the ability to dislodge the security granted in breach of the clause, which security will consequently have priority over the original lender's unsecured claim.[37]

A number of loan agreements drafted by American lawyers have attempted to increase significantly both the scope and purpose of the negative pledge clause, by incorporating within its terms an automatic security device. Such a clause basically provides that when the borrower grants third party security, in breach of the negative pledge, the borrower's obligations under the original lender's loan shall be secured upon the same assets, equally and rateably, with the third party obligations which are being secured. It is submitted that such a clause could not, under English law, give rise to a present equitable interest (which presumably is its primary intention), since the interest will only arise once the contingency in the clause is satisfied.[38] In other words, it can only advise when the borrower breaches the clause and grants third party security, at which point an equitable interest is immmediately created in favour of the original lender. This interest may be a present right for value,[39] (value being an essential ingredient if a security interest is to be created) in appropriate circumstances, for example, where the original lender is able to suspend future drawdowns unless the security interest is created in its favour. Providing the ingredient of value is present, another *caveat* relates to the question of intention[40] and the wording of the clause must clearly indicate that it was the borrower's intention to grant an equitable interest in favour of the lender.[41]

If one accepts the foregoing argument, a further *caveat* which must be satisfied (if the clause is to give rise to a security interest) is that the clause must identify the assets over which the future security interest is being prospectively offered by the borrower. Where the wording of the clause specifically states that the original lender's security interest will attach to *those assets* over which the third party creditor is given security, equally and rateably, the problem of identification is removed. However, if the clause states that upon the grant of such third party security, the original lender is to be given matching security, equal in value to the third party security, but over different assets, no security interest is created since the assets (over which

6.42

---

[37] It would, of course, be possible to dislodge third party security which is either not perfected (*i.e.* because it has not been registered) or is in breach of local insolvency rules (*i.e.* a floating charge granted within six months of a winding-up). See generally, Vol. 1, Chap. 22 of this work.

[38] See Goode, "Legal Problems of Credit and Security" (1982) pp. 48–51; Gabriel, pp. 84–90.

[39] See *Re Jackson & Bassford Ltd.* [1906] 2 Ch. 467, p. 479; *Re Gregory Love & Co. Francis v. Gregory Love & Co.* [1916] 1 Ch. 203, p. 211, cited in Gabriel, pp. 87–88; *cf.* Goode *loc. cit.*, above. n. 38, where he suggests that the value must be given at or after and in consideration of the security, and that money advanced by the lender prior to the date the contingency is met will not satisfy the "value" requirement. Goode, therefore, concludes that the negative pledge gives nothing more than a contractual right.

[40] *William Brandt's Sons & Co.* v. *Dunlop Rubber Co. Ltd.* [1905] A.C. 454; *Norman* v. *Federal Cmmr. of Taxation* (1962) 109 C.L.R. 9, cited in Gabriel, p. 90.

[41] *Ibid.*

the original lender's security will attach) have not been identified.[42] Before the contingency is satisfied, by breach of the negative pledge, there seems little doubt that the lender is only entitled to an equity which is not an interest in any of the borrower's assets.[43] However, as we have indicated, once the contingency is met, and providing the conditions mentioned above can be satisfied, it would seem that the negative pledge can give rise to an equitable security interest, namely an equitable charge.

6.43   One may argue that talk of equitable charges in relation to the negative pledge is all very well, but in the final analysis such arguments are purely academic, since negative pledge clauses, when drafted by English lawyers, do not attempt to create equitable charges. In practice, this may no longer be the case, and it has been evident from a number of recent international banking law conferences that the technique of incorporating an automatic security device within the terms of the negative pledge clause is becoming more common. What is not clear, however, is whether lenders appreciate that any equitable charge which may be ultimately created will only give priority if it is perfected by registration under section 395 of the Companies Act 1985.

An alternative equitable interest to which the clause may give rise is the equitable lien which is not based on possession of the relevant asset(s) and is enforceable in similar ways to a mortgage by equitable charge. There is some authority in the United States supporting the argument that the negative pledge gives rise to an equitable lien,[44] but little support exists for this in England, and even in the United States a greater preponderance of authority is of the opinion that the negative pledge is not enforceable against third parties.[45]

WHAT PROTECTION DOES THE NEGATIVE PLEDGE GIVE THE LENDER?

6.44   Even if one accepts the argument that the negative pledge may, in appropriate cases, give rise to an equitable interest, the fact remains that such interest may not afford any real protection in favour of the lender. This is because the lender's equitable interest will only relate to property which has been secured in favour of a third party in breach of the clause. It is difficult to imagine how such property could be "equally" secured as between the third party creditor and the lender, and at least one commentator suggests that the negative pledge may therefore fail to create an interest in the property due to lack of certainty.[46]

---

[42] See *National Provincial and Union Bank of England* v. *Charnley* [1924] 1 K.B. 431, cited in Gabriel, p. 85. See also Goode, *loc. cit.*, n. 38 above, pp. 49–50.

[43] As to the distinction between an equitable interest and a "mere equity" see Goode, *Commercial Law* (1982), p. 72.

[44] *Coast Bank* v. *Minderhout*, 61 Cal 2d 311, 392 P 2d 265, 38 Cal. Rptr. 505 (1964), cited in Wood, p. 151.

[45] *Equitable Trust Co.* v. *Imbesi* 287 Md, 249, 412 A. 2d 96 (App 1980); see also *Kelly* v. *Central Hanover Bank & Trust Co.* 85 F 2d 61 (2d Cir. 1936).

[46] See Gabriel, p. 86. In most cases the contingency will only be satisfied when a legal interest, in the form of a security, is granted in favour of a third party. It is difficult to see how such legal interest could rank equally with the lender's equitable interest even when the clause specifically states that the same security will be automatically given to the eurocurrency lender.

Since there is no doctrine of constructive notice with regard to negative pledge clauses contained in eurocurrency loan agreements, the clause will become subordinated to a third party who breaches it by purchasing a legal interest in good faith without notice. Only if the third party creditor has actual notice would he be bound by the terms of the clause. In such a situation the lender's only effective remedy would, therefore, be a contractual right to demand security equal to that given in favour of the third party. Alternatively, the lender could, of course, accelerate the facility and demand repayment, since breach of the negative pledge will invariably be an event of default under the loan.[47]

If it can be shown that the third party creditor took his security with notice of the negative pledge clause, it may be possible for the lender to bring a claim against the creditor in tort for interference with the eurocurrency loan contract, although this is remote and would depend to a large extent on the precise wording of the negative pledge and the manner in which it was breached.[48]

4. The pari passu covenant[49]

The *pari passu* covenant is a companion of the negative pledge clause and is sometimes referred to as if it were part of the negative pledge covenant. This is erroneous since the negative pledge relates to secured indebtedness whereas the *pari passu* covenant covers only unsecured indebtedness. The *pari passu* covenant is normally worded in such a way that the borrower warrants[50] that its obligations under the loan will not be subordinated to any unsecured creditor. In other words, that the rights of the eurocurrency lender will always rank at least *pari passu* with the rights of the borrower's other unsecured creditors.

6.45

The *pari passu* covenant is normally expressed as a continuing covenant, hence the words . . . "will at all times." Furthermore, the obligations owed to the lender are expressed to rank "at least" *pari passu* in order to provide for the possibility of the borrower incurring unsecured indebtedness which is subordinated to the lender's claim. Clearly, the lender would not wish to elevate such subordinated debt to the same position as its own.

Many jurisdictions provide that certain classes of unsecured creditors will rank in priority to others,[51] and since the clause has no effect on third parties, it is common to qualify the scope of the clause in favour of those creditors who are thus afforded priority. The efficacy of the clause once again lies in the fact that it is invariably linked to an event of default which permits acceleration and the right to demand repayment, preferably before the borrower becomes insolvent. Whether the clause therefore achieves its desired

---

[47] If it is possible to effectively "police" the negative pledge, the lender may be able to prevent breach by obtaining an injunction against the borrower. However, in practical terms such a degree of knowledge on the part of the lender is most unlikely.

[48] See Goode, *loc. cit.*, n. 38 above, p. 51 and the cases cited therein.

[49] See clause 15(i) in the specimen agreement, Chap. 17 below.

[50] *Ibid.*

[51] See, for example, Part XII, Insolvency Act 1986.

purpose will depend upon how effectively it can be "policed," and this should be borne in mind by those drafting the agreement.

Additional covenants commonly found in eurocurrency loans

5. Use of proceeds

6.46   . . . We have already seen that in certain circumstances it may be necessary to impose restrictions on the use or purpose of the loan.[52] Whenever this is deemed necessary it is common to reinforce the purpose clause[53] with a specific covenant linked to an event of default permitting acceleration in the event of any breach. Once again, however, it may be very difficult to "police" such a covenant, and if the loan is used for an *ultra vires* purpose in breach of the covenant dire consequences will still follow for the lender.[54]

6. Anti-merger covenants

6.47   Anti-merger covenants are relatively common where the borrower is a corporate entity and the primary purpose of such a covenant is to maintain the identity of the borrower. In rare cases the scope of the covenant may go much further than maintaining the identity of the borrower, and may require key management figures to remain in office or to be replaced by persons approved by the lender.

7. Anti-disposal covenants[55]

6.48   Just as it may be important to maintain the identity of the borrower, it is likely that the lender will want to preserve the borrower's assets, which will be available for any future distribution. The clause may be drafted very widely to prevent any "creeping" disposals of all assets, or may relate only to a small number of assets which the lender perceives as fundamental to the borrower's credit-worthiness. Where the covenant is very restrictive it is common to incorporate numerous exceptions which permit the borrower to carry on its day to day business. The clause may be reinforced by a covenant requiring the borrower to maintain a certain level of insurance cover over specified assets and against such risks as prescribed by the lender. The anti-disposal covenant obviously operates hand in hand with both the financial covenants and the negative pledge, the general purpose being to prevent the depletion of funds to which the lender must look for eventual repayment.

---

[52] Above, para. 6.09.
[53] See clause 3 in the specimen agreement, Chap. 17 below.
[54] Above, paras. 6.09 and 6.10.
[55] See clause 14 (a)-(f) in the specimen agreement, Chap. 17 below.

Remedies for breach of covenant

As we have already indicated[56] the loan agreement will normally provide **6.49** specific remedies for any breach of covenant by linking the covenants to an event of default.[57] The wording of such an event of default will typically read as follows: "The Borrower defaults in the due performance or observance of any of its covenants, undertakings or obligations under this Agreement."

Breach of the covenants will therefore normally permit the lender to suspend and/or cancel the facility and accelerate the borrower's obligation to repay. However, this may prove to be of little practical effect if the borrower's financial condition has deteriorated so badly that it is unable to repay. The lender's only hope is that the covenants will act as an early warning system which may enable the lender to recover its funds before the situation is completely lost.

---

[56] Above, para. 6.33.
[57] For a fuller discussion of the remedies which may be available, see Chap. 9 below.

7. Syndicated Loans[1]

Introduction

7.01 The business of syndicating loans[2] developed principally because many international loans became so large that no single financial institution had either the capacity or the desire to lend the entire sum on its own.[3] There were many other factors which led to syndicated loans becoming the predominant financing vehicle during the late 1960s and throughout the 1970s for many borrowers needing to raise large amounts of debt in a relatively short time,[4] but in so far as the lenders were concerned the major attraction which the instrument gave was the ability to spread the credit risk.

The process of syndication which we will consider in this chapter is the "true" syndication. That is to say the process by which a group of banks lends directly to the borrower under a single loan agreement. The lending banks have always perceived the "true" syndication as nothing more than a collection of individual loan contracts conveniently documented in one single agreement. This perception is of fundamental importance and will be considered in detail later.[5] The "true" syndication can be compared with the participation agreement which is sometimes erroneously referred to as a syndicated loan agreement. As we will see in a later chapter of this work,[6] the technique employed in a participation agreement is for a single bank to lend directly to the borrower and then sell all or part of its interest in that loan to other lenders. The confusion in terminology has no doubt arisen because many "true" syndications enable the lending banks (the participants) to sell all or part of their interest in the syndicate loan to other lenders, who may, or may not, be party to the original syndicated loan.[7]

The syndicated loan is built upon the same structural skeleton as the single lender eurocurrency term loan agreement,[8] the main difference being those clauses within the syndicated loan agreement which set out the legal relationship as between the participating banks.[9] Further, as in the case of a single lender international term loan agreement, there is no such thing as a

---

[1] See generally, Gabriel, Chap. 7; Wood, Chap. 11; Rendell (ed.) Chap. 2; McDonald, *International Syndicated Loans* (1982); Slater, "Syndicated Bank Loans" [1982] J.B.L. 173.

[2] It is also possible to syndicate other bank facilities, namely, contract guarantees and bank acceptance credits; for a fuller exposition of the techniques which might be adopted in such syndications, see Chap. 12 below.

[3] See Wood, p. 256.

[4] For an excellent exposition of these factors, see McDonald. *loc. cit.* n. 1 above, pp. 1–58.

[5] See para. 7.33 below.

[6] See Chap. 8 below.

[7] The practical and legal implications of such a course of events is considered in detail in Chap. 8 below.

[8] On international term loan agreements generally, see Chap. 6 above.

[9] Another important difference relates to the contractual provisions within the syndicated loan agreement which deal specifically with the role of the agent bank. On the role of the agent, see para. 7.20 below.

standard syndicated loan. The number of participating banks can vary enormously as can the amount being advanced. Some syndicated loans may be underwritten, some may be secured, some evidenced by notes and some guaranteed, some are neither. All these factors will have a major impact on the documentation which evidences the transaction, but the basic underlying legal issues remain constant.[10] It is upon these underlying legal issues that we will now concentrate our attention.

THE STEPS IN ARRANGING A SYNDICATED LOAN

The procedure most commonly adopted in arranging a syndicated loan is **7.02** for the borrower to authorise a single bank, known as the lead manager or managing bank, to arrange the loan on the borrower's behalf.[11] The lead manager will then settle in outline with the borrower the basic terms upon which the loan is to be promoted to potential participants. It is normally the lead manager which actually promotes the loan by approaching other banks in the market or otherwise generally soliciting interest. It is common practice for the lead manager to provide detailed information relating to both the loan agreement and the borrower, as part of the promotion exercise. The final, and some would say most onerous, obligation which is normally placed upon the lead manager is for it to negotiate the terms of the syndication agreement, which will ultimately evidence the contract upon which the funds are to be advanced.[11a] We will consider each of these steps in turn.

A. Obtaining the mandate

As we have already indicated[12] the syndication process effectively com- **7.03** mences when a bank obtains a mandate from a prospective borrower. The commitment placed upon the lead manager within the terms of the mandate can vary, although lead managers do not normally secure the mandate on a fully underwritten basis. Most mandates simply require the lead manager to use its "best efforts" to arrange a suitable syndicate. The problem with such mandates is that the wording used to describe the obligation placed upon the lead manager often defies any precise legal definition. One might be tempted to say that it would, therefore, be safer to leave the mandate silent. Nothing, in fact, could be further from the truth, at least under English law, because there is a rebuttable presumption[13] that a commercial agreement is

---

[10] See Slater, *loc. cit.*; n. 1 above, pp. 173–174.
[11] An alternative technique is for loose consortia of banks to bid against each other in order to obtain the borrower's mandate. Much will obviously depend upon the prevailing market conditions and the credit standing of the borrower. See generally on this topic, McDonald. *loc. cit.* n. 1 above, Chap. 5.
[11a] Strictly speaking, the lead manager is also normally obliged to arrange the signing ceremony at which the agreement is executed.
[12] See para. 7.02 above.
[13] It would appear that the burden placed upon the defendant in rebutting this presumption is a heavy one; see *Edwards* v. *Skyways Ltd.* [1964] 1 All E.R. 494, p. 500.

intended to give rise to legal relations between the parties.[14] It is clear then, at least under English law, that if the lead manager is to limit any obligations which the mandate may impose, this must be achieved by express wording within the terms of the mandate itself. The wording must be carefully chosen, however, for as one commentator indicates,[15] "A condition such as "subject to formal documentation" may not be enough to prevent a court from holding the bank to the bargain set out in the letter, even though it was never formalised."[16]

The requirement contained in most mandates is, as already indicated, for the lead manager to use its "best efforts." It would seem that there is at least some dispute as to the precise meaning of this phrase,[17] and it would be preferable for the lead manager to state, quite specifically, that the parties do not intend to enter into any legal relations. If such a course of action were adopted the court would treat the mandate as binding in honour only.[18] The words "subject to contract" would achieve this desired purpose, at least under English law.

B. The promotion stage

7.04   Once the basic terms and conditions of the loan have been agreed with the borrower, the lead manager will start to solicit interest from potential participants.[19] Rather than send out details indiscriminately, the lead manager will normally carefully target possible participants[20] and then (usually by telex) send out "term sheets" to those banks selected. These "term sheets" are basically a synopsis of the borrower, the actual proposal and the fee structure applicable to different levels of the syndicate.[21]

Those possible participants which indicate an interest to the lead manager's original telex are then circulated with an information memorandum, which contains pertinent information regarding the borrower's financial, economic and political situation. In many respects, it is the information memorandum which presents the most serious legal implications for the lead manager. As one commentator indicates[22] "no other syndicate docu-

---

[14] *Ibid.*

[15] See Wood, p. 256.

[16] See *Branca* v. *Cobarro* [1947] K.B. 854, cited in Wood, *ibid.*

[17] Phillip Wood indicates (p. 257) that such wording may be construed as a near absolute commitment, whereas Peter Gabriel suggests that the English courts seem to have treated "best" as "reasonable," see Gabriel, p. 118.

[18] See, for example, *Appleson* v. *Littlewoods Ltd.* [1939] 1 All E.R. 464; *Rose and Frank Co.* v. *Crompton & Bros., Ltd.* [1925] A.C. 445; *Jones* v. *Vernons' Pools* [1938] 2 All E.R. 626.

[19] Where the loan is particularly large or is likely to be difficult to arrange it is common to find various levels of management groups, namely, the lead management group and the management group. Each grouping will perform different functions and such a structure will add significantly to the cost of setting up the facility. The various fees which may be payable under such a facility are considered in Chap. 6 above.

[20] The number of banks targeted can vary enormously and can range from less than a dozen to almost a thousand. On the factors which influence the group of banks ultimately selected, see McDonald, *loc. cit.*; n. 1 above, p. 116.

[21] On the fees which may be payable, see generally, Chap. 6 above.

[22] See McDonald, *loc. cit.*; n. 1 above, p. 125.

ment is more controversial, or has less certain utility, than the information (or placement) memorandum."

POTENTIAL LIABILITY ARISING FROM THE INFORMATION MEMORANDUM

The information memorandum is, basically, a selling document,[23] and its legal status and the obligations to which it gives rise will depend upon the nature of the information which it contains, and the circumstances surrounding its distribution. In the vast majority of cases, the information contained in the memorandum will have been supplied by the borrower, and only in rare cases will the lead manager attempt to verify such information. It would appear that a rather casual approach has traditionally been taken towards the preparation of most information memoranda, and lawyers are rarely involved.[24] The memorandum commonly incorporates wide disclaimers, which are intended to protect the lead manager against any potential claim from a participant relating to information contained in the memorandum which might transpire to be incorrect. At least one American case has dramatically indicated how significant such potential claims might be. In the case of *Re: Colocotronis Tanker Securities Litigation*,[25] a claim was brought by several American regional banks, which had participated in syndicated loans to the Colocotronis shipping group, against the lead manager of the syndicate (the European–American Banking Corporation (EABC)). The plaintiffs alleged that EABC held itself out to be skilled in international finance and expert in investigating, analysing and recommending potential participations in syndicated loans, such as those granted in favour of the Colocotronis shipping group. It was further alleged that EABC had a duty to the plaintiffs to advise them of all material facts relevant to the Colocotronis loans, and that EABC was guilty of both untrue statements of material facts[25a] and of the omission to state material facts, which had induced the plaintiffs to participate in the syndicated loans.

All actions arising out of the Colocotronis litigation were subsequently settled, but only after EABC agreed to remit to each participant the full amount of their participation. In effect EABC, as lead manager, agreed to underwrite the entire transaction. As McDonald points out,[26] " . . . the action stunned the Eurobanking community" which as a consequence began to look much more carefully at the potential liability for incorrect information contained within the information memorandum.[27]

7.05

---

[23] See Cates, "Role of managers and agents" (1982) I.F.L.R. 21, p. 22.

[24] See Slater, *loc. cit.* n. 1 above, pp. 175–176.

[25] 420 F.Supp. 998 (S.D.N.Y. 1976).

[25a] Namely, that EABC had thoroughly examined the financial condition and operations of the Colocotronis group.

[26] See McDonald *loc. cit.*; n. 1 above, p. 126.

[27] Since the information contained within the memorandum is provided by the borrower and the lead bank simply circulates such information on behalf of the borrower, there can be little doubt that potential liability would attach primarily to the borrower. However, as the Colocotronis litigation clearly shows, when the borrower becomes insolvent, or is otherwise unable to satisfy any potential claim, the participating banks will turn their attention towards the lead manager(s).

In so far as English law is concerned, the potential heads of liability would be as follows:

i. Fraudulent misrepresentation

7.06   Where the lead manager has been party to the preparation of an information memorandum which contains a statement which it knows to be false, or is reckless as to whether or not a statement is true,[27a] then civil and criminal liability may attach.

ii. Negligent misrepresentation

7.07   The lead manager may, in appropriate circumstances, be liable for damages for negligent misstatements contained in the information memorandum on the basis of a line of cases commencing with *Hedley Byrne & Co. Ltd.* v. *Heller & Partners Ltd.*,[28] that is, on the basis that negligent advice/information is given (by the lead manager), to a person(s) who relies on it (the participating bank(s)), in a situation where a special relationship of trust or confidence exists between the parties, and that person(s) (the participating bank(s)) suffers foreseeable loss in consequence of that reliance.

There are clearly a number of important *caveats* which must be satisfied before the *Hedley Byrne* doctrine can expose the lead manager to liability for negligent misrepresentation,[29] not least the need to establish a "special relationship" between the lead bank and the participating banks. In *Hedley Byrne* itself, none of their Lordships was willing to lay down precise criteria for the existence of the "special relationship," preferring to rely on broad statements of general principle capable of being applied to a wide range of factual situations.[30]

It must also be established that the participating banks actually relied on the misrepresentation,[31] and that their loss was caused by the misstatements contained within the memorandum.[32]

An important aspect of the *Hedley Byrne* decision is that the statement

---

[27a]   See *Derry* v. *Peek* (1889) 14 App. Cas. 377.

[28]   [1964] A.C. A65; see also *Mutual Life and Citizens' Assurance Co. Ltd.* v. *Evatt* [1971] A.C. 793; *Esso Petroleum Co. Ltd.* v. *Mardon* [1976] Q.B. 801. The lead manager may also in appropriate circumstances be liable under s.2(i) of the Misrepresentation Act 1967.

[29]   As to the general conditions of liability for misrepresentation, see Treitel, *The Law of Contract* (6th ed., 1983) Chap. 9.

[30]   Of particular importance in determining whether such a "special relationship" exists will be the degree of involvement of the lead manager in the preparation and distribution of the information memorandum, the degree to which the lead manager is identified in the memorandum as a source of information (or otherwise), the complexity of the transaction, the access which ordinary participants have to the source of information, the extent to which the lead bank is involved in soliciting potential participants to join the syndicate, and whether it derives any benefit from the borrower for promoting the loan. This final element was specifically referred to in *Mutual Life and Citizens' Assurance Co. Ltd.* v. *Evatt* [1971] A.C. 793 (P.C.) and will be present in most syndicated loan agreements. On the type of commission which might be payable to the lead manager(s), see Chap. 6, para. 6.27 above.

[31]   It will not be enough to show that a reasonable man would have relied on the misrepresentation; there will be no liability if the participating banks did not, in fact, rely on it. See *JEB Fasteners Ltd.* v. *Marks Bloom & Co.* [1983] 1 All E.R. 583; *The Lucy* [1983] 1 LLoyd's Rep. 188. This will obviously be the case if the information memorandum never came to the participants' attention.

[32]   See *JEB Fasteners Ltd.* v. *Marks Bloom & Co.*, n. 31 above.

containing the misrepresentation need not be one of fact[32a] but can be one of opinion or advice (*Hedley Byrne* itself concerned a banker's reference) and, therefore, a potential plaintiff could rely on negligent misrepresentation in circumstances where an action for misrepresentation may otherwise not lie because the statement in question is one of opinion.

Whether the lead bank will be so liable for negligent misrepresentation will depend on all the circumstances. Factors of particular importance will be the extent to which the lead manager was involved (if at all) in the preparation and distribution of the memorandum and the manner in which it was used as a selling document to solicit interest from potential participants. The complexity of the overall transaction will aslo be important as will the access which syndicate members had to the source of information contained in the memorandum. These latter two factors will be particularly important where an unsophisticated participant is endeavouring to show that in a complex agreement, and with little or no access to the information, it relied almost exclusively on the skill and expertise of the lead bank.[32b]

PRECAUTIONS TO BE TAKEN BY THE LEAD BANK

Notwithstanding the conditions which must be satisfied before a lead manager can be liable for misstatements made within the information memorandum, the potential liability, as indicated by the *Colocotronis* litigation, can be substantial, and appropriate precautions should be taken by the lead manager to safeguard its position.   **7.08**

As Wood points out,[33] ". . . there may be a case for having no information memorandum at all, especially where the borrower is well known or where potential participants can be expected to have sufficient credit information of their own, notably in the case of government loans." This sound advice does not appear to have been heeded, and information memoranda are still commonly used to promote syndicated loans, in addition to a number of other financial instruments which are now commonly used to raise funds in the euromarkets.[34]

DISCLAIMER NOTICES/EXCULPATORY CLAUSES

Rather than dispense with the information memorandum in appropriate cases, the market has developed a practice whereby the memorandum is specifically deemed to have been prepared by the borrower, and in addition contains fairly extensive exculpatory provisions, which attempt to relieve the lead manager of any potential liability. Whether this achieves its desired

---

[32a] As a general rule for an action in misrepresentation to lie, the statement must be one of fact and not of law, advice, opinion or intention unless it can be shown that the defendant did not actually hold the opinion or intention, for which purpose the plaintiff may produce evidence of circumstances known to the defendant. See *Edgington* v. *Fitzmaurice* (1885) 29 Ch. D. 459 where Directors were held liable for representing that the proceeds of a debenture issue were to be used to buy new equipment whereas in fact the company was insolvent and the proceeds were needed for the payment of pressing debts.

[32b] Such factors would also be important in the participant bank's attempt to establish the existence of a "special relationship" of trust or confidence.

[33] See Wood, p. 260.

[34] On the importance of the information memorandum to a number of different finance instruments commonly employed in the euromarkets, see generally, Chap. 10 below.

purpose will depend, to a large extent, upon the circumstances surrounding the promotion of each individual syndicated loan. No two cases will ever be the same and, therefore, our attention must focus on fundamental principles rather than specific examples.

7.09   As we have already seen,[35] the lead manager will normally prepare the information memorandum from information supplied by the borrower, and only in rare circumstances will the manager attempt to verify the information supplied.[36] In many cases, therefore, it could be argued that the lead manager acts as nothing more than a "conduit" (at least in so far as the information memorandum is concerned) through which information passes from the borrower to the prospective participants. The lead manager will normally seek to reinforce this notion by expressly providing (normally in the front cover of the information memorandum) that the information supplied in the memorandum is merely intended to provide " . . . the basis for each bank to make its own independent economic and financial evaluation of the borrower, or encourages prospective lenders to seek additional supporting information from sources it deems appropriate."[37] This basic approach is also normally reflected within the terms of the loan agreement itself by the inclusion of a clause which might read as follows:

> Each Bank has made its own independent investigation and evaluation of the creditworthiness of the Borrower and the Guarantor (if appropriate) as it has judged to be appropriate and prudent in connection with the making of its loan.[38]

Whether this type of exculpatory clause will be effective, will depend upon the law of the particular jurisdiction concerned.[39] The laws of most jurisdictions would not recognise such a clause if it were shown to be a sham or if it were contrary to the applicable law.[40] Under English law, (and most other common law jurisdictions) liability cannot be excluded for fraudulent misrepresentation. In so far as negligent misrepresentation is concerned, a clause which attempts to exclude such liability will only be upheld by an English court if it is deemed "reasonable."[41] The requirement of reasonableness will make it difficult to foretell whether an exculpation clause will be upheld, and without more this would place the lead bank in an invidious position. Fortunately, however, the Unfair Contract Terms Act 1977 (UCTA) contains a number of provisions which reduce this uncer-

---

[35] See para. 7.05 above.

[36] For a fuller exposition of the potential duties of the lead manager, see Clarke and Farrar, "Rights and Duties of Managing and Agent Banks in Syndicated Loans to Government Borrowers" [1982] U. of Ill. L.Rev. 229.

[37] McDonald, *loc. cit.*, n. 1 above, p. 125.

[38] As to the wording which might be included within the information memorandum, see Calhoun, "Eurodollar Loan Agreements: An Introduction and Discussion of Some Special Problems" 32 The Business Lawyer (July 1977) 1785, p. 1791. See also the Encyclopedia, para. 5250.

[39] The local laws of the jurisdictions where the information memorandum is sent will be important in this respect.

[40] See Wood, p. 261.

[41] See the Misrepresentation Act 1967, s.3, as amended by the Unfair Contract Terms Act 1977, s.8. See generally, the UCTA s.11 and Schedule 2.

tainty, some of which are particularly relevant to the situation we are presently considering.

Of particular importance will be the strength of the bargaining positions **7.10** as between the lead manager and the participating banks. Where all parties are relatively sophisticated it may be easier to satisfy the test of reasonableness, but the lead manager should be wary of potential participants which are unsophisticated, in the sense of having had little exposure in syndicated lending.

DUE DILIGENCE

Whilst appropriate disclaimer notices and exculpatory clauses within the information memorandum might go some way to protecting the position of the lead manager, they should not be relied on exclusively. Extreme care should be taken in the preparation of the information memorandum. In essence, the lead manager should exercise appropriate "due diligence"[42] during the performance of all its duties, from the time at which the mandate is obtained to the execution of the syndicated loan agreement itself. What constitutes due diligence will depend on the circumstances of each particular case. Of particular importance will, once again, be the relative sophistication of the banks involved, their access to independent information, (as noted earlier the less access the participants have to the relevant information, the higher will be the standard of care expected of the lead manager) and the extent to which the participants rely on the information memorandum.[43] A clear distinction can be made between sovereign credits, where the relevant information will often be readily available and certain corporate credits (particularly those in relation to project financing), where the entire transaction will normally be much more complex, with little public knowledge available.[44]

Opinions or future projections should whenever possible be avoided, and **7.11** if it is necessary to include them they should be substantiated. Projections are commonly required in the case of project loans, and in such cases they should be prepared by experts and furnished to the participants in substantially the same, if not the identical, form in which they were prepared by the expert. The lead manager should also make it clear within the terms of the information memorandum that the projections have been prepared by independent experts, and that the lead manager itself will not be responsible for their accuracy.

There are other important principles of disclosure of which the lead manager should be aware, namely:

(i) The difficulties posed in the event that the lead manager acquires confidential information about the borrower which is material to the credit proposal.

(ii) The difficulties posed in the event that the lead manager finds itself in

---

[42] On due diligence generally, see Wood, pp. 261–262.
[43] *Ibid.*
[44] For an excellent practical outline of some of the issues which the lead manager should consider in the case of both a sovereign and a corporate syndicated loan information memorandum, see McDonald, *loc. cit.* n. 1, above, pp. 207–213.

a position where different departments of the bank possess different types of information about the borrower, some of which has not been made available to the other participants. Such a situation may, in appropriate cases, give rise to a conflict of interest arising insofar as the lead manager is concerned.[45]

(iii) The difficulties posed in the event that the lead manager becomes aware of certain events, after the information memorandum has been circulated (but before the loan agreement is executed) which affect the truthfulness of statements made within the memorandum. As Wood points out,[46] failure to make the participants aware of such events may make the misrepresentation fraudulent,[47] though presumably it would be possible for the original memorandum to state specifically that particular statements, for example, projections, could change with time.

These difficulties are considered elsewhere in this work[48] and will not trouble us further here.

7.12   One final comment which can be made regarding the precautions which the lead manager(s) might consider appropriate, concerns syndicated loans in which there are different management groups.[49] A participating bank should not seek to be included as a co-manager unless it is actually functioning as such. It has become relatively common in recent years for a large number of participants to be named in one of the numerous management groups. There have been two main reasons which have prompted many banks to desire such listing. First, to enhance the bank's reputation in the international market place, and secondly, to enable the bank to share in the management fee (if applicable).[50] It should be possible, however, for the banks to arrange the fee structure in such a way that the banks do not have to become named managers in order to obtain their share of any relevant fees which are payable,[51] and, as one commentator points out, the participants' disappointment "at forgoing the prestige inherent in being listed as a co-manager can be assuaged by some other prestigious but less perilous listing."[52]

Will the information memorandum be construed as a regulated prospectus?

7.13   An additional problem which the information memorandum poses for the lead manager is that it may, in certain jurisdictions, be construed as a regulated prospectus. Many jurisdictions impose special liability in respect of the

---

[45] On conflicts of interest generally, see Goode (ed.) *Conflicts of Interest in the Changing Financial World* (1986).

[46] Wood, p. 262; see generally, pp. 261–263.

[47] *Davies* v. *London and Provincial Marine Insurance Co.* (1878) 8 Ch.D. 469, cited in Wood, p. 262.

[48] See generally, Chap. 10 below.

[49] See n. 19 above and accompanying text.

[50] On the management fee generally, see Chap. 6 above.

[51] See Chap. 6 above for a fuller exposition of the fees which might be payable.

[52] See Calhoun, *loc. cit.*, n. 38 above, p. 1791.

distribution of certain documents[53] relating to certain types of securities.[54] However, as Wood points out,[55] almost invariably the information memorandum will benefit from an exemption, depending on the circumstances, on one or more of the following grounds:

(i) The offer contained in the memorandum was not a public invitation.
(ii) The memorandum was only circulated to sophisticated investors.[56]
(iii) The borrower was a state or state-controlled entity.[56a]
(iv) The participation in the loan agreement does not constitute "securities" or "debentures" under the relevant statute.[57]
(v) The memorandum was issued outside the jurisdiction to foreign residents or nationals.

The position in the United Kingdom is comprehensively dealt with elsewhere in this work,[58] suffice it to say here that the information memorandum will not fall foul of the Companies Act 1985 if it is not deemed to be a "debenture"[59] within the meaning of section 58 of the Act,[60] nor if the offer contained in the memorandum is not being made to "the public" as defined in sections 59 and 60 of the Act.[61] The prospectus provisions of the Companies Act will also be avoided if the information memorandum is issued by an overseas company to so-called "professionals" under the Act.[62]

In addition to the prohibition contained in the Companies Act, the Prevention of Fraud (Investments) Act 1958 imposes a general prohibition on the distribution of "circulars" containing, amongst other things, offers of securities or information calculated to lead directly or indirectly to the sub-

---

[53] The type of document covered by the prohibition will obviously depend upon the precise wording of the statutes which regulate the marketing of securities. In the U.K. the Companies Act 1985 refers to "debentures" whereas the Prevention of Fraud (Investments) Act 1958 refers to "circulars." As to how these two terms have been defined, see Penn, "Sterling Commercial Paper" [1986] B.F.L.R. p. 195, pp. 201–209. In the U.S.A. both the Securities Act 1933 and the Securities Exchange Act 1934 define securities to include "any note . . . or any certificate of interest or participation in . . . any of the foregoing." It would appear that weight of authority in the U.S.A. now holds that notes and participation agreements issued in commercial bank loans do not come within the various prohibitions; see Clarke and Farrar, *loc. cit.*, n. 36 above, p. 236. It would appear, however, that the position might not be as settled as one would like; see, for example, *United California Bank* v. *THC Financial Corp.*, 557 F. 2d 1351, 1357 (9th Cir. 1977).

[54] *Ibid.*

[55] See Wood, p. 257

[56] Notwithstanding what has been said earlier in this chapter about some banks being more sophisticated than others (see para. 7.10 above), it is most unlikely that a bank participating in a syndicated loan agreement would not be classed as a sophisticated investor.

[56a] As to the definition of a "state" and a "state-controlled entity" under English law, see generally, Chap. 3 above.

[57] As to the likely position in both the U.K. and the U.S.A., see n. 53 above; see also Chap. 10 below.

[58] See Chap. 10 below; see also, Penn, *loc. cit.*, n. 53 above, pp. 201–208; Goodall, "Offers of Commercial Paper in the U.K." I.F.L.R. (April 1984) pp. 15–19. For an account of the position in the U.S.A., see Wood, pp. 258–259; Clark and Farrar. *loc. cit.*, n. 36 above.

[59] For a fuller exposition of what may or may not constitute a debenture under the terms of section 58 of the Companies Act 1985, see Penn. *loc. cit.*, n. 53 above, pp. 201–202 and the cases cited therein.

[60] Companies Act 1985.

[61] *Ibid.* For a fuller exposition of what may or may not be construed as an "offer to the public" see Penn, *loc. cit.*, n. 53 above, pp. 202–203.

[62] See s.79(2) of the Companies Act 1985.

scription or purchase of securities.[63] The prohibition in section 14 of the Act relates to a wide variety of matters[64] and would certainly cover an information memorandum used in a syndicated loan agreement. There are, however, two exemptions available. The first of these is that documents may be distributed by licensed or authorised dealers.[65] The second is that documents may be issued to so-called "professionals" which would include most banks.[66] If the information memorandum is issued on behalf of a state or state entity it would also be exempt.[67]

The regulatory framework in the United Kingdom is undergoing fundamental change at present following the recent enactment of the Financial Services Act 1986. Unfortunately, at the time of writing, the Act is not fully operative, although some of its implications are considered elsewhere in this work.[68]

C. Negotiation of the loan documentation

7.14 Another matter of concern to the lead manager will be the extent to which it may owe duties and liabilities to the participants during the negotiation and drafting of the syndicated loan documentation.[69]

Academic writers appear to hold the view that no duties arise during this phase of the syndication process. Gabriel, for example, expresses the following view[69a]:

> "Then arises the question of negotiation of the loan contract itself. As pointed out above in this role the lead is acting in its own right. It is felt that in such a situation when the loan document is being negotiated the lead only needs to have its own rights in mind. It is not acting as agent for the participants. So far as the participants also only getting the benefit, or disadvantage of the lead's negotiation with the Borrower, it is actually a matter extraneous to the lead manager. The Borrower here is only willing to extend to the participant the terms it has negotiated with the lead. The participants may not have any recourse against the lead on the basis of agency, but only against the Borrower in contract."

This view is supported by Clarke and Farrar in the following terms[69b]:

> "Although conservative financial lawyers will counsel their Manager clients that they should expect to be held to the fiduciary standard, the better view is that the syndication process represents the classic arm's length transaction and, therefore, fiduciary obligations should not be

---

[63] Prevention of Fraud (Investments) Act 1958, s.14.
[64] See ss.14(1), (2) and (3).
[65] The term "authorised dealer" is used conveniently to denote a dealer not required by the 1958 Act to obtain a licence; this includes most banks.
[66] The "professional" exemption under s.14(2) of the Prevention of Fraud (Investments) Act is wider than that contained in s.79(2) of the Companies Act (see n. 62 and accompanying text). For a fuller exposition of the potential scope of this exemption, see Goodall, *loc. cit.*, n. 58 above.
[67] See s.14 of the Prevention of Fraud (Investments) Act 1958.
[68] See generally, Chap. 10 below.
[69] See generally, Clark and Farrar, *loc. cit.*, n. 36. above, pp. 238–244.
[69a] n. 1 above, at p. 147.
[69b] n. 69 above, at p. 234.

imposed on the Manager. The members of a syndicate are "buying" a product developed, marketed, and serviced by the Manager/Agent. While the members undoubtedly rely on the reputation and experience of the Manager, the relationship is not fundamentally different from the relationship between IBM and the purchaser of a large computer system."

It is submitted that both these views are inconsistent with market practice and current legal trends.

Insofar as market practice is concerned, there can be little doubt that during the negotiation process it is now well recognised that the lead manager acts on behalf of the participating banks. Whether the lead manager owes fiduciary obligations to the participants during the negotiation process is, however, much less certain.

The question of who is a fiduciary is not easily answered,[70] however, it would seem that fiduciary obligations can arise not only in the traditional relationships,[71] but also in any case where one party (the lead manager) undertakes to perform some task on behalf of another (the participants).[72] Recent case law indicates that courts are prepared to extend the traditional principles to cover relationships which previously might not have been thought to give rise to a fiduciary relationship.[73] In the light of these decisions it now seems more likely (although it should be emphasised that there has never been an English case directly on this point[73a]), that a lead manager would (in appropriate circumstances) be held to be in a fiduciary relationship with the participating banks.[74] The argument in favour of such a relationship would, however, be more credible if it could be shown that the lead manager acted on behalf of the participants during the negotiation process in a specific way,[75] (for example, in cases where only the lead manager had access to the borrower at the relevant time), or where the lead manager was in a position of advantage, due to its close relationship with

---

[70] On fiduciary relationships generally, see Meagher, Gummow and Lehane, *Equity, Doctrines and Remedies* (2nd ed., 1984) Chap. 5; Shepherd, *The Law of Fiduciaries* (1981); Finn, *Fiduciary Obligations* (1977); Sealy, "Fiduciary Relationships" (1962) C.L.J. 69 and "Some Principles of Fiduciary Obligations" (1963) C.L.J. 119.

[71] The traditional relationships include: trustee and beneficiary; executor and beneficiary; solicitor and client; agent and principal; director or promoter and the company; as between partners, and perhaps even in a joint venture situation, see Meagher, Gummow and Lehane, *loc. cit.* n. 70 above, p. 124 and the cases cited therein.

[72] See *Re Coomber* [1911] 1 Ch. 723.

[73] See, for example, *Brian Pty. Ltd.* v. *U.D.C.* [1983] 1 N.S.W.L.R. 490; *United States Surgical Corporation* v. *Hospital Products International Pty. Ltd.* [1983] 2 N.S.W.L.R. 157; *Coleman* v. *Myers* [1977] 2 N.Z.L.R. 255.

[73a] The only English authority which considers the relationships under a syndicated loan, namely, *UBAF* v. *European American Banking Corporation* [1984] 2 All E.R. 226 does not examine the issue of fiduciary relationships.

[74] The traditional view in relation to commercial contracts was that a fiduciary relationship, as between substantial corporations who enter into commercial arrangements at arm's length, would only be recognised after a most painstaking analysis of the facts of a particular case. See, for example, *Keith Henry & Co. Pty. Ltd.* v. *Stuart Walker & Co. Pty. Ltd.* (1958) 100 C.L.R. 342; *Walden Properties Ltd.* v. *Veaver Properties Ltd.* [1973] 2 N.S.W.L.R. 815; *Amalgamated TV Services* v. *TV Corporation* [1969] 1 N.S.W.L.R. 65.

[75] Above, n. 73.

the borrower, which effectively forced the participants to rely on the lead manager's expertise.

The following extract from the judgment of Dawson J. in *United States Surgical Corporation* v. *Hospital Products International Pty. Ltd.*[75a] conveniently summarises some of the relevant factors which the court may take into account in deciding whether a fiduciary relationship exists.

> "It is usual—perhaps necessary—that in such a [fiduciary] relationship one party should repose substantial confidence in another in acting on his behalf or in his interest in some respect. But it is not in every case where that happens that there is a fiduciary relationship . . . . There is, however, the notion underlying all the cases of fiduciary obligation that inherent in the nature of the relationship itself is a position of disadvantage or vulnerability on the part of one of the parties which cause him to place reliance upon the other and requires the protection of equity acting upon the conscience of that other."[75b]

If one accepts the argument that the lead manager may, in appropriate circumstances, be in a fiduciary relationship with the participating banks, it remains to determine the nature of the obligations to which such a relationship gives rise.

1. NO-CONFLICT

7.15 The lead manager will not be allowed to enter into engagements in which it has, or can have, a personal interest conflicting, or which possibly may conflict, with the interest of those it is bound to protect.[76] This principle may cause particular difficulty for a lead manager which holds participations in some of the borrowers' other credits which conflict with the provisions in the loan agreement in which it is acting as lead manager.

2. NO PROFIT RULE

7.16 The lead manager will not be allowed to use its position for the purpose of gaining personal profit.[77] Without more, this would cause grave difficulties for the lead manager, since the compensation it receives, by means of the lead management fee,[78] is one of the main reasons why many banks desire to act in the capacity of lead manager.[79]

3. DUTY TO DISCLOSE

7.17 The lead manager will be under a duty to disclose information which is relevant to a potential participant's decission as to whether it should join the syndicate.[80] A participant seeking to rely on this duty would need to establish that a reasonably prudent lead manager would have disclosed the infor-

---

[75a] (1984) 58 A.L.J.R. 587.
[75b] *Ibid.* at p. 628.
[76] *Aberdeen Ry. Co.* v. *Blaikie Bros.* [1854] 1 Macq. 461, 471 *per* Lord Cranworth L.J.; see also, *Phipps* v. *Boardman* [1967] 2 A.C. 46.
[77] *Ibid.*, p. 105.
[78] See Chap. 6, above.
[79] See para. 7.03 above.
[80] See *Brian Property Ltd.* v. *U.D.C.*, n. 73 above.

mation in question. Expert evidence will often be required to show what a reasonably prudent lead manager would have disclosed. The importance of expert evidence was highlighted in a recent civil fraud case[80a] in which Steyn J. cited[80b] the following passage in *Cross on Evidence* (6th ed.), p. 25:

"Whenever it is necessary to determine whether someone's conduct complies with some objective standard, as where negligence is alleged, evidence is admissible to show how others might be expected to behave in similar circumstances."

In addition to the fiduciary obligations outlined above, the lead manager, in its capacity as the participant's agent,[81] will be under a duty to exercise due care and skill in negotiating the loan agreement with the borrower.[82] It has been suggested that a paid agent might be under a higher duty than a gratuitous agent, but this principle would seem to be of dubious validity under English Law.[83] It is clear, however, that no action will lie against the lead manager unless its failure to exercise reasonable care is the effective cause of loss suffered by the participant(s).[84]

Exculpatory Clauses

The potential obligations arising out of the fiduciary relationship between **7.18** the lead manager and the participating banks may appear considerable, but in practice such obligations (at least those outlined above) are either qualified or completely negated within the terms of the loan agreement.

A typical clause might read as follows:

Neither the Agent nor any Manager, nor any director, officer, employee or agent of any of them shall be responsible to any Bank for:

(i) any failure by the Borrower or the Guarantor (if relevant) to fulfil any obligation under this Agreement: or

(ii) any recitals, statements, representations or warranties contained in this Agreement or in any certificate or other document referred to, or provided for, or received, under this Agreement: or

(iii) for the value, validity, effectiveness, genuineness, enforceability or sufficiency of this Agreement.[85]

As the above example indicates, the clause will be drafted very widely, but without more, such a clause would not be enough to protect the lead manager against all potential liability and a number of additional precautions may be necessary, in appropriate circumstances.

If the manager is to obtain a fee (as is common), this should be disclosed[86] and consented to by the participants either in the agreement itself or in some ancillary document.

[80a] *Banque Keyser Ullman S.A.* v. *Skandia (UK) Insurance* [1987] 2 Lloyds Rep. 69.

[80b] *Ibid.* at p. 88.

[81] See para. 7.09 above.

[82] See *Keppel* v. *Wheeler* [1927] 1 K.B. 577; *Heath* v. *Parkinson* (1926) T.L.R. 693.

[83] See Powell, *The Law of Agency* (2nd ed., 1961) p. 304; Friedman, *The Law of Agency* (4th ed., 1976); pp. 127–130; *Bowstead on Agency* (14th ed., 1976) p. 117.

[84] See *O'Connor* v. *B.D.B. Kirby & Co.*, [1971] 2 All E.R. 1415.

[85] See also, clause 19(1) in the Specimen Agreement, Chap. 17 below.

[86] See clause 20(2) in the Specimen Agreement, Chap. 17, below.

Whenever possible the participants should be given time to consider the documents themselves and be encouraged to take independent legal advice on their sufficiency.

One final precaution which the lead manager may wish to take is to obtain a specific warranty from the participants (normally within the terms of the agreement) that they will be responsible for making their own independent investigation into the sufficiency of the loan documentation and that they will continue to be so responsible.[87]

Providing the lead manager takes the precautions which have been outlined above, it is reasonable to assume that an English court would find that banks which participate in syndicated lending are capable of looking after their own interests, and therefore would not be allowed to obtain redress in the courts against the lead manager[88] should events not turn out as the participants would have wished.[89]

D. Execution of the agreement

7.19   The final responsibility of the lead manager is to arrange for the execution of the loan agreement itself, and as we have seen in an earlier chapter of this work the precise location of execution can have a significant impact on the legal obligations to which the agreement may give rise.[90] Once the loan agreement has been executed the lead manager effectively drops out of the picture, since its obligations have been met and the responsibility of administering the loan falls upon the agent bank, to which our attention will now turn.

THE AGENT BANK

The duties of the agent

7.20   The distinction between the lead manager and the agent bank[91] is blurred in many syndicated loan agreements due to the fact that the same bank fulfils both functions. Nevertheless, most loan agreements make a clear distinction between the two roles, and in practice the responsibilities of the agent

---

[87] For an example of how such a clause might be worded, see Cates, *loc. cit.*, n. 23 above, pp. 22–23.

[88] Although a case has yet to come before the English courts on the question of a lead bank's potential liability, an interesting case has been decided in the U.S.A. In *NBI Mortgage Investment Corp.* v. *Chemical Bank* [1976–1977] Fed.Sec.L. Rep (CCH) para. 95.632 (S.D.N.Y. 1976) cited in Wood, p. 263, a participating bank was prevented from claiming that it relied upon the lead manager in circumstances where the loan agreement included a clause disclaiming collectability and where the participants had been given the right to examine the loan documentation.

[89] This assumption is, of course, subject to the earlier discussion in relation to potential liability for misrepresentation; see para. 7.07 above. See also, *George Mitchell (Chesterhall) Ltd.* v. *Finney Lock Seeds Ltd.* [1983] 2 All E.R. 737.

[90] See Chap. 6 above.

[91] It should be pointed out that some syndicated loan agreements provide for the appointment of a number of agent banks. This is particularly common in sovereign credits; see clause 19(1) in the specimen agreement, Chap. 17 below.

only come into operation after those of the lead manager have ceased, namely, upon execution of the agreement. The agent bank is the agent of the participating banks and most agreements include a clause which states that the agent has been appointed by banks to fulfil certain functions.[92]

The functions of the agent are, basically, administrative and it is normally paid an appropriate fee for carrying out its obligations.[93] Its obligations should be clearly spelt out within the agreement in the hope of limiting any potential liability; however, as recent developments in international banking have indicated, the position may not be as straightforward as one would wish. Of particular concern will be the fact that the laws of certain jurisdictions impose obligations upon agents which may bear little resemblance to those to which the agent assumed it would be subject.

In so far as English law is concerned an agent owes a number of implied duties or obligations to his principal,[94] some of which are particularly relevant in the context of international syndicated loan agreements.

I. DUTY TO EXERCISE REASONABLE CARE AND SKILL

This aspect of an agent's obligations has already been considered with regard to the obligations imposed upon the lead manager.[95] There can be little doubt, however, that it poses a much more significant threat to the agent bank, because of the nature of the agent's obligations under the loan agreement. The agent may find itself in a particularly difficult position when the borrower is approaching insolvency or where an event of default has occurred. In addition, where a loan agreement gives the agent a discretion,[96] with regard to the performance of its obligations, such discretion must be exercised with due care and skill. **7.21**

II. DUTY TO ACT PERSONALLY

Unless the agent bank has been expressly or impliedly authorised to delegate some or all of its obligations to a third party, it owes the participants a duty to act personally.[97] This prohibition on sub-delegation is normally covered by a clause in the loan agreement, which permits the agent bank to perform its duties by or through its agents or employees.[98] **7.22**

III. DUTY NOT TO PERMIT A CONFLICT OF INTEREST

The agent bank will be under a strict duty not to allow its own interests to come into conflict with those of the participating banks, unless those banks, with full knowledge of the material circumstances, consent. Since many agent banks also hold a participation in the credit facility being syndicated, **7.23**

---

[92] See clause 19(1) in the specimen agreement, Chap. 17 below.

[93] See clause 20(2) in the specimen agreement, Chap. 17 below. For a discussion of the fees which may be payable, see generally, Chap. 6 above.

[94] It could also be argued that in appropriate circumstances an agency may give rise to fiduciary obligations, since an agency relationship is, of necessity, one in which one party is to act on behalf of another; see para. 7.14 above. See also, *Re Coomber*, n. 72 above.

[95] See para. 7.17 above.

[96] A discretion may be given over the right to accelerate or to grant waivers; see Wood, p. 264.

[97] See *John McCann & Co. v. Pow* [1975] 1 All E.R. 129.

[98] See the specimen clause at para. 7.18 above.

or may have separate facilities outstanding in favour of the borrower, it is not difficult to envisage how such a conflict of interest could arise. As Wood points out,[99] the agent bank may find itself in a difficult position should it allow a conflict of interest to arise, and notwithstanding all-embracing exculpation clauses, the only safe course of action might be " . . . to disclose the interest to the syndicate and leave it to decide whether or not to appoint another agent."[1]

IV. DUTY NOT TO MAKE ANY SECRET PROFIT

7.24 The agent bank is in a similar position to the lead manager[2] with regard to the fees which are normally paid for the agent's services. It is common practice, therefore, to include an appropriate clause within the terms of the agreement (or some accompanying document) whereby the participants are made aware of any fees which are so payable.[3] In addition, the clause should be worded so as to permit the agent to engage in banking business with the borrower. Such business would technically be in breach of the secret profit duty unless relaxed by the agreement.

Protecting the agent bank within the loan agreement

7.25 Because of the onerous implied obligations which may, in appropriate circumstances, be imposed upon the agent bank, it is common practice for banks appointed as agents to insist upon elaborate protective clauses being incorporated within the loan agreement. We have considered some of the clauses that may be included, but there are others which merit our attention.

Agent's responsibilities under the terms of the agreement

7.26 The loan agreement will normally seek to define, as closely as possible, the agent's duties. Some may go further and provide that the agent shall not be under any duties except for those expressly set out in the agreement.[4] The duties commonly include[5]; the duty to administer payments and receipts as between the borrower and the syndicate,[6] the duty to examine any relevant documentation which is required from the borrower[7]; and the duty to inform the syndicate members if it becomes aware of a default (this duty has

---

[99] See Wood, p. 269.

[1] *Ibid.*

[2] See para. 7.16 above.

[3] See clause 20(2) in the specimen agreement, Chap. 17 below.

[4] See clause 19(1) in the specimen agreement, Chap. 17 below. Some agreements attempt to circumvent the possibility of the agent being subject to the implied obligations outlined in para. 7.20 above, by calling the relevant bank by some other name, for example, the servicing bank. It is most unlikely, however, under English law that such wording would achieve its desired purpose.

[5] See generally, the Encyclopedia, para. 5352.

[6] The agent is normally under a duty to distribute any receipts pro rata the syndicate members.

[7] This would include documents required under the conditions precedent and conditions subsequent. See generally, Chap. 6 above as to the documents which might be required.

been the subject of great debate since the Iranian hostages crisis and is considered in greater detail below).[8] Most loan agreements also place the agent bank under a duty to determine the prevailing interest rate on the appropriate interest dates, normally by consultation with the reference banks.[9]

Some of these duties might be exercised at the discretion of the agent bank, but when a discretion is allowed it should be clearly defined in order to avoid any future disagreement between the agent and the participants as to its precise scope and purpose. The extent of any discretion varies enormously, both in respect of the loans in which a discretion may be granted, and also specific clauses over which the discretion may operate. The discretion may be limited by a typical provision which reads:

> In the exercise of all its rights powers and obligations under this Agreement the Agent shall act in accordance with the instructions of the Majority Banks, but, in the absence of any such instructions, such Agent may (but shall not be obliged to) act as it shall deem fit in the best interests of the Banks and any such instructions and any such action taken by the Agent in accordance therewith shall be binding upon all the Banks.[10]

Some loans limit the discretion even further by requiring the agent to consult with the participants before taking any action. The problem with a discretion which is so limited is that it may operate against the interests of the participants in the event that the agent needs to act quickly to protect the participants' interests. This problem may be particularly acute on the occasion of a default, where, as we shall see, it may be crucial for the loan to be terminated and accelerated as quickly as possible if the syndicate is to have any hope of recovering monies owed by the borrower.[11]

7.27

The acceleration clause, together with the discretionary rights of the agent bank came under close scrutiny following the American hostage crisis in Iran.[12] A large number of the Iranian loan agreements which were outstanding at the time of the crisis had American banks as agents and permitted such agents to accelerate the loan, at their own volition, subject only to the proviso that they must accelerate if so instructed by the majority banks. Though no American bank actually accelerated on its own volition, many foreign banks were nervous about the discretion which had been granted. As a consequence greater attention is now taken in most syndicated loan agreements to curb any discretionary authority given to the agent. Unfortunately, as we have already indicated,[13] this may actually operate against the interests of the participants, particularly where they are spread over a wide geographical area, thus making it more difficult for the agent to obtain authority to act quickly should a situation so require.[14]

---

[8] See para. 7.27 below.
[9] See generally, Chap. 6 above.
[10] See also, clause 19(1) in the specimen agreement.
[11] See generally, Chap. 9 below.
[12] On the impact of the hostage crisis generally see Nichols "Lessons from the Iranian Experience: Impact on loan syndications and other international transactions" [1981] Journal of Comparative Law and Securities Regulation, pp. 89–100.
[13] See para. 7.26 above.
[14] The presence of a discretion may also make the chances of a conflict of interest much more likely, see para. 7.23 above.

CLAWBACK PROVISIONS

7.28 In the event that the agent bank makes a repayment (of either interest or principal) to a participant before it has obtained the relevant funds from the borrower (normally because of time differences between different countries) it is commonly given authority, within the terms of the loan agreement, to "claw-back" such moneys in the event the borrower fails to make the relevant payment.[15] The clause is normally worded to permit claw-back of payments made in the opposite direction. In other words, where payments have been made to the borrower (for example, on a drawdown date) before the appropriate funds have been obtained from the participant banks.[15a]

REPLACEMENT OF AGENT

7.29 The agreement will normally make provision for the replacement of the agent bank should this prove necessary. If a replacement is required because of the agent's insolvency any moneys paid to the agent, but not distributed before its insolvency, will be traceable in equity under English law.[16] A syndicate may, however, insist on greater protection against the agent's insolvency and require it to hold all moneys received under the syndicated loan in a separate trust account[17] until such moneys are distributed to the participants in accordance with the agreement.

EXCLUSION OF LIABILITY

7.30 In addition to the various provisions outlined above, most syndicated loan agreements will also contain elaborate and extensive exculpation clauses.

A typical example might read as follows:

> Neither the Agent nor any of its directors, officers, employees or agents shall be under any liability or responsibility of whatsoever kind to any of the Banks.
>
> (i) arising out of or in relation to any failure or delay in performance or breach by the Borrower of any of its obligations hereunder or by any party under any of the documents referred to hereunder, or
>
> (ii) for any statements representations or warranties in this agreement or under any document referred to herein or for the validity effectiveness enforceability or sufficiency of this agreement or any of the other documents referred to herein or be obliged to enquire as to the performance by the borrower or any other party hereto or thereto of any of the terms or conditions hereof or thereof, but the Agent shall promptly notify each Bank by telex of any event of default of which the personnel of the Agent having the conduct of the matter the subject of this agreement have actual knowledge, or
>
> (iii) for any inaccuracy or deficiency in or omission from any information furnished to any Bank by any Agent or the managers or any of them and without prejudice to the generality of the foregoing any

---

[15] See clause 19 in the specimen agreement, Chap. 17 below.
[15a] *Ibid.*
[16] On tracing generally, see Vol. 1 of this work.
[17] On trust accounts generally, see Vol. 1 of this work.

inaccuracy deficiency or omission which renders any information so furnished misleading, or

(iv) for any action taken or omitted to be taken hereunder or in connection herewith unless caused by its own gross negligence or wilful misconduct.[18]

As we have indicated earlier in this chapter,[19] exculpation clauses will be subject to strict interpretation and an English court would construe such a clause against the agent bank which relied on its terms. Whether such a clause would effectively protect the agent will be subject to those observations made in respect of exculpation clauses incorporated for the benefit of the lead manager,[20] and this topic need not trouble us further here.

GENERAL INDEMNITY FOR AGENT BANK

In addition to the all-embracing exculpation clause previously mentioned, most syndicated loan agreements will include a clause whereby the participants agree to indemnify the agent, rateably in accordance with their respective participations, for any losses incurred by the agent in the performance of its duties.[21] The right to an indemnity will obviously be lost if the agent acts outside the scope of its authority or performs its duties negligently.[22]   **7.31**

ARE THE DUTIES EXTENDED IN THE DEFAULT SITUATION?

One final issue worthy of mention relates to the obligations of both the lead manager and the agent bank in a default situation. It has been suggested by a number of commentators[23] that additional, and more onerous, obligations might be assumed in such a case. It is submitted that such a duty is remote, at least under English law, and would, in any event, be restricted to giving information, concerning the default, to the participating banks.[23a] This rather interesting issue is considered in greater detail later in this work.[24]   **7.32**

The relationship between the syndicate members

We identified at the commencement of this chapter the traditional perception that a syndicated loan is nothing more than a number of quite separate credits advanced to the borrower under one single loan agreement. Bankers   **7.33**

---

[18] See Cates, *loc. cit.* n. 23 above, p. 24.

[19] See para. 7.09 above.

[20] *Ibid.*

[21] See clause 19(5) in the Specimen Agreement, Chap. 17 below.

[22] See Wood, p. 270.

[23] See, for example, Clarke and Farrar, *loc. cit.*, n. 36 above, pp. 242–244; Horn, "The Restructing of International Loans and the International Debt Crisis" (1984) I.B.L., pp. 400–409.

[23a] Since the lead manager effectively drops out of the picture once the agreement has been executed it is difficult to imagine how such a bank could be under a duty at some point, perhaps years, after the agreement has been signed. If the same bank performs the dual function of both lead manager and agent bank the position would clearly be different, but even in such a case duties, if any, which arise on a default, would seem to attach to that bank in its capacity as agent, not as lead manager.

[24] See Chap. 9 below.

and their lawyers have viewed the loan documentation as a convenient means of pulling together the various credits which comprise the entire loan. Few have ever doubted that each individual lending bank has a quite separate and independent contractual relationship with the borrower.

It is also well recognised that as well as having contractual relationships with the borrower, the syndicate members have contractual relations as between themselves. Such relations are governed exclusively[25] by the clauses contained within the agreement, and provisions such as the sharing clause and the set-off clause are examples of how the loan documentation is structured in such a way as to bind the banks together. Notwithstanding the various "binding" clauses contained within the agreement, banks have always perceived their obligations with the borrower as being several, and this view is normally reinforced within the terms of the documentations along the following lines:

> The rights and obligations of each Bank under this Agreement are several to the intent that
>
> (i) failure of a Bank to carry out its obligations under this Agreement shall not relieve any other party hereto of any of its obligations hereunder.
>
> (ii) no Bank shall be responsible for the obligations of any other Banks or Agent hereunder, and
>
> (iii) each bank may, subject as expressly stated herein, exercise its rights and pursue its remedies hereunder independently of the Agent and the other Banks.[26]

COULD THE RELATIONSHIP BE CONSTRUED AS A PARTNERSHIP OR A JOINT VENTURE?

7.34   A recent decision of the Supreme Court of New York,[27] which held that a syndicated loan agreement amounted to a joint venture, has, however, cast a shadow over many of these previously held views. This decision[28] is of considerable importance and its facts are worthy of mention.[29]

The case arose out of an action which had been brought by Crédit Français International (CFI), a French banking corporation, against Sociedad Financiera de Comerco (SFC), a Venezuelan financial institution, to recover U.S.$ 2 million which had been loaned under the terms of a U.S.$ 25 million syndicated loan agreement. The borrower had defaulted on the payment of interest instalments in the face of the Venezuelan government's restrictions on the use of foreign currency to pay external debts. The crucial issue was whether CFI would be able to bring an action against the borrower for unpaid interest, notwithstanding that the other syndicate members chose not to join the cause.

The borrower defended the claim on a number of grounds, the most

---

[25] The question of whether such clauses do in fact evidence all the potential rights and obligations of the participants will be considered later in this chapter. See para. 7.36 below.

[26] See clause 2(2) in the specimen agreement.

[27] See *Credit Français International, S.A.* v. *Sociedad Financiera de Comerco.* C.A. 3491/84 490 NYS 2d 670 (Sup.Ct. NY. 1985). For an excellent article on some of the interesting implications of the case see Buchheit, "Is syndicated lending a joint venture?" I.F.L.R. (August 1985) pp. 12–14.

[28] *Ibid.*

[29] See Buchheit *loc. cit.*, n. 27 above.

important for our purpose being that CFI was *not* a proper party to bring an action because it was not representing the syndicate, or even a majority of the syndicate, in the proceedings.

The judge hearing the case found that the lending syndicate of banks " . . . may properly be construed as a joint venture" and, therefore, individual members of the syndicate would not be permitted to proceed against the borrower to recover debts owed to the syndicate as a whole. The court also concluded that the lending banks had *intended* to surrender their autonomy in relation to the right to bring proceedings, and for that matter any other important issue, to the agent bank.

It should be pointed out that the documentation which evidenced the loan in *Crédit Français*[30] was poorly drafted and failed to minimise the risk that a court might construe the agreement as a joint venture. However, the broader ramifications of the decision cannot be easily dismissed. The court based a significant part of its judgment on general principles of syndicated lending, which the court felt could properly be construed as a joint venture. General principles of partnership law were identified by the court in support of this finding. This effectively ruled out any possibility of an individual syndicate member proceeding against the borrower on its own.[1] **7.35**

It is generally acknowledged that the decision in *Crédit Français* is incorrect and would not be followed in England, since under the Partnership Act 1890 a syndicate will not constitute a partnership by reason of the fact that the banks share gross, not net, returns.

Notwithstanding the universal condemnation which the decision in *Crédit Français*[32] has received, it has focused attention on the loan documentation, and in particular those provisions which should be included to negate any possible suggestion that the agreement is a partnership/joint venture. It is submitted that the wording of the specimen clause above[33] covers the precautions which the participants should take in order to avoid the syndicate being construed as a partnership/joint venture. However, such precautions may not completely extinguish the risk of such construction, particularly when one considers the lengths to which the court in *Crédit Français* was prepared to go in order to completely misconstrue the intentions of the contracting parties.

The impact of the sharing clause

One of the most effective "binding" clauses found within a syndicated loan agreement is the sharing or redistribution of payments clause which reinforces the underlying philosophy of syndication, namely, that each lender should receive pro rata payments and that the borrower should not be permitted to discriminate in making such payments. **7.36**

The precise wording of the clause[34] will, however, be crucial in order to determine whether this basic philosophy is in fact upheld. The recent Ira-

---

[30] n. 27 above.
[31] See the Encyclopedia, para. 5280.
[32] n. 27 above.
[33] See para. 7.33 above.
[34] See clause 27 in the Specimen Agreement, Chap. 17 below.

nian and Falklands crises serve to illustrate how important the precise wording of the sharing clause is likely to become in the event that its activation becomes necessary.

THE IRANIAN SHARING CLAUSE

7.37 Two banks were commonly employed as agent banks in syndicated loans to Iran during the 1970s, namely, Chase Manhattan and the Iran Overseas Investment Corporation (IOIC). These banks fulfilled the agent's role for fundamentally different reasons. As one commentator points out,[35] Chase was an aggressive American bank with large deposits eager to lend at the right margin, whereas IOIC was closely connected to the Iranian government and was committed to raising funds for Iranian projects. The sharing clauses used in their agreements reflected these differences. Chase had incorporated a clause requiring payments made by the borrower to be shared, but not deposits which any bank might use to set-off against the borrower's indebtedness. The IOIC loans contained a full sharing clause which covered both receipts and set-off rights. When the Iran crisis broke Chase set-off the large deposits it held on behalf of the Iranian government and refused to apply such deposits under the sharing clause. Chase may not have made many friends as a consequence of their action but many lawyers probably admired their tough draftsmanship.[36]

Before the Iran crisis, sharing clauses were commonly referred to as set-off sharing clauses. This was undoubtedly a misconception. Some clauses certainly are set-off sharing clauses since they provide for the sharing of any conceivable method of repayment. Some, however, (as the Chase example above demonstrates) cannot be classified in such a way.

The precise wording of the sharing clause has come under greater scrutiny since the Iran crisis with lenders being particularly anxious to prevent any single lender elevating its position *vis à vis* other lenders. In essence the market is simply seeking to maintain the pari passu philosophy which lies at the heart of the eurocurrency market.

THE FALKLANDS CRISIS

7.38 Rather different problems arose during the Falklands crisis, where, basically, a number of French banks refused to share with British banks, whom the Argentinians were refusing to pay, moneys received from Argentina. The French banks claimed that the crisis was a *force majeure* which thereby prevented the sharing clause from operating. This plea was rejected by the British banks and it soon became clear that the French banks, presumably because of the close relations between France and Argentina, were simply stalling for time. The crisis once again highlighted the strains which are placed on the sharing clause when its activation becomes necessary, and the importance of specific wording defining how the clause will operate is now perceived as being of fundamental importance.[37] Whether specific wording will be of any real assistance in a highly politicised situation (as was the case during both the Iran and Argentine crises) remains a debatable point.

[35] See Brown, "Sharing strains on Euromarket syndicates," I.F.L.R. (June, 1982) p. 4.
[36] *Ibid.*
[37] For a fuller exposition of the impact which the Falklands crisis had on sharing clauses, see Brown, *loc. cit.*, n. 35 above.

Other important clauses covering the relationship between the syndicate members

The agreement should also clearly identify those rights over which control **7.39**
is vested with the majority banks,[38] and the mechanical procedures which
are to be used to identify the wishes of the majority should be spelt out.
Some clauses permit participants to proceed on their own, (for example, the
ability to bring proceedings against the borrower) without the consent of
the majority; however, the agreement will normally limit this freedom by
requiring the bank to notify all other participants before taking independent
action. This will thereby enable the syndicate to keep abreast of all developments and take such action as is deemed necessary to protect its interests.

In conclusion, it can be said that the relationship between the syndicate
members is an uneasy balance between independent and collective rights
and obligations. A balance clearly has to be struck by those drafting the
agreement in order to satisfy the needs of both the syndicate as a whole and
the individual participants thereto.

---

[38] See generally, the Encyclopedia, para. 5300.

8. Transferability of Loans and Loan Participations

Introduction

8.01   Asset sales have existed as long as banks and other financial institutions have been putting loans and other assets on their balance sheets. It is, however, only in the last decade that this activity has risen to prominence in the international financial markets. The principal reason for the increase in this activity has been the shifting regulatory and economic conditions under which banks are required to operate.

It may be helpful at the commencement of this chapter to define what is meant by "asset sales" in this context. At the simplest level it is the process by which a bank disposes of a loan to another bank in a manner which will allow the selling bank to remove the loan from its balance sheet as an asset.[1] Central to achieving this objective is the ability of the selling bank to demonstrate that it has successfully transferred the credit risk of the borrower to the buying bank.[1a]

Throughout the course of this chapter we will use this simple model as the basis for legal analysis, although it is misleading to assume that this is by any means the only type of activity which properly comes under the broad umbrella of the term "asset sales." Commitments to lend and "contingencies," such as the risk under swap contracts[2] or the risk of non-reimbursement under letters of credit[3] or bankers' acceptances, can and are often "sold" by banks.[4] However, to avoid unnecessary repetition, and in order to assist interpretation of the terminology used throughout the chapter, we shall use the expression "seller" or "selling bank" to denote the person disposing of the risk in question, the expression "buyer" or "buying bank" to denote the person assuming the risk and the expression "sale" or "disposal" (and cognate expressions) to refer to the method of passing risk whether by assignment, novation, participation or otherwise.

There are various reasons why a bank may want to sell an asset. Historically, banks have always needed from time to time to free up internal or external lending limits to allow new credits to be provided to particular customers. Further, the imposition or simply the possibility of adverse tax consequences or reserve requirements, capital adequacy ratios or similar restrictions are often recognised in the loan documentation itself as a reason

---

[1] Banks are increasingly concerned with the removal or "hedging" of risk attached to contingent liabilities which are not reflected "above the line" in the balance sheet. See below at 8.28 for why this should be so.

[1a] This would appear to be the common factor for most sophisticated accounting regimes. It will not necessarily be the only factor, *e.g.* in the United States the risk participation of a funded credit may not achieve off-balance sheet treatment because the responsibility for funding has not been passed to the buyer.

[2] See Chap. 11, below.

[3] See Chap. 13, below.

[4] Some or all of the asset sale techniques discussed in para. 2 below can apply to most forms of receivables and contingent liabilities—the examples given are by no means exhaustive.

for transferring a loan asset. Particular instances may arise where the enforcement or recovery of debts is facilitated by the transfer of a loan, as, for example, where a need arises to establish a jurisdictional link[5] with a defendant obligor or to enable set-off rights[6] to be fully utilised.

In recent years the stimulus for the asset sales market has derived from the international debt crisis and the subsequent reaction of regulators and bank controllers to the management and control of a bank's assets and liabilities. The market's impetus is increasingly provided by the need for banks to continue to satisfy their customer's needs for new credits, whilst staying within externally and internally imposed ratios imposed on the use of capital and the return on assets and equity. The ingenuity shown by banks in achieving these often competing goals is a tribute to their inventiveness. One need only consider the burgeoning market in the sale or swapping of rescheduled debt and other weaker credits to appreciate the level of ingenuity which has been employed to develop novel financial instruments.

METHODS OF SALE

What, then, are the legal techniques that may be employed by a bank to achieve the sale of a loan? Three principal techniques are commonly employed under English law.   **8.02**

1. Assignment[7]

An assignment of a debt may take the form of a legal or an equitable assignment. The starting point for a consideration of these two forms of assignment is section 136 of the Law of Property Act 1925, which states in sub-section (1) that:—

> "Any absolute assignment by writing under the hand of the assignor (not purporting to be by way of charge only) of any debt or other legal thing in action, of which express notice in writing has been given to the debtor, trustee or other person from whom the assignor would have been entitled to claim such debt or thing in action, is effectual in law (subject to equities having priority over the right of the assignee) to pass and transfer from the date of such notice:—
> (a) the legal right to such debt or thing in action;
> (b) all legal and other remedies for the same; and
> (c) the power to give a good discharge for the same without the concurrence of the assignor . . . "

In simple terms, a legal assignment is an assignment which satisfies the conditions in section 136, an equitable assignment is one which does not. Although it may not be apparent at first glance, many assignments entered into by banks for the sale of assets will not satisfy the conditions necessary for the creation of a legal assignment. This will often be the case because

---

[5] See Chap. 2, above.
[6] See Chap. 9, below.
[7] See generally, Vol. 1, Chap. 11 of this work.

part only of the debt is to be assigned to the buyer or because the assignment is not (initially at least) perfected by notice being given to the obligor or, occasionally, because the assignment is not in writing.[8]

8.03　In broad terms it may be said that, provided notice of assignment is given to the underlying obligor, the differences between a legal and an equitable assignment are, so far as English law is concerned, more apparent than real. A legal assignment is, as we have seen, operative to give the assignee the full legal and beneficial interest in the debt with the result that the assignee will be able to sue the borrower directly without any need to rely upon the assignor to assist in the enforcement of the debt. An equitable assignee will, as beneficial owner of the debt being assigned, also enjoy the same right, although purely as a procedural matter he must join the assignor as party to such action.[9]

It is the giving of notice to the debtor which is more significant than technical distinctions between legal and equitable assignments. This is because (a) until notice is given the borrower may continue to discharge the debt by making payments to the assignor with all the practical problems of tracing which this may present on liquidation of the assignor, (b) priorities as between competing equitable assignees may turn on the order in which notice is given and (c) notice prevents the debtor from setting-up any new rights of set-off, counterclaim or other equities which it may have against the assignor.

It has been suggested[10] that a significant defect of the notified equitable assignment as compared to a legal assignment is that a bona fide legal purchaser of the debt without notice of the prior equitable interest may rank ahead of the equitable assignment in terms of priority. The preferred view, however, is that the bona fide purchaser is displaced by section 136, which subjects legal assignment to "equities having priority over the right of the assignee."[11] Of course, the granting of a legal assignment after an equitable assignment has previously been granted by the selling bank assumes fraud on the part of the selling bank. It is believed that the risk of such a fraud is normally discounted by buying banks in the asset sales market.

On the question of notices, although it will often be more in the interests of the assignee, and, therefore, it is often the assignee who will give notice of the assignment to the debtor (and the agent bank in a syndicated credit), it is surprising that the right to give or the responsibility for giving notice is not expressly given to or imposed by English law on the assignor or assignee. It would appear that either can give notice and that notice need not be given formally or in writing (unless section 136 applies, in which case it must be in writing). Indeed it is sufficient that the debtor is aware of the assignment although his awareness may be derived from sources other than the assignor or the assignee.[12]

---

[8] For why an assignment may not be in writing, see below.

[9] Either as co-plaintiff if the assignor consents or as co-defendant if he does not. R.S.C. Ord. 15, r. 6 now provides that non-joinder cannot defeat a cause of action, although the court may direct that the assignor be made a party to the case.

[10] See the Encyclopaedia, para. 3778.

[11] The preferred view, therefore, is that the rule in *Dearle* v. *Hall* (1828) 3 Russ. 1, governs.

[12] *Lloyd* v. *Banks* [1868] Ch.App. 488, where notice was acquired by the debtor reading a newspaper.

A final word on assignments. Unless the other parties to the loan contract agree otherwise, an assignment will only operate to transfer rights and benefits.[13] It will not operate to transfer obligations. The selling bank will, accordingly, remain obliged even after the assignment to perform any obligations owed to the borrower which remain to be performed. These obligations may be significant with, say, a revolving loan or even with a fully-drawn term loan where, say, a multicurrency option exists which may require "top-up" payments[14] on interest payment dates or, sometimes, the repayment and re-advance of the loan where currencies are switched.

2. Novation

Novation in the context of the sale of a loan is the name given to an arrangement whereby the mutual rights and obligations of the selling bank (and the other parties to the underlying loan documentation) are relinquished and discharged, in consideration of the establishment of new rights and obligations, on identical terms, between the buying bank and such other parties.[15] In other words, the novation gives rise to an entirely new contract between the original parties to the loan (other than the seller) and the buyer. **8.04**

It could be argued that the novation produces the ideal result from the perspective of both buyer and seller. The seller relieves himself of his obligations to the borrower (this may be particularly important when a bank is selling commitments to lend) which is something it will be unable to achieve by an assignment or the granting of a participation. The buyer, on the other hand, puts itself in the same position as the original lender. It will have a direct contractual relationship with the borrower and will have all the rights and benefits which it would have had if it had been a party to the original facility.

A major difficulty with a novation, however, is the fact that it can be a cumbersome method of selling a loan asset since it requires the agreement of all the original parties to the loan. Such agreement may be particularly difficult to obtain in a conventionally structured syndicated loan agreement.[16] As Collins M.R. pointed out in a leading case in this area of law: "A debtor cannot relieve himself of his liability to his creditor by assigning the burden of the obligation to somebody else; this can only be brought about by the consent of all three, and involves the release of the original debtor."[17]

---

[13] See, for example, *Trendtex Corp.* v. *Credit Suisse* [1980] Q.B. 629; *Tolhurst* v. *Associated Portland Cement* [1902] 2 K.B. 660; and *United Dominions Trust* v. *Parkway Motors* [1955] 2 All E.R. 557.

[14] A "top-up" payment will be required from a bank, for example, where the loan is to be outstanding in one of the optional currencies for successive interest periods and the optional currency has weakened as against the base currency of the loan. The bank will have to advance a further amount in the optional currency to bring it up to the applicable base currency equivalent.

[15] The establishment of consideration does not present a problem as some commentators have suggested (see, for example, "Selling Loan Assets under English law: a basic guide," *International Financial Law Review*, (May, 1986) p. 29). The agreement by the borrower to repay the new debt which it owes to the buying bank provides the consideration for the original lender's release of the old debt.

[16] See Chap. 7, above.

[17] *Tolhurst* v. *Associated Portland Cement Manufacturers (1900), Ltd.*, [1902] 2 K.B. 660, p. 668.

8.05   Notwithstanding the practical problems which it may pose, novation is alive and flourishing as a means of disposing of assets especially where the "asset" takes the form of a contingent liability such as that under a backstop loan facility or a revolving credit. This is largely the result of the practice of including in the loan document "transfer" language, setting out procedures for the future novation by lenders of their respective rights and obligations under the loan document.[18] A modified example of such language is contained in Clause 25(2) of the Specimen Loan Agreement.[19] A fuller example of the language which may be included in a syndicated back-stop facility might read as follows:—

"(A) If any Bank wishes to transfer all or any of its rights, benefits and obligations hereunder, then such transfer shall be effected by the delivery to the Agent of a duly completed and duly executed Transfer Certificate in the form set out in the Schedule hereto whereupon, to the extent that in such Transfer Certificate the Bank party thereto seeks to transfer its rights and obligations hereunder:—

> (i)   the Borrower and such Bank shall each be released from further obligations to the other hereunder and their respective rights against each other shall be cancelled (such rights and obligations being referred to in this Clause as "discharged rights and obligations");
>
> (ii)   the Borrower and the Transferee party thereto shall each assume obligations towards each other which differ from the discharged rights and obligations only in so far as the obligations so assumed and the rights so acquired by the Borrower are owed to and constituted by claims against such Transferee and not such Bank; and
>
> (iii) The Agent, such Transferee and the other Banks shall acquire the same rights and assume the same obligations between themselves as they would have acquired and assumed had such Transferee been an original party hereto with the obligations assumed by it as a result of such transfer.

(B) The Agent shall promptly notify the other parties hereto of the receipt by it of any Transfer Certificate and shall deliver a copy of such Transfer Certificate to the Borrower."

The transfer language of this specimen clause simplifies the process of novation by obtaining the agreement in advance of all parties to the loan document to any future novation. In doing so it takes advantage of the principle of English law that an offer may be made "to the public at large" which was established in the well-known case of *Carlill* v. *Carbolic Smoke Ball Co.*[20] Such an offer may be accepted by anyone who satisfies the conditions specified in the offer.

The novation itself is facilitated by the scheduling to the loan document of a short form of transfer certificate. The execution of the certificate by the

---

[18] For a detailed analysis of the various forms of transfer mechanisms and their uses, see further Bray, "Developing a Secondary Market in Loan Assets," *International Financial Law Review*, (October, 1984) and Hughes, "Transferability of Loans and Loan Participations," *Journal of International Banking Law*, 1987.

[19] See Chap. 17, below.

[20] [1892] 2 Q.B. 484; *affd.*, [1893] 1 Q.B. 256.

selling and buying bank and the delivery to the borrower or the agent bank of the executed certificate will complete the novation. The transfer method has, therefore, borrowed the old-established principle of English law that an offer may be made to the public at large without it being necessary for the offeror to know the identity of the other party to the contract.[21]

3. Participation

The third and perhaps the most popular legal technique used in the off-balance sheet disposal of assets is the funded "participation" or "sub-participation."[22] The term has no technical legal meaning in English law but is normally used to describe a funding arrangement between the seller and the participant under which the participant places funds with the original lender on terms that those funds will only be repaid to the participant together with interest thereon as and when corresponding amounts of principal and interest are received from the borrower under the loan to which the participation relates. The participation is thus "non-recourse" to the selling bank in the sense that the seller is not liable to make payments to the participant if corresponding amounts are not received from the borrower.[23]

8.06

The term "participation" when used to describe an English law non-recourse funding arrangement should not be confused with its U.S. counterpart, which by no means shares all the characteristics of its English cousin.[24]

The important distinction between a participation and an assignment or a novation is that the participation is an entirely separate contractual arrangement from the underlying loan agreement and there is, accordingly, no contractual *nexus* between the participant and the borrower. In basic legal terms this means that the participant will not be able to sue the borrower in the event of default by the borrower in performing its obligations under the loan agreement. It will have to rely on the original lender to take recovery action, although as we will see later in this chapter, it may be able to exercise some influence over the actions taken by the lender following a default.[25]

From this legal distinction between participations, assignments and novations flows an equally significant commercial distinction. The party taking a loan participation acquires a double credit risk—that of the borrower and of the original lender. If the original lender goes into liquidation,

---

[21] By way of example we have considered only one of the various transfer mechanisms used in loan documentation. Other structures are outlined in the articles referred to in n. 18.

[22] For a comprehensive review of the topic of sub-participations under English law, see Hughes and Palache, "Loan participations—some English law considerations," *International Financial Law Review*, 1984 I.F.L.R. (November, 1984).

[23] There is no reason in English law why such a contractual arrangement should not be upheld. Loans repayable on a contingency are valid contracts under English law, see *Waite Hill Holdings* v. *Marshall* [1983] 133 N.L.J. 745.

[24] For a considered review of the U.S. participation agreement, see Reade Ryan, *International Financial Law Review*, 1984 I.F.L.R. (October, 1984).

[25] Typically, the participant will have contractual right *vis-à-vis* the seller to veto or, at least, be consulted before the seller exercises certain rights or discretions under the loan facility being participated. It is, for example, common for the participant's consent to be required before extending payment dates or reducing interest rates.

the participant will find that monies subsequently recovered from the borrower will not be applied in satisfying the original lender's liabilities under the participation, but rather towards the liabilities of the original lender owed to its general body of creditors.[26]

The popularity of the loan participation will, double-credit risks notwithstanding, appear less surprising due to the impact of non-U.K. legal aspects of asset sales, in addition to contractual restrictions in loan documentation which may impede the disposal of loan assets.

4. Other methods of sale

8.07 Considerations of space prevent a detailed discussion of other methods employed to dispose of other usual types of bank credit.[27] Two other techniques are, however, worthy of a brief mention.[28]

A. RISK PARTICIPATION

Where the underlying risk which the bank is seeking to lay off takes the form of a non-funded asset then the document used to dispose of the risk is sometimes described as a "risk" participation. This type of instrument would commonly be used where the bank has a contingent liability (such as under a guarantee) or where it is contemplated that its legal liability will effectively be funded by its customer (as with liabilities under letters of credit or accepted bills of exchange). Under the risk participation the participant receives a fee for compensating the bank in the event of default in the performance by the bank's customer of its obligations. As such, the risk participation might well be viewed under English law as a contract of insurance[29] and, accordingly, in certain jurisdictions may be *ultra vires* for the risk participant.[30]

B. BROKING

This is something of an umbrella title which describes contractual arrangements having differing legal characteristics. In its most simple form it involves a bank acting as an intermediary in an agency capacity for either the seller or the buyer of an asset.[31] In other cases it may describe the process by which a bank takes an asset as agent or trustee for the benefit of a third party.

---

[26] Below.

[27] Sale as agent for an undisclosed principal or the declaration of a trust of the benefit of the relevant asset being two of more obvious alternative methods.

[28] For a fuller discussion of alternative methods of sale and some of the potential legal problems, see Tempselt, "Interbank relations in loan participation agreements" 1984 B.L.J. 31 and Behrens, "Classification of loan participations following the insolvency of the lead bank" 1984 62 T.L.R. 1115.

[29] Note that the U.K. Insurance Companies Act 1982 s.2(2) permits banks to carry on insurance business if it is carried on solely in the course of carrying on, and for the purposes of, banking business.

[30] This would appear to be true for French banks, for example. In other jurisdictions the risk participation could, perhaps, be treated as a guarantee.

[31] As, for example, where a bank enters into an acceptance facility on terms that it might procure the acceptance of relevant bills by a third party.

Comparison between sale methods

Mention has already been made of the attraction and popularity of the sub-   **8.08**
participation as a method of disposing of assets. This derives essentially
from the legal nature of the sub-participation, which establishes a distinct
and separate legal relationship between seller and buyer. Accordingly, participation does not involve a transfer of the beneficial ownership in the underlying loan debt or indeed any of the rights of the seller in respect of the
underlying loan facility.[32]

For these reasons it is unusual to find in a loan document any express
attempt to restrict the granting of sub-participations (see the Specimen Loan
Agreement annexed hereto, for example). Further and equally importantly,
it is rare for the law of the borrower or any guarantor (where they are non-
U.K. entities) to seek to impose conditions on or otherwise seek to regulate
the granting of a sub-participation. Nor will a sub-participation normally
attract adverse tax consequences in the borrower's or the guarantor's jurisdiction.[33]

It may be gathered from the previous paragraph that the position is otherwise with novations or assignments. Clause 25(2)(a) of the Specimen Loan
Agreement[34] is not untypical in its approach to assignments and transfers
nor in its requirement for the consent of the borrower (not to be unreasonably withheld or delayed) for assignments or transfers of rights and/or obligations outside the selling bank's own group. Where obligations are
novated it is invariably the case that the borrower's consent will be required
as the borrower will be taking a credit risk on the transferee. As we will see
later an assignment or novation may also have disastrous consequences for
the buyer if full regard is not had to the position under local law.

Notwithstanding these difficulties there are an increasing number of situ-   **8.09**
ations where assignment or novation will be the preferred route. Assignment and novation both give the buyer a beneficial interest in a debt (the
debt owed to the seller, in the former case, or the new debt arising from the
novation, in the latter case). This may be vital where the buyer is seeking to
take advantage of an available tax credit in its own jurisdiction.[35] With
weaker credits (and certainly where rescheduled or potentially reschedulable
debt is involved), the buyer will often wish to have a directly enforceable
claim against the borrower. Indeed, the wishes of seller and buyer will
usually coincide in such a situation since the seller will want the consequences of, and the responsibility for, handling any default or restructuring
which may fall upon the buyer.

A buyer which is interested in establishing a banker-customer relationship with the borrower may refuse to accept a sub-participation as it prevents him from having a contractual nexus with the borrower. Indeed, it is
often the desire to maintain a legal and contractual relationship with the

---

[32] For a fuller discussion of the legal relationships to which the sub-participation may give rise,
see the articles referred to in n. 28 and also, McLaughlin, "Underlying relationships in bank
participations 1984 I.F.L.R. (November) p. 8.
[33] There are exceptions, the United States for example, see below.
[34] See Chap. 17, below.
[35] The U.K. Revenue, for example, will generally only recognise the beneficial owner of the
debt as being entitled to tax credits.

borrower which drives sellers towards the use of the sub-participation as a sale instrument. Where relationship factors are less relevant a seller may defer to the buyer's wishes for an assignment or novation.

Of course, where a need arises to transfer the seller's obligations under a loan facility to the buyer (as with a revolving or back-stop facility), then novation provides the only solution. It is normal both in assignments and sub-participations to impose an obligation on the assignee or sub-partici-pant to fund future payment obligations of the seller. Such undertakings will, however, only normally operate contractually between seller and buyer.[36] If the buyer defaults, the borrower can still insist on the seller per-forming its contractual obligations to the borrower under the terms of the loan facility. Under a novation the borrower agrees to discharge the legal obligations owed by the seller in consideration of the buyer assuming iden-tical obligations.

A further disadvantage in the assignment method has been the threat that stamp duty would be imposed under the Stamp Act 1891.[37] It would appear that this threat is receding due to recent statements made by the U.K. Revenue which indicate that loans of any tenor may be treated by the Revenue as being loan capital and thus within the exemptions from stamp duty for assignments of loan capital.[38]

English law considerations

8.10 Having described the legal nature of the various sale techniques it might be helpful at this juncture to isolate a number of specific English law issues which a prudent seller or buyer should consider before concluding any asset sale.[39] These issues will be considered under the following headings:—

    (a) credit risk;
    (b) contractual restrictions;
    (c) confidentiality;
    (d) liability of seller to buyer; and
    (e) the rights and obligations of the buyer.

a. Credit Risk

8.11 Consideration of credit risk might conveniently be looked at both from the viewpoint of the credit risk of the borrower and the credit risk of the selling bank.

The principal objective of the selling bank is to transfer the borrower's credit risk to the buying bank. As we have seen, this is generally achieved either by assigning or novating the debt to the buyer or by passing the risk to the buyer by means of a "non-recourse" sub-participation.

One must consider, however, the situation where the borrower seeks to

---

[36] An assignment or participation will not normally be effective to transfer the selling banks obligations to the buyer as discussed above.

[37] The impact of stamping requirements is considered in greater detail in Chap. 6, above.

[38] See below.

[39] See further Allen, "Asset Sales—an analysis of risk for buyers and sellers; *Journal of Inter-national Banking Law*, 1987.

restructure or refinance the original loan facility either because he has run into financial difficulties and needs time to pay or, conversely, because he is now able to obtain better terms from other lenders.

In such a situation we see, at a practical level, the distinction between a participation and an assignment or novation. As the seller of a participation remains the legal "lender of record" and beneficially entitled to receive repayment of the underlying debt, it will be to the original lender that the borrower (and, where they are involved, central banks and other regulatory authorities) will look to agree the restructuring or refinancing of the loan.

Typically, the participation will contain protective language along the following lines:—

> "It is further agreed that the Original Lender is and shall remain entitled to:
> (i) exercise or refrain from exercising any or all of its rights and powers arising under or in connection with the Loan Agreement or any document relating thereto; and
> (ii) agree to any amendment or waiver of the terms of the Loan Agreement or any other such document.
> Provided that, in exercising or refraining from exercising such rights and powers or agreeing to such amendment or waiver, the Original Lender shall have regard to all relevant circumstances including the interests of the Participant and the Original Lender shall not be entitled under this Clause to agree to any such amendment or waiver which would directly result in the reduction of the Loan otherwise than by repayment."

The limits of the protection which this language may afford the original lender can be seen if we take the example of a refinancing of the old loan. In such a case the existing lenders will be required to make a new loan to the borrower on the revised terms and this new loan will be applied in or towards repayment of the old loan. The irony here is that repayment of the old loan will trigger an obligation on the part of the original lender to pay out his participant under the participation. Thus, it may be that just at the point at which the borrower's credit deteriorates the participant finds that his participation is paid out. It is no consolation to the original lender to say that he is not legally obliged to enter into any rescheduling arrangements. The rescheduling may represent his only realistic hope of recovering his money and the political pressures to co-operate may in any event prove difficult to resist.

8.12 It is to counter the possibility of the borrower's credit risk returning to the original lender in this way that banks selling participations have sought to protect their position on rescheduling. A typical clause may read as follows:

> "If the persons to whom is owed at least fifty per cent. of the Borrower's indebtedness, or any class of the Borrower's indebtedness of which the Advances outstanding under the Participated Facility form part, agree to any readjustment or rescheduling (howsoever described) of such, or such class of such, indebtedness, then the Original Lender may agree to, or participate in, such readjustment or rescheduling on

such terms as the Original Lender thinks fit and, for these purposes, the Original Lender shall be entitled, *inter alia*, to:

(i) agree to any release, novation or payment of any of the Borrower's indebtedness under the Participated Facility;

(ii) undertake on its own behalf any obligations in connection with such readjustment or rescheduling;

(iii) treat any principal amounts advanced to it by the Participant hereunder as if the same had been advanced to it by the Participant in respect of the Original Lender's obligations in relation to such readjustment or rescheduling and, to the extent that the Original Lender so treats such amounts, retain for its own account any principal amounts which would otherwise have been payable to the Participant pursuant to [relevant clause];

(iv) treat any amounts (other than amounts of principal) which would otherwise have been payable to the Participant pursuant to [relevant clause] as if the same had been principal amounts advanced to it by the Participant in respect of its obligations in relation to such readjustment or rescheduling; and

(v) convert, at such rates as may be determined by it, any amount treated by it as having been advanced to it by the Participant in respect of its obligations in relation to such readjustment or rescheduling into such currencies as such obligations may from time to time be denominated

Provided that in agreeing to, or participating in, such readjustment or rescheduling the Bank shall have regard to all relevant circumstances including the interests of the Participant.''

8.13   Having established that the rescheduling will not entitle the participant to be paid out under the terms of the participation the clause will normally continue by providing that the original lender's sole obligation thereafter is to pay to the participant amounts corresponding to monies received under the rescheduling which are attributable to the amounts paid by the participant to the seller under the original terms of the participation.

Consideration of the selling bank's credit risk again turns on the distinction between assignment and novation on the one hand and participation on the other.

An assignee (whether legal or equitable) of a loan or a person taking a novation of that loan will be beneficial owners of a debt, being the debt assigned to the assignee or that created by the novation. Their claims in respect of that debt and monies paid by the borrower in respect of that debt will take precedence over those of a trustee in bankruptcy or liquidator of the selling bank.[40] Any monies recovered by the seller from the borrower (as where, for example, monies are routed through the seller under an undisclosed assignment) will be monies received on trust for the buyer and, as such, will not be available to the general body of creditors of the seller.

The participant does not enjoy such an enviable position. He will take the double credit risk of the seller and of the borrower, for, as we have seen, he had no enforceable claim against the borrower in respect of the loan. He will

---

[40] See *Re Wallis, exp. Jenks* [1902] 1 K.B. 719; *Re Anderson* [1911] 1 K.B. 896.

rank with the other unsecured creditors of the selling bank and monies recovered from the borrower will simply be added to the general pool of funds available for distribution to these creditors.[41]

b. Contractual Restrictions

As assignment involves the transfer of rights arising as against the borrower **8.14** under the relevant loan facility it is not surprising that the well-advised borrower will seek to regulate when and upon what conditions assignments may occur. The borrower's case will be even stronger where the transfer of obligations owing to the borrower is contemplated. As an example of the type of restrictions which will commonly be negotiated clause 25(2) of the Specimen Loan Agreement presents a fairly standard set of provisions,[42] consent of the borrower (not to be unreasonably withheld) being required unless the assignment or transfer of the lender is "intra-group."[43]

The consequences of failing to observe such contractual restrictions are clear. The assignment or novation will be invalid as against the borrower and may involve the seller in an action for breach of contract. Indeed the failure by the seller to deliver to the buyer what had been bargained for might mean that the assignment or novation would not even survive as a contractual arrangement binding seller and buyer alone.

Although it is relatively common to find contractual restrictions on assignment within the terms of a loan document, effective restraints on the granting of participations are rare.[44] This has been due to the fact that the participation does not involve any transfer of rights or obligations arising under the loan facility and, therefore, the view has traditionally been taken that the granting of participations is a private matter between lender and participant and of no concern to the borrower. Whilst this may be correct from a strict legal point of view, the extent to which participants may influence the way in which the lender exercises its rights under the loan facility occasionally leads to a requirement that the borrower's consent be obtained or at least that notice of the participant's name be given. Of greater concern in this context is the question of confidentiality, a matter to which we will now turn our attention.

c. Confidentiality

Whatever the express contractual restrictions set out in the loan documen-   **8.15** tation the ability of a lender to assign, novate or participate may be effectively restricted by considerations of confidentiality.

A relationship of banker and customer exists between borrower and lender, and under English law (as well as in most other jurisdictions) a bank

---

[41] Nor will a participant be able to apply any deposits of the borrower which it holds by way of set-off against monies unpaid to the participant. There is no mutuality, the borrower owes the loan to the original lender. The same conclusion was reached in the U.S. case of *In re Yale Express System* Inc. 245 F. Supp. 790 (SDNY 1965).

[42] See Chap. 17, below.

[43] Subject to what is said below, contracts are normally assignable in the absence of express prohibition.

[44] A court might well take the view that the contract could be rescinded on the grounds of misrepresentation or because of a breach of a fundamental term of the contract.

owes a duty of confidentiality to its customers.[45] Consequently, any disclosure by the lender to third parties of the terms of or, indeed, even the existence of any loan facility may well constitute a breach of this duty. Disclosure of information provided to the lender pursuant to or in connection with the facility would also clearly give rise to a claim for breach of this duty. Since the sale of a loan asset will normally necessitate the disclosure, at the very least, of the terms of the underlying loan, a seller may find the path to such sale blocked even where the loan documentation does not expressly prohibit sale in the manner proposed.

The duty of confidentiality under English law is, thankfully for sellers of assets, not an absolute one.[46] The most relevant qualification of the duty for our purposes is where disclosure is made with the express or implied consent of the borrower. A glance at Clause 25(4) of the Specimen Loan Agreement[47] will reveal the type of express disclosure language that a well-drafted loan agreement might contain. Implied consent is a concept which is a little more difficult to focus upon. Is there implied consent where the loan agreement expressly allows assignments and participations without consent? The answer is not obvious, although the case of holding that there is implied consent is strengthened where the salient terms of the facility are revealed publicly in the press with the consent of the borrower or where the borrower is made aware of the possibility of sales occurring and assents thereto.

In some cases, where the facility has been well publicised and where the disclosure is limited to the basic terms of the loan document and financial statements, there may not, even in the absence of consent, be a breach of the duty of confidentiality. Arguably in such circumstances the information disclosed is in the public domain and, for the reasons advanced above, it may additionally be viewed as the subject of an implied consent by the borrower.

Breach of the duty of confidentiality will give rise to an action for damages in respect of loss arising from the breach. In the majority of cases, however, it will be difficult to discern precisely what loss has been suffered. However, in a situation where, for example, defaults under the loan agreement or other facilities are revealed to third parties or where details of more favourable terms are disclosed to competitor banks, it will be much easier to identify the potential loss which may be suffered by the errant bank.

d. Potential Liability of Seller to Buyer

8.16   The absence of any substantial case law on this subject makes analysis of the potential liability of a seller to the buyer most difficult.

In so far as the assignment or participation agreement is concerned, the responsibility of the seller to the buyer in relation to the borrower's financial condition and the adequacy and legalities of the underlying loan documentation will largely be disclaimed.

---

[45] For a fuller discussion of the extent of this duty under English law, see Vol. I, Chap. 3 of this work.

[46] See the leading case of *Tournier v. National Provincial and Union Bank of England* [1924] 1 K.B. 461.

[47] See Chap. 17, below.

The scope of disclaimer provisions in most agreements should leave the buyer in no doubt that the principle of *caveat emptor* is alive and well. The language of a typical disclaimer clause might read as follows:

> "The Original Lender makes no representation or warranty and assumes no responsibility with respect to (i) the due execution, legality, validity, adequacy or enforceability of the Loan Agreement or any document relating thereto, (ii) the financial condition of the Borrower or any other party to the Loan Agreement or any document relating thereto or (iii) the performance by the Borrower or any other such person of its obligations under the Loan Agreement or any other such document; in particular but without limitation, if the Borrower or any other person shall fail to perform any of its obligations under the Loan Agreement or any document relating thereto, the Participant shall have no recourse to the Original Lender in respect of such failure."

Whether such a provision would be upheld where the seller suspected or had reason to believe that all was not well so far as the loan documentation or the financial condition of the obligor was concerned is another matter. Further, such a provision will not necessarily assist where the seller has made contrary oral or written representations or warranties at or prior to the time of sale. Where the seller was subsequently discovered to have no title to the underlying debt there must also be a real risk that the sale would be set aside on the ground that there is a total failure of consideration.[48]

Less clear, however, would be the situation where the debt sold is, for example, subject to equities (such as set-off claims) or where prior defaults had occurred or, indeed, were subsisting at the time of sale. In the absence of express provisions a court would have to find some representation or warranty made by the seller outside the terms of the sale agreement[49] or read some implied term into the contract by reference, perhaps, to an established market practice of only selling loans free of such claims or defaults. Much would turn on the state of the seller's knowledge of such circumstances at the time of sale.

Where, as is often the case with an assignment, the sale is as "beneficial owner" the relevant covenants set out in the second schedule to the Law of Property Act 1925 will by virtue of section 76(1) of that Act be deemed to be given by the seller. These include covenants as to the power to convey, absence of encumbrances and so forth.[50]

An assignor will also be under a duty, on a continuing basis, not to do any act in derogation of its grant.[51] If the assignment is equitable the assignor as holder of the legal interest in the debt for the assignee may also be subject to the duties of a fiduciary.[52]

In the case of a participation the original lender does not have a relationship of trust or agency with the participant. Any claim which a participant might bring for actions of the original lender which effectively deprive him

---

[48] *Marnham* v. *Weaver* [1899] 80 L.T. 412.

[49] See Chap. 6, above.

[50] For a fuller discussion of the importance of s.76 of the Law of Property Act, see Vol. I, Chap. 17 of this work.

[51] *Gerard* v. *Lewis* [1867] L.R. 2 C.P. 305.

[52] These include duties of due diligence and disclosure.

of what he had bargained for would most likely have to be founded in contract.

e. Rights and Obligations of the Buyer

8.17 A useful starting point for a discussion on the rights and obligations of the buyer is an examination of the often heard statement that an assignee acquires the rights but not the obligations of the assignor.[53]

Taking the statement in reverse order, it is true, as previously discussed, that in the absence of the consent of all parties to the original loan agreement the assignor will *vis-à-vis* the borrower remain obliged to perform all the obligations which it originally contracted to perform, although it is invariably the case that any assignee will be required in the assignment to agree to fund the assignor's payment obligations.

On a more practical level, however, circumstances will arise when it will be desirable, or even critical, that the assignee perform the obligations of the assignor. Most obviously this will be the case where the assignor defaults in the performance of an obligation which is a condition to the assignor obtaining some benefit under the loan agreement. Similarly, where defaults by the assignor under the loan facility will potentially give rise to a consequence adverse to the interests of the assignee, such as a termination of the loan contract or action for breach of contract with the attendant possibility of set-offs and counterclaims. In such a case the assignee may find that performance of the contract is a small price to pay to protect his interests.

Nor is it true that the assignee of a loan will necessarily acquire all the rights of the seller under the loan facility being sold. Two overriding principles may come into play which may make any assignment ineffective or restrict the rights transferred by such assignment. These are the principles that a debt is not assignable if the debtor is put in a worse position than he would have been but for the assignment, and the principle that personal contracts are not assignable.

As the borrower under a loan which has been assigned need not have consented to the assignment it would be clearly unfair if the burden on the borrower under the loan contract were to be increased by the assignment. For this reason it is doubtful whether an assignee would (unless the loan agreement otherwise provides) acquire the benefit of such protective provisions as grossing-up provisions in tax clauses or indemnities under increased cost clauses or, indeed, the benefit of any indemnity under the loan agreement.

8.18 A simple example will help to illustrate why this should be so. A Spanish borrower may have entered into a loan facility with a group of international and domestic banks, all of whom, for this purpose, book the loan through their local branches in Madrid. Under current Spanish law no withholding tax should apply to interest payments under this loan. If, however, one of the lenders were to assign its interest in the loan to a bank which does not have a Spanish branch and which books the loan outside Spain, a withholding tax will arise, the rate of which will usually depend upon the terms of the applicable double tax convention between Spain and the country of the

---

[53] See above, n. 7.

assignee.[54] In such circumstances the borrower may well find that it has to gross-up the withholding tax even though it had deliberately invited the original banks to join the facility in order to avoid any withholding tax problems.

The prudent borrower should be able to avoid the disastrous consequences of the example outlined above by making it clear within the terms of the loan documentation that it is not liable to gross-up for taxes or indemnify against increased costs where no such liability would have arisen but for the assignment. Clause 25(2)(b) of the Specimen Loan Agreement[55] represents the type of compromise often reached by borrower and lenders on this issue.

To return to our original point of discussion, the reason why a borrower may find its position prejudiced by an assignment is that it is often the case that the loan documentation will make it clear that the benefit of all rights under the loan facility extend to assignees or transferees. If so, the principle that the debtor cannot be put in a worse position by an assignment will clearly be displaced. It is important, therefore, for an assignee to check the loan documentation closely to establish what rights it will actually acquire irrespective of what the assignment agreement may purport to say on the subject. Conversely assignors should beware writing assignments which assign "all the assignor's rights, benefits and title in, to and under" the relevant loan agreement, as to do so may make the assignor potentially liable to the assignee in contract or in an action for misrepresentation.

The principle that personal contracts are not assignable is a related but different principle from that just discussed. Here, the focus is not so much on an increase in the debtor's burden under the loan contract, but the degree to which the contractual relationship between the parties involves personal skill or confidence. The question is whether "it can make no difference to the person on whom the obligation lies to which of the person he is to discharge it."[56] As the courts appear to apply an objective test in answering this question and do not examine, for example, whether one creditor is more likely to pursue his rights and remedies more vigorously than another,[57] it is a principle which will probably be of limited application in the context of the assignability of loan agreements.

One can, nonetheless, imagine circumstances where the continued involvement in a loan of a particular bank might give rise to the implied non-assignability of the loan. This might be the case, for example, in a complicated project financing where a particular bank might have an important monitoring or administrative function. It is more likely, however, that this role would be carried out by a bank in a capacity other than as lender and in such a case there should be no reason why its rights as a lender could not be assigned.

From what has been said earlier in this chapter it is hardly surprising that **8.19** the assignee will normally take the contract assigned as he finds it. In other words he will not, by virtue of the assignment be put in a better position

---

[54] For a fuller discussion of the impact of double tax treaties, see Chap. 5, above.
[55] See Chap. 17, below.
[56] *Tolhurst* v. *Associated Portland Cement Manufacturers (1900) Ltd.* [1902] 2 K.B. 660, 688.
[57] See *Fitzroy* v. *Cave* [1905] 2 K.B. 364.

than the assignor. If a debt is mistakenly or fraudulently assigned at a time when it has already been paid or if such debt is void or unenforceable, then the assignee will have no choice but to look to the assignor for his remedy.

The rights and obligations of a participant or a transferee under a novation are capable of simpler analysis. The participant will owe no obligations to the debtor but will normally contractually undertake with the original lender to fund any payment which the original lender has to make to the borrower under the terms of the loan facility. Under a novation the transferee will normally assume obligations identical to those which remain to be performed by the original lender.

A participant will not be able to claim the direct benefit of any of the lender's rights under the loan contract. Any protections required by the participant against such matters as taxes, increased costs, illegality, reserve asset costs and so forth will have to be separately negotiated with the selling bank. It is unlikely that the seller will be prepared to accord the participant the same protections which the borrower will give to the seller. At best a seller may agree to pass on amounts corresponding to those recovered from the borrower under the loan agreement. In some cases it will be far from certain precisely what the original lender will be entitled to claim under these provisions, following the granting of a participation.

Another example may help to illustrate the principle at issue. An English bank makes a sterling loan to an English borrower. The rate of interest payable by the borrower includes an element based on the cost to that bank of complying with Bank of England primary liquidity requirements.[58] The bank grants a sub-participation in respect of the loan to another English bank. If the element of interest referable to primary liquidity requirements is based on the cost to each lender of compliance, then it is highly likely that the original lender will not be entitled to claim the additional rate of interest following the granting of the sub-participation and, accordingly, will have nothing to pass on to the participant. It will be otherwise where, as is more usual with syndicated credits, the test is objective by reference to the cost of compliance of certain designated banks on certain assumptions.

The rights of the transferee under a novation will in most cases be identical in content to those of the original lender.

Local law

8.20   Our consideration of the legal aspects of asset sales has so far centred on the English law aspects of such transactions. Where the asset being sold is a loan made by an English incorporated bank to an English borrower, the buyer is an English incorporated bank also and the sale takes place in London, there is generally from a legal perspective no reason to look outside the realms of English law to conclude a sale to the satisfaction of both seller and buyer.

Unfortunately, few asset sales are as simple as this and cross-border elements abound. At one level the issue is one of conflict of laws—what is

---

[58] See Vol. I, Chap. 1 of this work.

the proper governing law of the particular aspect of the asset sale at issue?[59] At another level the issue is how tax authorities, central banks and other regulatory authorities in other countries will view the changed circumstances brought about by the sale of the asset.

Aside from English law the other jurisdictions which are chiefly relevant to any consideration of the legal, tax and regulatory aspects of a sale include:—

(a) the jurisdiction of the borrower and any guarantor;
(b) the jurisdiction of the place of sale; and
(c) the jurisdiction of the buyer.

The jurisdiction of the borrower or any guarantor will be relevant in a number of respects, the most obvious being in relation to questions of enforceability.[60] Irrespective of compliance with the requirements of the loan documentation, it may not be possible for, say, an assignee or transferee to enforce his claim against the borrower in the borrower's or the guarantor's own courts unless any consents have been obtained or notices given which are required to be obtained or given as a matter of the borrower's or guarantor's own law.[61]

Perhaps the best known example of such a requirement is that under French law where the Civil Code specifies that formal notice of assignment must be served on the debtor by a *huissier* (process agent) and the documentation evidencing the notification registered.

Whether an English court would take cognisance of such local law requirements is another matter. An English court might well apply conflicts rules and take the view that the assignment of a loan governed by English law would be valid notwithstanding failure to comply with French procedural formalities. On a practical level the French courts may not take the same view when asked to give or enforce an English judgment if notice of assignment had not been duly served.

Failure to observe local rules which require the buyer to obtain exchange control or other consents from regulatory authorities may effectively prevent a borrower from meeting its obligations to the buyer of the debt.[62] Priorities as against the borrower may turn on the technical requirements of the borrower's law as to such matters as formalities or the nature of the instrument of sale.[63]

The attitude of the tax authorities to the sale of a loan made to a borrower in their jurisdiction is the issue which most emphasises the importance to seller and buyer of considering the wider implications of the sale. In many jurisdictions the method of sale used and the location of the buyer will be critical in determining such questions as whether any withholding tax[64]

---

[59] Conflict of laws principles are considered in greater detail in Chap. 1, above.
[60] See Chap. 2, above.
[61] See Chap. 1, above.
[62] France and Italy are examples. Much depends on the wording of the approval obtained.
[63] In Spain preferred creditor status under an "escritura publica" may be lost if, say, the debt is novated. See also, Chap. 1, above.
[64] For a fuller discussion of withholding tax implications, see Chap. 5, above.

which exists in relation to the original loan will increase as a result of the sale, whether any withholding tax which previously did not exist will arise and whether any exemption from withholding tax which has been given will continue to run for the benefit of the buyer.

8.21 Aside from the strict legalities, many central banks and exchange control authorities require certain information relating to the transfer of assets for which they regard themselves as being responsible. Whether it is the borrower, the seller or the buyer who should give the requisite information is sometimes open to interpretation, as are the consequences of failing to notify. It is most important, however, for both the seller and the buyer to appreciate the implications of displeasing such authorities.

The place of sale and the jurisdiction of the buyer will be particularly relevant when considering tax issues such as stamp duty or withholding taxes.[65] The concern here is more in relation to stamp duties attracting to the sale instrument or taxes arising on payments to be made by the seller to the buyer.

Two examples may be considered in this context. First, the seller of a loan outside Switzerland will find that the sale is potentially liable to a Swiss turnover tax (stamp duty) on the sale irrespective, it seems, of whether the method of sale adopted is assignment or participation. The tax attracts because the asset is being sold out of Switzerland, not because a Swiss borrower is involved or because the currency of the asset is Swiss Francs. Secondly, the seller of a loan made to a U.S. borrower may find himself liable as a paying agent to deduct withholding tax on payments of interest made by the borrower through the seller (as with a non-notified assignment) or by the seller to the buyer under a back-to-back arrangement (such as a participation). Whether the tax is deductible will in the main depend on the location of the buyer and whether he is able to book the asset in a jurisdiction where he is able to claim the benefit of any applicable double taxation treaty.

Although it is not possible to generalise, as the preceding two examples demonstrate, it would be fair to state that it is unusual for a participation to have implications outside the country of both the selling bank and that of the governing law of the underlying loan facility and the sale contract. The opposite might be said of assignments and novations and this is another important reason for the enduring popularity of the participation as a means of sale. The distinction is perhaps understandable when one considers the nature of the various sale methods. Assignment and novation involve a transfer of rights and give the buyer beneficial ownership of a debt directly enforceable against the borrower and any borrower. A participation does not involve any dealing in the underlying rights and simply establishes a separate contractual relationship between buyer and seller. The participation is clearly, therefore, less significant in relation to matters of enforceability and the payment obligations of the borrower. Revenue authorities will however, as we have seen, be more likely to look through the strict legal relationship and accord assignments and participations similar treatment.

---

[65] *Ibid.*

Taxation

The tax aspects of an asset sale are critical from the point of view of both **8.22**
buyer and seller as any adverse tax consequences will usually result in a tax
liability in excess of the profit that either party can expect to make on the
asset sale. The U.K. tax aspects of any asset sale can conveniently be considered under three headings:—

    (a) stamp duty;
    (b) withholding tax; and
    (c) distributions.

a. Stamp Duty

An assignment of a debt is prima facie chargeable with *ad valorem* stamp **8.23**
duty under the heading "Conveyance or Transfer on Sale" in the Stamp Act
1891. The current rate of assessment is 1 per cent. on the amount or value of
the consideration for the transfer.[66] Stamp duty must be paid within 30 days
of the relevant transfer although this date can be postponed if the assignment is executed outside the jurisdiction, in which case the assignment must
be stamped within 30 days of the relevant instrument entering the country.
Failure to stamp on or prior to the due date gives rise to a liability to pay
interest on the unpaid duty in addition to certain specified penalties.[67]

The principal consequence of not paying stamp duty is not that the
instrument effecting the assignment is invalid but that it cannot be produced
in evidence in an English Court.[68] This has led to the practice for many
banks of executing and keeping assignments off-shore and thus delaying the
liability to pay stamp duty and avoiding penalties and interest running. The
duty itself is not avoided but will only have to be paid if and when proceedings are brought in the English courts, as where, for example, an assignee
suing a borrower has to show title to bring his claim. Indeed, where a suitable alternative venue can be found English stamp duty may not be relevant
as a foreign court may disregard the requirement to pay the duty.

Before proceeding further it should be mentioned that the duty does not
apply to all assignments of debts. The ambit of the duty is established in section 14(4) of the Stamp Act 1891, which limits the applicability of the duty
to " . . . an instrument executed in any part of the United Kingdom, or
relating wheresoever executed, to any property situate, or to any matter or
thing done or to be done, in any part of the United Kingdom. . . . "

The difficulty for any person relying on this wording is in showing that
the applicable assignment does not relate to any property situate in the
United Kingdom or to any matter or thing to be done there. These
expressions have been given a broad interpretation by the courts[69] and it
may be fatal, even if the only connection with the United Kingdom is that

---

[66] Where the benefit of loans which have not been made are sold, stamp duty will normally be
payable on the maximum amount of the consideration payable, *i.e.* the maximum amount
of the loans agreed to be made, see *Underground Electric Railways Co. of London Ltd. and Glyn,
Mills, Curries & Co.* v. *I.R.C.* [1916] 1 K.B. 306.

[67] s.15, Stamp Act 1891.

[68] s.14(1), Stamp Act 1891.

[69] In *Faber* v. *I.R.C.* [1936] 1 All E.R. 617 the mere carrying on by one of the parties of a business in the U.K. was sufficient connection. See also, *I.R.C.* v. *Maples & Co. (Paris) Ltd.*
[1908] A.C. 22.

the borrower is in the United Kingdom or that the agency function under a syndicated credit is carried out here. Certainly, the connection would probably be sufficiently established if obligations under the loan facility have to be performed in the United Kingdom as with a loan denominated in sterling.[70]

8.24   Some attempts to bring an assignment outside the charge to stamp duty have focused on the fact that stamp duty is a tax on instruments. If the assignment is effected otherwise than by use of an instrument of transfer then no stamp duty will arise. One method of achieving this is for the seller to make an offer to assign to the buyer which is accepted by the buyer making payment of the requisite purchase price. Even if one ignores, as it is probably correct to do, concerns of an extension of the *Furniss* v. *Dawson* principle[71] to this type of scheme there may be practical difficulties in the way of its success. This is because any subsequent written record of the transaction may attract stamp duty. Within this category may come subsequent written acceptances of the offer made by the seller and even the giving of notice of assignment to the debtor.

The whole issue has recently been further complicated by certain interpretations placed by the Inland Revenue on the meaning of the words "loan capital" as used in section 79 of the 1986 Finance Act. As assignment of loan capital within the meaning of section 79 is exempt from stamp duty, it has previously been thought that although loan capital is defined as including "funded debt" issued by a body corporate or other body of persons it referred to what one eminent judge called debt which "has some degree of permanence or long-term character."[72]

When the Bank of England gave the green light to the sterling commercial paper market in 1986[73] it did so with Revenue assurances that no liability to stamp duty on sterling bearer instruments would arise. This assurance was apparently given on the basis that sterling commercial paper and its sale came within the exemption from bearer duty provided for the "issue of an instrument which relates to loan capital or on the transfer of loan capital constituted by, or transferable by means of, such an instrument.[74] If sterling commercial paper is capable of constituting loan capital surely the tenor of a loan, however short, should not prevent a loan constituting loan capital. It would appear, therefore, that banks can with some confidence rely on the exemption from stamp duty for assignments of loan capital.

Some doubts nevertheless still linger on. Can an overdraft ever constitute loan capital? Is a sovereign borrower or a state agency a "body corporate" or "other body of persons"? Resolution of this last question is of great

---

[70] It is argued that the mere possibility that suit may subsequently be brought in the English courts is not sufficient as the words "done or to be done" require a greater element of certainty than would be present in these circumstances.

[71] The principle was applied to stamp duty in the case of *Ingram* v. *I.R.C.* [1986] 2 W.L.R. 598.

[72] Lord Wilberforce in *Reed International* v. *I.R.C.* [1975] 3 All E.R. 218.

[73] For a detailed discussion of the circumstances in which sterling commercial paper was given approval by the Bank of England see, Penn "Sterling Commercial Paper" 1986 2 B.F.L.R. pp. 53–68. Those interested in a practical discussion of the tax implications of sterling commercial paper should see Edge "Tax aspects of sterling commercial paper" 1986 I.F.L.R. (June) pp. 10–13.

[74] s.79(2), Finance Act 1986.

importance especially for those engaged in the debt swap market. Certainly, a state is capable of being a body politic, but can a state which is embodied in the form of its president or ruler be viewed as a body of persons?[75]

Neither novations nor participations involve the transfer or assignment of a debt. Both simply involve the establishment of contractual relations between borrower and transferee and seller and buyer respectively and, for this reason, neither should attract any liability to pay stamp duty.

b. Withholding Tax[76]

8.25 The withholding tax position in the United Kingdom will, as with stamp duty, depend in part on the nature of the sale instrument being used. With a participation the question is simply whether the payments of interest made by a U.K. tax resident seller to the buyer can be properly categorised as interest paid by the seller in the ordinary course of the seller's U.K. banking business and thus, within the exemption from U.K. withholding tax[77] contained in section 54(2)(*b*) of the Income and Corporation Taxes Act 1970 ("The Taxes Act"). This test will be applied irrespective of the residence of the borrower or of the buyer.

What is in the ordinary course of a seller's banking business would seem to be a question of fact notwithstanding Inland Revenue indications that where a loan has a tenor of more than five to seven years interest paid under a participation of that loan may not be in the ordinary course of the seller's U.K. banking business. The basis for such a contention is difficult to establish and would appear to be an historical view based on Revenue perceptions of the typical tenor of borrowings in the markets. As loans now frequently extend beyond five to seven years the Revenue's attitude cannot be supported on these grounds.[78] Of course, with longer-term participations (as might be necessary if, say, a mortgage portfolio were to be sold) a legitimate distinction might be drawn between fund raising which is to be regarded as being in the ordinary course of *banking* business and capital raising which might not be so regarded.

Withholding tax issues in relation to assignments are even more difficult to decipher. We shall take the assignment of the loan made to a U.K. tax resident borrower first. Where payments are made direct to the assignee the Revenue appear to consider that the advance on which interest is paid, is made by the person for the time being to whom the interest is owed, that is, the assignee. Accordingly, where the assignee is a bank carrying on a bona fide banking business in the United Kingdom, the payments of interest made to the assignee will be within the exception from withholding tax contained in section 54(2)(*a*) of the 1970 Act.[79]

---

[75] Other exemptions from stamp duty which may be applicable in the asset sales market include assignments of certain secured and guaranteed debts and certain transfers *intra* group.

[76] See generally, Chap. 5, above.

[77] Imposed by s.54(1) of the Income and Corporation Taxes Act on day "yearly interest of money chargeable to tax under Case III of Schedule D" paid by specified persons.

[78] Most recent pronouncements by the Revenue on the subject do seem to indicate that loan of longer tenor may now be participated free of withholding tax.

[79] *i.e.* The Income and Corporation Taxes Act 1970, the exception being to the effect that no withholding tax will attach to "interest payable in the United Kingdom on an advance from a bank carrying on a bona fide banking business in the United Kingdom.

If payments are not made direct to the assignee but routed through the assignor, then both the borrower and the assignor may in the Revenue's view have a liability to deduct tax. This will certainly be the case where the assignee is a non-U.K. tax resident as the Revenue do not accept the argument that if the loan has at the outset the character of an "advance made by a bank carrying on a bona fide banking business in the United Kingdom" it maintains that character throughout the life of the loan notwithstanding any subsequent assignment. Where the assignee is a U.K. resident bank the assignor should, if the Revenue's view is consistently applied, be entitled to make interest payments gross.

8.26   In any event there would appear to be a strong case for arguing that section 54 of the 1970 Act[80] should not apply at all in relation to payments made by an assignor under an equitable assignment. The assignor is in effect simply acting as a collecting agent handing over monies to its principal. If the agent merely accounts for money to his principal he is not paying interest and should not, therefore, be under an obligation to deduct basic rate tax under section 54.[81]

If the borrower is a non-U.K. resident and payments are made direct to the assignee no U.K. withholding tax will be applicable and it will be necessary to look to the laws of the borrower to check whether any withholdings arise.

If payments are routed through the assignor (as with an undisclosed assignment) section 159 of the Taxes Act[82] will come into play. Sub-section (2) of that section provides that:—"Where foreign dividends are entrusted to any person in the United Kingdom for payment to any persons in the United Kingdom, they shall be assessed and charged to income tax under Schedule D. . . ."

Consequently if the assignee is a U.K. resident, the assignor will be obliged to make a withholding. If the assignee is a foreign resident, then section 159[83] does not apply although the assignee must "prove" its non-residence on a "claim" made to the Revenue.[84]

Novation, involving as it does, the creation of new contractual rights and obligations, does not give rise to a tax treatment of interest payments different from that applicable to interest payments made by the borrower to the original lenders. I do not propose to say anything more on this subject as it is outside the scope of this chapter.[85]

c. Distributions

8.27   Although at first sight its relevance may be doubted section 233 of the Taxes Act[86] must be borne in mind by any seller granting a participation in a loan made to a U.K. tax resident. That section defines a "distribution" in relation to a company as including "any interest or other distribution out of

---

[80] *i.e.* The Income and Corporation Taxes Act 1970.
[81] Of the Income and Corporation Taxes Act 1970.
[82] *i.e.* The Income and Corporation Taxes Act 1970.
[83] *Ibid.*
[84] Sub-section (4) of s.159.
[85] ss.54 and 159 of the Income and Corporation Taxes Act 1970 as extended by certain extra-statutory concessions will again be the relevant provisions to consider.
[86] *Ibid.*

assets of the company in respect of securities of the company . . . where the securities are . . . securities under which the consideration given by the company for the use of the principal secured is to any extent dependent on the results of the company's business or any part of it. . . . "[87]

The difficulty for the seller derives from the breadth of the wording of the section. There is clearly an argument that the payments made to the participant are dependent on the results of the seller's business (or at least part of it) as they are dependent on payments being made by the borrower and the seller's business will, by definition, include the lending of money.

The consequences of the section applying are fairly disastrous for the seller. He will be unable to deduct the payments to its participant from his income in computing his taxable profits and will be required to account for advance corporation tax in respect of the distribution. Where the participant is within the charge to U.K. corporation tax, section 60 of the Finance Act 1982 does, however, provide relief by providing that interest payments to such a person will not, subject to certain exceptions, be viewed as a distribution for the purpose of section 233.

In those circumstances where section 233 potentially still has application it is to be hoped that the Revenue will take a common sense view and hold that payments made to participants should be regarded as an expense incurred in the earning of profits rather than a distribution of those profits. This contention may have less chance of success, however, where, for example, the seller of the asset is a special purpose vehicle whose sole business is the making of loans in order to sell them off. Even here it is hardly the case that payments to participants represent disguised distributions of profits, but the wording of the section is more apposite and presents the Revenue with a stronger chance of succeeding with an argument based on section 233.

Regulation of asset sales

Perhaps one of the most significant factors contributing to the continued growth and innovation in the asset sales market in the United Kingdom has been the refusal of regulatory authorities to impose any significant restrictions on the activities of banks involved in this market. Typical of the attitude of the Bank of England, for instance, was a comment in a recent discussion paper on syndicated credits in which the Bank simply noted that "several large banks have recently developed active asset sales programmes, which suggests that activity may be increasing—or, at least, that secondary trading of participations is becoming an explicit balance sheet management tool."[88] **8.28**

In the United States, where the asset sales market was born, the hand of the regulators is more clearly in evidence[89] and the activities of banks buying and selling participations is circumscribed by the guidelines laid down

---

[87] *Ibid.*

[88] Bank of England Discussion Paper No. 22, dated March 1985 on Syndicated Credits Market.

[89] See Ryan, "Participations in Loans under New York Law," 1984 I.F.L.R. (October) pp. 40–47.

by the Office of the Comptroller of the Currency (OCC) as to prudent practices for banks operating in this market.[90]

The OCC circular containing these guidelines is chiefly directed at buying banks and puts an onus on these banks to ensure that they obtain adequate documentation, make their own credit analysis and maintain proper controls during the life of the participation. The circular nevertheless has an indirect impact on sellers in that buyers will request the provision of information and the giving of warranties and assurances to enable them to comply with their responsibilities under the OCC guidelines.

There is no reason to suppose that the regulators will continue to do anything but support banks in their attempt to reduce and manage balance-sheet exposure.[91] However, what is clear from the recent rash of consultative papers[91a] produced by central banks and other regulatory bodies on both sides of the Atlantic is that greater attention is being focused on the proper treatment of off-balance sheet items where it is felt that a bank retains a commitment or other form of contingent liability in relation to such item. While accountants devote their energies to questions of whether a balance sheet should more properly reflect the substance rather than the form of transactions,[92] central banks are turning their minds to the imposition of risk ratings and capital adequacy requirements in respect of off-balance sheet items which represent commitments or a potential credit exposure.

In the context of asset sales it is likely, therefore, that sales carrying some element of recourse may not in future be given a risk rating by the Bank of England for the purpose of capital to risk asset ratios. Within this category of asset sale might come (i) risk participations, where the risk of default by the obligor is effectively "guaranteed" or "insured" by a third party, (ii) sales of assets on the basis that they will be "repurchased" at some future date or (iii) the sale of "strips" of loans carved out of what is in reality a medium term commitment.

8.29 Items (ii) and (iii) provide an interesting contrast between the U.K. and the U.S. approach to maximising profitability from asset sales. It is self evident that a buyer is more likely to buy a less desirable credit if the tenor of the risk is short rather than medium or long term. Similarly, the seller will be able to retain a greater portion of any interest payable if he sells a loan priced as a medium term credit on the basis that the buyer takes the credit risk inherent in that loan for a period less than the full term of the loan.

United Kingdom incorporated banks have achieved some success in per-

---

[90] OCC Banking Circular 181 originally issued December, 1983 amended August, 1984.

[91] Recently there has been more evidence in relation to structural asset sales (such as the sale of mortgages) that the Bank of England is looking at the legal and commercial notes associated with such sales. Whether this will lead to a more general re-examination of the risks associated with all forms of asset sale is not yet clear.

[91a] See, for example, March, 1986, Paper of Committee on Banking Regulations and Supervisory Practices on "The Management of Banks' Off-Balance Sheet Exposures," March 1986, Consultative Paper of Bank of England on the "Off-Balance Sheet Business of Banks," and the January, 1986, "Agreed proposal of the United States Federal Banking Supervisory Authorities and the Bank of England on Primary Capital and Capital Adequacy Assessment."

[92] See the Institute of Chartered Accountants December, 1985 Technical Release on "Off-Balance Sheet Finance and Window Dressing."

suading their auditors that where an asset is sold on the condition that it will be "repurchased" at some future date by the seller the credit risk lies with the buyer until repurchase and accordingly until repurchase the off-balance treatment for the asset could be claimed by the seller.

Auditors of U.S. banks on the other hand have tended to take the opposite view and, thus, arose the search for other means of carving out a short-term sale of a medium term asset. The answer to this problem was found in the technique of "stripping" loans. Loans were rewritten so that monies advanced were repayable at the end of each interest period albeit that they would, subject to the satisfaction of certain conditions, be re-advanced on that date so that no actual transfer of funds occurred. The conditions referred to are typically that no actual or potential event of default has occurred and that any representations made continue to be true and correct. The argument, so it goes, is that the credit risk has been successfully passed to the buyer as the seller is not obliged to re-advance if there has been a deterioration in the seller's credit risk as evidenced by the occurrence of events of default or misrepresentations.

The American Institute of Certified Public Accountants (AICPA) has recently[93] doubted the wisdom of such an approach arguing that deterioration in financial standing may not necessarily be reflected in the occurrence of events of default or misrepresentations unless they include specific financial ratios or something akin to a "material adverse change" provision.

What is more interesting are the comments[94] of the Office of the Comptroller of the Currency (OCC) and the Board of the Governors of the Federal Reserve given in response to the AICPA recommendations. Both the OCC and the Federal Reserve found it hard to imagine any circumstances where the sale of a "strip" loan should count as taking an asset off-balance sheet. Indeed it was suggested that the taking by the seller of a mere option to buy back in the future might prejudice off-balance treatment. The concerns of the regulators as to re-sale difficulties if buyers could not be found for future "strips" point to the real reason for volumes of assets would return to their balance sheets and the appearance of a well-managed balance sheet complying with all requisite ratios would appear somewhat illusory.[95]

This, of course, is a fair point although it should come down to a question not of whether an item is on balance sheet or not but whether a particular risk-rating or weighting should be applied to an asset for capital adequacy purposes where some element of recourse is divined. This indeed is the approach which has been adopted by the Bank of England and the U.S. Supervisory Authorities in their recent joint proposals[96] although a fair assessment of the risk involved in selling assets on a repurchase or"strip" basis is a far from simple task. Nevertheless, the move to a common

---

[93] AICPA Proposed Practice Bulletin: "Accounting for Sales of Loans under Committed Facilities," August 8, 1986.

[94] Above, n. 90.

[95] This concern is echoed by the Committee on Banking Regulations and Supervisory Practices (see n. 91, above) in the following terms " . . . where the asset in question is certain to come back to the selling bank at some predetermined date, the credit risk on the asset sold remains essentially with the selling bank."

[96] See n. 91, above.

approach by regulators is to be welcomed as a way of avoiding the artificial practice of "parking" of assets for sale in unregulated jurisdictions thereby giving certain banks an unfair advantage over competitors.

8.30   Turning briefly to United Kingdom securities law we will find that asset sales makes little impact. The prospectus requirements of the Companies Acts[97] will not normally apply as the sale document will not constitute a debenture.[98] This is so even if the sale is by way of novation using a transferable loan certificate or transfer certificate as the certificate of transfer does not contain any acknowledgement of indebtedness or covenant to pay but is merely the means of effecting the novation.[99] The Prevention of Fraud (Investments) Act 1958 may, however, be relevant although an exemption from its provisions will normally be available.[1]

Again the U.K. position may be contrasted with the United States where sub-participations as passive investment contracts, may be viewed as "securities" for the purposes of the Securities Act of 1933[2] and the Securities Exchange Act of 1934.[3] More relevantly for the future development of the asset sales market the sale of assets may run foul of the Glass-Steagall Act[4] to the extent that the sale is out of step with traditional bank practices in this area. This is because even if a loan participation is a security for Glass-Steagall purposes U.S. banks have an express statutory power to discount and negotiate promissory notes. It is thought that this power includes the granting of participations but this argument loses much of its power once sales are contemplated which cannot be viewed as within traditional bank practices.[5]

Equally important from the seller's perspective may be the treatment of the asset sale for the purpose of reporting requirements and lending limits and similar requirements imposed by regulatory bodies. In the U.K. the Bank of England will normally recognise a sale, even by way of participation,[6] as passing the responsibility for reporting a loan which has been sold from the seller to the buyer. Where limits exist (such as informal limits on the volume of sterling acceptances permitted to be outstanding) sale

[97] Prospectus requirements are considered in greater detail in Chap. 10, below.

[98] As to what may or may not constitute a debenture see Penn, "Sterling Commercial Paper," *loc. cit.* n. 73, above.

[99] Contrast the use of Transferable Loan Instruments (a technique more fully discussed by Bray in the I.F.L.R. article referred to in n. 18 above) which are deliberately designed to be securities, but will often be within the "professional investor" exemptions in s.79 of the Companies Act 1985 and s.195 of the Financial Services Act 1986 (to be replaced by Part V of the Financial Services Act 1986 under which the Secretary of State for Trade and Industry has power to make orders exempting from prospectus requirements advertisements relating to securities issued to persons sufficiently expert to understand any risks involved). Where the T.L.I. relates to a sterling loan, timing consent under the Control of Borrowing Order 1958 may also be necessary.

[1] Because the seller is a licensed or exempt dealer.

[2] Even if so viewed the private placement exemption should be available.

[3] Selling banks are, accordingly, potentially subject to the anti-fraud provisions and disclosure standards contained in that Act.

[4] The name commonly given to four sections of the U.S. Banking Act of 1933 which demarcates the line separating commercial and investment banking. Note that Glass-Steagall will also apply to the activities of a non-U.S. branch of a U.S. bank.

[5] This point is particularly relevant when considering transferable participations and sales to corporates, see below, paras. 7.1 and 7.3.

[6] See Bank of England Paper General/P2 (December) 1982.

methods should be examined to see if they will be effective to free up those limits. Risk participations, for example, will not normally stop an acceptance liability from counting towards Bank of England limits but the procuring of a third party acceptance will.[7]

DEVELOPMENT OF THE MARKET

By way of conclusion we will briefly turn our attention to some current developments in the asset sales market and identify the legal and regulatory issues surrounding these developments.   **8.31**

Secondary market

The introduction of concepts of transferability into loan documentation was principally designed to encourage the completion of the process of securitisation for loan assets by simplifying secondary market trading of the loan. This was achieved by the same method which enabled the initial sale of the loan. The first (and indeed any subsequent) buyer of the loan was issued with a transfer certificate or transferable loan certificate which facilitated subsequent novations of the loan.   **8.32**

In some cases this method of sale will not be attractive or desirable. Novation of the loan will involve the co-operation of the borrower both in accepting the principle of transferability in the original loan documentation and, often, in approving individual transfers. Furthermore, novation may have unfortunate legal consequences because it involves the creation of a new contract. Exchange control consents may have to be renewed. Priorities may be lost. Withholding tax problems may arise. In other words the insertion of a transfer mechanism simplifies the process of transfer but does not avoid those disadvantages which a novation has compared with, say, a participation.

It is hardly surprising, therefore, that some institutions have seen an alternative or additional path to securitisation in the transferable participation. Making a participation transferable simply involves applying to a participation the same techniques as are applied to a loan to make it transferable. Similarly, subsequent sales can be facilitated by delivering to each new buyer a form of transfer certificate which can be used for any re-sale. The original lender has thus "securitised" the loan without the need for any involvement or, indeed, knowledge on the part of the borrower. From a regulatory and securities perspective the transferable participation should not be treated any differently from a transfer certificate or a transferable loan certificate.[8] The tax treatment of the transferable participation is similarly straightforward. Stamp duty will not attach to tranfers as they operate by way of novation. No withholding tax will arise in the U.K. merely because of a change in participant provided that the provisions of section 54(2)(*b*) of the Income and Corporation Taxes Act apply.

[7] Contrast the U.S. position where a participated acceptance will under certain conditions cease to count towards the limits of the selling bank.
[8] Although the element of transferability might in the U.S. strengthen the argument that the sale is outside traditional banking activity and is, therefore, caught by Glass-Steagall limitations on the investment bank activities of commercial banks.

Although the selling bank will have assisted secondary market trading of the underlying loan it will be at a cost, namely, that the seller remains lender of record and will continue to have a contractual relationship with the participant originally holding the participation. A subsequent sale does not allow him to "drop out of the picture."

The transferable participation will still be a useful tool for any seller or buyer even in the absence of a genuine secondary market in assets. The purchase of assets for re-sale, the trading of sovereign debt in the debt swap market and the booking of assets sold or bought to satisfy short-term needs and requirements or under ever-green or re-newable facilities are all examples of transactions where the element of transferability will greatly assist the subsequent management of the asset sold. Another area where its use may be invaluable is in the area of "pooling" which is a topic worthy of separate consideration.

Pooling

8.33   The current vogue for the repackaging and, if necessary, the securitising of assets having some degree of commonality seems to know no bounds. At a simple level the assets may simply be loans having a common link (mortgages, ECGD backed credits, credit card loans) but at a more complex level may be any form of receivable having some common point of reference (*e.g.* property rentals).

Repackaging these assets will often involve the use of a special purpose vehicle which will acquire the necessary assets and fund the acquisition by issuing securities. Conventional asset sale techniques may, however, prove a simpler and equally efficient method of securitising assets in this manner.

The use of off-balance sheet vehicles may be unsatisfactory in a number of respects. Cost is one, but another more significant concern lies in the correct accounting treatment for the architect of such a structure (normally the entity which presently holds the assets on its balance sheet). Will the sale to the vehicle achieve off-balance sheet treatment where, as is usual, some element of recourse is given to the original owner of the assets or a related company, or where the substantial benefit derived from the original assets still remains with the original holder of the assets?

The funding of the acquisition might be more simply achieved by the use of, say, a participation than by the issue of securities, particularly where the investor base is banks or other financial institutions. The need for the paraphanelia of a securities issue, such as listing and the satisfaction of attendant requirements can be avoided. If an element of liquidity is desired use can be made of the concepts of transferability discussed earlier in this chapter.[9]

Corporate investors

8.34   Traditionally, the asset sales market has been a bank to bank market. The increasing sophistication of corporate investors and the attraction of the relative size of yields on loan assets as compared to those available to such

---

[9] Above.

investors in the bond or commercial paper market has led to the corporate market showing a great deal of interest in the sale of assets.

The prudent seller will have to proceed cautiously when considering an advance into such a market. While it is true that corporates have been for some time participants in the securities markets as investors, much emphasis is placed by those regulating these markets on the provision of proper investor protections. These include both the proper provision of information to investors as well as restrictions on the type of investors who participate in such markets. Similarly, the type of borrower who will have access to such markets will often be limited in terms of the borrower's credit rating.

None of these protections exist in the asset sales market and there is no doubt that the regulators would view with interest, if not concern, any substantial growth in this market. In certain circumstances the regulators might, if they saw fit, make use of whatever weapons are presently at their disposal to curtail the activities of the selling banks.

In the United Kingdom this might take the form of introducing appropriate regulations under the Financial Services Act 1986 or, indeed, taking a restrictive view as to what was a payment of interest in the ordinary course of U.K. banking business for the purpose of section 54(2)(b) of the Income and Corporation Taxes Act. The possibility of an attack on the basis that the participation was a "debenture" for prospectus purposes should not be ruled out, although for reasons previously explained[10] such an attack should fail.

In the United States investor protection has historically been regulated for to a greater extent. The obvious risk of an extension of the asset sales market to corporate investors is that this will be seen as involving a breach of the Glass-Steagall Act.

---

[10] Above.

9. Events of Default and Remedies

Introduction

9.01 The events of default clause[1] in a eurocurrency loan agreement is perceived by most lenders as being the cornerstone of the entire agreement, since it is the events of default which give the agreement "teeth," by describing the circumstances in which the lender can demand repayment.[2] As one commentator succinctly puts it[3] . . .

> "A prudent bank lender, before committing to lend for a term to any borrower, sovereign or private, considers and determines those possible events which, if they occurred, would impair the prospect of repayment. Those events are typically specified in the loan agreement with the borrower as events of default."

The events of default clause is often the most vigorously contested clause in the entire loan agreement, and it is crucial for those negotiating the loan to appreciate both its scope and practical significance. A very extensive clause, covering many different events of default, may be viewed as highly desirable in so far as the lender is concerned, but if such restrictions make it impossible for the borrower to use the funds for their intended purpose, the clause may very well operate against the lender's interests. It is obvious, therefore, that a fair balance should be struck between the interests of the lender and the borrower. This balance will vary enormously from one loan agreement to another, since it will depend upon the particular circumstances of the parties' to the agreement. For this reason, the default clause, like many other clauses in a eurocurrency loan, should always be "tailor-made." There is no such thing as a "standard" events of default clause.

As in earlier chapters of this work, reference will once again be made to the specimen syndicated loan agreement to be found in Chapter 17, in order to facilitate a fuller and more practical understanding of this topic.

Alternative clauses will also be highlighted to illustrate how the precise wording can be altered to meet the specific needs of the contracting parties.

The commercial and financial objectives of the clause

9.02 The principle objective behind the events of default clause has already been identified, namely, to describe those circumstances in which the lender can terminate the loan agreement and demand immediate repayment. In practice, however, the problem is usually more subtle and lenders, particularly

---

[1] As to events of default generally, see Wood, Chap. 7; Donaldson and Donaldson, Chap. 10; Kalderen & Siddiqi, pp. 176–189; Clark and Taylor, "Events of default in Eurocurrency loan agreements" (1982) I.F.L.Rev. September 15; Gabriel, Chap. 6; Ryan, "Defaults And Remedies Under International Bank Loan Agreements With Foreign Sovereign Borrowers—A New York Lawyer's Perspective," [1982] 1 U.Ill.L.Rev. 89; Youard, "Default in International Loan Agreements" [1986] J.B.L. 276.

[2] See clause 16 in the Specimen Agreement, Chap. 17 below.

[3] Ryan, *loc. cit.*, n. 1 above, p. 89.

bank lenders, will normally only demand repayment in extreme cases. This is because banks are in the business to, among other things, lend money and if the borrower is able to repay most bankers would not (despite a technical default) wish to terminate the loan and demand repayment. Such action would, at the very least, seriously prejudice relations between bank and borrower and may, in certain circumstances, have more far reaching consequences.[4]

There are undoubtedly many different categories of default, some more serious than others, and not all of them necessarily bring about a termination of the loan. The default may be nothing more than a technical default, in which case the lender is unlikely to terminate the loan and demand repayment. Alternatively, it may be the first sign that the borrower is experiencing financial difficulties, for example, a late payment of interest, thereby acting as an early warning device to the lender which may consequently decide to monitor the borrower's activities more closely, rather than terminate and demand repayment immediately. In an extreme case, default may be so serious that the borrower is unlikely to fulfil its financial commitments. In such a situation it will be most important that the lender is able to act quickly in order to recover as much as possible from the borrower and/ or any guarantor.

It must be appreciated, therefore, that an event of default does not necessarily bring about a termination of the loan. Indeed, it can be said with some confidence that termination and acceleration of a eurocurrency loan, because of an event of default, is the exception rather than the rule, in practice. The principle reason for this is that lenders are rarely able to recover fully the total indebtedness owed by the borrower. Experience has shown that at best the existing loans of the borrower will be re-negotiated,[5] but this will be a time consuming and expensive business and may involve writing off either unpaid interest and/or capital. It may also, as we have already suggested, lead to irreparable damage in the relationship between the lending bank and its borrowing customer. At worst the default may precipitate the liquidation of the borrower, in which case there will be little hope of the lender recovering anything more than a small proportion of the amount owing.[6]

9.03

Notwithstanding the fact that breach of an event of default rarely triggers the acceleration of a eurocurrency loan, one cannot overemphasise the importance of drafting appropriate events of default within the terms of the agreement, which, on the one hand recognise a balance of interest between the parties, but on the other, enables the lender to speak from a position of strength should anything go wrong. The lender will, at the very least, be able to use the threat of acceleration as a leaverage device during restructuring negotiations, at which time it will be most important for the lender's

---

[4] As to the consequence which may follow, see Donaldson and Donaldson, *loc. cit.*, n. 1 above.

[5] Re-negotiation or restructuring, as it is more commonly called, is considered in greater detail later in this chapter, see para. 9.34 below.

[6] In most cases the lender in eurocurrency loan will rank as an unsecured creditor in the borrower's liquidation. Obviously if the loan is guaranteed or secured in some way, the chances of recovery will be far greater. As to the efficacy of security in international loan agreements, see generally, Chap. 14 below.

rights to be on a par with those of other unsecured creditors, thereby preventing the borrower from preferring those creditors to the eurocurrency lender.

CLAUSES COMMONLY FOUND IN INTERNATIONAL TERM LOAN AGREEMENTS

DISTINCTION BETWEEN ACTUAL BREACH AND ANTICIPATORY BREACH

9.04   Events of default fall into two basic categories,[7] namely, actual default, such as non-payment of principal or interest, and anticipatory default. The fundamental difference between these two categories is that in the former, the contract will almost certainly have been breached, whereas in the latter, the clauses operate primarily as an early warning device putting the lender on notice that an actual default, *i.e.* non-payment, is imminent. The anticipatory default clauses will, hopefully, enable the lender either to terminate the loan and obtain repayment before the borrower's financial position worsens, or to obtain some form of security to safeguard its position.[8]

We will now turn to consider some specific clauses which are commonly incorporated into international loan agreements.

A. Failure to pay[9]

9.05   The most basic event of default is failure by the borrower to pay principal and/or interest on the loan as and when it falls due. Such failure is prima facie inconsistent with the continuation of the lender's commitment, and a clause covering such an event should obviously be incorporated into every loan agreement. It must be appreciated, however, that there are a variety of reasons which may lie behind the borrower's failure to pay, and the clause should be worded in such a way as to take account of this. Where the failure to pay arises because the borrower does not possess the necessary funds, this is a clear indication that the borrower is experiencing serious financial difficulties and non-payment is likely to recur. In such a situation the lender would not wish to qualify its ability to terminate the loan and call for repayment before the borrower becomes completely insolvent. Few cases, however, will be so clear cut. The borrower may be experiencing a temporary cash flow problem or the failure may be due to inadvertence. Worse still, the failure may be due to an administrative error on the part of the lender or within the international banking system.[10] In such cases immediate termi-

---

[7] See Wood, p. 164.

[8] There will always be a risk, however, of such security being struck down under the laws of the borrower's jurisdiction. Most countries, including England, have rules governing the validity of security granted within a short period of the borrower's liquidation. See generally, Vol. 1, Chap. 28.

[9] See clause 16(*a*) in the specimen agreement, Chap. 17 below.

[10] Failures due to the international banking system are not as uncommon as one might imagine, particularly when complicated multicurrency options are involved, see Donaldson & Donaldson, p. 137.

nation of the loan would be inappropriate and may have catastrophic consequences for an otherwise financially sound borrower, due to the impact of
cross-default clauses.[11]

In order to safeguard the borrower against such harsh consequences some **9.06**
lenders are prepared to incorporate grace periods within the agreement.
Where a grace period is included, the default will be deemed not to have
occurred (in so far as the triggering of remedies is concerned) until a specified number of days has elapsed since the payment fell due. The period of
grace given must be long enough to enable the borrower to remedy a technical default but not too long so as to prejudice the position of the lender. It
follows that the parties' may agree different grace periods for different types
of payment, for example, principal, interest, fees and duties etc., each
period reflecting the importance attached to each type of payment. In so far
as eurocurrency loan agreements are concerned grace periods for non payment tend to be very short[12] and they are rarely given for non-payment of
principal.[13]

B. Breach of representations and warranties[14]

Since the borrower's representations reflect the basic legal and factual **9.07**
assumptions upon which the lender extends the loan facility, it is hardly surprising that breach of those assumptions would be deemed an event of
default. Indeed, as we indicated in an earlier chapter of this work,[15] the
primary purpose of the representations and warranties is to trigger an event
of default, not to provide a means of obtaining damages should they turn
out to be untrue.[16]

An event of default linked to the breach of a representation or warranty
will afford greater protection to the lender if the representations are deemed
to be continuing,[17] and in such a case the borrower will commonly seek to
mitigate against the harsher implications of the clause.

One way in which this and other clauses may be softened is by the incorporation of a "materiality test," *viz*;

> "Any representation or warranty made or deemed to be made by the
> Borrower under this Agreement or in any certificate, document or
> financial or other statement furnished at any time under or in connec-
> tion with this Agreement shall prove to have been incorrect or mislead-
> ing in any material respect when made or deemed to be made . . . then
> such an event shall be deemed to be an event of default."

The problem with such a clause is that it begs the question, "what is

[11] The impact of cross-default clauses is considered in greater detail later in this chapter, see
para. 9.10 below.
[12] It is rare to see grace periods of more than five days and most are for three days or even less.
See Clark and Taylor, *loc. cit.*, n. 1 above, p. 12.
[13] For a fuller discussion on how and why a lender may differentiate between different types of
non-payment, see Donaldson and Donaldson, pp. 159–161.
[14] See clause 16(*c*) in the specimen agreement, Chap. 17 below.
[15] See Chap. 6 above.
[16] They also serve a useful investigative function, see Chap. 6 above.
[17] See clause 13(2) in the specimen agreement, Chap. 17 below.

material?" This problem may be overcome by specifying a financial limit whereby materiality is to be gauged. Unfortunately, however, representations and warranties do not normally lend themselves to such a test. In practice, therefore, the ambiguity inherent in materiality tests will, at best, lead to uncertainty between the parties and at worst, litigation on its precise meaning.[18] For this reason many lawyers will discourage the use of materiality tests[19] and advocate in their place appropriate grace periods which should, of course, only operate in relation to those breaches of the loan agreement which can be remedied.[20]

C. Breach of covenants

9.08 The importance of the covenants given by a borrower in an international loan agreement has been considered earlier in this work,[21] and it is common, as in the case of representations and warranties, to link their breach to an event of default.

A typical clause might read:

"The Borrower shall default in the performance or observance of any covenant contained in this Agreement and such default shall continue for a period of 10 days."

9.09 The example given provides for a blanket grace period of 10 days for all covenants which, it is submitted, is unrealistic in most loan agreements. As we have already seen,[22] the covenants given by a borrower cover a wide variety of its activities, and it is likely that the lender will perceive some as being more important than others. Indeed, it is common practice in eurocurrency loans for the lender to consider some covenants so fundamental or incurable that any breach would be deemed an automatic event of default. Precisely which covenants the lender considers fundamental will obviously depend upon the circumstances of each individual case.[23]

Most lenders recognise that any leeway given to the borrower, in the form of grace periods, must be considered very carefully. Breach of a single covenant may signify that the borrower is on the verge of collapse, and in such a case it will be crucial for the lender to act as quickly as possible in the hope of obtaining repayment before the borrower falls into liquidation. As an alternative to grace periods a materiality test may be included in respect of those covenants which the lender does not consider fundamental to the

---

[18] The courts would determine the meaning on an objective basis and presumably evidence would be heard from experienced bankers in the eurocurrency markets as to the real materiality in question. See, *Docker* v. *Hyams* [1969] 1 Lloyd's Rep. 333; aff'd [1969]. See also, Youard, *loc. cit.*, n. 1 above, p. 381.

[19] See Clark and Taylor, *loc. cit.*, n. 1, p. 12.

[20] Notwithstanding the uncertainty inherent in the materiality test, many lenders insist upon its incorporation.

[21] See Chap. 6 above.

[22] *Ibid.*

[23] Examples of fundamental covenants may include: the borrower's covenant to notify the lender of any event of default; the covenant not to dispose of its assets; the covenant not to change its business without the consent of the lender; the covenant not to enter into any merger or consolidation; the ratio covenants; the negative pledge and the *pari passu* ranking covenant.

protection of its interests. The same problem, that of uncertainty, will once again apply, however, to the operation of the materiality test, and it is submitted that such a test is even less appropriate in the case of covenants than for breach of representations and warranties.[24]

D. Cross default[25]

9.10 The cross default clause is the principal anticipatory event of default and is an essential safeguard for the lender, since it provides a most effective "early warning" device providing it is appropriately drafted.

A typical clause might read:

> "The Borrower shall default in any payment of principal or of interest of any other indebtedness, or any other indebtedness which becomes due or capable of being declared due prior to its scheduled maturity as a result of a default thereunder."

Such a clause is intended to prevent the bank from being placed at a disadvantage in the event of the borrower defaulting under one of its other credit facilities. A lending bank will normally want to play an active part in any decision which is made concerning the fate of a borrower. The cross default clause should provide for this by enabling the lender to accelerate its own facility whenever this is necessary to obtain a seat at any subsequent creditors' meeting, which is convened to discuss the borrower's future. The clause also strengthens the *pari passu* principle that all creditors in the same class should be treated alike. Lenders in the eurocurrency markets have always attached a great deal of importance to this principle and it is recognised as the primary purpose of the cross default clause.

I. WHAT ARE THE IMPLICATIONS OF THE CLAUSE?

9.11 The cross default clause is generally recognised as being the most important anticipatory event of default,[26] but its consequences can be catastrophic for both the lender and the borrower due to the "domino effect" which the clause may set into motion. Those negotiating the clause must appreciate these consequences, and it is hardly surprising that the precise wording of the clause is often one of the most contentious aspects of the negotiation process.

Most creditworthy borrowers should, in the event of an emergency, be in a position to repay a small percentage of their outstanding indebtedness, but the domino effect brought about by the operation of the cross default clause (which will normally have been included in all of the borrower's international credits) is likely to ruin any borrower. The effect, which the clause is likely to have, significantly enchances the impact of the default sanction, but its implications are so severe that they may operate against the lenders' interest in a potential default situation. The knowledge that the clause, if triggered, will almost certainly bring about the total collapse of the borrower may effectively prevent it from being employed.

---

[24] See para. 9.06 above.
[25] See clause 16(*d*) in the specimen agreement, Chap. 17 below.
[26] See Wood, p. 166.

9.12 Notwithstanding the comments made above, the sanction of the cross default clause remains severe and the borrower will normally seek to mitigate its effect. Grace periods and materiality tests are often requested, but the lender should be aware of the problems which such softening techniques pose.[27] Lenders should resist grace periods which start to run, not when the default occurs or when the borrower becomes aware of the default, but when the lender informs the borrower. Delay in triggering any event of default may have serious consequences for the lender's position and, therefore, grace periods, if granted, should be for a very short period of time, should start to run at the earliest possible time, and should only cover technical defaults or administrative delays on the part of the borrower.

Another way in which the borrower may seek to "soften" the clause is by requiring that it can only be "triggered" if the borrower's default on the third party credit is above a certain threshold figure or that the default is under a particular type of facility.

Any restriction imposed upon the operation of the clause may put the lender at risk, particularly where third party creditors of the borrower are not subject to similar restrictions. In such a case the restrictions should be resisted by the lender, and in any event, many experienced negotiators would argue that it is crucial to keep one's options, in the event of a default, as flexible as possible.

2. THE WORDING OF THE CROSS DEFAULT CLAUSE

a. What Should the Clause Cover?

9.13 Because of its importance, many lenders seek to word the clause in the widest possible terms. An example of how this can be achieved is seen in the specimen clause given above,[28] which includes the phrase "any other indebtedness." Without more, such wording would cover all financial obligations owed by the borrower, from the $3 milk bill to the $3 million syndicated loan agreement. Such a clause is clearly unrealistic insofar as both lender and borrower are concerned, since it would almost certainly change the term loan into a demand loan and may trigger an event of default in a number of the borrower's other credit obligations because of the "domino effect" of the clause. It is hardly surprising, therefore, that borrowers normally resist such widely drafted clauses and attempt to restrict their scope to well defined classes of indebtedness, such as borrowed money, unsecured credits or to commercial bank credits.[29] Sovereign borrowers will be particularly anxious to limit the scope of the clause,[30] and it is relatively common in such cases to restrict its operation to the external indebtedness of the borrower. External indebtedness is normally defined as indebtedness owed to non–residents or indebtedness, which is denominated in a currency other than that of the borrower's own country.

Another important consideration with regard to corporate borrowers is

---

[27] See para. 9.06 above.

[28] See para. 9.10.

[29] Borrowers may also seek to include a de-minimis provision within the terms of the cross default clause specifying that the clause will only be "triggered" if the third party default is over a certain amount.

[30] See Carroll, "The Worst Clause in the Euromarkets" *Euromoney*, June, 1981; Youard, *loc. cit.*, n. 1, p. 387.

whether the clause should cover subsidiaries. Where the lender takes such subsidiaries into account, when taking the credit analysis decision, they should be included, as should any guarantor where relevant. However, where the borrower is being analysed in isolation it may be totally inappropriate to widen the scope of the clause unnecessarily.

b. When Should the Clause Crystallise?

Since it is in the lender's interest to negotiate as wide a cross default clause as **9.14** possible, most clauses are drafted in such a way as to enable the lender to terminate and accelerate its own loan even though the borrower's other credits are not accelerated. This type of clause is often referred to as the "capable of" cross default clause, since it permits the lender to accelerate its own loan in the event that any of the borrower's other credits are *capable of being accelerated*. Whether or not the other credits are in fact accelerated is irrelevant, indeed, most lenders would argue that to limit the cross default clause in such a way would be tantamount to placing the operation of the clause in the hands of the borrower's other creditors.

The "capable of" formulation places the lender in the strongest possible position, since it enables the lender to be the master of its own destiny. A borrower which accedes to such a clause will consequently find itself in a perilous position, since the clause will, of necessity, nullify the effect of any grace periods operating over events of default in its other loan agreements. Such a clause may also prejudice the borrower's relations with its other creditors, who will undoubtedly be less than happy if they themselves have agreed upon cross default clauses which can only be triggered in the event of actual acceleration of a third party credit.

The obvious danger with any cross default clause that may be triggered prior to actual acceleration of other indebtedness, or which does not take into account grace periods, is that it may set the "domino effect" into motion whilst the borrower is making a bona fide attempt to remedy the breach. As we indicated earlier, such a course of events is likely, without more, to drive almost any borrower into liquidation.

3. CAN THE CLAUSE BE EFFECTIVELY POLICED?

One final problem posed by the cross default clause is that in practice its **9.15** usefulness may be curtailed due to the standards of secrecy which euro-market lenders, particularly banks, are expected to maintain.[31] As with many clauses in an international loan agreement, the clause must be capable of being effectively policed, in other words the lender must have fairly full information on the position with regard to the borrower's other indebtedness, and in particular, whether it has defaulted upon such indebtedness. Without such information the cross default clause is useless as an early warning device, and it will fail to maintain *pari passu* treatment if third party creditors are able to enforce against the borrower without the lender becoming aware.

In conclusion, it can be said that although the cross default clause is perceived as crucial to protect the position of the lender in most international loan agreements, its limitations should not be overlooked. Furthermore,

---

[31] See Clark and Taylor, *loc. cit.*, n. 1 above, p. 13.

those negotiating its precise wording must be aware of the serious consequences to which the clause may give rise. As we have already indicated, lenders will obviously want as wide a clause as possible,[32] but this may place the borrower in default virtually from the moment the loan agreement is executed. Such a consequence can hardly be in the interests of either the borrower or the lender.

E. Liquidation or Moratorium[33]

9.16 The laws of most countries recognise that bankruptcy or liquidation of the borrower will constitute an event of default regardless of what is stated in the loan agreement. However, such an eventuality should still be specifically covered within the events of default, since the relevant legal procedures in the country of the borrower's domicile[34] may be disadvantageous to the lender or at least not as advantageous as the lender would wish.

A typical clause covering this type of default might read:

> "The Borrower or any subsidiary or any guarantor shall enter into voluntary or involuntary liquidation or dissolution, or shall be adjudicated to be bankrupt or insolvent, or if a receiver shall be appointed over any of the assets of the Borrower or any subsidiary or any guarantor, of if the Borrower or any subsidiary or any guarantor admits in writing its inability to pay its debts as they mature or makes any assignment or proposal for the benefit of creditors."

Once again, this particular clause tends to be drafted very widely, but unlike the cross default clause it will rarely be a contentious issue as between the parties. Where the borrower falls into liquidation or specifically states that it is unable to pay its debts, there can be no question of the loan being continued. Similarly, where subsidiaries or guarantors have been included as part of the credit, they also should be included within the ambit of the clause.

F. Bankruptcy of sovereign borrowers

9.17 Sovereign states are not generally subject to bankruptcy or insolvency proceedings since there is no international regime governing states which are unable to pay their debts. However, quasi-government entities and government owned corporations[35] do normally fall within the scope of such proceedings and, where relevant, it is common to incorporate such entities within the terms of the clause.

The equivalent to bankruptcy in so far as a sovereign state is concerned is the declaration of a moratorium on the repayment of its debts, and although formal proceedings are rarely involved the practical effect for the lender is, if anything, even more catastrophic, since under a moratorium all payments

---

[32] For an example of just how widely the clause may be worded, see clause 16(*c*) in the specimen agreement, Chap. 17 below.

[33] See clause 16(*f*) in the specimen agreement, Chap. 17 below.

[34] As to the significance of the borrower's domicile generally, see Chap. 2 above.

[35] As to the distinction between states and state controlled entities, see Chap. 3 above.

are frozen, whereas in a bankruptcy there is always a chance of receiving a percentage of the sums owed. Because the threat of moratorium is so serious it is common to include an appropriate event of default either when lending to a sovereign or where a sovereign is guaranteeing the loan.

Such a clause might read:

> "the Borrower declares any general moratorium on its indebtedness or upon any indebtedness assumed or guaranteed by it."

In practical terms, the clause is unlikely to be of any assistance, since acceleration after the moratorium has been declared will rarely enable the lender to obtain repayment,[36] and in most cases the declaration will be followed by lengthy rescheduling negotiation.[37]

Nevertheless, it will be important for the bank to retain the ability to accelerate upon such an occurrence, otherwise it may not have a voice during the rescheduling process.

G. Changes in the control of the borrower

The lender may have made its credit decision on the assumption that the **9.18** borrower will continue to be controlled by some larger entity. This will commonly arise when the loan is being advanced to a government-owned corporation or a subsidiary of a large company. In such a situation the lender will want to review its position in the event of control by the parent being severed. An appropriate event of default will permit the lender to make such a review, *viz*:

> "the Borrower ceases to be a subsidiary of . . . . . . or ceases to be under the voting control of . . . ."

Where the parent exercises a significant degree of control over the borrower it will be crucial for the lender to insist upon a guarantee from the parent.[38] Some lenders prefer to take matters one stage further and require the parent or state to join the borrower as principal debtor, particularly where the lender is fearful that the borrower may be nationalised or expropriated,[39] as is often the case with companies engaged in the exploitation of natural resources.[40]

H. Disposal of assets

Disposal of all or part of the borrower's assets is a common event of default **9.19** in corporate loans, although it is common to incorporate practical limitations which ensure that the borrower will be able to carry on with its nor-

---

[36] For an excellent discussion of how the moratorium may be enforced, see Du Plessis, "Exchange Control: South Africa's Debt Standstill Provisions" [1986] 23 J.I.B.L. 87.

[37] Some of the problems posed by the rescheduling process are considered later in this chapter, see para. 9.34 below.

[38] Whenever a loan is guaranteed it will be most important to draft the agreement in such a way that the guarantor is linked with the borrower throughout the relevant events of default. For a fuller discussion of guarantees in international banking, see Chap. 15 below.

[39] See Chap. 3 above.

[40] For a fuller discussion of this problem, see Clark and Taylor, *loc. cit.*, n. 1 above, p. 13; Wood, p. 168.

mal trading activities. The lender will be particularly concerned to prevent the borrower from disposing of assets which form the underlying basis of the loan,[41] or from disposing of assets which are essential for the continuing viability of the companies business. In order to safeguard the lender's position still further an event of default should also be linked to an anti-disposal covenant.[42]

I. IMF membership

9.20   Where the borrower is a sovereign state, it has become increasingly common to provide that it shall be an event of default if the borrower ceases to be a member of the International Monetary Fund (IMF) or is unable to use the IMF's resources.[43] It is well recognised that a healthy relationship between a state borrower and the IMF is a sign that the borrower is conducting its financial affairs in a prudent fashion. Continued membership is, therefore, a source of great comfort to many state lenders in the eurocurrency markets. On the other hand, a breakdown in relations between the borrower and the IMF usually signifies that all is not well and will, at the very least, put the lender "on enquiry."

9.21   Of more practical significance is the fact that IMF membership may give the state borrower access to direct financial assistance which may help the borrower to overcome a short-term liquidity crisis, though it should be remembered that the IMF will only assist its members during temporary difficulties. If the borrower's problems are deep-rooted IMF membership may be of little practical help.

Additional protection may also be afforded to the lender by requiring the borrower to maintain a stand-by arrangement with the IMF.[44] Such an arrangement enables a member to make purchases of foreign currency from the IMF at regular intervals. Since lack of foreign currency is one of the main factors behind many sovereign loan defaults, the ability to obtain such currency may be perceived as crucial for the continuation of the loan.[45]

J. Material adverse change[46]

9.22   The "material adverse change" clause is another contentious event of default which is commonly drafted into international loan agreements. The purpose of this clause, as its name suggests, is to permit the lender to

---

[41] This issue will be particularly important in relation to project finance loans.

[42] See Chap. 6 above.

[43] IMF membership may also be a condition precedent and continued membership a condition subsequent. Rather than incorporate IMF membership as a specific event of default many loans include such membership within the representations and warranties breach of which will, as we have seen, trigger an event of default, see clause 13(1)(*l*) in the specimen agreement, Chap. 17 below.

[44] See Ryan, *loc. cit.*, n. 1 above, pp. 97–98.

[45] For a detailed account of the IMF's stand-by facility, see Gold, "The legal character of the Fund's stand-by arrangements and why it matters" (IMF Pamphlet Series No. 35 1980); "Order in International Finance, the promotion of IMF stand-by arrangements and the drafting of private loan agreements" (IMF Pamphlet Series No. 39, 1983).

[46] See clause 16(*h*) in the specimen agreement, Chap. 17 below.

accelerate the loan in the event that a material and adverse change occurs in the financial condition or operation of the borrower. A typical clause might read as follows:

> "there shall occur any other event which in the judgment of the Bank would materially and adversely affect the ability or willingness of the Borrower to perform its obligations under this Agreement."

The clause operates as a safeguard of last resort, a "sweeping-up" provision which, it is hoped, will give some protection to the lender if all else fails. Its inclusion should not, however, lure the lender into taking a soft approach to the more specific events of default,[47] some of which have been outlined above. There is no substitute for appropriately drafted events of default, and it could be argued that where such events are included within the loan there should be no need to incorporate an all-embracing material adverse change clause. Nevertheless, many lenders perceive the clause as crucial and as the specimen clause indicates it is typically drafted in the widest possible terms. The intention being to cover any conceivable circumstance which may affect the borrower's willingness or ability to perform its obligations under the loan. This intention is normally reinforced by giving the lender sole discretion in determining whether a material adverse change has in fact occurred. The problem with the clause lies in the generality of its language which poses obvious difficulties of proof, and this problem may not be solved simply by placing any discretion solely in the hands of the lender, particularly if the discretion is exercised unreasonably.[48]

REMEDIES

The remedies available to a lender in the event of a borrower defaulting on its obligations can be conveniently divided between those which are commonly included within the terms of the loan documentation (the internal remedies) and other remedies existing under general principles of law which may, or may not, be specifically referred to (the external remedies). **9.23**

A. The internal remedies

TERMINATION OF THE AGREEMENT AND ACCELERATION OF THE MATURITY[49]

The most basic sanction available to the lender in the event of a borrower's default is the right to declare the outstanding portion of the loan immediately due and payable and to cancel any commitment to provide further loans.[50] The ability to exercise this right swiftly, in other words, with no grace period, will be fundamentally important in certain circumstances[51] **9.24**

---

[47] See Youard, *loc. cit.*, n. 1 above, pp. 390–391.
[48] See Wood, p. 168; Gabriel, pp. 58–62. For an excellent discussion of how many banks view the material adverse change clause, see Donaldson and Donaldson, p. 164 *et seq.*
[49] See clause 16(*h*)(i) and (ii) in the specimen agreement.
[50] See Wood, p. 50.
[51] Some interesting circumstances are considered by Phillip Wood in "Sudden Death Accelerations" (1982) I.F.L.R. September 22, p. 23.

and, therefore, the precise wording of the clause should be carefully considered. A typical example might read as follows:

> "Then in any such event and at any time thereafter if such event is continuing, the Bank[52] may, by notice in writing to the Borrower cancel any undrawn amount of the facility and declare the loan forthwith due and payable, together with all interest accrued thereon and all other amounts payable hereunder.[53]"

Such a clause should enable the lending bank to act quickly in the event that circumstances so require, subject to the proviso that the event of default must be continuing. In other words, the event of default which triggers the termination/acceleration clause must not only have been breached but must also be continuing at the time the right to terminate and accelerate is exercised. If the borrower cures the event of default before such right is exercised, the bank will have lost its right (at least in so far as that particular event of default is concerned), but once the right has been exercised by the bank, the borrower loses its ability to cure.[54]

9.25 Another possible limitation which may operate upon the lenders contractual right to terminate and accelerate the loan relates to the application of equitable principles. The application of such principles has been confirmed in a number of American cases, although it would appear that appropriate cases to which equitable principles can be applied to prevent termination/acceleration will be rare.[55] The most likely equitable principle which may operate against the interests of the lender is the equitable principle of good faith which has been applied to the enforcement of acceleration clauses, particularly in New York.[56] In that State it would appear that the courts will prohibit acceleration in cases where the lender's conduct is "oppressive," "unreasonable" or "unconscionable" or "where a trivial default is entirely out of proportion to the harshness of the acceleration clause."[57] In other cases the courts have looked at the materiality of the event of default in order to establish whether the lender's acceleration is in such bad faith as to require equitable intervention by the courts.[58]

In so far as English law is concerned the courts have made it clear that cer-

---

[52] Where the loan is a syndicated facility the agent bank is sometimes given discretionary authority to declare an event of default and accelerate the loan. The alternative approach is to vest the right of acceleration with the majority banks, although for the sake of administrative convenience it is normally the agent bank which actually notifies the borrower, *viz*: "the agent bank will declare a default when so instructed by the majority banks and declare the loan due and payable." A hybrid clause may also be used which combines both approaches, *viz*. "the agent may (and if so instructed by the majority banks must) declare a default. . . . " The significance of each type of clause is considered in greater detail in Chap. 7, above.

[53] For an example of how the wording of the clause may be varied, see clause 16(*h*)(i) and (ii) in the specimen agreement, Chap. 17 below.

[54] As to whether loan agreements, which do not provide that the default must be continuing, can be accelerated after the default has been cured, see The Encyclopaedia, para. 3562.

[55] See *Fifty States Management Corp.* v. *Pioneer Auto Parks Inc.*, 46 NY 2d 573, 577, 389 NE 2d 113, 116, 415 NYS 2d 800, 803 (1979), cited in Gruson (ed.), p. 164.

[56] See Gruson, (ed.) pp. 163–165.

[57] See *100 Eighth Avenue Corp.* v. *Morgenstern* 4 AD 2d 754, 164 NYS 2d 812 (1957).

[58] See *Domus Realty Corp.* v. *3440 Realty Co.* 179 Misc. 749, 40 NYS 2d 69 (1943), aff'd mem., 226 AD 725, 41 NYS 2d 940 (1943), cited in Gruson, p. 164. It would appear that the equitable principle of good faith may be statutorily applied in the State of New York, especially to the material adverse change clause, under the Uniform Commercial Code S. 1–208.

tainty and predictability of clauses negotiated between commercial parties must be upheld and therefore, the application of equitable limitations upon the lender's right to terminate/accelerate is much less significant.[59] Where the lender's right to accelerate is discretionary all that seems to be required is that the discretion is exercised honestly, in good faith.[60]

WAIVER

The lender's use of waivers may also place a significant limitation upon its **9.26** ability to terminate/accelerate the loan.[61] In practice, most lenders will explore every possible avenue before terminating the loan and enforcing its remedies and, notwithstanding an event of default, where the borrower is essentially credit-worthy it is common for the lender to grant an appropriate waiver.

Whenever such a waiver is granted it should be dealt with in writing in order to bring certainty both to the circumstances in which it was granted and to the manner in which it will operate.

Waivers which are granted orally, or by conduct, for example, where the lender permits the borrower to draw down the loan in full knowledge that breach of an event of default has occurred, pose particular problems. This is because it will be extremely difficult to ascertain the circumstances in which the waiver will operate.[62] The parties may ultimately find themselves in disagreement, the borrower arguing that its default is covered by the lender's oral or implied waiver, and the lender arguing that it is not so covered. A lender should never allow itself to fall into this position and in order to avoid any such possibility, it is common practice to send out a no-waiver letter whenever there has been a breach of the loan agreement by the borrower. This practice should safeguard the lender against any future contention by the borrower that certain clauses in the loan have been continually waived.[63] It will also encourage specific negotiation between the parties on the question of whether, and in what circumstances, any waiver will operate.

ACCELERATION MAY ACTUALLY REDUCE THE PROSPECT OF REPAYMENT

One final, and very practical limitation on the lender's right to terminate/ **9.27** accelerate, is that by exercising such a right the lender may cause the borrower's other international credits to be accelerated due to the impact of cross-default clauses.[64] As we have already indicated,[65] it is most unlikely

---

[59] See *The Brimnes* [1974] 3 All E.R. 88; *The Laconia* [1977] 1 All E.R. 545; *The Chikuma* [1981] 1 All E.R. 652, cited in Wood, *loc. cit.* n. 51 above, p. 22.

[60] *Ibid.*, see also, *Docker v. Hyams* [1969] 3 All E.R. 808.

[61] See generally, Wood, pp. 172–173; The Encyclopaedia, paras. 3639–3672; Gruson (ed.), p. 165.

[62] See *Birmingham and District Land Co. v. London and North Western Rail Co.* (1888), cited in Wood, p. 172.

[63] In appropriate cases however such a course of events may lead to an estoppel arising, see The Encyclopaedia para. 3639.

[64] See para. 9.10 above.

[65] *Ibid.*

that the lender will recover anything more than a small percentage of the sums owing, if the "domino effect" of the cross default clause is activated. In the majority of cases it is likely that such a course of events will culminate in lengthy, and expensive rescheduling negotiations.

DEFAULT INTEREST[66]

9.28   International loan agreements invariably make specific reference to default interest which the borrower must pay in the event that it fails to make payment of any amount on the due date. Default interest will normally be payable whenever there is delay in payment, regardless of whether or not the loan is terminated/accelerated.

The rate of default interest can, in some cases, be significantly higher than the normal rate charged on the loan, thereby acting as a penal measure. In most loans, however, the figure will be a modest increase above the normal rate. Lenders should be particularly wary of default interest provisions which operate as a penal measure, since a number of jurisdictions, including England, refuse to admit penal rates of interest and permit only the recovery of costs.[67] Where a small increase is made in respect of default interest, the lender could properly contend that the clause operates as a compensatory device against additional expenses which may be incurred in the event of the borrowers default.

GENERAL DEFAULT INDEMNITY

9.29   In addition to the clause specifically covering default interest, most loan agreements also require the borrower to indemnify the lender against any loss which the lender sustains because of the borrower's default. Such a clause might read as follows:

> "The Borrower shall indemnify the Bank against any loss or reasonable expenses which the Bank may sustain or incur as a consequence of any default in the payment of principal or interest on the loan, or any other amount due under the loan, or as a consequence of the occurrence of any event of default under the loan"[68]

As the wording of the specimen clause indicates, the lender will normally seek to draft the clause as widely as possible, in order to cover any loss associated with the default.[69]

---

[66] See clause 17 in the specimen agreement, Chap. 17 below.

[67] It would appear that an English court would certainly strike out a clause which acted as a penalty, aimed at pressurising the borrower against breaching the loan agreement; see *Dunlop Pneumatic Tyre Company Ltd.* v. *New Garage and Motor Company Ltd.* [1915] A.C. 79. It would seem that under English law the increase must genuinely compensate the lender for the additional cost incurred in dealing with the defaulted loan.

[68] Where the loan agreement is syndicated the relevant clause normally provides that the Agent bank shall quantify the loss, see clause 17 in the specimen agreement, Chap. 17 below. See also, Chap. 7 above.

[69] The clause may also, in appropriate cases, make specific provision for currency loss. For a fuller exposition of how such a clause might operate, see Donaldson and Donaldson, p. 180.

SET–OFF

As Phillip Wood points out[70] . . . "Potentially one of the most useful rem-   **9.30**
edies available to a bank lender on a default by the borrower is the ability to
use deposits of the borrower placed with the bank to pay out the defaulted
loan by a set-off."

Set-off is a remedy which bridges the gap between the internal and external remedies since a clause covering the lender's right to set-off may be
incorporated within the terms of an international loan agreement. Rights of
set-off also exist in equity, but only where given conditions are fulfilled.[71]

The English law of set-off has been comprehensively dealt with earlier in
this work[72] and here our attention will focus upon the set-off clause, which
usually seeks to confer broader rights of set-off than would be given in
equity.

Such a clause may read as follows:

> "The Lender may set-off against any obligation of the Borrower due
> and payable by it hereunder any monies held by the lender for the
> account of the Borrower at any office of the lender anywhere and in
> any currency exchanges as are appropriate to implement such set-off."

It is debatable whether the courts in either England or New York would
permit set-off where the funds to be set-off are in another jurisdiction or in a
currency other than that specified in the agreement. Set-off in such cases
would certainly not be allowed in equity and the specimen clause serves to
illustrate how the loan agreement may attempt to extend the lender's rights.
The problem with such a clause is that under English law it may constitute
the creation of a charge over the borrower's deposits, and if so construed
will be void under section 395 of the Companies Act 1985 unless it is registered.[73] Such a construction, however, now appears unlikely following the
decision of Millet J. in *Re Charge Card Services*.[73a]

B. External remedies

SPECIFIC PERFORMANCE

An English court will not normally grant an order for specific performance   **9.31**
where damages would be an adequate remedy. Nor will the court normally
grant specific performance where the loan agreement makes provision for a
more suitable remedy, for example, termination and acceleration. The English approach is also followed in New York[74] and would suggest that specific performance will rarely be available to remedy the borrower's breach of
an event of default.

---

[70] See Wood, p. 173.

[71] See generally, Goode, *Legal Problems of Credit and Security* (1982), pp. 100–122.

[72] See Vol. 1, Chap. 10; see also, Hapgood, "The Law of set-off in England" I.F.L.R. (1983)
(June) pp. 22–25. For a comparison with New York law, see Mortimer, "The law of set-off
in New York" (1983) I.F.L.R. (May), pp. 24–33.

[73] See *In Re Charge Card Services Ltd.* [1986] 3 W.L.R. 697, [1986] 3 All E.R. 289. See also, *Re
Brightliffe Ltd.* (1986) 2 B.C.C. 99, 359. For an interesting discussion of the set-off principles
in both of these cases, see Shea [1986] 3 J.I.B.L. pp. 192–201.

[73a] *Ibid.*; see in particular the remarks of Millet J. at pp. 307–314.

[74] See Gruson (ed.), p. 167.

PROHIBITORY INJUNCTION[75]

9.32   Although an English court would be reluctant to grant an order for specific performance which would require a positive act on the part of the borrower, it would be much more favourably disposed towards the grant of an injunction which restrains the borrower from performing acts which are in breach of its obligations under the loan agreement.[76] Thus, the borrower may be restrained from breaching an undertaking or covenant, providing the lender can act quickly, before the breach occurs. This once again highlights the importance of incorporating undertakings/covenants within the loan agreement which can be effectively policed by the lender.[77]

OTHER EXTERNAL REMEDIES

9.33   There are a number of other remedies which may be available to the lender in the event that the borrower breaches the loan agreement, and most of these are considered elsewhere in this work.[78] They include: the right to repudiate the contract and accelerate the sum outstanding; the right to sue the borrower for damages; the right to sue for outstanding amounts of interest and/or principal; the right to rescind the loan agreement and claim damages.

As we have seen,[79] the availability of such remedies will depend upon the circumstances surrounding the borrower's breach, and although they may provide the lender with a number of important safeguards, their availability will normally be subject to significant limitations. They should never be relied upon as a substitute for express remedies, which must always be incorporated into the loan agreement in order to bring a degree of certainty and predictability to the rights of the lender in the event that the borrower subsequently breaches the agreement.

RESTRUCTURING

Introduction

9.34   Where the borrower encounters difficulties so that it is no longer able to meet its liabilities as they fall due, the lender may agree to open restructuring negotiations in the hope that the borrower will pull through its present financial difficulties. Such a course of action may be perceived as being more attractive than winding-up proceedings which, as we have already seen[80] will realise for the lender only a small proportion of the sums owed. Restructuring agreements are particularly common in so far as sovereign

---

[75] See generally, Goode, *Commercial Law* (1982), p. 117.
[76] Again, a similar approach is taken in New York; see Gruson, n. 74 above.
[77] See generally, Chap. 6 above.
[78] See generally, Chaps. 6 and 7 above.
[79] *Ibid.*
[80] See para. 9.03 above.

borrower's are concerned and such agreements tend to be even more complex than corporate restructurings.[81]

Insofar as the lender's are concerned, the most important components of the restructuring process will be:

(i) the rescheduling of the borrower's existing debt;

(ii) the provision of new money;

(iii) the need to conclude formal arrangements for the maintenance of inter-bank lines of credit.

One of the main advantages of restructuring is that control stays with the lenders, but there are a number of major problems which such a course of action pose for the lenders, not least the need to provide new money. It is hardly surprising that many lenders resent the need to provide new money, seeing it as a case of "throwing good money after bad." As a consequence, the documentation evidencing restructuring agreements tends to be drafted heavily in favour of the lenders.

Before we consider some specific aspects of the restructuring process it **9.35** must be pointed out that no two restructurings are ever the same. There are no international guidelines governing the process of restructuring and our discussion of this topic will, therefore, concentrate on general principles rather than specific examples. Many of the inherent difficulties in a restructuring exercise arise out of the sheer complexity of the negotiations which are necessary. A typical sovereign restructuring[82] will involve tens, if not hundreds, of individual borrowers in both the public and private sector, with a corresponding number of separate credit instruments. The credits themselves will have been advanced in a multitude of different currencies at varying maturities, interest rates and margins. The documentation evidencing such credits will be equally diverse, ranging from one paragraph promissory notes to voluminous syndicated loan agreements. It is hardly surprising that the most difficult question is often the first "which of the borrowers' debts will be rescheduled?"

The restructuring process

A. DECLARATION OF A MORATORIUM

Insofar as sovereign restructurings are concerned the restructuring process **9.36** has generally commenced following an announcement by the state of a specific cut-off date upon which it proposes to suspend payment of its obligations, accompanied by an announcement of the opening of negotiations to reschedule.[83] The major problem facing a corporate borrower should it

---

[81] For a short, but interesting, exposition of some comparisons between corporate and sovereign restructurings, see Karat, "Corporate and sovereign restructurings compared" (1983) I.F.L.R. November, pp. 35–36.

[82] For an excellent exposition of the various approaches to the restructuring of sovereign debt, see Clark and Hughes in Gruson (ed.), pp. 131–137. See also, Horn, "The Restructuring of International Loans and the International Debt Crisis" (1984) I.B.L., pp. 400–409; Clark, "Problems, and Solutions, to sovereign debt restructuring" (1984), I.F.L.R. (October), pp. 4–8.

[83] See Wood in Kalderen and Siddiqi, pp. 134–138. For an excellent exposition of how the recent South African restructuring commenced, see E. D. Du Plessis, "Exchange Control: South Africa's Debt Standstill Provisions," [1986] 2 J.I.B.L., pp. 87–99.

decide to commence restructuring negotiations by the declaration of a so-called moratorium, is that individual creditors, with minimal exposure, may feel that their interests are best served by taking independent legal action against the borrower to enforce the debts they are owed. Such a course of action may have serious implications for the borrower's prospects, since its major creditors may be disinclined to restructure in a case where many minor creditors are actively seeking to enforce their rights by means of attachment or otherwise. Nevertheless, many corporate borrowers do survive this vulnerable stage, and the bankruptcy laws of both England and the United States provide various procedures which may help to achieve a work-out situation.[84]

Rather than declare a moratorium the borrower, and likewise the lender(s), may prefer the restructuring to be conducted privately, as between an individual debtor and an individual lender, or syndicate of lenders. Such a procedure will be unrealistic, however, when the borrower has many different creditors with whom it must negotiate.

B. ADMINISTRATION OF THE RESTRUCTURING

9.37   In most of the recent major restructurings, the negotiations from the lending bank's side have been led by a so-called "steering committee." The members of this committee are normally drawn from the leading bank creditors of the borrower and each committee is the product of the specific restructuring in question. No two steering committees have ever comprised the same banks, but although their members are appointed on an ad hoc basis, the manner in which these committees are formed and work on the restructuring has, to some extent, been formalised. In many of the recent sovereign restructurings, for example, the steering committee has comprised between 10 to 14 banks with a permanent chairman.[85] A number of sub-committees have usually been appointed to deal with particular aspects of the rescheduling and these sub-committees have tended to work with the steering committee in supervising the drafting of the documentation for the rescheduling and new-money agreements, and generally, in implementing the restructuring itself.

C. IS THERE A DUTY UPON ANY OF THE BANK CREDITORS TO TAKE A MAJOR ROLE IN THE RESTRUCTURING EXERCISE?

9.38   It has been suggested by at least one learned commentator[86] that certain banks may be under a contractual duty to assume a leading role in the restructuring negotiations. Those principally cited are the lead managers

---

[84] The Insolvency Act 1986 contains two new procedures, namely, the Administration and the Voluntary Arrangement processes which provide mechanisms for assisting corporate rehabilitation and reconstruction. These new procedures do not, however, go as far as Chapter 11 proceedings in the United States. See generally, Vol. 1, Chap. 20 of this work.

[85] For an excellent exposition of the practical problems behind some of the recent sovereign debt restructurings, see Mauger, "Sovereign Debt Restructuring: The Practical Background" [1986] 2 J.I.B.L., pp. 100–118.

[86] See Horn, *loc. cit.*, n. 82 above.

and/or the agent banks in syndicated loan agreements. Professor Horn contends[87] that since both the lead managers and agent banks have acted for and on behalf of the other syndicate members in both the formation of the syndicate and thereafter during the life of the loan, one may conclude that in a crisis (for example in a restructuring exercise) such banks will be obliged to take leading roles on behalf of the syndicate. Professor Horn accepts, however, that such a duty is remote, and would, in any event, be restricted to giving information about the crisis to the other syndicate members.

It is submitted that such a conclusion must be correct, since if one closely **9.39** examines the contractual relationships which exist between the parties to a syndicated loan agreement[88] it is clear that no such duty can be found to exist. The duties of the lead manager/managers, for example, will be confined to forming the syndicate and drafting the loan documentation. Such banks will cease to occupy any special position in the syndicate (unless they also act as agent banks) once the loan agreement has been executed. In so far as the agent bank[89] is concerned, its duties will only commence once the loan has been executed and, as we have seen,[90] the loan documentation will usually restrict its duties, largely to administrative matters. The agent bank will normally be bound to inform the syndicate members of the events which give rise to the need for a restructuring operation. Few loan agreements, however, will give the agent bank power to conclude restructuring negotiations on behalf of the syndicate and even if the agent bank is prepared to participate in such negotiations it may, before so participating, require the express approval of each syndicate member.[91]

It will be most important for the members of the steering committee to ensure that they do not become agents of the banks on whose behalf they are acting in the restructuring negotiations. As we have already seen in an earlier chapter of this work,[92] being construed as an agent under both English and New York law will impose significant duties upon the members of the committee.[93]

A further problem for the steering committee is that it may come to acquire certain confidential or inside information concerning the borrower. If such information is material, the members of the steering committee should insist upon the borrower disclosing it to the other bank creditors. English law would also take a stern view towards any secret deals which may be agreed between the members of the steering committee and the borrower.[94]

---

[87] *Ibid.*

[88] See generally, Chap. 7 above.

[89] There may, of course, be more than one agent bank appointed by the syndicate, see Chap. 7 above.

[90] *Ibid.*

[91] Some loan agreements actually give the agent bank authority to negotiate during a restructuring exercise, others require consent from a majority of the syndicate. In the vast majority of cases, however, express approval will be required from each syndicate member.

[92] See Chap. 7 above.

[93] These would include duties of due diligence, disclosure, avoidance of conflicts of interest, and accounting for profits received from the agency.

[94] See, for example, *Re EAB* [1902] 1 K.B. 457; *Re Milner* (1885) 15 Q.B.D. 605; in *Re Hodgson* (1851) 4 De G & SM 354.

D. IDENTIFYING THE DEBTS WHICH ARE TO BE RESCHEDULED

9.40 As we indicated earlier,[95] the first, and perhaps the most difficult issue to resolve in a sovereign restructuring is precisely which of the borrower's debts are to be included in the negotiations. In most cases it will only be necessary to restructure part of a country's debt, the problem is "which part?" The category of debt ultimately selected must be sufficiently broad to enable the sovereign debtor to re-establish itself, yet not so broad as to prejudice the co-operation of the banks which are to participate in the rescheduling. The state debtor will have additional motives for keeping the rescheduled package as small as possible, since margins and fees will generally be higher than those found in the credits originally advanced.[96]

The restructuring negotiations will normally be restricted to the state's external debt; few sovereigns would countenance external interference over local currency obligations. External debt is generally recognised as debt payable in a currency other than the debtor's local currency, to creditors who operate outside the jurisdiction of the debtor.

9.41 Identifying the external debt will give a basis upon which the rescheduling negotiations can commence,[97] although as we have already indicated, no two restructurings are ever the same. Furthermore, although the external debt will provide a starting point, it will still be necessary to distinguish, amongst the external debts identified, those that will be rescheduled and those that will not.

A further criterion commonly applied is that of rescheduled maturity. In other words, the rescheduling is often limited to those credits originally scheduled to mature within a given period of time.[98]

In many recent sovereign reschedulings a critical division has been made between those debts having a term of more than twelve months to run and those with less than twelve months remaining.

E. THE NEW MONEY AGREEMENT

9.42 An essential component of most large restructuring arrangements is the need to supply the borrower with new medium term credits or, as it is often called, "fresh" money. The amount so required is often expressed as a percentage of the lending banks current exposure to the borrower, although it should be emphasised that there is no legal obligation upon any of the creditors to provide funds for the new money agreement. Most banks recognise, however, that they will have to carry rescheduled debt for several years, particularly in the case of sovereign debt. In addition, they recognise the need to provide fresh credits to various state and corporate borrowers, until more stable repayment positions can be achieved. Without the new money agreements it is difficult to see how many of the recent rescheduling agreements could have been reached.

---

[95] See para. 9.35 above.

[96] In the present climate, however, the difference may not be all that significant.

[97] It is most unlikely that all external debt will be rescheduled. Examples of external debt which is normally excluded include: public bonds, government guaranteed loans, short term credits and privately placed securities.

[98] Other important criteria which have been used to identify the debt to be rescheduled include identifying the purpose of the outstanding credits or the nature thereof.

The "fresh" money is normally provided in pre-determined stages and, for obvious reasons, a considerable degree of control is exercised over the borrower's ability to draw-down the "fresh" money. For this reason the new money agreement is normally kept as an independent obligation, entirely separate from the "old money" documents.

F. KEY PROVISIONS IN THE RESTRUCTURING AGREEMENTS[99]

The documentation evidencing both the rescheduling and new money **9.43** agreements will contain many of the clauses commonly found in international loan agreements, although the precise wording of the various clauses may differ to reflect the bargaining position of the respective parties. In most cases, therefore, the documentation will be drafted heavily in favour of the lenders.

A fundamental principle exposed by these agreements is that the lenders which acquiesce to the restructuring arrangement will, in return, be repaid on a fair and reasonable basis. In other words, they will be given parity of treatment *viz à viz* those creditors with "comparable indebtedness" whose debts have not been included within the rescheduling. Comparable indebtedness, therefore, encompasses any other debt which satisfies the criteria used to identify the debt being rescheduled, but which, for some reason, is not so rescheduled on similar terms. In addition, the borrower will be expected to meet its non-rescheduled obligations in the terms outlined during the restructuring negotiations. Preferential payment of such debt will obviously be disadvantageous to those lenders which agree to reschedule their own credits.

In order to promote parity of treatment, certain contractual provisions have become a common feature of the restructuring documentation. The precise wording of these clauses will obviously be tailor-made for each particular restructuring and, for present purposes, we will merely highlight some general principles.

i. Comparable Indebtedness Covenants

One method of achieving parity of treatment for different categories of **9.44** comparable indebtedness is to ensure that the debtor expressly undertakes, within the restructuring agreements, not to pay comparable indebtedness[1] without the consent of the lenders whose credits are rescheduled.

A major practical problem with this type of clause is that it will be difficult to monitor. Additionally, it may not be feasible for the debtor to comply with such a clause, since it may have the effect of disrupting its trading activities and thus be counter-productive in so far as the rescheduling lenders are concerned.

The clause may also pose legal problems in that any attempt to enforce such a covenant may, under English law, lay the lenders open to an action in tort for inducing the debtor to breach contractual obligations owed to third party creditors.

---

[99] See generally, Clark and Hughes, *loc. cit.* n. 82 above, pp. 133–134.

[1] The term "comparable indebtedness" would need to be clearly defined within the documentation in order to prevent future uncertainty as to its precise meaning.

ii. Mandatory Prepayment Provisions

9.45   Another method by which the lenders may attempt to impose parity of treatment is by incorporating mandatory prepayment provisions within the restructuring documentation. Such provisions are similar to the sharing clauses which are commonly found in syndicated loan agreements[2] and require that a reduction in the exposure of third party creditors must be accompanied by a pro-rata reduction in the exposure of those lenders whose credits have been rescheduled. The precise wording of the pro rata clause may vary and in some cases a mandatory prepayment will only be required if so requested by the lenders (or the majority of them).

iii. Other Clauses which Seek to Maintain Parity of Treatment

9.46   In addition to the clauses already identified most restructuring agreements will contain, negative pledge clauses, *pari passu* sharing clauses and cross-default clauses, the purpose of which will be to prevent discrimination and preserve equality as between creditors of the debtor. All of these clauses have been considered in detail elsewhere in this work[3] and will not be dealt with any further here.[4]

G. AVAILABILITY OF FOREIGN EXCHANGE

9.47   In the case of most sovereign restructurings the crisis which led to the need to restructure will usually have been precipitated by an insufficient supply of foreign exchange to service the country's external debt. The immediate response of most governments when faced with a major debt crisis is to impose exchange control regimes with varying degrees of stringency.[5] A sovereign state will obviously control the movement of foreign exchange following the introduction of such a régime and it will, therefore, be open to the sovereign to manipulate the allocation of foreign exchange to various state entity borrowers (for example, public corporations). It will be crucial in such a case for the lenders to inhibit the sovereign's power of discrimination with regard to foreign exchange, although in practical terms few sovereigns will be prepared to guarantee the availability of foreign exchange.

H. IMPORTANCE OF SUPRA–NATIONAL ORGANISATIONS

9.48   There are at least three supra-national organisations[6] which play an important role in sovereign restructuring negotiations. The Bank for International Settlements is often called upon to provide bridging finance whilst the recovery plan is being worked out and the World Bank has over the years developed a high level of expertise in supervising sovereign restructurings.[7]

---

[2] See generally, Chap. 7 above.

[3] See generally, Chap. 6 above.

[4] For an exposition of how the wording of these clauses may be altered in the case of a sovereign restructuring, see Wood, para. 4.13 *et seq.*

[5] See Du Plessis, *loc. cit.*, n. 83 above.

[6] The Paris Club also plays an important role in restructuring, "official" debt, see Suratgar (ed.), pp. 125–129.

[7] See Mauger, *loc. cit.*, n. 85 above, pp. 107–109.

It is without doubt, however, the International Monetary Fund (IMF) which plays the most important role.[8]

IMF membership will be vital to enhance a sovereign debtor's credit standing, and it is common for IMF membership to be a condition precedent in restructuring arrangements. Acceptance of any IMF recovery plan will also normally be a condition precedent and compliance with its terms a condition subsequent. The IMF will also play an important role in the dissemination of information concerning the debtor's financial condition, and its recovery scheme often becomes the cornerstone of the restructuring negotiations, with events of default in the new agreements commonly linked to the debtor's performance under its terms.

Despite all the criticisms which have been levelled at the IMF's role in the international debt crisis its importance within the restructuring process cannot be over-emphasised, and in many cases official creditors and commercial banks will simply refuse to commence restructuring negotiations until a recovery programme has been agreed between the IMF and the debtor country.

Conclusion

There can be little doubt that restructuring arrangements pose innumerable problems for those conducting negotiations on behalf of commercial bank creditors. In this chapter we have considered but a few of these difficulties, an extensive treatise being impossible owing to the ad hoc manner in which the arrangements are usually conducted. Each particular debtor, be it a corporate or a sovereign state, will have its own peculiar problems, and it will be the job of the bankers, together with their lawyers, to address these problems in the restructuring agreements which are finally worked out. **9.49**

---

[8] See Suratgar (ed.), pp. 131–136; Gold, "Relations between banks' loan agreements and IMF stand-by arrangements" (1983) I.F.L.R. (September) pp. 28–35; Manger, *loc. cit.*, n. 85 above, pp. 109–110.

10. Euronotes and Commercial Paper

Introduction

10.01 Most legal documents begin by endeavouring to define words and phrases used within them. To avoid confusion throughout this chapter the terms "Euronotes" and "Commercial Paper" will be used as if they had the following definitions:

> "Euronotes" means notes issued pursuant to a facility under which banks or other financial institutions have a *commitment* to purchase them[1]; and
>
> "Commercial Paper"[2] means notes issued pursuant to a facility under which, *ab initio*, there is *no* commitment either to issue or purchase notes.

In so far as the Euromarket is concerned the Euronote emerged, in volume terms, before Commercial Paper. The concept of commercial paper as used in the United States predates its use in the Euromarket, but this chapter will not touch upon the United States market though some of the legal issues which arise for United Kingdom companies will be equally relevant to commercial paper issued in the United States.

A useful starting point is to compare the Euronote with some of the common characteristics found in the Eurobond.[3] The principal distinctions, some of which we will consider in greater detail later in this chapter, are that Eurobonds are generally listed instruments (Euronotes are generally not listed); Eurobonds are generally issued in small denominations (between US$1,000 and US$10,000 each), whereas Euronotes are generally issued in large denominations (US$250,000 or more); Eurobonds generally have maturities of between three years and, say, 15 years, depending on current market conditions (Euronotes generally have maturities of up to one year); and, in view of their longer maturities, Eurobonds almost universally have extensive terms and conditions relating to their repayment and constitution. While some of the legal characteristics, such as negotiability, and some of the legal constraints, in terms of offering them for sale, are the same, this chapter will not touch upon Eurobonds generally but we will simply refer to them by way of contrast.

---

[1] On Euronotes, see generally, Fabozzi, *Floating Rate Instruments* (1986); Ugeux, *Floating Rate Notes* (1985); Bankson and Lee (ed.) *Euronotes* (1985); Henderson, "Structuring and Documenting Euronotes" (1985) (May) I.F.L.R. p. 18; Beaumont, "The difference between NIF's and RUF's" (1985) (June) I.F.L.R. p. 31; "Euronote Offer Documents under U.K. Law" (1985) (August) I.F.L.R. p. 32.

[2] On Commercial Paper, see generally, Penn, "Sterling Commercial Paper" [1986] B.F.L.R. pp. 195–209; Johnson and Keslar, "Here comes Euro C.P." (1985) (June) *Euromoney Corporate Finance*; Goodall, "Offers of commercial paper in the U.K." (1984) (April) I.F.L.R. p. 15.

[3] On Eurobonds generally, see Wood, Chaps. 8 and 9.

The Euronote market[4]

Short-term lending activities in the Euromarkets following the oil crisis in **10.02**
1973 until approximately 1980 were largely carried out by direct commercial bank lending. However, increasing competition amongst banks to
lend Eurodollars to their customers led to a steady decline in lending margins and this was coupled during the same period with a rapid increase in
the number of banks involved in the market. Large syndicated loans
became typical financing structures as we have seen elsewhere in this
work.[5]

It was out of this competitive environment that the Euronote market
developed and which led in due course to the emergence of the Euro-
commercial paper market.

It is readily accepted by most market participants that the first facility
which used the Euronote as a means of borrowing was one arranged in late
1978 by Citicorp Investment Bank Limited for New Zealand Shipping Corporation. It is important to appreciate the commercial environment in
which the structure was put together. First, there existed a healthy and
active Certificate of Deposit market in London which was used by prime
banks for raising short to medium term funds. There seemed no reason why
another prime credit like New Zealand Shipping Corporation, whose debt
was guaranteed by Her Majesty in Right of New Zealand, should not be
able to attract funds from the same investors as were buyers of Certificates
of Deposit. Secondly, New Zealand Shipping Corporation, which had
hitherto borrowed through the syndicated loan market, was keen to cut its
cost of funds as much as possible. The principal aim of the bank was to put
together a structure which would not cut its overall lending margin but
would still achieve the borrower's objective. The logic, therefore,
demanded that investors would be attracted by an instrument which to all
commercial intents and purposes was identical to a Certificate of Deposit
but issued by a prime credit rather than a bank. The product of the thinking
was the Note Purchase Facility.

Definitions (or rather the lack of legal definitions) and the use of differ- **10.03**
ent names to distinguish one bank's product from another's has often
caused confusion to those who participate in the Euronote market. A
plethora of names have been used—Note Purchase Facility; Note Issue
Facility ("NIF"); Revolving Underwriting Facility ("RUF"); Grantor
Underwritten Notes ("GUN") and so on. To the extent that these facilities involve the issue of Euronotes, the definition used at the beginning
of this chapter will continue to apply. For ease of reading, however, the
term RUF will be used throughout his chapter to describe a Euronote
facility.

Before examining the structure of a RUF in detail one can see from the
following table the rapid increase in the volume of transactions during the
period 1981–1984.

---

[4] See generally, Bullock, *Euronotes and Euro-commercial Paper*, (1987); Bankson and Lee (ed.)
loc. cit., n. 1 above.
[5] See Chap. 7 above.

10.04   FIG. I. THE GROWTH OF THE EURONOTE MARKET (BY VOLUME, US$M)[5a]

Issuer category	1981	1982	1983	1984
Sovereign	700	856	650	8,355
Corporate	100	605	320	7,191
Bank	490	745	2,425	2,480
Supranational	100	100	—	500
Total	1,390	2,306	3,395	18,256

The table is somewhat misleading in that it only records the maximum volume of Euronotes *capable* of being issued—it does not record actual volumes issued. Many facilities which have been signed have never been used as they are designed as back-stop facilities.

The Euro-commercial paper market

10.05   With the exception of one or two isolated facilities arranged in the early 1980's, there was essentially no eurocommercial paper market until mid-1985 onwards. Its emergence at this time is in part attributable to the Bank of England's attitude towards RUFs. Banks had, until the mid 1980's, treated their underlying commitments in RUFs as an off-balance-sheet risk. Given the potential volume of these commitments, as shown in the table above, the Bank of England set in train a review of the range of off-balance-sheet risks in order to assess them and as a provisional measure (still in operation, but subject now to consultation both with banks and regulators elsewhere) treated all such obligations as contingent liabilities for capital adequacy purposes and included them at a weight of 0·5 in the calculation of the risk asset ratio.[6]

This had the potential effect of increasing the level of underwriting fees payable by Issuers under RUFs and bankers once again sought for an alternative structure. The solution was Commercial Paper—where no underwriting commitment was entered into, rather banks used their placing power to sell paper to investors. Clearly, from the issuers point of view this was, to a certain extent, less satisfactory since the absence of underwriters meant they had no guarantee of funds at a fixed margin. On the other hand if they were of good credit standing and chose banks with placing power they could achieve essentially the same result and not suffer any increase in costs. As a result the Commercial Paper market grew very rapidly as the following table shows:

[5a] See Bankson and Lee (ed.), n. 1 above.
[6] See Bank of England Notice of April 3, 1985.

FIG. 2. EURO–COMMERCIAL PAPER PROGRAMMES   **10.06**

Volume and Number by Type of Issuer

	1985		1986 (until mid-July)	
	$m	No	$m	No
Corporate	7661	(52)	9610	(67)
Sovereign	3600	(22)	2554	(12)
Supranational	—	(—)	200	(1)
Bank	5950	(20)	14575	(51)
TOTAL	17211★	(94)	26939†	(131)

★ includes 9 amount unspecified/unlimited
† includes 14 amount unspecified/unlimited

Revolving underwriting facilities: documentation

The facilities syndicated in the Euronote market have taken many forms.   **10.07**
However, underlying each of them is an obligation on the part of certain
banks and financial institutions to subscribe for Euronotes at a price which
will give the Issuer funds at a fixed margin over, say, LIBOR. This obligation only arises in circumstances where the Euronotes cannot initially be
sold to others.

The greatest variations in documentation arose because of the methods
adopted by different banks for initial sales. Some have involved a tender
panel (a group of banks, brokers and dealers assembled to bid for the
Issuer's Euronotes); others have permitted only the arranger of the facility
to place the Euronotes at a fixed price (known as sole placing agency).

Because of the basic legal obligation, RUFs borrowed heavily for their
legal structure from the syndicated loan agreement[7] and therefore, many of
the legal and commercial issues which present themselves in a syndicated
loan agreement also fall to be considered when a RUF is being documented.

As with the syndicated loan agreement, the conditions precedent[8] to each
issue of Euronotes are particularly important to those undertaking the
underwriting commitment. On the one hand the Issuer will want to be
assured that it will receive the funds, particularly when it may be more difficult to place a public issue. On the other hand the underwriters, as with
banks in a syndicated loan agreement, will not want to take an unqualified
risk. In particular, they will be reluctant to take the risk of external factors
which might make the Issuer's paper less attractive to investors who, in

[7] On the basic structure of the syndicated loan agreement, see Chap. 7 above.
[8] For a general discussion of the importance of conditions precedent in international term loan
agreements, see para. 6.23 above.

normal circumstances, would be relied upon to purchase Euronotes which the underwriters would otherwise be obliged to purchase.

EXTERNAL RISK FACTORS

10.08 The usual risks which are dealt with in RUF documentation are the same as those for a syndicated loan, namely, illegality, increased costs and withholding tax provisions. In so far as illegality is concerned, it is commonly provided that the underwriters' commitment to purchase Euronotes will be subject to cancellation in the event of such illegality.[9]

Similarly, as regards increased costs (such as the cost of maintaining additional capital to cover the off-balance-sheet risk weighting given by the Bank of England and referred to earlier), the clause will be very similar to that found in the specimen agreement.[10]

As regards withholding tax provisions, and in particular the imposition thereof, it will be necessary to include a clause[11] obliging the Issuer to gross-up for any amounts which it is required to deduct either under the facility (whether in respect of fees payable thereunder or otherwise) or, on occasions, in respect of the Euronotes themselves as a separate obligation from any grossing-up obligation which may appear on the form of Euronote itself.[12] Each of these circumstances would increase the cost to the banks of purchasing the paper and make that paper less attractive in the market, thereby reducing the banks' potential earnings.

In addition to the factors which have been outlined (which affect principally the banks), there may be others which prejudice the ability of the banks to sell the Euronotes to potential investors. These would include conditions relating to a change in the Issuer (such as its creditworthiness or the validity of its obligations) and these are normally dealt with in the documentation by way of cross reference to the representations and warranties.[13]

Perhaps the most important warranty will relate to the Information Memorandum[14] which, in the context of a RUF, as opposed to a syndicated loan agreement, takes on greater significance and a slightly different form. It is important to take a slightly closer look at information memoranda generally and the additional liabilities that this may incur for underwriters.

INFORMATION MEMORANDA AND OTHER OFFERING MATERIAL

10.09 The basic intention of underwriters in a Euronote facility is to on-sell to investors the Euronotes which they are obliged to purchase under the facility. Consequently they will normally wish to have at their disposal an Information Memorandum and (or at the very least) the Issuer's latest financial statements to distribute to potential purchasers. Unlike a Eurobond

---

[9] This, in effect, will have the same impact as the clause covering illegality which is commonly incorporated into a syndicated loan agreement, see clause 11(2) in the specimen agreement. Chap. 17 below.

[10] See clause 11(1), Chap. 17 below.

[11] See clause 10(2), Chap. 17 below.

[12] See Sched. 1, Pt. I of Specimen Dealer Agreement in Chap. 18 below.

[13] See clause 12(2) in the specimen agreement, Chap. 17 below. The arguments for retaining all/or omitting some or all of these representations and warranties will be identical to those considered in para. 6.28 above.

[14] See clause 13(1)(h) in the specimen agreement, Chap. 17 below.

(which as stated earlier is generally a listed instrument) Information Memoranda prepared for prospective purchasers of Euronotes are not, as yet, subject to any statutory or regulatory requirements as to their contents.[15] The distribution of any such information may well give the implication that the information may be relied on by the potential purchaser and this may incur liability on the distributor of the information. It is common to include on the inside cover of all such memoranda specific langauge[16] displacing any implications as to the reliability of the information.

MISREPRESENTATION AND NEGLIGENCE

Under English law, if a person makes a representation as to a matter of fact **10.10**
to another person who, in reliance on it, is induced to enter into a contract with the former, the former is liable under the Misrepresentation Act 1967 to compensate the latter for any damage suffered by him as a result, unless the former proves that he had reasonable grounds to believe, and did believe, that the fact as represented was true.[17] Alternatively, the liability would be in damages for breach of warranty if the person who suffered the damage could show that it was an express or implied term of the contract between them that the matter of fact represented was true, when in fact it

---

[15] But see the discussion of Pt. V of the Financial Services Act 1986 and the EEC Directive on prospectuses referred to in paras. 10.28 and 10.29 below.

[16] A typical disclaimer might read as follows:

"The Issuer confirms that at the date hereof the description of the Issuer contained in this Information Memorandum is true and accurate in all material respects and does not contain any untrue statement of a material fact and that, to the best of its knowledge, information and belief after having made all reasonable inquiries, this Information Memorandum does not omit to state any fact which is material in the context of the issue of the Notes or the omission of which makes any statement in this Information Memorandum misleading in any material respect.

This Information Memorandum does not constitute an offer or invitation by or on behalf of the Issuer or the Banks to subscribe or purchase any Notes. No person has been authorised to give any information or to make any representation not contained in this Information Memorandum or any supplement hereto, and if given or made, such information or representation must not be relied upon as having been authorised.

The delivery of this Information Memorandum at any time does not imply that the information contained herein is correct as of any time subsequent to the date hereof. The Banks have no responsibility, express or implied, to update the Information Memorandum.

None of the Banks makes any representation, express or implied, as to the accuracy or completeness of any information in this Information Memorandum.

This Information Memorandum should be read in conjunction with the Issuer's latest Annual Report and is not intended to provide the basis of any credit or other evaluation. Each potential purchaser should determine for itself the relevance of the information contained in this Information Memorandum as supplemented from time to time and its interest in the purchase of the Notes should be based upon such investigation as it deems necessary.

The distribution of this Information Memorandum and the offering of the Notes in certain jurisdictions may be restricted by law; persons into whose possession this Information Memorandum comes are required by the Issuer and the Banks to inform themselves about and to observe any such restrictions. No application will be made at any time to list the Notes on any stock exchange."

[17] Liability for misrepresentation in relation to statements made in an information memorandum are considered in greater detail in Chap. 7 above.

was not. In these circumstances the claimant does not have to prove reliance on the fact represented as a factor inducing him to enter into a contract.[18]

It follows that it is generally safer, from a legal point of view, for no representation whatsoever to be made and no information to be distributed. If some information is given, however innocently and however helpful the provider of that information is trying to be, if it subsequently turns out to be incomplete while appearing to be complete, the law will treat the omission as misrepresentation. This is clearly of importance to intermediaries which, in the case of RUFs, would include the banks who are underwriting and also the members of any tender panel who themselves will wish to on-sell Euronotes for which they successfully tender. It is advisable therefore, in addition to the specific disclaimers[19] that are included on the inside cover of Information Memoranda to incorporate further protective provisions within the RUF documentation which would oblige the Issuer to confirm on each occasion that Euronotes are to be issued, the accuracy and completeness of the Information Memorandum and, if necessary, the latest financial statements, and oblige the Issuer to indemnify each of the intermediaries for any damages, etc., suffered by them as a result of distributing the Information Memorandum containing inaccuracies or misrepresentations.

In addition, any arranger who distributes such information to members of the tender panel or other banks will normally want to include a specific provision within the documentation which limits the extent of his responsibilities.[20]

To add to these concerns, consideration must also be given to the Companies Act 1985, the Prevention of Fraud (Investments) Act 1958, the Banking Act 1979 (and, following its introduction, the Banking Act 1987 which will repeal the 1979 Act) and various subordinate legislation enacted under the Banking Act 1979. Before addressing these questions, which form part of the overall regulatory environment in which Euronotes and Commercial Paper are issued, it is important to examine the structure of Euro-commercial Paper documentation and to consider the nature of the instruments themselves.

Euro-commercial paper documentation

10.11   A specimen Euro-commercial Paper Dealer Agreement is provided in Chapter 18 of this work, together with a number of other agreements which would normally be required in order to establish a Euro-commercial Paper Programme. We will now turn to consider some of the issues to which these documents give rise.[21]

THE DEALER AGREEMENT

The common form of Dealer Agreement originally borrowed heavily from the form and content of the Revolving Underwriting Facility and simply

---

[18] On damages for breach of warranty, see generally, Chap. 6 above.

[19] The significance of such disclaimers is considered in Chap. 7 above.

[20] Such a clause would be very similar to clause 19(1) in the specimen agreement, see Chap. 17 below.

[21] The clauses referred to hereafter will relate specifically to the specimen Euro-commercial Paper Agreement in Chap. 18 below.

omitted those sections which attempted to protect the banks against the various underwriting risks which have already been discussed.[22] As a result the documentation is much shorter than that found in a typical Revolving Underwriting Facility.[23]

The principal parties to the Dealer Agreement are the Issuer itself and the dealers.[24] Some agreements also include a guarantor, if so required, and an issue agent. In so far as the issue agent is concerned it is not uncommon for him to be party only to the Agency Agreement and not the Dealer Agreement.

The specimen agreement in Chapter 18 only contemplates the issue of U.S. Dollar denominated commercial paper, and we will consider later in this chapter the important changes which would need to be made to the form of Dealer Agreement and the form of note in order to adapt this specimen agreement to one which caters for the issue of Sterling Commercial Paper.   **10.12**

Clause 4 of the specimen agreement[25] deliberately fails to set out any specific mechanics for reaching agreement to issue Commercial Paper but rather leaves it to the parties to decide on what terms and by what means such an agreement is reached. The only limitations placed on the parties are as follows:

(i) that no issue can take place until the conditions precedent are satisfied (Clause 3);

(ii) that the aggregate amount outstanding under the programme shall not exceed a specified amount (Clause 4(2));

(iii) that the minimum denomination of Notes (at least initially) is not less than US$500,000 (Clause 4(2));

(iv) that the dealer must take delivery of Notes either in global form or in definitive form but cannot split his allocation between the two. (This provision is included so as to avoid any problems arising in the European clearing systems of identifying the owners of the global and definitive notes in relation to a particular series of Notes, by virtue of the fact that the European clearing systems treat all Notes of a particular series as fungible with each other whether they are represented in one form or two);

(v) the method by which the subscription price will be calculated (Clause 6). (It is also possible to issue Commercial Paper on an interest-bearing basis (which would lead to the purchase price formula being calculated on a different basis and the form of the note varying slightly to incorporate a reference to the payment of interest) but it is fair to say that the majority of issues are now done on a discounted basis);

(vi) the dealers will not offer, sell or deliver the Notes except in accordance with the detailed restrictions contained in the Agreement (see Schedule 3); and

(vii) perhaps most importantly, the basis on which each agreement to

---

[22] See para. 10.08 above.

[23] The Euronote Association, through its Documentation sub-committee, is presently seeking to achieve uniformity in the market for Dealer Agreements.

[24] The specimen agreement in Chap. 18, below, also includes a guarantor, which may or may not be required, depending upon the circumstances surrounding the issue, and also an issue agent.

[25] See Chap. 18 below.

issue and purchase notes is entered into under the Agreement (see Clause 10).

Generally speaking very little negotiation need take place over the terms of this Agreement and the only areas in which the dealers generally feel the need to be protected are first, those in relation to funding costs, should agreement be reached to purchase Notes and the representations and warranties subsequently not turn out to be true (see Clause 10(3)), and, secondly, those in relation to any liabilities they may incur as a result of distributing the Information Memorandum on behalf of the Issuer and the Guarantor to third parties arising out of some statement in that Information Memorandum being untrue, etc.[26]

FORMS OF COMMERCIAL PAPER

10.13 The principal considerations (aside from those mentioned elsewhere in this chapter[27]) are (i) whether or not to give the option to the Issuer of issuing global notes (which is now the predominant method); (ii) whether or not to make any global note exchangeable for definitive notes; and (iii) if the global note is to be exchangeable, when it is to be exchangeable.

The specimen agreement[28] contemplates that either globals or definitives can be issued, but it is not uncommon for globals alone to be issued.

The form of the global note (contained in Part 2 of Schedule 1 to the specimen agreement) will be lodged with one or other of the clearing systems or a common depositary on behalf of both. In order to give those persons which have entries in their accounts in the clearing systems direct rights against the Issuer, it is necessary for the Issuer and, if there is a Guarantor, the Guarantor to enter into a Deed of Covenant (see Schedule 5 to the specimen agreement) upon which they can sue directly without involving the clearing systems, as holders of the global note, in having to sue on behalf of their accountholders.

DEED OF COVENANT

10.14 As stated above the purpose of the Deed of Covenant is to give accountholders in the European clearing systems direct rights against the Issuer. The Deed operates as a unilateral declaration by the Issuer to pay "relevant accountholders" should the global note not be paid and it becomes void pursuant to its terms (i.e. it is not exchanged for definitive notes subsequent to a failure to pay thereon).

The use of a Deed Poll is an ancient method under English law for conferring benefits on third parties provided it is, of course, executed under seal.

While there are a number of foreign jurisdictions in which corporate entities do not have seals, this has not generally presented an obstacle to the use of Deeds of Covenant, provided that a wafer seal is affixed and due authority is given by the corporation for the entry into of such a deed.

The same principles as regards sealing and third party benefits apply to the giving of a Deed of Guarantee which is the commonly adopted method

---

[26] See para. 10.10 above, and also, clause 11 in the specimen agreement, Chap. 18 below.
[27] See para. headed "The Note" below.
[28] See Chap. 18 below.

for giving guarantees whether the notes are issued either in global or definitive form and obviates the necessity to print and execute a full-blown guarantee on the back of each definitive note.

The purpose behind the adoption of these methods is twofold, namely:—

(i) to reduce the costs of issuing paper under a Commercial Paper Programme; and

(ii) to acknowledge the reality of the market in which this paper is issued, sold and traded, namely through clearing systems by sophisticated financial institutions who have accounts in clearing systems.

Unfortunately, there have been a number of difficulties in co-ordinating the subscription arrangements with the clearing systems but, happily, the Euronote Association has this under review and is presently in discussion with the European clearing systems in the hope that, in due course, a common payment and settlement procedure can be adopted against the delivery of global notes.

It is against this background that a variety of Issuing and Paying Agency Agreements have been drafted to accommodate the particular procedures adopted by these agents, and it is for this reason no specimen is included, as each agent tends to have its own particular style of wishing to enter into the documentation and conforming changes between that agreement and the Dealer Agreement will need to be made where necessary.

In summary, therefore, the documentation is comparatively simple, not in need of significant negotiation and capable of being produced and signed in a short time frame.

Having said this, however, the dealers will want to be able to solicit interest for these Notes by being able to distribute an Information Memorandum. A discussion of the effects of such an Information Memorandum and potential liabilities incurred in distributing the same have already been considered.[29]

The Note

Set out in Schedule 1, Part I of the Specimen Euro-commercial Paper Dealer **10.15**
Agreement[30] is a common form of Commercial Paper note.

In spite of the sheer volume of Commercial Paper in the market and its short form, there is still a lack of consistency both in the format and the terms upon which it is issued. Over the past few years, however, the lack of consistency has been reduced and the emergence of a documentation sub-committee made up of members of the Euronote Association may reduce this still further by the development of an accepted market format (similar to that issued by the British Bankers' Association in relation to Sterling Commercial Paper and sterling certificates of deposit). Notwithstanding this lack of consistency, the following features invariably appear in the form of the Commercial Paper itself.

---

[29] See para. 10.10 above. See also the general discussion of potential liability with regard to information memoranda in Chap. 7 above.

[30] See Chap. 18 below.

"PAYABLE TO BEARER"—NEGOTIABILITY

10.16   It is essential that the holder or bearer of Commercial Paper should be in possession of a negotiable instrument. The advantages of this type of instrument over other types of chose in action, such as loan participations (in whatever form),[31] is that a "holder in due course" (*i.e.* a bona fide purchaser for value without notice of any defect in title or other intervening equity) obtains for himself perfect title even though his predecessor may not have held such a title.[32]

Both the Euronote and Commercial Paper come closest in their format to a "promissory note." Under English law a promissory note is defined in section 83 of the Bills of Exchange Act 1882, as follows:

> "a promissory note is an unconditional promise in writing made by one person to another, signed by the maker, engaging to pay, on demand or at a fixed or determinable future time, a sum certain in money, to, or to the order of, a specified person or to bearer."

The question which falls to be determined, therefore, is whether a Euronote or Commercial Paper are promissory notes under the Bills of Exchange Act. The form of Euronote and Commercial Paper which we have been considering throughout this chapter has most of the characteristics required. Unfortunately, the example,[33] by reason of the obligation to gross-up in respect of taxes required to be deducted and, in particular, the exceptions to that obligation, means that the common Euronote or Commercial Paper are not "a . . . promise . . . to pay . . . *a sum certain.* . . . " Indeed any provision which qualifies in any respect either the time for payment or the amount payable, or which imposes any condition on payment, will prevent a note from being a "promissory note" for the purposes of the Bills of Exchange Act.

Accordingly, whether a Euronote or Commercial Paper, which are themselves "promissory notes," will be regarded under English law as negotiable instruments will depend on whether by the custom of the market they are regarded as being negotiable. Ultimately, the question as to the custom of the market will need to be decided by a court based on evidence provided by experts particularly as to the existence of an active secondary market. It would now seem inconceivable that Euronotes or Commercial Paper were not regarded by the financial community as negotiable or that a court would hold them not to be negotiable instruments. While doubts were raised in the early days of the market, the volume of issues now undertaken would make a contrary view quite unacceptable. A number of other elements, however, need to be considered when deciding whether or not a particular form of Euronote or Commercial Paper is likely to be negotiable. These include the following:

(i) A number contain legends restricting the right of the holder to offer, sell or deliver them in the United States, subject to limited exceptions.[34] The view is generally held, however, that even with a restrictive legend, if

---

[31] On loan participations generally, see Chap. 8 above.
[32] On the rights of a holder for value, see generally, Vol. 1, Chap. 18 of this work.
[33] See Chap. 18 below.
[34] Such a legend can be found in the specimen agreement at Chap. 18 below.

the custom of the market is to treat the Euronote or Commercial Paper as negotiable then that is what it is.

(ii) Cash Payments—it has been suggested that negotiability requires that the holder be able to obtain cash, but that, given the constraints which have been placed on such a provision, by reason of foreign laws and settlement procedures which may preclude or obviate the necessity for cash payments, it is no longer common to give a cash payment option and that this does not, today, destroy negotiability.

(iii) Conflicts of Laws—the laws of the jurisdiction of the Issuer of the Euronote or Commercial Paper may in some way conflict with the laws governing the Euronote or Commercial Paper themselves which, in our example,[35] is English law.[36]

SECURITY PRINTING

It has become common for all Euronotes and definitive Commercial Paper **10.17** to be security printed in order to avoid difficulties relating to forged instruments. The general standards which are commonly applied are those suggested by the British Bankers' Association relating to the printing of Certificates of Deposit and which are described in their guidelines as "minimum requirements for London Good Delivery." These requirements dictate the type of paper, the method of printing, the characteristics of the note, their methods of issue together with strong recommendations as regards additional security options and office practices which should be carried out by those responsible for the issue of notes. Unfortunately, this requirement has proved to be expensive and, as we have seen earlier in this chapter,[37] there has been a significant move over the past few years away from security printed notes to global notes which are lodged with the European clearing systems and traded entirely through those systems.

DISCOUNT/INTEREST BEARING

Whether or not Euronotes or Commercial Paper are issued at a discount **10.18** from their face value (giving them a yield to maturity) or in interest bearing form, will depend upon the particular nature of the investors to whom the banks or dealers which purchase them are directing their sales effort. It is common in today's markets to provide for both types of notes and, with the exception of United Kingdom companies (who will be subject to the deep discount securities legislation contained in the Finance Act 1984[38]), there is no intrinsic legal difference between the two types of instrument.

CURRENCIES

Euronotes and Commercial Paper are only freely capable of issue in major **10.19** currencies if denominated in United States Dollars, European Currency Units (ECU), Canadian Dollars or Australian Dollars. It is possible to issue Euronotes and Commercial Paper denominated in other currencies but in so

---

[35] See Chap. 18 below.
[36] On the rules of private international law generally, see Chaps. 1 and 2 above.
[37] See para. 10.13 above.
[38] See para. 10.40 below.

far as sterling denominated notes are concerned, these are subject to the restrictions set out both by legislation and by the Bank of England and, in so far as they relate to notes of less than one year, discussion of the relevant requirements is dealt with later in this chapter when we focus on Sterling Commercial Paper.[39]

GUARANTEES

10.20 It is common also to find that Issuers are mere finance vehicles and that therefore, for credit purposes, a guarantee is necessary. These can be given in one of two ways, namely, to set out the form of guarantee (duly signed by the Guarantor) on the form of the Note (normally on its reverse) or to have the Guarantor execute a Deed Poll (a unilateral declaration in favour of holders of all notes) that it guarantees all payments due by the Issuer under the notes. An example of such a Deed of Guarantee is set out in more detail in Schedule 4 to the Specimen Euro-commercial Paper Dealer Agreement.[40]

The regulatory and legal framework

10.21 Much of the regulatory and legal framework with which bankers, issuers and lawyers are concerned is directed towards the protection of investors. No clear definition exists as to whom the investors in Euronotes or Commercial Papers are, but most likely they are banks, building societies, central government agencies and the treasury departments of large corporations. Unfortunately, the regulatory and legal framework is not drafted with these types of investors in mind. Rather they are directed towards the "widows and orphans" category of investor. It is debatable that many "widows and orphans" (or even their trustees) have US$500,000 to invest short-term!

The distinction between regulation and legal framework is at times difficult to draw. The most obvious example where the two merge is in the Banking Act 1979, to which our attention will now turn.

THE BANKING ACT 1979[40a]

10.22 Section 1(1) of the Banking Act provides that "no person may accept a deposit in the course of carrying on a business which is a deposit-taking business" unless it is a recognised bank, a licensed deposit-taker or otherwise exempt. The definitions of "deposit"[41] and "deposit-taking business"[41] are wide and their effect is that an issuer which issues Euronotes or

---

[39] See para. 10.30 below. For a description of the regulatory and legal restrictions applicable to Sterling Euronotes having a maturity of one year or more, see Bank of England Notice dated March 19, 1985 and "Medium Term Notes," (1986) (December) *Corporate Briefing* Vol. I, No. 2.

[40] See Chap. 18 below.

[40a] This Act will be replaced by the Banking Act 1987. The implications of this new piece of legislation are considered in Vol. I, Chap. I of this work.

[41] As to the meaning of "deposit" and "deposit-taking business" under the Banking Act 1979, see *S.C.F. Finance Co. Ltd.* v. *Masri* [1986] 1 All E.R. 40 (Q.B.); see also, *S.C.F. Finance Co. Ltd.* v. *Masri* (No. 2) (1987) 131 S.J. 74. For an interesting discussion of the decision of Leggatt J., see Welch, "Meaning of Deposit and Deposit-Taking Business under the Banking Act 1979—Whether Contract Unlawful and Monies Paid Recoverable," (1986) 1 J.I.B.L. 54. See also, Penn, *loc. cit.*, n. 2 above, pp. 196–198.

Commercial Paper on a regular basis would in almost all cases be "carrying on a deposit-taking business" (the deposit being the proceeds of the issue of the notes).[42]

In the early days of RUFs the method by which the parties sought to avoid this problem was to make use of one of the exemptions contained in section 1(5) of the Act. This subsection provides, *inter alia*, that " . . . in this Act 'deposit' does not include . . . a loan made by . . . a recognised bank or a licensed institution. . . . " Accordingly, it was thought that if the Issuer sold its Euronotes to a recognised bank, licensed deposit-taker or other exempt institution under the RUF as principal, even if it was known that the exempt person would be on-selling to other parties, it was possible to avoid the difficulties set by section 1 of the Act and its wide definitions.

This structure, even if it did not infringe the strict wording of the Banking Act, was frowned on by the Bank of England. As a result banks were, not surprisingly, reluctant to enter into transactions which the Bank of England regarded as "artificial." The effect of the Bank of England's view, however, was to exclude the ability of United Kingdom companies to enter into such facilities, other than through an offshore finance vehicle.

However, in order to provide a solution to this problem the Bank of England expressed the view that a breach of section 1 of the Act could only occur if an Issuer accepted the deposits in the United Kingdom. Whilst welcoming this interpretation, most practitioners were surprised as the Act contains no apparent territorial limitation. By way of explanation the Bank of England stated that, in their view, a deposit is accepted in the place where it is *first* received by the deposit-taker. Therefore, if payment is made to a bank account of the deposit-taker outside the United Kingdom, the Bank of England will not construe this as an acceptance of a deposit in the United Kingdom even if a deposit-taker is carrying on business in the United Kingdom or the arrangements for the taking of the deposit are made in the United Kingdom.

As a matter of banking practice, payment to the Issuer for securities denominated in a particular currency will almost invariably be made to a bank account in the principal financial centre of the country of that currency. Accordingly, issuing dollar denominated securities, payment for which is received in a bank account in the Issuer's name in New York, will not, under the Bank of England's interpretation, infringe section 1 of the Act.[43]

THE COMPANIES ACT 1985

In due course the relevant parts of the Companies Act which relate to Euro- **10.23**
notes and Commercial Paper will be replaced by the Financial Services Act 1986. The contents of this section of this chapter are therefore relevant as at the date of publication but consideration will need to be given in due course to the provisions of the Financial Services Act as and when they become operative, and a discussion of some of their implications is contained later in this chapter.[44]

The first section of the Companies Act which we must consider (and the

---

[42] See Penn, *loc. cit.*, n. 2 above, pp. 197–198.
[43] As regards the position relating to Sterling Commercial Paper, see para. 10.30 below.
[44] See para. 10.28 below.

one which is often overlooked) is section 81 which states that it is unlawful for any private company (as distinct from a public limited company) incorporated in the United Kingdom to offer debentures to the public or to allot or agree to allot debentures with a view to them being offered for sale to the public. In so far as United Kingdom companies are concerned, therefore, it is important to ensure that the Issuer of the paper is a public limited company (p.l.c.). Some United Kingdom financing subsidiaries of large corporations are not p.l.c.'s and this point should be investigated early in any proposal.

Other important sections of the Companies Acts which affect those concerned with Euronotes and Commercial Paper are the relevant provisions concerning prospectuses. At first glance this may not seem to be relevant (prospectuses are usually only issued in relation to listed instruments which Euronotes and Commercial Paper are not) but the definition of "prospectus" contained in the Companies Act[45] is very wide and would include any type of *written* offer to which the appropriate legal liabilities contained in the Companies Act legislation would apply.

10.24   Two approaches can be used to ensure that no "prospectus" is issued. The first approach, which was commonly used by United Kingdom incorporated companies prior to the enactment of the Financial Services Act, was to ensure that all offers of the securities were made orally. The reason for this was that a "prospectus" must be in writing[46] and this route was considered to be a practical possibility in the context of a market which primarily conducted its business on the telephone. Unfortunately, great care needed to be taken to ensure that no document, whether an Information Memorandum (*which did not itself contain an offer*) or any subsequent telexes confirming transactions concluded on the telephone, would constitute a prospectus. Concern was also expressed that quoting prices on a Reuters screen (which is common practice in the market) might constitute that form of communication as a "prospectus" if, as a matter of fact, persons could purchase notes at the prices quoted on the screens. Much would seem to depend on whether the screen facility provides a price which can be accepted electronically via screen back-up.[47] Such a facility may well constitute a document, whereas one which simply advertises the name of the company issuing the paper, yet does not *offer* the paper at a specific price, would not seem to come within the terms of section 58(1).[48] Where the screen actually provides a paper feed-out, there can be little doubt that the feed-out would be construed as a document for the purposes of section 58.[49]

---

[45] See Companies Act 1985, s.744.

[46] Strictly speaking under s.58(1) it is the "documents making the offer to the public" which by definition must be "in writing."

[47] The Companies Act 1985, s.58(1) specifically covers documents which *offer* debentures for sale to the public, so at the very least the screen facility must make an offer of sale if it is to be deemed a prospectus.

[48] *Ibid.*

[49] Although the use of a screen facility may not bring an issue within prospectus requirements under s.58, one need also consider whether it would be construed as a circular for the purposes of s.14(1) of the Prevention of Fraud (Investments) Act 1958. The 1958 Act does not define "circular," however, it is the author's opinion that ordinary usage of the term connotes a meaning incompatible with screen facilities. Both pieces of legislation are palpably out of date as far as this issue is concerned.

For the moment at least it would appear to be the case that prices quoted on screens are not "offers." Attempts by the Securities and Investment Board to persuade the Eurobond market to adopt a more up-to-date, screen-based, trading system have failed. The Association of International Bond Dealers (AIBD) has been persuaded by its members that prices quoted should not be capable of acceptance—in other words are only indicative and dealers should be free to deal at another price.

Given these uncertainties the Commercial Paper market was commonly **10.25** tapped by United Kingdom companies through their offshore finance vehicles as these vehicles were able to take advantage of the second approach, namely to ensure that there was no "offer to the public".

Section 79(2) of the Companies Act provides an exclusion from what may constitute an "offer to the public," namely, that if the Issuer is a company incorporated outside Great Britain (even if the notes are guaranteed by a British company), an offer made to a person whose ordinary business it is to buy or sell shares or debentures (whether as principal or agent) is not deemed to be an offer to the public and, therefore, falls outside the prospectus requirements of the Act. This left a situation in which United Kingdom companies and foreign companies were in a different position until the enactment of the Financial Services Act which, in section 195, now states that section 79(2) of the Companies Act 1985 shall apply for the purposes of Chapter I of Part III of the Companies Act as well as for those of Chapter II of that Part, provided that the offer was in respect of "debentures"[50] which, under the terms of issue, must be repaid within less than one year of the date of issue (*i.e.* 364 days). Accordingly, whilst there may need to be a distinction as to the maximum maturity commonly inserted in documentation[51] in general terms United Kingdom companies and foreign companies are now in the same position in so far as issues of short-dated securities are concerned.

The exemption, however, raises the question as to exactly which persons fall into the category of persons whose "ordinary business it is to buy or sell shares or debentures (whether as principal or agent)." The test is one of fact, namely, what is the ordinary business of the legal entity to which the offer is made? There may be circumstances in which the corporate treasurer of an entity seeking to invest in short-term securities whilst being himself experienced in investing in these types of instruments, cannot have an offer made to him in his capacity as representative of the legal entity, as the test relates to the ordinary business of the legal entity. In these circumstances, therefore, whether the Issuer is a United Kingdom company or a foreign company the prospectus provisions will be back in place and the first approach, the oral offer approach, would be the only safe haven.

It is to be hoped that, in due course, when Part V of the Financial Services Act comes into force (the section of the Financial Services Act dealing with unlisted securities) that this debate, as to whether or not the corporate treasurer of a large corporation is deemed to fall within the "professionals exemption," will be resolved.

---

[50] For a fuller exposition of what constitutes a debenture, see Penn, *loc. cit.*, n. 2 above, pp. 201–202 and the cases cited therein.
[51] See the specimen agreement, Chap. 18 below.

PREVENTION OF FRAUD (INVESTMENTS) ACT 1958

10.26   As with the relevant sections of the Companies Act discussed above, the provisions of the Prevention of Fraud (Investments) Act 1958 still apply but will also be replaced by the provisions of Part V of the Financial Services Act in due course.

However, for the present, section 14 prohibits the distribution, or possession for distribution, in or from the United Kingdom of "circulars" (which will include any information, including Information Memoranda, whether or not they constitute prospectuses within the meaning of the Companies Act) containing among other things, offers of securities or information calculated to lead, directly or indirectly, to *the subscription or purchase of securities.*[52]

There are, however, two exemptions to this rule which enable the majority of transactions to steer clear of the provisions of this Act. The first exemption enables circulars to be distributed to persons "whose business involves the acquisition and disposal, or the holding, of securities (whether as principal or as agent)."[53] This exemption, the so-called "professionals" exemption, is wider than that contained in section 79(2) of the Companies Act 1985,[54] although its precise scope has never been determined by the Department of Trade and Industry which oversees the enforcement of the Act.[55] The crucial issue would seem to be whether or not the entity to whom the information is sent is as a matter of fact in the business of acquiring and disposing or holding of securities. There can be little doubt, however, that if a person is regarded as a "professional" for the purposes of section 79(2),[56] that person would also come within section 14(5).[57] Accordingly, the safer and more commonly relied on exemption is the one which allows "circulars" to be distributed by or on behalf of a person who is exempt under one of the categories described in section 14(3),[57a] namely, a member of any recognised stock exchange or recognised association of dealers in securities or by or on behalf of the holder of a principal's licence. Most banks and financial institutions operating in this country fall within one or other of these categories though the matter should always be checked against the lists published by the Department of Trade and Industry.

THE LICENSED DEALERS (CONDUCT OF BUSINESS) RULES 1983

10.27   These rules were published in 1983 pursuant to powers given to the Board of Trade by section 7 of the Prevention of Fraud (Investments) Act 1958. They apply to the conduct of business by licensed dealers and, while it is not

---

[52] Prevention of Fraud (Investments) Act 1958 (PFI), s.14.
[53] P.F.I. 1958, s.14(5).
[54] The extent of s.79(2) is discussed in para. 10.23 above.
[55] For a discussion of the potential scope of this exemption, see Goodall "Offers of commercial paper in the U.K." (1984) April I.F.L.R. pp. 15–19.
[56] Companies Act 1985.
[57] PFI 1958.
[57a] *Ibid.*

expressly stated in the rules, exempt dealers are expected to comply with them in spirit. The rules, which include provisions regarding the disclosure of material interests, the contents of written offers and the circumstances in which "cold calling" is permitted, will be replaced by the provisions of the Financial Services Act 1986.[58]

FINANCIAL SERVICES ACT 1986

Part V of the Financial Services Act which, on the assumption they are not **10.28** listed, is relevant both to Euronote and Commercial Paper issues is expected to come into force towards the end of 1987, depending on how long it takes for the subordinate legislation, which is very important, to be promulgated. Before such legislation is brought into effect one can only hazard a guess at the scope and effect of the Financial Services Act 1986.

Part V of the Act prohibits the issue of advertisements offering securities unless a prospectus is filed or unless certain exemptions are available.[59] An advertisement "offers" securities in very wide terms, to cover not only a straight offer but any invitation or statement which is calculated to lead to people acquiring securities. An advertisement issued outside the United Kingdom is treated as issued in the United Kingdom if it is directed to or made available for persons in the United Kingdom.[59a] The advertisement need not necessarily be in writing. It could be by word of mouth or it could be displayed on a screen.

There are three exemptions, to which a fourth may be added. One exemption is that an order may be made by the Secretary of State to exempt advertisements issued to persons appearing to him to be sufficiently expert to understand any risks involved, *i.e.* an exclusion for professionals, but it is to be hoped that the wording will be much wider and cover corporate treasurers and others.

The second exemption, and one that is possibly more important, looks at the nature of the instrument rather than the person to whom the advertisement is addressed and will cover advertisements issued in whatever circumstances if they relate to securities appearing to the Secretary of State to be of a kind that can be expected normally to be bought or dealt in only by persons sufficiently expert to understand any risks involved. It seems likely bearing in mind that Sterling Commercial Paper is a short-term instrument and is issued in denominations of £500,000 or more, there will be an exemption which will be most helpful to the Sterling Commercial Paper market.

The third exemption can arise where the issuer already has its securities dealt on an approved exchange—which would include The Stock Exchange in London—and that exchange certifies that persons likely to consider acquiring the securities under offer will have sufficient information to enable them to decide whether to do so, having regard to the issuer's compliance with the rules of the exchange, to the nature of the securities under

---

[58] See para. 10.28 below.
[59] See Financial Services Act 1986 (FSA), s.160.
[59a] See F.S.A., s.207(3).

offer and to the circumstances of their issue, *i.e.* a Stock Exchange exemption. It is doubtful whether any approved exchange will be prepared to take the risk of saying that it is in order to offer the securities to the public under this exemption in case the issuer fails to meet its obligations in respect of that paper. Further, the exemption would not generally be available to an issue by a subsidiary since such an entity does not normally have its paper listed on The Stock Exchange.

The fourth possible exemption is in respect of Sterling Commercial Paper. It is to be hoped that the government can be persuaded to use its powers under section 2 of the Act and decide to take Commercial Paper out of Part V of the Financial Services Act altogether. This can be done under certain conditions and it is possible that the exemption could be given under this head, but presumably it would be subject to certain restrictions as to size of issues and persons to whom offers could be made.

In conclusion it should be mentioned that section 56 of the Financial Services Act also prohibits cold-calling on investors, although there are exemptions for cold-calling on certain forms of business investors which would help with most Euronotes and Commercial Paper.

EEC DIRECTIVE ON PUBLIC OFFER PROSPECTUSES

10.29   There has been in existence for some years now a draft Council Directive "on the prospectus to be published when transferable securities are offered to the public" for adoption and subsequent implementation by Member States of the EEC. This directive, which has been dormant until the beginning of 1987, has recently received considerable attention, not least from the Euromarkets.

While its effect in relation to Eurobonds and Euro-equities may be far-reaching and significant, it is hoped that the provisions of the directive will enable the Euronote and Commercial Paper markets to continue to operate with relative freedom.

The directive applies to "transferable securities which are offered to the public for the first time in a Member State" (Article 1). It is clear from this article that the directive is premised on three critical concepts, namely, "transferable securities" which are "offered to the public" for "the first time in a Member State." Unfortunately, the directive states that it is neither possible nor expedient to endeavour to have a common definition of "offer to the public" and it therefore remains a possibility that each Member State will implement the directive with its own interpretation of this phrase.

In so far as the Euronote and Commercial Paper markets are concerned, however, the provisions of Article 2 of the directive may be sufficient to avoid any necessity for a prospectus to be published in a Member State. These state that the directive shall not apply to (a) transferable securities offered in individual denominations of at least [40,000] ECU; (b) transferable securities offered to persons in the course of their trade or profession; or (c) transferable securities offered to a restricted circle of persons. While each of these exemptions leaves a certain amount to be desired in terms of their drafting, given the fact that Euronotes and Commercial Paper are commonly traded only in multiples of US$250,000 (or its equivalent), it is thought that the directive will not apply to these types of instruments.

Sterling Commercial Paper

Before April 29, 1986, there were two principal obstacles to the ability of **10.30** companies to issue Sterling Commercial Paper. The first was the Banking Act 1979, which as we have already seen prohibits anyone (apart from banks and licensed deposit-takers and certain other exempt institutions) from taking deposits in the course of carrying on a deposit-taking business. The definition of "deposit" under the Act[60] is so wide that it was thought that the issue of Commercial Paper denominated in sterling could amount to "carrying on a business which is a deposit-taking business" for the purpose of this Act.[61] Perhaps more importantly the Bank of England were of the opinion that such activity infringed the Act.[62] In order to alleviate this problem the Bank of England issued a notice on April 29, 1986, setting out the arrangements whereby companies would be able to issue Sterling Commercial Paper. This notice was followed in May by a regulation[63] under the Banking Act which effectively removed the constraints outlined above.

The notice issued by the Bank of England outlined the requirements which would have to be met in order to bring Sterling Commercial Paper issues within the exemption.[64] Those requirements relate to the following:

a. Eligible Issuers

The Bank of England has stated that an issuer, wherever incorporated, must **10.31** have net assets of at least £50m, with shares listed on The Stock Exchange in London, or be a wholly-owned subsidiary guaranteed by a parent which fulfils those criteria. In addition, if the company is incorporated in England, it must be a public limited company because under the Companies Act it is an offence for a private company to issue debentures to the public.[65] If the issuer is incorporated overseas, local advice must be sought to ensure compliance with local requirements.

It is also important to note that the Bank of England has made it clear that it did not wish to see issues of Sterling Commercial Paper being made by recognised banks or licensed deposit takers, nor by building societies, who are themselves able to issue certificates of deposit.

---

[60] Banking Act 1979.

[61] See Penn, *loc. cit.*, n. 2 above, pp. 196–198.

[62] Banking Act 1979, s.1.

[63] Banking Act 1979 (Exempt Transactions) (Amendment) Regulations 1986 (S.I. 1986 No. 769).

[64] Notwithstanding the exemption from the Banking Act given by the notice, there may still remain the need to comply with the Banking Act 1979 (Advertisements) Regulations 1985 (S.I. 1985 No. 220). These apply to any advertisement which invites the making of deposits, unless the issuer is taking deposits only at offices in the U.K. or another EEC member state, or the only invitees are all recognised banks, licensed deposit-takers or other exempt institutions. Thus, if an overseas issuer is used, it should either comply with the requirements (which include, for example, giving a summary balance sheet in the offer) or have the office through which it is taking the money located in an EEC member state, or restrict the invitees to banks, licensed deposit-takers or other exempt institutions. There is an argument that if the Bank of England's view on what constitutes a "deposit-taking business" is correct as a matter of law, then by definition the Regulations cannot apply to issues of Sterling Commercial Paper. The basic rule must be, however, that if one does not fall clearly within one of the exemptions, the position should be carefully considered.

[65] See Companies Act 1985, s.81.

The Bank of England, as a matter of policy, intended to keep the two markets separate, at least for the present. Banks can, however, guarantee issues of Sterling Commercial Paper.

b. Describing the Paper

10.32 The new legislation requires Sterling Commercial Paper to have three statements or "rubrics" on the face of it:

(1) that it is issued in compliance with Regulation 15 of the Banking Act 1979 (Exempt Transactions) Regulations 1986;

(2) that the issue is not guaranteed by any recognised bank or licensed deposit-taker or, if it is, to state the name; and

(3) if no prospectus is issued—and none normally would be—a statement by the company that it is in compliance with its obligations under the listing rules in respect of its shares listed on the Stock Exchange and that, since its last publication of information in compliance with the listing rules, having made all reasonable enquiries, it has not become aware of any change in its circumstances which could reasonably be regarded as significantly and adversely affecting its ability to meet its obligations on the paper as they fall due.[66]

One of the conclusions which can be drawn from these three requirements is that one cannot have "paperless" sterling commercial paper, although presumably it is possible to make issues using global notes. The paper issued must be transferable in minimum face value amounts of £500,000 with a maturity of less than a year but not less than seven days after the date of issue. If an overseas issuer is used, then it must, in addition, obtain consent under the Income and Corporation Taxes Act 1970[67] if it has a United Kingdom parent. Fortunately, such consent tends to be something of a formality.

c. Management of Issues

10.33 Issuers may issue Sterling Commercial Paper either directly to investors or through an intermediary who may distribute the paper and/or underwrite the issue itself. The Bank of England recognises that different kinds of intermediaries may at present be subject to differing regulatory arrangements in relation to their management activities in Sterling Commercial Paper. To avoid the unfair competitive environment to which this could give rise, the Bank has indicated that the intermediary should be a recognised bank or licensed deposit-taker, incorporated in the United Kingdom for whom the Bank has established capital adequacy and liquidity requirements.[68]

It is envisaged that other types of intermediaries will be allowed to manage issues once the Financial Services Act becomes fully operative.

---

[66] The Regulation does not impose any sanctions against a company which makes a false representation, though in most cases civil liability for misrepresentation would normally attach. See generally, Chap. 7 above.

[67] s.482.

[68] Underwritten elements of Sterling Commercial Paper will be treated by the Bank of England as contingent liabilities of the underwriting institutions, subject to a weighting of 0·5 in assessing capital adequacy.

NEGOTIABLE/DEBENTURE

As with Euronotes and Commercial Paper, it is most important that Ster- **10.34**
ling Commercial Paper is negotiable. The analysis earlier in this chapter[69]
relating to the issue of negotiability is also applicable with regard to Sterling
Commercial Paper.

It will also be important to determine whether sterling commercial paper
constitutes a debenture within the meaning of section 58.[70]

Precisely what constitutes a debenture within the meaning of section 58
has defied any precise legal definition.[71] Nevertheless, though it may be difficult to determine what is and what is not a debenture, as Gower points
out, "the juristic nature of the underlying transaction is never in doubt".[72]
The description which has received most favour was given by Chitty J. in
Edmonds v. *Blaina Furnaces Co.*,[73] where he described it as a term which
imports or acknowledges a debt. This definition was given wider interpretation the following year in the *Levy* case,[74] where Chitty J. remarked " . . .
in my opinion, a debenture means a document which either creates a debt or
acknowledges it, and any document which fulfils either of these conditions
is a debenture".

Applying these, and more recent interpretations,[75] to Sterling Commercial Paper, it is difficult to argue that such instrument is not a debenture.
Certainly, it is clear that the regulatory authorities have assumed this to be
the case, and seem to expect those in the market to treat Sterling Commercial Paper as if it were a debenture.

THE COMPANIES ACT 1985

The Companies Act prohibits a company offering its debentures to the pub- **10.35**
lic unless, in essence, one of the following circumstances applies: (i) the
company offers its debentures only by word of mouth and not in writing;
(ii) the company files a prospectus; (iii) the company files listing particulars;
or (iv) in the case of a foreign company[76] the company offers its debentures
only to professionals, *i.e.* persons whose ordinary business it is to buy or
sell shares or debentures.[77]

The real difficulty with these exemptions arises not at the time of the

---

[69] See para. 10.16 above.

[70] Companies Act 1985.

[71] See *Levy* v. *Abercorris Slate and Slab Co.* (1888), 37 Ch.D. 260 where Chitty J. remarked
(p. 264) " . . . I cannot find any precise legal definition of the term [debenture], it is not
either in law or commerce a strictly technical term, or what is called a term of art," see also,
N.V. Slavenburg's Bank v. *Intercontinental Natural Resources Ltd.* [1980] 1 W.L.R. 1076, where
Lloyd J. said " . . . I note that . . . [many judges] of great eminence have declined to
attempt a definition of what is meant by a debenture. I certainly do not propose to rush in
where they have feared to tread . . . there is no hard and fast definition."

[72] Gower L.C.B., *Gower's Principles of Modern Company Law* (4th ed., 1979) p. 401.

[73] (1887) 36 Ch.D. 215; see also, *Topham* v. *Greenside Glazed Fire-Bricks Co.* (1888) 37 Ch.D.
281, where it was held that a memorandum or a deposit of title deeds was not a debenture,
since the memorandum contained no acknowledgement of a debt or covenant to pay.

[74] *Levy* v. *Abercorris Slate and Slab Co.*, n. 71 above.

[75] See, for example, *Lemon* v. *Austin Friars Investment Trust Ltd.* [1926] 1 Ch. 1; *N.V. Slavenburg's Bank* v. *Intercontinental Natural Resources Ltd.*, n. 71 above.

[76] *cf.* Financial Services Act 1986, s.195 in relation to short-term instruments.

[77] For a fuller discussion of these exemptions, see Penn, *loc. cit.* n. 2 above, pp. 202–204.

primary issue but with secondary issues or secondary trading. Thus, if an offer of commercial paper is made with the intention that it will be re-offered to the public—and, since it is in tradable form, it would be difficult to argue that that is not the intention—if it *is* re-offered within six months, then it is deemed to have been the intention at the outset. Any subsequent offer will also have to comply with one of the exemptions outlined above. In practice, the original or primary issue will not be accompanied by a prospectus or listing particulars and, therefore, the only two realistic choices are either to limit offers to professionals[78] or else to make offers only by word of mouth.

A further exemption which is sometimes suggested is the "private placing" exemption,[79] but this is almost certainly not available for Sterling Commercial Paper, for two reasons. First, there is clearly an intention to create a secondary market, and secondly, the only major decision in this area, namely, *Governments Stock and other Securities Investment Co. Ltd.* v. *Christopher*[80] indicates that that exemption is not available for *bearer* instruments but only registered instruments.

PREVENTION OF FRAUD (INVESTMENTS) ACT 1958

10.36 As we indicated earlier in this chapter,[81] section 14 of the PFI Act prohibits the distribution of circulars relating to the sale of securities. It also prohibits the distribution of offers to take part in arrangements where the purpose is to make a profit. Therefore, even if one argues that Commercial Paper is not a debenture and therefore not a security, an issue of Sterling Commercial Paper is still likely to be within section 14 of the PFI Act.

There are, however, two exemptions available under the PFI Act. The first of these relates to debentures only and covers documents distributed by a licensed or exempt dealer in securities.[82] The second relates to documents distributed to persons whose business involves the acquisition and disposal, or the holding, of securities whether as principal or as agent. As we have already seen,[83] this definition is slightly wider than the definition found in the Companies Act[84] and probably would extend to corporate treasurers. The second exemption is also available whether or not Commercial Paper constitutes debentures.

One final point worthy of mention is that the PFI Act introduced a criminal offence[85] in respect of any person who makes a reckless or deliberately misleading or false statement or dishonestly conceals information in inducing or attempting to induce another person to enter into an agreement relating to securities. In addition, there are the usual contractual and other misrepresentation liabilities, liabilities for negligence, breach of statutory

---

[78] Unfortunately, it seems likely that the definition of "professionals" probably excludes corporate treasurers.

[79] See ss.59 and 60 of the Companies Act 1985.

[80] [1956] 1 W.L.R. 237.

[81] See para. 10.26 above.

[82] The term "authorised dealer" is used conveniently to denote a dealer not required by the 1958 Act to obtain a licence.

[83] See para. 10.26 above.

[84] Companies Act 1985, s.79(2).

[85] See PFI Act, s.13.

duty, fraud and so on, which are applicable on an offer of Commercial Paper as they are on an offer of any other form of security.

CHANGES TO SPECIMEN DOCUMENTATION

With the exception of the obvious changes to the face of the note referred to above, the principal change usually made to adapt a typical Euro-commercial Paper Dealer Agreement to one relating to Sterling Commercial Paper is the incorporation of additional warranties confirming that (i) the shares of the Issuer or, as appropriate, the Guarantor are listed on The Stock Exchange in London; (ii) the net assets of the Issuer or, as appropriate, the Guarantor are not less than £50,000,000; (iii) the Issuer or, as appropriate, the Guarantor is in compliance with its listing obligations and not aware of any material adverse change in its financial position; and (iv) the Issuer and, if appropriate, the Guarantor is not a bank or other licensed institution under the Banking Act 1979 nor a building society, all of which merely reflect the contents of the Bank of England's notice relating to eligible issuers.   **10.37**

TAX ON SHORT-TERM INSTRUMENTS

We will now turn to consider some of the taxation aspects of short-term debt issues (such as Commercial Paper) in the United Kingdom for the run-of-the-mill United Kingdom industrial or commercial company.   **10.38**

The three principal questions to be addressed are as follows.

(1) Will there be a withholding tax?

(2) Will the issuer get tax relief for any financing costs, whether they are borne as interest or in discount form?

(3) What is the position on currency gains and losses if the issue is of paper denominated other than in sterling?

Three supplementary points also often arise.

(1) Is the issuer going to get tax relief for its legal fees and other front-end costs that will be borne?

(2) Is VAT going to be a problem?

(3) Is stamp duty going to be a problem?

1. Will there be Withholding Tax?

In so far as the securities which have been considered in this chapter are concerned, namely, fixed short term securities, interest will usually be short interest. Short interest in the United Kingdom, paid by United Kingdom issuers, is never subject to United Kingdom withholding tax. United Kingdom withholding tax provisions on United Kingdom-source interest apply only to annual interest (interest in respect of obligations which have a clear life in excess of one year or which have a life that may exceed one year) (see s.54, I.C.T.A. 1970). However, it is more common for securities to be issued on a discount basis.   **10.39**

Further, it is equally clear that original issue discount, when paid out at maturity by an issuer, is not subject to withholding tax (since it will almost invariably be a "deep discount" within section 36 of F.A. 1984) and that applies both with short-term notes and with long-term notes, thus the length of the notes' maturity is of no relevance *vis-à-vis* withholding tax on an original discount.

Having a committed facility does not turn what would otherwise be short interest, free of withholding tax, into annual interest, subject to withholding tax—so long as it is not wholly contrived (*e.g.* if the securities will almost always end up with the same holders).

Additionally, if the paper is issued on a discounted basis the 1984 Finance Act requires a legend to go on the notes which broadly states, " . . . This is a deep discount note. The amount of the discount is X and you will pay tax on that amount".

It was thought at one time that, if this legend was not included on the note, then the note was not of deep discount. This issue presented some practical difficulties in the market.

In general, issuers make a token effort to comply with this particular requirement and incorporate a legend which acts as a health warning that it is a deep discount note. It is thought that the Revenue has no sanction against issuers who do not incorporate such a legend on a note and the issue is probably perceived as a matter between the note issuer and the investor.

2. Will the Issuer get Tax Relief?

10.40   The answer to this question varies significantly between discount notes and interest-bearing notes.

The basic rules relating to short interest are that, if you are an investment company—for example, a group holding company or an investment trust— you will get no relief whatsoever for short interest that you pay unless you pay it to a United Kingdom bank (section 248 of I.C.T.A. 1970). However, as the Commercial Paper market is all about getting paper out into the wholesale markets, and not about banks lending money, the banking exemption will not apply. If, therefore, the issuer, is an investment company or a group holding company, (*i.e.* somebody who is not trading) it should not issue interest-bearing notes.

Short interest, by contrast, will be tax-allowable for trading companies. There may be difficulties with those holding companies carrying on a hybrid activity: partly trade, partly investment holding company activity. They will have to be able to show that the money being raised was being used for the purposes of their trading activity rather than for putting more money into a subsidiary, for example. If the money is being used for investment purposes, this would effectively mean that the company has been split into two parts. The money would have gone to the investment side of the company's activities and in those circumstances interest would not be allowable.

If interest-bearing notes are important for the particular market into which the paper is being sold a United Kingdom issuer must be a trading company using the money for trading purposes. If such a situation does not exist and it is still a commercial requirement that the notes bear interest, then an offshore vehicle should be used as the issuer.

By contrast, the rules relating to discount notes are altogether easier. The rules state that original issue discount is tax-allowable; no distinction is made between trading borrowers or investment borrowers (see Schedule 9 of F.A. 1984).

The only point to note is that the tax relief usually comes not on an accruals basis, over the life of the particular notes, but in the accounting period in which the particular issue of notes *matures*. It is not a good thing, if the company's tax year ends in December, to make an issue which is going to mature on January 2 because in such a situation tax relief will have to be put off for a full year. It is far better to make an issue where the notes mature on December 30 and thus get the tax relief in the early period. It is effectively a cash basis of taxation.

3. Tax Position of Investors

The Inland Revenue issued a paper through the Bank of England in 1986 **10.41** stating that, in their view, short-term notes fell to be taxed in exactly the same way as certificates of deposit. The result was that, regardless of the deep-discount rules and regardless of the amount of interest received, any profit that was made by an investor in buying a note and then selling it or holding it to maturity would be taxed as an income profit.

While this position may be arguable, most investors have accepted the position. Thus, from the investor's point of view, the basic assumption is that whatever commercial profit is made will be taxed as income and in most cases will be taxed as income when received, which will be at maturity.

4. Relief for the Front-end Costs?

The answer to this question will depend on whether the transaction is on **10.42** circulating capital account. For an original discount issue, there are no problems in obtaining relief for front-end costs. They will be tax-deductible in full (para. 3(6) Schedule 9, F.A. 1984), as and when paid, and if a long-term facility is being set up there is no requirement, therefore, to amortise over the life of the issue the costs of setting up a longer-term facility. Full tax relief can be taken up-front.

5. Will any of the Various Commissions Paid be Subject to VAT?

The issue of the notes itself will not give rise to any VAT charges, nor will any commissions chargeable by the selling groups or by the dealers who are setting up the particular programme for the company be subject to VAT.

6. Is Sterling Commercial Paper Subject to Stamp Duty on Transfer?

The Inland Revenue have confirmed generally that there will be no stamp duty on issues of Sterling Commercial Paper.

7. Issues Denominated in a Foreign Currency

Unfortunately, we have here to consider the anomalous areas that exist in **10.43** the United Kingdom tax system. Let us take as an example a United Kingdom industrial or commercial company which raises a foreign currency borrowing. It has been told by its bankers that the best thing to do is to borrow dollars and enter into a currency swap[86] back into sterling, thereby getting cheaper sterling than if it had borrowed sterling directly.

From a tax point of view, this has to be broken down into three transactions. First of all there is the dollar loan. Secondly, there is the swap under which dollars have been initially sold for sterling and ultimately dollars will be acquired back at a fixed sterling price. Thirdly, there is the sterling investment.

These three transactions will, in most cases, be treated as transactions on capital account, whether the borrower is a trading or an investment company. If this sort of facility is being set up, it is being set up for the long term and for use for the long term.

The company, therefore, has a dollar borrowing which is a liability; it has a currency swap which is an asset under which it can buy dollars forward at a fixed price and which may turn out to be very cheap when they are bought; and there is a sterling investment.

10.44 There are no problems on the sterling investment in terms of currency movements. There are no problems at all on the dollar borrowing if it is on capital account; if the company makes a currency gain on such borrowing it is not chargeable. The problem area comes with the swap. If, under the swap, the company is able to buy dollars cheaply, by comparison with the spot rate at the time the transaction is closed out, the Revenue will undoubtedly conclude that those dollars are an asset for capital gains purposes— foreign currency is an asset for capital gains purposes. They will conclude that the company has a base cost for that asset equal to the forward price which, if the swap has done its job, will be less than the current spot price. The profit, the comparison between the forward price and the spot price, will be taxed as a capital gain at maturity—30 per cent. off the top unless you have current year or carried forward capital losses or current year trading losses.

This may not seem fair as there is a corresponding loss on the dollar borrowing. The resulting position therefore is that the company has a sterling asset which will not attract problems, but it also has a currency swap, which is an asset that may give rise to a tax charge. There is also a loss on the dollar borrowing for which there is no relief.

The result of this state of affairs has been to force United Kingdom companies to issue foreign currency denominated paper with a swap attached through offshore vehicles. United Kingdom companies can issue the dollar paper in the Netherlands, write the swap in the Netherlands and then lend sterling back to the United Kingdom under a long-term facility, so that the interest paid out of the United Kingdom on that facility is annual interest with no withholding tax under the United Kingdom double-tax convention.

While there are no tax problems in the Netherlands there are some incidental costs; administering a Dutch company; paying tax to the Dutch authorities on the margin that they will require, at their tax rate of 46 per cent. The tax charge at 46 per cent. in the Netherlands on the extra eighth or a quarter per cent. will be matched out by a tax deduction in the United Kingdom on the extra eighth or a quarter per cent. at our present rate of 35

---

[86] On currency swaps generally, see Chap. 11 below.

per cent. So, although people tend to say that the 46 per cent. charge in the Netherlands is daunting, in fact it comes down to an 11 per cent. charge, and may well be a little less than that.

The only residual point on raising loans through the Netherlands is that the tax scheme outlined above will work only if the company is genuinely managed and controlled in the Netherlands.

11. Swaps and Related Instruments

CURRENCY AND INTEREST RATE SWAPS[1]

Evolution of the currency swap/back-to-back and parallel loans

11.01 The international swap market grew out of the sterling/dollar back-to-back[2] and parallel loans[3] which were entered into between U.S. and U.K. entities during the 1970s. These loans arose in response to the restrictive U.K. exchange controls and the limited availability to the U.K. subsidiaries of U.S. companies of fixed rate sterling funds. A parallel loan essentially involves two separate loan transactions. As fig. 1 below illustrates, a parallel loan might involve a U.K. parent and a U.K. subsidiary of a U.S. parent on one side of the transaction and a U.S. parent with a U.S. subsidiary of a U.K. parent on the other. In our example the U.K. parent would make a sterling loan to the U.K. subsidiary of the U.S. parent in parallel with a dollar loan made by the U.S. parent, at the prevailing dollar/sterling exchange rate, to the U.S. subsidiary of the U.K. parent. The maturity of both loans would be identical and the result would be that exchange rate fluctuation could be hedged and U.K. exchange controls circumvented. The sterling loan and the dollar loan would each constitute separate loan transactions and would normally be documented in separate and independent loan agreements.[4]

FIG. 1 PARALLEL LOAN

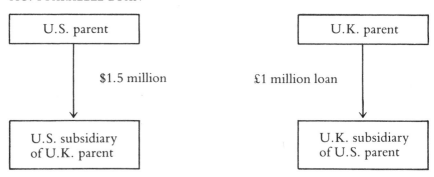

Essentially, back-to-back loans are parallel loans but between two parties only. As fig. 2 on page 225 indicates, in the back-to-back loan the two subsidiary companies have been dropped out of the direct loan transactions and the U.S. and U.K. parent companies lend their respective currencies direct

---

[1] On currency and interest rate swaps generally, see Price and Henderson, *Currency and Interest Rate Swaps* (1984).
[2] See fig. 2, p. 225.
[3] See fig. 1.
[4] In some cases the parent companies might be expected to guarantee the loans of their respective subsidiaries.

to each other. If the funds are actually required by the subsidiary companies they will simply be on-lent as a domestic group transaction as indicated by the broken lines in our example.[5]

These arrangements gave rise to complex issues in relation to set-off (par-   **11.02** ticularly in relation to four party parallel loans) and the giving of security as well as creating potential liability to tax on notional currency gains. Back-to-back and parallel loans constituted borrowings for the purpose of borrowing restrictions and were "on balance sheet."

The currency swap involving only a single agreement solved a number of these problems whilst producing identical cash flows. Instead of loans being made in sterling and dollars (as under the back-to-back and parallel loan structures) the parties entered into a spot exchange transaction for the sale of one currency for the other and a forward exchange transaction under which the original sale and purchase were reversed. As no loans had been made, interest was not paid, but, at periodic intervals, fees corresponding to interest payments on the relevant currency amounts were exchanged. The currency swap had the further advantages of not constituting borrowings and of falling into the category of "off-balance sheet" items for accounting purposes.

FIG. 2 BACK–TO–BACK LOAN

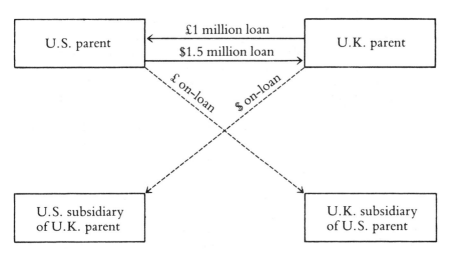

Currency swaps: basic structure

The basic structure of a currency swap (or, more accurately, a cross cur-   **11.03** rency interest rate swap) is as outlined above.[6] The parties agree to exchange equivalent amounts (at the then current spot rate of exchange) in

---

[5] See fig. 2.
[6] See also, figs. 4 and 5 below, pp. 227 and 228.

two different currencies. This initial exchange is effected on the commencement date of the swap. Additionally, the parties agree to effect a re-exchange (or reverse foward exchange contract) of the same principal amounts on a specified future date. During the term of the swap the parties make periodic payments to each other, the amounts of which are calculated by reference to the principal amounts exchanged and to fixed and/or floating rates of interest. It will not necessarily be the case that the respective payments are made on the same periodic basis, for example, the fixed rate payer may make annual payments whilst the floating rate payer makes payments on a semi-annual basis.

Arbitrage: the birth of the rate swap

11.04   At the time of its inception the principal economic justification for a currency swap was that it enabled an investor to acquire a foreign currency denominated investment, whilst at the same time entitling it to re-acquire the amount of its investment in its domestic or other currency of account at a specific future date, thereby eliminating any exchange risk which might otherwise have been incurred on such foreign currency investment. Although the abolition of exchange controls in the U.K. in 1979 removed one of the original justifications of currency swaps, the volume of currency swaps transacted continued to increase rapidly as corporate treasurers saw the arbitrage opportunities which currency swaps offered. A borrower can raise funds denominated in a foreign currency but bearing a lower interest rate than would be payable on its domestic borrowings, and, by swapping the proceeds of such foreign currency borrowing into its domestic currency, can obtain funds at a lower overall cost of borrowing, even when the expenses of the swap are taken into account. In today's market the underlying motivation for most swaps is arbitrage, and, accordingly, it is usually the case that at least one party has access to a particular capital market or source of funds to which the counterparty either does not have access or can only gain access on relatively less attractive terms. Where that party, notwithstanding having access to the particular market or source of funds, wants funds from another market or source to which the counterparty has access, the respective requirements of both entities can be met by a swap.

11.05   It is from arbitrage that the interest rate swap evolved,[7] the first rate swaps being transacted during 1982. In our specimen example in fig. 3, one entity ("B") can borrow fixed rate funds more cheaply than another entity ("A") but wishes to raise floating rate funds; A is able to raise floating rate funds at a lower margin than the margin which it pays when raising fixed rate funds. A and B therefore independently borrow identical principal amounts in the same currency (in our example, dollars) for the same period from different markets and/or funding sources, A paying a floating rate of interest and B a fixed rate. Through a rate swap (which may either be a direct contractual arrangement between A and B (as in our example) or be through intermediaries) A and B "swap" interest obligations. A agrees to

[7] See fig. 3 on p. 227.

pay to B periodic payments calculated by reference to the principal amount and to a fixed rate of interest whilst B agrees to pay to A amounts calculated by reference to the principal amount and a floating rate of interest. The result is that both parties have obtained funds priced in the desired way and since the difference between the rates at which A and B can raise fixed rate funds is greater than the difference between the rates at which they can raise

FIG. 3 INTEREST RATE SWAP

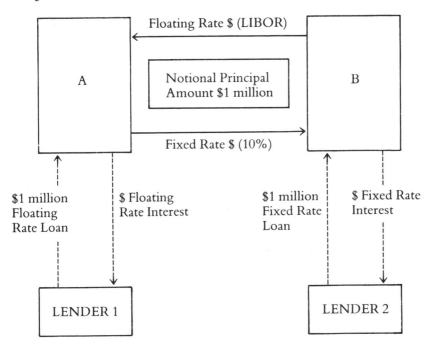

FIG. 4 CURRENCY SWAP

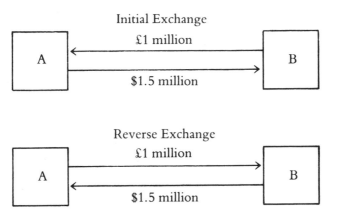

FIG. 5 CROSS CURRENCY INTEREST RATE SWAP

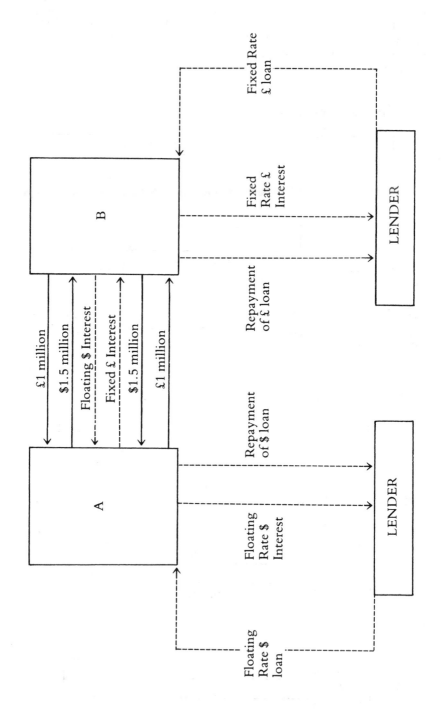

floating rate funds, by splitting, or arbitraging, both parties will effectively be paying interest at a lower rate than that at which the funds would otherwise have been available. The currency swap has become an extension of this arbitrage where not only interest but also currency is swapped.[8]

Documentation and related issues[9]

The rapid expansion of the swap market and the increased volume of transactions has given rise to several important developments in the area of documentation. As the number of market participants and the level of competition have increased, so swap transactions have been concluded more quickly and control has shifted from the transaction originators to the dealers. The terms of swaps are now agreed by dealers over the telephone and confirmed by telex with a subsequent exchange of formal documentation governing the transaction. Notwithstanding these changes, swap transactions are still documented in reasonable detail in view of the desirability of dealing comprehensively with the events (both fault-related and non-fault related) which might give rise to an early termination and with the determination of the compensation upon early termination. Participants have become increasingly aware, however, of the advantages of standardising documentation so as to minimise the exposure between the time when the terms of a particular transaction are agreed and the time when the formal documentation is signed so as to minimise the costs associated with a swap. The emergence of master agreements and standard form documentation and codes is a response to this awareness. Before returning to look at master agreements and standard codes in more detail, we will consider the principal provisions commonly found in single currency and/or rate swap agreements.

11.06

I. DEFINITIONS

Where, as is often the case, a swap is being entered into in connection with another transaction (a borrowing or an investment, for example), the definitions section will serve to reflect the nature of the underlying transactions being hedged by the swap. Particular attention should be paid to drafting the definitions so as to ensure that the provisions of the swap match those of the underlying obligations; for example, floating interest rates should be calculated by reference to the same underlying rates and in respect of identical calculation periods so as to ensure that the floating payments under the swap so far as possible equal the relevant payments under the underlying obligation. Care should also be taken to check that the various "business day" definitions conform so as to ensure that the relevant amounts are

11.07

---

[8] See fig. 5 on p. 228.
[9] For an annotation of sample clauses in a complete swap agreement, see Gooch and Klein, *Swap Agreement Documentation* (1987). See also, Price and Henderson, *loc. cit.* n. 1, esp. Chap. 7; House, "Documenting and implementing a loan swap" I.F.L.R. (October, 1984) pp. 29–32; Gray, Kurz and Strupp, "Structuring and documenting interest rate swaps" (September, 1983) I.F.L.R. pp. 14–19.

received on the same dates as the underlying obligations are to be discharged.

It is in the area of definitions that standard codes for swaps have had a particular impact. The "Code of Standard Wording, Assumptions and Provisions for Swaps" published by the International Swap Dealers Association (the "ISDA Code") is designed to establish a "uniform vocabulary" for dollar rate swap agreements. The ISDA Code contains a comprehensive set of definitions which can be incorporated into a particular rate swap agreement by cross-reference thereby shortening, and hopefully simplifying, the documentation, whilst at the same time giving swap dealers and their lawyers a common vocabulary. The provisions of the ISDA Code are discussed in more detail below.

2. PAYMENTS

11.08 The payments clause will contain the provisions for the making of, in the case of a currency swap, the principal exchanges and, in the case of both currency and rate swaps, the fixed and/or floating periodic payments.

In the case of a rate swap under which all payments are being made in the same currency, it is considered advantageous where the payment dates coincide, to provide for the payments to be netted off against each other with only an amount equal to the excess of the larger amount over the smaller amount being paid. There are two principal advantages arising from payments being made on a net basis:

(i) it is safer from a credit exposure point of view and avoids the problem of the conditionality of payments, since the parties do not need to be concerned as to whether the other party has made its payment; and

(ii) in the case of a cross-border swap, netting of payments has the advantage of reducing or, in some cases, eliminating, payments which might otherwise be subject to withholding taxes.

Under a currency swap, payments will usually be made gross, since they are denominated in different currencies; netting can, however, be achieved by converting one of the amounts due into the currency of the other amount at the then current spot rate of exchange and requiring only the excess of the larger amount over the smaller amount to be paid by the party owing such larger amount.

11.09 This clause will also contain the payment mechanics, designating the time and place at which, and specifying the relevant bank accounts to which, payment is to be made. Whether or not payments are being made on a net basis, it is customary to include a provision to the effect that the obligations of the parties to make each payment shall be conditional upon the other party having already made, or contemporaneously making, all payments then due from such party, thereby at least attempting to reduce the risk of one party being required to pay in circumstances where the counterparty has failed to pay. Although it is the desire of both parties to a swap to ensure that neither one is required to make payment unless and until it receives the corresponding payment due from the counterparty, in certain circumstances this will not be possible. For example, in the case of a dollar/yen currency swap it is inevitably the case that the party making the yen payment on any particular payment date will be required to make such payment prior to the corresponding dollar payment being made by the counter-party. This will be the case in any currency swap where the time difference between the financial centres in the countries of issue of the relevant curren-cies is such that at no time are banks open for business in both financial centres at the same time.

The safest way, from a credit point of view, of eliminating the exposure risk for the party making the first payment is for the parties to establish escrow arrangements with one or more banks. Such an arrangement would require each party to pay the amount due to be paid by it to the escrow bank and to give to the escrow bank instructions to pay that amount to the coun-terparty upon receipt by the escrow bank of the amount payable by the counterparty on such payment date. One difficulty with such an arrange-ment is that the party paying in the financial centre which opens later will be required to pay the relevant amount to the escrow bank on the previous business day in order to ensure that payment can be made at the specified time in the other financial centre. The current practice appears to be to avoid such cumbersome and expensive payment mechanisms, particularly where one of the parties is a bank. In currency swaps, where the exposure risk is increased as a result of the amounts of principal to be re-exchanged at maturity being considerably greater than the periodic payments, the parties may be given the right to request such an arrangement.

An alternative method of dealing with the exposure risk is to provide that a party receiving any payment in advance of the time at which it is required to make the corresponding payment to the counterparty will be deemed to hold such amount in trust for the counterparty until such time as it makes its own payment to the counterparty. Due to difficulties in relation to the equitable remedy of tracing and the creation/registration of charges there are doubts as to the enforceability of such a provision.

3. GROSSING–UP

Since any reduction in the amount received by either party to a swap will **11.10** adversely affect the economic viability of the transaction for the recipient it is customary to include in swap documentation (particularly in relation to cross-border swaps) a grossing-up provision requiring the parties to gross-up payments in the event of any withholding tax being applicable so as to ensure that the payee receives the full amount which it would otherwise have received.[10] However, a requirement to gross-up will almost invariably result in the transaction becoming uneconomic from the point of view of the party required to pay the additional amounts. Accordingly, under a swap agreement, it is customary to include a right whereby the party required to gross-up can terminate the swap. Such right will usually require the parties to negotiate in good faith, initially in order to seek a substitute basis for making payments which will avoid the necessity for payments to be made subject to taxes and for the affected party to gross-up. Only where the parties are unable to agree upon such an alternative basis (*e.g.* by one of the parties changing its booking office) will the affected party be entitled to terminate the swap.

[10] On withholding tax and grossing-up generally, see Chap. 5 above.

4. JUDGMENT CURRENCY

11.11 A judgment currency clause is normally included in order to protect the parties against foreign exchange losses which might be incurred as a result of payment being made by the counterparty otherwise than in the currency of obligation (whether pursuant to a court judgment or otherwise). Such a provision should always be included in currency agreements and in any cross-border rate swap. Generally speaking, such provisions are in similar form to the currency indemnity provisions found in loan agreements[11] and, accordingly, their enforceability is subject to the same uncertainty.

5. CONDITIONS PRECEDENT[12]

11.12 The parties may require that the relevant agreement only becomes effective upon delivery of specified documents and evidence as to the due authorisation and execution of, and the obtaining of all consents in connection with, the relevant agreement. Unlike a conventional loan agreement, the conditions precedent will frequently apply to both parties. Many agreements include delivery of documentation evidencing the authority of the person who executed the swap as a covenant which must be complied with within a specified period of the agreement being signed. Where both parties to a swap are banks it is less usual to find conditions precedent. Legal opinions[13] are not normally required in connection with inter-bank swaps although it is common practice for banks to take opinions in respect of corporate counterparties. Corporate counterparties may also be required to deliver a copy of their latest financial statements as a condition precedent.

6. REPRESENTATIONS AND WARRANTIES[14]

11.13 Limited representations and warranties are normally given by each party in relation to its corporate capacity, the due authorisation, execution and delivery of the relevant agreement, the obtaining by it of all necessary governmental and other consents and non-continuance of events of default. A representation may also be included as to the non-applicability of withholding taxes to swap payments. Representations and warranties on the part of one party only may be required in certain circumstances: for example, a corporate counterparty may be required to represent and warrant as to the accuracy of the financial statements delivered as a condition precedent. It is not usual in a single swap agreement to provide for repetition of representations and warranties.[15]

---

[11] See clause 26 in the specimen agreement, Chap. 17 below.
[12] On the legal significance of conditions precedent generally under English law, see Chap. 6 above.
[13] On legal opinions generally, see Chap. 16 below.
[14] For a comparison of how representations and warranties in loan agreements differ from those found in swap agreements, see Chap. 6 above.
[15] Such a clause is common in loan agreements, see Chap. 6 above. See also, clause 13(2) in the specimen agreement, Chap. 17 below.

7. COVENANTS[16]

Covenants in swap agreements are usually of limited scope. Those which   **11.14**
are included customarily provide for maintenance of all necessary governmental and other consents, an obligation to notify the counterparty of the
occurrence of an event of default and a covenant that the obligations under
the swap will continue to rank *pari passu* with all other unsecured and unsubordinated indebtedness. Swap agreements involving a corporate counterparty may contain additional covenants on the part of such party.

8. SUPERVENING ILLEGALITY: IMPOSITION OF WITHHOLDING TAXES

In addition to the events of default entitling the non-defaulting party to ter-   **11.15**
minate the swap, there will usually be at least two further events entitling
the parties to terminate prior to the end of the term. Supervening illegality
is included as an event entitling the parties to terminate a swap in cross-
border rate swaps and in almost all currency swaps (in view of the risk of
imposition of foreign exchange controls which may have the effect of rendering unlawful foreign currency denominated payments). The right is
usually expressed to be exercisable by either party so as to enable the affected party (*i.e.* the party for whom performance has become illegal) to terminate prior to the occurrence of an event of default which would otherwise
inevitably arise upon its first failure to make payment, or so as to enable the
non-affected party to terminate prior to it being required to make a payment at a time when it knows the affected party will be unable to perform
its future obligations. The latter case would be particularly relevant if the
affected party is paying on an annual basis whilst the non-affected party is
paying on a semi-annual basis. It may be the case that the effect of the supervening illegality is to render the compensation provisions themselves unenforceable. However, inclusion will still be of value (a) where the illegality is
prospective and payment of the compensation amounts can be made before
the change in law takes effect, or (b) in a currency swap which provides for
conversion and netting out of compensation amounts, when payment by
the affected party in its currency of obligation has been rendered illegal.

As discussed previously,[17] in the event that either of the parties is
required to gross-up as a consequence of the imposition of withholding
taxes, subject to any requirement to negotiate in good faith in order to seek
acceptable means of re-arranging the transaction, the affected party will
usually be entitled to terminate the swap.

One further change in circumstances which may give rise to an early ter-   **11.16**
mination option exercisable by the affected party is change in reserve, liquidity and risk/asset ratio requirements. The effect of such change may be to
impose upon banks additional costs in connection with swaps. In the past an
increased costs clause such as that customarily found in Eurocurrency loan
documentation has only occasionally been included in swap documentation.
However, in view of the proposals put forward in March 1987 by the Bank
of England in relation to "credit equivalent amounts for interest rate and

---

[16] For a comparison of how the covenants in a loan agreement differ from those found in swap
  agreements, see Chap. 6 above.
[17] See para. 11.10 above.

foreign exchange rate related instruments" and the action being taken by banking regulatory authorities in other jurisdictions the authors expect that provisions in relation to reserve, liquidity and risk/asset ratio costs will be included more frequently in swap documentation in the future. Any such obligation to indemnify in respect of increased costs imposed on the parties will probably be accompanied by a right exercisable by the party required to make the indemnity payment to terminate the swap, such right only being exercisable if good faith negotiations (as referred to above in the context of grossing-up) have not provided an acceptable substitute basis enabling the transaction to be restructured so as to avoid such additional costs. The proposals of the Bank of England referred to above are discussed in more detail below.

11.17   Each of the foregoing events can be described as non-fault related. Where a swap is terminated as a result of the occurrence of an event of default in respect of one of the parties, it is the majority view that the defaulting party should be required to compensate the non-defaulting party for any losses which it has suffered as a consequence of the early termination, but that the non-defaulting party should not be required to make any payment to the defaulting party even in circumstances where movements in currency exchange rates and/or interest rates mean that the non-defaulting party enjoys a "windfall" profit upon such early termination. In the case of non-fault related terminations, it is common practice to regard the relevant termination as being of a neutral character and whilst the non-affected party will always be compensated for any losses, it may be required to make payment to the affected party in respect of the losses incurred by the affected party upon the early termination to the extent only that the non-affected party makes a gain. Where both parties to a swap are affected parties, it is usual practice, provided at least one of the parties will incur losses upon the early termination, to provide for sharing of the losses/gains. Usually no payments are made if neither party has incurred any loss.

9. EVENTS OF DEFAULT

11.18   The events of default found in swap documentation are usually relatively limited in scope when compared with those found in conventional loan documentation.[18] Under a conventional loan agreement, once the facility has been drawn down by the borrower there are few, if any, remaining obligations to be performed by the lender. Accordingly, it is in the lender's interests to ensure that the events of default are drafted so as to enable it to accelerate the loan as soon as it becomes apparent that the borrower is in financial difficulties.[19] But contrast, under a swap the parties will both have continuing obligations and, accordingly, the events of default (or the majority thereof) will be reciprocal, both parties having the benefit (and, if too strictly drafted, the burden) thereof. The events of default customarily contained in swap agreements are non-payment of amounts due under the

---

[18] See generally, Chap. 9 above. See also, clause 16 in the specimen agreement, Chap. 17 below.
[19] For a fuller exposition of how the events of default clause might be worded to achieve this purpose, see Chap. 9, para. 9.24 above.

agreement, breach of covenant (which is not remedied within any agreed grace period), material breach of representation or warranty and insolvency. Swap agreements may also include a cross-default, although this is frequently limited either to other swap transactions or to other transactions between the parties (or their affiliates). Care should be taken to ensure that any cross-default clause does not catch swaps prematurely terminated as a result of the occurrence of a non-fault related event.

In relation to default remedies, the swap agreement should entitle the non-defaulting party either to leave the agreement in place and sue the counterparty for breach of contract or to terminate the future payment obligations of both parties under the agreement, thereby giving rise to the right to receive compensation determined in accordance with the compensation provisions contained in the agreement.

10. COMPENSATION

Almost all swap agreements provide for compensation on early termination **11.19** to be determined in one of the following ways[20]:

(i) A general indemnity by the defaulting party in favour of the non-defaulting party; or

(ii) Payment calculated by reference to a formula to determine the discounted value of replacement cash flows by a combination of borrowing and investment; or

(iii) Payment based on the cost of replacing the terminated swap with a swap (having a term equal to the unexpired term of the terminated swap) with a counterparty who undertakes rights and obligations the same as those of the defaulting party.

The method for calculating compensation payments in the event of early termination has evolved as the swap market has developed. At the outset compensation was usually payable on an indemnification basis, *i.e.* the defaulting party indemnified the non-defaulting party for its losses and damages occasioned by the premature termination of the agreement, without specifying how such losses and damages should be calculated. The development of the swap market brought about a slightly more "scientific" approach to the calculation of compensation payments in the form of compensation formulae. As the depth of the market continues to increase, the formula based approach is itself being replaced by an "agreement value" approach whereby compensation payable is measured by reference to the cost to the non-defaulting party of entering into a replacement swap.

Certain points should be borne in mind in the context of an indemnification approach. Under the principles laid down in *Hadley* v. *Baxendale*[21] it was held that unless the party in breach of a particular contract was aware of another transaction or agreement to which the non-defaulting party was a party, the defaulting party would not be responsible for any loss of profit or other damages incurred by the non-defaulting party as a consequence of its

---

[20] For an interesting exposition of various approaches for computing damages upon early termination of a swap, see Gooch and Klein, "Damages provisions in swap agreements" (October, 1984) I.F.L.R. pp. 36–40.

[21] (1854) 9 Exch. 341.

inability to fulfil such other transaction or agreement. It was held in a later case[22] that if at the time of entering into the contract the parties were aware of other contracts the performance of which was dependent upon the fulfilment of the first contract, in the event of a default under the first contract the defaulting party would be liable in respect of any losses or damages suffered by the non-defaulting party as a consequence of the non-defaulting party being unable to fulfil its obligations under the other contract. In the context of swaps this is particularly relevant given that both parties will usually be entering into transactions under which their obligations are hedged by entering into the swap or which are substantially the reverse of the swap. This will almost invariably be the case for intermediary banks which have "matching" swaps on either side. Accordingly, in the context of an indemnification approach, it has become the practice to make specific reference to matching transactions entered into by each party in order that any loss or damage incurred by such party in relation to such matching transactions may be brought into account in the event that the swap is prematurely terminated. Whilst such a provision entitles the parties to bring into account transactions entered into prior to the termination date, it is uncertain whether it would entitle the non-defaulting party to enter into a replacement swap at the time of breach/termination. Accordingly, further provisions are usually incorporated within the indemnification provisions, entitling the non-defaulting party to attempt to enter into arrangements in order to cover its exposure (by virtue of termination of the existing swap) and to mitigate losses which might otherwise be incurred.

11.20   Notwithstanding the breadth of indemnification provisions, there remain considerable difficulties in determining and reaching agreement as to the costs and losses which should be taken into account on an early termination. In the interests of greater certainty it has become increasingly common to determine the amount of compensation payable on an early termination by reference to a pre-agreed formula incorporated in the agreement.

A formula approach determines compensation by reference to the cost to the non-defaulting party of re-creating for the non-defaulting party the cash flows under the terminated swap by reference to a combination of borrowing and investment made at the market rates prevailing on the termination date.

Various arguments are put forward as to the merits of the indemnity and formula approaches. Whilst the indemnity is relatively simple, to draft it does give rise to potential difficulties in relation to the treatment of non-fault related terminations. In practice, in order to prove the loss or damage incurred as a consequence of early termination it will be necessary for a party to carry out a calculation not wholly dissimilar from the formula approach. Indeed, one argument advanced in favour of the formula approach is that it reflects the various steps which the non-defaulting party would actually take in order to re-create its position under the now terminated swap and, accordingly, is more likely to result in payment of compensation equating to its actual losses. A further argument advanced in favour of the formula approach is that it lends greater certainty in relation to

---

[22] *Victoria Laundry (Windsor) Ltd.* v. *Newman Industries Ltd.* [1949] 2 K.B. 528.

the amount which will be payable on termination; a claim under an indemnity is open to potential defences based both on questions of fact and law (*e.g.* failure on the part of the indemnified party to mitigate its losses), whereas a formula is a pre-agreed express contractual provision which should be subject to fewer uncertainties and defences.

As the liquidity of the swap market has increased it has become possible **11.21** to determine damages by reference to the cost to the non-defaulting party of entering into a replacement swap with another counterparty on substantially the same terms as those applicable to the terminated swap. The cost to the non-defaulting party of arranging such a replacement swap is usually determined by reference to "quotes provided by leading dealers in the relevant swap market" (as in the ISDA Code). One advantage of an agreement value approach over a formula is that it is considerably simpler from a documentation viewpoint and the amount is considerably easier to calculate. It is also argued that an agreement value approach more accurately reflects the action which would be taken by a non-defaulting party in the event of termination of a swap and, accordingly, is more likely to produce a figure which corresponds to its actual losses or gains. However, this is clearly only likely to be the case in circumstances where there is a market of sufficient depth; there is an implicit assumption in the agreement value approach that the swap market will continue at the same level throughout the term of the relevant swap. However, in relation to any type of swap in respect of which quotations are not readily available, an alternative approach is recommended. In any event, it is advisable to include a "fall back" approach which will apply in the event that it is not possible to obtain any or a sufficient number of quotations for a replacement swap. Whilst it is fairly widely accepted that the non-defaulting party should obtain more than one quotation, there is no uniform practice as to how the market value should then be determined on the basis of such quotations, *e.g.* the average of such quotations. It may well be argued that if the non-defaulting party is to mitigate its losses, the agreement value should correspond to the lowest quotation obtained. The agreement value approach does not make any allowance for any differences in the credit standing of the original counterparty and the replacement counterparty. Supporters of the agreement value approach argue however that the variation in credit standing is unlikely to be as high as that under a formula approach which will usually replace the fixed rate payer with a government obligation.

One risk which is common to the various approaches is that where the **11.22** terms of the relevant agreement provide for one-way compensation payments (*i.e.* only the defaulting party is required to make payment upon premature termination) there is a greater likelihood of the provision being construed as a penalty and accordingly, not being enforceable. The English courts will however seek to give effect to freely negotiated contractual terms and would probably give effect to a provision in a swap agreement entitling the innocent party to retain any "windfall" profit provided that retention of such profit did not of itself constitute a penalty. It is thought to be the case however that where compensation provisions may result in payment being made by either the defaulting or the non-defaulting party (two-way payments) the chances of such provisions being construed as a penalty are more remote.

11. INDEMNIFICATION

11.23   Swap agreements will usually provide for reimbursement by the defaulting party of all costs and expenses incurred by the non-defaulting party in suing for any amount due under, or in connection with enforcement of, the relevant agreement.

12. ASSIGNMENT: TRADING IN SWAPS

11.24   As the volume of swap business has increased, greater attention has been focused on the "trading" of swaps. As interest and/or exchange rates move, so the benefit which a party derives from a particular swap will increase or decrease and such party may prior to the expiry of the term of the swap wish to realise its gain or, alternatively, restrict its exposure. Furthermore, a party which has entered into a swap in connection with a matching investment or borrowing may, because it has decided to reduce its investment or has prepaid its borrowing, wish to terminate the swap. To date, it has been comparatively rare for swap agreements to confer upon either party a voluntary early termination right (other than in the specific non-fault related circumstances discussed above). However, as confidence in the depth and continuity of the swap market increases, the possibility of incorporating optional termination rights becomes more likely. A party's right voluntarily to terminate a swap will be subject to payment of an early termination payment calculated in accordance with a pre-agreed formula. In the absence of such a right, a party may seek to realise its gain/terminate its exposure under a particular swap by way of "assignment." Swap agreements usually contain contractual restrictions on the right of the party to assign and/or transfer its rights and obligations under the relevant swap and, therefore, the prior consent of the other party will usually be required.

Some banks, in their standard form swap documentation, attempt to include a right to transfer both their rights and obligations to third parties or, where more restrictively drafted, to third parties which fulfil specified criteria, *e.g.* the transferee is in the same group of companies or is a recognised bank. From an English law viewpoint, it is incorrect in the context of a swap to talk in terms of an "assignment." In view of the mutual obligations of the parties to a swap to make future payments, transfer of a swap requires not only an assignment of rights but also an assumption of obligations—*i.e.* a novation is required to which the other original counterparty must be a party.[23] Accordingly, it will be necessary to obtain the concurrence of the original counterparty to such arrangement. The proposed transferee may have an inferior credit standing to the transferor or, even if the transferee has a similar credit standing, there may be other valid reasons why the original counterparty would wish to withhold its agreement. Clearly, the counterparty would not be willing to consent if such transfer or assignment were to give rise to withholding taxes or other increased costs, *e.g.* as a result of different treatment for the purposes of permitted exposure or adequacy requirements imposed by the Bank of England or other relevant regulatory authority.

---

[23] On the general principles of English law in relation to assignment and novation, see generally, Chap. 8 above.

Where a party wishes to extricate itself from a swap arrangement where there is no voluntary early termination right or possibility of novating, it is open to such party to enter into another swap by which it effectively reverses the original swap whilst locking into any profit which has arisen as a consequence of movements which have occurred in exchange and/or interest rates since the commencement of the swap. By such an arrangement, the party will inevitably increase its exposure as it then carries the risk of default by both the original swap counterparty and the new swap counterparty.

13. GOVERNING LAW AND JURISDICTION

The governing law will usually be either English or New York law and the **11.25** appropriate submission to the jurisdiction will usually be included,[24] including appointment of a process agent to receive service. Although there are stylistic differences between English law and New York law governed agreements, most swap agreements will be enforceable under the laws of either jurisdiction. Where appropriate, a waiver of immunity clause should also be included.

Whilst the chosen governing law will govern the contractual obligations of the parties,[25] the laws of other jurisdictions will continue to be relevant; the effect of the insolvency of one of the parties will be determined by the law of the jurisdiction in which the insolvency proceedings are commenced.[26] Questions of the corporate capacity of a party to enter into and perform a swap and of the authority of the person signing the agreement will be determined by the law of the jurisdiction of incorporation of such party.

Master agreements: insolvency

One result of the increase in the volume of swaps transacted is the develop- **11.26** ment and increased use of master agreements by parties (particularly financial institutions) entering into more than one swap with one another. A master agreement creates a standard set of terms and conditions which can be incorporated into all swap transactions between the parties to such agreement. Such an agreement enables the parties to document subsequent swap transactions by way of a short confirmation (which may be given by telex) or written contract, the principal purpose of which is to set out the financial terms of the particular swap and, to the extent required, modify or supplement the terms of the master agreement.

One issue of particular interest in connection with master swap agreements is the relationship between the various swaps entered into pursuant to the agreement and, more particularly, whether they will be treated as part of a single transaction or as a series of related individual transactions having standard terms and conditions in common. One advantage of their being

---

[24] As the precise wording which such a clause may follow, see generally, Chap. 2 above.
[25] On the proper law of the contract generally, see Chap. 1 above.
[26] *Ibid.*

treated as wholly separate transactions is that, to the extent permitted by the terms of the master agreement, the parties will be able to dispose of individual swaps thereby promoting the growth of the secondary market. The alternative approach, namely to regard the subsequent swaps as part of the same transaction, has obvious credit analysis advantages and may also ensure that all swaps under the master agreement are afforded the same treatment in the event of the insolvency of the relevant counterparty. Given the executory nature of a swap (*i.e.* under which both parties have obligations remaining to be performed), treating the various swaps as a single transaction would be of value in preventing a trustee or liquidator from adopting those swaps under which the insolvent counterparty has gained a benefit as a consequence of movements in interest and/or exchange rates whilst repudiating those which have moved to the disadvantage of the insolvent party (and in respect of which the non-defaulting party would be required to claim in the liquidation of the insolvent party as an unsecured creditor). A master agreement under which the various swaps are regarded as a single transaction may enable the solvent non-defaulting party to have all swaps showing a benefit to the insolvent party netted out against those which show a benefit to the non-defaulting party.

11.27   As discussed above, a master agreement has obvious attractions from a credit exposure point of view. Where the payment dates under different swaps coincide it is usually the case that the master agreement will provide for netting of all payments due in the same currency on the same day and it is only to the extent that the aggregate amount payable by one party exceeds the aggregate amount payable by the other party that payment will actually be made. It is customary under the terms of a master agreement to provide that an early termination will apply simultaneously to all swaps under the master agreement and for liquidated damages to be calculated on an aggregate net basis. Notwithstanding the credit exposure advantages, it is desirable to include a degree of flexibility; for example, in relation to cross-border or currency swap master agreements, it should be borne in mind that circumstances may arise in which only some of the swaps are affected, *e.g.* illegality in relation to specified, but not all, foreign currencies. Additionally, the likelihood of one of the parties wishing to assign or novate individual swaps should not be ignored.

A recurrent concern in many banking transactions is: what happens if the borrower becomes insolvent? In the case of a simple loan, the position is normally straightforward; the lender can prove in the insolvency for a liquidated sum equal to the outstanding amount of the loan. In the case of both rate and currency swaps, there will potentially be future flows of funds to both parties. As previously discussed, a rate swap under which all payments are being made in the same currency may provide for payment on a net basis and for only the balance to be paid one way or the other. However, in the case of a currency swap, netting off, although possible, will not normally apply and there will be periodic payments both ways in addition to the final payments on maturity of the swap of the principal amounts exchanged. If one party to a swap becomes insolvent, the last thing that the solvent party will wish to do is to have to continue making payments to the insolvent party with no prospect of receiving corresponding payments from the other party.

Under English insolvency law neither the making of an administration **11.28**
order or a winding up order nor the passing of a resolution by a company to
be voluntarily wound up will, of itself, terminate contracts to which the
insolvent company is a party.[27] However, whilst an administrator has
power to carry on the business of the company of which he is appointed
administrator[28] he is not bound to perform contracts to which the company
is a party. Such a failure is, however, likely to result in a repudiation of the
contract. Similarly, a liquidator can perform a contract to which the company of which he is appointed liquidator is a party but is not bound to do so
and can repudiate the contract or application can be made to the court for
the contract to be rescinded.[29]

Whilst on the basis of current interest or exchange rates it might appear to
an administrator or liquidator that it would be to the benefit of the insolvent
company for a swap to be continued, there will be a risk that if rates subsequently move the other way, the liquidator or administrator will ultimately end up in a negative position. The liquidator or administrator may,
therefore, decide not to perform the swap and in the case of a liquidator
repudiate it or seek its rescission, even if, at the relevant time, the swap is
showing a benefit to the insolvent company.

As has been described above, swap agreements normally contain events
entitling either party to terminate the obligations of both parties to make
future payments which would have been made in the ordinary course, on
the occurrence of specified events of default which will invariably include
insolvency proceedings in relation to the other party. Upon termination of
the future payment obligations of the parties by the non-defaulting party,
the relevant compensation provisions will apply. Where the operation of
such provisions can only result in a payment to the non-defaulting party,
the payment will be expressed to be by way of liquidated damages and to
represent a pre-estimate of the losses which will be incurred by such party as
a result of the early termination. If, however, the calculation could result in
a payment either way, it will be more difficult to categorise it as anything
other than a pure contractual obligation. In the former case, the liquidator
or administrator might seek to avoid the payment on the basis that it represents a penalty and not a genuine pre-estimate of the loss suffered by the
non-defaulting party. If the argument succeeded the solvent party would be
left having to prove its actual loss. If the payment consists of no more than a
bare contractual payment obligation, then the repudiation of the contract by
the liquidator will result in a repudiation of the obligation to make the payment contracted for and the other party will then have to prove in the liquidation for its actual loss. The liquidator could, acting in this way, seek to
have some other method of calculating the loss used.

The making of an administration order will not of itself prevent the non- **11.29**
defaulting party from exercising its rights to terminate its obligation to
make future payments under the swap, but it may prevent such party from
taking any action to recover any amounts expressed to be payable to it as a

---

[27] For a fuller exposition of the impact of insolvency upon a company's affairs, see Vol. 1,
Chap. 28 of this work.
[28] See Insolvency Act 1986, Sched. 1.
[29] Insolvency Act 1986, s.186.

242 SWAPS AND RELATED INSTRUMENTS

result of the early termination, since under section 16 of the Insolvency Act 1986, during the period when the administration is in force "no . . . proceedings and no execution or other legal process may be commenced or continued . . . against the company or its property except with the consent of the administrator or the leave of the court. . . . " These restrictions would not however appear to restrict the exercise of rights of set-off.

11.30   Rule 4.10 of the Insolvency Rules which have been made under the Insolvency Act 1986 provides that where there are mutual debts between a company in liquidation and a solvent company the smaller debt shall be set-off against the larger debt and that only the balance shall be accounted for by the solvent company or shall be proved for by the solvent company in the insolvency of the other company. This rule replaces the provisions previously contained in section 31 of the Bankruptcy Act 1914. The effect of these provisions should be that, where two parties have entered into several swaps some of which show a benefit to one party and others show a benefit to the other party, the solvent (non-defaulting) party should be able to set-off any amounts payable by it to the insolvent party against the amount payable to it by the insolvent party. To the extent they apply, these provisions are mandatory.[30] Probably the set-off provisions not only apply to amounts immediately due and payable at the commencement of the winding up, namely, in the case of a voluntary winding up, at the time the resolution is passed or, in the case of a winding up by the court, when the petition for the winding up is presented,[31] but also to other amounts payable provided they could be ascertained when the account was taken. However, the wording of Rule 4.90(3) could be interpreted to mean that if at the time the termination provisions under the swap were triggered the non-defaulting party knew a meeting had been convened to pass a resolution for the defaulting party to be wound up or that a winding up petition had been presented, any contractual payments which flow from the termination may not be capable of being set-off. Where currencies other than sterling are involved they probably have to be converted into sterling at the time when the winding up commenced.[32] Amounts owing by one company in a group cannot be set-off against amounts due to another company in the same group even if both are in liquidation.

The foregoing description of the effect of insolvency is based on English insolvency law. However, this will not always be applicable, even if the relevant swap agreement or agreements are governed by English law. The law to be applied in any insolvency proceedings will be the law of the place where the proceedings are instituted.[33] If, therefore, an English bank enters into a swap with an Italian company in respect of which insolvency proceedings are commenced in Spain, the effect of the insolvency on the contractual rights and obligations of the parties will generally be determined in accordance with Spanish law. The law of the relevant jurisdiction in which the insolvency proceedings are taking place may be substantially different from that of England. For example in the United States, unless it can be

---

[30] See *National Westminster Bank Ltd.* v. *Halesowen Presswork & Assemblies Ltd.* [1972] A.C. 785.
[31] See s. 129(1) of the Insolvency Act 1986.
[32] See *Re Lines Bros. Ltd. (In Liquidation)* [1982] 2 W.L.R. 1010, [1982] 2 All E.R. 183.
[33] See generally, Chap. 1 above on the private international law principles which govern such issues.

shown that the swap constitutes "financial accommodation," provisions in the agreement entitling the solvent party to terminate its obligation to make future payments because of the insolvency proceedings may not be effective.[34]

STANDARD DOCUMENTATION

In June 1985 the International Swap Dealers Association published the first **11.31** edition of the Code of Standard Wording, Assumptions and Provisions for Swaps for the purpose of establishing a "uniform vocabulary for dollar rate swaps." In 1986 this was succeeded by the 1986 Edition which expands the coverage of the ISDA Code (by, inter alia, including limited representations and warranties, covenants and events of default) but leaves the basic mechanics and provisions of the 1985 Edition unchanged and is still applicable only to rate swaps. The ISDA Code is neither a guide to swaps nor a standard form of agreement[35] but is a comprehensive set of definitions and presumptions. The parties to a swap may either adopt the ISDA Code in its entirety or may simply incorporate it into an agreement (whether a master agreement or a single swap agreement—the 1986 Edition distinguishes between a swap agreement which may govern one or more swaps transactions and a single swap transaction) particular provisions of the ISDA Code. The parties are at liberty to amend or supplement the provisions of the ISDA Code as they think fit. Express provisions in the agreement between the parties will apply to the extent that they are inconsistent with the terms of the ISDA Code.

In certain matters the ISDA Code creates a presumption which will apply **11.32** in the absence of any express statement by the parties, *e.g.* as to time and manner of payment, rounding up of averages of quotations and the effect of payments falling due on non-business days. On other matters the ISDA Code contains a number of different options one of which must be selected by the parties. In relation to floating rates, the ISDA Code contains definitions for seven basic types of floating rates and permits choice between obtaining those rates from published sources (*e.g.* the Reuters Monitor system) or calculating the same on the basis of quotations obtained from reference banks or dealers. By indicating the option selected, the relevant term or presumption is incorporated into the particular agreement. In other areas the ISDA Code simply provides a framework and the parties must provide the details in the relevant agreement. For example, the ISDA Code contains references to a default rate but it is left to the parties to specify what that rate should be. Similarly, although the ISDA Code refers to "Events of Default" and defines certain types of event of default (*e.g.* "Breach of Covenant") the parties themselves must specify the relevant events.

The ISDA Code contains formulae for calculating the fixed and floating amounts payable under rate swaps (including, in the case of the 1986 Edi-

---

[34] For a fuller discussion, see Henderson and Cates, "Termination provisions for swap agreements under U.S. and English insolvency laws" in *Swap Finance*, (Ed. Boris Antil) Vol. 2, Part VI, Chap. 3.

[35] The International Swap Dealers Association have since the time of writing published forms of master interest rate swap agreement (incorporating the ISDA Code, 1986 Edition) and of master interest rate and currency exchange agreement.

tion, mechanics for the compounding of floating amounts). There are detailed provisions in relation to the determination of the selected floating rate. By simply specifying either "Gross Payments" or "Net Payments" the parties can specify whether payments are to be made in full or on a netted basis. In relation to early termination, Article 12 of the ISDA Code provides three different approaches for calculating the compensation payable on termination of the relevant swap or swaps, namely, agreement value, formula and indemnification. In selecting the compensation basis the parties may provide either that the amount is to be recovered by whichever party suffers the greater loss by reason of the early termination or, alternatively, only by the non-defaulting party. Where the parties designate "Two Way Payments" payment will be made to the party suffering the greater loss without regard to the question of responsibility for the early termination. Where "Limited Two Way Payments" are specified the identity of the party entitled to receive payments will depend upon the nature of the event giving rise to the early termination. Where the termination has come about by virtue of the occurrence of an event of default in relation to one of the parties, the defaulting party will be obligated to make a compensation payment to the other party in an amount equal to such party's measure of damages. If, however, the early termination is attributable to the occurrence of a non-fault related termination event, payment will be made to the party suffering the greater loss in an amount equal to one-half of the difference between the parties' respective losses/gains.

11.33   In relation to governing law, the ISDA Code creates a presumption in favour of New York law and the submission to the jurisdiction of the New York courts. It is of course open to the parties to specify a different governing law and, accordingly, it is possible to incorporate the ISDA Code, or particular provisions thereof, into an English law governed rate swap or master agreement.

In August 1985 the British Bankers' Association published recommended terms and conditions for both interest rate and currency swaps (the "BBAIRS terms"). The BBAIRS terms are intended to be regarded as normal market practice for transactions in the London Interbank Market with maturities up to and including two years and which fall within the categories covered. It is stated in the introduction to the BBAIRS terms that banks and brokers in the London Interbank Market are expected to quote on the basis of the BBAIRS terms and should make it clear to potential counterparties if they wish to deal on any other terms. The statement that in the absence of such a contrary clarification banks and brokers in the London Interbank Market are expected to follow the normal custom of the market by quoting on the basis of the BBAIRS terms will not, without more, operate to incorporate the BBAIRS terms into a swap. Accordingly, any swap to be transacted on the basis of the BBAIRS terms should include an express statement to such effect. It is also open to the parties specifically to adopt the BBAIRS terms in relation to transactions having maturities in excess of two years.

Whilst the ISDA Code operates as a comprehensive definitions section, the BBAIRS terms constitute a set of standard agreements including events of default, representations and covenants. Whilst the ISDA Code contemplates that the parties may accept some but not all of the provisions and/or presumptions of the Code, the BBAIRS terms contemplate by way of additional documentation only an exchange of confirmations specifying the financial terms of the particular transaction. Clearly, whereas the stated purpose of the ISDA Code is to establish a "uniform vocabulary," the BBAIRS terms are seeking to influence general market practice.

Just as the basic approaches of the ISDA Code and the BBAIRS terms dif- **11.34–** fer, so there are a number of differences between the provisions and pre- **11.39** sumptions provided for in the two documents. Whilst the ISDA Code allows the parties to select any one of seven basic types of floating rate, the BBAIRS terms provide for the "BBA Interest Settlement Rate" which, broadly speaking, is determined on the basis of rates quoted to the "information vendor" by eight of the twelve member panel of BBA designated reference banks. Whereas under the ISDA Code the parties are free to select from the three specified approaches to compensation payments (and to provide for an appropriate "fall back"), the BBAIRS terms simply provide for compensation on an indemnification basis. The governing law applicable to the BBAIRS terms is English law. Whilst the ISDA Code is limited to dollar rate swaps, the BBAIRS terms provide for swaps denominated in dollars, sterling, deutschemarks, Swiss francs and yen as well as containing standard terms for cross currency swaps.

TAXATION

The taxing authorities in most jurisdictions have been reluctant to take a **11.40** formal position on the treatment of swap payments. The U.K. tax treatment for payments and receipts under currency and rate swap agreements is governed by Revenue practice in the absence of specific legislation or, as yet, case law.

In the case of a currency swap which provides for the payment of periodic payments calculated by reference to interest rates, such payments are not regarded by the U.K. Revenue as "yearly interest of money" for the purposes of section 54 of the Income and Corporation Taxes Act 1970 ("ICTA 1970"). The currency exchange is regarded as a sale of currency with a forward resale. Since there is no underlying loan, the periodic payments are not characterised as interest payments for U.K. tax purposes. Instead, the U.K. Revenue takes the view that the periodic payments constitute "annual payments" falling within section 53 of ICTA 1970. Accordingly, a U.K. party making such payments, whether to a U.K. party or to a non-U.K. party, is, subject to the exceptions discussed below, required to deduct income tax at the basic rate from such payments and to account to the U.K. Revenue for such deduction. In relation to a U.K. party making such payments, the payments will constitute either trading expenses or "charges on income" and, accordingly, they will either be taken into account in calculating, or allowable as a deduction against, total profits.

The exceptions to the requirement to withhold basic rate income tax are as follows:—

1. By way of concession, the U.K. Revenue has confirmed that if a "recog- **11.41** nised bank" (*i.e.* a bank carrying on a bona fide banking business in the U.K. and which is formally recognised as such by the U.K. Revenue) enters

into a currency swap acting as principal (and not merely as an arranger), swap payments paid by or to such recognised bank may be made gross without deduction of income tax under section 54(2) of ICTA 1970. The foregoing concession applies not only in relation to U.K. incorporated banks but also to the U.K. branches of overseas incorporated banks.

The Deputy Chairman of the Board of Inland Revenue set out the following guidelines in a letter to the Bank of England in September 1979:—

(i) Where a bank carrying on a bona fide banking business in the U.K. enters as principal into a currency swap agreement, periodic payments paid to the bank or by the bank may be made gross without deduction of tax;

(ii) Periodic payments will be treated as normal expenses or receipts of the banking business and will enter into the computation of its trading profits;

(iii) Where periodic payments are paid to such a bank by a U.K. trading company they will constitute a normal trading expense of that company under Schedule D Case I, and where paid by an investment company will be allowed as a "charge on income" under section 248 of ICTA 1970; and

(iv) Periodic payments received by a U.K. trading or investment company will be chargeable under Schedule D Case III.

The foregoing concession does not apply where a U.K. party (not itself being a "recognised bank") makes a payment to a non-U.K. branch of a U.K. or foreign bank and in such circumstances any periodic payments would be paid under deduction of tax (subject to any relief afforded by any applicable doubt tax treaty).

It should also be noted that the concession referred to above only applies where the U.K. bank is acting as principal and not where it acts as an arranger. In such circumstances the U.K. party making payment to the arranger bank is regarded as making payment directly to the other party to the transaction and accordingly must pay under deduction of tax (subject always, in the case of payment to a non-U.K. resident, to any applicable double tax treaty relief).

11.42 2. It may be possible under an applicable double tax treaty to obtain relief from withholding tax pursuant to section 53 of ICTA 1970 provided that the requisite formalities are complied with. The position is somewhat unclear in view of the fact that whilst many treaties deal with "interest payments," some treaties do not deal with "annual payments." Other provisions which may be relevant are a "business profits" article or an "other income" article (e.g. Article 22 of the U.S./U.K. Treaty).

Swap payments received by a U.K. counterparty (other than the recognised bank acting as principal) from a non-U.K. counterparty will be taxable under Schedule D Case V.

In the case of rate swaps, although no formal statement has been made by the U.K. Revenue, its approach has been the same as that adopted in relation to currency swaps. Accordingly, it appears that the concession granted to U.K. banks acting as principal in currency swaps applies in the same manner in relation to rate swaps.

In relation to currency swaps the question of the potential liability under U.K. tax legislation to corporation tax on income or chargeable gains on foreign currency gains is an area of considerable complexity which falls outside the scope of this chapter. However, careful consideration should be given to this problem by swap parties.

FORWARD RATE AGREEMENTS

What are they?

The classic rate swap involving a series of payment flows in two directions **11.43** (or, at least, the potential for payment flows in two directions) represented the earliest form of the modern, sophisticated approach to interest rate risk management. Further developments followed and one of the products to emerge was the "forward rate agreement."

A "forward rate agreement" is an essentially simple concept. Two parties are involved and the following elements are agreed: (i) a notional principal amount; (ii) a future "settlement date"; (iii) a "maturity date" (which will typically be a specific number of months after the "settlement date"); (iv) a fixed rate of interest (for the payment of which one party ("X") is responsible); and (v) a floating rate of interest (for example, LIBOR) for the payment of which the other party ("Y") is responsible.

Having agreed these items, the parties await the arrival of the settlement date. On that date, the agreed fixed rate of interest is compared with the LIBOR quoted by prime banks in the London Interbank Market for deposits in the currency of the agreed notional principal amount for delivery on the settlement date and for a period equal to the period between the settlement date and the maturity date.

If the relevant LIBOR proves to be lower than the agreed fixed rate, then **11.44** the shortfall (expressed as a percentage rate per annum) is multiplied by the agreed notional principal amount and by a fraction the numerator of which is the number of days between the settlement date and the maturity date and the denominator of which is 360 (if the currency of the transaction is not domestic sterling) or 365 (if it is). The result of that multiplication then falls due as a debt owed by X to Y.

Of course, it is possible that market rates of interest will have moved in a different direction: the relevant LIBOR might have proved to be higher than the agreed fixed rate of interest. In this case, the excess if multiplied as described above and the result falls due as a debt from Y to X.

Three critical areas need to be examined by lawyers when advising clients about forward rate agreements: they are (i) the implications of the Gaming Act 1845; (ii) documentation; and (iii) tax.

The Gaming Act 1845

Section 18 of this charming piece of nineteenth century legislation renders **11.45** null and void any contract of "gaming or wagering." Is a forward rate agreement such a contract?

The expressions "gaming" and "wagering" are not defined in the Gaming Act and one must therefore have recourse to the leading case on the topic, namely the Court of Appeal's decision in *Tote Investors, Ltd.* v. *Smoker.*[36]

The facts of this case are worthy of mention. Mrs. Smoker placed a bet on credit with the Totalisator. She was unable to pay the stake and was sued. She argued that the transaction was a wager. Her argument failed. The terms of her contract with the Totalisator were that the stake moneys placed by all the punters betting on a particular race were aggregated and divided between those who had betted on the winner, after deducting the Totalisator's fixed profit and expenses. Whilst an individual punter could win or lose on the race's outcome the Totalisator (the punter's counterparty) could not. As a result, the transaction was not a wager.

As the Court of Appeal put it, it takes two to make a bet.

On the face of the contract constituting a forward rate agreement, we appear to have a major problem; depending on the way market interest rates move, one of the two parties to the transaction is bound to "win" and the other is bound to "lose" (save for the mathematically unlikely circumstance of a "draw," *i.e.* where the fixed interest rate payable by X turns out to be equal to the LIBOR fixed on the settlement date). The key element of the *Smoker* case[37]—the inability of one of the parties to suffer a loss or make a profit on the result of the race—is missing.

Before despair sets in, it is important to examine why the parties to the forward rate agreement have entered into it. Clearly, if the purpose of both parties is genuinely to "take a punt" on interest rate movements in the market during the period between the agreement date and the settlement date, one has little sympathy: it is a contract with the clearest possible gaming/wagering motives for both parties.

11.46 In fact, most forward rate agreements are entered into for genuine, proper commercial purposes, *i.e.* hedging underlying interest rate exposure. Essentially, a forward rate agreement would allow (in our example) X (the "payer" of the fixed rate interest) to hedge against the risk of LIBOR rising above the selected fixed rate between the agreement date and the settlement date: conversely, it would allow Y to hedge against the risk of LIBOR falling below the selected fixed rate between those two dates. If both X and Y had entered into the contract for these genuine commercial reasons, then the contract should not be regarded as gaming or wagering.

Typically, however, at least one of X and Y will not be entering into the transaction for hedging purposes, but will do so in order to provide (in effect) a service to its customer, the other party. In this case, the party providing the service will no doubt have separately hedged its exposure under the agreement, but its motive for entry into the agreement is profit, not hedging.

The profit, however, will not be a function of the outcome of the agreement, but will be a function of the cost of the separate hedge: it is a fixed

---

[36] [1968] 1 Q.B. 509.
[37] *Tote Investors Ltd.* v. *Smoker* [1968] 1 Q.B. 509.

profit, rather like the fixed profit made by the Totalisator in the *Smoker* case.[38] In this case too, neither party can truly be said to be wagering or gaming.

As a result, whilst on the face of the transaction the Gaming Act poses significant difficulties for forward rate agreements, the practical circumstances in which such an agreement will amount to a wager will be few. Nevertheless, the sanction of unenforceability is draconian and the means of its avoidance—establishing that you had an acceptable motive for the transaction—is scarcely to be regarded as an objective cast-iron certainty in every case.

Section 63 of the Financial Services Act 1986

Fortunately, many of the problems which have been identified above may no longer be relevant now that section 63 of the Financial Services Act 1986 has come into force. Under this provision, no contract to which the section applies will be unenforceable by virtue of the gaming/wagering legislation. Are forward rate agreements one of those contracts? **11.47**

Subsection (2) of section 63[39] provides that the section applies to any contract entered into by either or each party "by way of business and the making or performance of which by either party constitutes an activity which falls within paragraph 12 of Schedule 1 to this Act. . . ."

The first element is that at least one of the parties must be entering into the agreement "by way of business." One trusts that the courts will take a robust view of this rather curious expression: hopefully, the argument that speculation cannot amount to a genuine "business" activity will be given short shrift.

Assuming that that hurdle is overcome, the next question is whether the "making or performance" of the forward rate agreement falls within paragraph 12 of Schedule 1 to the Act[40]—namely, "buying, selling, subscribing for or underwriting investments or offering or agreeing to do so. . . . " It seems that a forward rate agreement is an investment: it is a "contract for differences" within the meaning of paragraph 9 of Schedule 1. **11.48**

However, does the "making or performance" of the forward rate agreement amount to "buying, selling, subscribing for or underwriting" rights under a contract for differences? If one were to give these expressions their natural meanings, the answer would probably be no. However, the Financial Services Act contains some language which should save the day. Paragraph 28(1)(d) of Schedule 1 provides that "references to buying and selling include references to any acquisition or disposal for valuable consideration"; paragraph 28(2) then explains further: a "disposal" includes the assumption of liabilities under a contract corresponding to the relevant rights.

[38] *Ibid.*
[39] Financial Services Act 1986.
[40] *Ibid.*

The net effect is that, when X undertakes to pay Y if market rates move in one direction, X is assuming a liability which corresponds with the rights Y acquires to receive that sum; that assumption amounts to a "disposal"; it is a disposal "for valuable consideration" (namely, Y's undertaking to pay X if, in fact, rates move in the opposite direction) and such a disposal is thus to be treated as "selling" under paragraph 12. As a result, the entry into, and performance of, a forward rate agreement is free of the taint of gaming/wagering now that section 63 has come into force.

"FRABBA" terms

11.49 Historically, documentation for forward rate agreements tended to be on the brief side as lawyers were not normally involved in the drafting. Eventually, the British Bankers' Association came to grips with the issue and, in August 1985, a booklet containing the intended market norm emerged under the charming title of "FRABBA" terms.

FRABBA terms contains a statement in the Introduction that "the Working Party has mainly confined itself to the London Interbank Market, and has not been directly concerned with the terms and conditions which individual banks may elect to quote to their customers or to banks abroad, although FRABBA terms could be utilised in such circumstances."

Clearly, one of the most important questions which a bank needs to consider is whether FRABBA terms are adequate for forward rate agreements entered into with non-bank or foreign customers. One would assume that most banks would be of the view that FRABBA terms are adequate if the counterparty is creditworthy, but, particularly with non-bank/foreign customers, two additional legal/documentation issues arise, namely legal capacity and taxation.

As regards legal capacity, Gaming Act considerations have been rather obliquely addressed in paragraph 1.3 of FRABBA terms, with the apparently gratuitous statement that "it is understood that both parties have entered into this f.r.a. in accordance with normal banking practice." This was included in an attempt to ensure that on Gaming Act grounds no argument of unenforceability could be raised in an interbank transaction; with a bank to customer transaction, a provision of equivalent (and probably limited) legal value might be "it is understood that both parties have entered into this f.r.a. for genuine commercial purposes and not for speculation." In any event, the existing paragraph 1.3 is inappropriate for use with non-bank counterparties and needs always to be changed or excluded by express term.

11.50 For the general question of legal capacity of corporate counterparties, the practice in the swap market has been to obtain an appropriate legal opinion: being essentially for interbank transactions, FRABBA terms do not contemplate this. The usual representation that the agreement is valid and binding and that all necessary approvals have been obtained is, however, included in paragraph 2. With non-bank customers, it would normally be wise to check the truth of these representations with legal counsel at least at the time of the first transaction with that customer.

Taxation is also addressed in paragraph 2 of FRABBA terms, with the bald representation that "as at the date of this f.r.a., all payments to be made . . . hereunder may be made free and clear of, and without deduction for or on account of, any taxes whatsoever."

Whether this statement is true or not will depend upon the local law applicable to the customer. In relation to a U.K. customer (*i.e.* a customer resident in the U.K. or a non-resident entering into the agreement through a U.K. branch or agency), the Inland Revenue Technical Division confirmed to the authors' firm in October, 1985 that no deduction or withholding on account of tax need be made from payments made under forward rate agreements. This was based on the understanding that forward rate agreements involve one net payment only on the selected settlement date: the absence of any element of recurrence was considered critical. This is because, if there were any element of recurrence, the possibility arose that the payments could be "annual" payments within section 53 of ICTA 1970, attracting a requirement to deduct at source, and to account for, basic rate tax.

11.51 The above probably remains good law, but two points are worthy of note. The first is that the representation on tax in FRABBA is given as at the date the f.r.a. was entered into: it is not repeated thereafter. Second, FRABBA terms do not contain any provision for grossing-up (nor, for that matter, any provision for termination due to the post-agreement imposition of withholding tax—a surprising ommission). This exposes the two parties to a risk of a change in law during the life of a given f.r.a., with no right to compensation, whether in the form of gross-up or termination compensation. The risk is, to some extent, proportional to the length of time between the agreement date and the selected settlement date. Presumably, the omission of this protection is intended to reflect the "one-off," and normally short-term, nature of a forward rate agreement.

The termination provisions of FRABBA terms are similarly brief and, to some eyes, scanty. They consist of the following events of termination: (i) winding-up by the court is ordered or a resolution for voluntary winding-up is passed (excluding an approved reconstruction or amalgamation); (ii) the initiation of insolvency or bankruptcy proceedings which are not discharged within 30 days of the appointment of a receiver of all or any part of the counterparty's assets; or (iii) any representation made under paragraph 2 (also on the scanty side, being limited to the capacity, approvals and tax matters referred to above) being untrue when made.

Clearly, the absence of an event of termination directed at a breach of a payment obligation under the agreement itself is of no concern—after all, only one sum is due and that at the settlement date (the effective maturity of the transaction). However, the absence of a cross-default provision might be of some concern to credit officers (compare the omission of such a provision from the BBAIRS terms).

The consequences of termination of a forward rate agreement governed by FRABBA are similar to those contained in the BBAIRS terms and operate on a general indemnity basis.

Unlike the BBAIRS terms, however, FRABBA terms do not contain a provision requiring termination in the event of it becoming unlawful for either party to continue the transaction. As with the absence of a grossing-up clause this deliberate omission reflects the perception of forward rate agreements as "one-off" short-term transactions, consequentially involving less risk than a swap with the same counterparty.

"FLOOR/CEILING" AGREEMENTS

11.52 "Floor" agreements, "ceiling" (or "cap") agreements and "floor-ceiling" (or "collar") agreements are the newest entrants to the interest rate risk management scene and were introduced by the American investment banks into the euromarkets during late 1985.

A "floor" agreement is one entered into by a bank and a customer under which, in return for an up-front (and one-time only) fee, the bank provides the customer with protection against a fall in interest rates. The essential elements of the agreement are: (i) a notional principal amount (*e.g.* $100mm); (ii) a "floor" rate below which the customer does not wish to see market interest rates fall (*e.g.* 10 per cent. per annum); (iii) the market base interest rate to be used (*e.g.* LIBOR); (iv) the tenor of the agreement (*e.g.* 10 years) and the reference periods to be used (*e.g.* six months).

On each agreed reference date, there are compared (a) the "floor" rate and (b) the base rate quoted in the market for deposits in the currency of the notional principal amount for delivery on the reference date and for a period equal to the reference period in question. If the market rate is lower than the "floor" rate, then the bank pays the customer a sum calculated at an annual rate equal to the shortfall (expressed as a percentage rate) for the relevant reference period on the agreed notional principal amount. For example, LIBOR for a $100MM notional principal amount is 10 per cent. on a given reference date for a six month (183 days) reference period. Using an 11 per cent. "floor" rate, the bank pays to the customer an amount calculated as follows:

$$\$100MM \times 1\%\star \times \frac{183}{360} = \$508,333.33$$

★ The difference between LIBOR (10%) and the 11% "floor" rate.

If, in fact, on a given reference date, LIBOR is equal to, or more than, the "floor" rate, no payment is made by either party.

11.53 A customer might use a "floor" agreement in order to protect himself against (say) a situation where he owned a floating rate investment, but had funded that investment on a long-term, fixed-rate basis. A "ceiling" agreement provides inverse protection, *i.e.* against the risk of a rise in interest rates. The structure of a "ceiling" agreement is identical to that of a "floor" agreement, save that the bank pays the customer in the event that market rates of interest are *higher* than the chosen reference rate. A "ceiling" agreement might be used to enable the customer to "hedge" a fixed-rate investment which has been funded by means of floating-rate funds.

Both "floor" and "ceiling" agreements involve the payment to the bank by the customer of up-front fees. These fees are not cheap and the "collar" agreement has been designed to reduce the fees and to tailor the product more precisely to the customer's requirements. Under a "collar" the bank would (say) "sell" to the customer a "ceiling" (*i.e.* the bank would grant "ceiling" protection in return for an up-front fee) and simultaneously the customer would "sell" to the bank a "floor" for an up-front fee on terms involving potential payments by the customer using a notional principal amount, reference dates and periods and a base market rate identical to those applicable to the "ceiling" it had "purchased" from the bank. The net effect would be that (i) the two fees are netted out, producing (normally) one fee payable to the bank of an appropriately low figure and (ii) payments would move from the bank if the market rate exceeded the chosen "ceiling" and from the customer if the market rate fell below the chosen "floor"; if the market rates were somewhere between the two, then no payments would be made.

The customer has thus effectively "collared" his interest costs between the "floor" and the "ceiling": he does not suffer if market rates rise above the "ceiling" but nor can he benefit if they fall below the "floor."

Insurance law considerations

To the non-lawyer, the three instruments, namely, "floors," "ceilings," **11.54** and "collars" might well be viewed as contracts of insurance. After all, in return for an up-front fee (the premium), the bank (the insurer) is undertaking with the customer (the insured) that, upon the happening of a specified contingency (market rates of interest moving above or below an identified fixed rate), the bank (insurer) will indemnify the customer (insured) against loss by paying the customer an amount sufficient to cover the customer against the excess or shortfall rate calculated on a pre-agreed principal amount.

Are the three instruments to be regarded by the lawyer as contracts of insurance? The area of doubt seems to concern the question of whether the payment being made by the bank on each reference date is truly an indemnity against loss. It is submitted that the mere fact that the calculation of the amount of that payment is by reference to external market factors (current interest rates), rather than to the customer's specific individual circumstances, is not sufficient to prevent the transaction being regarded as an indemnity.

The argument, in insurance's favour, would be that, since the protection is being purchased to hedge against the contingency of adverse rate movements, if the protection were not there, loss would follow if that contingency occurred—e.g. the customer might be obliged to pay to the person funding it on a LIBOR basis an amount of interest exceeding the yield on its fixed-rate investment.

On this basis, the three instruments could be viewed as contracts of insur- **11.55** ance. The matter is far from clear, however, as many of the normal business characteristics of an insurance arrangement are absent and the court will take such absence into account. This can be seen from a dictum of Romer J. in *Seaton v. Heath*,[41] where the learned judge said,

" . . . contracts of insurance are generally matters of speculation where the person desiring to be insured has the means of knowledge as to the

[41] [1899] 1 Q.B. 782.

risk, and the insurer has not the means or not the same means. The insured generally puts the risk before the insurer as a business transaction and the insurer on the risk stated fixes a proper price to renumerate him for the risk being undertaken. . . . "

One could scarcely argue that a bank selling a "floor" understands less well than the customer the nature of the risks of LIBOR falling below a particular rate during a specific period. Equally, the idea of the customer "putting" these risks before the bank "as a business transaction" does not really ring true as a description of the three instruments.

As a result, the position has to be regarded as unclear. If, however, the three instruments were to be regarded as insurance contracts, what are the consequences?

The first is that the contract would be one "of the utmost good faith," requiring the "insured" to disclose to the "insurer" all material facts which would influence a prudent insurer. Frankly, where the insurer is a bank active in the interest rate risk management market, the idea of such a duty to disclose being imposed on a corporate customer seeking to control its interest costs is almost laughable. The area of worry would be in the context of a "floor/ceiling" or "collar," where one might argue that there are two insurance contracts; the "floor" (where the customer is the insurer) and the "ceiling" (where the bank is the insurer). The risk would be that the customer's obligations under the "floor" could be prejudiced by the absence of "full disclosure" by the bank of all "material facts," *e.g.* historical frequency of interest rates falling below the chosen "floor."

11.56 The other area of risk concerns the statutory requirements governing insurance business. Essentially, if a person "carries on" any "insurance business" in the U.K., an offence is committed by that person, unless he is authorised to do so by the Department of Trade: section 29(1) of the Insurance Companies Act 1982 (the "Act").

Clearly, "business" denotes some element of continuity although there is some authority for the argument that an isolated transaction may, in some circumstances, amount to "business." If the sale by a bank of a "floor" or a "ceiling" is a contract of insurance, then if that bank sells such protection sufficiently frequently for it to become a "business," then, on the face of section 2(1) of the Act, an offence is committed.

Fortunately, section 2(4) of the Act provides that subsection (1) does not apply to "general business of class 14, 15, 16 or 17 if it is carried on solely in the course of carrying on, and for the purposes of, banking business."

Would a "floor" or a "ceiling" fall within one of those classes? The answer seems to be yes, on the basis that the wording of class 16(c) is so wide as to catch anything not mentioned elsewhere in classes 1 to 17. As to the remaining requirements of subsection (4), it is submitted that they are to be regarded as duly satisfied provided one is prepared to view "banking" as going beyond the activities of taking deposits and lending money and as encompassing all those activities nowadays common to commercial and investment banks.

11.57 For a non-bank customer which frequently sells "floors" as part of "floor-ceiling" (or "collar") arrangements, the exemption provided by subsection (4) is not available. As a result, there would be a risk of criminal sanctions (section 14). However, of more immediate relevance, will the breach of the criminal law prejudice any party's obligations under the "collar" by tainting the same with inherent illegality/unenforceability?

The answer, on the face of it, is to be found in section 132 of the Financial Services Act 1986. This would have the effect of making any "contract of insurance" entered into by any person (*i.e.* the customer) in the course of carrying on an insurance business in contravention of section 2 of the Act unenforceable against the other party (*i.e.* the bank); that other party can, however, enforce the insurer's (customer's) obligation, if it so wishes, or rescind the contract and sue for damages.

If the relevant "contract of insurance" is the "floor" element, rather than the whole "collar," then section 132 of the Financial Services Act will have little practical effect. After all, the bank has no obligations under the "floor" element which are capable of being rendered unenforceable; further, the bank has no incentive to rescind. If, however, the "contract of insurance" is the whole "collar," the (ludicrous) result may be that the bank's obligations under the "ceiling" element cannot be enforced by the customer! One can scarcely believe that the draughtsman of the section meant that banks should be able to use it to this effect.

However, it may well be that section 132 of the Financial Services Act in fact does not provide the answer. The section expressly does not apply to any agreement "to which Section 5(1) above applies." These words were included to ensure that life assurance contracts were not caught by section 132. This is because life assurance is to constitute an "investment" for the purposes of the 1986 Act and there was a desire to have all "investments" dealt with separately. **11.58**

Unfortunately, the wording used has a wider effect than intended. The effect of section 5(1) of the Act is that a contract entered into by a person in the course of carrying on an investment business is unenforceable against the counterparty, unless the first-mentioned person is duly authorised. "Collars," "floors" and "ceilings" are "investments" within the meaning of the Act (paragraph 9, Schedule 1). If the customer is selling "floors" sufficiently frequently for this to constitute a business—and if it does not constitute a "business," then the difficulties posed by the insurance legislation fall away anyway (see above)—then the "floor"/"ceiling"/"collar" will be "an agreement to which section 5(1) above applies" and thus section 132 will not apply!

As a result, the answer to our original question—is the contract unenforceable—has to be found elsewhere. Eventually, it will be found in section 5(1) (with essentially the same results as described above for a contract within section 132), *but* section 5(1) is not yet in force! This causes us to return to the law in force before the 1986 Act. The relevant law is to be found in the Court of Appeal's 1986 decision in *Phoenix General* v. *Administratia Asiguraritor de Stat*[42] and the answer seems to be (as the court put it) "unfortunate": namely, the whole of the relevant contract is illegal and unenforceable. If the "contract" in question is just the "floor" element, then the customer cannot be sued; if the whole "collar" is affected, then neither bank nor customer can be sued.

---

[42] [1986] 1 All E.R. 908.

Taxation

11.59 The principal taxation concerns with the three instruments are (i) withholding tax: is either party obliged to deduct tax from any payment made under the agreement, and (ii) deductibility: can the "seller" of the protection deduct any payments it makes thereunder from its profits in computing its tax liability and can the "buyer" of the protection deduct the up-front fee in computing its tax liability?

As usual, these questions are normally to be determined by reference to the tax law of the jurisdiction in which the taxpayer incurs the expenditure. In the case of a U.K. taxpayer, the Inland Revenue has explicitly described floor/ceiling agreements as essentially "insurance type" agreements. This view is rather surprising as it is not difficult to argue that a "floor/ceiling" instrument is merely a rate swap where one of the parties has commuted its obligations into an up-front fee. The net effect of the Revenue's position is as follows:—

(i) withholding tax: none. Neither the fee nor any payments under the agreements would be regarded as "annual payments" or "yearly interest" and so there is no requirement to deduct tax under sections 53 and 54 of ICTA 1970; and

(ii) deductibility: deductible as an expense of the payer's trade and not as a charge on income. For customers who are investment companies for tax purposes, payments will not be regarded as deductible as expenses of management.

11.60 The position as stated in paragraph (ii) above is very unfortunate for non-bank customers. This is because the determining factor as regards the deductibility of the significant fees paid for this form of protection (or the deductibility of any payments made under the "floor" element of a "collar") will, as the Revenue put it, "depend upon the circumstances," *i.e.* why was the expenditure incurred: if for trading purposes, there may be an opportunity to deduct; if for other purposes (*e.g.* to hedge interest rate exposure itself incurred to fund long-term capital requirements), there will not be an opportunity to deduct. This is not helpful as it makes deductibility dependent upon the factual circumstances surrounding the transaction being hedged, which may not be easy to assess.

For banks and other financial institutions, the Inland Revenue accepted that any payments made should be deductible under Case I of Schedule D to ICTA 1970.

Documentation for "collar" agreements

11.61 Documentation for a "collar" agreement tends to follow the documentation applicable to rate swaps. The rationale behind this is clear: although, on a given date, the nature of the obligations of the parties is such that a payment can only move from one of them (and not the other), each of them have a contingent future claim (or series of contingent future claims) on the other which has a business value and with respect to which the usual range of protections would be appropriate, *e.g.* grossing-up and compensation on termination.

For "floor" or "ceiling" agreements, one might take the view that the position is rather different. After all, only one of the parties (the customer) has the benefit of a series of future and contingent claims on the other (the bank): the bank received on inception of the transaction all the money that it is going to receive (the fee) and has accordingly no further interest in the inclusion in the document of any extra protections beyond the bald statement of its obligations to pay money to the customer in the event that interest rates move in the appropriate direction.

Some banks have exploited this distinction between their exposure on "collar" agreements and the other two of the three instruments by drafting a standard form "collar" agreement which gives the full range of protections to both parties and a separate "floor" and "ceiling" agreement of much shorter length including little or no protection for the purchasing customer. Other banks have indicated a desire to show the market that they are prepared to sell protection on the same basis as they insist on when purchasing protection. In the view of each of these banks, it is right that a customer purchasing "floor" or "ceiling" protection from it should be given the full range of ancillary legal rights, e.g. grossing-up and compensation on termination. This approach has the added benefit of allowing these banks to prepare one standard form framework document which can be used for each of the three instruments.

The two different approaches mentioned above should provide the reader with assistance in understanding why it is that some documents for the three instruments in the market are so short and others seem to be so much longer. In advising a purchaser of protection, the right approach is to seek the full range of ancillary legal protections notwithstanding the extra length that this gives to the document.

CAPITAL ADEQUACY

Over recent years the supervision of U.K. banks by the Bank of England **11.62** has become progressively more formalised.[43] There has also been a continuing dialogue between the banking supervisory authorities in the main financial centres of the world with a view to establishing some uniformity in the prudential requirements imposed on banks.

Historically, supervision was based on an examination of a bank's balance sheet. Did the bank have adequate capital in relation to the size of its loan portfolio? Did it have sufficient liquidity? Whilst the principal business of most commercial banks today continues to be the taking of deposits and the lending of money, a number of their activities may not be reflected in their balance sheets. There are also many financial institutions which have banking status but whose principal business is in other areas of activity which are essentially off-balance sheet transactions, such as underwriting. Included in off-balance sheet activities are swaps, forward rate agreements and "floor/ceiling" arrangements.

As previously discussed, whilst a currency swap has, broadly speaking, the same economic effect as a back-to-back loan arrangement, a currency swap is an off-balance sheet transaction. Although the principal amounts

---

[43] On supervision by the Bank of England generally, see Vol. 1, Chap. 1 of this work.

exchanged (or the asset into which they have been converted or invested) will appear in the respective balance sheets of the parties at the end of the year in which the initial principal exchanged are effected, the re-exchange obligations will not appear as a loan liability nor will the amount receivable upon such re-exchange show as an asset in the balance sheet. In the case of a rate swap, neither the amounts payable nor the amounts receivable by the parties over the term of the swap will be reflected in the parties' respective balance sheets. The net amounts received or paid will simply be reflected in their profit and loss accounts. A swap however always involves the credit risk of the counterparty. What happens if the counterparty becomes insolvent or is otherwise unable or fails to pay? The worst scenario would be if the solvent party is forced to pay and left to prove as an unsecured creditor for the amount due to it. A less draconian situation is the one in which some set-off can be effected so that the exposure is limited to the difference between, in the case of a currency swap, the difference between the rate of exchange reflected in the swap and current exchange rates or, in the case of an interest swap, the difference between the amounts payable under the swap an current interest rates.

11.63   In a consultative paper published by the Bank of England in March, 1986 entitled "Off Balance Sheet Business of Banks" it was stated:

> "Counterparty failure in a foreign exchange or interest rate contract exposes a bank to a potential loss (or profit). The same applies to sale and repurchase transactions and other forward sales and purchases, particularly of fixed rate assets. . . . However, in these transactions the bank is not exposed on the whole of the underlying principal amount of the contract (except on settlement date for most contracts where principal is exchanged—*e.g.* some currency swaps, forward foreign exchange contracts and forward asset sales and purchases). Should a counterparty fail during the life of the contract, the bank is left with an unexpected or unintended foreign exchange or interest rate exposure. The magnitude of any profit or loss can be measured in terms of the cost of replacing the contract at current market rates ("replacement cost"). This may involve purchasing an equivalent contract or generating the same stream of cashflows by mean of cash market transactions. Prudent management requires an estimate, on a cautious basis, at the beginning of the contract and throughout its life of the likely replacement cost which might be incurred in the case of counterparty failure. This estimate will reflect, *inter alia*, the volatility of the particular interest rates or foreign exchange rates involved, the maturity of the contract and the depth of the markets in or through which any lost cash flows might be replaced."

11.64   The Bank of England and other banking supervisory authorities, such as the U.S. Federal Banking Regulatory Authorities, have adopted the approach that the credit risk arising from off balance sheet items should be included in calculating the exposure which a bank may have in the context of its capital. A consultative paper on the Convergence of Capital Adequacy Assessment in the United Kingdom and the United States was published in January 1987 by the Board of Governors of the Federal Reserve System, the Office of the Comptroller of the Currency, the Federal Deposit Insurance

Corporation, all of the U.S., and the Bank of England. Off balance sheet items specifically addressed by the paper include financial guarantees, standby letters of credit, acceptances, commitments such as revolving underwriting facilities and interest rate and foreign exchange rate related transactions (*e.g.* swaps). Certain of these items were already included in the Bank of England's capital adequacy requirements. For example, underwriting obligations are included in the Notice published by the Bank of England BSD/1985/2 (April, 1985).

In March 1987 the Bank of England published a consultative paper on Credit Equivalent Amounts for Interest Rate and Foreign Exchange Rate Related Instruments to form part of the joint paper published by the U.S. Federal Banking Supervisory Authorities and the Bank of England in January 1987. This paper sets out the proposed approach for converting notional principal amounts into balance sheet equivalents for risk asset calculation purposes. The paper distinguishes between single currency rate swaps, forward rate agreements, interest rate options purchased, cross currency swaps (including cross currency interest rate swaps), forward (not spot) foreign exchange contracts, foreign currency options purchased and any other instruments of a similar nature that give rise to similar credit risks. This last item clearly recognises that the inventiveness of bankers has not yet been exhausted! Specifically excluded, however, are instruments traded on futures and options exchanges which require daily marking-to-market an payment of variation margin.

The paper indicates that in assessing the risk value of the various types of instrument two factors will be taken into account. These are described as the "current exposure" and the "potential exposure." Current exposure will represent what the cost would be to the bank in replacing the payment stream anticipated by the transaction if the counterparty were to default by reference to current interest or exchange rates, translated, if not in sterling, into sterling. Thus in the case of a currency swap which provides for the bank to pay to the counterparty £100 in six months' time in exchange for US$150 and the current rate of exchange is £1 = US1·30, the bank has a US$20 or £13·84 exposure. Similarly, in the case of a rate swap, if the bank is due to receive from the counterparty in 12 months' time LIBOR on a notional amount of £100 and the fixed amount payable by the bank under the swap is calculated by reference to a fixed rate of 10 per cent. and the current LIBOR rate is 5 per cent. the bank has an exposure of £5. Potential exposure recognises the fact that over the remaining duration of the contract the relevant currency or interest rates may fluctuate. Conversion factors based on the principal amount involved have been calculated depending on the unexpired period of the contract based on statistical models of interest and exchange rate fluctuations.

11.65

The Bank of England in common with other banking supervisory authorities imposes exposure limitations on banks which include both country exposure limits and exposure limits to particular entities. These are discussed in a paper entitled Large Exposures Undertaken by Institutions Authorised under The Banking Act 1979 issued by the Bank of England in February 1987. The paper distinguishes between exposure to banks and non-banks. It also requires, in calculating the exposure which a bank has to another entity, that there be taken into account interest rate contracts, including interest rate swaps, forward rate agreements and interest rate options purchased and foreign exchange rate contracts, including cross currency swaps, forward foreign exchange rate contracts and foreign currency options purchased.

There are a number of areas in which the Bank of England has adopted a conservative approach for the purpose of making the relevant calculations. For example, it will not normally be possible to take security into account in determining exposure and exposure will have to be calculated taking into account connected persons, such as companies in the same group. So far as swaps and related transactions are concerned, it would appear that they will have to be considered individually and it will not be possible where a bank has entered into two or more swaps with the same counterparty for them to be netted off in calculating the total exposure (even though the relevant master agreement might provide otherwise, as previously discussed).

12. Contract Guarantees and Standby Letters of Credit

Introduction

Contract guarantees and standby letters of credit are relatively recent devel- **12.01** opments which are encountered primarily in international supply or construction contracts. They are used in construction contracts to ensure the financial standing of a contractor and his ability to fulfil an obligation into which he has entered. They are also commonly used in international contracts of sale where the buyer wishes to insure against the seller being unable to supply the goods sold, or where the seller wishes to insure against the failure of the buyer to pay the purchase price, or meet his other obligations under the contract of sale.

The documents which are used to guarantee the obligations outlined above are described by a variety of names and there is little uniformity in the use of terms. The distinction between a contract guarantee and a contract bond would seem to be one of words and/or form rather than of substance, and for the purpose of this chapter the words guarantee and bond will be used synonymously.

As a general rule bonds or guarantees are used by English bankers, whereas the standby letter of credit is a product of banking practice in the United States. This chapter will initially examine the bond or guarantee under English law and conclude with a brief discussion of the standby letter of credit.

THE BONDS OR GUARANTEES WHICH MAY BE GIVEN UNDER ENGLISH LAW

There are a number of different bonds or guarantees which a bank's cus- **12.02** tomer[1] may be called upon to provide in favour of his overseas buyer or seller. The principal ones being: performance bonds, bid or tender bonds, advance payment bonds and retention money bonds.[2] Each of these may be given in either first demand or conditional form.

---

[1] The emphasis in this chapter will relate to bonds or guarantees issued by banks rather than surety companies. However, it should be pointed out that banks are not the only institutions which provide such instruments, although in terms of volume they are by are the most significant.

[2] Other bonds which may be issued include: maintenance bonds; customs bonds; transportation bonds; equipment bonds; working capital replenishment bonds; and completion bonds. For a practical discussion of how such bonds operate, see Gmür (Ed.) Trade Financing (2nd ed., 1986) Chap. 12.

FIG. 1 SPECIMEN TENDER BOND

National Westminster Bank PLC ↻

International Banking Division
Bonds and Guarantees Department · Overseas Branch

OUR GUARANTEE GU (GUARANTEE NUMBER)

We understand that (APPLICANTS NAME) ("the Applicant") (APPLI-CANTS ADDRESS) are tendering for the (DESCRIPTION OF GOODS) under your invitation to Tender (TENDER/CONTRACT NUMBER ETC) and that a Bank Guarantee is required for (AGREED PERCENTAGE/OF CONTRACT) % of the amount of their tender.

We, NATIONAL WESTMINSTER BANK PLC, Overseas Branch, London HEREBY GUARANTEE the payment to you on demand of up to (AMOUNT IN FIGURES) (say, (AMOUNT IN WORDS)) in the event of your awarding the relative contract to the Applicant and of its failing to sign the Contract in the terms of its tender, or in the event of the Applicant withdrawing its tender before expiry of this guarantee without your consent.

This guarantee shall come into force on (COMMENCEMENT DATE) being the closing date for tenders, and will expire at close of banking hours at this office on (EXPIRY DATE) ("EXPIRY").

Our liability is limited to the sum of (AMOUNT IN FIGURES) and your claim hereunder must be received in writing at this office before Expiry accompanied by your signed statement that the Applicant has been awarded the relative contract and has failed to sign the contract awarded in the terms of its tender or has withdrawn its tender before Expiry without your consent, and such claim and statement shall be accepted as conclusive evidence that the amount claimed is due to you under this guarantee.

Claims and statements as aforesaid must bear the confirmation of your Bankers that the signatories thereon are authorised so to sign.

Upon Expiry this guarantee shall become null and void, whether returned to us for cancellation or not and any claim or statement received after expiry shall be ineffective.

This guarantee is personal to yourselves and is not transferable or assignable.

This guarantee shall be governed by and construed in accordance with the Laws of England.

A. Bid or tender bonds (see fig. 1)

12.03   Bid or tender bonds will be given in support of a customer's tender for a particular contract, as assurance of the customer's intention to sign the contract and comply with the terms of such contract in the event of his tender being accepted.

   If the tender is accepted and the customer fails to proceed as planned, the party to whom the bond has been advanced (the beneficiary) will simply make demand under the terms of the bond. The purpose of such a bond is to compensate the beneficiary for the additional costs he may bear in re-awarding the contract to another party. These costs may be significant in circumstances where the beneficiary is forced to publish new tender conditions and commence the tender process afresh. Depending on the circumstances, a bid bond may be issued for a fixed sum of money or a fixed percentage of the submitted tender.

Once the tender has been accepted, and assuming that the customer is willing to proceed, it will normally be necessary to replace the bid or tender bond with a suitable performance bond. Some bid bonds, however, are drafted in such a way that they automatically become performance bonds once the bid is accepted. If the customer fails to furnish an appropriate performance bond within the requisite time, the beneficiary will be at liberty to cancel the contract and call on the bid or tender bond originally given. The bid bond should be returned once the contract has been signed and the appropriate performance bond issued and in addition, all bid bonds covering the unsuccessful bids should be returned to the appropriate parties.[3]

A common problem with bid or tender bonds is that they are nearly always unilaterally extended. Such bonds tend to be issued for a period of 90 days in the first instance, but especially in construction contracts, the overseas employer is hardly ever ready to award the contract after 90 days, and accordingly seeks to have the bond extended. Further extensions are often necessary with major contracts and in many cases the employer is simply stalling for time until he secures the best possible deal for himself. Negotiations often proceed for many months and this may well have serious cost implications for the bidder. For example, the effect of inflation during lengthy negotiations may make the final contract price prohibitive, as may currency exchange movements. Whenever possible, the bidder should negotiate suitable conditional wording within the terms of the bond to give some degree of protection against the problems which have been highlighted above.[4]

B. Performance bonds (see fig. 2 on page 264)

Performance bonds are the most common instruments issued and are given **12.04** by a bank in support of a customer's obligation to fulfil a specified contractual commitment. In many situations, the overseas party will be uncertain whether, for example, the seller will be able to supply the goods sold, or to satisfy his other obligations under the contract. In such a case the performance bond, especially when issued in first demand form,[5] will safeguard the buyer's position. Should the seller fail to meet his obligations, the buyer will simply make demand on the bond under whatever terms have been agreed between the parties.

---

[3] It does not necessarily follow that all bid bonds supporting unsuccessful bids will be returned. Some countries require banks to extend their bid bond even though the contract has been awarded to a party other than the one on whose behalf the bank issued its bond, see Stumpf, *Frequent Abuse of Contract Guarantees and Attempts at Remedying Such Abuses*, Liber Amicorum, Hommage Frederic Elsemann, ICC. (Paris, 1978.).

[4] Examples of clauses which might be included within the terms of the bond to give some degree of protection to the bidder can be found in the CBI booklet entitled *Contract Bonds and Guarantees* (2nd ed., 1983).

[5] The distinction between "first-demand" and "conditional" bonds is considered later in this chapter. See para. 12.7 below.

FIG. 2 SPECIMEN PERFORMANCE BOND WITH ARBITRATION CLAUSE

National Westminster Bank PLC

International Banking Division
Bonds and Guarantees Department - Overseas Branch

OUR GUARANTEE GU(GUARANTEE NUMBER)

We understand that you have entered into a Contract (TENDER/CON-TRACT NUMBER ETC) (the Contract) with (APPLICANTS NAME) (the Applicant) (APPLICANTS ADDRESS) for the (DESCRIPTION OF GOODS) and that under such Contract the Applicant must provide a Bank Performance Guarantee for an amount of (AMOUNT IN FIGURES) being (AGREED PERCENTAGE OF CONTRACT) % of the value of the Contract.

We, NATIONAL WESTMINSTER BANK PLC, Overseas Branch, London HEREBY GUARANTEE the payment to you on demand of up to (AMOUNT IN FIGURES) (say, (AMOUNT IN WORDS)) in the event of the Applicant failing to fulfil the Contract, provided that your claim hereunder is received in writing at this office accompanied by:

    (a) your signed statement that the Applicant has failed to fulfil the Contract, together with either:—

    (b) the written admission of the Applicant that it has failed to fulfil the Contract, or

    (c) a copy of an Arbitration Award in your favour, certified by a Notary Public as a true copy of the original of such Award expressed to be made (i) pursuant to the Contract; and (ii) in your favour.

and such a statement together with either the written admission of the Applicant or a copy Arbitration Award as above shall be accepted as conclusive evidence that the amount claimed is due to you under this guarantee.

Claims and statements as aforesaid must bear the confirmation of your Bankers that the signatories thereon are authorised so to sign.

This guarantee shall expire at close of banking hours at this office on (EXPIRY DATE) ("EXPIRY") so that any claim and statement hereunder together with the written admission of the Applicant or copy Arbitration Award must be received at this office before Expiry in the manner stipulated hereinabove and after expiry this guarantee shall become null and void whether returned to us for cancellation or not and any claim and statement together with the written admission of the Applicant or copy Arbitration Award received after Expiry shall be ineffective.

This guarantee is personal to yourselves and is not transferable or assignable.

This guarantee shall be governed by and construed in accordance with the Laws of England.

Performance bonds are normally required within a few weeks of the contract being awarded, although in some cases, particularly in negotiated contracts, the bond may be required at the moment the contract is executed. In the event of the bond being required before the contract is signed, the issuing bank should qualify its commitment in order that it will only become effective once the underlying contract has been executed.

A common problem with performance bonds is that they are often issued for 10 per cent. of the full contract price[6] and there is rarely any provision made within the terms to reduce liability under the bond in relation to the progress of work under the contract. This is because the overseas employer will generally view the bond as covering the complete contract and, therefore, the contractor/seller will be at risk until total performance has been rendered. Experience has shown that unscrupulous beneficiaries are quite prepared to make demand on such bonds even though the underlying contract has been virtually completed. Whenever possible, the contractor should seek to protect himself by including suitable wording within the terms of the bond, whereby his liability is reduced in accordance with work carried out on the underlying contract. It is essential in such cases to provide for some independent party, for example, a building surveyor, who will conclusively certify the amount of work which has been carried out. The independent third party will play an important role in cases of dispute which frequently arise between the parties to the underlying contract.

C. Advance payment bonds (see fig. 3 on page 266)

Advance payment bonds are issued in circumstances where the overseas buyer makes advance payments to the seller of a given percentage (anything between 10 and 20 per cent.) of the full contract value. They are particularly common in construction contracts where an employer advances money to the contractor to enable him to commence work (order equipment and materials, engage personnel and sub-contractors, begin drawings, etc.).   **12.05**

The taking of the bond will safeguard the position of the buyer/employer, enabling him to obtain repayment of the sum advanced in the event that the seller/contractor fails to carry out his obligations in the underlying contract. The bond so issued may provide for the liability of the issuing bank to be reduced (usually *pro rata*) in accordance with performance by the seller/contractor, and it is common in such a situation to insist on progress certificates which not only give evidence that proper use is being made of the advance payment, but also indicate the work which has been carried out.

D. Retention money bonds (see fig. 4 on page 267)

Retention money bonds are given in support of contracts which call for a percentage of each payment to be withheld until the contract has been completed and accepted by the overseas buyer/employer. The bond will enable   **12.06**

---

[6] The value of the performance bond will obviously reflect the strength of the parties' bargaining position; however, in some countries the value may be fixed by local law. For example, in Saudi Arabia the percentage is fixed at 5 per cent. for publicly tendered contracts.

FIG. 3 SPECIMEN ADVANCE PAYMENT GUARANTEE WITH
REPRODUCTION AND OPERATIVE CLAUSE

National Westminster Bank PLC ♻

International Banking Division
Bonds and Guarantees Department · Overseas Branch

OUR GUARANTEE GU (GUARANTEE NUMBER)

We understand that you have entered into a Contract (TENDER/CON-
TRACT NUMBER ETC) with (APPLICANTS NAME) (the Applicant)
(APPLICANTS ADDRESS) for the (DESCRIPTION OF GOODS) and that
under the Contract the sum of (AMOUNT IN FIGURES) being (AGREED
PERCENTAGE OF CONTRACT) % of the total contract value is payable
in advance against a Bank Guarantee.

In consideration of your making an Advance Payment of (AMOUNT IN
FIGURES) (the Advance Payment) to the Applicant we, NATIONAL
WESTMINSTER BANK PLC, Overseas Branch, London, HEREBY
GUARANTEE to refund to you on demand up to (AMOUNT IN
FIGURES) (say, (AMOUNT IN WORDS)) in the event of the Applicant
failing to fulfil the Contract.

Our maximum liability hereunder shall automatically reduce by (REDUC-
TION PERCENTAGE) % of the value of (SERVICE/GOODS TO
EFFECT REDUCTION) as evidenced by presentation to us by (PRE-
SENTER FOR REDUCTION) of (DOCUMENTS FOR REDUCTION)
showing the (EVIDENCE PRESENTED BY DOCUMENTS) which we
shall be entitled to accept as conclusive evidence that the (CONCLUSIVE
EVIDENCE OF) has been effected.

This guarantee shall remain valid until reduced to nil in accordance with the
foregoing procedure or until close of banking hours at this office on (EXPIRY
DATE) ("EXPIRY") whichever shall first occur. Any claim hereunder must
be received in writing at this office before Expiry accompanied by your signed
statement that the Applicant has failed to fulfil the Contract, and such claims
and statement shall be accepted as conclusive evidence that the amount
claimed is due to you under this guarantee.

Claims and statements as aforesaid must bear the confirmation of your
Bankers that the signatories thereon are authorised so to sign.

*This guarantee shall become operative upon issue of our amendment making
it effective, which will be issued upon receipt by us of written confirmation
from the Applicant that the latter has received the Advance Payment.

Upon Expiry, this guarantee shall become null and void, whether returned to
us for cancellation or not and any claim or statement received after expiry shall
be ineffective.

This guarantee is personal to yourselves and is not transferable or assignable.

This guarantee shall be governed by and construed in accordance with the
Laws of England.

Alternative
*This guarantee shall become operative automatically on receipt of the
Advance Payment of (AMOUNT IN FIGURES) on the account of (APPLI-
CANTS NAMES) at our (BRANCH) Branch.

FIG. 4 SPECIMEN RETENTION MONIES BOND WITH OPERATIVE
CLAUSE

National Westminster Bank PLC ♻

International Banking Division
Bonds and Guarantees Department · Overseas Branch

OUR GUARANTEE GU (GUARANTEE NUMBER)

We understand that under the terms of your Contract (TENDER/CON-
TRACT NUMBER ETC) with (APPLICANTS NAME) (the Applicant)
(APPLICANTS ADDRESS) for the (DESCRIPTION OF GOODS) you are
retaining the sum of (AMOUNT IN FIGURES) being (AGREED PER-
CENTAGE OF CONTRACT) % of the contract value by way of retention
monies (the Retention Monies) and that you are prepared to release the said
retention monies against a Bank Guarantee.

In consideration of your releasing the sum of (AMOUNT IN FIGURES) to
the Applicant we, NATIONAL WESTMINSTER BANK PLC, Overseas
Branch, London, HEREBY GUARANTEE the repayment to you on
demand of up to (AMOUNT IN FIGURES) (say, (AMOUNT IN
WORDS)) in the event of the Applicant failing to fulfil the Contract.

This guarantee shall remain valid until close of banking hours at this office on
(EXPIRY DATE) ("EXPIRY"). Any claim hereunder must be received in
writing at this office before Expiry accompanied by your signed statement
that the Applicant has failed to fulfil the Contract, and such claim and statement shall be accepted as conclusive evidence that the amount claimed is due
to you under this guarantee.

Claims and statements as aforesaid must bear the confirmation of your
Bankers that the signatories thereon are authorised so to sign.

★This guarantee shall become operative upon issue of our amendment making
it effective, which will be issued upon receipt by us of written confirmation
from the Applicant that the latter has received the Retention Monies.

Upon Expiry, this guarantee shall become null and void, whether returned to
us for cancellation or not and any claim or statement received after Expiry
shall be ineffective.

This guarantee is personal to yourselves and is not transferable or assignable.

This guarantee shall be governed by and construed in accordance with the
Laws of England.

ALTERNATIVE
★This guarantee shall become operative automatically on receipt of the Reten-
tion Monies of (AMOUNT IN FIGURES) on the account of (APPLICANTS
NAME) at our (BRANCH) Branch.

the seller/contractor to receive the total amount of each "work in progress" payment made by the buyer/employer, thus improving his cash flow position. The bond will obviously protect the overseas beneficiary, who will simply make demand should the seller/contractor fail to meet his contractual commitments.

Retention money bonds are normally issued for either the full amount of expected retentions or a fixed percentage of the contract value. In either case the bank's actual liability should be limited to the progress payments actually released by the overseas buyer/employer.

First demand or conditional?

12.07   Bonds or guarantees can be given in either first demand or conditional form and it will be necessary to examine the precise wording in order to determine the nature of the commitment which is being made by the issuing bank to the overseas beneficiary.[7]

If the bond is given in first demand form (known to many bankers as the "suicide form") the obligation to make payment under its terms arises on first demand without proof or conditions. The advantage of such a bond is obvious, since it can be called on by the beneficiary without proof of loss caused by breach of the underlying contract, or any other form of breach.

The documentation evidencing such bonds is usually unambiguous. For example, in the case of *Edward Owen Engineering Ltd* v. *Barclays Bank International*[8] the relevant clause in the bond simply read " . . . payable on demand without proof or conditions."

In the case of a conditional bond or guarantee the obligation to make payment will be conditional upon the party to whom the bond is issued (the beneficiary), proving default by the party who is to perform the subject matter of the bond (the seller/contractor).[9]

First demand bonds are normally provided by banks on behalf of their customers, whereas surety or insurance companies are presently the most important source of conditional bonds. Such companies are generally unwilling to issue first demand bonds, believing them to be commercially unsafe. The banks, on the other hand, have traditionally preferred first demand commitments which, as we shall see, enable the bank to stand clear of any contractual dispute which may arise between the parties to the underlying contract.

Conditional bonds

12.08   Although conditional bonds have traditionally been provided by surety and insurance companies in more recent years, banks have moved into this field and a number of banks now issue conditional bonds when so required by

---

[7] See Williams, "On demand and Conditional Performance Bonds" [1984] J.B.L.8, Arora, "The Legal Position of banks in Performance Bond cases" [1981] L.M.C.L.Q.

[8] [1978] 1 All E.R. 976.

[9] This will normally be the seller in a sale of goods contract or the contractor in an international construction contract.

the contracting parties. Conditional bonds afford considerable protection to the seller/contractor, as payment under its terms will normally be conditional upon the beneficiary proving:

(i) an unremedied breach of contract by the seller/contractor and
(ii) loss caused by such breach.

Unlike the position in first demand bonds, it will be necessary for the bank issuing the conditional bond to become involved in the underlying contract in order to be satisfied that the "conditions" of payment have been met. This poses a number of significant problems for the bank, and in order to safeguard its position, the bank will normally require appropriate provisions to be drafted within the bond documentation relieving the bank of any need to involve itself in any contractual dispute between buyer and seller.

The provisions commonly adopted require documentary evidence of breach before the payment obligation can be triggered. Bonds containing such provision cannot be described as truly conditional, nor first demand, and they will be considered in detail later in this chapter.[10]

In 1978 the International Chamber of Commerce (ICC) published *Uniform Rules for Contract Guarantees*[11] which propose a set of internationally acceptable rules for certain types of contract guarantees. The rules seek to secure a uniformity of practice between the parties and endeavour to balance their respective interests without losing sight of the commercial purpose which underpins these instruments. The most significant areas covered by the rules include: the definition of terms commonly used in bonds or guarantees, the liability of the guarantor to the beneficiary, the latest dates for claims under bonds, the documentation required in support of claims, the termination date of the instrument, and the settlement of disputes and arbitration procedures.

Unfortunately, the usefulness of the ICC rules is, to say the least, questionable. For example, they are not expected to prevail over any foreign law which prescribes the text of any given bond or which stipulates the time period on which a claim can be made.[12] A further drawback to the rules is that they were not drafted so as to apply to first demand bonds, and, therefore, they have no relevance to the type of instruments which are most commonly issued by banks.

Not surprisingly, few buyers have found the ICC rules acceptable, and there has been considerable reluctance to make use of them. The ICC has now recognised the problem and is currently working on a code of practice to deal specifically with the problems arising from first demand bonds or guarantees. A uniform set of rules covering these instruments is long overdue and it is to be hoped that the ICC proposals, once formulated, will be

---

[10] See para. 12.9 below.
[11] I.C.C. Publication No. 325 (1978).
[12] Article 1 specifically provides that where a rule is contrary to a provision of law applicable to the bond/guarantee from which the parties cannot derogate, that provision prevails. If a guarantee does not indicate an express governing law, the applicable law is that of the guarantor's place of business (Article 11).

considerably more effective than the present rules covering conditional instruments.

The documentary bond

12.09   The party who originally requested the issue of the bond (the seller/contractor) has no protection against unilateral, unfair and/or capricious demand by the beneficiary when the bond is issued in first demand form.[13] This has led to financial catastrophe for many contractors in recent years,[14] and in order to mitigate against the harsher implications of first demand bonds it is becoming increasingly common to see protective clauses drafted within the terms of the documentation, affording a degree of protection against the unscrupulous beneficiary.

The first demand bond can be mitigated in a number of ways by linking the bond to performance of the underlying contract. Even the most absolute undertaking inevitably contains some reference to the underlying contract, even though it may only be a reference to the contract number. However, bankers who are prepared to mitigate must do so with caution lest they find themselves embroiled in any ensuing dispute which arises between their customer (the contractor) and the beneficiary with regard to the underlying contract.[15] One way in which the bank may attempt to soften a first demand bond is by incorporating a clause requiring documentary proof of the contractor's default before payment can be made to the beneficiary. Arbitral awards and surveyors' reports are examples of documents which may be required in such cases. Whenever such a clause is included the bank must ensure that all parties will be bound by the documentary evidence. In other words, the findings of the surveyor or arbitrator must be conclusive and not subject to appeal, otherwise the bank will be placed in the invidious position of not knowing whether to pay when the beneficiary produces the documentary evidence required.

12.10   As Goode points out,[16] bonds which are triggered solely by presentation of one or more documents to the issuing bank are in fact unconditional undertakings, because proof of default is not a condition of the bank's duty to pay, which must be fulfilled as soon as the stipulated documents are presented. The documentary requirement clearly prevents the bond from being triggered by a simple demand and, therefore, affords a considerable degree of protection for the contractor, who cannot complain when the bank makes payment following an independent report[17] that the contractor is in

---

[13] The relationships arising under a first demand bond are considered in detail later in this chapter, see para. 12.14 below.

[14] See Rendell, "The Iranian Revolution Continues in the Courts" (June 1979) *Euromoney* p. 7 *et seq.*; Lord, "The No-Guarantee Rule and the Standby Letter of Credit" (1979) 96 Banking L.J. 46; Driscoll, "The Role of Standby Letters of Credit in International Commerce: Reflections After Iran" 20 (1980) Va J.Int'l.L. 459; Briggs, "Defusing the danger of bonds," *Euromoney, Trade Finance Report*, (August 1984) p. 32.

[15] For an interesting discussion on how this might be achieved, see Nelson, "How to Make a Standby Credit Worth More than the Paper It's Written On" (November 1979) *Euromoney* p. 113; Jordan, "Guarantee Bonds; Their Use in International Contracts"; (June 1980) Int'l Cont. L. & Fin. Rev. p. 201.

[16] See Lloyd (ed.), *The Liability of Contractors* (1986) p. 99 *et seq.*

[17] By a local surveyor, for example.

default of the underlying contract. The documentary requirement will also enable the bank to stand clear of the underlying contract, providing, as we have already seen, that the document presented is deemed to be conclusive proof of default by the contractor.

It would appear that such bonds are a half-way house, since they cannot be classified as "first demand," nor are they truly "conditional." Perhaps it is now time to alter the terminology and classify bonds as either "documentary" (*i.e.* triggered solely by the presentation of documents) or "non-documentary" (*i.e.* dependent upon proof of actual default).[18]

Even in circumstances where no documentary evidence is required, it is common for the issuing bank to insist upon the beneficiary making a formal statement, within his demand, that the contractor has breached some term of the underlying contract.[19] It has been suggested by commentators in some jurisdictions that such an "effective clause" entitles the bank, in cases of doubt, to request further information.[20] This is unlikely to be the position under English law, provided that the beneficiary makes his demand on the terms provided for within the bond.[21] The issuing bank may, of course, seek clarification where compliance is not made by the beneficiary, although it would be quite within its rights simply to reject the claim without further enquiry.[22]

The legal position of banks issuing first demand bonds on behalf of their customers

When issuing a first demand bond on behalf of its customer to an overseas beneficiary, the bank enters into an absolute undertaking, and must meet its obligations under the bond, even if its customer objects and contends that the beneficiary's demand is unjustified.[23] The bank will not be concerned with the relations between its customer and the beneficiary, nor whether its

12.11

---

[18] See Goode, above, n. 16, p. 99. The writer accepts that such terminology may not cater for the true "on-demand" bond which is triggered by simple demand. However, even in extreme cases it is usual to require the demand to be made in writing with or without a formal statement that breach has materialised.

[19] See *Esal (Commodities) Ltd. and Relton Ltd.* v. *Oriental Credit Ltd.* and *Wells Fargo Bank* [1985] 2 Lloyd's Rep. 546; *Siporex Trade* v. *Banque Indosuez* [1986] 2 Lloyd's Rep. 146.

[20] This would appear to be the position in West Germany. See Horn, "Burgoschaften und Garantien zur Zahlung auf erstes Anfordern" (1980) N.J.W. p. 2153 *et seq.*

[21] This view is supported by the judgment of Ackner L.J. in *Esal (Commodities) Ltd.* v. *OCL* above, n. 19, p. 550, where he said " . . . in addition to the beneficiary making the demand, he must also inform the bank that he does so on the basis provided for in the performance bond itself. This interpretation not only gives meaning and effect to the words "in the event that the supplier fails . . . " which otherwise would be mere surplusage, but in no way imposes an extravagant demand upon the bank." See also, the observations of Kerr J. in *R. D. Harbottle (Mercantile) Ltd.* v. *National Westminster Bank Ltd.* [1978] 1 Q.B. 146, p. 150.

[22] *Ibid.*

[23] Under English common law a "guarantee" is a secondary obligation securing an underlying debt and, therefore, dependent upon conditions and defences in the underlying contract (see Chitty, *The Law of Contracts*, (25th ed., 1983)). A bond on the other hand is " . . . an instrument under seal, usually by deed poll, whereby one person binds himself to another for the payment of a specified sum either immediately or at a fixed future date" (*Halsbury's Laws of England* (3rd ed.) Vol. 3, pp. 329, 330).

customer is in default of contractual commitments.[24] This is because under English law the first demand bond is a primary obligation on the part of the bank, comparable to an indemnity rather than to a true guarantee.[25] A truly conditional bond,[26] however, which requires proof of default in the underlying contract, will be a secondary obligation.

This distinction is of the utmost importance, since in the case of a secondary obligation the bank will be under no liability at all in the event that the principal obligation does not come into being or if it has already been discharged. In the case of a primary obligation the bank will be liable, notwithstanding that the underlying contract never comes into being or is null and void.

This principle was called into question, however, by the Court of Appeal in *Potton Homes Ltd.* v. *Coleman Contractors (Overseas) Ltd.*[27] The salient facts of this case were that Potton Homes had agreed to supply Coleman Contractors with prefabricated building units which were to be shipped to Libya. There were altogether three contracts and the total purchase price was about £1,300,000. The plaintiffs, Potton Homes, secured on-demand performance bonds covering all three contracts for approximately £68,000. Differences arose between the parties and the defendants made demand under the terms of the performance bonds after alleging a number of defects in the buildings which had been delivered. The plaintiffs claimed that £89,621 was due under the three contracts and judgment for this sum was later given by the official referee, Judge Hawser, Q.C., who ordered a stay of execution and allowed the defendants to pursue their counterclaim. As regards the performance bonds the learned judge held that he had no power to restrain the defendants from making calls upon them. He further found that the case was not an appropriate one for him to award a Mareva injunction.[27a] He did, however, conclude that in view of the plaintiffs' undoubted entitlement to over £89,000, it would not be right that the defendants should be paid £68,000 to do with as they wished. He ordered that the payments under the performance bonds should be frozen until the issues in the action were tried. The defendants appealed.

12.12 The Court of Appeal (Eveleigh and May L.JJ.) allowed the appeal and held that the defendants were duly entitled to obtain payment under the terms of the performance bonds. From the point of view of the bank, the underlying contract was said to be irrelevant and, therefore, the bank was

---

[24] The question of whether a bank should be satisfied that there has been some form of default before honouring a first demand bond was considered in *Howe Richardson Scale Company Ltd.* v. *Polimex—Cekop and National Westminster Bank Ltd.* [1978] 1 Lloyd's Rep. 161. In this case the Court of Appeal made it clear that a bank which gives "first demand type" bonds is under no obligation to enquire whether there has been performance of the underlying contract. Any dispute on that contract would have to be settled at a later stage. Indeed, this appears to be the main reason why bankers prefer such bonds to those having a conditional nature.

[25] A line of cases decided by the English courts has consistently upheld the autonomy of the first demand bond, see Penn, "Performance bonds: are bankers free from the underlying contract?" [1985] L.M.C.L.Q. 132, and the cases cited therein.

[26] See para. 12.08 above.

[27] (1984) 128 S.J. 282. This case is also discussed in Penn, above, n. 25.

[27a] For a discussion of the grounds upon which an English court will grant a Mareva injunction, see Chap. 2, para. 2.05 above.

obliged to honour the bond when demand was made, notwithstanding the plaintiffs' counterclaim for a sum in excess of that being claimed under the performance bonds.

As between buyer and seller, however, Eveleigh L.J. observed that the underlying contract could not be disregarded so readily. The facts of each case would have to be considered, and where the underlying contract had been lawfully avoided or where there was failure of consideration between buyer and seller, for which the seller undertook to procure the issue of the performance bond, there was no reason why, as between buyer and seller, the seller should be unable to prevent a call upon the bond. This point was not discussed by May L.J., who adopted the doctrine of strict autonomy and would not admit such additional defences.

It is submitted that the stricter approach of May L.J. is likely to prevail. **12.13** The decisive test is the intention of the parties, and if they agree to a first-demand bond they intend, necessarily, to give the beneficiary the benefit of an autonomous commitment from the issuing bank. The commitment as between the issuing bank and the beneficiary requires no consideration[28] and, therefore, cannot fail for want of consideration in the underlying contract. Under English law the first demand bond is closely associated with the irrevocable letter of credit, with regard to which it has been held[29] that the irrevocability of the credit extends to the buyer-seller relationship. This was a necessary conclusion because if the seller had been prohibited from drawing under the credit, the irrevocable obligation of the bank would be indirectly undermined.[30] Precisely the same problem would arise in the case of first demand bonds if the beneficiary were to be prevented from making a successful demand because of problems arising from the underlying contract.

No reference has been made in subsequent cases[31] to the approach suggested by Eveleigh L.J.; all of these cases[32] have emphasised the traditional approach that only fraud would suffice to ground injunctive relief.[33]

The relationships created by first-demand bonds

The legal relationships created by the issue of a first-demand bond amount **12.14** to three or four distinct contracts, depending upon whether a correspondent bank is used in the transaction. Overseas beneficiaries normally insist upon the bond being issued by a national bank based in their own country and,

---

[28] The theoretical problem under English law that the beneficiary gives no consideration to the bank in return for the promise received does not appear to have been raised seriously in practice. The same theoretical problem arises in relation to letters of credit, see generally, Chap. 13 below.

[29] *Hamzeh Malas & Sons* v. *British Imex Industries Ltd.* [1958] 2 Q.B. 127.

[30] For a fuller discussion of the relationships created by letters of credit, see Chap. 13 below.

[31] Goode argues that the approach of Eveleigh L.J. deserves serious consideration, but following such consideration concludes that it is unlikely to be followed, see n. 16 above.

[32] See *GKN Contractors Ltd.* v. *Lloyds Bank plc and Another* (1985) 30 Build.L.R. 48: *Esal (Commodities) Ltd. and Relton Ltd.* v. *Oriental Credit Ltd. and Wells Fargo Bank* [1985] 2 Lloyd's Rep. 546; *Siporex Trade* v. *Banque Indosuez* [1986] 2 Lloyd's Rep. 146.

[33] The fraud exception is considered later, see para. 12.19 below.

therefore, for the purpose of this discussion we shall consider the four party scenario. The first contract is that between employer and employee in a construction contract, or buyer and seller in a sale of goods contract. This is the underlying contract pursuant to which the bond is issued. The second contract reflects the relationship between the employee and his own bank, the instructing bank. The employee will normally instruct his own bank to cause the correspondent bank to issue the first-demand bond in favour of the beneficiary. The instructing bank, before effecting such instructions, will require a counter-indemnity[34] from the employee, the terms of which normally permit the bank to debit the employee's account for all claims received and paid to the correspondent. The third contract reflects the relationship between the instructing bank and the correspondent bank which ultimately issues the bond to the beneficiary. This relationship is frequently characterised as a "counter guarantee" or counter-indemnity, given by the instructing bank in favour of the correspondent bank. The precise wording of the guarantee will be as crucial as that in the bond itself because of the knock-on effect which it has for both the instructing bank and the employee. The fourth and final contract is the most fragile in the entire structure and relates to the bond itself, which is issued by the correspondent bank to the beneficiary.

The importance of private international law

12.15   As in all international banking contracts, principles of private international law will play a crucial role in determining the rights and obligations of the various parties described in the above scenario. In order to highlight the importance of private international law we need only add hypothetical jurisdictions to our scenario, for example, an English contractor/supplier instructs his own bank, which is based in London, to procure the issue of a first-demand bond through a correspondent bank, based in Syria, in favour of a Syrian beneficiary.

Such a scenario will, of necessity, bring into play private international law principles (should any dispute arise), and it is, therefore, surprising that choice of law and forum clauses are rarely found in any of the four contracts outlined above. One reason for this may be due to the fact that the relevant documents are often nothing more than short letters or telexes with few standard clauses. However, the significance of such clauses cannot be over-emphasised, and they are omitted at one's peril.[35]

In determining the parties' obligations under a contract, English courts apply the proper law concept, under which the court will apply the law selected by the parties within the contract documentation, as the law governing their particular contract.[36] Where no express choice is made, the

---

[34] The form of the counter-indemnity is discussed at para. 12.23 below. See also, Fig. 5.

[35] See Penn & Cashel, "Choice of Law Clauses under English and New York Law; (1986) J.B.L. 333; Wood, "External Governing Law—Fortress or Paper House" (July 1982) Int'l Fin. L. Rev. 11.

[36] See Penn & Cashel, above n. 34, and the cases cited therein.

courts will endeavour to find an implied choice[37] and if there is none, they have come to accept that the proper law is that law with which the transaction has its closest and most real connection.[38]

Although only considered in one reported case, the proper law also appears to be the formula used by the courts in order to ascertain the law of first demand bonds.[39]

In the case of *Edward Owen Engineering Ltd.* v. *Barclays Bank International Ltd.*,[40] Brown L.J. stated that in the absence of express provision, the proper law (of first demand bonds) is that with which the transaction has its closest and most real connection. This approach has been favoured for some time in relation to letters of credit and it is hardly surprising that the courts should use identical criteria to ascertain the proper law for both instruments.[41]

12.16 If the proper law principle is applied to the four-party situation outlined above and it is assumed that no express or implied choice has been made in any of the contracts, the significance of such a clause, or lack of it, becomes readily apparent. The contract between the contractor/supplier and its own bank, the instructing bank, will be governed by English law, whereas the contract between the instructing bank and the issuing bank may be governed by either English or Syrian law, depending upon the significant contacts which that contract has with England and Syria. The contract between the issuing bank and the beneficiary will obviously be governed by Syrian law, but the law governing the underlying contract will not be so easily identifiable.[42]

It is not inconceivable that of the four contracts outlined, three may be governed by different systems of law. Consequently, the parties may find themselves bound by terms quite different from those originally intended. The seriousness of such a situation can best be identified by considering a problem which regularly arises in practice.

12.17 Each of the four contracts within our typical scenario outlined above should contain an expiration date on which the obligations of the various parties cease. It is not uncommon, however, to find the beneficiaries of "on-demand" bonds insisting upon repeated extensions and threatening to make

---

[37] *Ibid.*

[38] See Dicey and Morris, p. 755 *et seq.* The principles followed by the English courts in determining the proper law of a contract are also considered in Chapter 1 of this work.

[39] The proper law approach is not universally accepted, however, and at least one learned writer suggests an alternative approach. Professor Horn contends "It appears to be an internationally established conflicts rule that the law of the bank which obliges itself by issuing the bond, guarantee or standby letter governs (*lex bancae*)." Professor Horn does, however, accept that this will be overridden where an express choice of law is made by the parties. See Horn, "Securing International Commercial Transactions: Standby Letters of Credit, Bonds, Guarantees and Similar Sureties" 9 I.J.G.U. 3 at p. 283.

[40] [1978] 1 All E.R. 976.

[41] See also, *Offshore International SA* v. *Banco Central SA* [1977] 1 W.L.R. 399; [1976] 3 All E.R. 749; *Power Curber International Ltd.* v. *National Bank of Kuwait SAK* [1981] 1 W.L.R. 1233; [1981] 3 All E.R. 607.

[42] It cannot be said with any certainty that this contract would be governed by either English or Syrian law. The contract may have closer and more significant connections with a completely different legal system.

demand if such extensions are not granted. This has the effect of keeping the bond alive for many years and is further compounded by the fact that the laws of some countries do not recognise the expiration of the issuing banks' obligation until the beneficiary has surrendered the instrument or issued a declaration of release.[43] This is precisely the position under Syrian law. Thus, even though the bond issued in our example may incorporate an expiry date, if both the contract between issuer and beneficiary, and that between instructing bank and issuing bank, are found to be governed by Syrian law, then the instructing bank may find itself obligated under its counter-indemnity long after the supporting counter-indemnity, which it took from the employee, has expired.[44] The instructing bank should obviously try to avoid such problems by incorporating an English governing law clause within the terms of the counter-indemnity which it gives to the issuing bank.[45] A specific expiry date may afford little protection in the event of the indemnity being governed by Syrian law.

Where the bond is actually issued by an English bank to an overseas beneficiary the problem remains the same and unless the bank takes appropriate precautions within the bond documentation it may find itself bound by completely inappropriate legal provisions.[46]

The terms of the bond should also incorporate a clause stipulating which courts will have jurisdiction to hear any dispute relating to the bond.[47] The principal objective behind such a clause is to confer effective jurisdiction upon the desired courts by fulfilling all the necessary procedural requirements, thereby minimising the risk that the chosen forum might decline jurisdiction.[48]

Arbitration is an obvious alternative to litigation and has frequently been used in bond issues. Here again, however, it will be crucial to stipulate where arbitration will take place, and also that the arbitrator's findings will be binding on all parties. The bank which pays in accordance with an arbitral award will not want to be concerned about the prospect of an appeal being made by the losing party.

---

[43] Under Syrian law the bond will remain valid until it is physically surrendered. The position is even more problematic under Turkish law where a beneficiary is entitled to claim for up to ten years after the expiry date. But in doing so he must prove that the default of the contractor/supplier occurred before the expiry date of the bond. It is possible in Turkey to include a choice of law clause which would exclude Turkish law and the extended right to claim, although it is most unlikely that Turkish beneficiaries would agree to such a clause.

[44] This will obviously be the case if the bond is not surrendered by the beneficiary on its expiry date and the indemnity contract between employee and instructing bank, which has the same expiry date, is governed by English law.

[45] Alternatively, it should make sure that the counter indemnity it takes from the employee covers all claims made on the counter indemnity which it gives to the issuing bank.

[46] The significance of the choice of law clause is particularly apparent when the transaction is closely connected with banks and beneficiaries based in the Middle East. Many countries in that part of the world have little established law on the interpretation of first-demand bonds, and to omit and express choice of law is to run the risk of a legal vacuum in the event of litigation.

[47] For a fuller discussion on the validity of jurisdiction clauses and the position where no express clause is incorporated, see Chap. 2 above. See also, Wood, Chap. 3 et seq.

[48] Wood considers the factors influencing forum selection and also the self imposed restrictions on the exercise of jurisdiction by various courts above, n. 47.

Abusive calling

Over the last decade the international business community has become **12.18** increasingly concerned about abusive calls on guarantees by overseas beneficiaries. This abuse has been particularly prevalent in the case of first demand bonds, and injunctions are regularly sought in the English courts to prevent the banks from making payment, when the demand is deemed unjustified. Banks, however, have long been aware that timid submission in the face of such an injunction will seriously devalue their own international paper. Bankers place their international reputation on the line when giving first demand bonds, and it has become a basic proposition in international trade that nothing, or nothing much, should come between a bank and its obligation to make payment when demand is made. The English judiciary have taken a harsh approach to the enforcement of these instruments, and it is now well settled that the only exception to the general rule, that banks must honour first demand bonds "without proof or condition," is in cases where the bond is called on fraudulently, and the bank has knowledge of such fraud.

The question of fraud

Fraud, however, is extremely difficult to establish under English law and it **12.19** is worth considering the attitude of the English courts where fraud has been at issue.

The first case to consider the fraud exception with regard to first demand bonds was *Harbottle* v. *National Westminster Bank Ltd.*[49] The facts of this case were that the plaintiffs had entered into three contracts of sale with Egyptian buyers. Each contract required the plaintiffs to provide performance bonds, equal to 5 per cent. of the full contract price, in favour of the Egyptian buyers. The first demand type performance bonds were issued by an Egyptian bank, following the buyers' insistence that they be issued locally, and were supported by a counter-indemnity issued by Harbottle's own bank, the National Westminster Bank. The plaintiffs sought an injunction restraining the National Westminster from making any payment under the terms of the counter-indemnity, alleging that the demands made by the buyers were fraudulent and without justification. The plaintiffs also claimed that the buyers had not performed their obligations under the contracts, as they had failed to open the necessary letters of credit for payment of the purchase price. The case came before Kerr J. in the High Court, when the National Westminster Bank applied for the injunction to be set aside on the grounds that the bank had no option but to pay on demand. In his judgment, Kerr J. stated that the courts will rarely interfere with such irrevocable obligations undertaken by banks, and will not be concerned with disputes relating to the underlying contract of sale. This effectively ruled out as irrelevant the plaintiffs' contention that the buyers had failed to open the necessary letters of credit. That, in other words, did not constitute fraud sufficient for any exception to be made. The learned judge drew an analogy

---

[49] *R. D. Harbottle (Mercantile) Ltd.* v. *National Westminster Bank Ltd.* [1978] Q.B. 146; [1977] 2 All E.R. 862.

with cases dealing with confirmed letters of credit, suggesting that such cases applied equally to first demand performance bonds. The injunctions were consequently dismissed, thus permitting the bank to make payment under the counter-indemnity. It was also made clear in the court's judgment that any claim by the seller for breach of the buyers' obligations on the underlying contract must be the subject of a separate action.

Two Court of Appeal cases[50] quickly followed the *Harbottle*[51] decision and both placed first demand bonds on a similar footing to irrevocable letters of credit, in so far as the position of the issuing bank is concerned. Lord Denning went even further by declaring them to be . . . "virtually promissory notes payable on demand."[52]

12.20   A more recent case to consider the question of fraud is *United Trading Corporation SA v. Allied Arab Bank Ltd.*[53] where the Court of Appeal held that interlocutory injunctions restraining a bank from honouring its obligations under the bond would only be granted where the only realistic inference to be drawn from the evidence is that the beneficiary calls on the bond fraudulently, and the bank has actual knowledge of the fraud. The relevant date for establishing knowledge of fraud on the part of the bank is the date on which the bank makes payment.[54] A bank could be liable in negligence if it complied with a demand which it knew to be fraudulent[55] but no liability would attach in cases falling short of "actual knowledge."

The judgment of Ackner L.J. in *United Trading*[56] crystallises the difficulty facing a party seeking to establish the fraud exception

" . . . The evidence of fraud must be clear, both as to the fact of fraud and as to the bank's knowledge. The mere assertion or allegation of fraud would not be sufficient. We would expect the court to require strong corroborative evidence of the allegation, usually in the form of contemporary documents, particularly those emanating from the buyer. In general, for the evidence of fraud to be clear, we would also expect the buyer to have been given the opportunity to answer the allegation and to have failed to provide any, or any adequate answer in circumstances where one could properly be expected."[57]

Following the *United Trading* case it would now seem that the employee (if he is to have any chance of success) would be well advised to institute proceedings against the beneficiary, thereby giving notice of the fraud allegation and providing an opportunity for the beneficiary to respond. However, this in itself will not be enough, and the employee will also have to institute separate proceedings against the instructing bank in order to pre-

---

[50] *Howe Richardson Scale Co. Ltd. v. Polimex-Cekop and National Westminster Bank Ltd.* [1978] Lloyd's Rep. 161; *Edward Owen Engineering Ltd. v. Barclays Bank International Ltd.* [1978] Q.B. 159 [1978]; 1 All E.R. 862.

[51] Above, n. 49.

[52] Above, n. 50, p. 878.

[53] *United Trading Corporation SA and Murray Clayton Ltd. v. Allied Arab Bank Ltd. and others* [1985] 2 Lloyd's Rep. 554.

[54] *Ibid.*, p. 560.

[55] *Ibid.*, p. 560.

[56] Above, n. 53.

[57] See also *Bolivinter Oil SA v. Chase Manhattan Bank N.A.* [1984] 1 Lloyd's Rep. 251.

vent payment from being made. A major problem presents itself here, since, as we have already seen, the instructing bank has no contractual relationship with the beneficiary, and in order to prevent the instructing bank from making payment to the issuing bank (under their indemnity agreement), the employee must adduce clear evidence that the issuing bank's claim upon the instructing bank is also fraudulent. In almost every conceivable case this will be impossible to prove. The employee's only alternative would be to bring proceedings directly against the issuing bank. This would again be doomed to failure since as we have already seen, no contractual relationship exists between these parties and any attempt to bring an action in tort by claiming that the issuing bank owed the employee some duty of care would undoubtedly fall on deaf ears in a foreign court.[58]

It is, therefore, arguable that the judgment of Ackner L.J. in *United Trading*[59] has rendered the fraud exception impotent. This must certainly be the case wherever a correspondent bank is used and those seeking bond support should be clearly informed of the potential risk they face. **12.21**

Bankers should also be aware of the risk they run should they refuse to make payment once demand is made. It is an oft-used saying that a banker's word is his bond, and a bank which is prepared to break its word will find few people prepared to accept its international paper.

In order to prevent such difficulties arising, many banks will only advise their customer (the employee) of the position *after* payment has been made. This will prevent him from bringing proceedings against the bank unless he becomes aware of a potential claim from an independent source. In so far as English law is concerned the bank which adopts such an approach is quite safe, since there is no obligation to inform the customer either before or after payment has been made.[60]

The position would obviously be different if the bank had expressly agreed to inform its customer before making payment. This would place the bank in an invidious position since its customer, upon being informed by the bank, may take immediate steps to prevent payment from being made, whereas the primary obligation of the bank would be to make immediate payment under the terms of either its bond or counter-indemnity. Consequently, the bank would be forced to resist any attempt by its customer to prevent payment. This is a course of action to which few, if any, customers would be agreeable.

It is essential, therefore, that the customer seeking first demand bond support should understand the obligations which arise upon the issue of a first-demand bond. To this end, the bank should make certain that the relevant information is given to its customer before issue.[61] Well-informed customers can have no cause for complaint should they insist upon bond support and ultimately find themselves paying a heavy price. **12.22**

---

[58] It is assumed that proceedings would have to be brought in the jurisdiction of the issuing bank, since relief obtained outside that jurisdiction would, no doubt, not be recognised within it.

[59] Above n. 53.

[60] *Esal (Commodities) Ltd. and Relton Ltd.* v. *Oriental Credit Ltd. and Wells Fargo Bank N.A.* [1985] Lloyd's Rep. 546, *per* Ackner L.J., p. 553.

[61] It could be argued that the bank owes its customer a fiduciary obligation in such a situation to make him aware of the inherent risk which arises on the issue of a first demand bond.

The *United Trading*[62] decision is also noteworthy for highlighting a problem which has troubled bankers for some time. In his judgment Ackner L.J.[63] said that a bank could arguably be liable in the tort of negligence if it complied with a demand by the beneficiary which it *knew* to be fraudulently made. It is submitted, however, that in cases falling short of "actual knowledge" the position of the paying bank should not be prejudiced in any way by the decision.

Safeguarding the position of the issuing bank
FIG. 5 SPECIMEN COUNTER INDEMNITY

National Westminster Bank PLC ౭

International Banking Division
Bonds and Guarantees Department · Overseas Branch

**Complete in appropriate currency

You at the request of the undersigned having given or agreed to give the

for**   (say   )*Insert description of document eg Bond Guarantee Indemnity &c

†Insert description of contract &c for which the Bank has accepted liability

(the Beneficiary) in respect of†

Delete as appropriate

in such form as the Beneficiary may require
in the terms endorsed hereon
the undersigned hereby agree(s) to keep you indemnified from and against all actions proceedings claims and demands which may be brought or made against you and all losses costs charges damages and expenses which you may incur or sustain or for which you may become liable by reason either directly or indirectly of your having undertaken such obligation and you are hereby irrevocably authorised and directed to pay forthwith on any demand appearing or purporting to be made by or on behalf of the Beneficiary any sums up to the limit of your said liability which may be demanded of you from time to time without any reference to or any necessity for confirmation or verification on the part of the undersigned if being expressly agreed that any such demand shall as between the undersigned and you be conclusive evidence that the sum stated therein is properly due and payable and you are further authorised to debit any account of the undersigned and where the undersigned is more than one any account or accounts of all or any of the undersigned with the whole or any part of the amount of any payment which you may make thereunder whether any such account or accounts shall be overdrawn or may become overdrawn by reason of any such debit provided that if the credit balances in the currency of the liability of the undersigned hereunder are insufficient to meet such liability or there are no credit balances in the said currency you shall have the right to purchase at the spot rate of exchange an amount in the currency of such liability not exceeding the amount of the deficiency and to debit the cost to any existing or new account of the undersigned and to apply the currency so purchased in or towards satisfaction of such deficiency.

---

[62] Above, n. 53.
[63] Above, n. 53, at p. 558.

And we agree that where the undersigned is more than one our liability hereunder and upon any account opened in our joint names in respect of our liability hereunder shall be joint and several.

This Counter Indemnity shall be construed in accordance with English Law and shall be additional to any other Counter Indemnity which you now or hereafter may hold.

Dated this   day of

One thousand nine hundred and

Signed by   _____

*Insert full name of Signatory

†

in the presence of:

†If given by a Company add Signed by Signature of
Witness _____

Director(s) of acting for and on behalf of the Company by   Name in full
virtue of a resolution of the Directors passed the (in Block Letters) _____

day
                          Address _____
of

19   _____

Occupation _____

If executed by a Company the acknowledgment should be signed by a Director or by the Company Secretary   I/We acknowledge receipt of a completed copy of this document.

_____

_____

                                        Signature(s)

NWB1039 Rev Feb 82–1

A. OBTAINING COUNTER–INDEMNITIES (SEE FIG. 5 ABOVE)

12.23 The attitude of the English courts to first demand bonds clearly shows that in the absence of fraud, the issuing bank will be bound to make payment when demand is made by the beneficiary. Issuing banks should therefore obtain counter-indemnities from either the instructing bank or the seller/contractor, depending upon the circumstances. Where the bond is issued by a correspondent bank (see fig. 7 on page 282), that bank will obtain an indemnity from the instructing bank which should cover all costs incurred as a result of the bond issuance. We have already seen how important it is to carefully word both the bond and counter-indemnity to ensure that one does not expire before the other.[64] The instructing bank will in turn obtain a counter-indemnity from its own customer, the seller/contractor, the terms of which will normally permit the bank to debit its customer's account for all claims received and paid. A simple diagram (fig. 6, on page 282) may help to clarify the position of the various parties.

[64] See para. 12.17 above.

FIG. 6.

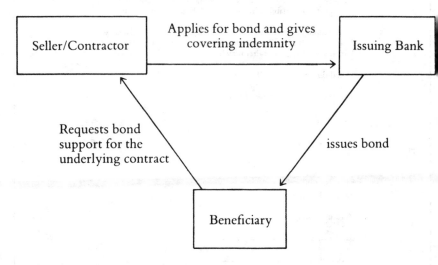

In Fig. 6 above, the bond is issued by the seller's/contractor's own bank.[65] The position will change whenever the bond is issued by a correspondent bank, *viz.*

FIG. 7.

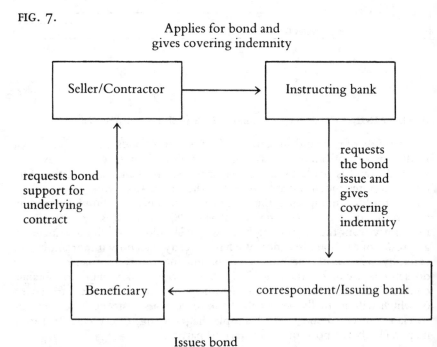

[65] It is not necessary for the seller/contractor to request the issue from his own bank but it is most common for him to do so.

B. SYNDICATION

In recent years contractors have become involved in very large overseas **12.24** contracts, often with foreign governments, which require the support of correspondingly large bonds. In many of these contracts individual banks have been unwilling to take the exposure on their own, preferring to syndicate the bond, thereby spreading the risk.[66]

The structure of the syndicated bond facility closely resembles a typical syndicated loan agreement,[67] apart from the fact that it is usually built on a first demand bond, issued in favour of the employer/beneficiary. The diagram (fig. 8) on page 284 may help to clarify the position of the various parties.

TWO RECOURSE OBLIGATIONS

As we can see from the diagram on page 284 there are in fact two distinct **12.25** recourse obligations under a syndicated bond facility. The first is between the issuing bank and the syndicate banks, (the participants) and this specifies the terms upon which the syndicate will severally reimburse the issuer for any loss it may suffer under the bond. The obligation of each participant will normally be *pro rata* its commitment under the syndicate facility.

The reimbursement obligation of each participant may take the form of standby letters of credit[68] issued by the participants to the issuer, rather than a simple clause in the facility agreement itself. Some bankers consider that standby letters of credit provide them with a greater degree of protection than would be the case under a contractual indemnity provision. This would not be the case under strict English legal principles. However, in a purely practical sense it may well be easier to obtain reimbursement when a standby letter of credit has been issued, particularly when the facility has become embroiled in a highly politicised environment.

THE RECOURSE OBLIGATION IMPOSED UPON THE SELLER/ CONTRACTOR

The second recourse obligation is that imposed upon the seller/contractor, **12.26** and may run either directly to the issuing bank or to the participants in reimbursement of payments they may have made to the issuer. The facility agreement commonly provides for the appointment of an agent bank which may collect payments made by the seller/contractor and apply them either to the issuing bank or the participants (*pro rata*), depending upon the terms of the agreement.[69]

---

[66] For an excellent article on bond syndication, see Kronfol, "The Syndication of Risk in Unconditional Bonds" (1984) J.B.L. 13.
[67] See Chap. 7 above.
[68] See para. 12.31 below.
[69] The seller/contractor will normally be required to pay interest either to the issuing bank or the syndicate members until full reimbursement has been made to such bank(s).

FIG. 8 SYNDICATED BOND ISSUE

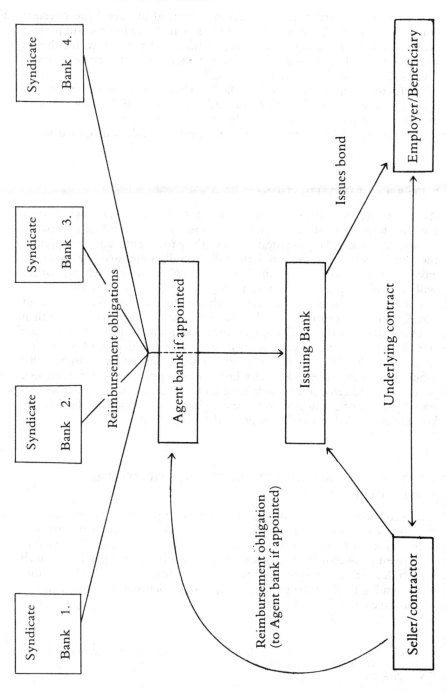

OTHER PROVISIONS IN THE SYNDICATED BOND AGREEMENT

The terms of the facility will also include many of the standard clauses   **12.27**
found in a syndicated loan agreement, including representations and warranties given by the seller/contractor, covenants and events of default. The
precise wording of these clauses will obviously depend upon the circumstances of each particular case and it will be vital to obtain the opinion of
local counsel to ensure that they impose valid and binding obligations upon
the seller/contractor.[69a]

Documentation of syndicated bond issues is obviously a complex affair
and will certainly add to the seller's/contractor's costs, probably making the
proposed contract much less attractive. In addition, where the bond is
required urgently, it may be impossible to arrange a syndicate quickly
enough.[70] Nevertheless, for banks wishing to spread the risk it is a most
effective mechanism, and may hold additional advantages for the seller/con-
tractor whose name will be publicised to a large market, thereby broaden-
ing exposure to the most important financial institutions.

Safeguarding the position of the seller/contractor

INSURANCE SUPPORT AND THE EXPORT CREDITS GUARANTEE
DEPARTMENT

a. Private Insurance

Insurance cover[71] can be obtained by the seller/contractor from the private   **12.28**
insurance market against the unreasonable or unjustified calling of first-
demand bonds. Such cover may protect the seller/contractor not only
against "unfair" calling but also where he defaults on the underlying contract for specified political reasons beyond his control.

Premium rates from the private market vary from country to country and
from contract to contract, with higher rates in higher risk countries, ironi-
cally where cover will be most wanted. There can be little doubt that, once
again, such cover will greatly add to the cost of the proposed contract, possibly pricing the seller/contractor out of serious contention.

b. Export Credits Guarantee Department

Additional support can be provided by the Export Credits Guarantee   **12.29**
Department (ECGD), which operates a bond support scheme as well as
providing for unfair calling of bonds.[72] The ECGD bond support scheme,
however, is restricted to contracts worth £250,000 or more, on cash or near
cash terms which are insured with ECGD against the normal credit risks.
Support is given by means of an indemnity to the issuing bank (see fig. 9 on
page 286) under which ECGD is unconditionally liable to reimburse the
bank in full for sums called under the terms of the bond. Any payment

---

[69a] The importance of legal opinions is considered in greater detail in Chap. 16 below.
[70] See Kronfol, above, n. 66, p. 17.
[71] Cover is available from Lloyd's underwriters, with the support of many of the major British
insurance companies, and from certain U.S. insurance groups.
[72] For fuller details of ECGD support, see *Contract Bonds and Guarantees* (2nd ed., 1983), published by the CBI.

made by ECGD becomes the subject of a separate claim against the seller/ contractor under the related recourse agreement. However, a refund will be made by ECGD if it is established that the seller/contractor was not in default under the terms the underlying contract, or that his failure was due to circumstances beyond his control.

Provision for unfair calling can be obtained from ECGD by means of an insurance policy fully covering any loss suffered by the seller/contractor, but in order to make a successful claim it must be shown that the seller/contractor was not in default on the underlying contract, or that failure was due to circumstances beyond his control.

FIG. 9 ECGD BOND SUPPORT SCHEMES

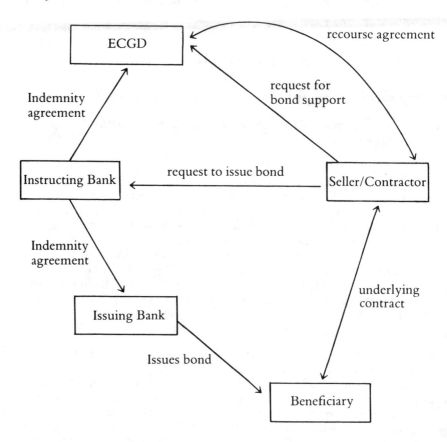

Correspondent banks

12.30 Overseas buyers/employers often insist upon bond support being issued by a national bank based in their own country. The difficulties facing the seller/ contractor in such a situation have already been highlighted,[73] and it will be

---

[73] See para. 12.20 above.

virtually impossible for him to prevent payment even where the demand is fraudulent.[74] Bankers should, therefore, encourage their customers to negotiate with the beneficiary and attempt to persuade him to take the bond directly from the customer's own bank. United Kingdom banks have many branches based overseas and these may be used where an overseas beneficiary insists upon the bond being issued by a bank based in the local jurisdiction, and if this can be achieved, much of the additional cost, delay, and most important of all, risk will be avoided.

The position in the United States

Nationally chartered banks in the United States are prohibited by Federal **12.31** and state banking laws from acting as guarantors or sureties for the obligations of third parties, and the prevailing authorities conclude that issuing such guarantees would be *ultra vires*.[75] As a consequence, performance type guarantees have become the business of an entirely separate industry, the surety bond industry. This industry is heavily regulated in the United States by the insurance commissioners, and as a consequence has always been very conservative in both its underwriting policies and geographical scope.

The prohibition on bank guarantees[76] and the conservatism of the surety industry created significant problems following the Second World War for America businesses wanting to increase international trade. The market was clearly in need of a viable instrument for guaranteeing performance under international contracts. The banks responded to this need by adapting the traditional commercial documentary letter of credit, which they were permitted to issue, to a new use. The new instrument, known as the standby letter of credit[77] thereby came into being.

Use of the standby letter of credit remained relatively infrequent until the late 1960's, due to concern over its legality. However, the use of this new instrument exploded during the 1970's with total facilities issued running into billions of U.S. dollars. A number of regulations were passed during this period by the U.S. Comptroller of Currency and in May 1977 formal approval was given to their use.

The standby letter of credit is built upon the same structure as the commercial documentary credit.[78] and is an obligation which arises upon presentation of documents.[79] In many cases, however, the underlying transaction does not generate documents and the only document which a

---

[74] *Ibid.*
[75] See Hartfield *Bank Credits and Acceptances* (5th ed., 1974), pp. 154–155; Lord, "The No-Guarantee Rule and the Standby Letter of Credit" (1979) 96 Banking L.J. 46; *Border Nat'l Bank* v. *American Nat'l Bank*, 282 F. 73 (5th Cir. 1922).
[76] The prohibition placed on nationally chartered banks does not extend to overseas branches of U.S. banks which can, and do, provide such guarantees.
[77] This new instrument was initially referred to as the "guaranty letter of credit" but its title was quickly changed because it was felt that the word "guaranty" was inappropriate bearing in mind the prohibitions placed on U.S. banks.
[78] See Chap. 13 below.
[79] See Gable "Standby Letters of Credit, Nomenclature has Confounded Analysis" (1980) 12 *Law and Policy in International Business*, No. 4, p. 903; Driscoll, "The Role of Standby Letters of Credit in International Commerce: Reflections After Iran," (1980) 20, Virginia J. Int'l Law, 459.

beneficiary must present is a written statement that the seller/contractor has failed to perform, or in some cases merely a written statement that payment is demanded under the standby facility.

12.32   Such statements will not provide the same sort of objective third-party evidence that a carriers' bill of lading provides where a commercial letter of credit is being used. Nevertheless, this type of triggering mechanism is common in many standby facilities.

The issuing bank's obligations under standby letters of credit can be closely compared with those arising in the case of first demand bonds, particularly where the triggering of the standby facility is by simple written demand. Furthermore, the standby letter of credit is an independent obligation on the part of the issuing bank, quite distinct from the underlying contract, so that/and accordingly, breach of that contract will not be an excuse permitting the bank to refuse payment, provided of course, that the proper documents (if required) are presented by the beneficiary in accordance with the terms of the standby letter of credit.

The only obligation placed upon the bank is to determine whether the documents presented conform "on their face." There is no duty to examine the subject matter of the underlying contract.[80]

The fraud exception

12.33   As with first demand bonds, the only circumstance in which a bank can be prevented from making payment under a standby letter of credit, when given in simple demand form, is where there is clear fraud. The problem in the United States has been the attitude of the courts in determining what is clear fraud.

The leading pre-Uniform Commercial Code case is *Szteijn* v. *J. Schroder Banking Corp*[81] in which the buyer sought to prevent the bank from honouring a letter of credit issued in connection with a sale of bristles from India to the United States. The problem arose over the fact that the seller had not shipped bristles, but rather crates of cowhair. Under traditional rules the court would not have interfered because the bank's letter of credit was quite separate from the underlying contract of sale. In this case however, the court said that if the buyer were able to show "intentional fraud on the part of the seller" then the court would prevent the bank from honouring the letter of credit. The court emphasised that the crucial ingredient was "active fraud on the part of the seller," a distinction which narrowly defined the fraud which would be allowed. More recent decisions[82] have defined fraud in broader terms than in *Szteijn*[83] and in the *American Bell*[84] case the court was favourably disposed to a broad concept of "fraud in the trans-

---

[80] See *Dynamics Corporation of America* v. *Citizens and Southern National Bank*, 356 F.Supp. 991 (N.D. Cal. 1973).

[81] 31 N.Y.S. 2d 631 (S.Ct.1941).

[82] See *Dynamics Corporation*, above, n. 80; *Intraworld Industries Inc.* v. *Girard, Trust Bank*, 461 Pa. 343, 336 A 2d 316 (1975); *Harris Corp.* v. *Nat'l Iranian Radio & Television*, 691 F. 2d 1344, 1353–8 (11th Cir. 1982); *American Bell International Inc.* v. *The Islamic Republic of Iran* 474 F.Supp. 420 (S.D.N.Y. 1979).

[83] Above, n. 81.

[84] Above, n. 82.

action."[85] It is submitted, however, that such a concept has no application in simple demand standby facilities and is unlikely to be followed.[86]

One final similarity which can be made between first demand bonds and standby letters of credit is that in both cases the bank will be liable if it makes payment, notwithstanding the fact that clear evidence of fraud has been brought to its attention.

Conclusion

The requirement to provide bonds and standby facilities in support of con-   **12.34** tractual obligations will continue to be an important factor in international trade. These instruments enjoy enormous popularity with overseas buyers as well as bankers who are constantly refining the documentation used, in order to satisfy market needs.

Whether such instruments maintain this popularity will depend to a large extent upon the attitude of the courts, and in particular their willingness to enforce contractual undertakings according to their terms. This explains, to some extent, the harsh attitude which has been adopted by both the English and United States courts to the fraud exception. In the event that the courts change their traditional approach it is likely that the instruments would soon lose their commercial efficacy.

---

[85] *Ibid.*, p. 424.
[86] It should be recognised however that in many of the Iranian Letter of Credit cases the courts appeared favourably disposed to the "fraud in the transaction" concept, see Getz "Enjoining the International Standby Letter of Credit: The Iranian Letter of Credit Cases" (1980) 21 Harv. Int'l. L.J. 189.

13. Commercial Letters of Credit

GENERAL

Characteristics of letters of credit

13.01 Commercial credits are most commonly used in connection with import and export transactions, where an exporter who contracts to sell goods to a foreign purchaser is unwilling to despatch them in reliance on the purchaser's personal credit, either because the purchaser is unknown to him or because his credit is uncertain. The purchaser, on the other hand may equally be uncertain about the exporter's reliability, and, therefore, unwilling to part with his money before the goods are registered. A transaction under a commercial letter of credit, therefore, presupposes the case of a seller or buyer whose reputation is sound in his own country, but who is not sufficiently known in foreign markets, to enable him to rely on his reputation when selling or purchasing goods abroad. A compromise, therefore, has to be reached whereby the purchaser agrees in a contract of sale to procure the opening of a commercial credit by a reliable bank in his own country in favour of the exporter, and when the bank notifies the exporter of the opening of the credit, the exporter has an assurance that when he despatches the goods and tenders the shipping documents to the bank, he will be paid the purchase price by the bank. Thus, the exporter has the certainty of being able to obtain payment on the agreed date, and the importer is able to postpone payment until he knows that the goods have been despatched and probably until an even later date so as to enable him to re-sell the goods before the issuing bank pays for the price of the goods under the credit.

A commercial letter of credit may be said to be an undertaking by a bank to pay a sum of money to the person in whose favour the credit is issued, or to accept or purchase a bill of exchange drawn or held by that person. The bank's undertaking is usually conditional on the presentation of certain specified documents to the bank showing that the goods described in the credit have been despatched to the beneficiary.

13.02 It is of the essence to a banker's commercial credit that there is an antecedent underlying contract for the sale of goods or other contract in which it is agreed that the price or other payment will be exchanged by means of a banker's letter of credit. The duty of arranging payment by this method rests on the buyer who makes an application in writing for the purpose to the issuing bank. This application is at the same time a mandate, a request and an indemnity undertaking. It requests the bank to issue or open a letter of credit and set out the conditions under which the bank is to pay the beneficiary or honour his bills of exchange. In the letter of application the applicant undertakes to reimburse the bank for all payments made by it under the letter of credit, and this forms the basis of the contract between the issuing bank and the applicant for the credit. Once the bank is satisfied that the letter of application is in order and the conditions in it are practicable, the bank issues the letter of credit in favour of the beneficiary. It may be sent directly to him, or it may be sent to the bank's agents in the beneficiary's country. The letter of credit may be in any form, but it should contain an undertaking by the issuing bank to pay the amount for which it is issued or to accept or purchase bills of exchange drawn by the beneficiary for that amount, provided the conditions set out in the letter of credit are fulfilled (*e.g.* presentation of shipping documents).

An agreement that payment should be by letter of credit involves several steps. These steps are traced below:

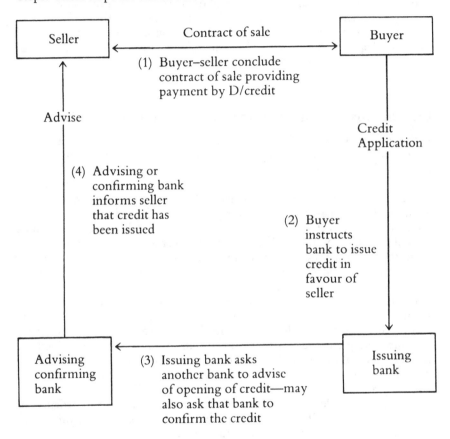

Although the courts have not attempted to define letters of credit, the effects these undertakings have has been enunciated by the courts. In *Equitable Trust Company of New York* v. *Dawson Partners Ltd.*[1] Scrutton L.J., said:—

> "The system is intended to allow the seller to obtain money as soon as he ships the goods by discounting bills drawn on the purchaser, while the purchaser has not to pay for the goods until some time after he has sold them. To do this the discounting bank must be furnished with some security satisfactory to it that if the shipment complies with certain conditions it will be paid for. This is obtained by the promise of

[1] (1926) 25 Lloyds L.R. 90, 93.

the bank giving the . . . credit to accept bills for the price if the shipment complies with the specified conditions . . . "

There have been attempts to standardise the conditions on which banks are prepared to issue and to act on commercial credits. The uniform *Customs and Practice for Commercial Documentary Credits*, now in their fifth edition (1983) were originally formulated in 1933 by the International Chamber of Commerce and are virtually universally applied. The uniform customs apply to all documentary credits unless the parties agree otherwise. However, there must be wording in the credit indicating that the credit is to be subject to the uniform customs and practices on documentary credits. In *Forestal Mimosa* v. *Oriental Credit*[2] a marginal note to the effect that the uniform customs were to be incorporated into the documentary credit was held to be sufficient.

Outline history of commercial documentary credits

13.03 Although transactions similar to banker's commercial credits were occasionally entered into during the middle of the eighteenth century, it was not until the middle of the nineteenth century that transactions similar to the modern commercial credit began to appear in the U.K. The earliest form of commercial credit was one by which a bank or firm of merchants authorised an intending purchaser of goods, or a person who needed to raise money or incur debts in connection with the manufacture or sale of goods, to draw bills of exchange on the bank or firm up to a certain amount, and the bank undertook to accept the bills when presented by the person in whose favour the credit was opened, or by persons to whom the bills were payable or to whom they had been negotiated.

In the earlier part of the nineteenth century an export transaction would be financed by a bank or other issuer of a credit issuing a letter of credit to the purchaser of the goods which authorised him to draw on the issuer for the purchase price and costs of transportation, and which contained the issuer's undertaking to accept a bill of exchange for the total amount when presented by the person in whose favour the bill was drawn. Under such a letter of credit the purchaser could either send a bill drawn on the issuer together with the letter of credit to the seller and leave him to procure the acceptance of the bills, or more simply, the purchaser could obtain the issuer's acceptance himself and send the accepted bill to the seller. In the 1870's and 1880's a change in the form of the letter of credit took place by the substitution of the creditor who was to be paid by means of the credit as the beneficiary, instead of the issuer's customer.

This form of credit also had the advantage that the creditor was brought into an immediate relationship with the issuing bank, and was not merely a third party with whom the bank came into contact as a result of issuing a letter of credit to the debtor. Two forms of letters of credit were common at this time, first, the negotiation credit which has now largely been superseded in the U.K., although it is still used and fairly popular in the Far East, and secondly, an authority given to the creditor to draw bills on the issuing

[2] [1986] 1 W.L.R. 631.

bank itself and containing an undertaking by the bank to accept or pay the creditor's bills on presentation.

This is the basic form of the modern banker's commercial credit, and developments since the First World War have merely elaborated this basic form of the credit and attached additional obligations to it, which have been developed by commercial practice as the needs of commerce have become more complex and sophisticated.

JUDICIAL BASIS OF THE LETTER OF CREDIT

The legal nature of the relationships arising under the letter of credit has **13.04** been treated as based on the ordinary principles of contract law and for that reason, the rights and obligations of the parties have been determined by the terms of the written agreement or implied under the rules of contract. In dealing with the relationship between the issuing bank and the seller there arises legal uncertainty, however, because at no point does the issuing bank enter into negotiations with the seller in order to conclude a contract with him, and seemingly, the issue of the letter of credit is simply an act done by the bank acting on behalf of the buyer. In addition to the underlying contract of sale where the purchase price is paid by means of a letter of credit, however, two further contracts must nevertheless arise, namely, (i) a contract between the buyer of the goods and the issuing bank by which it engages to issue the credit and (ii) a contract between the bank and the seller of the goods by which the bank undertakes to honour bills drawn by the seller under the credit and to pay the amount of the credit on presentation of the documents. In recent years the courts have assumed without comment that there exists a legal contractual relationship between the bank and the seller, and the decisions of the court have been exclusively concerned with the incidents of that contract. In order to establish the existence of a binding legal relationship between the issuing bank and the seller various theories have been suggested by legal writers. It is proposed to deal with these in outline.

Revocable credits

Where the parties to the sales contract require a revocable credit to be issued **13.05** no difficulty in determining the nature of the relationship between the issuing bank and the seller arises. The issuing bank in opening a revocable credit does not become legally liable until it accepts or negotiates the seller's drafts, so that the seller has no rights against the bank until his drafts are both tendered and accepted. The basis of a revocable credit is that the issuing bank is entitled to terminate the credit without notification to the seller. A person acting on the revocable credit is deemed to have notice of the fact that the credit can be revoked or altered at any time without notice.

In *Cape Asbestos Co. Ltd.* v. *Lloyds Bank Ltd.*[3] Bailhache J. held that when the credit is revocable the bank is under no legal obligation to give notice of the cancellation to the beneficiary, and if it did give notice it was as a matter of courtesy and not obligation.

---

[3] [1921] W.N. 274; see also, *Urquhart Lindsay* v. *Eastern Bank Ltd.* [1922] 1 K.B. 318.

Article 9 of the Uniform Customs provides that: "A revocable credit may be amended or cancelled at any moment without prior notice to the beneficiary . . . " so that if notice were required by law to be given before the issuing bank could terminate the credit, this would conflict with the essential feature of the revocable credit, namely, that it imposes no obligation on the issuing bank until the shipping documents are accepted by the bank and the bill of exchange tendered with them is accepted. Gutteridge and Megrah point out that a beneficiary relying on the revocable credit must be expected to realise that the credit can be terminated without notification, and so the beneficiary cannot contend that the issuing bank is estopped from cancelling the credit merely because he has acted on it.

Article 7(c) of the Uniform Customs deems all credits to be revocable in the absence of an express indication otherwise, and because the parties realise that no security is afforded to the seller under a credit which can be revoked whether it is stated to be revocable or not, they will in practice expressly agree that the credit is to be irrevocable, and the credit will itself state that it is irrevocable. Moreover, as between the buyer and seller, unless the latter expressly agrees to accept a revocable credit, he is entitled by implication in the contract of sale to have an irrevocable letter of credit issued by the buyer's bank as the court held in *Giddens* v. *Anglo African Produce Co.*[4] Juridically, therefore, a letter of credit which is expressed to be revocable, or which is not expressed to be irrevocable, is a mere unilateral statement of intention by the issuing bank on which the beneficiary is invited to act but entirely at his own risk. In fact, it is no more than a statement that the bank is authorised by the buyer to pay the price of the goods bought from the seller, but without prejudice to the right of the buyer to cancel the authority or the bank to renounce it.

Irrevocable credits

13.06   The relationship between the issuing bank and the seller has been the subject of more frequent judicial treatment when the issuing bank has opened an irrevocable credit in favour of the beneficiary-seller. Article 10 of the Uniform Customs provides: "irrevocable credits constitute definite undertakings of the issuing bank, provided that the terms and conditions of the credit are complied with . . . " and " . . . such undertakings can neither be amended nor cancelled without agreement of all parties thereto. . . . "

The purpose of an irrevocable credit is to provide the beneficiary of the credit with an unqualified obligation by the issuing bank to accept and pay bills drawn by him if he presents the documents called for by the credit to the bank. The banker's obligation under an irrevocable credit is, therefore, intended to be immediate and conditional only on the seller presenting the requisite documents. However, there are no direct negotiations between the issuing bank and the seller, and because of this the nature of legal relationship of the issuing bank and the seller, and of the bank's obligation to the seller are not obviously contractual.

The earlier letter of credit was more easily justified as being based on a contract, because it was issued to the buyer (or applicant of the credit) who

---

[4] (1923) 14 Ll.L.R. 230.

was thereby authorised to raise funds or purchase goods from third parties by drawing bills of exchange in their favour which would be accepted or purchased by the issuing bank. The letter of credit could, therefore, be considered as an open offer to prospective beneficiaries and they could accept this offer by giving credit to the applicant for the credit in return for bills drawn on the issuing bank.[5]

There is now no justification for treating the issuing bank's customer who has applied for the issue of the credit as the bank's agent to constitute a contractual relationship between it and the claimant, or to treat the claimant as an assignee of the customer's rights against the issuing bank. The modern letter of credit is issued as a result of a contract between the issuing bank's customer and the bank under which benefits are to be given by the bank to a third party, the beneficiary, and it is intended that his rights against the bank shall be determined, not by the terms of the contract between the bank and its customer, but by the terms of the letter of credit which is issued by the bank to the beneficiary. The letter of credit is, therefore, intended to constitute a separate contract, but the difficulty which arises in envisaging such a contract between the bank and the beneficiary is that there are no direct negotiations between the bank and the beneficiary preceding the issue of the letter of credit, and there therefore appears to be no offer made by the bank which is accepted by the beneficiary. Furthermore, there appears to be no consideration given by the beneficiary for the issuing bank's promise in the letter of credit. Because of the absence of these two essential features of any contract the juridical basis for the contract between the issuing bank and the beneficiary has been the subject of considerable doubt and ingenuity in finding a satisfactory explanation.

A number of theories have been advanced by legal writers to justify the conclusion that there is a contract between the issuing bank and the beneficiary. Additionally, juridical forms other than a contract have been resorted to, to explain the legal relationship between the issuing bank and the beneficiary. It is now proposed to examine these various theories.

Offer and acceptance theory

One of the main theories advanced to explain the nature of the relationship between the issuing bank and the seller or beneficiary of the credit is the Offer and Acceptance theory, the basis of which is that the letter of credit is an offer which the beneficiary may accept as the person to whom the offer is directed. On this basis, a letter of credit which requests S to sell and deliver certain goods to B and promises in return that the issuing bank will pay the price or accept or purchase bills of exchange for the price is such an offer. Alternatively, it is argued that if the buyer furnishes consideration to the issuing bank in the form of an executory promise to put the bank in funds by a specified date in return for the issue of a letter of credit which authorises the seller to draw on the issuing bank, the issue of a letter of credit is an offer to the designated seller made pursuant to the prior contract, and, therefore, is irrevocable and can be accepted by the seller acting on it. The second of these expositions of the offer and acceptance theory accords more

13.07

---

[5] *Union Bank of Canada* v. *Cole* (1877) 47 L.J.C.P. 100.

closely with practice, since letters of credit are normally issued only after the underlying contract which they are to finance has been entered into, and in any case they are not expressed to be issued in consideration of the beneficiary entering into or carrying out the underlying contract with the issuing bank's customer.

The contractual rules relating to Offer and Acceptance present no difficulties. There must be a specified offer capable of acceptance by the offeree assenting to it, and the person who accepts the offer must be the person or one of the persons to whom it is addressed. In the case of a letter of credit, the offer made by the issuing bank to the beneficiary must be communicated to him before he can accept it. It is not sufficient that the issuing bank has merely instructed its branch overseas or another bank to issue the credit, and the fact that the underlying contract of sale requires the credit to be issued by a named bank and that bank in fact issues the credit does not automatically impose an obligation on the bank toward the beneficiary.

A question on which opinions have differed radically is that if the issue of a letter of credit is an offer by the issuing bank to the seller, at which point of time does acceptance of the offer by the seller take place, so that the contract between them binding under English law can happen at one of two points of time, both of which have been treated as the material time by judicial decisions, namely:—

(1) when the bank opens and notifies the credit to the beneficiary; or

(2) when the beneficiary acts on the credit or notifies his acceptance of it to the issuing bank.

1. Conclusion of a contract when the bank opens and notifies the credit to the beneficiary

13.08   The parties here contemplate that the letter of credit constitutes an irrevocable obligation binding the issuing bank in favour of the beneficiary (normally the seller) from the moment it is issued and notified to him. In *Hamzeh Malas* v. *British Imex Industries*,[6] Jenkins L.J., in giving judgment, said: " . . . it seems to me plain enough that the opening of a confirmed letter of credit constitutes a bargain between the banker and the vendor of the goods which impose on the banker an absolute obligation to pay . . . "

If this view is accepted it appears to be established that the contract between the issuing bank and the seller comes into existence when the letter of credit is issued and notified to the seller.

If acceptance of the offer takes place at the time the issuing bank notifies the seller, it does not appear to be necessary for an acceptance of the credit to be given by the beneficiary to the issuing bank. In a unilateral contract where express acceptance of the offer made by one party is unnecessary, the other party's conduct in adopting the contract operates as acceptance and may also constitute the whole or part of the consideration.[7] But in such a situation where one party has the power unilaterally to bring a contract into existence it is necessary for him to fulfil the conditions which the offeror requires for the adoption of the contract he proposes, or at least to do an act

---

[6] [1958] 1 All E.R. 262.
[7] *Carlill* v. *Carbolic Smoke Ball Co.* [1893] 1 Q.B. 256.

which unequivocally shows his intention to adopt the contract. If the opinion of Jenkins L.J. in the *Hamzeh Malas* case is taken literally, however, it would mean that the contract under an irrevocable letter of credit becomes binding before the seller has done any act adopting the terms of the credit. This would shut out the possiblity of the bank withdrawing the credit by notifying the beneficiary to that effect before he had acted in reliance on it or otherwise adopted it.

The view that there is an acceptance and a binding contract conferring rights on the beneficiary of the credit when the issuing bank notifies him of its issue leaves unsolved the question of whether any consideration is given by the beneficiary in return for the bank's promise to accept or pay for his bills. The customer of the issuing bank who procures the issue of the letter of credit undoubtedly gives consideration for the bank's promise, but this does not mean that the beneficiary does so. The accepted rule in this respect is that two parties cannot by a contract confer rights upon a third person who is not a party to the contract and who, therefore, gives no consideration.

2. Conclusion of a contract when the beneficiary notifies the issuing bank of his acceptance of the credit or acts on it

An objection raised by Gutteridge and Megrah to the offer and acceptance theory is that if the letter of credit is merely an offer: " . . . there must be an intervening space of time (*i.e.* until the documents are tendered) during which the banker can withdraw the offer and cancel the credit, thus defeating the very object for which it was issued."   **13.09**

The objection is unanswerable if it is considered that the beneficiary's acceptance of the bank's offer takes place only when he tenders the documents called for by the credit, but there is authority to suggest that in fact acceptance may take place earlier. In *Urquhart Lindsay & Co. Ltd.* v. *Eastern Bank Ltd.*[8] Rowlatt J., in dealing with the legal position of the parties, said: "There can be no doubt that upon the plaintiff's acting upon the undertaking contained in the letter of credit, consideration moved from the plaintiffs which bound the defendants to the irrevocable character of the arrangement between the defendants and the plaintiffs."

The learned judge would seem to suggest that the contract was concluded by the plaintiff's "acting upon the undertaking" and that this was sufficient to constitute acceptance of the offer made by the defendant bank. However, the judge did not explain what he meant by "acting upon the undertaking." Davis[8a] suggests that in the particular circumstances the commencement of the manufacture of the goods to be financed by the credit is sufficient for this purpose and he rejects the view of Gutteridge and Megrah that only the tender of the documents called for by the credit amounts to acceptance, thus leaving the contract with the issuing bank inchoate until the completion of the manufacture of the goods and their shipment. It is submitted that the view put forward by Gutteridge and Megrah places the time of acceptance

---

[8] [1922] 1 K.B. 318.
[8a] (1936) 52 L.Q.R. 230.

at too late a point in the transaction and that if this view were correct the credit would be revocable by the issuing bank (and the seller would have no protection at all if the credit were revoked or cancelled before the tender by him of the requisite documents). In the case of irrevocable credits, however, this would destroy the whole purpose of making them irrevocable, since the whole basis of the credit is that it cannot be revoked once it has been issued.

If, on the other hand, the view of Davis is accepted, the contract between the issuing bank and the seller comes into existence when the seller-beneficiary commences to manufacture the goods covered by the credit.[9]

There is some support for the view that partial performance of the seller's obligation under the contract of sale or the commencement of such performance may be sufficient as acceptance of the credit by the seller and as consideration furnished by him under the ordinary rules of contract. In *Offord* v. *Davies*[10] and *Great Northern Railway* v. *Witham*[11] it was suggested that the contract was effective as soon as the offeree made an unequivocal start on the undertaking in question.

Gutteridge and Megrah prefer the view that the contract is concluded when the documents are presented to the bank; this view ensures certainty as to the time of acceptance, but it is submitted that it places the time of acceptance at too late a stage in the proceedings. The view is supported by Donaldson J., in *Elder Dempster Lines Ltd.* v. *Ionic Shipping Agency Inc.*,[12] where he said:

> "The best explanation of the legal phenomenon constituted by a banker's letter of credit is that it is an offer which is accepted by being drawn upon. Accordingly what matters is the offer which was made to the plaintiffs and not the way in which, as a matter of history, the individual parts of the offer came together . . . "

It may be concluded, therefore, that if acceptance by the seller is necessary, the contract is definitely complete and binding not later than the time when the shipping documents are presented to the issuing bank, but there is considerable judicial support for the view that acceptance takes place when the seller commences to manufacture the goods in question, although theoretically this would still give the bank the opportunity to revoke the credit after it is issued but before the seller commences manufacture.

13.10   Whether acceptance of the issuing bank's offer takes place when the issuing bank communicates the issue of the letter of credit to the beneficiary, or alternatively when the seller commences performance under the contract or presents the shipping documents for acceptance, the question of what amounts to the consideration furnished by the seller for the credit still has to be examined. The rule of English law was finally laid down in *Dunlop* v. *Selfridge*,[13] where the House of Lords held that in order for there to be a valid contract consideration must move from the promisee, and in the case of bankers' commercial credit it was held in *Morgan* v. *Larivière*[14] that con-

---

[9] See *Dexters Ltd.* v. *Schenter & Co.* (1923) 14 Lloyd's Law Rep. 586.
[10] (1862) 12 C.B.N.S. 748.
[11] 1873 L.R. 9 C.P. 16.
[12] [1968] 1 Lloyd's Rep. 529.
[13] [1915] A.C. 847.
[14] (1875) L.R. 7 H.L. 423.

sideration moves solely from the buyer of the goods and is consequently insufficient to support any promise made by the banker to the seller. However, in recent years the courts have not questioned what constitutes consideration for the credit moving from the seller or beneficiary but have assumed that there is valuable consideration given by him for the banker's promise.[15]

McCurdy[15a] submits that the consideration furnished by the seller is not the manufacture or commencement of manufacture of the goods, because that is not what the bank bargains for and because performance by the seller of an act which he is legally bound to perform under the contract of sale cannot be consideration for the bank's undertaking. However, a distinction has to be drawn between two situations, first, where the promise to perform the existing duty is made to a person to whom the promisor is already legally bound, and secondly, where the promise is made to a third party.

In the former case it is accepted that neither a promise to do a thing nor the actual doing of it will be a good consideration if it is something which the promisor is already bound to do, either by the general law or by a subsisting contract with the other party.

However, where a promise is made by one person to another to do what he is already bound to do by a contract with a third party, that constitutes valuable consideration for a promise by the other. A promise by A to B to do what A is already bound to do by a contract with C constitutes good consideration for a promise by B to A.[16]

The guarantee theory

In order to determine the legal nature of the relationship that arises between **13.11** the issuing bank and the seller, various other theories have been put forward. The Guarantee Theory construes the banker's commercial credits as subordinate contracts by which the issuing bank guarantees the payment of the price of the goods or other sum payable under the contract between the beneficiary and the bank's customer. However, this supposes that the bank's obligation to the seller is not an independent one, but is dependent on the buyer defaulting in paying the amount he owes the beneficiary.

This theory does not stand up to criticism. First, it should be noted that the liability of the issuing bank to pay is a primary one under a letter of credit, and not a liability dependent on the buyer's default; on the contrary, the seller can only resort to the buyer for payment of the price of the goods if the bank defaults under the letter of credit. Secondly, the letter of credit cannot be construed as complying with the provisions of section 4 of the Statute of Frauds, which requires a guarantee to be evidenced by a note or memorandum in writing identifying the principal debtor and the debt he owes. Furthermore, under the law relating to a guarantee, the issue of the letter of credit would preclude the seller and buyer from altering the terms of the original sales contract if the letter of credit were to remain in force,

---

[15] See *Urquhart Lindsay* v. *Eastern Bank Ltd.* [1922] 1 K.B. 318; and *Re Agra & Mastermans Bank* [1867] L.R. 2 Ch.App. 391.
[15a] "Commercial Letters of Credit" (1921–22) 35 Harvard Law Review 539.
[16] *Shadwell* v. *Shadwell* (1860) 9 C.B.(N.S.) 159.

and it is clear that a letter of credit continues to be effective according to its terms notwithstanding such an alteration.

The estoppel or trustee theory

13.12 This theory is based on the principle enunciated in *Pickard* v. *Sears*[17] that:

> "Where one by his words or conduct wilfully causes another to believe the existence of a certain state of things, and induces him to act on that belief, so as to alter his own previous position, the former is concluded from averring against the latter a different state of things as existing at the same time."

The theory supposes that the issue of an irrevocable letter of credit amounts to a representation by the issuing bank that it has received an amount equal to the price and that it holds that amount to the issue of the seller. It is then deduced that the bank is estopped by this representation against the seller who acts in reliance on it from contending that it does not hold the money to his use. The basis of this theory is that it is usual for the buyer either to deposit money with the issuing bank to cover the amount to be paid to the seller, or if the buyer does not make such a deposit for him to arrange for a loan from the bank for the purpose. This is the only meaning which an irrevocable credit can have, and if a bank issues an irrevocable credit without these preliminaries having been completed, it is estopped from denying the receipt of the money after the seller has acted on the representation.

The argument has little support in case law, since the buyer rarely deposits the purchase money immediately (or arranges a loan from the issuing bank) as this would be contrary to the very basis of letters of credit, the purpose of which is to enable a bank to accept a time draft for the purchase price which the seller may discount and for the buyer to receive the goods before being obliged to pay for them. Furthermore, the issuing bank which issues an irrevocable letter of credit merely undertakes that a binding contract been made in favour of the seller and the bank promises to pay on certain conditions. Such representations are not sufficient to raise an estoppel in favour of the seller.

13.13 The estoppel theory has been rejected by the courts in *Morgan* v. *Larivière*[18] where the House or Lords held:

> " . . . I read this letter as being nothing more than this: a statement by bankers to a tradesman who supplies goods to a customer of the bankers that they, the bankers, on behalf of their customer, will act as paymasters to the tradesman up to a certain sum of money. . . . In a transaction of that kind there is nothing of equitable assignment, there is nothing on trust; and it appears to me that any banker who had given an undertaking of that kind would be very much surprised to find that it was held that a certain portion of the funds of his customer in his hands had been impressed with a trust, had been equitably assigned, and had, in fact, ceased to be the moneys of the customer. . . . "

---

[17] (1837) 6 A & E 469.
[18] (1875) L.R.7 H.L. Cas. 423.

In order for the funds in the hands of the bank to be impressed with a trust, the bank must not only have actual receipt of the money, but there must also be an express or implied admission that the funds are appropriated to a specific purpose. Furthermore, if the bank agrees to hold funds of the seller on trust or for a certain purpose, the trust or the use in favour of the seller does not arise until the letter of credit is actually issued by the bank and accepted by the seller, for a trust or use in favour of the seller cannot arise merely by the intention of the buyer that the issue of the letter of credit shall appropriate the funds held by the bank to the seller. There must actually be an agreement between the holder of the funds (the bank) and the intended recipient (the seller) for a use or trust to arise. In *Walker* v. *Rostron*[19] P sold goods to B taking his acceptance of certain bills and sent the goods to D as B's agent. P being in doubt of B's solvency required further security, and it was, therefore, agreed between P, B and D that B should write and deliver to D a letter authorising him to use the proceeds of the consignments in order to pay B's acceptances as they fell due if P had not previously been paid by B. The letter was delivered to D and he agreed to make payments in accordance with it. Before the bills matured for payment B became bankrupt and D refused to pay P. The court held that P could sue D for the money had and received and there was consideration for the new agreement between the plaintiff and the defendant because of the existence of a debt (owing to P).

The assignment and novation theories

McCurdy[20] advances two alternative theories to explain the binding effect **13.14** of letters of credit. First, he suggests that immediately the contract between the buyer and the issuing bank is entered into, it is assigned by the buyer to the seller with notice to the banker. There is some support for this theory in the earlier cases relating to letters of credit. In *Hindley & Co.* v. *Tothill Watson & Co.*[21] it was said: "The proposals contained in these letters are obviously made with the express intention of placing the company and the plaintiffs in direct relations and giving each reciprocal rights, and getting rid of the defendants as intervening parties."

The theory found judicial support in the earlier case of *Agra and Mastermans Bank ex p. Asiatic Banking Corp.*,[22] where on the question of assignment, Cairns L.J. said:

"But assuming the contract to have been at law a contract with Dickson, Tatham & Co. [the buyers] and with no other, it is clear that the contract was in equity assignable and that Dickson Tatham & Co. must be taken to have assigned (if assignment were needed) to the Asiatic Banking Corporation . . ."

However, it must be remembered that these cases were decided when letters of credit were issued to the buyer, and it is doubtful whether the theory would find support in the case of modern letters of credit, which are issued

[19] (1842) 9 M. & W. 411.
[20] "Commercial Letters of Credit" (1921–22) 35 Harvard Law Review 583.
[21] (1894) N.Z.L.R. 13.
[22] (1867) L.R. 2 Ch.App. 391.

directly to the seller. Indeed, the assignment theory has been disapproved in two cases. In *Citizens Bank of Louisiana* v. *Bank of New Orleans*[23] it was held that even if the debtor has funds in the hands of the bank, they are not impliedly assigned to the beneficiary of the credit upon it being issued. This was confirmed in *Morgan* v. *Larivière* in which the court further said that the bank is in no way made liable to the beneficiary by the debtor contracting the debt he owes to the beneficiary and promising that the bank will issue a credit in order to pay it.

The second theory advanced by McCurdy is the Novation Theory; that when the sales contract requires the buyer to procure the issue of an irrevocable credit, there is in it a term that, on the credit being issued, the buyer with the consent of the seller shall cease to be a party to the transaction and that by virtue of a novation, the issuing banker shall be substituted for the buyer as the other party to the contract.

McCurdy recognises that the assignment theory is not wholly satisfactory in that it confers upon the seller only equitable or derivative rights, so that any defences the bank might have against the buyer under its contract with him could be set up against the seller. For this reason he finds it "necessary to go a step further" and find a novation assented to in advance by the seller.

The theory of novation can be criticised on the ground that it involves the release of the buyer from his liability to pay for the goods in consideration for the bank assuming that liability. This does not in fact occur, for it has been clearly established that the issue of a letter of credit does not operate to release the buyer from liability for the price of the goods sold to him.

The theory that the buyer is the seller's agent

13.15   Gutteridge and Megrah advance the theory that there is, in the contract of sale, an implied authority from the seller to the buyer to arrange for payment of the price by the issue of credit. The authors[24] say:

> "The cardinal feature of the transaction is that the seller is not content to rely on the buyer's ability or readiness to pay the price. . . . The seller is, therefore, willing to make a contract of sale only on the basis that the buyer will procure an independent promise of payment made by a banker . . . "

McCurdy rejects the view that the buyer acts as an agent of the seller in procuring the issue of the letter of credit to be issued, but he does not give any reasons. Davis also rejects this view on the ground that if the buyer were the seller's agent, then under the rules of agency the seller would be responsible for all the acts of the buyer as his agent in negotiating the issue of the credit.

The agency theory would also produce the result that the contract between the issuing bank and the seller would be governed not by the terms of the letter of credit (as it undoubtedly is) but by the instructions to open the credit given by the buyer to the issuing bank and accepted by it.

---

[23] (1873) L.R. 6 H.L. 352.
[24] p. 32.

The seller's offer theory

13.16 This theory is based on the view that the seller by stipulating in the antecedent sales contract for the issue of an irrevocable credit undertakes to deliver the documents of title to the goods to the issuing banker (instead of to the buyer) in return for the bank's undertaking to honour the seller's drafts. The theory is obviously inapplicable to clean credits in which the banker does not require the delivery of documents to him. The theory also supposes that the seller is bound by a contract with the bank from the moment the credit is issued, since this would constitute the bank's acceptance of the seller's offer. The defect of the theory is that the seller is in fact under no obligation to deliver the shipping documents in respect of the goods to the bank and the only effect of him delivering them to the buyer is that he cannot then avail himself of the credit.

To conclude, the only theory that can explain the juridical basis of the modern letter of credit is the Offer and Acceptance theory, but under English Law this theory leaves unresolved the question of what constitutes valuable consideration for the contract between the issuing bank and the seller. Some of the other theories can be applied to explain the basis of the early kind of letter of credit, but they are inapplicable to the letter of credit in its modern context. While the development of the commercial credits has been due to a large extent to mercantile custom, the letter of credit is these days more the creature of contract than custom, and the courts readily hold it to be the subject of the rules of contract law.

VARIETIES OF LETTERS OF CREDIT

13.17 The law of commercial letters of credit has developed and changed as the needs of the commercial community have required. One of the illustrations of this fact lies in the various types of credit which have been devised to meet divergent circumstances. The nomenclature for the different kinds of credit has not always received judicial approval, and regard must, therefore, be given to the meanings attached to the terms used by the commercial community, or when they have received judicial recognition, by the judiciary. The modern form of credit is of recent growth. It is issued not to the issuing bank's customer, but to a third party named by the customer, with whom the customer has commercial dealings, in order to carry through a particular transaction. In effect, the name and solvency of the banker are substituted for those of the customer. It is now proposed to examine the various types of credit and the distinguishing names used for them.

General and special credits

13.18 A general letter of credit is one addressed by the issuing bank to the world generally, requesting that advances be made to a named person (the bank's customer) by anyone to whom it is shown. In *Re Agra and Masterman's Bank ex p. Asiatic Banking Corporation*[25] it was held that a general letter of credit

---

[25] (1867) L.R. 2 Ch. App. 391.

constitutes a continuing offer which is capable of acceptance by anyone who acts in reliance upon it.

Moreover, the court held that the letter of credit constituted a contract to the benefit of which all persons taking and paying for the bills on the faith of it were entitled in equity, without regard to the equities between the bank and the beneficiary and that the appellant was entitled to prove for the amount payable under the bills even though the bank had not accepted them.

A special letter of credit is one which is not addressed to the world generally, but instead to some specified person or persons, and only the person to whom the letter is addressed can acquire rights under it. The distinction is of little importance today, when the main object of a letter of credit is to assist a commercial concern to carry out a contract which he has already made.

Clean (or open) and documentary credits

13.19 In a clean or open letter of credit, the issuing bank undertakes to accept or negotiate drafts drawn by the beneficiary without any shipping or other documents being delivered to it. A bank issuing such a letter of credit lacks the security given by the possession of documents of title. For this reason, clean letters of credit will only be issued at the request of a customer whose financial standing is sound, and even then the bank will normally require the customer to lodge sufficient security to cover any bills which may be drawn under the credit.

A documentary credit is one in which the person or bank issuing it undertakes to honour bills drawn under the credit only if they have attached to them certain specified documents, such as bills of lading, insurance policies and invoices which the bank or person can hold as security for the advances made. In *Mann, Taylor & Co. Ltd.* v. *Royal Bank of Canada*[26] the court said that a documentary credit in that particular case meant a loan of money on the bank's credit to the borrower on the security of a document of title to the goods. Any document of title to goods would suffice unless particular documents were prescribed in the conditions set out in the letter of credit.

Revolving credit

13.20 A revolving credit is one the amount of which remains constant for a specified period, so that, whenever during that period it is drawn upon, it becomes automatically available again for the full amount of the credit. In *Nordskog & Co.* v. *National Bank*,[27] the meaning of a revolving credit was explained by the joint general manager of Lloyds Bank, who was called as an expert witness. He defined a revolving credit as: "a credit for a certain sum at any one time outstanding, which is automatically renewed by putting on at the bottom what you have taken off at the top."

---

[26] (1935) 40 Com.Cas. 267.
[27] (1922) 10 Lloyds L.R. 652.

Anticipatory credits

This term refers not to letters of credit themselves, but to advances made on **13.21** the strength of them. These advances are made by bankers abroad to enable suppliers or agents for purchasers to acquire raw materials or produce. The advances are made to the beneficiary of the letter of credit and the letter expressly provides that the goods for which anticipatory advances are made or the products into which they are incorporated shall be shipped and the relevant shipping documents delivered to the issuing bank.

Negotiation credits

The earlier form of credit, which was predominantly used in trade between **13.22** the United Kingdom and the Far East and Australasia, was the negotiation credit, by which the issuing bank undertook to purchase bills of exchange drawn by the creditor on the debtor. The bills were rarely accepted by the debtor before presentation to the issuing bank, and when the bank had paid the face value or the discounted value of the bill to the holder of the bill, it reimbursed itself by debiting the debtor's account as its customer, and not by relying on its rights as an indorsee of the bills.

Confirmed and unconfirmed credits

An exporter may insist either that a commercial credit in his favour should **13.23** be issued by a bank in his own country, or that a credit issued by a foreign bank in the purchaser's country should be confirmed or guaranteed by a bank in the exporter's country. The issuing bank in the purchaser's country will in such a case employ a second bank in the exporter's country not only to advise the exporter of the issue of the credit but also to undertake an obligation to pay the amount of the credit or to accept or negotiate bills drawn under it, whether or not the issuing bank places it in funds to make payment. Where the intermediary bank accepts a direct obligation toward the exporter to honour the credit, it is a confirmed irrevocable credit; otherwise, it is unconfirmed and the advising bank is not liable to the exporter. There can be no confirmation of a revocable credit.

Revocable or irrevocable credits

The Uniform Customs and Practice for Documentary Credits, article 9 **13.24** states: "A revocable credit may be amended or cancelled by the issuing bank at any moment and without prior notice to the beneficiary."

The main feature of a revocable credit is that the issuing bank reserves to itself the right to modify or cancel the credit, and a person acting in reliance on a credit of this nature is deemed to have notice that the credit may be withdrawn at any time. However, if an intermediatory bank acts on the credits before notice of cancellation is given to it, then that bank is entitled to be reimbursed for its expenditure.

By article 10 of the Uniform Customs and Practice an irrevocable credit "constituted a definite undertaking of the issuing bank, provided that the stipulated documents are presented and that the terms and conditions of the credit are complied with. . . . "

In such a case the issuing and confirming banks, if the credit is confirmed, cannot withdraw their undertaking to honour it once the credit has been communicated to the beneficiary.

Transferable credits

13.25   In addition to the types of credit here dealt with, certain other types of credit were devised, the purpose of which was to enable the beneficiary of the credit to transfer or assign the benefit to a third party. These will be dealt with separately in dealing with the transfers of the benefit of a commercial credit.

Technical terms

13.26   The technical names given to the various types of credits have already been dealt with, and here it is proposed to deal merely with the technical terms associated with commercial credits and the names assigned to the parties in a commercial credit transaction.

The bank which issues a commercial credit is known as the "opening bank" or the "issuing bank," the latter term being derived from the fact that the notification of the credit to the creditor is by a letter of credit issued to him by the bank.

The person in whose favour a credit is opened is known as "the beneficiary" and he alone can require the issuing bank to pay the amount of the credit or to accept bills drawn under it, but his rights under the contract can be assigned by a written instrument (see below).

The issuing bank often employs another bank to notify the issue of the credit to the beneficiary. The bank so employed is known as the "advising bank," and it acts as an agent for the issuing bank, which is, therefore, responsible for its acts or omissions under the ordinary rules of agency law. The advising bank is not a party to the credit itself, and so is not obliged to honour the credit if the issuing bank fails to do so, nor in the case of revocable credit is it liable to the beneficiary if the issuing bank cancels the credit. Where, however, the advising bank "confirms" a credit issued by another bank, it becomes responsible for the performance of the issuing bank's obligation to the beneficiary in addition to the issuing bank. In this situation the confirming bank accepts the bills drawn by the beneficiary, usually on its own account, or on behalf of the issuing bank if the beneficiary requests this to be done. The confirming bank then passes the shipping documents to the issuing bank so that it or its customer, at whose request the credit was opened, will be in possession of the documents by the time the goods covered by the credit arrive in the customer's country. Often, the presentation of the bills to the confirming bank for payment is anticipated by its purchasing them at their face value less interest to maturity when the beneficiary presents the bills drawn by him for acceptance by the confirming bank. In such a case the confirming bank either passes the bills unaccepted to the issuing bank for acceptance by it, or if the confirming bank both accepts and discounts the bills presented to it by the beneficiary, it retains them and debits the issuing bank with their amount on maturity. However, a bank which has not confirmed a credit does not become a confirming bank merely because the credit provides that bills drawn under it may be negotiated to that bank, and the bank in fact purchases them at their face or discounted value. Instead, it becomes a holder of the bills itself with the usual right of recourse against the drawer and payee if the issuing bank dishonours them, and it also has a right to claim from the issuing bank under the letter of credit if the benefit of it is assigned to the negotiating bank.

Transfers of the benefit of credits

Only the person who is expressly named in the letter of credit as the ben- **13.27** eficiary of it can draw bills under it, and it is he alone who can require the issuing bank to accept or negotiate those bills unless the credit otherwise provides. A beneficiary cannot, therefore, authorise another person to draw on the credit unless the letter of credit expressly permits him to do this. It is because of this that various types of credits have been devised which enable the beneficiary to transfer or assign the benefit of the credit to third parties (*e.g.* to sub-contractors from whom the beneficiary obtains goods to fulfil his obligations to the issuing bank's customer). Where the credit itself is not stated to be transferable, no transfer of the credit is permitted, because to do so would defeat the purpose of the credit, *e.g.* it would introduce an element of uncertainty.

However, article 55 of the Uniform Customs allows the rights of the beneficiary under the credit, as with any other contract to be assigned at law by a written instrument which is notified to the issuing bank, and in equity by an agreement to assign it for value.[28] As in the case of other similar instruments the assignment of rights at law does not have to be in any particular form, provided it is in writing and is signed by the beneficiary. The assignee can then present bills drawn by the beneficiary under the credit and require the issuing bank to accept or negotiate them. Unlike a novation, an assignment involves a transfer of the assignor's rights without the consent or agreement of the other party, but the assignee has no greater rights against the issuing bank than the beneficiary of the credit, and so if the issuing bank can repudiate the credit as against the beneficiary, it can refuse to accept or negotiate bills presented by the assignor, *e.g.* where the credit was obtained through misrepresentation.

Where the letter of credit expressly authorises the beneficiary to transfer **13.28** the benefit of a letter of credit, the credit is said to be "transferable." By article 54 of the Uniform Customs, the rights and benefits of a credit expressed to be transferable may be transferred to a third person or in fractions to several persons. In order to be divisible between several persons, a credit need not provide that it shall be divisible as well as transferable, since transferability implies divisibility as well. Transferable credits are mostly used where the seller of goods is not the manufacturer or supplier of those goods, but is a dealer or exporter who arranges with a manufacturer or supplier to supply

---

[28] Law of Property Act 1925, s.136(1).

goods to the ultimate purchasers at a higher price than the dealer or exporter pays for them, thus enabling the latter to obtain a dealing profit. The ultimate purchaser will procure a transferable credit in favour of the dealer or exporter and the latter then instructs the issuing bank to issue a credit in favour of the manufacturer or supplier for an amount less than the original credit and expiring a few days earlier than the original credit. In order to enable the beneficiary of the original credit to conceal the profit he is making by employing a manufacturer or supplier the agreement for the transfer of the credit often enables the beneficiary to substitute his own invoice for the goods supplied for those of the manufacturer or supplier, and to draw bills on the issuing bank in favour of the manufacturer or supplier for such part of that invoice price as he wishes and in his own favour for the balance.

The legal effect of a transfer of transferable credit is that the right to tender documents in return for payment of the price or the acceptance or negotiation of bills is transferred from the original beneficiary to the transferee or transferees. A transfer in this form is a substitution of the transferee for the beneficiary as the contracting party with the issuing bank and not an assignment of the original contract with the beneficiary. Once a transfer has taken place the beneficiary is under no further responsibility to the issuing bank. And in reality the substitution of the designated person as the drawer of the bills under the credit is a novation, *i.e.* the making of a new contract by which the original credit in favour of the beneficiary is discharged and a new credit is opened in favour of the designated person.

Professor Pennington[29] considers the terms "transferable" inept

> "because what really happens when a letter of credit permits transfers is that the person designated by the beneficiary accepts the offer by the issuing bank which arises from its undertaking in the credit that it will honour bills drawn by such a person instead of by the beneficiary. In reality the substitution of the designated person as the drawer of the bills under the credit is a novation, that is, the making of a new contract by which the original credit in favour of the beneficiary is discharged, and a new credit on the same terms is opened in its place in favour of the designated person. . . . "

13.29   Where, therefore, the credit (and not merely the rights under a credit) is transferred to a third party, there is a novation because, in fact, there is a change in the parties to the contract for the credit. This view accepts the argument that a letter of credit is a unilateral contract for which consideration is given by performance of the act (see discussion on the legal nature of documentary credits).

However, the transfer of the credit does not in itself amount to a novation of the underlying contract for the sale of goods. The buyer agrees to the substitution of a third party as the beneficiary of the credit where the latter has obtained the goods in question from the third party, but he does not agree to the substitution of the third party as the seller of the goods comprised in the underlying contract of sale, and if there is a breach of that contract by the third party failing to deliver the contract goods, it is the seller and not the third party whom the buyer must sue for the breach.

---

[29] See Pennington, Hudson & Mann, *Commercial Banking Law* (Macdonald and Evans, 1st ed.).

The same purpose of making a credit available to a third person is achieved by a back-to-back credit arrangement, and the advantage of such an arrangement is that the credit opened by the issuing bank need not be expressed to be transferable or divisible. Unlike transferable credit, which can only be transferred or novated once for the whole amount of the credit or for fractions of that amount, a back-to-back credit arrangement may be extended as many times as is necessary. This type of credit arrangement is usually used to finance a string of contracts for the sale of the same goods through several intermediaries, as well as the type of transaction for which a transferable credit is normally used, namely, to finance the acquisition of goods from sub-contractors. Under a back-to-back arrangement the obligations of the issuing bank to the beneficiary are used as security for the issue by the beneficiary's bank of a second credit in favour of a third party, and this credit in turn may be used as security for the third party's bank issuing a third credit in favour of a fourth party and so on. For example, if A sells goods to B, and B sells the same goods to C, and C to D, D's bank may open a credit in favour of C, which he uses as a security to induce his own bank to open a credit in favour of B, and B in turn may use this credit as a security for his own bank to open a credit in favour of A.

THE RELATIONSHIP BETWEEN THE DEBTOR AND THE BENEFICIARY

The underlying contract

A commercial credit is used to finance a contract for the sale of goods under **13.30** which the purchaser is obliged to make payment to the creditor by means of a documentary letter of credit. The rights and obligations of the buyer and seller are determined by the terms of the underlying contract, usually a contract for the sale of goods, and the contract of sale is in no way affected by the terms of the credit procured by the debtor. Consequently, once the commercial credit has been issued, this contract between the buyer and the issuing bank exists independently from the contract of sale of goods between the buyer and the seller. The result of this is that the bank is not concerned with any disputes that arise between the parties to the underlying contract concerning non-delivery or the quality or quantity of goods delivered. In *Hamzeh Malas* v. *British Imex Industries Ltd.*,[30] the court held a bank cannot refuse to accept or purchase a bill of exchange drawn by the beneficiary of a credit merely because the beneficiary has broken the underlying contract, even if the buyer is entitled to reject the goods delivered or proposed to be delivered by him because they are not of the contract description or quality. The American courts have gone even further an held in *Frey* v. *Sherbourne*[31] that the bank cannot refuse to accept the beneficiary's draft even if the bank's customer has rescinded the underlying contract of sale, or has terminated it because of a fundamental breach by the beneficiary. This, of course, assumes that the documents presented by the benefici-

---

[30] [1958] 2 Q.B. 127.
[31] (1920) 184 N.Y. Supp. 661.

ary to the bank are in proper order and fulfil any conditions under the letter of credit.

The payment of obligation

13.31   It is necessary to consider how far the rights of the buyer and seller are affected by reason of the fact that it is a term of the contract of sale that payment of the purchase price is to be made by means of a letter of credit.

If the underlying contract of sale requires the provision by the buyer of a letter of credit, then the opening of the letter of credit is a condition precedent to the performance by the seller of his part of the contract. The credit must be issued by the bank named in the underlying contract, (if any) and it must be opened and notified by the bank or its agent, to the creditor within the time agreed. If the underlying contract calls for a confirmed commercial credit the debtor must also ensure that the confirmation is given to the creditor within the same time limit. The buyer, therefore, has the obligation of complying with the method of payment and failure to do so discharges the seller from his obligations under the underlying contract.[32] Similarly, in *Garcia* v. *Page & Co.*[33] the court held that the opening of a confirmed credit was a condition precedent to the obligation of the sellers to ship the contract goods. In *Trans Trust S.P.R.L.* v. *Danubian Trading Co. Ltd.*,[34] Lord Denning said the duty of the seller to carry out the transaction is dependent on the buyer providing the letter of credit. The learned judge looked at the effect of a stipulation requiring a credit to be opened in advance and said:

> " . . . In these cases the provision of the credit is a condition precedent not to the formation of a contract, but to the obligation of the seller to deliver the goods. If the buyer fails to provide the credit, the seller can treat himself as discharged from any further performance of the contract and can sue the buyer for damages."

The time for opening the credit

13.32   Sometimes, the underlying contract may not specify the bank which is to open or confirm the credit, the kind of credit to be opened or the time within which it must be opened and notified to the creditor. In these circumstances, the court will have to construe the terms of the contract, and if necessary, make such implications as to the intention of the parties in order to determine the extent of their obligations and whether or not these obligations have been fulfilled. For example, in *Knotz* v. *Fairclough, Dodd and Jones Ltd.*[35] the underlying contract did not expressly require the seller to send a provisional invoice to the buyer so as to enable him to procure the opening of a credit for the amount set out therein, but the court implied a duty on the seller to do this since it was obviously the parties' intention.

Where, however, the sales contract contains a stipulation that the credit is

---

[32] *Dix* v. *Grainger* (1922) 10 Lloyds L.R. 496.
[33] (1936) 55 Lloyds L.R. 391.
[34] [1952] 1 All E.R. 970.
[35] [1952] 1 Lloyds Rep. 226.

required to be opened within a certain time, the seller is discharged if it is not opened and notified to him within that time. In the absence of such a stipulation, the buyer has a reasonable time within which to provide the credit. In *Garcia* v. *Page & Co. Ltd.*[36] a contract of sale required the buyer to open a "confirmed credit in London immediately" in favour of the sellers. There was a delay in providing the credit and the sellers notified the buyer that if the credit was not received in London by August 24, they would cancel the contract. The credit was opened in Spain by August 24 but not notified to the seller until a later date and the seller purported to repudiate the contract. The court held that a confirmed credit had to be opened immediately after the contract of sale was entered into, that is, within such a time as the buyer needs as a person of reasonable diligence to get the credit established. The buyer had failed to do this and the sellers were consequently entitled to repudiate the contract of sale.

In certain contracts, however, there may be no express stipulation as to the time within which the buyer must open the credit; in such cases the buyer has a reasonable time within which to obtain the opening of the credit. Alternatively, the contract may stipulate that it is to be opened within a reasonable time. In case of a dispute the court would have to decide, in both instances, what is a reasonable time and whether the buyer, in fact, was given a reasonable time to open the credit.

In *Kronman & Co.* v. *Steinberger*[37] the court said that where there is no stipulation that the credit should be opened at any particular time, it must be opened by the buyer within a reasonable time and that means that the buyer complies with his obligations to open the credit if within that time he has any error in the terms of the credit rectified.

By contrast, in *Baltimex Ltd.* v. *Metallo Chemical Refining Co. Ltd.*[38] a contract stated that payment for the goods was to be by a letter of credit "expected in a day or two." The court held that it could take into account the fact, known to the seller, that the buyer had sub-sold the goods to a Russian state trading corporation and intended to use a credit obtained by it to pay the seller and the period allowed for the opening of the credit was to be determined by the time it normally took a Russian state agency to procure the opening of a credit available in the United Kingdom. The court will, therefore, take into account any special facts of whch the seller is aware as likely to cause delay in opening the credit in order to determine whether a reasonable time has elapsed without the buyer opening the requisite credit.[39] In *Etablissements Chainbaux S.à.R.L.* v. *Harbormasters Ltd.*[40] an irrevocable letter of credit was to be opened in London within a "few weeks." The buyers delayed in opening the letter of credit because of an exceptionally long delay in obtaining exchange control permission from the French Government. An extension of time for opening the credit was granted, but the sellers later purported to repudiate the contract without giving notice to the buyer. The court held the plaintiffs had failed to procure the opening of

---

[36] (1936) 55 Lloyds L.R. 391.
[37] (1922) 10 Lloyds L.R. 39.
[38] [1955] 2 Lloyds Rep. 438.
[39] See Ellinger, "Reasonable Time for examination of documents" *Journal of Business Law* (1985) p. 406.
[40] [1955] 1 Lloyds Rep. 303.

a credit in time and were liable for breach of the underlying contract, even though the failure to comply was not attributable to any personal fault on their part. It is not a valid excuse for the debtor to say he has done everything possible to ensure that the credit was issued within the time permitted, and for him to show that the delay in the issue of a letter of credit was due to the carelessness of the bank or its agent.[41]

As to the question that a letter of credit had to be opened wthin a "few weeks" the judge said that the parties had in mind a period not exceeding a month. What is a reasonable time is to be assessed in the light of circumstances which prevail when the contract is entered into. He cited Lord Watson with approval in *Hick* v. *Raymond & Reid*,[42] who said:

> "reasonable time" . . . "has invariably been held to mean that the party upon whom it is incumbent duly fulfils his obligation, notwithstanding protracted delay, so long as such delay is attributable to causes beyond his control, and he has neither acted negligently nor unreasonably."

If, however, the plaintiffs obtain an extension of time for opening the credit from the defendants they must show that the extension of time allowed did not render time of the essence of the contract, so that the defendants could only terminate the contract after a further reasonable length of notice.[43]

Where, on the other hand, the debtor's failure to procure the opening of the credit is due to the creditor's acts or omissions, the debtor is not in breach of the underlying contract. In *Knotz* v. *Fairclough, Dodd & Jones Ltd.*[44] the seller failed to comply with his implied obligation to provide the buyer with an invoice so that the credit could be opened, and as a direct consequence of this the buyer failed to open the credit. The court held that the seller could not treat the underlying contract as terminated for that reason.

13.33   If the contract provides for shipment of the goods by the seller at any time during a stated period, the buyer, in the absence of an express stipulation, must open the credit and make it available to the seller at the beginning of the shipment period. In *Pavia & Co.* v. *Thurmann-Nielsen*[45] the contract provided for the sale of certain goods to be shipped from Brazil in February and/or March and/or April at the seller's option C.I.F. Genoa. The buyers were repeatedly pressed by the sellers to provide credit facilities but these did not become available until April 22. The buyers were held liable for failure to provide the credit as required by the contract. A confirmed credit must be made available to the seller at the beginning of the shipment period. The seller is entitled to be assured that he will receive payment on shipment. The seller is not bound to tell the buyer the precise date when shipment is to be made and whenever he decides to ship the goods within the shipment period (whether he ships at the beginning of the shipment period or later) he must be entitled to draw on the credit.

If the buyer does not want to put the credit machinery in motion until shortly before the seller is likely to ship, then he must make some provision

---

[41] *A. E. Lindsay & Co.Ltd.* v. *Cook* [1953] 1 Lloyds Rep. 328.
[42] [1893] A.C. 22.
[43] *Rickards Ltd.* v. *Oppenhaim* [1950] 1 All E.R. 420.
[44] [1952] 1 Lloyds Rep. 226.
[45] [1952] 2 Q.B. 84.

in the contract under which the credit shall be provided within a specified period from notification, *e.g.* 14 days after a cable communication from the seller, or something similar.[46] Similarly, in *Ian Stach Ltd.* v. *Baker Bosley Ltd.*[47] it was held that in a contract for the sale of goods F.O.B. which provided for shipment during a period within which the buyer was entitled to call for shipment of the goods at any time, the prima facie rule is that the credit called for by the contract of sale must be opened by the buyer at the latest by the first day of the shipment period.

The identity of the issuing bank

The underlying contract often does not specify the bank which is to open   **13.34** the credit, or the banks which are respectively to open and confirm it. There is no English case on this question, but it is submitted that if a letter of credit is required to be issued or confirmed by an English bank, the position under the Banking Act 1987 is clear, namely, that the institution which opens the credit must be an authorised institution within the terms of the Act, and the seller would be entitled to reject a credit issued or confirmed by any other institution or organisation.

The requirement of an irrevocable credit

If the contract of sale calls for a particular form of credit and if such a credit   **13.35** is not opened, the seller is under no liability. It was held in *Giddens* v. *Anglo-African Produce Co. Ltd.*[48] that if the underlying contract merely requires payment to be made by a "banker's credit" or "confirmed banker's credit," it is not sufficient for the debtor to procure the opening of a revocable credit, since the whole purpose of financing the transaction by a credit is to assure the creditor that he will be paid by a reliable institution which commits itself irrevocably to do so. The Uniform Commercial Code[49] provides that the debtor's obligation is to open an irrevocable credit unless the underlying contract of sale permits him to open revocable credit.

If the buyer in error provides a form of credit different from that stipulated for in the contract, he is entitled to rectify the error provided that the seller does not alter his position in reliance on the credit supplied. In *Kronman & Co.* v. *Steinberger*[50] a credit was opened by mistake, in dollars instead of sterling. The mistake was rectified within the time for opening the credit, but the sellers sought to take advantage of the mistake and cancel the contract. The court held that they were not entitled to do so, the sellers not having taken steps in pursuance of the credit originally provided. Consequently, if the buyer replaces a revocable credit by an irrevocable one within the time permitted by the underlying contract, he fulfils his obligations to the seller.

---

[46] *Sainson-Tiecher Grain Corpn.* v. *Oilcakes & Oilseeds Trading Co.* [1954] 3 All E.R. 468.
[47] [1958] 2 Q.B. 130.
[48] (1923) 14 Lloyds L.R. 230.
[49] Art. 2–325(3).
[50] (1922) 10 Lloyds L.R. 39.

The requirement of a confirmed credit

13.36 If by the terms of the underlying contract of sale the credit to be opened is to be a confirmed credit, it is not sufficient for the buyer to tender an irrevocable credit issued by the bank. The word "confirmed" has a distinct meaning from "irrevocable" and so if the credit is to be "confirmed" it must contain undertakings to honour the beneficiary's bills of exchange by at least two banks. In *Panoutsos* v. *Raymond Hadley Corporation of New York*[51] it was held that the seller is entitled to insist on strict compliance with the terms of the contract of sale and to require that a "confirmed credit" be made available, but he may waive this requirement by his conduct.

The purpose for which a seller normally requires a confirmed credit is that he thereby usually acquires an undertaking by a bank in his own country, of whose standing he has little doubt, that he will be paid if the issuing bank fails to do so; but, it becomes necessary to ask whether it is a condition of the contract that confirmation has to be by a bank in the seller's country. So if an American seller sells to a buyer in Chile who obtains a letter of credit by a bank in his own country and has it confirmed by a reputable English bank in London, the question is whether the seller can reject the letter of credit. If the contract requires "confirmation by a bank in the seller's country" then the seller can insist on strict compliance, but if the contract merely calls for a "confirmed credit" it is submitted the buyer is free to have another reputable bank, outside the seller's country confirm it, and the seller would probably have to accept the confirmation.

Waiver by the creditor

13.37 Where the buyer is in breach of a term inserted in the credit, the seller may waive strict compliance. This, however, does not mean that the seller can never avail himself of the condition in future, but he must give reasonable notice to the buyer of his intention to insist upon its future performance. If the buyer then fails to comply with the condition within a reasonable time, he is in default and the seller is entitled to cancel the contract without the buyer being entitled to damages.[52]

The seller may also lawfully terminate the contract after the buyer's initial default without giving him reasonable notice, if he can satisfy the court that the buyer would not have been able to procure the opening of the contract if further time had been granted. In *Etablissements Chainbaux S.à.R.L.* v. *Harbormasters Ltd.*[53] Devlin J. said he (namely, the seller) has to give a notice giving the other side reasonable time in the circumstances to comply with their obligations, and it is only after a failure to comply during this period that the seller is entitled to cancel the contract. However, the exception laid down in *Richards* v. *Oppenheim*[54] was held applicable on the facts of the case and the sellers held entitled to give peremptory notice.

The seller may waive strict compliance of the terms of the letter of credit expressly or impliedly. In *Panoutsos* v. *Raymond Hadley Corporation of New*

---

[51] [1917] 2 K.B. 743.
[52] See Reading C.J. in *Panoutsos* v. *Raymond Hadley Corp.* [1917] 2 K.B. 743.
[53] [1955] 1 Lloyds Rep. 303.
[54] [1950] 1 All E.R. 420.

York[55] the seller with knowledge of the fact that a confirmed credit had not been opened as required by the terms of the contract of sale shipped part of the goods under the contract. He later purported to cancel the sale contract, without notice, on the basis that the buyer had failed to open a confirmed credit. The court held that the seller, in continuing the shipments and actually drawing on the credit, must be held to have waived his right to strict compliance under the terms of the letter of credit. As regards future performance he was not entitled to repudiate the contract without giving the buyer a reasonable opportunity to comply with the exact terms of the credit and if a confirmed credit was not made available for the payment of balance of the price and future shipments, the seller would then be able to repudiate. Since the seller in this case had failed to do so, he was himself liable for damages. Similarly, in *Baltimex v. Metallo Chemical Refining Co.*,[56] it was held that the seller had waived a condition that the credit must be opened within a certain period by himself requesting for an extension of the time fixed for delivery of the goods. A waiver may therefore be implied from the facts of the case inferred from inaction on the part of the seller. In *Plasticmoda S.P.A.* v. *Davidsons (Manchester) Ltd.*[57] it was said that if the seller is guilty of inaction in response to the buyer's reasonable requests and allows the period during which the credit is to be made available to expire, then he has waived his right that the credit should be opened within a specified time.

Damages

If the buyer fails to fulfil his obligation under the underlying contract in respect of the opening, confirmation or notification of a banker's credit, he is liable to the creditor in damages for the consequential loss suffered by the seller, who may also treat the contract as terminated.   **13.38**

The measure of damages awarded by the court for breach of the underlying contract will normally be the same as for any other breach of contract. The test in assessing the measure of damages is that laid down in *Hadley* v. *Baxendale*[58] (as explained in *Victoria Laundry* v. *Newman Industries Ltd.*[59] namely, the loss suffered by the creditor as a direct and ordinary consequence of the buyer's breach of contract. If the underlying contract is for the sale of goods, such loss will usually be the difference between the contract price of the goods and the lower market price of similar goods on the last date by which the credit should have been opened, or on the later date when the creditor treats the contract as repudiated because of the buyer's breach. In *Ian Stach Ltd.* v. *Baker Bosley Ltd.*[60] Diplock J., dealing with the question of quantum, said that prima facie the measure of damages is the loss of profit on the transaction, but on the facts of the case because the seller did not treat the breach as terminating the contract until a later date, (*i.e.* towards the end of the shipment period by which time the buyers had failed

---

[55] [1917] 2 K.B. 743; see also *Ficon S.A.* v. *Sociedad Cadex Limitada* [1980] 2 Lloyd's Rep. 118.
[56] [1955] 2 Lloyds Rep. 438.
[57] [1952] 1 Lloyds Rep. 527.
[58] (1854) 9 Exch. 341.
[59] [1949] 2 K.B. 528.
[60] [1958] 2 Q.B. 130.

to comply with several demands for the credit to be opened) the amount of damages awarded would be the difference between the contract price and the market price at the time the seller accepted the buyer's repudiation.

The normal measure of damages is, therefore, the seller's loss of his bargain, but the circumstances in which the underlying contract is made may indicate that a different measure of damages is appropriate. In *Trans Trust S.P.R.L. v. Danubian Trading Co. Ltd.*[61] the plaintiffs contracted to sell to the defendants a quantity of steel which they themselves had contracted to purchase from Azur, a Belgian company. It was a term of the contract that payment by the defendants should be by a confirmed credit to be opened in favour of Azur, by an American Corporation to whom the defendants had in turn contracted to sell the steel. The defendants failed to procure the opening of the credit, and eventually repudiated the contract. The plaintiffs claimed from the defendants, as damages for breach of contract, the profit which they would have made if the transaction had been carried through. The market price of steel at the time of the repudiation was considerably higher than the contract price, and, therefore, the plaintiffs would only recover nominal damages if based on the difference between the contract price and the market value of the steel. The Court of Appeal, nevertheless, held that it must have been in the contemplation of the parties that in the event of a breach of the contract the loss to the plaintiffs would be their loss of profit on the transaction, namely, the difference between the purchase price the plaintiff agreed to pay Azur and the price the defendant had agreed to pay the plaintiff. The plaintiffs were, therefore, entitled to recover although the loss which resulted from their own impecuniosity, since they were known to depend on the opening of the letter of credit in order to be able to acquire the steel from Azur and the original suppliers.

The rule laid down in the *Liesbosch* case[62] and *Muhammad Issa el Sheikh Ahmad v. Ali*[63] that loss due to or aggravated by the plaintiff's impecuniosity is not generally recoverable was approved, but the court also approved the opinion of Lord Wright in *Liesbosch* "that damages due to impecuniosity may not be too remote if the loss might reasonably be expected to be in contemplation of the parties."

In *Pacific Overseas Corporation Ltd. v. Watkin Browne & Co. (N.Z.) Ltd.*[64] the court held that damages recoverable by the seller cannot be increased because, unknown to the buyer, he had a special opportunity to obtain goods to fulfil the contract at a lower price than the current market price and so could maximise his profit. On the other hand the seller is under a duty to mitigate the loss he suffers by taking advantage of any opportunity which comes to him to dispose of the goods at a better price than the current market price, and if he fails to do so, he can only recover the difference between that better price and the price agreed to be paid by the original buyer.

The fact that the courts have allowed the seller to recover damages for loss of the profit he would have made on a resale does not necessarily mean that damages will be recoverable under this head in every case where a

---

[61] [1952] 2 Q.B. 297.
[62] [1933] A.C. 449.
[63] [1947] A.C. 474.
[64] [1954] N.Z.L.R. 459.

buyer fails to provide a letter of credit. The question to be asked is whether the loss of profit would have been in the contemplation of reasonable businessmen as naturally flowing from the breach of contract in the circumstances.

The debtor's continuing liability for the debt

Once the debtor has procured the opening and notification of a commercial **13.39** credit in accordance with the underlying contract of sale, the issuing bank becomes liable to the creditor to accept and pay his drafts. A question of importance to the relationship which exists between the buyer and seller is whether the seller, by requiring payment by means of a commercial credit, agrees to release the buyer from liability for payment under the contract of sale once the credit is issued. This becomes especially important where the issuing bank becomes insolvent before it accepts or negotiates the seller's bills of exchange or before it pays bills it has accepted under the credit.

If the letter of credit were considered to be an absolute payment of the price owed to the seller, the buyer would be under no further liability to the seller once the credit was issued and the seller would have to accept a dividend in the bank's liquidation like any other of its creditors. This, however, would not be the situation where funds paid to the issuing bank were appropriated by the buyer for the purpose of honouring bills presented under the letter of credit.

The question as to whether the issue of a letter of credit constitutes absolute payment as between the buyer and seller was unclear until recently. It is now established that the issue of a letter of credit constitutes conditional payment only, and if the issuing bank fails to honour the seller's bill drawn in conformity with the credit, the rights of the seller against the buyer to insist on payment in cash will revive.

The English courts have dealt with the question of the buyer's liability in this situation in a number of cases. In *Newman Industries Ltd.* v. *Indo-British Industries Ltd.*[65] Sellers J. declined to rule whether the issue of a credit absolves the buyer from continued liability in all cases, but held on the particular facts of that case it did not do so, because the buyer would have remained primarily liable for the price if he procured the bank guarantee originally agreed upon in the contract of sale. The substitution by subsequent agreement of a bank commercial credit as the method of payment could not have been intended by the seller to terminate the buyer's personal liability.

The judge cited *Soproma S.P.A.* v. *Marine and Animal By-Products Corporation*,[66] where it was said by McNair J.:

> "Under this form of contract, payment by letter of credit, as it seems to me the buyer performs his obligations as to payment if he provides for the sellers a reliable and solvent paymaster from whom he can obtain payment—if necessary by suit—although it may well be that if the

---

[65] [1956] 2 Lloyds Rep. 219.
[66] [1966] 1 Lloyds Rep. 367.

banker fails to pay by reason of his insolvency the buyer would be liable . . . "

13.40   The same question was dealt with in *E.D. & F. Man Ltd.* v. *Nigerian Sweets and Confectionery Co.Ltd.*[67] where, under three separate contracts, the buyers agreed to buy 1,100 tons of sugar from the sellers, payment to be made in cash against documents presented in London under an irrevocable letter of credit. The bank failed to accept shipping documents duly tendered and the sellers brought an action against the buyers to recover amounts due under the contracts. The court held that as the buyer the respondent's liability, to the sellers was a primary liability but which was superseded by the issue of a letter of credit by the bank. However, the debtor's liability was superseded when the bank issued the credit during the period within which the issuing bank should have honoured the drafts but was activated again when the issuing bank defaulted.

Again, in *W. J. Alan & Co. Ltd.* v. *E.L. Nasr Export and Import Co. Ltd.*,[68] Lord Denning said that a letter of credit, when issued and accepted by the seller, operates merely as conditional payment; it does not operate to discharge the liability of the buyer, but the seller cannot look to the buyer personally for payment until the issuing bank has refused payment. Lord Denning went on to say that if the letter of credit is honoured by the bank when the documents are presented to it, the debt is discharged and the buyer is, of course, then absolved from liability. Furthermore, he indicated that acceptance of the seller's drafts by the bank under the credit might also discharge the buyer, since the seller thereafter looks exclusively to the bank for payment.

While the first part of this reasoning is a clear statement of the now generally accepted principle, it is questionable whether the second part, namely that acceptance of the drafts by a bank discharges the buyer, is likely to be followed. Furthermore, it is merely an *obiter dictum*, since the *Alan* v. *Nasr* case was decided on other considerations. In fact, in the recent cases of *Maran Road Saw Mill* v. *Austin Taylor & Co. Ltd.*[69] and *E. D. & F. Man Ltd.* v. *Nigerian Sweets and Confectionery Co. Ltd.*[70] it has been held that payment by means of a letter of credit becomes unconditional, and the debtor is discharged only if the issuing bank accepts and pays the bill drawn by the beneficiary, acceptance alone being insufficient. More recently, in *Re Charge Card Services Ltd.*[71] the court accepted the presumption that the "payment obligation under a letter of credit transaction was only conditional.

The High Court of Australia in *Saffron* v. *Société Minière Cafrika*[72] examined the question of whether the issue of a letter of credit discharges the buyer absolutely from the obligation to pay. It was held that, on the facts of the case, the provision of the letter of credit did not constitute absolute payment. The stipulation for payment by means of a letter of credit in the underlying contract of sale did not go beyond requiring the establishment of

---

[67] [1977] 2 Lloyds Rep. 50.
[68] [1972] 2 All E.R. 127.
[69] [1975] 1 Lloyds Rep. 156.
[70] [1977] 2 Lloyds Rep. 50.
[71] [1986] 3 All E.R. 289.
[72] (1958) 100 C.L.R. 231; see also, the New Zealand case of *Hindley* v. *Tothill, Watson & Co.* (1895) 13 N.Z.L.R. 13.

such a letter as a primary, but not the exclusive, method of payment and the seller was, therefore, entitled to recover the price from the buyer on the bank's default. As regards an irrevocable letter of credit the court expressed the view that a contractual term requiring an irrevocable, but not a confirmed credit, might "not unreasonably" be regarded as substituting liability under the credit (when issued) in place of the continued liability of the buyer.

There seems to be a difference of opinion in the United States as to **13.41** whether an irrevocable but unconfirmed credit operates as a discharge of the buyer. In *Greenhough v. Munroe*[73] the court held that the issue of an irrevocable credit does not discharge the buyer's liability for the price which is only discharged by payment of the bills accepted by the issuing bank under the credit. However, in *Vicacqua Irmaos v. Hickerson*[74] the court held that the issue of an irrevocable credit does discharge the buyer from liability. The question of whether the letter of credit is intended to be an absolute payment can only arise in special circumstances, namely, if the bank responsible for the credit were to be become insolvent, or as in the *Saffron v. Société Minière Cafrika* case, where, notwithstanding that the documents are not in conformity with the letter of credit, the seller loses control of the goods to the buyer. As such contingencies are unlikely to have been within the contemplation of the buyer or seller when the contract is entered into, any inquiry as to their intention must be artificial. Furthermore, regard must be paid to the terms and circumstances of the letter of credit for which the contract of sale provides in each individual case. An undertaking to provide a revocable credit cannot be an undertaking that the buyer will be discharged from his liability to pay, since a revocable credit by its nature provides no protection against cancellation. A buyer would undoubtedly encourage cancellation of the revocable credit if the seller accepted it as absolute payment.

THE RELATIONSHIP BETWEEN THE BENEFICIARY AND THE ISSUING AND CONFIRMING BANKS

The binding effect of the terms of the credit

The contractual obligations between the creditor and the issuing and con- **13.42** firming banks arise from the terms of the letter of credit. The issuing and confirming banks are, therefore, under a duty to the beneficiary to honour the credit, namely, to accept or negotiate bills presented to it by the beneficiary, either on demand if the credit is an open one, or if, as is more usually the case, the credit is a documentary letter of credit on fulfilment of the conditions set out in that letter of credit. The duty to honour the credit is unilateral and so the bank is bound to honour the credit if it is strictly complied with. There is no duty or obligation on the beneficiary to fulfil the terms of the credit, but if he wishes to benefit under it he must conform to

---

[73] (1931) 53 F. 2d 362.
[74] (1939) 190 So. 657.

the terms of the credit as a condition precedent to insisting on performance of the bank's obligations.

There are numerous cases in which the courts have held that only strict compliance with the terms of credit will suffice to activate the duty of the banks to accept or negotiate bills under it, and in *Equitable Trust Company of New York* v. *Dawson Partners*[75] Lord Sumner said: "There is no room for documents which are almost the same, or which will do just as well."

Indeed, the courts have refused to apply the *de minimis* rule to letters of credit as between the issuing or confirming bank and the beneficiary of the credit. Consequently, it has been held that a tender of documents for 4,997 kilos of sugar under a credit calling for 500 metric tons was bad.[76] Furthermore, the issuing bank need not accept substantial compliance even if the seller offers an indemnity. Article 43 of the U.C.P., however, does, allow a tolerance of 10 per cent. where words such as "circa" or "about" or other similar expression is used and unless the credit stipulates the quantity of goods must be exact, a tolerance of 5 per cent. is permitted. This provision does not apply where goods are sold in unit or as individual items.

13.43   There must, for two reasons, be strict compliance with the terms of the letter of credit if the beneficiary is to have a claim on the bank.

(1) If the issuing bank is to be entitled to reimbursement by its customer for the sum paid to the beneficiary under the credit, the documents it accepts must conform strictly to the terms of his instructions reflected in the letter of credit.

(2) The documents must be in proper order so that if the goods or other subject matter financed by the credit are non-existent, destroyed, lost or damaged, the bank and its customer would have documents which they could rely on to found claims against the responsible parties (*e.g.* the carrier who has issued the bill of lading, airway bill, etc.).

The letter of credit will specify the documents which the creditor is required to present under the credit. The documents required under an international sales contract are governed by the technical rules relating to C.I.F. and F.O.B. contracts. In the former instance, the seller is required to present to the buyer or his bank a clean bill of lading, an invoice and a marine insurance policy. The documents must be presented within the period specified in the credit, and the bank which has issued the credit is entitled to inist that the documents presented correspond exactly to the requirements of the credit. If they do not, the bank can refuse to take up the documents presented to it, although the goods actually shipped are of the description and quality required to fulfil the underlying contract of sale. The position of the seller and buyer under a C.I.F. contract has been set out by Devlin J. in *Kwei Tek Chao* v. *British Traders & Shippers Ltd.*[77] The seller has two distinct obligations, namely:

(a) to deliver the proper documents of title;

---

[75] (1926) 25 Lloyds L.R. 90; see also, *Bolivinter Oil S.A.* v. *Chase Manhattan Bank* [1984] 1 All E.R. 351; see Arora, "The Dilemma of an Issuing Bank: To accept or reject document tendered under a Letter of Credit" L.M.C.L.Q. (1984) pp. 81–90.

[76] *Moralice (London) Ltd.* v. *E. D. & F. Man* [1954] 2 Lloyds Rep. 526.

[77] [1954] 1 All E.R. 779; see also, *Lamborn* v. *Lake Shore Banking & Trust Co.* (1921) 188 N.Y.S. 162 (App.Div.).

(b) to ship the proper goods;
and the buyer in the event of the seller's failure has two distinct rights, namely,

(1) to reject the documents;

(2) to reject the goods.

Where the transaction is financed by a letter of credit the bank is only con-   **13.44**
cerned with (a) under the obligations of the seller and (b) under the rights of
the buyer. The credit transaction is not affected by the buyer's rejection of
the goods after his or his bank's acceptance of the shipping documents.

The bill of lading tendered by the seller under a letter of credit must conform to the description of the goods as represented in the terms of the
credit. In *Bank Melli Iran v. Barclays Bank (D.C.O.) Ltd.*[78] the defendants
issued a letter of credit for £40,000 representing the value of "100 new
Chevrolet trucks" against the presentation of a delivery order, insurance
policy invoice and a United States Government certificate that the trucks
were new. However, the documents accepted by the defendants described
the trucks as "100 new, good Chevrolet . . . trucks." The delivery order
described the trucks as "new (hyphen) goods." The court held that the
documents tendered and accepted by the defendants were defective, and
consequently the defendants were not entitled to debit the plaintiffs with the
amount paid against these documents.

In *Rayner & Co. v. Hambros Bank Ltd.*[79] a bank received instructions from   **13.45**
a customer to open a confirmed credit in favour of the plaintiffs covering a
cargo of "coromandel groundnuts." The bank opened the credit and notified the plaintiffs that it was available against an invoice and bills of lading
for "coromandel groundnuts." The plaintiffs presented bills of lading for
"machine-shelled groundnut kernels" accompanied by an invoice for "coromandel groundnuts." The bank refused payment, and the plaintiffs sued
for breach of the undertaking in the letter of credit. At first instance, Atkin-
son J. admitted evidence that "machine-shelled groundnut kernels" were
universally known in the trade to be "coromandel groundnuts" and gave
judgment for the plaintiffs. The bank appealed and the decision was
reversed. It was held that not only must the documents conform strictly
with the goods but that the defendant bank was under no obligation or duty
to acquaint itself with trade names. It is impossible to suggest that a bank is
to be affected with knowledge of the customs and customary terms of every
one of the thousands of trades for whose dealings it may issue letters of
credit.

The *Rayner* case has been the subject of much extra-judicial comment, but   **13.46**
it is clearly unreasonable to require the issuing bank to decide within the
short time it is given to accept or reject the documents whether certain
abbreviations in them are trade equivalent of the phraseology of the instructions it has received from its customer.

In both the *Bank Melli* case and the *Rayner* case the description in the
documents presented to the bank did not correspond to the description in
the letter of credit, and so the bank was under a duty to reject the documents. A bank issuing the letter of credit is entitled to reject the documents

---

[78] [1957] 2 Lloyds Rep. 367.
[79] [1943] 1 K.B. 37.

because 100 new-goods trucks are not the equivalent of a 100 new trucks, but clearly indicates second hand or used trucks, and similarly, coromandel groundnuts are not to the knowledge of the bank equivalent to machine shelled groundnut kernels, although in the trade they would be recognised as equivalent.

Where, however, in addition to the bill of lading, other documents are to be presented under a credit, it is sufficient if the description of the quality of the goods is contained in one of these documents, provided there is no need that the bill of lading should itself contain this description in order to fulfil its function as an undertaking by the carrier to deliver goods of the description in question. In *Guaranty Trust Company* v. *Van den Berghs Ltd.*[80] the defendants alleged that the documents accepted by the plaintiffs were not in order in that the bill of lading described the goods as "coco-nut oil" and not by the full description required under the credit namely "Manila coco-nut oil." They were, however, so described in a certificate of origin accompanying the bill of lading and there was no specific requirement that the bills of lading should include this description. The Court of Appeal held that assuming the documents required the goods to be described as "Manila coco-nut oil," the certificate of origin made it clear that the goods were of that nature and there was, therefore, sufficient compliance by the bank with the customer's instructions.

13.47   A full description of the goods obtained from a collective examination of the documents is, therefore, sufficient unless the letter of credit expressly requires each document to give a full description of the goods (see discussion on the form and nature of shipping documents). If the goods are described in the buyer's instructions to the bank by reference to weight or quantity and are consequently so described in the letter of credit, then the bill of lading must contain a corresponding statement of weight or quantity. This is so that the buyer will have an effective claim against the carrier for not delivering goods as described in the bill of lading.

In *London and Foreign Trading Corporation* v. *British and North European Bank*[81] the letter of credit required the bill of lading to be made out to the consignor's order endorsed in blank, and dated not later than October 1920. The plaintiffs contended that the bank had paid on an insufficient bill of lading, which stated that 5,895 bags of maize were shipped (this was in accordance with the contract) but which made no reference to the weight of the bags, as required under the credit. It was held that the bank had a limited authority to pay against a bill of lading which had to show that 500 tons had been shipped and under the invoice could not be used to satisfy the terms of the credit.

In *Midland Bank* v. *Seymour*[82] a confirmed irrevocable credit was issued by the plaintiff bank and it made payment against the tendered shipping documents. The invoice contained a full description of the goods, but the bill of lading described them simply as "12 bales Hong Kong duck feathers." The defendant alleged that the plaintiff bank had not complied with the mandate and refused to reimburse the bank on the ground that the

[80] (1925) 22 Lloyds L.R. 447.
[81] (1921) 9 Lloyds L.R. 116.
[82] (1955) 2 Lloyds L.R. 147.

bill of lading did not contain a full description of the goods. Devlin J. held that it was sufficient if the full set of documents contained all the particulars enumerated and called for in the letter of request, since the credit did not specifically indicate which particulars were to be put into each of the shipping documents.

Hence, it is sufficient that the set of documents as a whole should contain **13.48** all the particulars because the letter of request treated the document as a set, and provided that payment is made against an invoice, bill of lading and an insurance certificate collectively evidencing shipment of the goods in question, the bank is discharged from its obligation. Although the documents must be read together as demanded by the letter of credit, each document must be effectual in itself, that is, each document taken alone must be sufficiently detailed to fulfil the functions of that particular document.

The fact that the bill of lading need not give a full description of the goods as required by the credit, but must simply identify the goods, is supported by the Uniform Customs, Article 41(c), which states: "The description of the goods in the commercial invoice must correspond with the description of the credit. In all other documents the goods may be described in general terms not inconsistent with the description of the goods in the credit."

The effect of the proviso that the documents must be consistent with each other was clearly implied in the *Bank Melli* case where the credit called for "new Chevrolet trucks" and the bill of lading presented referred to the goods as "new-goods trucks" and the invoice specified "new trucks." The two documents read together clearly were inconsistent. The requirement that documents should be consistent had been adopted by Article 15 of the Uniform Customs which states: " . . . documents which appear on their face to be inconsistent with one another will be considered as not appearing on their face to be in accordance with the terms and conditions of the credit."

Discretion to accept non-conforming documents

It has been suggested that banks, in some instances, should be permitted to **13.49** exercise a certain discretion to accept non-conforming documents. In Germany a view which has emerged is to allow a bank to accept non-conforming documents on the principle that an agent has the discretion to deviate from his principal's instructions where it is necessary and in the interests of the principal (see Ellinger, *Documentary Letters of Credit* (1970)). This would allow the bank to accept non-conforming documents where their rejection would lead to a repudiation of the underlying contract.

A number of American courts have indicated support for the view that banks should have discretionary power of acceptance in such circumstances (see *Camp* v. *Corn Exchange National Bank*[82a]), although the general tendency of the courts is against permitting the banks to exercise a discretion and accept non-conforming documents.[82b]

[82a] (1926) 132A. 189, 191 (Pa).
[82b] Ellinger, *Documentary Letters of Credit*, p. 284.

SHIPPING DOCUMENTS: TECHNICAL RULES

Bills of lading, insurance policy and invoice

13.50   The law relating to tender of shipping documents is, as has already been said, technical, and a complete examination of it is outside the ambit of this chapter. However, it is proposed to deal briefly with some of the technicalities of whether or not the documents tendered under the letter of credit are sufficient. The beneficiary under a commercial credit issued by a bank to finance an import or export sale is normally required to present to that issuing bank a full set of clean, "on board" (or shipped) bills of lading for the goods indorsed in blank, an insurance policy or certificate covering war and marine risks and the beneficiary's invoice for the price of the goods, freight and insurance. If the goods are to be transported by land or air, the credit will require an appropriate bill of lading or airway bill and an insurance policy covering the carriage by land or air.

The duty of the beneficiary is to tender documents to which no reasonable exception can be taken under the rules governing C.I.F. contracts and under the Uniform Customs, if these are incorporated. Bills of lading are usually issued in sets of three and the letter of credit may require the beneficiary to present a "full set" of bills of lading.

However, in the absence of such an express term in the credit it has been held in *Sanders* v. *Maclean & Co.*[83] that the beneficiary need only tender one copy of a bill issued in a set and the issuing or confirming bank may only refuse to take up the documents if it can show that another copy of the set has been indorsed to another person. A bill of lading can be used by the issuing bank to collect the goods at the port of arrival only if it is made out to the bank's order (which is unlikely), or to the beneficiary's order and is indorsed by him in blank. The courts have held that a bill of lading is not good tender under a credit if it is made out in favour of the beneficiary or a third person and is not indorsed,[84] or if the bill does not name a person as entitled to the goods represented by it, but is simply made out "to order" and bears an illegible indorsement.[85]

13.51   The general law requires a bill of lading to be signed on behalf of the carrier and to be an "on board" bill, namely, one acknowledging that the goods have actually been loaded on the ship which is to transport them. A "received for shipment" or a forwarding agent's bill of lading will not be accepted under a credit requiring a "shipped" or "on board" bill of lading, for these merely indicate that the goods have been received for shipment but are not actually on board. In *Diamond Alkali Export Corp.* v. *Bourgeois*[86] the sellers tendered an invoice and a bill of lading in the following terms, namely, "received in apparent good order and condition from . . . to be transported by the S.S. Anglia," and a certificate of insurance in place of the policy. The court held that the buyers were entitled to reject the documents; the bill of lading did not acknowledge actual shipment of the goods and the

---

[83] (1883) 11 Q.B.D. 327.
[84] *National Bank of S. Africa* v. *Banco Italian di Sconto* (1922) 1 Lloyds L.R. 531.
[85] *Skandinavska Kreditakiebolagent* v. *Barclays Bank Ltd.* (1925) 22 Lloyds L.R. 523.
[86] [1921] 3 K.B. 443.

insurance document was not good tender of a marine policy under the ordinary rules governing C.I.F. contracts. Similarly, in *Enrico Furst & Co.* v. *W. E. Fischer Ltd.*[87] a bill of lading issued by a forwarding agent was held to be bad tender.

However, in order to accommodate bills of lading issued by forwarding agents in respect of goods loaded with other goods in containers before shipment, such bills are accepted as valid tender by the Uniform Customs. It is not proposed to deal with this matter here, which is one purely of shipping law.

The bill of lading tendered must be a "clean" bill of lading, namely, one which states that the goods were shipped in "apparent good order and condition" without qualification. An issuing or confirming bank is entitled to reject a bill of lading which has noted on the face of it or in the margin any description or reference to goods indicating that the goods are damaged or below standard. For example, the issuing bank was held entitled to reject documents where the bill of lading for a consignment of meat had the standard wording struck out and "misshapen and wet" inscribed by the shipowner (*Westminster Bank Ltd.* v. *Banco Nazionale di Credito*),[87a] and similarly where the bill of lading described the bags containing a consignment of onions as torn and resewn (*National Bank of Egypt* v. *Hannevig's Bank Ltd.*[87b] However, the fact the bill of lading requires the goods to be marked or packed in a certain way in order to make them easily identifiable at the port of discharge does not make the bill of lading unacceptable to the bank.[88]

A qualification which does not relate the shipowner's responsibility for the goods, but which entitles the issuing or confirming bank to reject the documents is a clause in the bill of lading allowing the shipowner to stow the goods on deck, instead of below deck, when the credit does not expressly permit carriage on deck. The Uniform Customs expressly permit the bank to reject a bill of lading which provides that the goods may or will be stowed on deck[89] or bills which are subject to the conditions of a charterparty when the conditions are not set out in the bill.

13.52

An issuing or confirming bank is not concerned with any general conditions in the bill of lading which are not required to be fulfilled by the letter of credit, but which the seller may have to comply with under the underlying contract of sale or which may affect the rights of the buyer against the carrier. In *British Imex Industries Ltd.* v. *Midland Bank Ltd.*[90] a bill of lading contained a clause providing that in the case of a cargo of iron and steel sheets and bars, the shipowner would not be responsible unless every piece was distinctly marked and secured. The issuing bank rejected the documents on the ground that there was no acknowledgement in the bill of lading that the term of the additional clause had been complied with and the beneficiary under the credit brought an action for the amount due. The court held that a clean bill of lading was called for and had been provided in conformity with the letter of credit, and the bank was wrong in rejecting

---

[87] [1960] 2 Lloyds Rep. 340.
[87a] (1982) 31 Lloyd's L.R. 306.
[87b] (1919) 1 Lloyds L.R. 69.
[88] *British Imex Industries* v. *Midland Bank* [1958] 1 All E.R. 264.
[89] Art. 28.
[90] [1958] 1 All E.R. 264.

the documents. The question of the sufficiency of the marking of the cargo was strictly related to the underlying sale of contract, and so the bank was not required to call for proof that the condition as to marking had been fulfilled. However, this would be otherwise if the letter of credit had expressly required evidence of conformity.

13.53   Finally, bills of lading must specify the port of shipment and arrival, and the bill must be a through bill of lading covering the whole of the voyage between those ports. If part of the journey is to be by road or air the bill must also cover that portion of the journey. The same applies to an airway bill. The Uniform Customs now provides in article 25 that if the letter of credit expressly permits the tender of a combined transport document for the transportation of goods partly by land and partly by sea or by air, the issuing bank may accept any form of transportation document (whether the document presented is a bill of lading, or an airway bill, or a road or rail consignment note or a combination of these) provided it covers the whole journey.

In certain cases, if the credit calls for the tender of a bill of lading it has been held that the beneficiary can compel the issuing or confirming bank to accept a ship's delivery order or a warehouse receipt instead, but only if he can show that the unloading of the ship named in the bill has begun or in the case of a warehouse receipt if the unloading has been completed, and in either case the bank must be able to obtain immediate delivery of the goods from the ship or warehouse. In *Forbes, Forbes Campbell & Co.* v. *Pelling, Stanley & Co.*,[91] the contract related to the sale of 11,000 cases of sultanas. The shipping documents which were tendered consisted of an invoice, a ship's delivery order and a certificate of insurance. The buyers rejected the documents as not being in order. It was held by the court, on appeal by the buyers, that the seller was entitled to present a delivery order or warehouse receipt in lieu of a bill of lading when the goods had been unloaded. On the other hand, however, in *National Bank of South Africa* v. *Banca Italiana di Sconto*,[92] it was held that if the credit requires a ship's delivery order or a warehouse receipt, the beneficiary cannot tender a bill of lading, although Atkin L.J. thought a bill of lading would have sufficed if it was shown that the ship had arrived at the arrival port and the goods covered by the credit were available for delivery.

13.54   The law relating to the sufficiency of the other documents which are required under a letter of credit is not so complex as the rules relating to bills of lading and will be dealt with briefly. The policy of insurance must, of course, cover all the risks expressly required to be covered in the letter of credit. Where the credit calls for an insurance policy, the tender of an insurance certificate which refers to the terms of an open policy under which the certificate has been issued but does not set them out is insufficient, and the bank will be entitled to reject the documents. In *Donald H. Scott & Co.* v. *Barclays Bank Ltd.*[93] the issuing bank opened a letter of credit, the terms of which were that it would honour the sellers' drafts for the amount of the purchase price, provided the drafts were accompanied by an approved

---

[91] (1921) 9 Lloyds L.R. 202.
[92] (1922) 1 Lloyds L.R. 531.
[93] [1923] 3 K.B. 1.

insurance policy covering the shipment of the goods. The sellers presented a draft for acceptance accompanied by a certificate of insurance which neither contained nor indicated any means of ascertaining the full terms of the insurance cover. The draft was dishonoured and the sellers brought an action against the bank. It was held that the certificate was not an "approved insurance policy" within the terms of the letter of credit, and the bank was justified in refusing to accept the documents. The court followed the rule laid down by Bailhache J. in *Wilson & Co. v. Belgian Grain Co.*[94] where it was held that the tender of a cover note was insufficient where the beneficiary has an open insurance policy covering all shipments made by him.

The court also approved the view of McCardie J. in *Diamond Alkali Corpn. v. Bourgeois*[95] that a certificate of insurance is not an insurance policy and does not purport to be one; it is a certificate that a policy has been issued which covers the goods mentioned in the certificate and it incorporates the terms of the policy, but it does not enumerate those terms of the policy or summarise the material terms, so that in order to discover those terms one has to examine the original policy.[96]

An insurance policy or certificate must cover all the risks specified in the **13.55** letter of credit, or all the risks which are usually insured against in the trade in question.[97]

Additionally, the beneficiary is required to tender an invoice stating the total price of the goods, and any adjustment which may have to be made should be effected by means of a claim on the buyer or a refund to him by the seller, and not by way of an addition to or a deduction from the price specified in the credit. In *Urquhart Lindsay & Co. Ltd. v. Eastern Bank Ltd.*[98] it was agreed between the parties that if the cost of labour for manufacturing the goods increased there would be a corresponding increase in the purchase price of the goods. The sellers accordingly presented invoices which, although within the limits of the credit, reflected the increased costs of manufacture. When the buyers discovered this they instructed the defendant bank to pay, in future, only the amounts representing the original prices. The defendants accordingly refused to pay or accept the documents for the next consignment, and the plaintiffs brought an action for damages against the issuing bank. The court held that the bank's refusal to pay the amount of the seller's invoices (within the limits of the credit) on the presentation of the proper documents constituted repudiation of the bank's obligations and the plaintiffs were entitled to damages. The bank, as between the buyer and seller must accept the invoices of the seller as correct provided they were within the limits of the credit and far from the letter of credit being qualified by the terms of the contract of sale the latter must accommodate itself to the letter of credit when determining the bank's obligations. The importance of the invoice is reinforced by the Uniform Customs and article 41(C) states that the description of the goods in the commercial invoice must correspond

---

[94] [1920] 2 K.B. 1.
[95] [1921] 3 K.B. 443.
[96] See *Wilson & Co.* v. *Belgium Grain Co.* [1920] 2 K.B. 1, and *Donald H. Scott & Co* v. *Barclays Bank Ltd.* [1923] 3 K.B. 1; *cf. Diamond Alkali Export Corpn.* v. *Bourgeois* [1921] 3 K.B. 443.
[97] *Borthwick* v. *Bank of New Zealand* (1900) 6 Com.Cas. 1.
[98] [1922] 1 K.B. 318.

to the description of the credit. In *The Lena*[99] the commercial invoice was required to describe the goods in terms corresponding with the description in the credit, but failed to do so. It was held that if specific items of description are included in the credit they must also be included in the invoice.

13.56   The letter of credit may sometimes require the beneficiary to present other documents, apart from a bill of lading, insurance policy and invoice, *e.g.* consular invoices, certificates of weight, quantity of analysis, or expert's certificates. The beneficiary, once again must comply strictly with these requirements. Consequently, in *Equitable Trust Co. of New York v. Dawson Partners Ltd.*[1] it was held that the tender of a certificate of quality by one expert was insufficient when the letter of credit required a certificate by experts in the plural, thus calling for at least two. Similarly, a certificate given by an expert whose qualifications are better than those of the expert named in the credit will not suffice.[2]

It is suggested in some cases that technical defects should not be grounds for rejecting documents (*Richard v. Royal Bank of Canada*).[2a] However, English courts do not support that view.

Rejection of documents tendered for extraneous reasons

13.57   The discussion so far has assumed that an issuing or confirming bank which refuses to accept the documents under a letter of credit does so either because the documents do not comply with the credit or because some condition in the letter of credit has not been fulfilled. It is now proposed to deal with the question whether or not the bank is entitled or bound to refuse to honour the credit on any other grounds unconnected with the terms of the credit, *e.g.* forgery of the documents presented or fraud on the part of the beneficiary.

A credit which is conditional on the presentation of shipping documents requires the presentation of genuine documents under which a real consignment of goods or their value may be collected from the carrier or the insurers. Forged documents confer no such rights and are worthless pieces of paper which the bank may reject.[3] The bank is required to accept the documents tendered only if all of them are genuine. It may reject the documents even if all but one are genuine documents and even though the bank itself will have no occasion to rely on that one document. Where, therefore, a forged bill of lading and a valid insurance policy are tendered and the goods are lost under circumstances which give the buyer the right to rely on the policy, the bank is entitled to reject the documents tendered because the bill of lading is a forgery. A document is a forgery not only if it bears a forged signature but if it purports to be a different kind of document from

---

[99] [1981] 1 Lloyds Rep. 68; See also, *Soproma SpA v. Marine and Animal By-Products Corpn.* [1966] 1 Lloyds Rep. 367, where it was held that there was no inconsistency between the description of the goods in the invoice and the description of the goods in the bill of lading.

[1] (1926) 25 Lloyds L.R. 90.

[2] *Basse and Selve v. Bank of Australasia* (1904) 20 T.L.R. 431.

[2a] (1928) 23F. 2d 430 (2nd Cir.).

[3] *Establishment Esekfa International Anstalt v. Central Bank of Nigeria* [1979] 1 Lloyds Rep. 445.

what it really is. In *Kwei Tek Chao* v. *British Traders and Shippers Ltd.*[4] bills of lading on which the shipment date had been falsified by showing the date of shipment as October 31, 1951 were presented to the issuing bank, together with other documents which were genuine. The bank accepted the documents in ignorance of the false shipment date and when the defect was subsequently discovered the buyers brought an action against the sellers for the repayment of the price, claiming that it was a condition of the contract of sale that only genuine bills of lading showing the real date of shipment should be presented. The court held that the bill of lading was a forgery because it showed the goods in question as having been loaded on the ship within the time specified in the credit, whereas in fact the loading had taken place afterwards. A bill of lading which bears a false shipment date deliberately entered in it is a forgery because it relates to a voyage which purports to have commenced on that date when in fact there is no such voyage. The court said the beneficiary does not warrant the genuineness of shipping documents unless he is the consignor named in them, but his moral blamelessness does not prevent the buyer from rejecting the goods on the ground of forgery when they are delivered, or alternatively from instructing the issuing bank not to accept bills drawn under the covering letter of credit. In *Guaranty Trust Company of New York* v. *Hanney & Co.*[5] it was likewise held that the beneficiary is not deemed to warrant the genuineness of any shipping documents attached to the draft when he was not the consignor named in them, and so no action lies against him either by the buyer or by the issuing bank to recover money paid under the credit unless he acted in bad faith and so was guilty of fraud.

If, however, the seller knows that the docments are forgeries when he **13.58** presents them and deliberately induces the bank to accept his draft, he will be liable to the bank in damages for fraud. In *Szteyn* v. *J. Henry Schroder Banking Corpn.*[6] the defendant issued an irrevocable letter of credit to a seller in India for the price of a consignment of bristles. The seller loaded fifty cases on board the ship and procured clean bills of lading and other documents from the shipping company. The documents described the goods in terms which complied with the letter of credit, but the cases in fact contained worthless rubbish. The sellers then presented the draft and documents to the issuing bank for payment. The plaintiffs, the buyers, on discovering the true state of affairs brought an action against the issuing bank and the beneficiary to restrain the issuing bank from paying against the draft. The court held that although the bank cannot reject documents because of a dispute between the parties relating to the quality of the goods supplied, the courts will grant an injunction to restrain the bank from making payment where the seller's fraud is called to the bank's attention before the documents are presented for payment. In this type of situation the buyer would not, if the bank were compelled to accept the documents, receive anything in the nature of the goods he contracted for.[7]

Even if the buyer can prove fraud on the seller's part that buyer cannot

[4] [1954] 2 Q.B. 459.
[5] [1918] 2 K.B. 623.
[6] (1941) 31 N.R. Supp. 2d. 631.
[7] See also, *Davis O'Brien Lumber Co* v. *Bank of Montreal* [1951] 3 D.L.R. 536.

obtain an injunction against the issuing or confirming bank to prevent it from honouring the credit unless the buyer makes the seller a co-defendant so that he will be bound by the judgment and finding of fraud on his part. In *Discount Records Ltd.* v. *Barclays Bank Ltd.*[8] all the parties (particularly the seller) were not before the court so as to be bound by its findings on the question of fraud and the court said that in order for an injunction to be granted to prevent the issuing bank from honouring the credit the buyer must make the seller a co-defendant in order to protect the bank against an action by the buyer for dishonour.

13.59   In *Royal Bank of Canada* v. *United City Merchants*[9] the House of Lords, however, held that in law there is only one ground for rejecting shipping documents which are formally in order, namely, the personal fraud of the beneficiary (*e.g.* where the beneficiary presents forged or falsified documents which he has all along known to be forged or falsified, or where he knowingly ships rubbish). The consequence of this is that if shipping documents are forged or falsified by a third party for whom the beneficiary cannot be held responsible (*e.g.* a loading broker or the original consignor of goods from whom the beneficiary has purchased goods afloat in good faith and in reliance on the forged or falsified documents) the issuing or confirming banks cannot reject the shipping documents and refuse to honour the credit. Lord Diplock justified this conclusion on the ground that the issuing or confirming bank has the right to be indemnified by the buyer, if whilst acting in good faith and with reasonable care to ensure that the documents are genuine, the bank accepts documents which although apparently in order turn out to be invalid; this right must correspond with an obligation on the bank to take up such shipping documents tendered by the beneficiary, because it would be impracticable for the bank's obligations to the beneficiary not to match exactly its right to an indemnity. This conclusion (with respect) is unnecessary and erroneous because whilst the issuing or confirming bank is entitled to an indemnity from the buyer if, as an agent, it accepts apparently conforming documents after a reasonable examination, it acts as principal in dealing with the beneficiary of the credit, however, and its obligation to him is limited to accepting documents which in fact are valid. It is not a necessary requirement, therefore, that a bank's right to an indemnity if it acts properly should in all respects be matched to the obligation it owes to the beneficiary to accept the documents. That obligation is sought to be qualified by the condition that the beneficiary must first present valid shipping documents.[10]

13.60   The House of Lords, in its judgment, treated the act of falsification and thereby invalidity of the shipping documents as amounting merely to personal fraud. The judgment, if followed in subsequent cases, would have the result that if the beneficiary presented documents which were insufficient because they set out the true facts (*e.g.* the bill of lading showed the correct date in which the goods were shipped and that date was after the last date of shipment specified in the letter of credit), the bank could quite properly

---

[8] [1975] 1 All E.R. 1071.
[9] [1982] 2 All E.R. 720.
[10] See A. Arora, "Fraud and Forgery in Commercial documentary credits," (1983) Vol. 9, No. 1, *Commonwealth Law Bulletin*, pp. 271–278.

reject the documents as non-conforming; on the other hand if the beneficiary presented falsified documents (*e.g.* the date of shipment was falsified so as to make it appear to be within the period allowed by the letter of credit), the bank could not reject the documents even it if knew of the falsity at the time the documents were presented. The judgment opens the gate to the seller who does not conform in fact to the terms of a letter of credit, by allowing him to enforce the obligations of the issuing or confirming banks under a letter of credit even though he tenders only apparently conforming documents, and grants him protection by removing the burden from the seller to ensure that the documents he tenders are not false or forged.

In exceptional circumstances the bank may also refuse to accept documents that are apparently in order on the ground that the goods actually shipped do not in fact conform to their description in the letter of credit, although their description in the shipping documents does conform to the credit. In *Société Metallurgique d'Aubrives and Villerupt v. British Bank for Foreign Trade*,[11] Bailhache J. ruled in an *obiter dictum* that the issuing or confirming bank would be justified in rejecting the documents and drafts of the beneficiary if he misdescribed the goods in such a way as to be guilty of fraud.

However, the bank is not entitled to reject the documents merely because **13.61** the seller has not fulfilled the terms of the underlying contract of sale, or if the buyer has repudiated the contract. The bank is entitled to reject the documents only if the seller fraudulently attempts to take advantage of the irrevocable nature of a commercial credit or if the bank has an interest in the quality of the goods. A bank which has paid the amount of the credit as the result of a fraudulent misrepresentation by the seller, can recover the amount paid, or if it discovers the fraud prior to payment, the seller cannot compel it to make payment.[12] However, if the documents conform to the letter of credit and are prima facie in order, the issuing bank is bound to pay, and the buyer cannot restrain it from making payment by countermanding his instructions. In *Hamzeh Malas v. British Imex Industries Ltd.*[13] the Court of Appeal held that an irrevocable letter of credit constituted a bargain between the issuing bank and the seller of the goods which imposed on the bank an obligation to pay if the conditions of the credit are fulfilled, irrespective of any dispute between the seller and buyer as to the quality of goods delivered under the underlying contract of sale. Similarly, the American courts have held in *Maurice O'Meara Co. v. National Park Bank of New York*[14] that whether the goods were of the quality which the purchaser contracted to buy did not concern the bank which issued the credit and in no way affected its liability to pay for them. Consequently, the bank was under no obligation to ascertain whether the goods to be delivered conformed to the contract between the buyer and seller. In *Frey v. Sherbourne*,[15] the New York Superior Court went even further, and held that the bank could not refuse to accept the beneficiary's draft even if the bank's customer has rescinded or terminated the underlying contract.

[11] (1922) 11 Lloyds L.R. 168.
[12] *O'Meara v. National Park Bank* (1925) 239 N.Y. 386.
[13] [1958] 2 Q.B. 157.
[14] (1925) 239 N.Y. 386.
[15] (1920) 184 N.Y. Supp. 661.

The relationship between indorsees of a bill of exchange drawn under a credit and the issuing and confirming banks

13.62   A letter of credit is not a negotiable instrument and the contract entered into under a letter of credit is made between the issuing and confirming banks and the beneficiary named in it. The credit cannot be transferred to a third party in order to enable that person to use it by drawing bills under it. However, under the ordinary rules relating to equitable assignments a bank which discounts a bill of exchange drawn by the beneficiary of a credit can, by joining the assignor to the action, sue the issuing or conforming bank for refusing to accept the bill of exchange if the letter of credit is delivered to it, since this clearly shows that the beneficiary intends the bank to take the benefit of the credit as an equitable assignee. By section 136(1) of the Law of Property Act 1925, the rights of the beneficiary under the credit (being a chose in action) can also be assigned at law by a written instrument signed by the beneficiary, provided the issuing bank is notified. In equity an agreement, whether written or oral, to assign the benefit of a credit for value suffices as an equitable assignment.[16] An assignment which fails to take effect under the Law of Property Act 1925 may, therefore, take effect in equity.[17] The language of the assignment is immaterial, provided its meaning is plain. It is merely necessary that the debtor should have notice that the debt has been made over by the original creditor to some third party and he is bound to pay it to that person.

However, not all acts of disposition amount to an assignment. For example, a person who draws a cheque on his bank in favour of a third person does not assign an amount out of his bank account equal to the amount of the cheque to the payee. The question whether a direction to the debtor to pay a third party is an assignment or merely a revocable mandate depends on the intention with which it is given, but in the case of an assignment of the benefit of a letter of credit when he indorses a bill drawn under it, the beneficiary's intention must always be to make an absolute assignment, since he ceases to have any interest in the credit when he has discounted the bill.

13.63   Certain types of credit have been devised which allow the benefit of the credit to be transferred to a third party. A negotiation credit is often expressed as being available not only to the beneficiary but also to all subsequent indorsees of the bills of exchange drawn by him under the credit. In this situation the contract under the letter of credit will expressly make the benefit of the credit available to all persons who act on it by negotiating bills drawn by the beneficiary. Under the common law rules of contract law the issuing bank makes a general and continuing offer to the world at large to honour such bills of exchange and an indorsee of a bill accepts the offer by acting on it and discounting the bill in the hands of the beneficiary or the present holder of the bill (see discussion on legal nature of a letter of credit). Where the issuing or confirming banks fail to honour drafts indorsed by the beneficiary, the indorsee, whether a discounting bank or an individual, has,

---

[16] *Sassoon (M.A.) & Sons Ltd.* v. *International Banking Corpn.* [1927] A.C. 771.
[17] *Holt* v. *Heatherfield Trust Ltd.* [1942] 2 K.B. 1.

therefore, a direct cause of action against the issuing and confirming banks for breach of contract.

When documents are presented to the issuing or confirming bank under a letter of credit, by a beneficiary who is consignor of the goods represented by the documents, he gives an implied warranty to the banks that the documents are genuine and not forged, falsified or altered. If, therefore, the bank is aware that the documents are forged, it can refuse to honour the credit. However, where a third party, such as an indorsee of the bill of exchange drawn under a credit, or a seller who acquires the contract goods from a supplier who ships them to the purchaser, presents shipping documents which have been procured by someone other than himself, he does not give any warranty as to the genuineness of the documents. In *Robinson v. Reynolds*[18] the court held that if the beneficiary negotiates his bill of exchange drawn under a credit to a holder in due course after the issuing bank has accepted the bill, the holder will be able to recover the amount of the bill from the bank and the bank will not be able to plead that its acceptance was obtained by the presentation of forged shipping documents. In *Leather v. Simpson*[19] L accepted and paid a bill of exchange against forged bills of lading tendered in good faith by the bank of Liverpool which had discounted the bill of exchange. The court held that the bank as indorsee of the bill did not warrant the regularity and genuineness of the documents presented with it and L had no equity to recover the amount paid. Similarly, in *Woods v. Thiedeman*[20] the defendant agreed to buy some wheat from one Homeyer, who was instructed to draw on the plaintiff's banking agents for the price, the drafts to be accompanied by an appropriate bill of lading. On advice from Homeyer that the wheat had been shipped, the defendant instructed the plaintiff (his bank) to request its London agents to accept Homeyer's drafts, but only on presentation of a bill of lading. The London agents accepted Homeyer's draft, as instructed, but before it became due, it was discovered that the bill of lading was a forgery and that no goods had been shipped at all. The London agents having paid the draft and debited the plaintiff with the amount, it was held that the plaintiff was entitled to recover the amount of the draft from the defendant. The plaintiff did not undertake to be responsible if it should turn out that the bill of lading was a forgery and that no goods were on board the ship.

A tender of a forged bill of lading is bad tender and can of course be **13.64** rejected, but if a bank or other person discounts a bill of exchange accompanied by the forged bill of lading and presents them to the buyer or the buyer's bank for acceptance or payment, the person presenting the documents does not by English law warrant or represent to the buyer the genuineness of the bill of lading, and if the bill of lading is a forged one, he is under no liability to the buyer or the buyer's bank to refund the amount paid on the strength of the documents. Likewise he does not warrant that the bill of exchange is genuine. In *Guaranty Trust Company of New York v. Hannay & Co.*[21] the court accepted the position of the holder of a bill of

---

[18] (1841) 2 Q.B. 196.
[19] (1871) L.R. 11 Eq. 398.
[20] (1862) 1 H. & C. 478.
[21] [1918] 2 K.B. 623.

exchange who presents it for payment as expressed by Dean Ames, of Harvard, in the Harvard Law Review, who said

> " . . . By presentment for payment he [the holder of a bill] does not assert, expressly or by implication, that the bill is his or that it is genuine. He, in effect says: 'Here is a bill, which has come to me, calling its tenor for payment by you. I accordingly present it to you for payment, that I may either get the money, or protest it for non-payment.' "

The person presenting the bill of exchange, furthermore, does not warrant the genuineness of the prior indorsements or acceptance on the seller's draft. In *Cocks* v. *Masterman*[22] and *London and River Plate Bank* v. *Bank of Liverpool Ltd.*[23] it was held that when a bill which becomes due and is presented for payment and is in fact paid, the fact that it is later discovered that the bill bore forged indorsements does not make the person who presented the bill liable to restore the amount paid (as money paid by mistake), if he has altered his position meanwhile (as he will have done by not exercising any right to recover the amount of the bill from prior holders of it). This rule is particulary important where bills are accepted or paid under letters of credit, since the issuing or confirming bank has no right of recourse under the bill of exchange against the person who presented it to the bank. This is so even in the case of a negotiation credit when the person presenting the bill for payment by the bank indorses the bill to it, because the bank by issuing or confirming the credit impliedly waives the right of recourse it would normally have against indorsers who have relied on the existence of the credit as security for payment of the bill.

Assignments

13.65   Article 55 of the Uniform Customs and Practices permits the beneficiary of a commercial credit to assign a debt which is due or will become due at some time in the future. In the latter case an assignment will be enforceable in equity provided that proper consideration has been given and that the debt materialises.

The rights of a beneficiary under a credit are a chose in action and normally assignable under section 136 of the Law of Property Act 1925, or by way of equitable assignment. A credit, to be transferable must be so designed (art. 54) but there would appear to be no reason why the beneficiary of a credit (not restricted in his favour) cannot transmit the benefit of the credit to a third party. This can be done by assignment if proper documents are tendered, since it is unlikely to make any difference to the issuing bank by whom the documents are tendered.

However, the question of assignment was examined in *Singer and Friedlander* v. *Creditanstalt Bankverein*[24] where the court held that the right to present documents under a non-transferable letter of credit cannot be assigned.

---

[22] (1829) 9 B. & C. 903.
[23] [1896] 1 Q.B. 7.
[24] [1981] Com.L.R. 69.

In the case of an assignment the bank may set up any defences against the assignee it could avail itself against the beneficiary (assignor). If, therefore, proper documents are tendered, the tenderer will be entitled to payment provided the issuing bank has no knowledge that the documents are either forged or fraudulent.

Assignment of the benefit of the credit

The mechanics of the assignment obviously depend on what is being **13.66** assigned and the terms on which the credit is payable. If the assignment is merely of the proceeds any clear intention to transmit will be sufficient provided the assignee notifies the bank which will be called upon to pay. The assignee will take subject to any set-off which the bank may be entitled to exercise against the assignor. Notice by the assignee must be given to the payer of the proceeds, whether that be the issuing bank or an intermediary bank called upon to confirm or pay the bank. If the intermediary bank were merely to advise the credit the assignee's notice must be given to the issuing bank. The notice of assignment should be clear and unequivocal and the bank should on receipt of notice verify the assignment with the beneficiary-assignor.

Assignment of the whole benefit of a credit

An assignment of the whole benefit of the credit must necessarily permit an **13.67** assignment of the moneys eventually payable under the credit; it includes all the rights that a beneficiary has and is subject to all the conditions he has to fulfil in order to become entitled. This amounts to a right to tender the documents if transmitted to the assignee to receive payment as the beneficiary and set-up any defences the payer could exercise (see assignments generally).

Measure of damages for breach—repudiation of a commercial credit

If the issuing or confirming bank wrongfully refuses to take up the docu- **13.68** ments tendered under a letter of credit, the seller may sue it either for the amount payable under the credit if the tendered documents are still available or alternatively, for the same amount as the seller could recover from the buyer for breach of the underlying contract of sale provided this does not exceed the amount of the credit.

In *Belgian Grain and Produce Co.* v. *Cox & Co.*[25] and *Larios* v. *Bonany y Gurety*[26] it has been held that the beneficiary may sue the bank for the actual amount payable to them under the credit without showing that he has suffered any loss by the bank refusing payment. However, the beneficiary can only bring an action of this nature if he still has the shipping documents required under the letter of credit and is prepared to deliver them to the bank.

[25] (1919) 1 Lloyds L.R. 256.
[26] (1873) L.R. 5 P.C. 346.

Instead of suing the issuing bank for the amount of the credit, the beneficiary under the credit may sue it to recover the same amount as would be recoverable from the buyer for breach of the underlying contract of sale.[27] These damages will normally be the difference between the amount payable under the credit and the lower market value of the goods covered by the credit, or if the bank repudiates the credit before the goods are shipped, damages are equal to the difference between the purchase price of the goods as set out in the letter of credit and the lower market value of the goods in the country from which they were to be shipped.

If the credit is issued in favour of a manufacturer and the bank repudiates the credit before the goods are completed, the measure of damages will be the expense already incurred by him and any profit which he would have made if the credit has been honoured. However, the amount of damages cannot exceed the total amount payable under the contract of sale or the maximum amount which the beneficiary was entitled to draw under the credit, whichever is less.

THE RELATIONSHIP BETWEEN THE BUYER AND THE ISSUING AND CONFIRMING BANKS

The documentary credit is opened at the request of the buyer and the relationship that arises between the buyer and the issuing bank is based on the contract and the Uniform Customs and Practices, if incorporated, under which the bank opens a letter of credit in consideration of certain promises made by the buyer, namely, to pay the issuing bank a commission and to put it in funds to meet the seller's drafts. The contract underlying the letter of credit not only determines the buyer's ultimate liability to the bank but also the bank's obligations to the buyer. It is proposed, therefore, to deal with the obligations imposed by this contract on the buyer and on the issuing bank. Where, however, the buyer requests the credit to be confirmed, the issuing bank will normally employ a bank in the seller's country to confirm the credit and advise the seller of the issue and confirmation of the credit. The relationship between the buyer and the confirming bank is more remote than his immediate contractual relationship with the issuing bank and this will also be dealt with in this section. Finally, the relationship between the issuing and the confirming banks will be dealt with.

The issuing bank's obligations to the buyer

13.69   As a result of the issuing bank undertaking to open a letter of credit, there arises a direct contractual relationship between the issuing bank and the buyer (the applicant for the issue of the letter of credit) and the obligations of the parties are determined not merely by the common law but also, if incorporated, the Uniform Customs and Practices. The issuing bank opens the credit in accordance with the instructions given to it by the buyer, and the bank's obligations are confined to honouring the drafts of the beneficiary when presented provided the shipping documents called for by the letter

---

[27] *Urquhart Lindsay & Co.* v. *Eastern Bank* [1922] 1 K.B. 38.

of credit are presented and the conditions to be inserted in the letter of credit comply with the buyer's instructions.

The common law rules

Although the obligation of the issing bank is simply to honour the letter of **13.70** credit it imposes both a positive and a negative duty on the issuing bank, and breach of either of these obligations will render it liable to the buyer. First, the issuing bank is liable to the buyer if it fails to issue the credit in accordance with his instructions and to honour drafts presented by the beneficiary (if the shipping documents accompanying the draft comply with the conditions of the letter of credit). Secondly, the issuing bank is liable to the buyer if it honours drafts presented by the beneficiary when the documents do not in fact comply with the credit.

In addition to the bank losing its right to reimbursement if it exceeds its mandate, the issuing bank is under a contractual duty to the buyer, the applicant of the credit, to obey his instructions and carry them out carefully. If it takes up documents which do not conform to the buyer's mandate, or if it refuses to take up documents which do conform to the mandate it is liable to the buyer in damages for any loss he suffers.

If the documents taken up by the issuing bank do not correspond to those required under the credit, it fails to conform to its mandate and it is also guilty of negligence, but if the disparity is not obvious, the bank is liable only if a competent bank exercising reasonable care would not have accepted the documents tendered. This sort of situation might arise where the description of the goods in the documents presented does not correspond to the description in the letter of credit, or the bill of lading tendered allows the goods to be carried on deck when the letter of credit does not permit this, or the insurance policy tendered contains an exclusion clause which is not usual in the trade. In *Borthwick* v. *Bank of New Zealand*[28] a bank took up shipping documents for a consignment of meat, including an insurance policy which excluded the insurer's liability for a total loss of the meat unless the ship carrying it was also lost. It was held that the bank had not fulfilled its obligations to ensure that the insurance policy covered the risk of loss of the meat as a competent banker would have done, and it was, therefore, liable in damages to the applicant of the credit.

However, the *Borthwick* case does not impose a duty on the issuing bank **13.71** to familiarise itself with the specialised terms and practices used in the trade. Indeed, the court held in *Rayner & Co. Ltd.* v. *Hambros Bank Ltd.*[29] that an issuing bank was justified in rejecting a bill of lading which described the goods in different terms from those used in the trade, although the goods shipped complied with the underlying contract of sale and a person familiar with the trade would have realised that this was so.

The issuing bank, it has been seen, is liable in damages if it disregards its instructions under the letter of credit or if it acts negligently in some other manner. However, the liability of the issuing bank may be extended to the acts of a third party, if the issuing bank employs the third party as its agent

---

[28] (1900) 6 Com.Cas. 1.
[29] [1943] K.B. 37.

to fulfil the whole or part of its functions under the credit. This arises where, for example the issuing bank employs another bank to advise or confirm the credit. The acts of such a bank or agent are attributed to the issuing bank, and the issuing bank is then liable to the buyer on this hypothesis, even though it exercised due care in selecting the other bank as its agent.

In *Equitable Trust Co.* v. *Dawson Partners Ltd.*[30] the court held that where a confirming bank took up shipping documents which did not conform to the buyer's instructions as a result of an error in the transmission of the instructions by the confirming bank to one of its own branches, the issuing bank was responsible to the buyer, its customer, but it was entitled to be reimbursed by the confirming bank for the amount for which it was liable. The court accepted the rule applied in *Ireland* v. *Livingston*[31] as to the liability of a principal for his agent's defaults and said that if a principal gives an order to an agent in uncertain terms so that it is capable of two different meanings, and the agent bona fide adopts one of two reasonable alternatives and acts upon it, the principal cannot repudiate the act of the agent as unauthorised because he meant the order to be read in a different sense. The issuing bank is, therefore, liable for the acts of its agents provided the confirming bank in adopting one of the possible interpretations acts in a manner it believes will benefit the principal. Similarly, in *Calico Printers Associaion* v. *Barclays Bank Ltd.*[32] it was held that when the applicant instructed the issuing bank to insure the goods to which the credit related, and the issuing bank transmitted these instructions to an advising bank carrying on business where the goods were delivered, the failure of that bank to insure resulted in the issuing bank being liable to the applicant for their value when the goods were destroyed.

13.72   Finally, the law may impose on the issuing bank a duty to pass on to its customer (the buyer or applicant of the credit), any information which it may acquire concerning the standing of the beneficiary, and which may effect the relationship between the buyer and the seller. In *Midland Bank* v. *Seymour*[33] the plaintiff bank, agreed at the request of the defendant to open a letter of credit in favour of a firm in Hong Kong with which the defendant buyer was dealing. The issuing bank made routine inquiries as to the financial standing of the Hong Kong firm, and the replies being satisfactory the issuing bank passed the information to the defendant. The issuing bank later received information which cast doubts on the integrity and financial standing of the Hong Kong firm, the beneficiary under the credit. The bank failed to pass this information on to the defendant, and was held liable for its failure to do so. The defendant could have prevented his loss by forestalling payment under the credit because of the Hong Kong firm's fraud. However, as the defendant was unable to prove such fraud he could only recover nominal damages.

Davis takes the view that a duty arises on the part of the issuing bank to pass on information about the beneficiary in all cases. However, it is sub-

---

[30] (1926) 25 Lloyds L.R. 90.
[31] (1872) 5 H.L. 395.
[32] (1939) 36 Com.Cas. 71.
[33] [1955] 2 Lloyds Rep. 147.

mitted that there is no general duty on the issuing bank to provide the buyer with any information it may have about the financial standing of the beneficary, and the case is an exception to the general rule, because the bank having voluntarily passed on to its customer information about the Hong Kong firm came under an obligation to transmit further information when it discovered that the beneficiary in fact was not as sound as the bank's original inquiries had led the buyer to believe. Moreover, there is no express undertaking in the letter of credit that the issuing bank will provide the buyer with information concerning the beneficiary's financial standing.

The obligations of the issuing bank to the beneficiary of the credit under the UCP

The Uniform Customs and Practices on Banker's Commercial Credits **13.73** codify the duties of an issuing bank towards an applicant for a credit and impose a lighter duty on the banks than that imposed by the Common Law. By article 15 of the Uniform Customs banks are required to examine " . . . all documents with reasonable care to ascertain that they appear on their face to be in accordance with the terms and conditions of the credit. . . . " and if the issuing bank takes up documents which appear on their face to be in accordance with the terms and conditions of the credit, the applicant must reimburse the bank.[34] Furthermore, the issuing bank assumes no liability "for the form, sufficiency, accuracy, genuineness, falsification or legal effect of any documents,"[35] nor for the consequences of delay and/or loss in transit of any messages, letters or documents[36] and issuing banks "utilising the services of another bank for the purposes of giving effect to the instructions of the applicant" are not liable for the acts or omissions of the other bank employed, who are deemed to act, not for the issuing bank but as agent for the applicant of the credit.[37] Under the Uniform Customs the issuing bank is, therefore, not liable for the acts of an advising or confirming bank; it has not yet been decided whether this provision is an exemption clause in a standard form of contract used by the issuing bank and, therefore, possibly invalid unless it can be justified as fair and reasonable under sections 2 and 3 of the Unfair Contract Terms Act 1977. Section 2 of the Act applies where issuing or advising bank act negligently and it requires neither a standard term be used in the contract nor a consumer. Whether the applicant of the credit can recover from the confirming bank for any wrongful acts will be dealt with when the relationship of the buyer and confirming bank is discussed below.

The buyer's obligations to the issuing bank

The discussion so far has dealt with the duties placed on the issuing bank **13.74** when the letter of credit is opened. It is now proposed to deal with the corresponding duties placed on the buyer if the issuing bank conforms to the letter of credit and fulfils its duties under it.

[34] Art. 16(a) UC & P.
[35] Art. 19.
[36] Art. 18.
[37] Art. 20.

The buyer is under a duty to put the issuing bank in funds to meet the seller's drafts before they become due. In *Reynolds* v. *Doyle*[38] the court held that a customer of a bank at whose request the credit is issued is under a duty to pay it the amount for which it has accepted bills of exchange a reasonable time before the bills fall due for payment. This is to ensure that the issuing bank has funds sufficient to meet the bill when it is required to pay them.

The customer is not required to put the bank in funds when the credit is actually issued, but the issuing bank can expressly stipulate that its customer must furnish it with the amount payable by it to the beneficiary of the credit before or at the time the credit is issued, so that the bank does not at any time risk its own funds. If the customer already has an account at the bank on which there is a credit balance, the bank usually requires that it be given power to debit the amount of the credit when the letter of credit is issued. Where, however, the customer does not have a balance sufficient to cover the amount of the credit, or where the credit is issued at the request of a bank, it may agree to advance the amount of the credit. The issuing bank will then rely on its right to be reimbursed the amount it pays under the credit together with its expenses and charges, and it may rely on any security interest it has over the shipping documents or in the goods they represent to recover the amount which the buyer owes it.

Where the applicant of the credit fails to provide the bank with adequate funds, so that it pays or purchases the beneficiary's drafts out of its own resources, the bank is entitled to charge the applicant the current rate of interest from the date the bill is paid or purchased by it.[39]

13.75 The obligation of the applicant to put the bank in funds is the counterpart of the bank's obligation to honour the credit. If the bank repudiates its obligation, either expressly or by implication, *e.g.* as a result of ceasing its business or by going into liquidation or having a receiver of its undertaking appointed, the applicant's corresponding obligation to provide it with funds is terminated, and subject to the claims of secured creditors of the bank any sums paid by the buyer for the purposes of the credit can be recovered.[40] If sums standing to the credit of the buyer's account have been specifically appropriated to the credit the buyer can recover the amount. Otherwise, he will recover the balance of his account as an ordinary creditor.

In *Greenhough* v. *Munroe*[41] an American court held that the buyer's obligation to put the bank in funds could not be enforced after the bank had ceased carrying on business and had stopped payment of its debts as they fell due. The consideration for the buyer's promise was the bank's obligation, not only to accept, but also to pay, the seller's drafts. The breach of its obligation to pay, by placing itself in a position where it was unable to make payment when called upon to do so resulted in a total failure of consideration (*i.e.* was a repudiatory breach) which precluded the bank from exercising any claim to be put in funds by the buyer. Furthermore, the buyer was entitled to use for his own purposes the shipping documents which the

---

[38] (1840) 1 M. & G. 753.
[39] *Re Ludwig Tillman* (1918), 34 T.L.R. 322.
[40] *Sales Continuation Ltd.* v. *Austin Taylor & Co. Ltd.* [1967] 2 All E.R. 1092.
[41] (1931) 53 F. 2d. 362.

bank had delivered to him under letters of trust and the trust in favour of the bank was terminated.

Finally, it remains to deal with the issuing bank's right to be reimbursed by the buyer. The bank's right to reimbursement is dependent on it having conformed strictly to the instructions given to it in the application for the opening of the credit. If, however, it exceeds its mandate in any respect, however slight, its right to be reimbursed is lost. Alternatively, if the applicant has put the bank in funds prior to the seller's drafts being presented, and the issuing bank departs from its mandate, the applicant is entitled to the return of his money (unless he waives his rights of strict compliance).

An issuing bank will exceed the mandate if it accepts or purchases a bill of exchange drawn by the seller without insisting on the beneficiary delivering the documents required by the applicant's instructions. This may happen because of a mistake by the issuing bank in transmitting instructions for the notification of the issue of a letter of credit by an advising bank. **13.76**

The Uniform Customs absolve the issuing bank from responsiblity for the consequences arising out of delay and/or the loss of messages, letters or documents, or for delay, mutilation or errors arising in the transmission of cables, telegrams or telex, or for the errors in the transaction of technical terms.[42] If the Uniform Customs are applied strictly the bank in the situation that arose in *Equitable Trust Co. of New York* v. *Dawson Partners Ltd.*[43] would not have been liable for the consequences of its mistake and it would have been entitled to reimbursement as though it had complied with the buyer's instructions. However, the Uniform Customs do not exonerate a bank which is guilty of negligence, because the issuing bank is under an overriding duty to be careful. Furthermore, it may be questioned whether the exoneration of the issuing bank under the Uniform Customs incorporated into its contract with the buyer can be impeached under sections 2 or 3 of the Unfair Contract Terms Act 1977 as not being fair and reasonable.

The rules governing the sufficiency of documents are the same whether the dispute is between the beneficiary and the issuing bank when the latter refuses to take up the documents tendered, or whether the dispute is between the issuing bank and its customer when it has taken them up and claims reimbursement by him. In *South African Reserve Bank* v. *Samual & Co.Ltd.*,[44] the plaintiff bank took up warehouse receipts for certain quantities of maize which did not specify the contracts under which they had been acquired by the beneficiary. The receipts were tendered under a credit which had been opened to cover the sale of a global quantity of maize to be shipped by several consignments, and the letter of credit contained an anticipatory credit clause by which the beneficiary could draw up to a stated fraction of the total amount of the credit on delivering warehouse receipts of warrants in favour of the bank as security. The Court of Appeal held that the anticipatory credit clause was not independent of the main credit, but merely a provision for advances to be made to enable the seller to purchase the maize from his suppliers. It was, therefore, necessary for the bank to ensure that the maize for which the warehouse receipts were delivered had

---

[42] Art. 18.
[43] (1926) 25 Lloyds L.R. 90.
[44] (1931) 40 Lloyds L.R. 291.

been acquired under the credit and would be represented by shipping documents. As this could only be done if the warehouse receipts identified the contracts under which the maize had been acquired by the beneficiary, the bank exceeded its mandate and its right to be reimbursed was consequently lost in accepting warehouse receipts merely for stated quantities of maize.

Conditions not relating to the contents of the shipping documents

13.77 If a bank takes up shipping documents and accepts or pays bills of exchange under a credit containing conditions not relating to the contents of the shipping documents, the question arises whether the bank may claim reimbursement from the buyer if those conditions are not in fact fulfilled. If the bank is negligent in failing to make adequate inquiries before deciding that the conditions have been fulfilled, it would lose its right to be reimbursed in any case. The Uniform Customs, however, protect the bank by providing that payment, acceptance or negotiation against documents which appear on their face to be in accordance with the terms and conditions of a credit binds the party giving the authorisation to take up the documents and reimburse the bank[45] and furthermore, the banks assume no liability or responsibility for the conditions stipulated in the document.[46] The effect of these provisions, (if they are valid, despite sections 2 or 3 of the Unfair Contract Terms Act 1977) is that the bank loses its right to be reimbursed only if it is negligent.

Where the Uniform Customs do not apply the courts have occasionally, but erroneously held that the issuing bank is entitled to proof by the beneficiary that all conditions contained in the credit which do not relate to the production of documents have been fulfilled. In *Union Bank of Canada* v. *Cole*[47] the defendants issued a letter of credit in favour of corn merchants, S. & Co., authorising them to draw bills of exchange against the defendants for shipments of grain, provided certain conditions set out in the credit as to the existence and identification of the grain to be shipped were complied with. The plaintiffs, with the knowledge that the conditions had not been complied with, advanced money on the security of bills drawn under the credit and the defendants refused to accept those bills. It was held that the contract between S. & Co. and the defendants on which the plaintiffs relied was subject to the conditions in the letter of credit being complied with and consequently the plaintiffs' claim failed. If the bank must make sure that these conditions are satisfied before it can debit its customer with the amount of the bills of exchange under the credit, the bank must have a corresponding right to insist on strict proof by the beneficiary that the conditions are satisfied before it accepts his draft. This goes against the basic rule of documentary credit that the issuing bank is only concerned to examine that the documents presented comply with the terms of the credit.

[45] U.C.P. 16.
[46] U.C.P. 17.
[47] (1877) 47 L.J.C.P. 100; See also, *Chartered Bank of India Australia and China* v. *MacFaydan* (1895) 64 L.J.Q.B. 367.

The letter of credit authorises only the beneficiary named in it to draw **13.78**
bills on the issuing bank. This imposes an obligation on the issuing bank to
honour bills of exchange only if they are actually drawn by the beneficiary
under the credit and not by a third person. In *Orr and Barber* v. *Union Bank of
Scotland*[48] and *British Linen Co.* v. *Caledonian Insurance Co.*[49] the issuing
bank paid bills of exchange drawn under a letter of credit to persons who
had fraudulently drawn cheques in the beneficiary's name and presented
them for payment under the letter of credit. The court held in both cases
that if an issuing bank accepts, purchases or pays bills of exchange drawn by
someone other than the beneficiary under the letter of credit, the bank cannot claim reimbursement from the applicant for the credit, even if it acts in
good faith and without negligence. In *British Linen Co.* v. *Caledonian Insurance Co.* the court took the view that a customer who deposited money with
the bank for the particular purpose of paying bills drawn by a named person
could treat money paid by the bank on bills forged by another person as not
having been paid out of the deposit, and therefore, as still being held by the
bank for the benefit of the real beneficiary. The beneficiary under a letter of
credit is, therefore, entitled to recover the amount of the credit even though
the bank had already paid it in good faith to a person not entitled to receive
payment.

However, the issuing bank does not exceed its mandate if it takes up
forged shipping documents from the beneficiary in good faith and without
negligence and it is then entitled to reimbursement by its customer. In
Woods v. *Thiedmann*[50] it was held that the mandate given by the applicant
under the letter of credit must be taken as authorising the bank to accept
documents which prima facie appear to be genuine. Consequently, the right
of the bank to reimbursement is not lost unless it was negligent and should
have realised that the documents were defective because they were forgeries. The Uniform Customs provide that the issuing bank assumes no
responsibility or liability for the genuineness, falsification or legal effect of
any documents presented[51] and as regards shipping documents (as distinct
from bills drawn under the credit) this appears to reflect the common law.

An issuing bank which exceeds its mandate retains the right to be reimbursed by the applicant of the credit if the latter ratifies what the bank has
done with full knowledge of the circumstances. The ratification may be
expressed or implied from the conduct of the applicant in going ahead with
the transaction once he has knowledge of the bank's breach of its obligations. In *Midland Bank* v. *Seymour*[52] it was held that the buyer ratified the
bank's conduct and its acceptance of drafts tendered under a credit which
had expired when the bank asked for and obtained the beneficiary's confirmation that the seller's invoice was correct. The customer's act relied on as
ratification must show that he approves of what the bank has done and if his
conduct is equivocal in this respect no ratification will be inferred.

---

[48] (1854) 1 Macq.H.L.Cas. 512.
[49] (1861) 4 Macq.H.L.Cas. 107.
[50] (1862) 1 H. & C. 478.
[51] Art. 17 U.C.P.
[52] [1955] 2 Lloyds Rep. 147.

The relationship between the buyer and the confirming bank

13.79   If a commercial credit issued by one bank is confirmed by another so as to make it liable to the beneficiary, there is a contractual relationship between the issuing and confirming banks, but no such relationship between the applicant for the credit and the confirming bank. Consequently, if the confirming bank exceeds its mandate by accepting or paying drafts when the conditions of the credit have not been fulfilled, it is not liable in damages to the applicant for the credit for breach of contract.

In *Orr and Barker* v. *Union Bank of Scotland*[53] it was held that the applicant for the credit could not sue the confirming bank when it had paid a forged draft and subsequently refused to honour a genuine draft presented by the beneficiary. Similarly, in *Calico Printers Association* v. *Barclays Bank Ltd.*[54] the court held that a confirming bank owes no duty of care to the applicant for the credit. In *Equitable Trust Co.* v. *Dawson Partners Ltd.*[55] the court furthermore held that there is no agency relationship between the buyer as principal and the confirming bank as his agent, so that an issuing bank cannot escape liability by arguing that the error committed by the confirming bank in accepting the documents was committed by that bank, as an agent of the buyer. On the contrary, the court held that the confirming bank acts as an agent of the issuing bank and so the issuing bank is liable as its principal to the buyer. Since the buyer is not responsible for any errors committed by the confirming bank he cannot be treated by the issuing bank as bearing the risk of the confirming bank's defaults, so it follows that the buyer cannot claim against the confirming bank for any default which operates to the buyer's detriment. If, therefore, the confirming bank acts negligently, it is not liable to the buyer, since the confirming bank owes the buyer no duty of care.[56]

13.80   However, the American courts have held in *Oelbermann* v. *National City Bank of New York*[57] that a confirming bank is liable to the applicant if it is guilty of fraud, for example, if it knowingly permits the beneficiary to draw under the credit for purposes not authorised by it. In that case the defendant bank confirmed a credit containing an anticipatory credit clause enabling the beneficiary to draw drafts on it in order to purchase raw materials to satisfy the underlying contract of sale, but the bank allowed the beneficiary to draw against the credit in order to reduce its overdraft on a general account with the confirming bank. The court held that the confirming bank was liable to the buyer for fraud, even though there was no direct contract between them.

It is submitted that the English courts, if faced with a similar situation would hold the confirming bank liable and it would not allow a bank which had deliberately committed a fraudulent act to rely on the defence that there

---

[53] (1854) 1 Macq.H.L. 512.
[54] (1930) 36 Com.Cas. 71.
[55] (1926) 25 Ll.L.R. 90.
[56] *Calico Printers Assn.* v. *Barclays Bank* (1930) 36 Com.Cas. 71.
[57] (1935) 79 F. 2d. 354.

was no direct contract between the buyer and itself. The confirming bank's liability would be a tortious one either for deceit or for conspiring with the beneficiary to obtain payment under the credit without being entitled to it. Furthermore, it is submitted that a confirming bank may now also be held liable for negligent misstatements to the buyer (either directly or through the issuing bank) under the principle laid down in *Hedley Byrne and Co.Ltd. v. Heller and Partners Ltd.*[58] and subsequent similar cases if it gives advice or information that it knows will be, or is likely to be, relied upon by the buyer. The liability is again a tortious one, since there is no direct contractual relationship with the buyer, but the fact that the buyer is intended to rely on the negligent statement imposes a duty of care on the confirming bank towards him.

The relationship between the issuing and confirming banks

The seller may make it a term of the contract of sale that the letter of credit **13.81** is to be issued not by a foreign bank in the buyer's country, but by a bank in his own country on whose solvency the seller is more inclined to rely. In these circumstances the buyer can request that his bank, or a bank in his own country make arrangements with the nominated bank so that that bank will open the credit in favour of the seller. The terms of this arrangement are a matter of private negotiation between the banks but it is proposed to deal with the relationship that arises, if any, between them. Alternatively, the issuing bank may issue the credit itself and procure the bank in the seller's country to confirm it. If the seller is content to accept a letter of credit issued by a bank in the buyer's country without confirmation by a bank in the seller's country, the issuing bank may employ a bank in the seller's country merely to advise the seller of the issue of the credit.

The relationship between the issuing (buyer's bank) bank and the intermediary bank whether the latter it issues, confirms or advises the credit, is that of principal and agent, so that when the intermediary bank has fully complied with the mandate it has a right to be reimbursed by the buyer's bank, and if it has suffered any loss, or may suffer any loss by reason of it complying with the mandate, it is likewise entitled to be indemnified by the buyer's bank. If the intermediary bank has accepted bills payable a fixed period after sight or on a specified date it is entitled to be reimbursed on paying the bills, whether or not there is any dispute between the buyer and seller, provided that the documents it has taken up are in conformity with the terms of its instructions. In *Bank Melli Iran v. Barclays Bank (D.C.O. Ltd).*[59] the Court of Appeal held that an issuing bank waives its right to reject documents taken up by the intermediary bank if it delays in exercising that right for an unreasonable length of time from the time the documents are tendered to it, or from the time it has knowledge that the documents

---

[58] [1964] A.C. 465.
[59] [1957] 2 Lloyd's Rep. 367.

taken up by the intermediary bank do not conform to the conditions in the credit. In *National Bank of Egypt* v. *Hannevig's Bank Ltd.*[60] it was held that if the issuing bank acnowledges the receipt of the documents without making any objection to them it waives its right to reject the document and the intermediary bank is then entitled to reimbursement. In *Westminster Bank Ltd.* v. *Banco Nazionale di Credito*[61] Roche J. said:

" . . . if the parties keep documents which are sent them, purporting to be sent them, or possibly sent them, in consequence of some mandate, which they themselves have issued, and keep them for an unreasonable time, that may amount to a ratification of what has been done as being done within their mandate . . . "

13.82   In the *Banca Nazionale di Credito* case, however, the court held there was no ratification by the applicant for the credit which affected the right of the issuing bank to reject the documents. The question in that case was whether the plaintiff bank which had issued a letter of credit on the instructions of the applicant's bank could claim on the indemnity given to it by the applicant to the credit on the applicant's failure to present complying shipping documents. The court held that if the applicant for the opening of the credit takes delivery of the goods, there is no automatic waiver of the issuing bank's independent right to reject the shipping documents. The issuing bank's right to reject the documents is distinct from the applicant's right to reject either the goods or the shipping documents under the contract of sale. There is no legal relationship between the applicant and the issuing bank acting on the applicant bank's instructions which entitles the applicant to treat the issuing bank as his agent so that it is, therefore, bound by his act. The same would apply if the plaintiff bank had been a confirming bank in this case. If the seller (beneficiary) is a customer of the confirming bank, it is deemed to have paid him when it credits him with the amount of the credit in its own accounts. The bills accepted by the confirming bank under the credit are then paid and discharged by it crediting the beneficiary's account and debiting the issuing bank's account with itself. The American courts have held in *Liberty National Bank and Trust Co.* v. *Bank of America National Trust and Savings Association*[62] that the bills are paid when such entries are made by the confirming bank, even though no money has passed between the parties. In this situation the confirming bank can enforce its right to an indemnity by the issuing bank despite the fact that the confirming bank reserves the right to reserve the credit entry in favour of the beneficiary if it fails to recover an indemnity from the issuing bank.

A further consequence of the confirming bank being in the position of an agent for the issuing bank is that a confirming bank is not entitled, on its own behalf and for its own benefit, to discount drafts drawn by the seller on the issuing bank. It would be guilty of a breach of duty in making a profit out of the transaction which it has entered into as an agent, and would be accountable for the amount of the discount to the issuing bank.

---

[60] [1919] 1 Lloyds L.R. 69.
[61] (1928) 31 Lloyds L.R. 306.
[62] (1955) 218 F. 2d. 831.

SECURITY INTERESTS UNDER LETTERS OF CREDIT

13.83 One common function of a letter of credit is normally to finance the sale of the goods and the bank which advances money to pay for the goods will either expressly or impliedly have a security over the shipping documents, and in certain cases the goods themselves, to safeguard its right to reimbursement of its advance by the customer at whose instance it issued the credit. The bank will have a lien, *i.e.* right to retain possession of the shipping documents and ultimately to sell the goods if the buyer fails to reimburse the bank. Furthermore, by express agreement, the bank may have a pledge over the goods or an equitable charge over them created by a letter of hypothecation or a letter of trust or a trust receipt signed by its customer. The method used by the bank to secure its right to reimbursement will govern the nature and extent of its interest in the shipping documents, the goods they represent and the remedies it may exercise whilst leaving the ownership of the goods vested in its customer.

The banker's lien

13.84 An issuing or confirming bank is entitled to hold the shipping documents which it receives from the beneficiary as security for the amount it has paid or committed itself to pay under the bills of exchange. The banker's lien arises by operation of law in consequence of the instructions given to the issuing bank to open the credit. The lien is independent of any other security the bank may take by express agreement. The ordinary right of the bank under its lien is a right merely to retain possession of the shipping documents, but in the case of such documents the lien carries with it the right to sell the goods represented by them and as such approximates more closely to a pledge than to a Common Law lien. In the case of other documents over which a bank has a lien there is no implied power of sale or realisation.

In *Brando* v. *Barnett*[63] Lord Campbell said: "Bankers most undoubtedly have a general lien on all securities deposited with them, as bankers, by a customer, unless there be an express contract, or circumstances that show an implied contract, inconsistent with lien . . . "

Again, in *Halesowen Pressworks and Assemblies* v. *Westminster Bank Ltd.*[64] the court distinguished between a lien and a right of set-off and accepted that banks have a general lien on all securities deposited with them by its customer.

13.85 The essential factor in deciding whether or not the documents are subject to a lien is whether or not they came into the hands of the bank in the course of its business as a banker. The bank has a general lien or right of retention over all kinds of documents belonging to its customer in its hands and the bank can hold them until all the amounts owed to it in respect of loans and advances have been paid back to the bank. The lien extends to all documents under which money may be obtained, whether they are negotiable or not, and in the case of documents relating to goods the lien extends to the goods

---

[63] (1846) 12 Cl. & Fin. 787.
[64] [1972] A.C. 785.

themselves so that if the customer fails to reimburse the bank, it can sell the goods and so realise the advance it has made on the customer's behalf. The bank may exercise a lien over cheques, bills of exchange, share certificates and securities generally, and in *Sewell* v. *Burdick*[65] securities were held to include bills of lading and other documents representing goods in transit. An issuing bank is therefore entitled to a lien over shipping documents taken up by it under a letter of credit as security for its right to reimbursement. A lien, therefore, gives the bank a security over the shipping documents, but it does not transfer the ownership of the goods to the bank.[66]

In *Aschkenasy* v. *Midland Bank Ltd.*[67] it was held that a bank which instructs another bank to make a payment to a third party is itself a customer of the other bank. It follows that a confirming bank may claim a lien over shipping documents taken up by it to enforce its right to be indemnified by its immediate customer, the issuing bank, and the fact that the applicant for the credit has put the issuing bank in funds does not in any way affect the confirming bank's lien.

Gutteridge and Megrah[68] on the other hand suggest that the intermediary bank has a pledge on the documents it accepts from the seller and is entitled to retain the documents against its principal, the issuing bank, until the intermediary is reimbursed, or alternatively, it may sell the goods represented by the documents if the issuing bank fails to reimburse it. Strictly speaking, what the intermediary bank has is a lien with a right to sell the goods if it is not reimbursed, and although they refer to it as a pledge, the authors in fact mean a lien.

13.86   The lien which a bank acquires over shipping documents delivered to it when it accepts or purchases a bill of exchange drawn by the beneficiary of a credit must be distinguished from the lien of the indorsee of an unspecified bill of exchange drawn under a credit. The beneficiary discounts the bill to a third bank instead of presenting it to the issuing or confirming bank for acceptance or negotiation; the person who takes the bill of exchange acquires a lien on the shipping documents if they are handed to him with the bill. In *Frith* v. *Forbes*[69] it was said that this lien may be enforced in the same way as a pledge by the indorsee selling the goods and using the shipping documents to effect the sale, or alternatively the bank may recover the proceeds if the goods are sold by the beneficiary. The lien, however, is only a security for obtaining the acceptance or negotiation of the bill of exchange by the issuing or confirming bank. In *Guaranty Trust Co. of New York* v. *Hannay & Co.*,[70] the Court of Appeal held that once the bill of exchange has been accepted, the indorsee has to rely exclusively on the credit of the issuing or confirming bank; his lien on the shipping documents is extinguished, and a new and separate lien arises in favour of the bank, giving the issuing or confirming bank security for its right of reimbursement. Lord Scrutton L.J. expressed himself as follows in the course of his judgment:

---

[65] (1884) 10 App.Cas. 74.
[66] *Halesowen Pressworks* v. *Westminster Bank* [1972] A.C. 785.
[67] (1934) 51 T.L.R. 34.
[68] p. 168.
[69] (1862) 4 De G.F. & J 409.
[70] [1918] 2 K.B. 623.

" . . . The bank will have the documents of title as security for its liability on acceptance, and the purchaser can make arrangements to sell and deliver the goods. Before acceptance and the documents of title are the security, and an unaccepted bill without documents attached is not readily negotiable. After acceptance the credit of the bank is the security. . . . "

Unpaid seller's right of stoppage in transit

The Sale of Goods Act 1979, s.44, provides that an unpaid seller who has **13.87** parted with the possession of the goods has a right to stop them in transit and to regain possession of them. The seller may resume possession of the goods while they are in transit (but not when the goods have actually been delivered to the buyer or his agent) and may then retain them until the purchase price is paid or tendered. A seller can exercise a right of stoppage in transit if the following conditions are satisfied:
(a) the seller must be unpaid; and
(b) the buyer must be insolvent; and
(c) the goods must be in transit.
The goods are in transit when they have passed out of the possession of the seller into the possession of a carrier but have not yet been delivered to the purchaser or an agent authorised to receive delivery. The seller will lose his right of stoppage when the goods are no longer in transit; for example, when they have actually been delivered to the buyer or if the carrier has attorned the goods to the buyer. The right of stoppage in transit may be exercised over some part of the goods where some of the goods have been delivered.

The right of stoppage may be lost by sub-dealings with the goods by the buyer. If, for example, the buyer mortgages or charges the goods, the seller can still exercise his right of stoppage notwithstanding that the goods have been pledged, but his rights will be subject to the rights of the secured creditor.

Position between the vendor and the carrier

If the carrier to whom a notice of stoppage has been delivered wrongfully **13.88** delivers the goods to the buyer, he is liable for conversion to the vendor. The carrier, however, has a lien on the goods for the freight due, and this will take priority over the seller's right of stoppage; the carrier can refuse to redeliver the goods to the seller unless the seller discharges the amount of the freight.

Unpaid seller's right of resale

The seller has a power of resale: **13.89**
(a) if he still has property in the goods;
(b) if the property in the goods has passed but the seller still has possession of the goods;
(c) if the property has passed but the seller has exercised his right of lien or stoppage in transit.

The 1979 Act, s.48(2), provides that where an unpaid seller has exercised his lien over the goods or his right of stoppage in transit, he may resell the goods and the buyer will acquire a good title as against the original purchaser.

The pledge

13.90 An applicant for a letter of credit may create different forms of security over the shipping documents representing the goods in favour of the issuing or confirming bank. The difference between these forms of security and a banker's lien is that the latter is created by operation of law without any agreement between the parties. However, the former arise only by the express agreement of the parties and their incidents are determined by agreement.

One of the forms of security available to the bank is a legal pledge of the goods in question and this is created by delivery of the subject-matter to the creditor, thereby giving him a legal right of possession until his indebtedness to the bank is discharged. The essence of a pledge is that the security vested in the pledgee consists exclusively of the possession of the goods in question and not any derivative proprietory interest in them. Consequently, if the goods are returned by the pledgee to the pledgor otherwise than as agent for the pledgee, the pledge comes to an end.[71] However, although the pledgee has no proprietory interest in the goods a pledge confers an implied right for the pledgee to realise his security by selling the goods, and shipping documents held by the pledgee may be used for this purpose.

At common law, a pledge can be created only by delivering either actual or constructive possession of the goods pledged, to the pledgee. If the goods are in the hands of the pledgor, he can effect the pledge by actual delivery; in other cases, he can give possession by some other sufficient act, such as handing over the keys of the warehouse where the goods are stored so as to vest control over them in the pledge. If, however, the goods are in the hands of a third party who holds them on behalf of the pledgor, a pledge may be effected by the pledgor instructing the third party to hold the goods for the account of the pledgee and by the third party attorning to the pledgee (*i.e.* acknowledging that the third party holds the goods on behalf of the pledgee) and the latter in such a case has constructive possession. Where, however, the goods are represented by documents, the mere delivery of the documents to the pledgee does not generally vest possession of the goods themselves in them, unless the person who had custody of them is notified of the arrangements and agrees to hold the goods on behalf of the pledgee. In the absence of such an agreement the pledge of the goods is incomplete and ineffective.

13.91 The House of Lords, however, recognised an exception to this rule in *Barber* v. *Meyerstein*[72] and held that a pledge of the goods by means of a deposit of documents relating to them is possible either if the document is a negotiable instrument or if it is a current bill of lading. The question in that case was whether the plaintiff, an indorsee for value of one copy of a bill of

---

[71] *North Western Bank* v. *Poynter* [1895] A.C. 56.
[72] (1870) L.R. 4 H.L. 317.

lading relating to goods which at the time of indorsement had been discharged from the ship which carried them on to a sufferance wharf on the River Thames, had priority by virtue of possession over the bill of lading over two stops which had been placed on them; one by the shipowner for unpaid freight and the other by certain mortgagees, and also whether he had priority over the claims of the third defendants who had subsequently accepted indorsements of the two other copies of the bills of lading and had obtained possession of the goods.

The court said that indorsement and delivery of a bill of lading while the ship carrying the goods represented by the bill is at sea operates in exactly the same way as the delivery of the goods themselves to the consignee or his indorsee after the arrival of the ship. Similarly, in *Sewell* v. *Burdick*[73] it was held that an indorsement and delivery of the bill of lading by way of pledge was equivalent to the delivery of the goods to the pledgee.

The rule has been recognised in subsequent cases, although its application has been somewhat restricted.

In *Official Assignee of Madras* v. *Mercantile Bank of India Ltd*. it was held **13.92** that the exception relating to bills of lading cannot be extended to railway consignment notes, warehouse warrants or other documents used in connection with the transport or storage of goods. Similarly, in *McEwan & Son* v. *Smith*[74] it was held that the issue or transfer of a delivery order calling on a warehouse keeper to deliver goods is not without an attornment by the keeper sufficient to bring about a constructive delivery of the goods to which it relates. In *McEwan & Sons & Co.* v. *Smith* a seller of sugar sold it to B, to whom he gave a delivery order addressed to his agent A, and the seller took B's bill of exchange in payment of the price. B sold the sugar to M and transferred the delivery order to him by indorsement. The sugar was stored in L's warehouse in whose books it was shown as having been received by him from A on account of the seller. Neither B nor M took any steps to act on the delivery order until a rumour arose of B's insolvency, when M presented the order to A and received from him in exchange a fresh order addressed to L, the warehouse keeper, directing delivery of the sugar to M. The sugar was subsequently removed from the warehouse by A on the orders of the seller before M could act on the delivery order and obtain delivery himself. The court held that possession of the goods had never passed from the seller, and consequently he could still enforce his lien over the goods as an unpaid vendor. The court observed that a transfer or pledge of documents of title to goods does not amount to a transfer or pledge of the goods themselves; a pledge of the documents is merely a pledge of the documents themselves regarded as physical objects, except in the case of a bill of lading. A delivery order does not transfer the ownership or possession of the goods, and even if it is indorsed the transfer of a delivery order is not sufficient to estop the owner from asserting his rights in the goods. Similar dicta are to be found in the *Official Assignee of Madras* v. *Mercantile Bank of India*[75] and more recently in *Inglis* v. *Robertson*.[76] In the latter case Lord Wat-

---

[73] (1884) 10 App.Cas. 74.
[74] (1849) 2 H.L. Cas. 309.
[75] [1935] A.C. 53.
[76] [1895] A.C. 616.

son said that in Scottish and English law the indorsement and handing over of delivery orders for goods as security for a loan along with a purported letter of hypothecation is sufficient in law and mercantile practice to constitute a pledge of the documents of title themselves under which the pledgee has a right to retain the documents of title until his advance is repaid, but the right of the pledgee to retain the documents does not give him any possessory or proprietary interest in the goods which the documents represent, subject of course to the exception in the case of bills of lading.

13.93   In *Kwei Tek Chao v. British Traders and Shippers Ltd.*[77] the court looked at the degree of protection given to a bank by a pledge of shipping documents, in particular the bill of lading, and held that

> " . . . All his [the buyer's] dealings with the documents are dealings only with that conditional [because of the seller's right of stoppage in transit if unpaid] property in the goods. It follows, therefore, that there can be no dealing which is inconsistent with the seller's ownership unless he deals with something more than conditional property. . . . "

In other words, the taking up of the bill of lading by the issuing bank and its delivery to the buyers will vest possession of the goods in the buyers in them, but the ownership of the goods had not been fully vested in the buyers.

If, in pursuance of an agreement by the buyer to give a charge on the goods to secure the bank's right to reimbursement, a bill of lading is delivered to the bank, then a pledge giving the bank the rights of a secured creditor is created, and the bank need do no more to safeguard its position. If, however, the goods are represented by documents such as delivery orders or dock warrants, it is essential in addition to the transfer of documents to the bank, that notice of the transfer should be given to the person who had physical possession of the goods and that he should attorn to the bank so as to vest constructive possession of the goods in it.

The common law rule, however, has been supplemented by legislation the purpose of which was to protect banks which made advances to mercantile agents. Under the Factors Act 1889 a pledge of any document of title to the goods, whether a bill of lading, rail or road consignment note, airway bill, dock or warehouse warrant or a delivery order creates a valid pledge if the pledgor is a factor.

By section 2(1) of the Factors Act 1889 it is enacted that:

> "Where a mercantile agent is, with the consent of the owner, in possession of the documents of title to goods, any sale, pledge or other disposition of the goods, made by him when acting in the ordinary course of business of a mercantile agent, shall, subject to the provisions of this Act, be as valid as if he were expressly authorised by the owner of the goods to make the same, provided that the person taking under the disposition acts in good faith, and has not at the time of the disposition notice that the person making the disposition has not authority to make the same."

---

[77] [1954] 1 All E.R. 779.

This is supplemented by section 3 of the Act, which provides that a **13.94** pledge of the documents of title to the goods is to be deemed a pledge of the goods, and for the purposes of the act the expression a "pledge" is to include "any contract, pledging or giving a lien or security" on the goods. In *Lloyds Bank Ltd.* v. *Bank of America National Trust and Savings Association.*[78] it was held that the statutory exception in respect of a pledge by a factor applies whether the factor acts as a mercantile agent for a third person or on his own account.

A further statutory exception was created by section 25(2) of the Sale of Goods Act 1893 (now the 1979 Act), which provides that a bank which makes an advance has a valid pledge if the buyer of goods has received the documents of title to them from the seller and has pledged the goods by delivering them or the documents of title to them before the latter's lien or right of stoppage in transit for the price payable under the contract of sale has expired. The section applies to a situation where A buys the goods from B who gives possession of the documents of title to them to A's or to his bank at a time when B has not received payment of the price because payment is due on the maturity of a bill of exchange which A or his bank has accepted. A then pledges the documents to C which creates a valid pledge under the section so that C gets priority over the seller who has not yet received the sale price.

The statutory exceptions raise uncertainties and, therefore, are rarely relied on in practice. Moreover, the unpaid seller's lien is suspended if he takes a bill of exchange for the purchase price and the right of stoppage *in transitu* will revive if the buyer becomes insolvent. Consequently, the creation of a statutory pledge over the documents is a security of doubtful effectiveness once the issuing or confirming bank has accepted the beneficiary's drafts under the credit unless the buyer subsequently becomes insolvent.

A pledge can only be created by the pledgee being given either actual or **13.95** constructive possession of the goods in question, and since a bank is not in the business of dealing in or storing goods, it is practically impossible for a bank to take actual possession of the goods. Where, therefore, a bank is owed money it will probably release the shipping documents to the buyer so that he can sell the goods and reimburse the bank. The question which is of importance for the bank is whether having released the documents to the buyer its charge or security over the goods is in any way affected. In *North Western Bank* v. *Poynter Son and Macdonald*[79] a Liverpool firm owned and held bills of lading of a cargo destined to Glasgow. The firm obtained an advance from a Liverpool bank to whom they indorsed the bill of lading as security. The bank returned the bill of lading, without indorsement, to the pledgors in Liverpool so that they could act as agents of the bank selling the cargo and receiving the price. The pledgors sold the cargo and a Scottish debtor to whom they owed a personal debt, arrested the unpaid price in the hands of the purchaser in Scotland and claimed a prior right to it, on the ground that in Scotland the pledgee had lost its right of property in the cargo in consequence of their having returned the bills of lading to them on

---

[78] [1938] 2 K.B. 147.
[79] [1895] A.C. 56.

a temporary basis for the purpose of selling the goods. The court approving *Tod and Son* v. *Merchant Banking Company*[80] held that the delivery of goods, either actual or constructive, destroyed the possibility of a pledge continuing or arising subsequently. However, on the facts of the case the bank took a pledge of the goods by delivery of the bill of lading to them and gave the applicant only a limited authority to sell them as its agent. This meant that the bank did not give up possession of the goods and its pledge continued so that it was entitled to the proceeds of sale in priority to general creditors of the pledgor. The limited authority of the buyer of goods whose purchase is financed by a letter of credit, to deal with the goods if the bank releases them to him so that he may sell them as the bank's agent, does not in any way prevent the pledge in favour of the bank from continuing, even though the buyer has physical control of the goods for the purposes of the sale.

13.96   The logical consequences of this rule were worked out by the court in *Re David Allester Ltd.*[81] where a company pledged bills of lading for imported raw materials to a bank to secure the company's overdraft. In order to sell the goods, the company subsequently obtained the bills of lading from the bank in return for a letter of trust undertaking to hold the goods and the proceeds of sale as trustees of the bank. The company then went into liquidation at a time when some of the goods had been sold and the proceeds of sale of the goods and the goods remaining unsold were still in the hands of the company. The liquidator claimed these for the general creditors and argued it had priority as pledgee. Astbury J. upheld the claim of the bank, and said:

> "The bank as pledgee had a right to realise the goods in question from time to time, and it was more convenient to them, as is common practice throughout the country, to allow the realisation to be made by experts, in this case by the pledgors. They were clearly entitled to do this by handing over the bills of lading . . . for realisation on their [*i.e.* the bank's] behalf without in any way affecting their pledge rights: see *North Western Bank* v. *Poynter*."

The *North Western Bank* v. *Poynter* case and *Re David Allester Ltd.* were approved by the Privy Council in *Official Assignee of Madras* v. *Mercantile Bank of India* where it was alleged that the respondent bank had terminated its pledge in respect of the goods by giving back possession of the railway receipts to the merchants. The Privy Council rejected this contention, and Lord Wright said: " . . . The respondents did not part with the possession of the goods in the juridical sense of the word, they merely parted with the custody; by entrusting the receipts to the insolvents as their agents or mandatories for the special purpose of convenient dealing with the goods. . . . "

Letters of hypothecation, letters of trust and trust receipt

13.97   In order to overcome the difficulties of the pledge as a form of security over the documents, two other forms of security are usually resorted to by banks which finance a purchase of goods, namely, the letter of hypothecation and

---

[80] (1883) 10 R. (Ct. of Sess.) 1009.
[81] [1922] 2 Ch. 211.

the letter of trust or trust receipt. A letter of hypothecation creates an equitable charge over the goods which ensures that if the goods are sold by the applicant the proceeds of sale are subjected to a first charge in favour of the bank. Consequently, if the applicant becomes bankrupt, or in the case of a company, if it is wound up, the bank ranks as a secured creditor and is entitled to be paid first out of the proceeds of sale. The letter of hypothecation, in practice, has largely been superseded by the letter of trust or trust receipt. The trust letter of receipt evidences an agreement between the bank and the customer that the bank will hand the documents of title to the goods to the customer so that he can obtain delivery of the goods and that the customer holds the documents of title, the goods when they are received, and eventually the proceeds of sale of the goods on behalf of the bank.

The letter of trust or trust receipt is either embodied in the application for the issue of a letter of credit by the bank, or is given separately by the applicant when the shipping documents have been taken up by the issuing or confirming bank and they are delivered to him so that he may collect the goods on arrival. Under the letter of trust, the buyer undertakes to hold the proceeds of sale as a trsutee for the bank absolutely and he is under a duty to pay the whole of the proceeds to the bank, which will deduct what is owed and return the balance to the applicant of the credit. If the applicant departs from the authority given to him to deal with the goods he is guilty of a breach of a trust. The trust relationship that arises is undoubtedly valid and is treated by the courts as creating a valid security interest in the goods in favour of the bank. In *Re David Allester Ltd.*[82] Astbury J. said: " . . . the bank as pledgee created a trust agency in the company for the purpose of the realisation of the bank's security. The trust agency was acknowledged and recorded in the letters of trust . . . "

13.98 The courts have recently given the bank even greater protection under letters of trust and trust receipts by holding that not only is the customer guilty of a breach of trust by wrongfully disposing of the goods, but that the bank may sue him and the disposee for conversion of the shipping documents in such a case. In *Midland Bank Ltd.* v. *Eastcheap Dried Fruit Co.Ltd.*[83] bills of lading relating to a contract for the sale of pepper were presented on July 2, 1960 to the plaintiff bank, which handed them to the purchasers with a collection note attached which stated that the documents were delivered to the defendants on trust for inspection of the goods and if the defendants failed to pay for the documents they were to be returned to the bank. The defendants, however, sold the documents to F. & Co. and the bank was unable to recover from the defendant either the documents or the payment received for them. The bank brought an action claiming to recover the value of the documents and alleged a breach of contract or conversion of the shipping document by the defendant. The court held that the defendants were in breach of the contract constituted by the delivery of the documents to them and they were also guilty of conversion of the documents, since they had interfered with the plaintiff's possessory right to the documents.

In this situation a person to whom the purchaser of goods wrongfully disposes of shipping documents which he has received under a trust letter or

---

[82] [1922] 2 Ch. 211.
[83] [1962] 1 Lloyds Rep. 359.

receipt is equally guilty of conversion of the documents, despite the fact that he gives value for them and acts in good faith so that in equity he has a good title to the goods themselves.

The nature of the relationship that arises between the bank and his customer under the letter of trust was examined by Davis,[84] who says the relationship is partly bailment, partly agency and partly trust. He continues: "It is a bailment in the sense that the documents are actually placed in the hands of the customer. It constitutes an agency in the sense that the customer is authorised to realise the goods and receive the purchase price for them . . . "

Davis[85] later adds: "The relationship created by a letter of credit constitutes a trust to the extent, and to the extent only, that the goods before sale and the proceeds of sale when received by the customer are 'earmarked' as belonging to the banker . . . "

13.99   Whatever the nature of the relationship that arises as a result of the letter of trust, the customer holds the goods or the proceeds of sale for the benefit of the bank to the extent of the bank's security, and failure by the customer renders him liable for breach of trust or if the breach relates to the shipping documents, to the tort of conversion. The liability of the customer has been recognised as arising not only when he deals with goods or with the proceeds of sale wrongfully, but also when the customer does any act which infringes the bank's security by dealing with the documents of title to them in a wrongful manner. In *Midland Bank Ltd.* v. *Eastcheap Dried Fruit Co.Ltd.*[86] the court held that the bank could recover the value of the goods in an action for conversion of the documents when its customer wrongfully and in breach of his obligations to the bank sold the documents to a third party.

As the interests of the bank under the letter of hypothecation and letter of trust are equitable in nature, anyone who acquires the goods, and the documents of title to them, while a charge subsists takes the goods or documents subject to the interest of the bank, except a purchaser or lender who acquires a legal interest in the goods without notice of the bank's equitable interest in them and without taking delivery of the shipping documents from the bank's customer. In *Union Bank of Canada* v. *Cole*[87] it was held that a person who purchases goods affected by letters of hypothecation or a letter of trust through a factor takes free from the bank's interest if he purchases the goods in good faith and without knowledge or suspicion of the existence of the bank's interest. However, this rule is subject to the qualification in *Midland Bank* v. *Eastcheap Dried Fruit* that, although the bank in this situation cannot recover the goods from a third party who bona fide bought them and took delivery of the shipping documents, the bank can recover damages from him equal to the value of the goods for the wrongful conversion of the shipping documents resulting from its own customer's breach of the conditions on which they were handed to him.

In reality banks will write "subject to trust receipt" or words to that effect

---

[84] *Law Relating to Commercial Letters of Credit*, p. 190.
[85] p. 193.
[86] [1962] 1 Lloyds Rep. 359.
[87] (1877) 47 L.J.(C.P.) 100.

on the documents and that will give a purchaser of the documents notice of the bank's interest.

The equitable proprietary interest of the bank over the goods and subsequently the proceeds of sale subsists only so long as the bank is in a position to fulfil its obligations to its customer. If the bank repudiates these obligations expressly or impliedly, for example, if it becomes insolvent, it loses its proprietary interest. In *Sales Continuation* v. *Austin Taylor & Co.*[88] it was said that in the circumstances the bank's proprietary interest in the goods ceases automatically and the applicant may keep the shipping documents, the goods or the proceeds of sale for his own benefit.

Registration of transactions

The Bills of Sale Acts 1878 and 1882 require the registration of documents   **13.100**
which create or transfer a proprietary interest in chattels. This includes mortgages (where ownership is transferred conditionally) and charges, but not absolute bills where ownership is transferred unconditionally (*i.e.* where goods are sold). The Bills of Sale Act 1878 contains the definitions of bills of sale and chattels, whilst the 1882 Act contains the registration provisions. The register kept under the Acts may be inspected, but unlike charges registered with the companies registry, however, registration of a bill of sale does not give notice of the charge and its contents (*i.e.* there is no "deemed" notice). Registrable bills are disliked by banks for a number of reasons, *e.g.* the bill must refer to a specified sum which is repayable on a specified date (excludes fluctuating overdraft balances); the Acts provide for the use of a statutory form and any deviation from the technicalities may avoid the security, the chattels in question must be specified in a schedule so that they can be identified.

There are a number of important exceptions to the registration requirements. It is intended to deal with the more important exceptions in connection with international trade:

(1) Securities given by companies. These are governed by the Companies Act 1985. Some of the provisions in that Act refer back to the Bills of Sale Act by requiring companies to register securities which, if given by an individual would be registrable under the Bills of Sale Act.

(2) Bills of Sale of goods abroad (in foreign parts) or at sea. This is a significant exception for bankers because a substantial amount of international trade is financed by giving security over goods abroad or at sea. A charge or mortgage of such goods is effective if given while they are not in this country.

(3) Letters of hypothecation of identified imported goods. A letter of hypothecation is an equitable charge either over goods in the owner's possession or over goods in a third party's possession. Again, this is a specific exception of relevance to the finance of international trade. However, it has recently been held that general letters of charge are not within this exception because the goods are insufficiently identified.

(4) Transfers of goods in the ordinary course of business, or bills of lading, delivery orders and other documents used in the ordinary course of

[88] [1967] 2 All E.R. 1092.

business as proof of possession or control of goods or authorising the possessor of the documents to transfer or receive the goods it represents. This exception (under section 4 of the 1882 Act) relates (a) to transfers and (b) to documents of title to goods, and is important where securities are given in conjunction with documentary credit transactions in international trade.

Appropriation of the bank's security in favour of the beneficiary

13.101 The beneficiary of a credit normally relies on possession of the shipping documents, or the acceptance of a bill of exchange by the issuing or confirming bank as his security for payment of the amount owed to him by the buyer. Before his draft is accepted by the issuing or confirming bank, he has a lien on the shipping documents, but this ceases and is replaced by the lien or other security interest of the issuing or confirming bank when the beneficiary's draft has been accepted by either of them. If both the buyer (the applicant for the issue of the credit) and the bank which issued or confirmed the letter of credit become insolvent, the beneficiary may appropriate any security the bank has for an indemnity from the buyer, its customer, in order to satisfy what is owed to him. The effect of this is that the beneficiary may sell the subject-matter of the security, and use the proceeds to pay the amount due to himself under the credit.[89]

Normally, the bank's security for an indemnity arises after it accepts the seller's or beneficiary's drafts and there is a pledge of the goods arising from possession of the shipping documents, or a letter of hypothecation or letter of trust or trust receipt in respect of the goods when the shipping documents have been released to the buyer. In this situation, the court held in *Re Suse ex.p. Dever*[90] that if both the bank and the buyer become insolvent, the beneficiary may recover the goods or the shipping documents and sell the goods in order to pay himself the amount of the bills that the bank has accepted in his favour.

However, the beneficiary can only appropriate the bank's security for an indemnity if both the bank and the buyer are liable to him. It is no objection to the application of the rule in this situation that the party sending the remittances was not a party to the bills as drawer or indorser, provided the bills were drawn in respect of a transaction upon which he is liable. In *Ex p. Waring, Inglis and Clarke*[91] it was said that the holders of bills have an equity to have the security, in the hands of the bank, applied specifically to the discharge of those acceptances on the ground that a person holding the bills which are the subject of an indemnity provision made by the principal debtor has a right to the benefit of the contract between the principal debtor and the party indemnified. This rule only applies where the bills drawn by the beneficiary and indorsed to a third party have been accepted by the bank before its insolvency and does not apply where the parties become insolvent before the drafts are accepted. Consequently, in *Vaughan* v. *Halliday*[92] it

---

[89] *Ex p. Smart, Re Richardson* (1872) L.R. 8 Ch.App. 220.
[90] (1885) 14 Q.B.D. 611.
[91] (1815) 19 Ves. 345.
[92] (1874) L.R. 9 Ch.App. 561.

was held that if an advising bank which has not confirmed a credit is put in funds to pay bills drawn and then both it and the applicant for the credit become insolvent, the beneficiary has no claim to those funds as the advising bank is under no duty to the beneficiary.

The rationale of this rule, by which the beneficiary may appropriate **13.102** securities held by the bank is that the insolvent bank cannot rely on its security for an indemnity by its customer as it has failed to carry out its undertaking under the credit; it has not paid and cannot pay the amount for which the credit was opened The debtor-buyer, however, cannot treat the security as a nullity because the bank will probably pay the beneficiary a dividend in its winding-up. In *Ex P. Waring* the security was treated as valid and existing for the benefit of the party able to fulfil his obligations, in these circumstances the beneficiary.

The rule appears to go against the contractual nature of the credit, which is that there is a direct relationship between the buyer and the issuing or accepting bank but that no liability extends to the beneficiary apart from the obligation to accept the documents if they conform to the credit. Furthermore, in the light of the decisions in *Sale Continuation Ltd.* v. *Austin Taylor*[93] and *Greenhough* v. *Munroe*[94] it seems likely that the bank's security for an indemnity by its customer will be treated as terminated when the bank becomes insolvent.

Indorsee of the draft under the credit

Finally, it remains to be discussed whether an indorsee to whom bills of **13.103** exchange drawn under a credit have been negotiated has any lien over the goods represented by the shipping documents unless the shipping documents are delivered to him when he discounts the bill of exchange.[95] In *Banner* v. *Johnson*[96] it was held that the holders of the bills drawn in respect of a consignment of cotton had no charge on the cotton for the amount of the bills. The indorsees who took the bills had no right other than to require the issuing or confirming bank to accept the bills, and if they were accepted, any security which the holders of the bills may previously have had comes to an end so as to make room for the security interest of the bank itself for its indemnity. In that case a Liverpool merchant purchased cotton and obtained from his bank a letter of credit in favour of the seller which authorised the seller (beneficiary) to draw on the bank for the price. The seller's drafts were accepted by the bank but before their maturity the issuing bank became insolvent. The court held the holders of the drafts had no charge on the cotton for the amount of the bills, and the bank did not become a trustee of the cotton "for every bill-holder." The same rule was enunciated in *Re Suse, ex. p. Dever*[97] where a bank in London, at the request of its customer issued a letter of credit in favour of a merchant in Shanghai for £20,000. The credit required the drafts to be accompanied by shipping documents relating to the purchase of tea. Under the letter of credit the bank agreed with the

---

[93] [1968] 2 All E.R. 1092.
[94] (1831) 53 F 2d. 362.
[95] *Guaranty Trust Co. of New York* v. *Hannay & Co.* [1918] 2 K.B. 623.
[96] (1871) 5 H.L. Cas. 157.
[97] (1884) 13 Q.B.D. 766.

beneficiary and also, separately with bona fide holders of the bills drawn under the credit, that the bills would be accepted on presentation and paid at maturity. The bills of exchange were discounted and the issuing bank after acceptance but before payment of the bills suspended business. The court held that the holders of the drafts could not claim any specific appropriation of the tea to meet the acceptances.

The same rule applies where the drafts, instead of being accompanied by the shipping documents are drawn against a particular consignment of the goods. In *Robey & Co.'s Perseverance Ironworks* v. *Ollier*[98] Brown consigned to the defendants by the ship "Acacia" a cargo which had been purchased at the joint risk of himself and the defendants, and advised them of the particulars of bills which he had drawn against the cargo, payable to his own order. The defendants, in their reply promised to protect the goods. Brown indorsed to the plaintiffs bills which were drawn: "Pay to the order of myself the sum of £ . . . sterling . . . [and] place to account cargo per Acacia." Brown stopped payment and the defendants sold the cargo. The plaintiffs brought an action claiming a lien on the proceeds of sale for the amount of the bills held by them. The action failed, and Mellish L.J. said:

> "The indorsement of a bill gives only a right to the bill, and I do not think that any mercantile man would suppose, because he saw in the bill the words 'place to account cargo per A,' that he would have a lien on that cargo. A mercantile man who is intended to have a lien expects to have a bill of lading annexed; if there is no bill of lading annexed he only expects to get the security of the bill itself."

13.104   An exception to the rule, namely, that a non-beneficiary holder of a bill has no security or charge on the goods if the buyer and issuing bank both become insolvent, arises where the seller and the accepting or issuing bank are insolvent. In these circumstances the rule in *Ex p. Waring*[99] will apply and the holders of the drafts will be able to claim the goods held as security, so far as they remain unrealised, to meet the drafts. In *Re Suse, ex p. Dever (No. 2)*,[1] bankers in London issued a letter of credit to merchants in Ceylon authorising them to draw on them for sums not exceeding £10,000 in one transaction. The bankers agreed with the merchants and also separately with bona fide holders of the bills that the bills would be duly accepted on presentation and paid on maturity. The merchants sent remittances accompanied with a letter stating they were sent to cover particular drafts mentioned in the letters. The bank paid the proceeds of the remittances into its general banking account, but before the drafts matured the bankers and the merchants stopped payment. At the date of liquidation acceptances under the letter of credit amounted to £11,000. The bank at that time held two bills of exchange in specie and received two further bills after it stopped payment, these having been posted by the merchants before they became aware of suspension of business by the bankers. The court held that the rule in *Ex p. Waring*,[2] applied and the proceeds of the four remitted bills held in specie at the commencement of the liquidation must be applied in paying

---

[98] (1872) L.R. 7 Ch.App. 695.
[99] (1815) 19 Ves. 345.
[1] (1885) 14 Q.B.D. 611.
[2] (1815) 19 Ves. 345.

those acceptances to which the bills had been appropriated. However, the rule had no application to any of the securities which had been realised by the bankers, whether the realisation was wrongful or not, for there then remained no security to which the rule could apply. Similarly, in *Ex p. Dewhurst*[3] the holder of a bill drawn in respect of a consignment of goods was entitled to the proceeds of the consignment when the drawer and the acceptor became insolvent. In that case the drawer and acceptor of a bill, which were distinct firms in India and England engaged in a joint venture. A bill was drawn specifically against a consignment of goods from the drawer to the acceptor. The holder was held entitled to the proceeds of the goods which under the joint venture agreement were to be applied primarily in indemnifying the acceptor.

---

[3] (1873) L.R. 8 Ch. App. 975.

14. Security for Borrowing[1]

14.01 In international transactions the taking of security is less common than with domestic borrowers. This is generally because international borrowers rely more upon their credit ratings than upon the security which they can offer. In addition, negative pledges are an ordinary feature of many loans, so that unless a borrower has no other creditors, his reply to any suggestion that he give security may well be that he is contractually prohibited from so doing. The major exceptions are when one is dealing with project finance, or with ship or aircraft finance. A few loans or bond issues may be secured, and with bonds, or syndicated loans, the security will be held by a trustee.

The primary purpose of taking security is that on the liquidation of the borrower the creditor will have priority over the unsecured creditors of the borrower. A sovereign borrower may be more reluctant than a corporate borrower to give security, but a sovereign may also become insolvent (unable to pay debts), or may simply be unwilling to repay debts, in which case the purpose of security is not to give a priority in repayment (as against other creditors) but is in order to provide a fund of assets (such as bullion, or investments, or trading debts) outside the borrower's country, to which the creditor may have recourse. In some cases, the purpose of the security is merely to allow the lender to take control of and to manage the property and perhaps the whole business of the borrower, if the latter is in difficulty. This, for example, would be permitted by the standard type of floating charge taken in this country. Additionally, a borrower may have given security to his domestic creditors: here, the security taken by a foreign lender is taken so that he will rank at least equally with, and not behind, those secured creditors. Conversely, the taking of a security by the lender may prevent other creditors from taking securities over those assets, and from thus posing any threat to the lender by reason of prior charges.

A. Conflicts of laws and securities

14.02 If a security is taken, what law applies to the security? The asset over which the security is taken may be movable (tangibles or intangibles) or immovable (such as land). Movable assets, moreover, may actually be moved, frequently, as is the case with ships or aircraft. These might be described as "ambulatory" assets.

As to immovables, in English law (as in most countries) most matters affecting land and other immovables are, sensibly, determined by the law of the place where the land is situated. This is a practical necessity, reflecting the difficulty of enforcing a security over immovable assets otherwise than in accordance with the law of the place in which the asset is situated. Simi-

---

[1] See Wood, Chap. 15.

larly, an English court would not order any direct remedy affecting land situated abroad[2] but might agree to the appointment of a receiver, (though he would have to seek recognition abroad).

Tangible movables are governed by the law of the place where the assets are at the time of transfer[3] and many jurisdictions take this view. We have examined this matter in the context of state expropriations of property,[4] and we have observed the following principles:

(i) That the validity of an expropriation or transfer of title (which would include the granting of a security interest) is governed by the law of the state in which the asset is situated at the time of the expropriation or other transaction, even if the asset is otherwise taken out of that state. This rule is subject to some exceptions, if the foreign law is penal or oppressive or morally repugnant.

(ii) That an English court will not recognise the validity of any expropriation, disposition or transaction affecting a proprietary interest in movables according to the law of one state if the asset is outside that state at the time of disposition, etc., unless the disposition, etc., also conforms with the law of the state in which the asset is at the time of the transaction.

As to those movables which in fact move (such as ships or aircraft) some **14.03** states (like the U.K.) may look to the law of the flag (treating the "ambulatory movable" as if it had a nationality, which determines questions of transfer).[5]

Even if the *lex situs* of an asset originally determines its transfer and the validity of a security, if the asset subsequently comes into the territory of another state, that state may treat its own rules as mandatory rules overriding the proper law of the security interest (the law of the original *lex situs*). Some states may do so in relation to any creditor in that jurisdiction, while others may do so only in relation (say) to *bona fide* purchasers of the asset. Some may do so only in relation to some further disposition in that new state, and others may do so even if there is no further disposition.

As to intangible assets, there is even less international certainty as to the applicable rules. The form of granting security is known (in the U.K., at least) as an assignment. The debt which is assigned may have been created by a contract with its own proper law, and the contract of assignment may also have a (possibly different) proper law. It must be determined (a) whether the assets are assignable at all by way of security, (b) what formal requirements are required, (c) what perfection requirements there are (*e.g.* registration, notification to debtor) (d) what is the general effect of the assignment, (e) what priorities there are between competing assignees. The first of these questions is generally determined by the proper law of the contract being assigned. The answer to the second question probably is that the assignment is valid if it complies either with the law of the state in which the

---

[2] Such as ordering a sale of it: *Grey v. Manitoba Railway Company* [1897] A.C. 254.
[3] See expropriations, above, and *Cammell v. Sewell* (1860) 5 H. & N. 728; *Inglis v. Robertson* [1898] A.C. 616.
[4] Above, Chap. 3.
[5] See *The Jupiter* [1924] P. 236; contrast *Republic of Spain v. National Bank of Scotland Ltd.* [1939] S.C. 413, mentioned above, Chap. 3, note 17 above.

assignment took place[6] or with the proper law of the contract of assignment. The perfection of a security interest (*e.g.* by notice to the debtor, or by registration) would seem to be a matter of essential validity, for the proper law of the contract of assignment, as would be the question of the general effect, and priorities.

14.04 A particular problem with the taking of securities in movables is that many states simply will not recognise the security interest unless the lender/mortgagee has taken possession of the asset. Non-possessory "chattel mortgages," that is, may simply be disregarded. In the U.K., for example, it is difficult for an individual to give a charge over chattels unless he complies exactly with the provisions of the Bills of Sale Acts, which make it difficult to take security unless all assets can be specifically described, and effectively impossible to take security over future assets. (This is, however, possible for companies, under the English "floating charge.")[7] Additionally, until it was abolished by the Insolvency Acts 1985–1986, the doctrine of "reputed ownership" meant that a debtor might be regarded as the owner of assets which were reputedly in his possession, even though he was not in fact the owner. Some countries will recognise a form of "constructive" possession, as where the mortgagee controls the *"indicia"* of possession (such as a key to a warehouse, or where the mortgagee takes a lease of the warehouse, licensing its use to the mortgagor). Similarly, possession may be recognised where a third party (such as a warehouseman) controls the movable and agrees to hold for the benefit of the mortgagee. (The third party "attorns" to the mortgagee). Sometimes, possession of documents of title to goods (such as bills of lading) is recognised as the equivalent of possession of goods, which is how, in England, the system of pledging such documents in international sales financing operations is able to operate. The goods may then be released to the debtor on trust receipt, maintaining the pledge. This transaction requires no registration in the U.K. It cannot, however, be assumed that all countries will recognise these various non-possessory devices, or that if they do, they will accord the same degree of priority to various claimants as would a U.K. court. Some countries may not recognise non-possessory securities at all. Others may recognise them only if the mortgage is satisfactorily registered (as is the case with floating charges in the U.K.).

The floating charge is a particular example of a type of security, familiar to the English lawyer or banker, which may not be recognised at all by foreign systems of law. English law recognises it as an equitable interest, and it is, of course, perfected by registration, and subject to fixed charges, even if those are taken later with knowledge of the prior floating charge. But even if an English court would recognise the charge, if the asset is abroad the question must be whether the foreign court will recognise the validity of the charge. Many common law jurisdictions will do so, but an investigation must be made even there as to whether there are differences in detail. Civil jurisdictions may or may not recognise the charge, and legal opinions should be sought.

---

[6] *Republica de Guatemala v. Nunez* [1927] 1 K.B. 669.
[7] Discussed in Vol. 1, Chap. 21.

B. General legal problems of taking security

So many problems may arise that it is not feasible to do anything other than give a checklist of the various problems which one may face in taking the security. **14.05**

(a) Does the borrower have good unencumbered title to the assets in question? For example, with land, any available registers should be checked. Ownership of ships and aircraft, registered securities, etc. should also be investigated.

(b) Has the borrower the power (if a corporation, government department, etc.) to give security? Has the giving of security been properly authorised by the company or principal?

(c) Does the security conflict with a contrary contractual agreement (negative pledge) given by the borrower to other creditors, which may either give those others priority, or render the borrower in default (and possibly in cross-default to others as well).

(d) Can the security be floating (as in the U.K.) or merely fixed? Some countries may not recognise anything but fixed charges over existing property. Others (as does the U.K.) may recognise securities over future (after-acquired) property. Some may recognise charges over future property subject to some minimum identification of it, and so on. Some may recognise the charge as a contractual obligation, but not as a property right conferring priority, etc.

(e) Does the security have to be registered, or are any governmental consents needed for the grant of security. What is the effect if it is not? We have examined the effect of section 395 of the Companies Act, in Vol. 1. Many countries have similar registration (or "filing") requirements, and sometimes (as in the U.K.) this will apply even if the company's property is not in the state in which it does business or is incorporated. Non-registration may make the charge void, or it may affect priorities.

(f) Should the security be held by a trustee? This may be essential in a bond issue, or where there is more than one lender, as in a syndicated loan. If there is a trustee, is his existence recognised? Some countries may not recognise the trust, and may treat the property (in case of the trustee's insolvency) as that of the trustee. Some countries may treat the relation between trustee and beneficiary as that of agent and principal. In that case, they may require evidence of the agent's authority.

(g) If there is a clause prohibiting prepayments, is this an unenforceable clog on the equity of redemption? English company law allows perpetual and irredeemable debentures to be given by companies. Other countries may allow the borrower to repay them when he chooses, so as to clear off his mortgage. **14.06**

(h) Are stamp duties payable on the security, and if so, who pays them?

(i) Will a court have jurisdiction to enforce the security interest? Generally, an English court would enforce a security over property given here, and this would be so even with sovereign borrowers, for the giving of security is clearly a waiver of immunity in relation to that asset.

(j) What remedies are there on default? Can the asset be sold, and if so, in a forced sale? May it be sold by private treaty or only by auction? What duties are imposed upon the seller in selling? Is foreclosure (where the lender becomes owner) available, or may the lender take possession, and keep the income (or must he account for it). Can proceeds of realisation be repatriated, or are there exchange controls?

(k) Maintenance of value clauses may be inserted so that additional property must be secured if the value of the collateral falls below a certain figure. Will this be effective? Some countries may not recognise it if particular assets, or classes of assets, are not specified. The subsequent security may be given at a time when the borrower is insolvent, or nearing insolvency, and may be affected by rules about preferences.

(l) Must the mortgage debt be expressed in currency local to the asset, even though the loan is otherwise denominated? Exchange rate problems may then arise (if the local currency declines in value) and in that case a maintenance of value clause may be required (borrower to give additional security), or an indexing technique may be adopted. Will such clauses be effective?

These problems are very significant, and the obvious practice is to take a legal opinion from counsel in the country in which the assets in question are situated.

15. Guarantees in International Transactions

The taking of guarantees was considered generally in Vol. 1 of this work.[1] In this Chapter, we consider policy matters and some general matters which may affect the guarantee.

GUARANTEES

1. Purposes of guarantees

The first purpose of a guarantee is, of course, to ensure that if the principal debtor (D) does not pay, another person (G) will pay. D may, for example, be a subsidiary of G. If an offshore subsidiary was used for the purpose of issuing commercial paper, for example, so as to avoid prospectus requirements, then the parent might be asked for a guarantee. Secondly, however, a guarantee may be taken so as to ensure that G exercises a supervisory function over D. Again, an obvious example is that of the parent company more closely supervising the subsidiary, or of the director more effectively managing the affairs of the company whose debts he has guaranteed. Thirdly, a guarantee may be taken in order to secure non–interference from G: as where G is a central bank with power to impose exchange controls (refuse permissions, etc.) or where G is a state with power to change municipal laws in a way which may detrimentally affect the ability of D to repay. **15.01**

2. Forms of guarantee

The guarantee may appear in a variety of forms. First, it may be a true guarantee, where G accepts a secondary liability dependent on D's liability and D's default. Alternatively, G may accept a primary liability independent of D's liability (an "indemnity" liability).[2] In some cases, "a letter of comfort" may be given which is not legally binding, though as observed,[3] so-called letters of comfort differ greatly in their wording, and some may amount to guarantees, or indemnities, or to other types of binding arrangement, such as an option. The formal method of taking a guarantee may be displaced with negotiable instruments with endorsements or avals. Under the Geneva system of bills and promissory notes, an aval by a stranger operates as a guarantee, and the signatory assumes the same liability as the person for whose honour he intervenes (e.g. that of the acceptor). Under the English common law system a person may[4] indorse a bill as a stranger (not to **15.02**

---

[1] Vol. 1, Chap. 20.
[2] Above, Vol. 1, para. 20.02.
[3] Above, Chap. 20.
[4] Under s.56 of the Bills of Exchange Act 1882.

transfer it, but to take on liability: he "backs" the bill, literally by signing on the back) and this has an effect similar to an aval, even if strictly it is not a guarantee. The indorser is liable only to subsequent parties (but may be liable to the drawer, if he becomes holder).[5] Quasi-guarantees may be given in some circumstances, so that G promises to see that D is sufficiently funded, or that if D defaults, G will purchase from the lender a loan made to D. Some guarantees are in the form of performance bonds, or standby credits.[6]

Where the guarantee appears is a matter of convenience. On sterling commercial paper, for example, the size of the instrument is such that it is usually more convenient for it to appear in a separate agreement, with the note stating whether it is guaranteed. In bond issues, it is often on the instrument itself, or may be contained in a trust deed with a reference being made to it on the bond. Such markings on the face of the instrument do not prejudice their negotiability, this being a matter for the custom of merchants.

3. Special terms of international guarantees

15.03 We have examined the various terms applicable to domestic guarantees. In a guarantee taken by an English lender, all of those may be expected to be found. Additionally, there may be terms which are peculiar to the type of transaction being guaranteed. In a guarantee of a term loan agreement, for example, G may also give covenants resembling those given by D, including negative pledge agreements, an undertaking to give financial and other information, representations and warranties, and grossing up clauses. If the loan is syndicated, there will be *pari passu* and sharing clauses, etc. Ordinarily, the guarantee will be made subject to the same law and forum as the loan agreement, so as to facilitate the bringing in a single forum of a single action against G and D, binding both.

If G is independent of D and cannot control him, certain additional terms may be included. One such term concerns grace periods, so that G is required to pay valid claims only at a specified time after their maturity. It may be that in that period D will have cured the default, perhaps on G's intervention, and G is reassured that his liability arises on a genuinely permanent default. G may also object if he is to be made liable for additional expenses (commissions, fees, or liability under indemnities and grossing up clauses) and the guarantee may, therefore, restrict his liability to principal and interest. In order to prevent the lender applying sums received from D first to the debts which G has not guaranteed, it may be provided that the lender must apply payments received (even if received, say, by way of set-off, or from some other security) first to those debts which G has guaranteed. Even where G is liable only for capital and interest, it may be unacceptable to G that he should be called upon to pay immediately the whole capital sum and interest outstanding at the date D's loan is accelerated. The guarantee, therefore, may provide for what is in effect the adop-

[5] *Byles on Bills of Exchange* (25th ed.), p. 187.
[6] See Chap. 12, above.

tion by G of the loan, so that he pays according to the original schedule of maturities, or as near as may be.

Further, a guarantor who otherwise has no control over D may wish to protect himself, or give himself a degree of control, through the guarantee itself. G may require to be kept fully informed about any matters which may affect his liability (the bank then requiring D's consent to disclose the information). Additionally, the lender may not be permitted to accelerate on D's default, without (say) calling on G first (this being coupled with the period of grace already mentioned). If there is a default, it may be provided that the lender shall take all steps to minimise his losses, and first shall proceed against D, perhaps on G's direction, and only then proceed against G. G may reserve the right to substitute himself as the creditor, by purchasing the debt from the lender at any time (so that, for example, if D is not yet in default, but may soon be, G can proceed against D's assets immediately, before they disappear). Finally, the identity of the lender (beneficiary of the guarantee) may be important to G, and assignments of the debt, therefore, may be prohibited.

4. Legal problems with guarantees

A. FORMALITIES

We have previously discussed the legal formalities required under English **15.04** law, such as that the guarantee (as opposed to an indemnity) must be in writing. An indorser or avaliser of a bill may become liable, of course, merely by signing his name on the bill. The formalities of any likely forum should be observed, though the English conflicts rule is to the effect that the document is valid if it conforms with the formalities either of the place of contracting or of the place of the proper law.[7]

B. CAPACITY OF D

In English law, if D is not liable and G has undertaken a secondary liability, **15.05** dependent on D's, then G will not be liable. This result may be avoided if it is the intention of the parties that G should be liable, regardless (the agreement then is an indemnity or at least not a true guarantee).[8] Generally, the lender will have taken great care, in any case, to ensure that D has the capacity to borrow.

C. CAPACITY OF G

The capacity of an individual depends upon his domicile, and for a com- **15.06** pany, it depends upon the law of the place of incorporation. In England, the matter has been affected by the *ultra vires* rule affecting corporations, and that rule has stated that the giving of the guarantee must be for the objects of the company (the true *ultra vires* question) and that a power to give guarantees must be exercised for the benefit of the company, since powers given to directors must be exercised in that way. In the latter case, the directors have

---

[7] Above.
[8] Above.

ostensible authority unless the party to whom the guarantee is given knows that it is not in the company's benefit.[9] The problem of group guarantees has been particularly acute. Problems of quorums of the board of directors may also arise, if, say, an interested director is prohibited from voting, and does so (the director might, for example, already have guaranteed the debts of the company whose debt is now guaranteed, and this makes him "interested").

In this work, however, we anticipate the abolition of the *ultra vires* rule in England, in which case the company may freely give guarantees, and the beneficiary will be affected only if he knows of some provision in the Articles (or some other limitation on the powers of the directors) which prevents the giving of the guarantee. Limitations may include the need for shareholder sanction, or a certain voting proportion of the board of directors, or a limit upon the amount of liabilities that may be guaranteed, and so on.

While this development will simplify the problems in the United Kingdom, and while many E.E.C. countries have already abolished the *ultra vires* rule, it is always necessary to obtain legal opinion from G's place of incorporation, as to G's ability to give the guarantee. At the same time, naturally, counsel will be asked to advise on the many other terms contained in English forms of guarantee.

D. EFFECT OF INSOLVENCY OF G

15.07   We have examined elsewhere the effect of taking a guarantee from G in circumstances where within two years G becomes insolvent. This may amount to a "preference" or undervalue and may be unenforceable. If the lender is "connected" the period for preferences (normally six months) may be extended to two years. Even if the guarantee is unaffected by such provision, if G becomes insolvent the lender is merely an unsecured creditor in the insolvency, and has no special priority.

E. OTHER CONSIDERATIONS IN DRAFTING GUARANTEES

15.08   We shall not repeat the discussion which occurs in Vol. 1 of this work, but the following matters may be considered when considering the terms of a guarantee.

(i) Governing law. The governing law should preferably be the same as that governing the main transaction.

(ii) Jurisdiction should preferably be the same as that governing the main transaction. This, together with a clause choosing the same proper law would facilitate a single set of actions in the forum in question.

(iii) The consideration should be stated, and should not be past consideration. Forms of consideration have already been considered.[10]

(iv) The guarantee is expressed as a continuing guarantee, covering all liabilities of the principal debtor. This avoids the effect of the rule in *Clayton's case*, by preventing the guarantor's liability becoming fixed when the debtor becomes liable for a particular sum.[11]

---

[9] Above, Companies, Vol. 1, Chap. 17.
[10] Vol. 1, Chap. 20.
[11] Vol. 1, Chap. 20, para. 20.09.

(v) There are protective clauses intended to allow the lender to modify the obligations of the debtor without discharging the guarantor. Without those clauses, any modification of the obligations of the principal debtor would discharge the guarantor.[12]

(vi) There are clauses which enable the lender to release a co-guarantor without discharging the guarantor.[13]

(vii) There are clauses enabling the lender to release security or to deal with security as he sees fit, without releasing the guarantor, and so that the security continues to be security for non-guaranteed debts, even though the guarantor may have paid off the guaranteed debts.[14] In other words, the guarantor's rights of subrogation are excluded.

(viii) There are clauses enabling the lender to pay sums received from the guarantor into a suspense account.[15]

(ix) There may be a "conclusive evidence" clause, enabling the lender to say what the guaranteed debt is, so that the guarantor cannot challenge this.[16]

(x) The guarantee may be for a limited sum or for the "whole debt," or for the whole debt with a proviso limiting liability.[17]

(xi) The guarantee may be for a limited duration, or for a specific transaction, or it may be continuing.[18]

5. Comfort letters

As already said,[19] a comfort letter comes in many forms and is an alternative to a legally binding guarantee. They are given generally because the person giving them does not intend legally to be bound (so that, for example, no contingent liability will appear on his balance sheet). Generally speaking, they begin with a statement that the comforter is aware of and approves the proposed loan or transaction, and then state that the parent agrees to maintain an interest in the borrower's share capital, and will give some financial support. They may promise to ensure good management, and not to asset-strip or take money from the subsidiary.   **15.09**

6. Legal problems with comfort letters

There is a tendency to think that such letters can never be binding, but it is clear that some so-called letters of comfort are so worded that in fact they create legally binding obligations. English law tends to presume that a commercial agreement is legally binding unless otherwise clearly stated[20] but other jurisdictions may react differently to the words "letters of comfort." Even in the U.K., an agreement between commercial parties may be   **15.10**

---

[12] Vol. 1, Chap. 20, para. 20.19 *et seq.*
[13] Vol. 1, Chap. 20, para. 20.44.
[14] Vol. 1, Chap. 20, para. 20.44.
[15] *Ibid.*
[16] *Ibid.*
[17] Vol. 1, Chap. 20, para. 19.18.
[18] Vol. 1, Chap. 20, para. 19.17.
[19] See para. 15.02 above.
[20] *Edwards* v. *Skyways Ltd.* [1964] 1 All E.R. 494.

deprived of legal effect if that is clearly stated,[21] but if the comforter makes what appears to be a clear promise, it may need words such as "this agreement is binding in honour only and does not constitute a legally binding contract" to achieve the result. Generally, however, the letter of comfort says "It is our intention (or policy) to do . . ." and this statement of intention is unlikely to amount to a promise to perform. On the other hand, some documents might be headed "Letter of Comfort" and yet contain the words 'We guarantee that in the following events we will see that the debts of our subsidiary not exceeding . . . will be paid in full . . ." and despite the introductory words, this might well constitute a legally binding agreement.[22]

A separate principle of English law requires that contract terms be expressed with such a degree of certainty that the court may know what obligations it is required to enforce. It may be that the letter of comfort will be expressed so vaguely that this certainty does not exist. For example, the letter may promise support if the subsidiary cannot meet its obligations, without saying what "cannot meet its obligations" means. The comforter may promise to "do all in our power" which is hardly capable of legal enforcement.

Additionally, English law will not hold an "agreement to agree" to be treated as a contract. If, say, the comforter agrees that if he ceases to own an interest in D, he will give a guarantee to the lender, this may be too vague, and is an agreement to agree. It could be made effective, if the terms of the guarantee were spelled out. It may additionally fall foul of the Statute of Frauds, which requires the terms of the guarantee to be in writing.

If there is no legally binding obligation on the comforter, its directors may be in breach of an obligation to their company if they pay. At present, they may act *ultra vires*, for payment may not be for the benefit of the company, and they might be restrained, and would be liable to the company. If the comforter company is insolvent, it may be wrongful trading to pay out the money,[23] or it may be a transaction at an undervalue.[24]

7. Standby credits

15.11 Standby letters of credit are discussed in Chapter 12 in this volume. They are used, particularly in the U.S., in order to fulfil the functions of a third party guarantee. A standby letter of credit is a document which has some of the characteristics of a documentary letter of credit, being a promise by a bank to pay a sum of money to a beneficiary on receipt of certain documentation. Sometimes that documentation is no more than a statement that the principal debtor has defaulted, coupled with a request to pay. Such credits are covered by the Uniform Customs and Practice for Documentary Credits (1983 revision) issued by the ICC. They are used particularly by U.S. banks because of legislative prohibitions on those banks giving guarantees, and because the U.S. courts have held that standby credits do not, in

---

[21] *Jones* v. *Vernon's Pools Ltd.* [1938] 2 All E.R. 626; *Rose & Frank Co.* v. *J. R. Crompton & Bros. Ltd.* [1923] 2 K.B. 657.
[22] See the *Chemco* case, Vol. 1, para. 20.46.
[23] Above, Vol. 1, Chap. 28, Section C.
[24] Above, Vol. 1, Chap. 28, Section E.

law, constitute guarantees. Nevertheless, they fulfil an identical function. In the U.S.A., credits are acceptable (*i.e.* it is accepted that they are not guarantees) if the bank which gives them receives a fee, and the credit contains an expiry date or is for a specific term, and is for a specific (not unlimited) amount, and calls for payment on receipt of documents only (so that the bank need not consider disputes between the parties), and the bank's customer has an unqualified obligation to reimburse the bank on the same condition as the bank has paid.[25]

Unlike a guarantee, consideration is not needed for standby credits[26] and the letter may be compared with an indemnity obligation (rather than a guarantee proper)[27] inasmuch as the issuer must pay even if the underlying transaction is void or unenforceable. In other words, as with an indemnity, the liability of the issuer/indemnifier does not depend upon the liability of the principal debtor.[28]

---

[25] Ruling of the controller of Currency of the U.S., 12 C.F.R., Article 7.7016 (1975).

[26] *Malas* v. *British Imex Industries Ltd.* [1958] 2 Q.B. 127; *Barclays Bank DCO* v. *Mercantile National Bank*, 339 F supp.457 (1972), affirmed 481 F.2d. 1224 (5th. Cir. 1973).

[27] Vol. 1, Chap. 20, para. 20.02.

[28] See *e.g. Savage* v. *First National Bank and Trust Co.* 413 F. Supp.447 (1976) and above, Vol. 1, Chap. 20, para. 20.02.

16. Legal Opinions

Introduction[1]

16.01 It is common practice in international banking transactions for the lenders to require formal legal opinions confirming the legal validity of the documentation which evidences their agreement with the borrower. The opinions are usually given by the lawyers who have been involved in the transaction, and they are addressed to the banks and underwriters who are involved in providing, or arranging the provision of, the finance. The practice of obtaining legal opinions originated in the U.S.A. where they were produced to satisfy the banks' auditors that the necessary legal procedures had been followed and that the loans could be enforced against borrowers. More recently, the practice of obtaining legal opinions has become widespread in international transactions and they are obtained in the course of good banking practice and not only to satisfy the banks' auditor's requirements. It has been pointed out in an earlier chapter of this work[2] that a number of legal systems may impinge on an international banking transaction and it is the function of the legal opinions to address the legal issues that arise under the laws of the various legal systems concerned, and to give the lenders some assurance that the issues have been met and do not cause any impediment to proceeding with the transaction. Alternatively, where there are difficulties, the lenders will be able to assess the risks which arise from the issues raised in the legal opinions.

16.02 Although legal opinions are important, their limitations should not be overlooked. A legal opinion is not an assurance that a good credit decision has been made in respect of a particular borrower, nor is it a guarantee that the borrower will be financially sound or able to repay the loan. The legal opinion speaks only of the transaction as documented and negotiated with the borrower. Accordingly, a legal opinion does not constitute an undertaking that the documents contain the perfect sledgehammer with which to browbeat a borrower in all possible situations that may arise. Nor does a legal opinion state that the document contains every possible provision which might apply in the future to any conceivable set of facts or circumstances. A legal opinion relates to the documents as entered into by the parties and states the validity and enforceability of the documents in the state in which they were executed.

As one commentator said: "If you cannot get a clean legal opinion you

---

[1] See generally, Fuld, "Legal Opinions in Business Transactions," (1973); 28 *The Business Lawyer*, 915; "Lawyers' Standards and Responsibilities in Rendering Opinions" (1978) 33 *The Business Lawyer*, 1295; Babb, Barnes, Gordon and Kjillenberg, "Legal Opinions to Third Parties in Corporate Transactions," (1977) 32 *The Business Lawyer*, 553; "Legal Opinions Given in Corporate Transactions" (1978) 33 *The Business Lawyer*, 2389; "Legal Opinions to Third Parties: An Easier Path," (1979) 34 *The Business Lawyer*, 1891; Jacobs, *Opinion Letters in Securities Matters* (1980); Wood Chap. 18; Youard, "And If You Want My Opinion" (1982) (September) *Euromoney*, 249; Meyrier, "Legal Opinions in Financial Transactions Involving Foreign Law" (1985) I.B.L. 410.
[2] See Chap. 1 above.

should not lend; if you get a clean legal opinion you still have to make the lending decision. And that is an entirely separate matter."[3]

A legal opinion should state that it addresses the law concerning a transaction as at the date on which it is given. A legal opinion cannot gaze into a crystal ball and predict what effect a change of law will have upon a given transaction, after it has been entered into.[4] The law to which the legal opinion speaks is the domestic law of the jurisdiction of the lawyer who is giving the legal opinion. Any comfort which the opinion gives is, therefore, local, not universal. A lawyer should not be asked to express a view on the law of another jurisdiction in which he is not admitted to practise. A lawyer can only be held out as an expert in the laws of his own jurisdiction and it would be foolish for a lender to insist upon a lawyer giving an opinion on the law of another jurisdiction.   **16.03**

The type of legal opinion which we will address in this chapter is one which covers the transaction generally. On some occasions a particularly difficult point of law might arise concerning a specific aspect of the transaction and in that case a lawyer might be asked to deal specifically with that aspect of law, most usually in a separate form of opinion.

Conditions precedent

As we indicated earlier in this work,[5] legal opinions are commonly required as a condition precedent to drawdown under the financing documents. The forms of opinions which are required to satisfy the condition precedent are often set out in schedules which are annexed to the loan documentation and these should be given careful consideration during the process of negotiating the loan documentation. If the forms of the proposed opinions are agreed at an early stage, before the form of the transaction has been settled, they will help to raise any legal issues which might cause difficulty. The negotiation and settlement of the forms of legal opinions should not be confused with or be traded as part of the negotiations of the terms of the loan transaction itself. The lawyer who gives a legal opinion does so as an expert and is giving his opinion in relation to the law as it affects the provisions in the documentation. What is said in the legal opinion should not affect the commercial terms or negotiations between the parties as to the transaction. That said, it is often the case that a party to a transaction might be asked to warrant or covenant as to a particular set of facts which the lawyer is unable to cover in his opinion.   **16.04**

Opinions should cover matters of law only, not matters of fact

As far as possible, legal opinions should be confined to matters of law and a lawyer should not be asked to give a warranty as to a state of facts, especially where the facts are not matters within his control or as to which   **16.05**

---

[3] Youard, *loc. cit.*, n. 1 above, p. 251.
[4] Since any system of law is constantly changing it will be impossible to "freeze" either the local law to which the opinion is addressed or the opinion itself. For a fuller exposition of how some lenders attempt to "freeze" the proper law of the contract, see Chap. 1 above.
[5] See Chap. 6 above.

he cannot be certain by investigation .[6] This applies particularly in the case of independent lawyers, although it might be modified in the case of in-house counsel employed by the borrower, who might be expected to have access to more information concerning the borrower, especially in relation to outstanding litigation, prior encumbrances and internal borrowing limitations. A borrower's independent legal advisers will not usually have access to such information and, if asked to give an opinion on such matters, will either qualify their opinion or refuse to express an opinion at all.[7]

A legal opinion will often state that certain facts have been assumed and the lenders will need to bear that in mind when reading the opinion because the onus is then upon them to check the assumed facts or to take the risk that the assumptions are not correct.

The jurisdictions in relation to which opinions should be obtained

16.06 There is usually more than one jurisdiction in relation to which it may be desirable to obtain a legal opinion. The relevant jurisdictions may include:

(i) The place where the borrower is incorporated or, in the case where the borrower is a sovereign state or state entity, the jurisdiction of the sovereign. Of particular concern in this regard will be legal matters concerning the existence, powers and capacity of the borrower and any necessary authorities that may be needed for the borrower to enter into the transactions contemplated and to perform its obligations. In addition, the legal opinion should cover the ability of the borrower to make the necessary repayments and other payments under the documentation, the question of taxation on interest and other payments by the borrower, such as withholding tax and interest payments, and the ability to sue the borrower and obtain and enforce judgment against the borrower in that jurisdiction.

If the borrower is an international organisation then there may be some difficulty in determining what the relevant law will be governing these issues and regard will have to be had to the principles of international law on these issues.

16.07 (ii) If the funds are being disbursed to the borrower or payments are to be made or other matters are to be performed in jurisdictions other than the jurisdiction of the borrower's incorporation or place of domicile, as for instance is often the case in capital market transactions or project financings, then legal opinions may need to be obtained from lawyers in the jurisdictions where those matters are to take place.

(iii) The jurisdiction of the proper law of the loan agreement. This opinion covers matters pertaining to the validity and enforceability of the documentation under the proper law of the documents and the ability to obtain a judgment in the courts of that jurisdiction. This opinion is usually in a briefer form than the opinions referred to in (i) and (ii) above and makes several assumptions on the matters covered by those other opinions.

(iv) In specific cases it might also be relevant to obtain legal opinions from

---

[6] For an interesting discussion of this problem, see Fuld, *loc. cit.*, n. 1 above.
[7] See Royal Bank of Canada Group Legal Department, "Comment" (1983) (January) I.F.L.R. p. 3.

other relevant jurisdictions if, for instance, security is being given over assets in another jurisdiction or, in the case of ship financings, in the jurisdiction of the flag of the vessel concerned. For example, such an opinion would cover the ability, under the *lex situs*, to take security over the assets concerned and any steps that may be necessary to perfect the taking of the security, such as registration procedures.[8]

From whom should the opinions be obtained?

The lenders will need to consider from whom the various legal opinions **16.08** covering the transaction should be obtained. In some cases there will be a duplication of opinions in that the lawyers retained by the borrower and the lawyers retained by the lenders will be asked to give separate opinions. To save on the costs of the transaction, the borrower may suggest to the lenders that its own lawyers should furnish the legal opinion in its jurisdiction concerning the matters referred to in (i) above. Alternatively, the lenders may insist that an independent lawyer should give the opinion or may indeed ask for both the borrower's own lawyers and an independent lawyer to give opinions. There is no hard and fast rule of practice on this but it is not unusual for one opinion in that jurisdiction to be given by the borrower's lawyers alone. If the borrower has its own in-house counsel then the borrower may suggest that that person should give the opinion but lenders sometimes feel that they would have better protection if the opinion was not given by an employee of the borrower. In the case of an international organisation established by treaty, it will often be the case that only the in-house counsel will be able or willing to give the opinion.

It is the usual practice for the lawyers appointed by the lenders to give the opinion referred to in (iii) above.

Liabilities of the lawyer

In giving an opinion, lawyers are expected to assume responsibility for the **16.09** views expressed in the opinion. Primarily, that responsibility will be to the persons to whom the opinion is addressed which, in most cases, will be the financial institutions providing or arranging for the provision of finance and also, perhaps, such a person as the trustee of any security that might be taken. The lawyers will need to consider who else might seek to hold them responsible on the opinion and, commonly, the lawyers will attempt to restrict their responsibility to the named addressees of the opinion. It is common for the opinion to conclude with a statement making it clear that it is only the persons to whom the opinion is addressed who may rely upon the opinion.[9] The opinion sometimes states, specifically, that the opinion may not be relied upon by assignees of the lenders or any other person who might have or acquire an interest derived through the lenders (such as a sub-participant).[10] Notwithstanding such an express limitation and disclaimer, a lawyer may find that some other person may seek to hold him responsible

---

[8] As to the various jurisdictions which may be relevant, see generally, Chap. 14 above.
[9] See Exhibit E of the specimen agreement, Chap. 17 above.
[10] See Chap. 8 above.

for the views that have been expressed or, more generally, for the way in which the transaction has been structured.

It is, therefore, necessary to consider the grounds upon which a lawyer will assume responsibility for the views that he has expressed in his opinion or, more generally, for his involvement in the transaction. To a large extent, this will depend upon the jurisdiction in which the lawyer has been working, but he may also find himself exposed to the laws of the jurisdictions in which his opinion was received or in which his advice was acted upon. What follows is limited to a brief and very general view of English law on these questions.[11]

16.10   The lawyer instructed by or on behalf of the lenders will have a responsibility to the lenders for the accuracy of his opinion. Where he has been retained directly by a lender then the responsibility will be a contractual responsibility arising from the retainer. In the case of a syndicated facility the lawyer will usually be retained by the agent and will not be retained separately by each of the lenders. In that case, the lawyer would have a contract with the agent but not with the lenders, unless it could be shown that each of the lenders expressly authorised the agent to retain the lawyer on behalf of the lenders. That may be difficult, especially if the documentation contains the usual provision by which the lenders acknowledge that they have not relied upon the agent for legal advice. To overcome any theoretical problems that this may give rise to concerning the reliance that the lenders in the syndicate may place upon the legal opinion, it will usually be addressed to the agent and to each of the lenders. In that situation, the responsibility of the lawyer would be governed by the law of tort which, at the end of the day, would be much the same as in the law of contract, namely, not to be negligent in giving the opinion.

In the absence of a legal opinion, a lawyer who knows that the lenders are relying upon his advice would have a general responsibility to advise correctly and not to give negligent advice. The duty would probably extend to pointing out any pitfalls in the documents and there would be a general responsibility to ensure that the lawyers were appraised of any legal risks to which they might be exposed by the transaction. In rendering his legal opinion, the lawyer will formally set out his advice and, in the qualifications and assumptions contained in the opinion, he will cover or limit most of the matters which he would otherwise need to advise upon generally, including the pitfalls. It is perhaps ironic that the rendering of a legal opinion has the practical effect of limiting the various matters which the lawyer would otherwise need to explain to the lenders in quite some detail.

16.11   If the legal opinion has been given by the borrower's lawyer as, for instance, with respect to the laws of the borrower's domicile, then that lawyer will have a responsibility in the law in tort to the lenders. That responsibility would be that he should not be negligent in giving his opinion and, again, the assumptions and qualifications stated in the opinion will limit the scope of his responsibility. He will not have a responsibility in contract as he was not instructed by the lenders.

In so far as third parties are concerned, the persons who might seek to establish some form of liability against a lawyer involved in a transaction

---

[11] For a detailed exposition of this topic, see Wood, para. 1804.

would be investors or assignees of the original lenders who have suffered a loss on the transaction and who have derived their interest in the transaction at some later time, usually through one of the original parties. This might, for instance, include a bond holder. They would not have a claim in contract and so they would seek to establish a claim in tort based upon a failure to take reasonable care in the legal work done by the lawyer, but it is difficult to imagine how such a claim could be successfully mounted, except in the most unusual of circumstances.[12] Such an investor would need to establish that he relied upon the lawyer in circumstances where it was reasonable to do so, that the lawyer ought to have known that a person such as the investor concerned would so rely on the lawyer and that such reliance played a significant part in the decision to invest. It is suggested that merely knowing the names of the lawyers who were involved would be insufficient.

The relevance of the distinction between a liability in contract and in tort will relate primarily to the time limits for instituting a suit against the lawyer if his advice or opinion has proved to be incorrect. Generally speaking, those time limits are calculated from the date from which the law deems the cause of action to have accrued.[13] The damages which could be recovered against the lawyer would be limited, basically, to the loss that the lawyer should reasonably have expected at the time that he gave his advice, to have resulted from his negligence. The lawyer would not be responsible for any other loss such as, for instance, resulting from a bad commercial decision which was not based upon the lawyer's advice.

Structure of a legal opinion[14]

Legal opinions are usually structured in four parts and are set forth in letter form on the headed notepaper of the lawyers concerned. The first part briefly describes the transaction and the documents to which the opinion relates. The second part sets forth the assumptions which the lawyers have made on matters of fact concerning the transaction. The third part of the opinion contains the actual matters upon which the lawyers are opining. The fourth part of the opinion sets forth the qualifications and exceptions as to the matters of law on which the opinion has been given. Each of those aspects of an opinion will now be dealt with separately. **16.12**

---

[12] In England the case of *Hedley Byrne & Co. Ltd.* v. *Heller and Partners Ltd.* [1964] A.C. 465 extended the tort of negligence for misstatements, where a duty of care was owed. Whether such a duty would exist, therefore, would depend upon the facts of the case at issue. There would need to be some "special relationship" between the parties which gives rise to a duty of care. It is unlikely that such a duty would arise in all but the most exceptional of cases. A further ingredient which would be necessary for liability in tort would be "reasonable forseeability." The lawyer giving the opinion could only be liable in tort to third parties if it was reasonably forseeable that such third parties would rely on his opinion. This is another reason why it is common to state within the terms of the opinion that no one other that the addressee may rely upon it. Since reliance would appear to be a necessary ingredient of liability in tort, by precluding third party reliance, expressly within the opinion, it is submitted that liability will be avoided.

[13] See the Limitation Acts and the Latent Damages Act 1986.

[14] See generally, the Legal opinions annexed to the specimen agreement, Chap. 17 below.

ADDRESSES AND DESCRIPTION OF TRANSACTION

16.13   The opinion should commence by setting out the parties to whom it is addressed. In the case of a syndicated loan, the opinion should be addressed to the agent and to each of the lenders. Where the lawyers giving the opinion have been retained specifically for the transaction and do not act generally for the lenders or the borrower, as the case may be, they may describe themselves as being specially retained in relation to the particular transaction, so as to negate any suggestion that they have any general knowledge of the party concerned or its affairs.

The opinion will then proceed to describe the transaction and the documents to which it relates. If there is time, the principal documents to be addressed will have been executed and the opinion will state this and be based on them. Sometimes, if time pressures do not permit the inspection of executed documents, the opinion will refer to drafts of the documents and there will then be a specific assumption set forth that the lawyers have assumed that the documents as executed were in the same form as in the draft documents that they have reviewed for the purposes of giving their opinion. Obviously, it is best if the lawyers are able to review the documents as executed so as to avoid any possibility of confusion, but it is often the case that time does not permit this to happen. The lawyers should then state that in giving their opinion they have examined the listed documents and that they have had regard to the laws of their jurisdiction as at the date of the opinion (but not the laws of any other jurisdiction) and "such other matters as they have considered relevant" in giving their opinion. The purpose of this additional statement, from the point of view of the addressees of the opinion, is to make it clear that the lawyers have not deliberately shut their eyes to any matter that they should reasonably have considered. The opinion should also state on whose behalf the lawyers have received instructions and sometimes they will also state that they have participated in discussions with the lender or agent for the lenders. In reviewing an opinion, the addressees should bear this in mind because the lawyers may have raised points on matters which are not strictly addressed in the opinion, for instance, the desirability of inserting certain provisions which have not appeared in the documentation in its final form.

ASSUMPTIONS

16.14   The next matter that will be referred to in the opinion is the assumptions that the lawyers have made in giving their opinion. The assumptions often relate to matters which are essential facts relating to the documentation and the transaction. The assumptions deal with such matters as the genuineness of signatures, conformity of copies of documents with the originals of those documents, the due execution of the documents by the parties, including the due authorisation of the persons who signed the documents on behalf of their principals, and the accuracy of the certificates that have been furnished (for instance, certificates concerning board resolutions). It would not, however, usually be proper for a lawyer giving an opinion with reference to a specific party to make all of those assumptions so far as they concern that party. For instance, if a lawyer acting for the borrower is giving an opinion relating to the borrower and its participation in the transaction, then the lawyer should not state as an assumption that the borrower has duly authorised the execution of the documents. Sometimes, lawyers prefer to state matters as assumptions rather than to insert them as qualifications at the end of their opinion, but this is usually a matter of style.

MATTERS OPINED UPON

Having stated the assumptions upon which the opinion is given, the opinion will then proceed to set forth the specific matters which are being opined upon. Set forth, below, are paragraphs commonly found in this section of legal opinions. The contents of this section will vary depending upon who is giving the legal opinion. Usually, it is the legal opinion furnished by the borrower's lawyers which is the most extensive, as it has a number of different matters to deal with concerning the borrower. For convenience of description, "Arcadia" will be the country in which the borrower is incorporated and England will be the country of the agreed proper law of the Loan Agreement. **16.15**

(1) *"The Borrower is a company duly incorporated for an unlimited duration and is validly existing under the laws of Arcadia, with power and authority to own its assets and conduct its business as presently being conducted and no administrator, receiver or trustee of the borrower, its business or assets, has been appointed"* **16.16**

These are matters principally concerning the jurisdiction of the domicile of the borrower and are usually opined upon in the opinion furnished by the borrower's lawyers. There are several different elements to this paragraph, as follows:

"Duly incorporated for an unlimited duration"—This refers to the setting up of the borrower as a corporation and will involve checking the relevant certificates of incorporation and other matters to ensure that the borrower was properly established. In some jurisdictions, corporations are established only for a limited period of time and if that is the case for a particular borrower then it would be relevant for this to be expressly covered. The language of this paragraph will be different if the borrower is not a corporation but, instead, a state instrumentality or an international organisation. In either case, the paragraph would need to refer to the basis upon which the borrower was established and continues to exist, such as the treaty under which the international organisation was established.

"Validly existing"—This refers to the continuing existence of the borrower as opposed to its original incorporation. It effectively means that the borrower has not been wound-up or dissolved. Most opinions do not deal with the situation where the borrower is about to dissolve, merge, or consolidate or where steps are being taken to such an end. If a lawyer is aware of such facts, he should disclose them in his opinion.

"In good standing"—This phrase originated in the United States of America and refers to the fact that the corporation has paid all of its taxes, non-payment of which might threaten its continuing existence. "Good standing" opinions are often supported by certificates from the relevant state authority which do not certify that the borrower is in good standing, but certify its existence and the absence of unpaid taxes. In jurisdictions **16.17** where the concept has no relevance, it would be best if this phrase were not used.

"Power and authority to own its assets and conduct its business as presently conducted"—This phrase is needed because without such authorisation the borrower would not be able to generate the funds necessary to service the loan. In certain cases, the lenders might request a wider statement to cover authority to carry on business in jurisdictions other than the jurisdiction of the lawyers giving the opinion. This should be resisted. If the lenders are particularly concerned about any particular jurisdictions then they should seek legal opinions from the lawyers in those relevant jurisdictions.

"No administrator, receiver or trustee of the borrower, its business or assets has been appointed"—This wording is intended partly to cover the situation where the borrower has sought protection from its creditors as, for instance, by the appointment of an administrator under the Insolvency Act 1986 or of a similar official under Chapter 11 of the U.S. Bankruptcy legislation. It also refers to certain, non-voluntary, appointments, for example, the appointment of a receiver or a trustee. These situations would not necessarily be covered by the phrase "validly existing."

16.18 (2) *"The Borrower has power to enter into and perform the Loan Agreement and to borrow thereunder"*

This establishes that the borrower is authorised by its certificate of incorporation or by local statute and by its constitutive documents, to enter into a particular agreement and, essentially, that the borrower will not be acting *ultra vires*. Again, this is a matter to be covered in the legal opinion of the borrower's lawyers, being a matter relating to the borrower's domicile. Generally speaking, these will be matters concerning the borrower's Memorandum and Articles of Association or Bye-laws and general principles of law concerning the corporate capacity of corporations under the relevant law. In the case of statutory bodies or international organisations, the relevant authorities will usually be found in the statutes, treaties or charters establishing the borrower.

Where security over assets is being given or a guarantee is being taken, then the legal opinion will need to address not only the power of the borrower to borrower, but also the powers and capacity of the guarantor to give the guarantee and the powers and capacity of the relevant corporation to create the security over the assets concerned. In addition, where security is being given over assets in a jurisdiction other than the corporation's domicile, the laws of the *lex situs* will be relevant to determine whether the assets concerned are of a type over which the relevant security can be given.[15] This may require a separate legal opinion from the lawyers of that jurisdiction.

16.19 (3) *"All necessary action to authorise the borrowing on the terms and conditions of the Loan Agreement and to authorise the execution, delivery and performance of the Loan Agreement in accordance with its terms has been taken"*

This refers to the procedural matters which are required with respect to

---

[15] See generally, Chap. 14 above.

the particular borrowing concerned. It will go to such matters as the authority of the directors or shareholders of the borrower to authorise the transaction and would also cover any particular limits on their powers, such as a limit on the power of the directors to commit the borrower to borrowing at any time in excess of a stated limit. It will also cover, in the case of state instrumentalities, any limits on the authority of that instrumentality to enter into the transaction and any ratification or additional authorities that may be required to commit the borrower, such as legislative, cabinet or other executive authorisations.

On the face of it, the lawyer giving the legal opinion will need to be satisfied that the necessary formalities were met when the decision was made to commit the borrower to the transaction. This means, for instance, the lawyers being satisfied that the meeting of the directors of the borrower who authorised the transaction was duly convened, that quorum requirements were met and that any requirements as to conflicts of interest and the like were satisfied. Some of these points, however, will come within the assumptions stated by the lawyers and it may be difficult to determine if they satisfied themselves that all of the procedural requirements for the borrower to act have been met. For instance, if they have assumed the correctness and validity of the certificates that have been given, then they will have assumed that the proper procedures were observed in convening and holding a board meeting and, indeed, that the board meeting was held and the necessary resolutions passed as set forth in the certified copy of the board minutes furnished to him. It is not usually practical to expect lawyers to go any further than this and it must therefore be a risk for the lenders to rely upon the correctness and accuracy of the certificates upon which the lawyers have relied. [15a]

(4) *"The Loan Agreement has been duly executed and delivered on behalf of the*   **16.20**
Borrower"

This refers to the authority of the individuals who purported to sign the documents on behalf of the borrower. The lawyers giving the legal opinion will need to be satisfied that the individuals were properly authorised under, for instance, the board resolutions of the directors of the borrower or under any relevant legislation. Sometimes, the relevant documents will be signed on behalf of a borrower under a power of attorney and if this is the case then the lawyers will need to check whether the borrower is entitled to give such a power of attorney and, if so, whether all the necessary formalities have been satisfied. The terms of the power of attorney will also need to be examined to ensure that in its scope they have permitted the attorney to act. Sometimes, a power of attorney will only authorise the attorney to execute a document in the form attached. In other instances, the power of attorney will be phrased more widely and will give the attorney power to negotiate some or all of the provisions of the documents or to agree amendments to those provisions. The lenders will need to be satisfied that under the law of

---

[15a] With regard to such matters it would normally be possible for the Lenders to rely on the rule in *Turquand's* case (*Royal British Bank* v. *Turquand* (1856) 6 E. & B. 327) that third parties dealing with a company are entitled to assume that the internal procedures of a company have been regularly conducted (in the absence of actual knowledge to the contrary).

the domicile of the borrower and under the law of the place where the power of attorney was executed, the attorney had been validly appointed to do what is described in the power of attorney.

16.21   (5) *"The Loan Agreement, as executed and delivered, constitutes a legal, valid and binding obligation of the Borrower enforceable in accordance with its terms"*

This statement should usually be contained in the opinion given by the lawyers in the jurisdiction of the proper law of the Loan Agreement. It would also be given, in a slightly varied form, in the opinion given by the lawyers in the jurisdiction of the domicile of the Borrower. The latter opinion would add that the statement is made on the assumption that it would be legally valid, binding and enforceable in accordance with its terms under the proper law of the contract. There are several different elements to this paragraph, as follows:

"Legal, valid"—To a large extent, these words overlap with other each other. What they mean is that there is nothing illegal or void in the document.

"Binding obligation enforceable in accordance with its terms"—The word "enforceable" should be distinguished from the words "in accordance with its terms." The word "enforceable" should not be taken as meaning specifically enforceable in the sense of being able to obtain an order for specific performance or some other equitable remedy requiring each obligation to be performed in the precise form set forth. Instead, what the word "enforceable" should mean is that proceedings could be taken before the courts for breach of the Agreement and that the courts would award some remedy. Usually, the remedy would be damages. However, the lawyers will not normally be able to predict what the quantum of damages will be for any particular breach.

There are many reasons why equitable remedies, such as an order for specific performance, would not be awarded to enforce positive action as required by the literal terms of the documents. For that reason and because the lawyers cannot predict the quantum of damages for all possible breaches, lawyers giving an opinion should avoid using the words "in accordance with its terms."

16.22   (6) *"The authorisations, approvals, consents, licences, exemptions, filings, registrations, notarisations and other requirements under the laws of Arcadia with respect to the Loan Agreement and the performance by the Borrower of its provisions, have been obtained and are in full force and effect"*

This will cover such matters as exchange control requirements and other licences and authorities imposed by the state authorities having jurisdiction over the borrower. It should be noted that in certain jurisdictions exchange control consents for the remittance of payments by the borrower may not be given on a blanket basis but might only be given with respect to payments due in the ordinary event. If the lenders sought to accelerate the loan due to default, the exchange control consents which were originally obtained may not permit the accelerated payment to be made. The lawyers should also check that the relevant exchange control consents cover not only principal and interest but other amounts such as fees and the like which might be payable.

(7) *"Under the laws of Arcadia, no deduction or withholding will be required to* **16.23**
be made from any payment due by the Borrower under the Loan Agreement."

If it is the case that withholding taxes might apply then that should be
specifically addressed in the opinion. It would not be good practice for the
lenders to rely on a grossing-up clause in a loan agreement and not require
an investigation as to the liability to pay withholding taxes and the like or
the rate at which those taxes are payable. The effect of a grossing-up obligation is to make the loan more expensive for a borrower and to increase the
amounts which the borrower may have to repatriate from its resources. The
lenders may need to take this into account in making their credit assessment
of the borrower.

(8) *"No stamp or registration or similar taxes or charges are payable under the* **16.24**
laws of Arcadia in respect of the Loan Agreement"

This provision is necessary as, under the laws of a number of jurisdictions, if stamp duty is not paid then the documents may not be enforceable
before the courts of the relevant country until the duty has been assessed and
paid. The other point to bear in mind about stamp duties is that there is
often a penalty duty payable if the stamp duty is not paid within the applicable period for payment and, practically speaking, it would be the lenders
in the first instance who would need to pay the penalty if they sought to
enforce the documents. Care should also be taken that there is no stamp
duty on security documents such as a mortgage. If stamp duty is payable
then the amount of the duty which is payable should be stated.

(9) *"It is not necessary under the laws of Arcadia in order to ensure the legality,* **16.25**
validity or enforceability of the Loan Agreement that it should be filed, registered or
recorded in any Public Office or elsewhere in Arcadia"

In some senses this provision overlaps with the provisions as to licences
and consents. A similar provision may also be of relevance to security documents where security is being given over assets within the jurisdiction. In
that case it might be advisable for this provision to be expanded to deal with
what action needs to be taken and the effect on priorities, *viz-à-viz* other
creditors, of taking such action.

(10) *"The execution and delivery by the Borrower of the Loan Agreement, the* **16.26**
borrowing thereunder and the performance by the Borrower of the terms of the Loan
Agreement will not conflict with or infringe the provisions of (1) the laws of Arca-
dia; (2) the Memorandum and Articles of the Borrower; (3) any order of any
judicial or other authority of Arcadia; or (4) any mortgage, contract or other under-
taking which is binding upon the Borrower or its assets"

This provision is very wide in its scope and to some extent overlaps with
the other provisions of the opinion. Lawyers should resist including in this
opinion the fourth limb of this paragraph as it requires them, effectively, to
undertake an audit review of the borrower's affairs and all of the transactions in which the borrower might have been involved or which may
have involved its assets (whether such transactions were public or private).
That wording might, for instance, cover negative pledges that might have
been agreed in a transaction of which the lawyers may not be aware. The

fourth limb is usually covered, instead, in representations and warranties given by the borrower in the Loan Agreement itself.

16.27 (11) "*There is no actual, pending or threatened litigation, arbitration or administrative proceedings concerning the Borrower or its assets before the Courts of or any other judicial or administrative tribunal in Arcadia*"

Again, this is a provision that lawyers should resist including in their legal opinion because it would require the lawyer to undertake a legal audit of all possible matters in which the borrower might be involved and indeed, of which the borrower itself may not be fully aware (especially so far as threatened litigation is concerned). Lawyers should also refuse to compromise by agreeing to insert in their opinion an additional statement relating to the materiality of such litigation because that would require the lawyers to form a value judgment as to the outcome of the litigation. Once again, this is a matter that should more appropriately be dealt with in the representations and warranties given by the borrower in the Loan Agreement.

16.28 (12) "*Under the laws of Arcadia the obligations of the Borrower under the Loan Agreement will rank pari passu with all its other unsecured indebtedness*"

This paragraph will be subject to the qualification as to insolvency, as to which see below. It should be noted that this paragraph does not purport to state what the position will be as regards any security that the borrower may have given either at the time of execution of the loan agreement or subsequently, as it would not be reasonable to expect the lawyers to know of all the possible security that might have been given (or may arise) whether in documentary form or as a matter of law (for instance, liens).

16.29 (13) "*The choice of English law to govern the Loan Agreement would be recognised and given effect to by the courts of Arcadia and accordingly if proceedings were brought against the Borrower before those courts, those courts would apply the laws of England as the proper law of the Loan Agreement*"[16]

This is an important provision from the lenders point of view because the lenders may wish to commence proceedings against the borrower in the courts of the borrower's jurisdiction and the lenders will need to know that those courts would apply the agreed proper law of the loan agreement in interpreting the obligations of the borrower.[17] Foreign lawyers will usually state as a qualification to their opinion that they have assumed that the English Courts would apply English law as the proper law of the loan agreement.[18]

16.30 (14) "*A judgment of the courts of England would be recognised and enforced in Arcadia by the Courts of Arcadia.*"

The purpose behind this provision is to ascertain whether a judgment obtained in the courts nominated as having express jurisdiction in the loan

---

[16] See generally, Chap. 1 above.
[17] As to the position in England and New York to this question of party autonomy, see Penn and Cashel, "Choice of Law Clauses under English and New York Law,"(1986) J.B.L. 333.
[18] For a discussion of the English law rules in ascertaining the proper law of a contract, see Chap. 1 above. Lawyers who give an opinion as to the validity of an express choice of English law as the proper law should consider if any qualification might be warranted by the dictum of Lord Wright in *Vita Food Products Inc.* v. *Unus Shipping Co. Ltd.* [1939] A.C. 277.

agreement, would be enforced in the local courts of the jurisdiction in which the borrower is situated. It is not normally the case that a court will automatically and without any qualification recognise and enforce the judgment of the courts of another jurisdiction and it would not be unusual for lawyers giving their opinion to qualify this paragraph.[19] What the paragraph seeks to ascertain is that it will not be necessary to have a complete re-trial of the merits of the case by the local courts.[20] Sometimes this matter is governed by a treaty between the two countries concerned dealing with the recognition and enforcement of the judgments of their respective courts, but it is not always the case that such a treaty will exist. In so far as the mutual recognition and enforcement of judgments within the E.E.C. is concerned, reference should be made to the Brussels Convention of September 27, 1968.[21]

The qualifications which are often found in an opinion dealing with this subject are that a foreign judgment will only be recognised if the following types of matter have been satisfied:

(i) that the procedural rules of the court giving the judgment had been observed,

(ii) that the foreign court had jurisdiction to determine the matter,

(iii) that the foreign court's judgment was final and conclusive,

(iv) that the decision of the foreign court was for a fixed sum,

(v) that the decision of the foreign court had not been obtained by fraud or a trick,

(vi) that enforcement of the decision of the foreign court would not be contrary in the local jurisdiction to public policy or constitute the enforcement of a judgment of a penal or revenue nature, and

(vii) that the decision of the foreign court was not contrary to natural justice.

(15) *"Under the laws of Arcadia neither the Borrower nor its assets is entitled to immunity from suit or enforcement of judgment with respect to any action or proceeding that might be brought in the courts of Arcadia arising out of or relating to the Loan Agreement"*   **16.31**

This paragraph addresses the question of sovereign immunity and is particularly important in a situation where the borrower is a state instrumentality. In that case, the statement may well need to be qualified at least in so far as it concerns execution of judgment against the assets of the borrower. It is also normal to qualify this statement by saying that diplomatic assets will be immune from enforcement proceedings.

(16) *"A judgment in the courts of Arcadia may be expressed in (the relevant currency of the Loan Agreement)"*   **16.32**

Until fairly recently, the courts of England were not prepared to award judgments in a foreign currency but insisted that any claim that was brought before them had to be converted into sterling. That line of reason-

---

[19] For a discussion of the circumstances in which an English court would recognise and enforce such a judgment, see Chap. 2 above.

[20] *Ibid.*

[21] The impact of both the Convention and the Civil Jurisdiction and Judgments Act 1982 is considered in Chap. 2 above.

ing was followed in many of the other common law jurisdictions. Recent decisions of the English courts now permit a judgment to be awarded in a foreign currency other than sterling both in situations where the proper law of the obligation to make the payment is a foreign law and where the proper law is English law.[22] It may not be the case, however, that all of the other common law jurisdictions will be prepared to follow the new line of reasoning of the English courts and so it is common to find qualifications inserted in opinions, to the effect that the courts of the relevant jurisdiction may not be prepared to award a judgment denominated in a foreign currency. Sometimes, this is further qualified by an express provision as to the effect of insolvency.[23]

16.33   (17) "*It is not necessary under the laws of Arcadia in order to enable the Lenders to enforce their rights under the Loan Agreement that they should be licensed, qualified, or otherwise entitled to carry on business in Arcadia*"

The purpose of this paragraph is to provide an assurance to the lenders that they will be able to enforce the loan agreement against the borrower in its jurisdiction without the necessity of having to establish for themselves a place of business, etc., in that jurisdiction.

16.34   (18) "*By reason only of the execution, delivery and performance of the Loan Agreement by the Lenders, they will not be deemed to be resident, domiciled or carrying on business in Arcadia or subject to taxation under the laws of Arcadia*"

This paragraph is of importance to the lenders in that it establishes whether they are likely to be deemed to be carrying on business and accordingly subject to taxation in a foreign jurisdiction only by reason of the loan agreement and their connection with it. Of course, they might already be so affected or the transaction might be taken in conjunction with other activities and that is a risk the lenders will have to bear.

Qualifications

16.35   Having set forth the matters which are expressly given as part of their opinion, the lawyers will then set forth the qualifications to which their opinion is subject. The qualifications will vary from one jurisdiction to another. Some of those matters have already been referred to above, but the following are qualifications that are commonly found in legal opinions:

16.36   (1) *Clause 8(4) of the Loan Agreement*[23a] *provides for default interest to be paid on overdue amounts.*[24] *Such interest may amount to a penalty under the laws of Arcadia and may therefore not be recoverable.*

We indicated in an earlier chapter of this work that some loan agreements provide for default interest to be paid on overdue amounts. Whenever default interest might be categorised as a penalty and thus not enforceable by the courts a qualification to this effect should be included within the opinion. There is increasing support, however, for the view that a provision

[22] See Goode, *Payment Obligations in Commercial and Financial Transactions* (1983), pp. 135 *et seq.*
[23] See *Re Lines Bros. Ltd.* [1983] Ch. 1.
[23a] See Chap. 17 below.
[24] See generally Chap. 9 above.

for increased rates of interest upon sums payable in an event of default should not be regarded as a penalty.[25]

(2) *"No opinion is expressed as to whether the Courts of Arcadia would give* **16.37** *effect to the currency indemnity contained in Clause [26] of the Loan Agreement"*

Currency indemnity clauses are commonly found in loan agreements but to date English lawyers have not been prepared to give opinions as to whether such a clause would be enforceable.[26] In any event, such a provision would not be likely to survive an insolvency.

(3) *"As regards Clause [29] of the Loan Agreement (jurisdiction) the Courts of* **16.38** *Arcadia may stay proceedings if concurrent proceedings are being brought elsewhere"*

This qualification might apply, at least so far as the English Courts are concerned, if they were presented with a claim at the same time as a similar claim is being heard in another jurisdiction or after it has been heard.[27]

(4) *"The Courts of Arcadia might not treat as conclusive those certificates and* **16.39** *determinations which the Loan Agreement states are to be so treated"*

This qualification is aimed at provisions in a loan agreement which provide that a certificate by a lender, as to an amount due or as to an interest calculation, is to be binding upon the borrower (save for manifest error and the like). Notwithstanding such a provision, the courts may require evidence to be given as to the facts upon which the certificate is based.[28]

(5) *"Equitable remedies, such as an order for specific performance or the issue of an* **16.40** *injunction, are available only at the discretion of the court and nothing in this opinion is to be taken as indicating that such a remedy would be available in respect of the obligations of the Borrower under the Loan Agreement"*

This qualification relates to the provisions in the opinion which go to the validity and binding effect of the loan agreement upon the borrower and should be taken in conjunction with the comments made above on those provisions.[29]

(6) *"The obligations of the Borrower may be limited by bankruptcy, insolvency,* **16.41** *liquidation, administration, reorganisation and other laws of general application relating to or affecting the rights of creditors"*

Under the laws of many jurisdictions, including most common law jurisdictions, insolvency and the like proceedings affecting the borrower may

---

[25] See Goode, *loc. cit.*, n. 22 above, p. 84.

[26] See *President of India* v. *Lifes Maritime Corp* [1987] 1 All E.R. 957.

[27] See *Spilianda Maritime Corporation* v. *Consulex Ltd.* [1986] 3 All E.R. 843; see also, *Mudurgolin Ltd.* v. *T.C. Ziraat Bankasi* [1986] 3 W.L.R. 606. As we indicated in Chap. 2 of this work, some loan agreements contain a waiver of a defence of *forum non conveniens*. Whenever such a waiver is present, it is common for the opinion to expressly qualify its enforceability.

[28] A "conclusive evidence" clause was attacked in *Bache & Co.* v. *Banque Vernes* [1973] 2 Lloyd's Rep 437 (C.A.) on the ground that it was contrary to public policy. However, the Court of Appeal upheld its validity. Lord Denning M.R. observed, at p. 440, that such a clause " . . . is only acceptable because the bankers and brokers who insert them are known to be honest and reliable men of business who are most unlikely to make a mistake." It is unclear precisely how far this line of reasoning would be extended by the courts.

[29] As to the extent to which such forms of equitable relief would be available under English law, see Chap. 9 above.

have a drastic effect upon its stated obligations under a loan agreement.[30] For instance, an obligation to pay interest may cease upon insolvency and a right to accelerate a loan agreement may be modified or otherwise affected. The claims of the lenders under a loan agreement may be converted into a right to prove as a creditor in the insolvency, but that may mean that only a dividend will be received and that damages for repayment of the whole amount advanced may not be available or enforceable. Insolvency may also mean that certain claims against the borrower may be payed in advance of those of the lenders (for instance, preferential claims for unpaid taxes).

16.42   (7) *"Claims may become barred under the Statute of Limitations or may be or become subject to defences of set-off or counterclaim"*

The first limb of this qualification is to the effect that the rights of a lender to bring an action against the borrower will be subject to the applicable limitation period of the jurisdiction in which the claim may be made. A claim will need to be brought within that period, otherwise it will be statute barred. The second limb relates to the right of the defendant in proceedings to set up a counterclaim or right of set-off to the action. The contractual provisions in a loan agreement, which purport to negate the borrower's right to do this, may not be given effect in certain jurisdictions.

16.43   (8) *"Where obligations are to be performed in a jurisdiction outside Arcadia they may not be enforceable in Arcadia to the extent that performance would be illegal or contrary to public policy under the laws of that jurisdiction"*

This qualification states that the courts of one jurisdiction may not be willing to enforce an obligation of the borrower which has to be performed outside that jurisdiction, if to do so would be illegal or contrary to the laws of the jurisdiction in which the obligation is to be performed.

16.44   (9) *"No opinion is expressed with respect to the laws of any jurisdiction other than Arcadia"*

This qualification reflects what was said above to the effect that the lawyers who give a legal opinion can only be expected to opine upon the laws of their own jurisdiction.

16.45   (10) *"The effectiveness of terms exculpating a party from a liability or duty otherwise owed are limited by law"*

This qualification means that a lender may not be able to bring a claim against the borrower if the lender is itself in breach or, alternatively, that a breach committed by the lender may be taken into account (for instance, by way of set-off or counterclaim), in reducing a claim taken against the borrower.

16.46   (11) *"Where a person is vested with a discretion to determine a matter in his opinion then the Courts of Arcadia may require that such discretion is exercised objectively and reasonably or that such opinion is based upon reasonable and objective grounds"*

In other words, the courts may refuse to give effect to an arbitrary decision of a lender which it purports to impose upon the borrower.

---

[30] As to the position under English law, see generally, Vol. 1 of this work.

(12) *"The enforceability of the Loan Agreement may be limited by the provisions* **16.47** *of Arcadian law applicable to contracts held to have been frustrated by events happening after their execution"*

In some jurisdictions this qualification may be amended to refer to the civil law doctrine of *force majeure*.[31]

(13) *"An Arcadian Court may refuse to give effect to a purported contractual obli-* **16.48** *gation to pay costs imposed upon another party in respect of the costs of any unsuccessful litigation brought against that party and such a court may not award by way of costs all of the expenditure incurred by a successful litigant in proceedings brought before that court"*

This qualification relates to clauses sometimes found in a loan agreement which purport to impose upon a borrower all of the costs incurred by the lenders in enforcing or attempting to enforce what they believe to be the obligations of the borrower. If in fact judgment is awarded in favour of the borrower then it is likely that the courts would refuse to impose upon the borrower the obligation to pay the unsuccessful lenders' costs of bringing the proceedings. Even in a situation where the lenders were successful, the courts may not oblige the borrower to pay all of the lenders' cost but only a proportion thereof and the ascertainment of that proportion will usually be subject to assessment by the courts.

(14) *"Provisions as to severability in the Loan Agreement may not be binding and* **16.49** *the question of whether or not provisions relating to invalidity may be severed from other provisions in order to save such other provisions would be determined by the Arcadian Courts at their discretion"*

This qualification relates to the clause often found in a loan agreement providing for severability of unenforceable or void provisions of the loan agreement. Effectively, the qualification states that the courts may take a different view and refuse to sever the tainted provisions so as to keep the other provisions intact.

Where security is being given then further qualifications may be inserted relating to the effectiveness of the security and as to matters concerning the priority of the security over other competing interests.

At least, in so far as English law and the other common law jurisdictions which follow English law are concerned, it is necessary in giving a legal opinion on security to consider in depth the matters relating to the security and the effectiveness of the security.[32]

Conclusion

Legal opinions perform a very useful function in international banking **16.50** transactions and it is surprising that such little attention has been focussed upon them until only a few years ago. An early attempt to consider the problems associated with legal opinions was made as recently as 1973[33] and

---

[31] See generally, Chap. 3 above.
[32] The issues to which an opinion might be addressed on the question of security are considered in Chap. 14 above.
[33] See Fuld, *loc. cit.*, n. 1 above.

since then a number of professional bodies, mainly in the U.S., have published various contributions on this important topic. Unfortunately, the U.S. lead has not been followed in many other jurisdictions and this has contributed to a somewhat confused understanding of many of the standard phrases outlined in the opinion clauses of this chapter. The problem is that many lawyers follow the U.S. practice without fully understanding the meaning of commonly-used U.S. phrases. A leading international lawyer cited an amusing example of this problem at a recent conference, namely that of a lawyer who, when asked to opine that a corporation was "in good standing" wrote: "The corporation is in very good standing. All directors are members of the best golf club in the city . . . ."[34]

This may have been rather an extreme example but it does emphasise the conceptual differences which undoubtedly exist between lawyers in different parts of the world.

Notwithstanding these conceptual difficulties and the different approaches which lawyers in competing jurisdictions take to the giving of opinions, a considerable degree of standardisation has already been achieved in a relatively short space of time. This process of assimilation and standardisation will no doubt continue as the number of international finance centres throughout the world increase and play their part in the evolution of market practice with regard to both the finance instruments themselves and the legal opinions which accompany such instruments.

---

[34] This, and other examples are given in Meyrier, *loc. cit.*, n.1 above, p. 140.

17. Specimen Syndicated Term Loan Agreement

Contents

17.02   THIS LOAN AGREEMENT is dated ...., 1987 and made

BETWEEN:

(1) THE REPUBLIC OF ....

(2) ....

as lead managers:
(3) ....   as managers:
(4) ....   as co-managers:
(5) THE SEVERAL BANKS and FINANCIAL INSTITUTIONS whose names and
     addresses appear in Exhibit A; and
(6) ....   as agents
WHEREAS pursuant to arrangements made by the Lead Managers, the Banks
have agreed to make available to the Borrower a loan facility of $...... and
ECU .... upon and subject to the terms and conditions of this
Agreement.

NOW IT IS HEREBY AGREED as follows:

1. Definitions

17.03   (1) In this Agreement:

Agent means, subject to Clause 19(12):

    (i) when designated $\dfrac{\text{``Dollar''},}{\text{England;}}$

    (ii) when designated $\dfrac{\text{``ECU''},}{\text{England;}}$

    (iii) when designated *relevant* and in relation to the Dollar Loans or the
    ECU Loans, the Agent in respect of such Loans; and

    (iv) without any such designation, the Dollar Agent or the ECU Agent
    (as the context requires).

Bank means:

(i) when designated *"Dollar,"* one of the Banks whose name appears in Part 1 of Exhibit A in its capacity as a *lender of participations* in the Dollar Loans (collectively the "Dollar Banks");

(ii) when designated *"ECU,"* one of the Banks whose name appears in Part II of Exhibit A in its capacity as a lender of participations in the ECU Loans (collectively the "ECU Banks");

(iii) when designated *"relevant"* and in relation to the Dollar Loans or the ECU Loans, one of the Banks participating in such Loans (collectively the "relevant Banks"); and

(iv) without any such designation, a Dollar Bank or an ECU Bank (as the contents require); and

Banks without any such designation means the Dollar Banks and the ECU Banks.

Borrower means the Republic of ....

Business Day means a day on which the relevant London financial markets are open for the transaction of the business contemplated by this Agreement and (in respect of a day on which a payment in Dollars is required hereunder) a day on which banks are also open for business in New York City and (in so far as a payment or calculation in respect of ECUs is required) a day on which banks and foreign exchange markets are open for business in the principal financial centre in the country of each component currency of the ECU.

Commitment means:

(i) when designated *Dollar*, the obligation of each Dollar Bank to con- **17.04** tribute to Dollar Loans hereunder up to the aggregate principal amount set opposite its name in Part I of Exhibit A (collectively the "Dollar Commitments");

(ii) when designated *ECU*, the obligation of each ECU Bank to contribute to ECU Loans hereunder up to the aggregated principal amount set opposite its name in Part II of Exhibit A (collectively the "ECU Commitments");

(iii) when designated *relevant* and in relation to the Dollar Loans or the ECU Loans, a Bank's Commitment in respect of such Loans; and

(iv) without any such designation, a Dollar Commitment or an ECU Commitment (as the context requires),

all subject to and in accordance with the terms hereof and to the extent not cancelled, reduced or terminated in accordance with the terms of this Agreement; the Dollar Commitments and the ECU Commitments are together referred to as the *Total Commitments*.

Commitment Period means the period from the date hereof until the day which is 90 days after the date hereof (both dates inclusive).

Default means any Event of Default and any event which, with the giving of notice and/or lapse of time and/or the fulfilment of other condition(s), would constitute an Event of Default.

Dollars or *$* means the lawful currency for the time being of the United States of America.

ECU means the European Currency Unit the value of which is equal to the value of the European Currency Unit as defined in Exhibit B.

Encumbrance includes any mortgage, pledge, lien, charge, assignment, hypothecation, security interest of any title retention, preferential right or trust arrangement or other agreement or arrangement the effect of any of which is the creation of security.

Event of Default means any of the events specified in Clause 16.

Information Memorandum means the Information Memorandum prepared in connection with this Agreement and dated

Interest Date in relation to each Loan means the last day or an Interest Period relative to such Loan.

Interest Period in relation to each Loan means each period ascertained in accordance with Clause 7 or 9 commencing:

> (i) in the case of the first Interest Period, on the date on which such Loan is first advanced; and
>
> (ii) in the case of subsequent Interest Periods, forthwith upon the expiry of the preceding Interest Period relative to such Loan.

Internal Indebtedness means any indebtedness denominated in....................

Lead Managers means the parties to this Agreement of the second part.

Lending Office means in relation to each Bank the office of such Bank whose address appears under its name in Exhibit A and/or any other office notified by such Bank to the relevant Agent in accordance with Clause 25(2)(*d*) as the office through which such Bank will perform its obligations hereunder and/or maintain its participation in the Dollar Loans or the ECU Loans, as the case may be, or any part thereof.

LIBOR means:

17.05   (i) in relation to each Dollar Loan, the arithmetic mean (rounded upward, if necessary, to the nearest one-sixteenth of 1 per cent. (1/16%)) of the rates, as supplied to the Dollar Agent at its request, quoted by the Dollar Reference Banks to leading banks in the London Interbank Market at or about 11.00 a.m. (London time) two Business Days prior to the commencement of the Interest Period to which the same is to apply, for the offering of Dollar deposits of an amount comparable to the Dollar Reference Banks' respective participations (or, in the case of a Dollar Reference Bank which is not also a Dollar Bank, to the participation of the Dollar Bank with which it is associated) in such Dollar Loan for a period equal to such Interest Period; and

(ii) in relation to each ECU Loan, the arithmetic mean (rounded upward, if necessary, to the nearest one-sixteenth of 1 per cent. (1/ 16%)) of the rates, as supplied to the ECU Agent at its request, quoted by the ECU Reference Banks to leading banks in the London Interbank Market at or about 11.00 a.m. (London time) two Business Days prior to the commencement of the Interest Period to which the same is to apply, for the offering of ECU deposits of an amount comparable to the ECU Reference Banks' respective Bank which is not also an ECU Bank, to the participation of the ECU Bank with which it is associated in such ECU Loan for a period equal to such Interest Period,

provided that, in either case, if any of the relevant Reference Banks shall be unable or otherwise fails so to supply such offered rates by 1.00 p.m. (London time) on such Business Day the same shall be determined, subject to Clause 9(1), on the basis of the quotations of the remaining Reference Banks.

Loan means, subject to Clause 7(2):

(i) when designated *Dollar*, the principal amount of each borrowing by the Borrower from the Dollar Banks hereunder or (as the context requires) the principal amount thereof from time to time outstanding;

(ii) when designated *ECU*, the principal amount of each borrowing by the Borrower from the ECU Banks hereunder or (as the context requires) the principal amount thereof from time to time outstanding; and

(iii) without any such designation, a Dollar Loan or an ECU Loan (as the context requires);

and *relevant Loans* means the Dollar Loans or the ECU Loans (as the context requires) and *Loans* means the Dollar Loans and the ECU Loans together.

Majority Banks means:

(i) when designated *Dollar*, Dollar Banks to whom more than 50 per **17.06** cent. (50%) in aggregate of the Dollar Loans is, at the relevant time, owing or, in the event that no Dollar Loan is then outstanding hereunder, Dollar Banks whose Dollar Commitments then aggregate more than 50 per cent. (50%) of all the Dollar Commitments;

(ii) when designated *"ECU,"* ECU Banks to whom more than 50 per cent. (50%) in aggregate of the ECU Loans is, at the relevant time, owing or, in the event that no ECU Loan is then outstanding hereunder, ECU Banks whose ECU Commitments then aggregate more than 50 per cent. (50%) of all the ECU Commitments; and

(iii) without any such designation, prior to the Term Date, Banks whose participations in the outstanding Loans and whose undrawn Commitments aggregate, at the relevant time, more than 50 per cent. (50%) of the total of the outstanding Loans and the undrawn amount of the Total Commitments or, after the Term Date, Banks to whom more than 50 per cent. (50%) in aggregate of the Loans is, at the relevant time, owing (and for the purpose of this paragraph (iii) $1 shall be deemed to be equal to ECUs 1·27).

Managers means the parties to this Agreement of the second, third and fourth parts.

Margin means:

    (i) for the period from the date hereof to (but excluding) the third anniversary of the date hereof, ... of one per cent. .... per annum; and

    (ii) thereafter, ... of one per cent. per annum.

Public Establishment means any agency, department or instrumentality of the Borrower or .... public enterprise or agency, state corporation, other public authority, and any domestic .... corporation or other legal entity the majority of whose capital or voting stock is owned directly or indirectly by the Borrower.

Public Financial Establishment means any Public Establishment which is a bank, insurance company or financial institution.

Reference Banks means, subject to the provisions of Clause 25(3):

17.07

    (i) when designated *Dollar*, the principal London offices of

    (ii) when designated *ECU*, the principal London offices of

    (iii) when designated *relevant* and in relation to the Dollar Loans or the ECU Loans, the Reference Banks in respect of such loans; and

    (iv) without any such designation, a Dollar Reference Bank or an ESU Reference Bank (as the context requires).

Repayment Date means each date for the payment of a Repayment Instalment.

Repayment Instalment means each instalment for repayment referred to in Clause 5.

Same Day Funds means Dollar funds settle through the New York Clearing House Interbank Payments System or such other funds for payment in Dollars as may at the time of the relevant payment be customary for the settlement of international Dollar transactions in New York City of the type contemplated by this Agreement.

Stamp Tax means the stamp tax (being at the date hereof at the rate of .... page) which would be payable if proceedings with respect to this Agreement were brought before the Courts of the Republic of

Taxes includes all present and future income and other taxes, levies, imposts, deductions, charges and withholdings whatsoever, together with interest thereon and penalties with respect thereto, if any, and any payments of principal, interest, charges, fees or other amounts made on or in respect thereof and "*Tax*," "*Taxation*" and similar words shall be construed accordingly.

Term Date means the last day of the Commitment Period.

(2) Unless the context otherwise requires, words importing the singular number shall include the plural and vice versa, persons shall include bodies corporate and vice versa. The index hereto and the headings herein are for convenience only and shall not affect the construction hereof. References herein to any agreement, licence or other instrument shall be deemed to include references to such agreement, licence or other instrument as varied or replaced from time to time and references herein to any enactment shall be deemed to include references to such enactment as re-enacted, amended or extended. References herein to a currency (howsoever expressed) shall include ECUs. References herein to Clauses and Exhibits are references, respectively, to clauses of and exhibits to this Agreement and the expressions "hereof," "herein" and similar expressions shall be construed as references to this Agreement as a whole and not limited to the particular clause or provision in which the relevant expression appears. Borrower, each Manager, each Bank, each Reference Bank, each Agent or the parties hereto shall, where relevant, be deemed to be references to or to include, as appropriate, their respective successors or assigns.

2. Loans/Commitments

(1) Subject to the terms of this Agreement and in reliance on the represen- **17.08** tations and warranties in Clause 13(1) each Dollar Bank and each ECU Bank agrees to participate in, respectively, Dollar Loans and ECU Loans to be made to the Borrower through its Lending Office up to an aggregate maximum principal amount not exceeding, respectively, its Dollar Commitment and its ECU Commitment.

(2) The rights and obligations of each Bank under this Agreement are several to the intent that (a) failure of a Bank to carry out its obligations hereunder shall not relieve any other Bank, either Agent or the Borrower of any of its respective obligations hereunder, (b) no Bank shall be responsible for the obligations of any other Bank or either Agent hereunder, and (c) each Bank may, subject as expressly stated herein, exercise its rights and pursue its remedies hereunder independently of the Agents and the other Banks.

3. Purpose

The proceeds of the Loans shall be applied in or towards providing financ- **17.09** ing for investments included in the economic plan of the Republic of .... for 1987 or other productive projects in the context of the stabilisation policy agreed between the Borrower and the International Monetary Fund. Without prejudice to the foregoing and the remaining provisions of this Agreement, none of the Agents, the Managers and the Banks shall be bound to enquire as to the applications by the Borrower of the proceeds of the Loans, nor shall any of them be responsible for, or for the consequences of, such application.

4. Draw-down

(1) COMMITMENT PERIOD

17.10   Subject to the terms of this Agreement (including but not limited to the conditions set forth in Clause 12), Loans will be made to the Borrower at any time and from time to time during the Commitment Period. Any amount of the Total Commitments unborrowed hereunder at the expiry of the Commitment Period shall automatically be cancelled at that time and shall not thereafter be available to the Borrower.

(2) DRAW-DOWN NOTICES

Whenever the Borrower desires to borrow hereunder it shall give notice, substantially in the form of Exhibit C, to the relevant Agent to be received by such Agent not later than 11.00 a.m. (London time) five Business Days prior to the proposed date for borrowing, specifying in respect of the proposed borrowing (a) the date thereof (which shall be a Business Day during the Commitment Period), (b) in the case of a Dollar Loan, the amount in Dollars (such amount being not less than $ .... and an integral multiple thereof if more or the undrawn balance of the Dollar Commitments) or, in the case of an ECU Loan, the amount in ECUs (such amount being not less than ECU .... and an integral multiple thereof if more or the undrawn balance of the ECU Commitments), (c) in any case where the same is not determined by Clause 7(2)(d), the duration of the first Interest Period relative thereto and (d) the payment instructions relative thereto to the extent that such instructions have not already been notified to such Agent by the Borrower. Subject to Clause 9, each such notice shall be irrevocable and the Borrower shall be bound to borrow in accordance with such notice. Promptly after receipt of such notice the relevant Agent shall notify the other Agent and each relevant Bank of such proposed borrowing. The Borrower may not serve notice of borrowing hereunder until after satisfaction of the conditions precedent set out in Clause 12(1).

(3) PARTICIPATIONS

Subject to the terms of this Agreement, each relevant Bank shall on the date specified in each notice given by the relevant Agent pursuant to Clause 4(2) make available to such Agent the amount of its participation in the Loan concerned in the proportion which its Commitment bears to the Dollar Commitments or the ECU Commitments, as the case may be.

(4) PAYMENT OF LOANS

17.11   All amounts to be made available by the Dollar Banks to the Dollar Agent under this Agreement shall be made available for value on the due date in Dollars and in Same Day Funds to the account of the Dollar Agent at .... U.S.A. (Account Number: ....) or at such other office or bank as the Dollar Agent may from time to time reasonably designate. All amounts to be made available by the ECU Banks to the ECU Agent under this Agreement shall be made available in ECUs and in immediately available funds not later than

11.00 a.m. (London time) on the due date to the account of the ECU Agent at England (Account Number: ....) or at such other office or bank as the ECU Agent may from time to time reasonably designate.

Each Agent shall forthwith transfer all such amounts so made available to it to such account or accounts of the Borrower at such bank or banks as the Borrower may reasonably designate and in like funds as they are received by such Agent.

(5) BREAKAGE COSTS

If the Borrower fails to borrow any Loan hereunder after notice of borrowing therefor has been served pursuant to Clause 4(2), the Borrower will pay to each relevant Bank such amount as such Bank may certify (such certification to be conclusive in the absence of manifest error) as necessary to compensate it for any direct losses on account of funds borrowed or contracted for in order to fund its participation in such Loan.

5. Repayment

The Borrower will repay the Dollar Loans in full by seven approximately **17.12** equal semi-annual instalments together equal to that of all the Dollar Loans borrowed hereunder and each being equal as nearly as possible to one-seventh of such Dollar Loans. The Borrower will repay the ECU Loans in full by seven approximately equal semi-annual instalments together equal to that of all the ECU Loans borrowed hereunder and each being equal as nearly as possible to one-seventh of the ECU Loans. The first such Repayment Instalment of the Dollar Loans and the ECU Loans shall be paid forty-eight months after the date hereof and subsequent Repayment Instalments shall be paid at six-monthly intervals thereafter with final Repayment Instalment on the seventh anniversary of the date hereof. Notwithstanding the above if any date for the payment of a Repayment Instalment would thereby fall on a day which is not a Business Day, such Repayment Instalment shall instead be paid on the immediately succeeding Business Day, and the provisions of Clause 6(3) shall be applied in establishing the amount and number of such Repayment Instalments in the event of any partial prepayment of the relevant Loans.

6. Prepayments

(1) VOLUNTARY PREPAYMENTS BY THE BORROWER

On giving not less than 30 days' prior notice to the relevant Agent (which **17.13** shall promptly give notice thereof to the relevant Banks), the Borrower may prepay the relevant Loans in whole or in part (but if in part in an amount of a minimum of $ .... or ESC .... as the case may be, and of an integral multiple thereof if more) on any Interest Date relative to the amount to be prepaid, provided always that, except in the case of a prepayment made by the Borrower to satisfy its obligations under Clause 4(6), the other Agent shall have received at the same time notice from the Borrower of its intention to prepay a portion of the other Loans in (having regard to the multiples of partial prepayments permitted above) approximately the proportion which the portion of the relevant Loans being prepaid bears to the relevant Loans at the date of the giving of such notice, such prepayment to be made on the next succeeding Interest Date(s) relative to the amount of the other Loans to be prepaid.

(2) INTEREST APPLIED TO PREPAYMENTS

Prepayments under this Agreement shall be made together with accrued interest thereon but, subject to Clause 10(3), without premium or penalty.

(3) APPLICATION OF PREPAYMENT

Amounts prepaid under this Agreement may not be re-borrowed hereunder. Each amount prepaid under Clause 6(1) shall be applied against any outstanding Repayment Instalments relative to the Loans to be prepaid in the inverse order of their maturity. Each prepayment of a Bank's participation under Clause 9 or 11 shall be applied against any outstanding Repayment Instalments relative to the Loans to be prepaid *pro rata*.

(4) IRREVOCABILITY OF NOTICE TO PREPAY

Any notice of prepayment given by the Borrower under this Agreement shall be irrevocable and the Borrower shall be bound to prepay in accordance with each such notice.

(5) LIMITATIONS ON PREPAYMENTS

The Borrower may not prepay all or any part of the Loans except in accordance with the express terms of this Agreement.

7. Interest Periods

(1) GIVING OF NOTICE TO SELECT INTEREST PERIOD

17.14 The Borrower shall prior to the beginning of each Interest Period relative to each Loan give notice to the relevant Agent, to be received by such Agent not later than 11.00 a.m. (London time) five Business Days prior to such Interest Period, specifying whether that Interest Period is to be of a duration of three or six months.

(2) FAILURE TO GIVE NOTICE

Subject always to the provisions of Clause 9, each Interest Period relative to a Loan shall be of a duration selected by the Borrower in accordance with the above, provided that:

(i) if the Borrower fails to select an Interest Period in accordance with the above, such Interest Period shall, subject to the following paragraphs below, be of a duration of six months;

(ii) if any Interest Period would end on a day which is not a Business

Day, such Interest Period shall be extended to the next succeeding Business Day;

(iii) subject to the other paragraphs of this Clause 7(2), any Interest Period, which commences on the last day of a calendar month or on a day for which there is no numerically corresponding day in the calendar month three or six months, as the case may be, after the commencement of such Interest Period, shall be the end of the last Business Day of the calendar month three or six months, as the case may be, after the commencement of such Interest Period;

(iv) the first Interest Period relative to each relevant Loan (other than the first such relevant Loan) shall end on the same day as the then current Interest Period relative to such first relevant Loan, as the case may be, (unless this would result in an Interest Period of less than five Business Days' duration, in which case such Interest Period shall end on the same day as the next Interest Period relative to such first relevant Loan) to the intent that on the expiration of such Interest Period such relevant Loans shall thereafter be treated as one relevant Loan and, subject to paragraph (e) below, all Interest Periods relative to the relevant Loans shall be coterminous; and

(v) if the selection of an Interest Period pursuant to the above procedures would result in any Repayment Date in respect of the relevant Loans falling otherwise than on the last day of an Interest Period relative thereto, the relevant Loans shall be divided into two parts, one part to be equal in an amount to the Repayment Instalment relative thereto to be paid on such Repayment Date and to have an Interest Period ending on such Repayment Date, and the other part to comprise the remaining amount of the relevant Loans and to have the Interest Period which would have applied to the relevant Loans but for this paragraph (v), and each such part shall be deemed to constitute a separate Loan.

(3) AGENT TO NOTIFY PARTIES

Each Agent will notify the Borrower and the relevant Banks of the duration of each Interest Period promptly after ascertaining the same.

8. Interest

(1) Subject always to Clause 9, interest shall be payable by the Borrower on **17.15** the Loans in accordance with this Clause 8.

(2) RATE OF INTEREST

The rate of interest applicable to each Loan for each Interest Period relative thereto shall be the rate per annum determined by the relevant Agent to be the aggregate of (i) the applicable Margin and (ii) LIBOR relevant to such Loan for such Interest Period.

(3) DUE DATES

Except as otherwise provided herein, accrued interest in relation to each Loan shall be payable on each Interest Date relative thereto.

(4) DEFAULT INTEREST

If the Borrower fails to pay any amount payable by it hereunder on the due date therefor, the Borrower shall on demand by the Dollar Agent if such overdue amount relates to a Dollar Loan or the ECU Agent if such overdue amount relates to an ECU Loan from time to time pay interest on such overdue amount from the due date up to the date of actual payment, as well after as before judgment and compounded quarterly, at a rate determined by the relevant Agent (after consultation with the relevant Reference Banks) to be ...... per cent ...... *per annum* above the higher of:

(i) the rate applicable to such overdue amount immediately prior to the due date (if of principal); and

(ii) the rate which would have been payable if such overdue amount had during the period of non-payment thereof constituted a Loan made hereunder for successive Interest Periods of such duration not exceeding six months as the relevant Agent may from time to time designate.

Any such designation by an Agent will be notified by it to the Borrower and the relevant Banks promptly. If an Agent (after consultation with the relevant Reference Banks) determines that Dollar or ECU deposits, as the case may be, in sufficient amounts are not being offered to leading banks in the London Interbank Market such rate shall be determined by reference to the cost of funds from such other sources as such Agent (after consultation with the relevant Reference Banks) may from time to time determine.

(5) CONCLUSIVE DETERMINATION BY AGENT

Each determination of the rate of interest by an Agent hereunder shall, in the absence of manifest error, be conclusive and binding upon all parties hereto and shall be promptly notified to the Borrower and the relevant Banks.

(6) Interest shall accrue from day to day and shall be computed on the basis of a year of 360 days and for the actual number of days elapsed.

9. Alternative Interest Rates and Non-Availability

17.16 (1) If and at any time prior to the commencement of any Interest Period relative to a Loan:

(i) the relevant Agent (after consultation with the relevant Reference Banks) shall have determined that, by reason of material circumstances seriously affecting the London Interbank Market, adequate and fair means do not exist for ascertaining LIBOR in respect of such Loan for such Interest Period; or

(ii) the relevant Majority Banks notify the relevant Agent that LIBOR would not accurately reflect the cost to such relevant Majority Banks of making or maintaining their respective participations in such Loan for such Interest Period; or

(iii) none, or only one, of the relevant Reference Banks notifies a rate to the relevant Agent for the purposes of determining LIBOR for such period,

the relevant Agent shall give notice thereof (an "alternative interest rate notice") to the Borrower and the relevant Banks. The Borrower, the relevant Agent and the relevant Banks shall then negotiate in good faith in order to agree a mutually satisfactory interest rate or rates, Interest Period or Periods and Interest Date or Dates (which shall be binding on all of the relevant Banks) to be substituted for those which would otherwise have applied pursuant to Clauses 7 and 8 and/or an alternative basis acceptable to all of them for funding or continuing to fund such Loan, whether with the same or some other currency or otherwise. If the Borrower, the relevant Agent and the relevant Banks are unable to agree upon an interest rate or rates, Interest Period or Periods and Interest Date or Dates and/or an alternative basis as aforesaid within a period of forty-five days from the date of the giving of the alternative interest rate notice (during which period no relevant Loan may be made hereunder), the relevant Agent shall promptly set an interest rate or rates, an Interest Period or Periods and an Interest Date or Dates in respect of the participation in such Loan of each relevant Bank (which shall be binding on such relevant Bank), all to take effect from the commencement of the Interest Period in respect of which the relevant Agent gave the alternative interest rate notice, which interest rate or rates shall be the aggregate of the applicable Margin and the cost to each relevant Bank of funding its participations in such Loan for the Interest Period or Periods so set. In the event that the state of affairs referred to above in this Clause 9(1) shall extend beyond the end of any Interest Period so agreed or set, the foregoing procedure shall be repeated as often as may be necessary. The Borrower shall pay to the relevant Banks interest of the amount of such Banks' participation in such Loan from time to time outstanding at the interest rate or rates so agreed or set on the Interest Date or Dates so agreed or set. Notwithstanding the foregoing, the Borrower shall be at liberty at any time after the relevant Agent shall have set an interest rate or rates as aforesaid and so long as such interest rate or rates continue(s) to be applicable, subject to its giving to the relevant Agent not less than five Business Days' notice, to prepay to the relevant Agent for the account of such Bank the whole (but not part only) of such Bank's participation in the relevant Loans, whereupon the liability of such Bank to participate in the relevant Loans shall forthwith cease.

(2) If any Bank shall certify to the relevant Agent that by reason of material **17.17** circumstances seriously affecting the London Interbank Market it is unable to obtain Dollars or ECUs in the London Interbank Market and that accordingly such Bank will not be able to participate or continue to participate in the relevant Loans or part thereof, such Agent shall despatch notice to the Borrower thereof whereafter the obligation of such Bank to participate in the relevant Loans shall forthwith cease and the Borrower shall prepay to such Agent for the account of such Bank the whole (but not part only) of such Bank's participation in the relevant Loans on the last day of the then current Interest Period(s) referable thereto. Notwithstanding the foregoing, in any such case the Borrower, such Agent and the Bank in question shall negotiate in good faith with a view to agreeing terms on which

such Bank's participation in the relevant Loans may be made available or funded in some other manner, provided that neither such Agent nor the Bank in question shall be under any obligation to continue such negotiations if terms have not been agreed within forty-five days of the certification by such Bank as aforesaid and provided further that no Bank shall be required to take any action which in its opinion is prejudicial to its interests.

(3) If at any time prior to the commencement of any Interest Period relative to an ECU Loan the ECU Agent (after consultation with the ECU Reference Banks) shall have determined that:

(i) deposits in ECUs are not freely available in the London Interbank Market; or

(ii) the ECU has ceased to be utilised as the basic accounting unit of the European Economic Community; or

(iii) the ECU has ceased to be used in the European Monetary System,

the Borrower, the ECU Agent and the ECU Banks shall then negotiate in good faith with a view to agreeing a basis on which the ECU Loans may continue to be made available in some other currency or currencies. If the ECU Agent, the Borrower and the ECU Banks are unable to agree upon a currency or currencies, an interest rate or rates, an Interest Period or Periods and an Interest Date or Interest Dates and/or an alternative basis acceptable to them within a period of forty-five days from the date of such notice (during which period no ECU Loan may be made hereunder), the ECU Agent shall promptly set Dollars as the currency of the ECU Loans in accordance with the provisions of Exhibit B (and for this purpose the Day of Valuation referred to in Exhibit B shall be the day two Business Days prior to the date on which the ECU Agent sets Dollars as the currency of the ECU Loans as aforesaid) and an interest rate or rates, an Interest Period or Periods and an Interest Date or Dates in respect of the ECU Loans (which shall be binding on the Borrower and the ECU Banks), all to take effect from the commencement of each Interest Period in respect of which the ECU Agent gave such notice. In the event that the state of affairs referred to above in this Clause 9(3) shall extend beyond the end of any Interest Period so agreed or set, the foregoing procedure shall be repeated as often as may be necessary. The Borrower shall pay to the ECU Agent for the accounts of the ECU Banks' interest on the amount of such ECU Banks' participations in each such amount of currency (or the relevant part thereof from time to time outstanding) at the interest rate or rates so agreed or set on the Interest Date or Dates so agreed or set. If, the ECU Agent having set Dollars as the currency of the ECU Loans, any Bank participating in the ECU Loans shall certify to the ECU Agent that, by reason of market conditions, it is unable to obtain Dollars and that accordingly it will not be able to continue to participate in the ECU Loans in Dollars, the provisions of Clause 9(2) shall apply to such Bank.

(4) The certificate of the relevant Agent or, as the case may be, the relevant Bank as referred to in this Clause 9 shall, in the absence of manifest error, be conclusive and binding on the Borrower.

(5) (i) When the liability of any Bank to participate in the relevant Loans

ceases pursuant to any of the provisions of this Clause 9 the Total Commitments and the relevant Commitment of such Bank shall both be reduced by the amount of such Bank's participation in the relevant Loans.

(ii) When the whole of the participation of any Bank in the relevant Loans is prepaid by the Borrower pursuant to any of the provisions of this Clause 9 the Borrower shall simultaneously with such prepayment pay to the relevant Agent for the account of such Bank accrued interest thereon and all fees and other amounts payable to such Bank hereunder.

10. Payments

(1) PLACE OF PAYMENT

All payments to be made by the Borrower hereunder shall be made, if they **17.18** relate to the Dollar Loans, to the Dollar Agent or, if they relate to the ECU Loans, to the ECU Agent. All such payments shall be made by the Borrower:

(i) if in Dollars, for value on the date upon which the relevant payment is due in Same Day Funds to the account of the Dollar Agent at .... U.S.A. (Account Number: ....) or

(ii) if in ECUs, not later than 11.00 a.m. (London time) on the date upon which the relevant payment is due in immediately available funds to the account of the ECU Agent at .... (Account Number: ....); or at such other office or bank as the relevant Agent may from time to time designate, provided always that if the Borrower is required to make a payment to the ECU Agent in Dollars in accordance with Clause 9(3) then such payment shall be made in Dollars for value on the date the relevant payment is due in Same Day Funds to such account of the ECU Bank at such office or bank as the ECU Agent may from time to time designate.

(2) PAYMENTS MADE FREE OF TAXES ETC.

All payments to be made by the Borrower hereunder shall be made without set-off or counterclaim and free and clear of and without deduction for or on account of any present or future Taxes imposed, levied or assessed by the Republic of .... or any other jurisdiction from or through which the Borrower may choose to make any payment hereunder (or any federation or organisation of which the Republic of .... or any such other jurisdiction is at the relevant time a member) or any political sub-division or Taxing authority of any of the foregoing, unless the Borrower is compelled by law to make payment subject to any such Tax. All such Taxes shall be paid by the Borrower for its own account prior to the date on which penalties attach thereto. The Borrower will indemnify each Agent, each Manager and each Bank in respect of all such Taxes. Should any such payment be subject to any such Tax and the above provisions either cannot be effected or do not result in an Agent, a Manager or a Bank actually receiving an amount equal to the full amount provided for hereunder, the Borrower shall pay to the relevant Agent for itself or for such Manager or such Bank, as the case may be, such additional amounts as may be necessary to ensure that such Agent, Manager or Bank receives a net amount in Dollars or ECUs, as the case may be, equal to the full amount which it would have received had payment not been made subject to such Tax. The Borrower shall deliver to the relevant Agent for itself or such Manager or Bank within fifteen days of each such payment by the Borrower of such Tax, evidence (including all relevant Tax receipts) satisfactory to itself or such Manager or Bank, as the case may be, that such Tax has been duly remitted to the appropriate authority.

(3) Any repayment or prepayment by the Borrower of the principal amount of any Loan or any part thereof which is made otherwise than on an Interest Date relative to such amount shall be made together with accrued interest on such amount and the Borrower shall further pay to each Bank to which such repayment or prepayment is made, on demand made by such Bank through the relevant Agent, such additional amount as such Bank may certify as necessary to compensate it for any loss, premium, penalty or expenses incurred or to be incurred by it (including loss of applicable Margin) on account of funds borrowed or committed for, to make, fund or maintain its participation in the amounts repaid or prepaid, such certification to be conclusive and binding in the absence of manifest error. For the purpose of this Clause 10(3), the last day of any Interest Period designated by an Agent pursuant to Clause 8(4) shall be deemed to be the Interest Date in respect thereof and the last day of any Interest Period established pursuant to Clause 9 shall be deemed to be the Interest Date in respect thereof.

(4) Whenever any payment hereunder shall become due on a day which is not a Business Day, the due date thereof shall be extended to the next succeeding Business Day. During any extension of the due date for payment of any principal of the Loans hereunder interest shall be payable accordingly.

(5) Except as otherwise indicated herein, all payments made to each Agent by the Borrower hereunder shall be promptly distributed by such Agent among the relevant Banks in the same proportion as their respective participations in the relevant Loans bear to the total outstanding amount of the relevant Loans and in like funds as they are received by such Agent.

11. Changes in Law

17.19 (1) If:

(a) any change in or introduction of any law, regulation, treaty or official directive (whether or not having the force of law) or in the interpretation thereof by any authority charged with the administration thereof or by any court of competent jurisdiction or any changes in any applicable direction, request or requirement (whether or not having the force of law) of any governmental, fiscal or monetary authority:

(i) subjects any Bank or either Agent to any Tax with respect to payments of principal of or interest on any Loan or any other amount payable by the Borrower for the account of or to any Bank or by either Agent to any Bank hereunder (other than Tax imposed, assessed, levied or collected on the overall net income of such Bank in the jurisdiction where such Bank's principal office or Lending Office for the time being hereunder is situated); or

(ii) changes the basis of Taxation of payments to any Bank or principal or interest on any Loan or any other amount payable by the Borrower for the account of or to any Bank or by either Agent to any Bank hereunder (other than a change in the statutory rate of Tax on the overall net income of such Bank imposed in the jurisdiction in which such Bank's principal office or Lending Office for the time being hereunder is situated); or

(iii) changes the basis of Taxation of any Bank in respect of any principal or interest paid by such Bank on, or otherwise in respect of deposits from third parties acquired or utilised to effect or maintain its participation in the relevant Loans or any part thereof; or

(iv) imposes, modifies or deems applicable any reserve, special deposit, cash ratio, liquidity or other requirement against or in respect of any, or any class of any, Dollar or ECU assets or liabilities of any Bank; or

(v) imposes on any Bank any other condition with respect to this Agreement or any Loan or any other amount payable under this Agreement;

or

(*b*) any Bank complies with any request, law, regulation or directive from any governmental, fiscal or monetary authority (whether or not having the force of law);

and as a result of any of the foregoing:

(a) the cost to any Bank of making, funding or maintaining its participation in any Loan or of maintaining its Commitment is increased by an amount which such Bank considers material; or

(b) the amount of principal, interest or other amount payable to any Bank or the effective return to any Bank hereunder is reduced (otherwise than as contemplated by Clause 10(2)) by an amount which such Bank considers material; or

(c) any Bank makes any payment or forgoes any interest or other return on or calculated by reference to any sum received or receivable by it from the Borrower or either Agent hereunder in an amount which such Bank considers material,

then and in each such case:

(I) such Bank shall notify the Borrower through the relevant Agent of such event promptly upon its becoming aware of the same and, in so far as it is permitted to do so, shall provide the Borrower with a copy of any relevant official documentation relating thereto; **17.20**

(II) upon demand from time to time by such Bank through the relevant Agent the Borrower shall pay to such Agent for such Bank such amount as shall compensate such Bank for such increased cost, reduction, payment or forgone interest or other return, the certificate of such Bank setting out the amount and basis for such amount shall, in the absence of manifest error, be conclusive and binding; it shall not be a defence to any such demand that the cost, reduction, payment, forgone interest or other return could have been avoided or reduced by such Bank; and

(III) the Borrower may prepay such a Bank's participation in the Loans, together with all interest accrued thereon and all fees and other amounts payable to such Bank hereunder (including any amount payable to the date of such prepayment pursuant to paragraph (II) above and any amount payable pursuant to Clause 10(3), on giving not less than thirty days' prior notice to the relevant Agent, provided that such notice is given within thirty days of the notification under paragraph (I) above; such Bank's Commitment shall be terminated on the giving of such notice.

(2) Notwithstanding anything to the contrary herein contained, if any change in law, regulation, treaty or regulatory requirement or in the interpretation or application thereof by any authority or agency charged with the administration thereof or by any court shall make it unlawful for any Bank to make or fund or maintain its participation in the relevant Loans or to give effect to its obligations as contemplated hereby, such Bank may, by notice thereof to the Borrower through the relevant Agent, declare that such Bank's obligations shall be terminated forthwith whereupon the Borrower will prepay forthwith (or if permitted by the relevant law, regulation, treaty or regulatory requirement) at the end of the then current Interest Period(s) in respect of the relevant Loans the then outstanding principal amount of such Bank's participation in such Loans, together with all interest accrued thereon and all fees and other amounts payable to such Bank hereunder and such Bank's Commitment shall be terminated on the giving of such notice. Notwithstanding the above, each Bank undertakes that, in the event that it becomes so unlawful for such Bank to make or fund or maintain its participation in the relevant Loans or to give effect to its obligations as contemplated hereby, it will use all reasonable efforts, for a period of forty-five days from the giving of the relevant notice by it, to transfer its participation in the relevant Loans and its obligations hereunder to another branch of such Bank or to another financial institution located in a jurisdiction in which it will not be so unlawful, provided that such Bank shall not thereby be required to take any action which in its opinion is prejudicial to its interests.

12. Conditions Precedent

(1) CONDITIONS TO ALL LOANS

17.21   The obligations of each Bank hereunder are subject to the condition that the Dollar Agent shall have received all of the following in form and substance satisfactory to the Dollar Agent not less than two Business Days' prior to the Borrower serving a notice to make the first borrowing hereunder:

(i) a copy of an extract from Law Number .... of ...., authorising the borrowing of loans in foreign currencies by the Borrower on conditions to be determined by Decree Law, certified as being true and in full force and effect as at a date no earlier than the date hereof;

(ii) a copy of Decree–Law Number .... of ...., of the Borrower, approving the terms of the facility governed by this Agreement and empowering the Minister for Finance and Planning (or a person or persons authorised by him) to execute and deliver this Agreement on behalf of the Borrower, certified as being true and in full force and effect as at a date no earlier than the date hereof;

(iii) a declaration of the Director General for Treasury, stating that the Total Commitments at the date hereof fall within the monetary limits from foreign currency borrowings by the Borrower presently authorised by law;

(iv) a certified true copy of the signatures of the person(s) authorised to execute this Agreement on behalf of the Borrower and of the persons authorised to sign all notices, certificates and other documents to be delivered by the Borrower hereunder;

(v) a copy of the exemption of the Ministry for Finance and Planning, exempting all payments to be made by the Borrower hereunder from .... Taxes on interest in accordance with Articles .... and of the Capital Tax Code, as introduced by Decree–Law Number .... of ...., certified as being true and in full force and effect as at a date no earlier than the date hereof;

(vi) a copy of all other authorisations, approvals, consents, licences and exemptions required in connection with the execution, delivery, performance, validity and enforceability of this Agreement, certified as being true and in full force and effect as at a date no earlier than the date hereof;

(vii) evidence that the Ambassador of the Republic of .... to the Court of St. James's and the Consul General of the Republic of .... in New York have agreed, for themselves and their successors to such offices, to act as the agent of the Borrower for receipt of service of process in England and New York respectively;

(viii) a legal opinion of the Attorney General of ....;

(ix) a legal opinion of .... addressed to the Agents, the Managers and the Banks, to the effect set forth in Exhibit D; and

(x) a legal opinion of ...., addressed to the Agents, the Managers and the Banks, to the effect set forth in Exhibit E.[1]

(2) CONDITIONS TO EACH LOAN

The obligations of each Agent and each Bank hereunder are subject to the further condition precedent that, both at the time of the request for and at

---

[1] The following conditions precedent may be included in the case of a corporate borrower: (a) conditions requiring copies of corporate documents to be produced, *viz.*: the memorandum; the articles of association; the board resolution approving the transaction in question and authorising certain individuals to execute the loan agreement on behalf of the borrower (b) a condition requiring *central bank authorisation* to be furnished. (It may be prudent in some cases to obtain a currency transfer undertaking direct from the central bank.)

the time for the making of each Loan, the representations and warranties of the Borrower set out in Clause 13(1) are true and accurate on and as of such times as if made at each such time and no Default has occurred and is continuing or would result from the proposed Loan.

13. Representations and Warranties

17.22   (1) The Borrower makes the following representations and warranties for the benefit of each Agent, each Manager and each Bank:

(*a*) *Powers and authority*

The Borrower has the power to enter into and perform this Agreement and to borrow hereunder and has taken all necessary action to authorise the borrowing of the Loans upon the terms and conditions of this Agreement and to authorise the execution, delivery and performance of this Agreement in accordance with its terms;

(*b*) *Legal validity*

This Agreement constitutes a legal, valid and binding obligation of the Borrower enforceable in accordance with its terms;

(*c*) *No conflict with laws relating to borrower*

The execution, delivery and performance of this Agreement will not violate in any respect any provision of (i) the constitution of the Republic of ...., (ii) any .... law, regulation or order applicable to the Borrower, or (iii) any mortgage, agreement or other undertaking, instrument or obligation to which the Borrower is a party or which is binding upon it or any of its assets, nor result in the creation or imposition of any Encumbrance on any of its assets pursuant to the provisions of any such mortgage, agreement or other undertaking, instrument or obligation;

(*d*) *No default*

There has not occurred any Default;

(*e*) *Consents*

All authorisations, approvals, consents, licences, exemptions, filings, registrations, notarisations and other requirements under those .... laws, regulations and orders which are applicable to the Borrower and required in connection with the execution, delivery, performance, validity and enforceability of this Agreement and, with the exception of the payment of the Stamp Tax, its admissibility in evidence in the Republic of .... have been obtained or effected and are in full force and effect, there has been no default in the performance of any of the terms or conditions thereof, no fees are payable in connection therewith and the Borrower has full authority to make all payments hereunder to each Agent in the currency required hereunder for the account of the relevant Banks to the accounts provided for in Clause 10(1);

(*f*) *No litigation*

17.23   No litigation, arbitration or administrative proceeding is pending or, to the best of the Borrower's knowledge and belief, threatened against or with respect to the Borrower or any of its assets which might materially and adversely affect the ability of the Borrower to perform its obligations under this Agreement;

(*g*) *No breach of obligations owed to third parties*

The Borrower is not in breach of or in default under any mortgage, agreement or other undertaking, instrument or obligation to which it is a party or which is binding upon it or any of its assets to an extent or in a manner which might materially and adversely affect the ability of the Borrower to perform its obligations under this Agreement;

(*h*) *Information memorandum*

As at the date of this Agreement the statements in the Information Memorandum are correct in all material respects and are not misleading and the Information Memorandum does not omit any material facts and, without prejudice to the generality of the foregoing, there has been no material adverse change in the financial condition of the Borrower from that disclosed by the Information Memorandum;

(*i*) *No immunity from suit*

The Borrower is subject to civil and commercial law with respect to its obligations under this Agreement; the execution and delivery by the Borrower of, and the borrowing of the Loans hereunder and exercise of its other rights and performance of its obligations under this Agreement constitute private and commercial acts rather than governmental or public acts and neither it nor any of its assets or revenues (save for assets in the public domain or in use for public utility purposes) enjoys under .... law any right of immunity from suit (including immunity based on grounds of sovereignty), judgment or execution on a judgment or attachment (whether before judgment, in aid of execution or otherwise) in respect of its obligations under this Agreement and the waiver contained in Clause 29(1) by the Borrower of any such right of immunity is irrevocably binding on the Borrower;

(*j*) *Not necessary to be licenced*

It is not necessary under the law and constitution of the Republic of .... (i) in order to enable any of the Agents, the Managers and the Banks to enforce its rights under this Agreement or (ii) by reason of the execution, delivery and performance of this Agreement by each of them that any of them should be licensed, qualified or otherwise entitled to carry on business in the Republic of ....;

(*k*) *No residence*

None of the Agents, the Managers and the Banks is or will be deemed to be resident, domiciled or carrying on business in the .... or subject to taxation in the Republic of .... by reason only of the execution, performance and/or enforcement of this Agreement; and

(*l*) *IMF membership*

The Borrower is a member in good standing of the International Monetary Fund and no limitation or restriction has been imposed on its use of the resources thereof.

(2) "EVERGREEN" REPRESENTATIONS AND WARRANTIES

17.24 The representations and warranties set out in Clause 13(1) shall survive the execution of this Agreement and the making of each Loan hereunder and shall be deemed to be repeated at the time of each request for a Loan and on each Interest Date with reference to the facts and circumstances then subsisting, as if made at each such time.

The following representations and warranties may be required in the case of a corporate Borrower: (i) a representation that the Borrower is duly incorporated and has power to execute the agreement under its terms (ii) a representation that the most recent audited accounts of the Borrower reflect a fair and true picture of its financial condition, (iii) a representation that the borrower or any of its subsidiaries is not in default under this or any other loan agreement.

14. Covenants

17.25 The Borrower undertakes that from and after the date hereof and so long as any amount payable hereunder is outstanding or any of the Total Commitments is in force:

(i) the Borrower shall furnish to the Dollar Agent in sufficient copies for all the Banks the printed annual report of Banco de .... for each of its financial years as soon as practicable;

(ii) the Borrower shall furnish to the Dollar Agent in sufficient copies for all the Banks within 120 days after the end of each calendar year a statement of its balance of payments for such period, prepared in accordance with the standard format of the International Monetary Fund, a statement of the composition of its holdings of gold, foreign exchange and Special Drawing Rights as of the end of such period and a description of any exchange restrictions affecting it in effect during such period;

(iii) the Borrower shall furnish to the Dollar Agent in sufficient copies for all the Banks from time to time, with reasonable promptness, such further information regarding the financial condition of the Borrower or any Public Establishment as either Agent or any Bank which the Dollar Agent may reasonably request;

(iv) the Borrower shall obtain and promptly renew from time to time all authorisations, approvals, consents, licences and exemptions as may be required under any applicable .... law or regulation to enable it to perform its obligations under this Agreement, or required for the validity or enforceability of this Agreement, shall comply with the terms of the same and will ensure the availability of sufficient foreign exchange to enable it to comply with its obligations under this Agreement; and

(v) the Borrower will notify the Dollar Agent (which shall promptly notify the ECU Agent and all the Banks) of any Default forthwith upon the occurrence thereof, and, in the case of the Borrower having notified the Dollar Agent of the commencement of negotiations with one or more of its creditors with a view to entering into any arrangement or composition with or for the benefit of its creditors or any of them (being an Event of Default pursuant to Clause 16(*f*)), the Borrower will use its best efforts to permit the Dollar Agent and the ECU Agent to participate in any such negotiations.

The following conditions may be required in the case of a corporate Borrower:

(*a*) a condition that neither the Borrower, nor any of its subsidiaries will dispose of any assets except with the prior written consent of the lending bank(s).

(*b*) a condition that neither the Borrower nor its subsidiaries will make any substantial change in its business, except with the prior written consent of the lending bank(s).

(*c*) a condition that neither the Borrower nor its subsidiaries will enter into any merger or consolidation, except with the written consent of the lending bank(s).

(*d*) a condition that the Borrower and its subsidiaries will maintain reasonable insurance covering its assets and business.

(*e*) a condition that the Borrower will maintain its corporate existence.

(*f*) a condition that the Borrower will maintain current assets, current liabilities, working capital, tangible net worth and total liabilities over or below a certain specified figure as the case may be.

15. Pari Passu and Negative Pledge

(1) The Borrower warrants and undertakes that its obligations hereunder **17.26** will at all times constitute direct, unconditional, unsecured, unsubordinated and general obligations of, and will rank at all times at least *pari passu* in all respects with all other present and future outstanding unsecured indebtedness issued, created or assumed by, the Borrower.

(2) The Borrower undertakes that from and after the date hereof and so long as any amount payable hereunder is outstanding or any of the Total Commitments is in force, the Borrower will not, and will procure that no Public Financial Establishment will, create or permit to exist any Encumbrance on or over any of the present or future assets (including the gold and foreign currency reserves of the Borrower) or revenues of any of them as security for any present or future loan, debt, guarantee or other obligation (whether of the Borrower, any Public Establishment or any other person, firm, body, company or other legal entity) unless all the Borrower's obligations hereunder (whether in respect of principal, interest or otherwise) either:

    (i) share (in a manner satisfactory to the Majority Banks) the security afforded by such Encumbrance equally and rateably with the loan, debt, guarantee or other obligation secured thereby, or

    (ii) receive (in a manner satisfactory to the Majority Banks) the benefit of an Encumbrance on other assets or revenues of the Borrower which the Majority Banks judge to be equivalent to that granted to such loan, debt, guarantee or other obligation.

Notwithstanding the above, there shall be disregarded for the purposes of this Clause 15(2):

   (i) pledges of or charges on the present or future assets or revenues of the Borrower or .... created or granted at any time hereafter in favour of the central government or central bank of any country or the Bank for International Settlements or the International Bank for Reconstruction and Development;

  (ii) any Encumbrance created or granted previously or at any time hereafter on any fixed asset of the Borrower or any Public Financial Establishment to secure the purchase price or cost of construction thereof or improvement or addition thereto or to secure any loan incurred no later than sixty days after such acquisition or after the completion of such construction, improvement or addition and which is used solely to pay such purchase price or cost; and

 (iii) liens which arose or may arise by operation of law, including tax or other statutory liens, to secure obligations incurred in the ordinary course of the affairs of any Public Financial Establishment which are either not due and payable or are being contested in good faith and with respect to which, in either case, adequate reserves are being maintained.

16. Events of Default

17.27 Upon the occurrence of any of the following events:

(*a*) the Borrower shall fail to pay when due any principal of or interest on any of the Loans hereunder or any other amount payable hereunder or under any agreement in connection herewith entered into with either Agent, any Manager and/or any Bank; or

(*b*) the Borrower shall default in the due performance and observance of any other provision contained in this Agreement and such default (if capable of remedy) shall remain unremedied for thirty days after notice thereof shall have been given by the Dollar Agent to the Borrower; or

(*c*) any representation, warranty or statement made or deemed to be repeated in this Agreement or in any notice, certificate, statement or the Information Memorandum delivered, made or issued by or on behalf of the Borrower hereunder or in connection herewith or any information provided by the Borrower to any of the Agents, the Managers and the Banks hereunder shall be at any time incorrect in any respect or any such representation, warranty or statement would, if made or repeated at any time with reference to the facts and circumstances then subsisting, be incorrect in any respect at that time; or

(*d*) there shall occur any default by the Borrower or any Public Establishment in the due and punctual payment of the principal of, or premium or prepayment charge, if any, or interest on, any other loan indebtedness or indebtedness in respect of monies raised by the issue of debentures, notes, bonds or other similar securities in a capital market, of or assumed or guaranteed by the Borrower of such Public Establishment (other than in respect of Internal Indebtedness of a Public Establishment which is not a Public Financial Establishment) when as the same shall become due and payable, and such default shall continue for more than the original period of grace, if any, applicable thereto, unless such payment is being contested in good faith by the Borrower or such Public Establishment and reserves at least equal to the amount of the contested payment are being maintained by it (the term "original period of grace" as used herein meaning that grace period fixed by the terms of the agreement or instrument under which such indebtedness was created, but specifically not including any extension in the time permitted for such payment or any waiver or delay in the requirement for such payment which has been separately agreed to between the obligor and obligee); or

(*e*) there shall occur any event (other than a default in payment) giving the creditor the right to demand repayment in respect of any other loan indebtedness or indebtedness in respect of monies raised by the issue of debentures, notes, bonds or other similar securities in a capital marker, of or assumed or guaranteed by the Borrower or any Public Establishment (other than in respect of Internal Indebtedness of a Public Establishment which is not a Public Financial Establishment) whether such event shall be acted upon or not, or any such loan indebtedness or other indebtedness as aforesaid shall become due and payable prior to its stated maturity; or

(*f*) the Borrower:

(i) shall be unable to pay its debts as they fall due; or
(ii) shall propose, commence negotiations with a view to or enter into any arrangement or composition with or for the benefit of its creditors or any of them; or
(iii) shall propose, declare or impose a moratorium on the payment of indebtedness of or assumed or guaranteed by it; or

(*g*) any encumbrance shall become entitled to attach, to foreclose or otherwise to realise any security interest in, or any judgment or other creditor shall become entitled to levy any execution on, any material part of the assets of any Public Establishment other than a Secondary Public Establishment (the term "Secondary Public Establishment" as used herein meaning any domestic corporation the majority of whose capital or voting stock is owned directly or indirectly by the Borrower and which is not a Public Financial Establishment or public utility, does not hold or enjoy a monopoly granted, sanctioned or otherwise provided by the Borrower directly or indirectly with respect to any goods or services, does not hold any concession or licence granted or provided directly or indirectly by the Borrower and is not organised or established directly or indirectly by the Borrower pursuant to any statute, regulation or authorisation other than the general corporation law of the Republic of ....), or any attachment, levy or similar measure shall be made in respect of any such assets and has not been discharged, cancelled or withdrawn within thirty days after the making thereof; or

17.28

(*h*) there shall occur any other event, of an extraordinary nature, which, in the reasonable judgment of the Majority Banks, would materially and adversely affect the ability of the Borrower to perform its obligations hereunder,

then and in any such event, and at any time thereafter if any such event shall then be continuing, the Dollar Agent may and shall if so directed by the Majority Banks by notice to the Borrower:

  (i) declare that the obligations of the Agents and the Banks hereunder and the undrawn amount of the Total Commitments shall be cancelled forthwith whereupon the same shall be so cancelled forthwith; and/or

  (ii) declare all the Loans immediately due and payable whereupon the same shall become immediately due and payable together with all interest accrued thereon and all other amounts payable hereunder.

17. Default Indemnity

17.29 The Borrower shall indemnify each Agent, each Manager and each Bank against any loss or reasonable expenses which such Agent, Manager or Bank may sustain or incur as a consequence of any default in payment of the principal amount of the Loans or any part thereof or interest accrued thereon or any other amount due hereunder or as a consequence of the occurrence of any Event of Default hereunder, including but not limited to loss of applicable Margin and any loss or expenses sustained or incurred in liquidating or employing deposits from third parties acquired to effect or maintain the Loans or any part thereof. A statement of the relevant Agent, Manager or Bank, as the case may be, of the amount of any such loss or expenses shall, in the absence of manifest error, be conclusive and binding on the parties hereto.

18. Control Accounts

17.30 Each Bank will maintain and keep accounts showing the aggregate amount of all sums advanced from time to time by such Bank hereunder together with the interest and other charges accrued thereon from time to time and all payments with respect thereto made by the Borrower from time to time pursuant to this Agreement. The accounts kept by each Bank shall constitute prima facie evidence of such Bank's participation in the relevant Loans, of such accruals and of such payments.

Each Agent will maintain a memorandum account showing the aggregate amount of the relevant Loans and all payments with respect thereto made by the Borrower from time to time pursuant to this Agreement.

19. The Agents and the Managers

(I) APPOINTMENT AND RESPONSIBILITY

17.31 Each Bank hereby irrevocable appoints and authorises each Agent to act as its agent hereunder with such powers as are expressly delegated to such Agent by the terms of this Agreement, together with such other powers as are reasonably incidental thereto. Neither Agent shall have any duties or responsibilities except those expressly set out in this Agreement. As to any matters not expressly provided for by this Agreement, each Agent shall act hereunder or in connection herewith in accordance with the instructions of the Majority Banks, but, in the absence of any such instructions, such Agent may (but shall not be obliged to act as it shall deem fit in the best interests of the Banks and any such instructions and any action taken by such Agent in accordance therewith shall be binding upon all the Banks, but in any event neither Agent is obliged or authorised (without first obtaining such Bank's consent so to act), by reason of this Agreement, to act on behalf of any Bank in any litigation, arbitration, claim, proceeding or any action of a similar nature whatsoever. Neither Agent shall, by reason of this Agreement, be deemed to be a trustee for the benefit of any Bank, the Borrower or any other person. Neither Agent nor any Manager nor any of their respective directors, officers, employees or agents shall be responsible to any Bank for any recitals, statements, representations or warranties contained in this Agreement, the Information Memorandum or in any certificate or other document referred to, or provided for in, or received by any of them under, this Agreement, for the value, validity, effectiveness, genuineness, enforceability or sufficiency of this Agreement or any other document referred to, or provided for, herein or any collateral provided for hereby or for any failure by the Borrower to perform its obligations hereunder. Each Agent may employ agents and attorneys-in-fact and shall not be responsible to the Banks for the negligence or misconduct of any such agents or attorneys-in-fact selected by it with reasonable care. Neither Agent nor any of its directors, officers, employees or agents shall be responsible to the Banks for any action taken or omitted to be taken by it or them under or in connection herewith, except for its or their own negligence or wilful misconduct. Each Agent may refrain from doing anything which would or might in its opinion (i) be contrary to the law of any jurisdiction or any official directive or (ii) render it liable to any person, and may do anything which in its opinion is necessary to comply with any such law or directive.

(2) DOCUMENTATION

Each Agent shall be entitled to rely upon any certificate, notice or other document (including any cable or telex) believed by it to be genuine and correct and to have been signed or sent by or on behalf of the proper person or persons, and upon the advice and statements of legal counsel, independent accountants and other experts selected by such Agent. Each Agent may deem and treat each Bank (or assignee of any Bank of which such Agent has received notice as provided in this sentence) as the holder of the participation in the Loan or Loans made by such Bank (or as the holder of such participation acquired by such assignee) for all purposes hereof unless and until a notice of the assignment or transfer thereof satisfactory to such Agent signed by such Bank (or such assignee) shall have been furnished to such Agent.

(3) KNOWLEDGE OF DEFAULT

Neither Agent shall be deemed to have knowledge of the occurrence of a **17.32** Default unless such Agent has received notice from a Bank or the Borrower describing such a Default and stating that such notice is a "Notice of Default." In the event that either Agent receives such a notice of the occurrence of a Default or officers of such Agent engaged in the performance of such Agent's functions hereunder otherwise have actual knowledge that a Default has occurred, such Agent shall give notice thereof to the other Agent, whereupon the Dollar Agent shall promptly notify all the Banks. The Dollar Agent shall use all reasonable endeavours to consult the ECU Agent and shall take such action with respect of such Event of Default as shall be reasonably directed by the Majority Banks, provided that, unless and until the Dollar Agent shall have received such directions and prior to any consultation with the ECU Agent, if such consultation should not prove to be practicable, the Dollar Agent may (but shall not be obliged to) take such action, or refrain from taking such action, with respect to such Event of Default as it shall deem advisable in the best interests of the Banks.

(4) ADDITIONAL RIGHTS

With respect to its Commitment and its participation in the Loans (if any), each of the Agents and the Managers in its capacity as a Bank shall have the same rights and powers hereunder as any other Bank and may exercise the same as though it were not an Agent or a Manager, and the terms "Bank" or "Banks" shall, unless the context otherwise indicates, include the Agents and the Managers in their individual capacities. The Agents and the Managers may accept deposits from, lend money to and generally engage in any kind of banking, trust or other business with the Borrower (and any Public Establishment) as if they were not, respectively, an Agent or a Manager and may accept fees and other consideration from the Borrower for services in connection with this Agreement and otherwise without having to account for the same to the Banks.

(5) INDEMNITY FOR AGENT

17.33 The Dollar Banks and the ECU Banks agree to indemnify, respectively, the Dollar Agent and the ECU Agent, in respect of the duties to be performed by such Agent on behalf of such Banks, and the Banks agree to indemnify the Dollar Agent, in respect of the duties to be performed by the Dollar Agent on behalf of all the Banks, (all to the extent not reimbursed by the Borrower hereunder but without limiting its obligations hereunder) rateably in accordance with their respective participations in the Dollar Loans, ECU Loans or Loans, as the case may be, (or, if no relevant Loan is outstanding hereunder at the relevant time, rateably in accordance with their respective relevant Commitments), for any and all liabilities, obligations, losses, damages, penalties, actions, judgments, suits, costs, expenses or disbursements of any kind and nature whatsoever which may be imposed on, incurred by, or asserted against, each Agent in any way relating to or arising out of this Agreement or any other document contemplated by or referred to herein or therein or the transactions contemplated hereby or thereby (including, without limitation, the charges, expenses and Taxes which the Borrower is obliged to pay under Clauses 21 and 22, but excluding, unless a Default has occurred, normal administrative costs and expenses incidental to the performance of its agency duties hereunder and any agency fee due to such Agent under Clause 20(2)(iii) or the enforcement of any of the terms hereof or of any such other documents, provided that no Bank shall be liable for any of the foregoing to the extent they arise from such Agent's negligence or wilful misconduct.

(6) REPORT

Promptly after its receipt thereof, each Agent will forward to the other Agent and each relevant Bank a copy of each report, notice or other document required by this Agreement to be delivered to such Agent by the Borrower for such Bank, provided that the Dollar Agent shall not be obliged to forward to any Bank a copy of any document received by it under Clause 12 unless such Bank so requests.

(7) INDEPENDENT INVESTIGATION

Each Bank acknowledges that it has independently and without reliance on **17.34** the Agents, the Managers or any other Bank, and based on such documents and information as it has deemed appropriate, made its own investigation of the affairs and financial condition of the Borrower and agrees that it will, independently and without reliance upon the Agents, the Managers or any other Bank, and based on such documents and information as it shall deem appropriate at the time, continue to make its own analysis and decisions in taking or not taking action under this Agreement. Neither the Agents nor the Managers shall be required to keep themselves informed as to the performance or observance by the Borrower of this Agreement or any other document referred to or provided for herein or in connection herewith. Except (in the case of the Agents) for notices, reports an other documents and information expressly required to be furnished to the Banks by either Agent hereunder, neither the Agents nor the Managers shall have any duty or responsibility to provide any Bank with any credit or other information concerning the affairs, financial condition or business of the Borrower which may come into the possession of any Agent or any Manager. Nothing in this Agreement shall oblige either Agent to disclose any information relating to the Borrower if such disclosure would or might in the opinion of such Agent constitute a breach of any law or duty of secrecy or confidence.

(8) AVAILABILITY OF PARTICIPATION

Unless the relevant Agent shall have received notice from a relevant Bank not less than one Business Day prior to the date for the making of a Loan that such Bank does not intend to make available to such Agent such Bank's participation in such Loan, such Agent, may assume that such Bank has made its said participation available to such Agent on the due date in accordance herewith and in reliance upon such assumption, such Agent may (but shall not be obliged to) make available to the Borrower a corresponding amount. If the amount of such participation is not in fact made available to such Agent by such Bank, such Agent shall be entitled to recover such amount (together with interest thereon at the rate determined by such Agent to be its cost of funds in the circumstances) on demand from such Bank or, if such Bank fails to reimburse such Agent therefore within five Business Days of such demand, from the Borrower, but without prejudice to the rights of the Borrower against such Bank.

(9) NOTICE OF PAYMENT

17.35 Unless the relevant Agent shall have received a notice from the Borrower not less than one Business Day prior to the date on which any payment is due to such Agent from the Borrower hereunder that the Borrower does not intend to make such payment, such Agent may assume that the Borrower has made such payment when so due and such Agent may (but shall not be obliged to), in reliance upon such assumption, make available to each relevant Bank on such payment date an amount equal to such Bank's *pro rata* share of such assumed payment. If the Borrower does not in fact make such payment to such Agent on such date, such Bank shall forthwith on demand repay to such Agent the amount made available to such Bank together with interest thereon at a rate determined by such Agent, in accordance with its usual banking practice, for advances in Dollars or ECUs, as the case may be, and for similar duration to a bank of like standing to such Bank.

(10) NO DUTY TO NOTIFY FAILURE TO PERFORM OBLIGATIONS

Neither Agent shall have any responsibility (i) to the Borrower on account of the failure of any Bank or the other Agent to perform its obligations hereunder, or (ii) to any Bank or the other Agent on account of the failure of the Borrower to perform its obligations hereunder. The Managers shall have no duties, responsibilities or obligations of any kind hereunder or in connection herewith.

(11) ALTERNATIVE INTEREST RATE

17.36   (*a*) If the relevant Agent serves an alternative interest rate notice on the relevant Banks in accordance with Clause 9(1), each of the relevant Banks shall, within three Business Days after the receipt of such notice or such longer period as such Agent may agree, notify the relevant Agent of the minimum rate of interest which would be acceptable to such Bank during such Interest Period in respect of its participation in the relevant Loans or the relevant part thereof and the relevant Agent shall rely upon that notification for all purposes when negotiating or setting the interest rate or interest rates for the relevant Interest Period or Interest Periods determined in accordance with Clause 9(1) and shall (when so setting) set and notify to the Borrower such rate for such Bank in accordance with Clause 9(1). In the event that any Bank fails to notify such Agent of such rate as aforesaid, such Agent shall be entitled to set such rate on behalf of such Bank as it considers reasonable.

(*b*) If the ECU Agent serves a notice on the Borrower in accordance with Clause 9(3), each ECU Bank shall, within three Business Days after the receipt of such notice (or such longer period as the ECU Agent may agree), notify the ECU Agent of the currency or currencies and the minimum rate(s) of interest and the Interest Period or Periods and Interest Date or Dates and/or an alternative basis which would be acceptable to such ECU Bank during the relevant Interest Period in respect of its participation in the ECU Loans (or the relevant part thereof) and the ECU Agent shall rely upon that notification for all purposes when attempting to agree with the Borrower a currency or currencies, an Interest Period or Periods and an Interest Date or Dates in accordance with Clause 9(3). In the event that any

Bank fails to notify the ECU Agent of such matters as aforesaid the ECU Agent shall not so reach agreement with the Borrower. If the Borrower and the ECU Agent are unable to agree upon a currency or currencies, an interest rate or rates, an Interest Period or Periods and an Interest Date or Dates and/or an alternative basis acceptable to them within a period of forty-five days from the date of notice from the ECU Agent in accordance with Clause 9(3), each ECU Bank shall, within three Business Days after the receipt of notice of such failure to agree (or such longer period as the ECU Agent may agree), notify the ECU Agent of its cost of funding its participation in the ECU Loans (or the relevant part thereof) in Dollars and the Interest Period or Periods and Interest Date or Dates which would be acceptable to such Bank during such Interest Period or Periods in respect of its participation in the ECU Loans (or the relevant part) being expressed in Dollars and the ECU Agent shall rely upon the notification for all purposes when setting an interest rate or rates, an Interest Period or Periods and an Interest Date or Dates in accordance with Clause 9(3) and shall set and notify to the Borrower all of such matters in accordance with Clause 9(3). In the event that such Bank fails to notify the ECU Agent of such matters as aforesaid, the ECU Agent shall be entitled to set such rate on behalf of such ECU Bank as it considers reasonable.

(12) RESIGNATION OF AGENT

Subject to the appointment and acceptance of a successor Agent as provided **17.37** below, each Agent may resign at any time by giving not less than thirty days' notice thereof to the Banks and the Borrower or may be removed by (i) in the case of the Dollar Agent, either the Dollar Majority Banks or the Majority Banks or (ii) in the case of the ECU Agent, the ECU Majority Banks and, in either case, at any time upon being given not less than thirty days' notice thereof by the relevant Majority Banks, which shall also notify the Borrower thereof. Upon any such resignation or removal, as the case may be, the Majority Banks, in the case of the Dollar Agent, or the ECU Majority Banks, in the case of the ECU Agent, shall have the right subject to the prior consent (not to be unreasonably withheld or delayed) of the Borrower to appoint a successor Agent. If no successor Agent shall have been so appointed by the Majority Banks or the ECU Majority Banks, as the case may be, and shall have accepted such appointment within thirty days after the retiring Agent's giving of notice of resignation or being given notice of removal, as the case may be, then the retiring Agent shall on behalf of the Banks, appoint a successor Agent, which shall be a reputable and experienced bank which has an officer (or a subsidiary with an office) in London and the Borrower's consent thereto shall not be required. Upon the assumption or acceptance of any appointment as Agent hereunder by a successor Agent, such successor Agent shall thereupon succeed to and become vested with all the rights, powers, privileges and duties of the retiring Agent, and the retiring Agent shall be discharged from its duties and obligations hereunder. After any retiring Agent's resignation or removal hereunder as Agent, the provisions of this Clause 19 shall continue in effect for its benefit in respect of any actions taken or omitted to be taken by it while it was acting as an Agent.

20. Fees

(1) COMMITMENT FEE

17.38 The Borrower will pay to the Dollar Agent and the ECU Agent for distribution to, respectively, the Dollar Banks and the ECU Banks a commitment fee computer at the rate of .... per cent., (......%) per annum on the daily undrawn, uncancelled amount of, respectively, the Dollar Commitments and the ECU Commitments during the period beginning thirty days after the date hereof and ending on the Term Date (both dates inclusive). Accrued commitment fee shall be payable on whichever is the earlier of the Term Date and the day on which the Total Commitments are fully utilised or cancelled. Commitment fee shall accrue from day to day and be calculated on the basis of a year of three hundred and sixty days and for the actual number of days elapsed.

(2) MANAGEMENT AND AGENCY FEES

The Borrower shall pay:

(i) to the Agents for the account of the Lead Managers, the management fee as agreed between the Agents, on behalf of the Lead Managers, and the Borrower in a letter of even date herewith;

(ii) to the ECU Agent for the account of the Agents and the Lead Managers, the expenses incurred by the Agents and the Lead Managers in connection with the negotiation, preparation, syndication and execution of this Agreement as agreed between the Agents, on behalf of the Agents and the Lead Managers, and the Borrower in a letter of even date herewith; and

(iii) to each Agent for the account of such Agent, the agency fee as agreed between the Agents and the Borrower in a letter of even date herewith.

21. Expenses

17.39 The Borrower shall reimburse the Agents, the Managers and the Banks on demand for the charges and expenses incurred by them in connection with the enforcement of, or the preservation of any rights under, this Agreement (including legal and out-of-pocket expenses and all Value Added Tax thereon).

22. Stamp Duties

17.40 The Borrower shall pay or indemnify the Agents, the Managers and the Banks against any and all stamp, registration and similar Taxes or charges imposed by law or by any governmental authority which may be payable or determined to be payable in connection with the execution, delivery, performance or enforcement of this Agreement. The Borrower shall indemnify the Agents, the Managers and the Banks against any and all liabilities with respect to or resulting from delay or omission to pay such Taxes or charges.

23. Waivers, Remedies Cumulative

No failure to exercise and no delay in exercising on the part of either Agent,   **17.41**
any Manager or any Bank any right, power or privilege hereunder shall operate as a waiver thereof, nor shall any single or partial exercise of any right, power or privilege preclude any other or further exercise thereof, or the exercise of any other right, power or privilege. The rights and remedies herein provided are cumulative and not exclusive of any rights or remedies provided by law.

24. Notices

All notices, requests, demands or other communications to or upon the   **17.42**
respective parties hereto shall be given or made in writing or by telex or cable and shall be deemed to be duly given or made when delivered (in the case of personal delivery or letter) and when despatched (in the case of telex) and on the first Business Day following despatch (in the case of cable) to the party to which such notice, request, demand or other communication is required or permitted to be given under this Agreement addressed as follows:

   (i) if to the Dollar Agent, at .... England (telex number: ....) attention: Loans Administration Department; or

  (ii) if the ECU Agent, at .... England (telex number: .... A/B G) attention: Loans Administration Department, reference Republic of .... /84; or

 (iii) if to any of the Dollar Banks, at its address or telex number, specified therefor in Part I of Exhibit A; or

 (iv) if to any of the ECU Banks, at its address or telex number specified therefor in Part II of Exhibit A; or

  (v) if to the Borrower, at ....

or at such other address or telex number as the relevant addressee may hereafter specify for such purposes to the others by notice, provided that any notice or other communication from the Borrower relating to draw-down, prepayment, repayment or details of payment, if made by telex, shall be made by tested telex. All such notices, requests, demands or other communications shall be effective upon receipt, provided that any notice, request, demand or other communication received on a non-working day or after business hours in the place of receipt shall be deemed received on the next following working day in such place.

A copy of any notice required to be given to either Agent by the Borrower shall at the same time be sent by the Borrower by telex to the other Agent. Notice by any party hereto to an Agent other than the Agent specified to receive such notice hereunder shall not constitute notice to the Agent so specified.

25. Assignments

(1) SUCCESSORS AND ASSIGNS

17.43 This Agreement shall be binding upon and inure to the benefit of the Borrower, the Banks, the Managers and the Agents and their respective successors and assigns, except that the Borrower may not assign or transfer all or any part of its rights or obligations hereunder without the prior consent of all the Banks.

(2) ASSIGNMENTS AND TRANSFERS BY BANKS

Each Bank may at any time change its Lending Office hereunder or, with the prior consent of the Borrower (such consent not to be unreasonably withheld or delayed), assign or otherwise transfer all or any part of its rights or obligations hereunder, provided that:

(*a*) no such consent shall be required in the case of an assignment or transfer to an affiliate, subsidiary or holding company (or subsidiary of such holding company) of such Bank or to another Bank or an affiliate, subsidiary or holding company (or subsidiary or such holding company) of such other Bank;

(*b*) if any assignment or transfer, which is made in accordance with paragraph (*a*) above, or any change of Lending Office is made, in either case, without the prior consent of the Borrower and results at the time thereof in additional amounts becoming due under Clause 10(2) or amounts becoming due under Clause 11(1), the assignee or transferee or Bank acting through such new Lending Office shall be entitled to receive such additional amounts or amounts only to the extent that the assignor or transferor or Bank acting through its previous Lending Office would have been entitled had there been no such assignment, transfer or change of Lending Office;

(*c*) the assignor or transferor shall be relieved of those obligations corresponding to the rights so assigned or transferred only upon:

   (i) the assignee or transferee confirming to the relevant Agent and the Dollar Agent (if the relevant Agent is the ECU Agent) and the Borrower that it undertakes to be bound by the terms of this Agreement and accepts all the terms hereof as if it had been an original Bank party hereto, in form and substance satisfactory to such Agent(s); and

  (ii) the assignee or transferee agreeing to pay to the relevant Agent and the Dollar Agent (if the relevant Agent is the ECU Agent) on demand all expenses certified by each such Agent as having been properly incurred by or in connection with the assignment or transfer in question by the assignor or transferor under this Clause 25(2); and

(*d*) any assignee or transferee or Bank which changes its Lending Office hereunder shall promptly give notice thereof to the Borrower (through the relevant Agent).

(3) REFERENCE BANKS

In the event that a relevant Reference Bank (or, in the case of a relevant **17.44** Reference Bank which is not also a relevant Bank, in the event that the relevant Bank with which it is associated) shall assign the whole of its rights hereunder or shall cease to be one of the relevant Banks, the relevant Agent will, in consultation with the Borrower, appoint a relevant Bank (or associated company of such Bank) to replace such Bank (or associated company of such Bank) as a Reference Bank.

(4) DISCLOSURE

Each Bank may disclose to a proposed assignee or transferee or sub-participant information in the possession of such Bank relating to the Borrower and furnished in connection herewith.

26. Currency Indemnity

(1) In the event of a judgment or order being rendered by any court or tri- **17.45** bunal for the payment of any amounts owing to any of the Agents, the Managers and the Banks under this Agreement or for the payment of damages in respect of any breach of this Agreement or under or in respect of a judgment or order of another court or tribunal for the payment of such amounts or damages, such judgment or order being expressed in a currency (the "Judgment Currency") other than the currency payable hereunder (the "Agreed Currency"), the Borrower shall indemnify and hold harmless each Agent, each Manager and each Bank against any deficiency and shall be entitled to be repaid any surplus in terms of the Agreed Currency of such Bank arising or resulting from any variation as between (i) the rate of exchange at which the Agreed Currency is converted into the Judgment Currency for the purposes of such judgment or order, and (ii) the rate of exchange at which such Agent, such Manager or such Bank, as the case may be, is able to purchase the Agreed Currency with the amount of the Judgment Currency actually received by such Agent, such Manager or such Bank.

(2) The above indemnity shall constitute a separate and independent obligation of the Borrower from its other obligations hereunder and shall apply irrespective of any indulgence granted by any of the Agents, the Managers and the Banks.

(3) The term "rate of exchange" shall include any premiums and costs of exchange payable in connection with the purchase of, or conversion into, the relevant currency, by the relevant Agent, Manager or Bank, as the case may be and the relevant Agent shall advise the Borrower of the details of the relevant rate of exchange.

27. Redistribution of Payments

If at any time the proportion which any Bank (the "receiving Bank") has **17.46** received or recovered (whether by set-off or otherwise) in respect of its portion of any sum due from the Borrower hereunder is greater (the amount of excess being herein referred to as the "excess amount") than the proportion thereof received or recovered by the relevant Bank receiving or recovering the smallest proportion thereof (which shall include a nil receipt), taking into account any earlier payment which has fallen due under this Agreement but has not been satisfied in full (whether or not due from the Borrower to the Banks participating in the same Loans), then the receiving Bank shall promptly notify the relevant Agent and the Dollar Agent (if not the relevant Agent) and:

(i) the receiving Bank shall promptly and in any event within thirty days of receipt or recovery of the excess amount pay to the Dollar Agent an amount equal to the excess amount;

(ii) the Dollar Agent (after consultation with the ECU Agent) shall treat such payment as if it were a payment by the Borrower on account of a sum owed to the Banks (whether or not participating in the same Loans), and, if made in Dollars but in respect of a sum due in respect of the ECU Loans, as if it were the ECU Agent and the sum was due from the Borrower in Dollars under the terms of this Agreement; and

(iii) as between the Borrower and the receiving Bank the excess amount shall be treated as not having been paid, while as between the Borrower and each Bank it shall be treated as having been paid to the extent receivable by such Bank,

provided that:

(i) where such amount referred to in paragraph (i) above is in respect of the ECU Loans, it shall be paid in Dollars, the amount of which shall be calculated in accordance with the provisions of Exhibit B and as if the Day of Valuation (as therein defined) was the second Business Day prior to the date of such payment;

(ii) where a receiving Bank has recovered any amount as a consequence of the satisfaction or enforcement of a judgment obtained in any legal action or proceedings to which it is a party, this Clause 27 shall not apply so as to benefit any other Bank which (being entitled so to do) did not join with the receiving Bank and did not give prior notice of its involvement in such action or proceedings to the relevant Agent and the Dollar Agent (if not the relevant Agent) for disclosure to the other Banks; and

(iii) where a receiving Bank is subsequently required to repay to the Borrower any amount received or recovered by it and dealt with under paragraphs (i), (ii) and (iii) above, each Bank shall promptly repay to the Dollar Agent for the receiving Bank the portion of such amount distributed to it, together with interest thereon at a rate sufficient to reimburse the receiving Bank for any interest which it has been required to pay to the Borrower in respect of such portion or such amount.

Each Bank shall promptly give notice to the relevant Agent and the Dollar Agent (if not the relevant Agent) of (i) the institution by such Bank of any legal action or proceedings hereunder or in connection herewith prior to such institution and (ii) the receipt or recovery by such Bank of any amount received or recovered otherwise than through the relevant Agent. Upon receipt of any such notice the Dollar Agent will as soon as practicable thereafter notify the ECU Agent (unless it has been notified by such Bank) and all the other Banks.

28. Governing Law

This Agreement and the rights and obligations of the parties hereunder shall **17.47** be governed by and construed in accordance with English law.

29. Waiver of Immunity and Jurisdiction

(1) The Borrower agrees that should either Agent or any Bank bring a legal **17.48** action or proceedings against it or its assets in relation to any matters arising out of this Agreement no immunity from such legal action or proceedings (which shall be deemed to include, without limitation, suit, attachment prior to judgment, other attachment, the obtaining of judgment, execution of other enforcement) shall be claimed by or on behalf of the Borrower or with respect to its assets, the Borrower hereby irrevocably waiving any such right of immunity which it or its assets now has or may hereafter acquire and the Borrower hereby consents generally in respect of any legal action of proceedings arising out of or in connection with this Agreement to the giving out of any relief or the issue of any process in connection with such action or proceedings including, without limitation, the making, enforcement or execution against any property whatsoever of any order or judgment which may be made or given in such action or proceedings.

(2) Any legal action or proceedings with respect to this Agreement against the Borrower or its assets may be brought in the Courts of England or of the Republic of .... or in any of the State Courts or Federal Courts sitting in New York City or elsewhere as any Bank or either Agent may elect, and, by execution and delivery of this Agreement, the Borrower hereby accepts, for itself and in respect of its assets, generally and unconditionally the non-exclusive jurisdiction of the aforesaid Courts and hereby designates, appoints and empowers, in the case of the Courts of England, the Ambassador of the Republic of .... to the Court of St. James's (or, in his absence from London, the person for the time being in charge of the .... Embassy in London) and, in the case of the State or Federal Courts sitting in New York City, the Consul General for the Republic of .... in New York (or, in his absence from New York, the person for the time being in charge of the .... Consulate in New York) to receive, for and on behalf of itself, service of process in such jurisdiction in any legal action or proceedings with respect to this Agreement and agrees that failure by such Process Agent to give notice of such service of process to the Borrower shall not impair or affect the validity of such service or of any judgment based thereon. The Borrower irrevocably waives any objection it may now or hereafter have to the laying of venue of any such action or proceedings in the aforesaid Courts and any claim it may now or hereafter have that any such action or proceedings have been brought in an

inconvenient forum. The Borrower further irrevocably consents to the service of process out of the aforesaid Courts in any such action or proceedings by the mailing of copies thereof by registered or certified airmail, postage prepaid to the Borrower at its said address. Nothing herein shall affect the right to serve process in any other manner permitted by law.

30. Language

17.49 Each document, instrument, notice, certificate and statement referred to herein or to be delivered hereunder shall be in the English language or accompanied by an English translation thereof certified by an officer of the Borrower as accurate. In the case of conflict and unless the Dollar Agent otherwise specifies, the English language version of any such document shall prevail.

31. Severability of Provisions

17.50 Any provision of this Agreement which is prohibited or unenforceable in any jurisdiction shall, as to such jurisdiction, be ineffective to the extent of such prohibition or unenforceability without invalidating the remaining provisions hereof or affecting the validity or enforceability of such provision in any other jurisdiction.

32. Counterparts

17.51 This Agreement may be executed in any number of counterparts and all of such counterparts taken together shall be deemed to constitute one and the same instrument.

IN WITNESS whereof the parties hereto have caused this Agreement to be duly executed on the date first written above.

EXHIBIT A

Part 1: Dollar Banks

17.52 BANKS AND LENDING OFFICES   COMMITMENT
ADDRESSES FOR NOTICES $

Telex No:

Telex No:

Telex No:

Total $

Part 2: ECU Banks

BANKS AND LENDING OFFICES   COMMITMENT   **17.53**
ADDRESSES FOR NOTICES   ECU

Telex No:

Telex No:

Telex No:

Telex No:

Total ECU   ———

EXHIBIT B

Definition of the ECU

(1) For the purposes of this Agreement and subject to paragraph (2) below,   **17.54**
"ECU" means the unit of account known as the ECU that is at present used
in the European Monetary System. The ECU is at present valued on the
basis of specified amounts of the currencies of nine of the member states of
the European Communities as shown below. This basis may be changed by
the European Communities from time to time, including changes in the
components, in which event the basis of valuation of the ECU will change
accordingly. Pursuant to Council Regulation (EEC) No. 3180/78 of
December 18, 1978 the ECU is at present defined as the sum of the following components:

0.828	German Mark
0.0885	Pound Sterling
1.15	French Francs
109.00	Italian Lire
0.286	Dutch Gilder
3.66	Belgian Francs
0.14	Luxembourg Franc
0.217	Danish Krone
0.00759	Irish Pound

(2) In the event that the ECU is not being used in the European Monetary
System or the ECU ceases to be utilised as the basic equivalent of the ECU
in Dollars as of any day on which a calculation pursuant to this Exhibit falls
to be made (the "Day of Valuation") shall be determined as follows:

The components of the ECU for this purpose (each a "Component" and
together the "Components") shall be the currency amounts that were components of the ECU when the ECU was most recently used in the European Monetary System, provided however that, if the ECU is being used

for the settlement of transactions by public institutions of or within the European Economic Community, or was so used after its most recent use in the European Monetary System, the Components shall be:

(i) the currency amounts that are components of the ECU as so used as of the Day of Valuation, or

(ii) the currency amounts that were components of the ECU when it was most recently so used, as the case may be.

The equivalent of the ECU in Dollars shall be calculated by the ECU Agent as the sum of the equivalents in Dollars of the Components. The rates to be used by the ECU Agent for the foregoing purposes shall be the rates of the ECU Agent for the purchase in the London Foreign Exchange Market of Dollars with each of the Components at or about 11.00 a.m. (London time) on the second Business Day prior to the Day of Valuation for value on the Day of Valuation.

EXHIBIT C

Notice of Borrowing

17.55   TO: ....

For the attention of Loans Administration Department

[Date]

Pursuant to Clause 4(2) of the Loan Agreement dated ....
1984 (the "Loan Agreement") between ourselves as Borrower, the Managers and the Banks (as defined therein) and yourselves and
★ ....
as Agents in respect of the Loan facility of $............. and ECU ....,
we hereby give you notice of the following proposed borrowing:

(a) Date: [...................]

(b) Amount: ★$[.......................]/ECU [....................]

(c) Duration of first Interest Period★★: [....
........................]

(d) Payment Instructions★★★: [....]

We confirm that the representations and warranties made by us and set out in Clause 13(1) of the Loan Agreement are true and accurate on the date hereof as if made on such date and that no Default (as defined in the Loan Agreement) has occurred and is continuing or would result from the proposed borrowing.

THE REPUBLIC OF ....

By: ....

Notes

★   Delete as appropriate.
★★   Only in respect of the first Dollar Loan or ECU Loan, as appropriate.
★★★ If not already notified to the relevant Agent.

EXHIBIT D

Legal Opinion   17–56

To:

    as Agents for the Banks herein referred
    to, and to such Banks and the Managers
    referred to below.

[Date   ]

Dear Sirs,

I have acted as legal adviser in .... in connection with the Loan Agreement (the "Loan Agreement") dated .... , 1984 between the Republic of .... (the "Borrower"), the Managers therein defined, the banks and financial institutions therein referred to (the "Banks") and ....
.... and .... as
Agents, under which the Banks have agreed to make available to the Borrower a loan facility of U.S.$ .... and ECU .... upon the terms and conditions therein contained.

Words defined in the Loan Agreement have the same meanings when used herein.

I have examined the following documents:

  (i) an executed copy of the Loan Agreement;
 (ii) Law Number .... of ...., authorising the borrowing of loans in foreign currencies by the Borrower on conditions to be determined by Decree Law;
(iii) Decree Law Number .... of ...., of the Borrower, approving the terms of the facility governed by the Loan Agreement and empowering the Minister for Finance and Planning (or a person or persons authorised by him) to execute and deliver the Loan Agreement on behalf of the Borrower;
(iv) a declaration of the Director General for the Treasury, stating that the Total Commitments under the Loan Agreement fall within the monetary limits for foreign currency borrowings by the Borrower presently authorised by law;
 (v) a letter dated [............], 1984 from the Minister for Finance and Planning, authorising a named person or persons to execute and deliver the Loan Agreement on behalf of the Borrower and to give and sign all notices, certificates and other documents to be delivered by the Borrower thereunder, together with certified specimen signatures of such persons;

(vi) the exemption of the Ministry for Finance and Planning, exempting all payments to be made by the Borrower under the Loan Agreement from .... Taxes on interest in accordance with Articles .... and .... of the Capital Tax Code, as introduced by Decree–Law Number .... of ....;

(vii) a declaration of the Director General for the Treasury, stating that the Ministry of Foreign Affairs has issued instructions to the Ambassador of the Republic of .... to the Court of Saint James's and the Consul General of the Republic of .... in New York authorising them to act as agents for the receipt of service or process in, respectively, England and New York; and

(viii) the opinion of the Attorney General of .... referred to in Clause 12(1)(viii) of the Loan Agreement,

and such other documents as I have considered necessary for the purposes of this opinion.

17.57   Accordingly I am of the opinion that:

(a) The Borrower has the power to enter into and perform the Loan Agreement and to borrow thereunder and has taken all necessary action to authorise the borrowing of the Loans upon the terms and conditions of the Loan Agreement and to authorise the execution, delivery and performance of the Loan Agreement in accordance with its terms.

(b) The Loan Agreement as executed and delivered constitutes a legal, valid and binding obligation of the Borrower enforceable in accordance with its terms.

(c) The execution, delivery and performance of the Loan Agreement will not violate in any respect any provision of (i) the constitution of the Republic of .... or (ii) any .... law, regulation or order applicable to the Borrower.

(d) All authorisations, approvals, consents, licences, exemptions, filings, registrations, notarisations and other requirements under those laws, regulations and orders which are applicable to the Borrower and required in connection with the execution, delivery, performance, validity and enforceability of the Loan Agreement and, with the exception of the Loan Agreement and, with the exception of the Stamp Tax, its admissibility in evidence in the Republic of .... have been obtained or effected and are in full force and effect, there has been no default in the performance of any of the conditions thereof, no fees payable in connection therewith and the Borrower has full authority to make all payments under the Loan Agreement to each Agent in the currency required under the Loan Agreement for the account of the relevant Banks to the accounts provided for in Clause 10(1) of the Loan Agreement.

(e) To the best of my knowledge and on the basis of the declaration referred to in paragraph (iv) above, the borrowing of the full amount of the Total Commitments will not cause any monetary limit for foreign currency borrowings by the Borrower to be exceeded.

(f) An exemption from the payment of capital tax having been granted by the Ministry for Finance and Planning in accordance with Articles

.... and .... of the Capital Tax Code, as introduced by Decree–Law .... of .... the Borrower will not be required under the present law or regulation of the Republic of .... or any Taxing authority thereof or having jurisdiction therein to deduct or withhold any sum from any payment (whether of principal, interest or otherwise) due or to become due from it under the Loan Agreement. Should any deduction or withholding be required in the future the obligation of the Borrower to pay such additional amounts as may be necessary to ensure that each Bank receives a net amount equal to the full amount which it would have received, had payment not been made subject to such deduction or withholding, contained in Clause 10(2) of the Loan Agreement, would be valid and enforceable. If the Borrower were required to make any deduction or withholding for or on account of Taxes from payments to be made under the Loan Agreement and failed to do so, then under the present law, there are no grounds upon which the Tax authorities in the Republic of .... would be entitled to assess any of the Agents, the Managers and the Banks for such Taxes or otherwise to recover such Taxes from any of the Agents, the Managers and the Banks.

(g) [Name of person(s) executing the Loan Agreement] has the right, power and authority to execute the Loan Agreement on behalf of the Borrower and any one of [............] has the right to give any certificates or notices to the Agents and the Banks, all in accordance with the provisions of the Loan Agreement.

(h) No stamp or registration or similar Taxes or charges are payable in the Republic of .... in respect of the Loan Agreement, except for the Stamp Tax.

(i) It is not necessary or advisable, in order to ensure the legality, validity or enforceability of the Loan Agreement or the admissibility in evidence thereof in the Republic of ...., to file, register or record the Loan Agreement or any other instrument relating thereto in any public office or elsewhere in the Republic of .... or to take any other action in relation thereto.

(j) The Borrower can sue and be sued under its own name. It is not **17.58** under .... law entitled to plead sovereign immunity from the jurisdiction of the Courts of the Republic of ...., and none of its assets (save for assets in the public domain or in use for public utility purpose) would be immune from attachment in aid of execution or from execution in any action or proceeding which might be brought in any competent Court of the Republic of .... with respect to any claims arising out of or relating to its obligations under the Loan Agreement.

(k) If the Loan Agreement were sued upon before a Court in the Republic of ...., such Court would recognise and give effect to the provisions of the Loan Agreement whereby the Loan Agreement is expressed to be governed by and construed in accordance with English Law, contained in Clause 28 of the Loan Agreement, and any judgment against the Borrower obtained in the Courts of England or the State or Federal Courts sitting in New York City will, after being duly reviewed and confirmed by the Court of Appeal in .... in accordance with the provisions of Article .... of the .... Code of Civil Procedure, be enforceable in the Republic of .... The conditions for confirmation of a foreign judgment, as set out in Article .... of that Code, are, in outline (i) that the foreign judgment is final and conclusive and given by a competent court (and the English Courts and the State or Federal Courts sitting in New York City will be so regarded, provided that the requirements of Article .... of the .... Code of Civil Procedure are satisfied), (ii) that the defendant was validly served with process and (iii) that the judgment does not contravene .... public policy. In my opinion the procedures for service of process set out in the Loan Agreement are valid for this purpose (provided that they are valid under the laws of England, in the case of proceedings in England, and the relevant State or Federal laws, in the case of proceedings in New York City) and there is nothing in the Loan Agreement which it would be contrary to .... public policy to enforce. If these conditions are fulfilled, the .... Courts would not re-examine the merits of the case, except to the extent necessary to ascertain that such conditions have been fulfilled. The provisions for submission by the Borrower to the jurisdiction of the English Courts and the Federal or State Courts sitting in New York City and the provisions for substituted service (including the appointment of the respective persons named therein to accept service on behalf of the Borrower in any proceedings in such Courts) are valid, binding and effective under the law of the Republic of ....

17.59   (*l*) A judgment in a Court of the Republic of .... for payment of a sum due under the Loan Agreement in Dollars or ECUs may be expressed in such currency.

(*m*) The indebtedness of the Borrower under the Loan Agreement ranks and will rank at all times at least *pari passu* with all other outstanding unsecured indebtedness, present or future, of the Borrower.

(*n*) It is not necessary under the law of constitution of the Republic of .... (i) in order to enable any of the Agents, the Managers and the Banks to enforce its rights under the Loan Agreement or (ii) by reason of the execution, delivery and performance of the Loan Agreement by each of them that any of them should be licensed, qualified or otherwise entitled to carry on business in the Republic of ....

(*o*) None of the Agents, the Managers and the Banks is or will be deemed to be resident, domiciled or carrying on business in the Republic of ...., or subject to taxation in the Republic of .... by reason only of the execution, performance and/or enforcement of the Loan Agreement.

The above opinion is expressed only with respect to the laws of the Republic of ....

Yours faithfully
[signature]

EXHIBIT E

English Legal Opinion   17.60

To:

as Agents for the Banks herein
referred to, and to such Banks and
the Managers referred to below.

[Date]

Dear Sirs,

We have acted as legal advisers in England in connection with the Loan Agreement (the "Loan Agreement") dated ...., 1984 between the Republic of .... (the "Borrower"), the Managers therein defined, the banks and financial institutions therein referred to (the "Banks") and .... and ....
.... as Agents, under which the Banks have agreed to make available to the Borrower a loan facility of U.S.$ ....: and ECU .... upon the terms and conditions therein contained.

We have received instructions from and participated in discussions with ....
.... (one of the Managers referred to above) about the provisions contained in the Loan Agreement.

We have examined the following documents:

(a) an executed copy of the Loan Agreement; and
(b) copies of the opinions referred to in paragraphs (viii) and (ix) of Clause 12(1) of the Loan Agreement.

For the purposes of giving this opinion, we have assumed that the Loan Agreement has been duly authorised, executed and delivered by each of the parties thereto.

Based upon the foregoing and subject to any matters not disclosed to us, we are of the opinion that, so far as the laws of England are concerned and subject to the qualifications set out below, the Loan Agreement constitutes a valid and legally binding obligation of the Borrower in accordance with its terms.

Further, we are of the opinion that no stamp, registration or other similar taxes or charges are payable in the United Kingdom in respect of the execution or delivery of the Loan Agreement.

The qualifications to which this opinion is subject are as follows: 17.61

(i) Clause 8(4) of the Loan Agreement provides for interest to be paid on overdue amounts. Such interest may amount to a penalty under English law and may therefore not be recoverable.

(ii) We express no opinion as to the enforceability of Clause 26 of the Loan Agreement (Currency Indemnity). However, an English Court would probably not give judgment for a monetary amount, due in a currency other than sterling, in such other currency. However, whilst we know of no authority, we consider it likely that an English court would give judgment in one or more of the component currencies of the ECU rather than in ECUs.

(iii) We express no opinion as to Clause 27 of the Loan Agreement (Redistribution of Payments).

(iv) As regards Clause 29(2) of the Loan Agreement (Jurisdiction), an English court may stay proceedings if concurrent proceedings are being brought elsewhere.

(v) Certain property of the Borrower will be immune from legal proceedings by virtue of diplomatic privilege.

(vi) There could be circumstances in which an English court would not treat as conclusive those certifications and determinations which the Loan Agreement states are to be so treated.

(vii) Nothing in this opinion is to be taken as indicating that the remedy of an order for specific performance or the issue of an injunction would be available in an English court in respect of the obligations arising under the Loan Agreement in that such remedies are available only at the discretion of the court.

(viii) The obligations of the Borrower are subject to all laws affecting creditors' rights generally.

(ix) The effectiveness of terms exculpating a party from a liability or duty otherwise owed is limited by law.

(x) No opinion is expressed with respect to the laws of any jurisdiction other than England. It is assumed that no foreign law affects the conclusions stated above.

This opinion is given for the sole benefit of the Agents, the Managers and the Banks which are the original parties to the Loan Agreement and may not be disclosed to any other person.

Yours faithfully,
[signature]

SIGNATORIES

17.62   The Borrower:

THE REPUBLIC OF

By:

The Lead Managers:

By:

By:

By:

The Managers:

By:

By:

By:

By:

By:

By:

By:

The Co-Managers

By:

By:

The Banks:

By:

By:

By:

By:

By:

By:

18. Specimen Euro-Commercial Paper Dealer Agreement

18.01   THIS AGREEMENT is made on ...., 19   Between:—

(1) .... (the "Issuer");

(2) .... (the "Guarantor");

(3) .... and

.... (together the "Dealers"); and

(4) .... (the "Issue Agent").

(A) The Issuer proposes from time to time to borrow money denominated in U.S. Dollars available in the Euromarkets by issuing and selling bearer Notes, to be guaranteed by the Guarantor and in an aggregate principal amount outstanding at any time not exceeding [............];

(B) The Dealers are willing to act as dealers pursuant to the terms of this Agreement; and

(C) The Issue Agent is willing to act as agent of the Issuer and the Guarantor for the purposes of issuing the Notes and for making payment on behalf of the Issuer or, as the case may be, the Guarantor of amounts due in respect of the Notes.

1. Interpretation

18.02   (1) In this Agreement, except where the context otherwise requires:—

Business Day means a day on which (a) dealings in Dollar deposits are carried out in the London inter-bank market and (b) commercial banks and foreign exchange markets are open for business in the City of London and, if on that day a transfer of funds is to be made under this Agreement, are not required or authorised to close in New York City;

Deed of Covenant means the deed of covenant of even date herewith made by the Issuer substantially in the form of Schedule 5;

Deed of Guarantee means the Deed of Guarantee of even date herewith made by the Guarantor and substantially in the form of Schedule 4 hereto;

Definitive Notes means bearer definitive notes of the Issuer substantially in the form of Part I of Schedule 1 and includes notes issued in exchange for Global Notes in accordance with the terms thereof;

Dollars and *$* means the lawful currency of the United States of America;

Global Notes means bearer global notes of the Issuer substantially in the form set out in Part II of Schedule 1;

Issue Date in relation to any Note means the date of issue and purchase of such Note;

Information Memorandum means the information memorandum prepared by the Issuer and the Guarantor, together with their respective latest accounts from time to time supplied to the Dealers for distribution in connection herewith;

Maturity Date in relation to any Note means the date for payment thereof;

Note Agency Agreement means the Agreement between the Issuer, the Guarantor and the Issue Agent relating to the issue of the Notes as the same may be amended from time to time;

Noteholders means the holders from time to time of Notes;

Notes means Definitive Notes and Global Notes;

outstanding means, in relation to the Notes, those which have been duly issued pursuant to this Agreement and the Note Agency Agreement other than:—

   (i) those which have been paid;

   (ii) those which have matured and the moneys for the payment of which have been duly paid to the Issue Agent in the manner provided in the Note Agency Agreement and remain available for payment to Noteholders upon presentation and surrender of the relevant Notes pursuant to the terms thereof;

   (iii) those in respect of which replacement Notes have been issued in accordance with Clause .... of the Note Agency Agreement;

18.03

and means, in relation to any Series, that the Notes comprising such Series are outstanding;

Paying Agent means the paying agent for the time being appointed pursuant to the Note Agency Agreement;

Purchase Price means, in respect of any Note purchased by any Dealer, the price, calculated in accordance with this Agreement, payable by such Dealer for such Note;

Series means Notes having the same Tenor and Maturity Date and which shall have been purchased on the same Issue Date;

Tenor in relation to any Note means the period from (and including) the Issue Date thereof to (but excluding) the Maturity Date thereof.

(2) The headings in this Agreement are inserted for convenience only and shall be ignored in construing this Agreement.

2. Appointment of Dealers

18.04   The Issuer hereby appoints the Dealers, and the Dealers hereby agree to act, as dealers pursuant to this Agreement. The Issuer may at any time appoint other or further Dealers. Any such Dealer appointed hereunder shall execute, acknowledge and deliver to the Issuer and the Guarantor an instrument (in form and substance satisfactory to the Issuer and the Guarantor) accepting such appointment and thereupon such Dealer, without any further act, deed or conveyance, shall become vested with all the authority, rights, powers, duties and obligations as if originally named as a Dealer hereunder. The Issuer shall forthwith notify the Issue Agent and the other Dealers of any such appointment.

3. Conditions of Issue

18.05   Before the Issuer first issues any Series, each of the conditions set out in Schedule 2 hereto shall have been fulfilled.

4. Facility and Issue Requests

(1) While neither the Issuer nor any of the Dealers shall at any time be obliged to issue or purchase any Notes, any Notes which the Issuer agrees to issue, and a Dealer agrees to purchase, or procure purchasers for, shall be purchased and paid for on the relevant Issue Date at the applicable Purchase Price.

(2) Notwithstanding the foregoing, the aggregate principal amount of Notes outstanding at any one time shall not exceed U.S.$ [............]. If for any reason Notes are issued which cause such limit to be exceeded this shall not prejudice the validity of such Notes or the guarantee of the Guarantor thereon. Notes shall be issued in denominations of US$500,000 or such other denominations as may be agreed between the Issuer, the Guarantor and the relevant Dealer.

(3) Any Series may be issued in the form of either a Global Note or Definitive Notes, as the Issuer and the relevant Dealer may agree, but no Series shall be represented at any one time by both a Global Note and Definitive Notes. Where in respect of any Series agreement has been reached between the Issuer and any Dealer purchasing Notes comprising such Series that the Notes to be purchased by such Dealer should be represented by Definitive Notes, all Notes to be issued in respect of that Series shall be Definitive Notes.

5. Notification to the Issue Agent and the Dealers

18.06   (1) The Issuer shall, as soon as is practicable after any agreement is reached with any Dealer for the issue and purchase of Notes notify the Issue Agent and the other Dealers of the aggregate principal amount of Notes to be issued on the relevant Issue Date, the Issue Date and Maturity Date of those

Notes and the Series of those Notes, whether Definitive Notes or a Global Note is to be issued and the identity of the Dealers purchasing or procuring the purchase of those Notes.

(2) The Issue Agent shall not (except in order to fulfil its obligations under the Note Agency Agreement in accordance with its normal commercial practices) disclose to any Dealer or any other party (other than the Issuer and the Guarantor) and no Dealer shall be entitled to require the Issuer, the Guarantor, the Issue Agent or any other Dealer to disclose to that Dealer any yield bid by, or any Purchase Price payable for any Notes by, any other Dealer or any yield agreed between the Issuer and any other Dealer in respect of any Notes.

6. Purchase and Issue of Notes

(1) The Purchase Price payable for any Note to be purchased by any Dealer **18.07** or for which any Dealer has procured purchasers shall be either the Purchase Price agreed between such Dealer and the Issuer or, where tenders are made on a yield basis, determined by that Dealer (and forthwith notified to the Issuer) by application of the following formula to the yield in respect of that Note pursuant to this Agreement:—

$$SP = \frac{FA}{1 + \frac{(D \times Y)}{360}}$$

where:—

SP is the Subscription Price

FA is the face amount of such Note

Y is the yield in respect of such Note

D is the number of days in the Tenor of such Note.

(2) Each Dealer shall (if necessary) forthwith determine the Purchase Price in respect of the Notes to be purchased by it or for which it has procured purchasers on any Issue Date and shall notify the same to the Issuer and the Issue Agent as soon as practicable after the determination thereof, but in any event prior to the Issue Date of such Notes.

(3) (a) On the Issue Date of any Note the Dealer purchasing that Note shall pay the applicable Purchase Price therefor in accordance with Clause 8 and the Issuer and the Guarantor shall procure that the Issue Agent shall, on behalf of the Issuer, issue and deliver that Note in accordance with the provisions of the Note Agency Agreement against payment as aforesaid.

(b) The Issuer will, in connection with each purchase and issue of Notes, give to the Issue Agent such information as it may require to enable it to perform the functions to be performed by it in relation to each such issue under the Note Agency Agreement.

7. Agreement of the Dealers

Each of the Dealers agrees that it will not offer, sell or deliver or procure the offer, sale or delivery of any Note or distribute the Information Memorandum or any other document relating to the Notes to any person or in any jurisdiction except in such manner and in such circumstances as will, to the best of its belief, result in compliance with any applicable laws and regulations. In particular, and without prejudice to the generality of the foregoing, each of the Dealers agrees that it will comply with the restrictions set out in Schedule 3 hereto.

8. Payments

18.08 (1) On each date on which any Dealer is obliged or procures persons to purchase any Note hereunder it shall pay or cause to be paid the Purchase Price for that Note in Dollars and in New York same day funds on the relevant Issue Date (against delivery of the Notes to or to the order of Morgan Guaranty Trust Company of New York (Brussels office) as operator of the Euro-clear System of CEDEL S.A. or a depositary of both for credit to such account or accounts with the Euro-clear System or CEDEL S.A. as such Dealer may direct) to such subscription account with the Euro-clear System or CEDEL S.A. as the Issue Agent shall have designated.

(2) The Issue Agent shall pay amounts so paid to it by each Dealer to the Issuer in Dollars and in New York same day funds on the relevant Issue Date by transfer to such account with a bank in New York City as the Issuer may designate.

(3) The Issue Agent shall not be obliged to make available to the Issuer any sum which it is expecting to receive from any Dealer for the account of the Issuer until it has been able to establish that it has received that sum. However, it may do so if it wishes. If and to the extent that it does so but it transpires that it had not then received the sum which it paid out:—

> (a) the Issuer (whom failing, the Guarantor) shall (without prejudice to its rights against such Dealer) on request refund it as soon as practicable to the Issue Agent; and
>
> (b) the Issuer (whom failing, the Guarantor) shall (without prejudice to its rights against such Dealer) on request pay to the Issue Agent the amount (as certified by the Issue Agent) which will indemnify the Issue Agent against any funding or other cost, loss, expense or liability sustained or incurred by it as a result of paying out that sum before receiving it.

(4) The obligation of any Dealer to purchase Notes shall be satisfied in full by payment of the Purchase Price in respect thereof to the Issue Agent pursuant hereto and no Dealer shall be concerned as to any subsequent application of the proceeds thereof by the Issue Agent or any other person.

9. Fees and Expenses

(1) The Issuer (whom failing, the Guarantor) shall pay to the Issue Agent   **18.09**
such fees as may be agreed between the Issuer and Issue Agent in writing.

(2) The Issuer (whom failing, the Guarantor) agrees to pay (a) to each of the
Dealers on demand, all costs and expenses (including taxes or duties thereon
and legal fees) reasonably incurred by the Dealers in connection with the
preparation and delivery of this Agreement, the Note Agency Agreement,
the Deed of Covenant, the Deed of Guarantee and the Information Memorandum, and (b) promptly, and in any event before any penalty becomes
payable, any stamp, documentary, registration or similar duty or tax payable in [...........], the United Kingdom or [...........] in connection with
the entry into, performance, enforcement or admissibility in evidence of
this Agreement, the Note Agency Agreement, the Deed of Covenant or the
Deed of Guarantee, or the issue, performance, enforcement or admissibility
in evidence of the Notes, and the Issuer (whom failing, the Guarantor) shall
indemnify the Dealers against any liability with respect to or resulting from
any delay in paying or omission to pay any such duty or tax.

10. Representations and Warranties

(1) The Issuer and the Guarantor jointly and severally represent, warrant   **18.10**
and agree to and with each of the Dealers that as of the date hereof and on
each Issue Date:

(a) the Information Memorandum as of the date thereof contains, having
regard to the particular nature of the Issuer, the Guarantor and of the
Notes, the information which is necessary to enable investors and their
investment advisers to make an informed assessment of the assets and liabilities, financial position, profits and losses and prospects of the Issuer and
of the Guarantor and of the rights attaching to the Notes; the information
contained in the Information Memorandum and in the most recent Annual
Report of each of the Issuer and the Guarantor delivered to the Dealers, is
true and accurate in all material respects and is not misleading; there are no
other facts the omission of which would make any statement or information or either of such Annual Reports misleading in any material
respects and that all reasonable enquiries have been made to ascertain such
facts and to verify the accuracy of all such statements and information and
the Issuer and the Guarantor shall promptly notify each Dealer in writing
of any change (actual, contemplated or threatened) in the assets and liabilities, financial position, profits and losses and prospects of the Issuer or
the Guarantor or in any material fact, whether or not contained in the
Information Memorandum, which is of such a nature as to render untrue
or misleading any statement of a material fact contained therein;

(b) save as disclosed in the Information Memorandum there has been
no material adverse change in the financial position or prospects of the
Issuer or of the Guarantor or of either of them and their respective subsidiaries taken as a whole since [...........];

(c) the execution, issue and delivery of the Notes, the execution and delivery by the Issuer and the Guarantor of this Agreement, the Note Agency Agreement, the Deed of Covenant and the Deed of Guarantee and the consummation of the transactions contemplated by the Notes, this Agreement, the Note Agency Agreement, the Deed of Covenant and the Deed of Guarantee, and compliance with their terms:—

(i) do not, and on the issue of any Note will not, violate, conflict with or result in a breach of any terms, conditions or provisions of any law or administrative regulation of [............] or political sub-division thereof, or court judgment or decree in [............] or any political sub-division thereof applicable to the Issuer or the Guarantor, or any agreement or other instrument to which the Issuer or the Guarantor is a party or by which the Issuer or the Guarantor is bound or to which any of their respective assets are subject;

(ii) have been duly authorised by the Issuer and the Guarantor; and

(iii) have the approval of [............]

so that this Agreement constitutes, and upon due execution, issue and/or delivery as aforesaid the Notes, the Note Agency Agreement, the Deed of Covenant and the Deed of Guarantee will constitute valid and legally binding obligations of the Issuer and the Guarantor in accordance with their respective terms;

18.11   (d) all authorisations, approvals or consents and all filings and registrations required by the Issuer and/or the Guarantor for the entering into of this Agreement, the Note Agency Agreement, the Deed of Covenant and the Deed of Guarantee and for the issue of the Notes and the consummation of all other matters contemplated hereby have been obtained or made and are in full force and effect;

(e) neither the Issuer nor the Guarantor is involved in any legal or arbitration proceedings which may have or have had during the past 12 months a significant effect on its financial position, nor is it aware of any such proceedings pending or threatened;

(f) no event exists or has occurred in relation to the Issuer or the Guarantor which would be (after the issue of any of the Notes) an event of default under the terms and conditions of any indebtedness of the Issuer or the Guarantor or which, with lapse of time or notice or both, would (after the issue of any of the Notes) be capable of becoming such an event of default;

(g) each of the Issuer and the Guarantor is duly established and has full power and authority to execute and deliver and comply with the terms and conditions of this Agreement, the Notes, the Note Agency Agreement, the Deed of Covenant and the Deed of Guarantee;

(h) each Dealer may provide to actual and potential purchasers of Notes copies of the Information Memorandum, as from time to time updated or revised, of any accounts of the Issuer and/or the Guarantor and of any information relating to the Issuer and/or the Guarantor supplied to such Dealer from time to time, and of the form of Note;

(i) neither the Issuer nor the Guarantor will, without the prior consent of the Dealers, amend or terminate the Note Agency Agreement, terminate the appointment of the Issue Agent or the Paying Agent thereunder or permit any change in the specified office of any Paying Agent;

(*j*) the payment obligations of the Issuer and the Guarantor under the Notes and the Deed of Covenant or the Deed of Guarantee (as the case may be) rank and will at all times rank *pari passu* as to priority of payment with all other unsecured and unsubordinated obligations of the Issuer and the Guarantor, present and future, subject only to laws affecting creditors' rights generally.

(2) The obligations of the Dealers to pay or procure the payment for Notes agreed to be issued pursuant hereto is conditional upon the representations and warranties contained in sub-clause (1) above being true and correct on the Issue Date of such Notes.

(3) The Issuer and the Guarantor, jointly and severally will on demand indemnify each Dealer against any costs, loss, expense or liability (including without limitation legal fees and any losses and expenses incurred in liquidating or otherwise employing moneys or deposits from third parties acquired to purchase or fund the purchase of such Notes as mentioned below) sustained or incurred by any such Dealer as a result of (i) any Notes not being purchased by reason of non-fulfilment of the condition in sub-clause (2) above, or (ii) any breach of any of the representations, warranties, agreements or obligations of the Issuer or the Guarantor in this Agreement or the Notes.

11. Indemnification

The Issuer and the Guarantor jointly and severally will indemnify and hold **18.12**
harmless the Dealers and each of them against any loss, claim, damages, liability or expense (including reasonable costs of investigation and defence) arising out of or based upon any untrue statement or alleged untrue statement of any material fact contained in the Information Memorandum or any other information made available by the Issuer or the Guarantor to the Dealers or any of them pursuant hereto or for use in connection with the offer or sale of any Note or the omission or alleged omission to state therein a material fact necessary in order to make the statements therein in the light of the circumstances under which they were made, not misleading. The obligations of the Issuer and the Guarantor under this Clause 11 shall survive the termination of this Agreement.

12. Communications

(1) All communications under this Agreement shall be by telephone (but only where specifically provided) or by facsimile transmission, telex or in writing delivered by hand.

(2) Each communication shall be made to the relevant party at the telex number or address or telephone number, and in the case of a communication by telex or in writing, shall be marked for the attention of, and in the case of a communication by telephone shall be made to, the person, from

time to time designated by that party to the others for the purpose of this Agreement. The initial telephone number, telex number, address and person so designated by the parties are set out on the execution pages of this Agreement.

(3) A communication will be deemed received (if by telex) when a confirmed answerback is received at the end of the transmission, (if by telephone) when made and (if in writing) when delivered, in each case in the manner required by this Clause 12. A communication may only be revoked if prior to such revocation being received, or being deemed to have been received as aforesaid, it shall not have been acted upon.

13. Amendment, Termination and Assignment

18.13 (1) The terms of this Agreement shall not be amended in any manner whatsoever except by written instrument signed by all the parties hereto.

(2) The Issuer may terminate this Agreement with respect to any Dealer and any Dealer may terminate this Agreement with respect to itself upon not less than 30 days' prior notice to the other parties hereto. No such termination shall, however, affect any rights or obligations in respect of Notes agreed to be purchased or outstanding on the effective date of such termination or any other rights or obligations of the parties hereto in relation to any indemnity contained herein.

(3) No person shall be entitled to assign or transfer all or any part of its rights or obligations under this Agreement.

14. Counterparts

This Agreement may be signed in any number of counterparts, all of which taken together shall constitute a single agreement.

15. Governing Law

18.14 (1) This Agreement is governed by, and shall be construed in accordance with the laws of England. The Issuer and the Guarantor each irrevocably submits to the jurisdiction of the Courts of England for the purposes of any legal action or proceedings arising out of or in connection with this Agreement ("Proceedings") and waives any objection to Proceedings in such courts whether on the grounds that the Proceedings have been brought in an inconvenient forum or otherwise.

(2) The foregoing submissions are made for the benefit of each of the Dealers and shall not affect the right of any Dealer to take Proceedings in any other jurisdiction nor shall the taking of Proceedings in any jurisdiction preclude any party from taking Proceedings in any other jurisdiction.

(3) The Issuer and the Guarantor each irrevocably appoints [............] (now of [..........]) to receive, for it and on its behalf, service or process in any

Proceedings in England. Such service shall be deemed completed on delivery to such agent whether or not it is forwarded to and received by the Issuer or the Guarantor as the case may be.

(4) The Issuer and the Guarantor each irrevocably consents to any process in any Proceedings anywhere being served by delivering a copy to it at its address applicable for communications sent to it in accordance with Clause 12(1) hereof.

(5) Nothing herein shall affect the right to serve process in any other manner permitted by law.

　　IN WITNESS whereof each of the parties has caused this Agreement to be executed by its duly authorised officers as of the day and year first above written.

[ISSUER]   By:

[address]   By:

Telephone No:
Telex No. and answerback:
Persons authorised:

[GUARANTOR]   By: **18.15**

[address]

Telephone No:
Telex No. and answerback:
Persons authorised:

[DEALER]   By:

[address]

Telephone No:
Telex No. and answerback:
Persons authorised:

[DEALER]   By:

[address]

Telephone No:
Telex No. and answerback:
Persons authorised:

SCHEDULE 1

Part I

Form of Definitive Note

18.16　[On the face]

[............]
(Incorporated with limited liability in [..........])

No. ....

U.S.$ [.........]

Series No. ....　　　　　Issue Date .... 19....
　　　　　　　　　　　　　　Maturity Date .... 19....

For the value received, [..............] (the "Issuer") promises to pay to the bearer on the above-mentioned Maturity Date the sum of [...................] thousand United States Dollars upon presentation and surrender of this Note to [..........................] (the "Paying Agent"), such payment to be made by U.S. dollar cheque mailed to an address outside the United States, its territories and possessions and all areas subject to its jurisdiction or, at the option of the bearer, by wire transfer to a U.S. dollar account with a bank located outside the United States, its territories and possessions and all areas subject to its jurisdiction.

The payment due under this Note shall be made without set-off or counterclaim and free and clear of, and without deduction for, any taxes, levies, duties, charges, deductions or withholdings, of any nature now or hereafter imposed, levied, collected, withheld or assessed in any jurisdiction unless such withholding or deduction is required by law. In that event the Issuer shall pay such additional amounts as would be necessary in order that the net amounts received by the bearer of this Note after such withholding or deduction shall equal the amount which would have been receivable hereunder in the absence of such withholding or deduction, except that no such additional amount shall be payable in respect of this Note:—

(*a*) to, or to a third party on behalf of, the bearer of this Note who is subject to such taxes, levies, duties, deductions or withholdings in respect of such Note by reason of his being connected with [................] otherwise than merely by holding this Note; or

(*b*) if it is presented for payment more than 30 days after the Maturity Date (if the full amount due in respect of this Note is duly received by the Paying Agent on or prior to the Maturity Date), except to the extent that the bearer of this Note would have been entitled to such additional amount on presenting the same for payment on the thirtieth such day.

Payment of this Note is guaranteed by [.......................] pursuant to a Deed of Guarantee dated [..............................], a copy of which may be inspected during normal business hours at the above-mentioned office of the Paying Agent.

[The income element for the income period from the Issue Date to the Maturity Date for the purpose of Section 36 of the Finance Act 1984 is the difference between the face amount and the issue price hereof.]

This Note shall not be validly issued unless authenticated by [..................], as Issue Agent.

This Note is governed by, and shall be construed in accordance with, the laws of England.

IN WITNESS whereof the Issuer has caused this Note to be duly signed manually or in facsimile on its behalf.

[...............................]

By: ....
(Authorised Signatory)

By: ....
(Authorised Signatory)

Certificate of authentication
[...................................],
as Issue Agent (without recourse, warranty or liability)

By: ....
(Authorised Signatory)

By: ....
(Authorised Signatory)

THIS NOTE HAS NOT BEEN REGISTERED UNDER THE UNITED STATES SECURITIES ACT OF 1933 AND MAY NOT BE OFFERED, SOLD, RESOLD OR DELIVERED, DIRECTLY OR INDIRECTLY, IN THE UNITED STATES OF AMERICA, ITS TERRITORIES AND POSSESSIONS AND ALL AREAS SUBJECT TO ITS JURISDICTION ("UNITED STATES") OR TO ANY PERSON WHO IS A CITIZEN, NATIONAL OR RESIDENT OF THE UNITED STATES, ANY CORPORATION, PARTNERSHIP OR OTHER ENTITY CREATED OR ORGANISED IN OR UNDER THE LAWS OF THE UNITED STATES OR ANY POLITICAL SUBDIVISION THEREOF OR ANY ESTATE OR TRUST THAT IS SUBJECT TO UNITED STATES FEDERAL INCOME TAXATION REGARDLESS OF THE SOURCE OF ITS INCOME (ALL OF THE FOREGOING BEING "UNITED STATES PERSONS").

ANY UNITED STATES PERSON WHO HOLDS THIS OBLI-

GATION WILL BE SUBJECT TO LIMITATIONS UNDER THE UNITED STATES INCOME TAX LAWS INCLUDING THE LIMI-TATIONS PROVIDED IN SECTIONS 165(j) AND 1287(a) OF THE INTERNAL REVENUE CODE.

SCHEDULE 1

Part II

Form of Global Note

18.17   [On the face]

[................................]

(Incorporated with limited liability in [....................])

Clearance System No. ....
No. ....
U.S.$[............]
[Issue Price ....]   Issue Date .... 19....
                                      Maturity Date................... 19....

For value received, [...................] (the "Issuer") promises to pay to the bearer on the above-mentioned Maturity Date the sum of [....................] thousand United States Dollars upon presentation and surrender of this Note to [............................] (the "Paying Agent"), such payment to be made by U.S. dollar cheque mailed to an address outside the United States, its territories and possessions and all areas subject to its jurisdiction or, at the option of the bearer, by wire transfer to a U.S. dollar account with a bank located outside the United States, its territories and possessions and all areas subject to its jurisdiction.

The payment due under this Note shall be made without set-off or coun-terclaim and free and clear of, and without deduction for, any taxes, levies, duties, charges, deductions or withholdings, of any nature now or hereafter imposed, levied, collected, withheld or assessed in any jurisdiction unless such withholding or deduction is required by law. In that event the Issuer shall pay such additional amounts as would be necessary in order that the net amounts received by the bearer of this Note after such withholding or deduction shall equal the amount which would have been receivable here-under in the absence of such withholding or deduction, except that no such additional amount shall be payable in respect of this Note:—

(a) to, or to a third party on behalf of, the bearer of this Note who is subject to such taxes, levies, duties, deductions or withholdings in respect of such Note by reason of his being connected with [...............] otherwise than merely by holding this Note; or

(b) if it is presented for payment more than 30 days after the Maturity

Date (if the full amount due in respect of this Note is duly received by the Paying Agent on or prior to the Maturity Date), except to the extent that the bearer of this Note would have been entitled to such additional amount on presenting the same for payment on the thirtieth such day.

If default is made in the payment referred to above, the Issuer hereby undertakes that upon presentation and surrender of this Note to it at [........ ....], on any business day on or after the Maturity Date the Issuer will issue to the bearer hereof duly executed bearer Notes in denominations of U.S. $500,000 and having an aggregate principal amount equal to the principal amount hereof in the form of this Note with the omission of this paragraph.

The issue price for each such definitive Note shall be the sum equal to the issue price of this Note [specified above] divided by the number of definitive Notes so issued. If definitive Notes are not issued in exchange for this Note before 5.00 p.m. (London time) on the thirtieth day after presentation and surrender as aforesaid, this Note (including the obligation hereunder to issue definitive Notes) will become void and the bearer hereof will have no further rights in respect of the aggregate principal amount due and payable under this Note (but without prejudice to the rights which the bearer hereof or any other person may have under a Deed of Covenant dated [.............] entered into by the Issuer). A copy of the said Deed of Covenant may be inspected during normal business hours at the above-mentioned office of the Paying Agent.

Payment of this Note is guaranteed by [......................] pursuant to a Deed of Guarantee dated [...............], a copy of which may be inspected during normal business hours at the above mentioned office of the Paying Agent.

[The income element for the income period from the Issue Date to the Maturity Date for the purpose of Section 36 of the Finance Act 1984 is the difference between the face amount and the issue price hereof.]

This Note shall not be validly issued unless authenticated by [.............], as Issue Agent.

This Note is governed by, and shall be construed in accordance with, the laws of England.

IN WITNESS whereof the Issuer has caused this Note to be duly signed manually or in facsimile on its behalf.

[...............................]

By: ....
  (Authorised Signatory)

By: ....
  (Authorised Signatory)

Certificate of authentication
[....],
as Issue Agent (without recourse,
warranty or liability)

By: ....
(Authorised Signatory)

By: ....
(Authorised Signatory)

THIS NOTE HAS NOT BEEN REGISTERED UNDER THE UNITED STATES SECURITIES ACT OF 1933 AND MAY NOT BE OFFERED, SOLD, RESOLD OR DELIVERED, DIRECTLY OR INDIRECTLY, IN THE UNITED STATES OF AMERICA, ITS TERRITORIES AND POSSESSIONS AND ALL AREAS SUBJECT TO ITS JURISDICTION ("UNITED STATES") OR TO ANY PERSON WHO IS A CITIZEN, NATIONAL OR RESIDENT OF THE UNITED STATES, ANY CORPORATION, PARTNERSHIP OR OTHER ENTITY CREATED OR ORGANISED IN OR UNDER THE LAWS OF THE UNITED STATES OR ANY POLITICAL SUBDIVISION THEREOF OR ANY ESTATE OR TRUST THAT IS SUBJECT TO UNITED STATES FEDERAL INCOME TAXATION REGARDLESS OF THE SOURCE OF ITS INCOME (ALL OF THE FOREGOING BEING "UNITED STATES PERSONS").

ANY UNITED STATES PERSON WHO HOLDS THIS OBLIGATION WILL BE SUBJECT TO LIMITATIONS UNDER THE UNITED STATES INCOME TAX LAWS INCLUDING THE LIMITATIONS PROVIDED IN SECTIONS 165(j) AND 1287(a) OF THE INTERNAL REVENUE CODE.

SCHEDULE 2

Conditions Precedent

18.18 (1) Certified copies of the Memorandum and Articles of Association or other constitutional documents of the Issuer and the Guarantor.

(2) Certified copies of all resolutions and other action required to be taken by the Issuer and the Guarantor to approve this Agreement, the Note Agency Agreement, the Deed of Covenant and the Deed of Guarantee and the issue of the Notes and to authorise appropriate persons to execute the same and take any other requisite action.

(3) A list of the names, titles and specimen signatures of the persons authorised to take action on behalf of the Issuer and the Guarantor as specified in (2) above.

(4) Certified copies of all consents required by the Issuer and the Guarantor for the issue of the Notes and the execution, delivery and performance of this Agreement, the Note Agency Agreement, the Deed of Covenant and the Deed of Guarantee.

(5) Legal opinions dated on or after the date of this Agreement from [............], [............] and from [............] each with such content as the Dealers may reasonably require.

(6) Evidence of acceptance by the process agents specified in this Agreement, the Note Agency Agreement, the Deed of Covenant and the Deed of Guarantee of their appointment as such.

(7) The Note Agency Agreement having been executed and delivered by all parties thereto.

(8) The Deed of Guarantee having been executed by the Guarantor and original executed copies thereof having been delivered to the Paying Agent and each of the Dealers.

(9) The Deed of Covenant having been executed by the Issuer and original executed copies thereof having been delivered to the Paying Agent and each of the Dealers.

(10) A sufficient stock of executed but uncompleted and unauthenticated Notes being held by the Issue Agent.

SCHEDULE 3

Sales Restrictions

(A) (1) The Notes have not been and will not be registered under the **18.19** United States Securities Act of 1933. Accordingly the Notes may not be offered or sold directly or indirectly in the United States of America, its territories and possessions and all areas subject to its jurisdiction ("United States"), or to any citizen, national or resident thereof, any corporation, partnership or other entity created or organised in or under the laws of the United States or any political subdivision thereof or any estate or trust that is subject to United States federal income taxation regardless of the source of its income ("U.S. persons").

(2) Each Dealer represents that it is not acquiring any of the Notes purchased by it for the account of any U.S. person. It also agrees that it has not offered, sold or delivered and will not, as principal or agent, offer, sell or deliver any Notes (whether acquired by it as part of the initial distribution or otherwise) directly or indirectly in the United States or to U.S. persons. It also agrees to deliver to each purchaser from it of Notes, at or prior to the confirmation of sale of such Notes, a written confirmation stating substantially the following:

These Notes have not been registered under the United States Securities Act of 1933 (the "Securities Act") and, accordingly, by your purchase and acceptance of these Notes, you represent, warrant and agree that:

(i) you are not a U.S. person (as defined below) and are not purchasing the Notes for the account of any U.S. person;

(ii) you will not offer or sell such Notes directly or indirectly in the United States or to any U.S. person; and

(iii) you will deliver to any purchaser of such Notes from you, at or prior to the confirmation of sale thereof, a written confirmation in the form hereof whereby such purchaser by its purchase and acceptance of Notes, represents, warrants and agrees to the effect set forth herein.

As used herein, "United States" means the United States of America its territories and possessions and all areas subject to its jurisdiction; and "U.S. person" means any person who is a citizen, national or resident of the United States, any corporation, partnership or other entity created or organised in or under the laws of the United States or any political subdivision thereof or any estate or trust that is subject to United States federal income taxation regardless of the source of its income.

(B) Prior to the repeal of Part III of the Companies Act 1985 pursuant to the Financial Services Act 1986, Notes may not be offered or sold in Great Britain, by means of any document, other than to persons whose ordinary business it is to buy or sell shares or debentures (whether as principal or agent), otherwise than in circumstances which do not constitute an offer to the public within the meaning of the Companies Act 1985), nor, prior to the repeal of the Prevention of Fraud (Investments) Act 1958 pursuant to the Financial Services Act 1986, may any offering material relating to the Notes be distributed in or from Great Britain (except by persons permitted to do so under the securities laws of Great Britain), otherwise than to persons whose business involves the acquisition and disposal, or the holding, of securities (whether as principal or as agent). Upon the coming into force of Section 159 and/or Section 160 of the Financial Services Act 1986 insofar as they may relate to Notes, no advertisement shall be issued or caused to be issued in the United Kingdom in contravention of those Sections or whichever of them shall have come into force.

(C) [Other selling restrictions (if any)].

(D) Each Dealer will observe all applicable laws and regulations in any jurisdiction in which it may offer, sell or deliver Notes. It will not directly or indirectly offer, sell or deliver Notes or distribute or publish any prospectus, circular, advertisement or other offering material in any country or jurisdiction except under circumstances that will result in compliance with any applicable laws and regulations, and all offers, sales and deliveries of Notes by it will be made on the foregoing terms.

(E) Without prejudice to the foregoing provisions, neither the Issuer nor the Guarantor shall have any responsibility for, and each Dealer will obtain any consent, approval or permission required by it for, the subscription, offer, sale or delivery by it of the Notes under, and it will comply with, the laws and regulations in force in any jurisdiction to which it is subject or in which it makes any subscription, offer, sale or delivery.

(F) Reference in this Schedule 3 to Notes shall be deemed to include any interest in any Global Note.

SCHEDULE 4

Deed of Guarantee

[Guarantor]

Deed of Guarantee

THIS DEED OF GUARANTEE is made on [..........................], 19.. by **18.20** [Guarantor] (the "Guarantor") a company incorporated under the laws of [....] and whose [head] [registered] office is situated at [...........................].

WHEREAS:—

(A) [Issuer] (the "Issuer") has entered into a Euro-Commercial Paper Programme Agreement (the "Programme Agreement") dated [...............] with the Guarantor and [......................] and [.....................] as dealers (each a "Dealer") and [.............] as Issue Agent under which the Issuer proposes, from time to time, to issue bearer promissory notes in global and definitive form with the benefit of the guarantee of the Guarantor herein contained.

(B) The Issuer has also executed a Deed of Covenant dated [..........] (the "Deed of Covenant") relating to Global Notes issued pursuant to the Programme Agreement.

(C) The Guarantor has determined to execute this Deed of Guarantee for the protection of the rights and interests of Relevant Account Holders (as defined in the Deed of Covenant) and the holders for the time being of the Notes (each a "Holder").

NOW THIS DEED WITNESSETH AND THE GUARANTOR DECLARES as follows:

(1) (A) As used herein, "Termination Date" means the date on which:—

(i) complete performance of the obligations contained in the Deed of Covenant and in all Notes outstanding from time to time occurs;

(ii) complete performance of the obligations contained in this Deed of Guarantee occurs; and

(iii) termination of the Programme Agreement in respect of all Dealers occurs,

whichever shall be later.

(B) Terms defined in the Programme Agreement or the Deed of Covenant have the same meaning when used herein.

(2) (A) The Guarantor hereby unconditionally and irrevocably guarantees to each and every Holder the due and punctual payment by the Issuer of all amounts payable under the Deed of Covenant and under all Notes outstanding from time to time when and as the same shall become due and payable in accordance with the terms thereof.

(B) If the Issuer fails to make payment as aforesaid, the Guarantor agrees to cause any such payment to be made as if such payment were made when due and payable by the Issuer.

(C) The liability of the Guarantor under this Deed of Guarantee shall not be lessened, affected or impaired by any time or indulgence granted to the Issuer by any Holder or by any other person or by any compromise, scheme or arrangement affecting the Issuer or dealings or transactions between the Issuer and any Holder or any other person, or by the dissolution, liquidation or bankruptcy of the Issuer or by any change in the status, functions, control of or ownership of shares in the Issuer.

(D) The Guarantor agrees that its obligations hereunder shall be unconditional, irrespective of the legality, validity, regularity or enforceability of the Deed of Covenant or of any of the Notes outstanding from time to time, the absence of any action to enforce the same, the waiver or consent by any Holder with respect to any provision of the Deed of Covenant or of any of the Notes, the obtaining of any judgment against the Issuer or any action to enforce the same or any other circumstance which might otherwise constitute a legal or equitable discharge or defence of a guarantor (other than payment in full of the relevant amount due) provided that the Guarantor shall be under no liability whatsoever hereunder in respect of or to the Holder of any Global Note which has become void in accordance with its terms other than by way of the Guarantor's guarantee hereunder of the obligations of the Issuer under the Deed of Covenant.

(E) The Guarantor hereby waives, with respect to the Deed of Covenant and all Notes and the indebtedness owed thereby and its obligations hereunder, diligence, presentment (other than of the Notes in accordance with their terms), objections or defences arising in respect of the Deed of Covenant and/or the Notes, filing of claims with the court in the event of merger, insolvency or bankruptcy of the Issuer, any right to require a proceeding first against the Issuer, protest, objections, notice and all demands whatsoever and covenants that this Deed of Guarantee will be a continuing guarantee which will not be discharged until the Termination Date.

18.21   (F) All payments by the Guarantor under this Deed of Guarantee shall be made without set-off or counterclaim and free and clear of, and without deduction for, any taxes, levies, duties, charges, deductions or withholdings, of any nature now or hereafter imposed, levied, collected, withheld or assessed in any jurisdiction unless such withholding or deduction is required by law. In that event the Guarantor shall pay such additional amounts as would be necessary in order that the net amounts received by the relevant Holder after such withholding or deduction shall equal the amount which would have been receivable hereunder in the absence of such withholding or deduction, except that no such additional amount shall be payable:—

(a) to, or to a third party on behalf of, a Holder who is subject to such taxes, levies, duties, deductions or withholdings in respect of its rights in the relevant Note by reason of his being connected with [........] otherwise than merely by holding its rights in the relevant Note; or

(b) in respect of any demand made more than 30 days after the Maturity Date of the relevant Note (if the full amount due in respect of such Note is duly received by the Paying Agent on or prior to such Maturity Date), except to the extent that a Holder would have been entitled to such additional amount on making such demand on the thirtieth such day.

(G) The Guarantor shall not be subrogated to the rights of any Holder against the Issuer in respect of amounts paid by the Guarantor pursuant to the provisions of this Deed of Guarantee until the Termination Date.

(H) As a separate and alternative stipulation, the Guarantor unconditionally and irrevocably agrees that, subject to the proviso to paragraph (D) above, any sum expressed to be payable by the Issuer under any Note or the Deed of Covenant but which is for any reason not recoverable from the Guarantor hereunder on the basis of a guarantee shall nevertheless be recoverable from it as if it were the sole principal debtor.

(3) The records of CEDEL and/or the Euro-clear Operator, as the case may **18.22** be, shall in the absence of manifest error be conclusive evidence of the identity of the Relevant Account Holders and the principal amount of rights in respect of Global Notes credited to the securities account of each Relevant Account Holder at any time.

(4) Any statement issued by CEDEL or, as the case may be, the Euro-clear Operator to any Relevant Account Holder relating to a specified Global Note or Global Notes and stating the principal amount of rights in respect of Global Notes which are credited to the securities account of such Relevant Account Holder shall in the absence of manifest error be conclusive evidence of the records of CEDEL or, as the case may be, the Euro-clear Operator for the purposes of this Deed of Guarantee (but without prejudice to any other means of producing such records in evidence). Each Global Note will bear the clearance system number allocated to such Global Note by CEDEL and/or the Euro-clear Operator, as the case may be. It shall be conclusive evidence that any entry in any securities account relates to any particular Global Note if the clearance system number allocated to such Global Note and the number identifying such entry are identical.

(5) The Guarantor hereby covenants to and agrees with the Holders that:

(A) its payment obligations under this Deed of Guarantee rank and will at all times rank *pari passu* as to priority of payment with all its other unsecured and unsubordinated obligations, present and future, subject only to laws affecting creditors' rights generally;

(B) it will pay promptly, and in any event before any penalty becomes payable, any stamp, documentary, registration or similar duty or tax payable in [............] or the United Kingdom in connection with the entry into, performance, enforcement or admissibility in evidence of this Deed of Guarantee and/or any amendment of or waiver in respect thereof, and shall indemnify the Holders against any liability with respect to or resulting from any delay in paying or omission to pay any such tax.

(6) (A) This Deed of Guarantee shall be deposited with and held by the Paying Agent (as defined in the Notes) until the Termination Date and for so long thereafter as any claim made against the Issuer or the Guarantor by any Holder in relation to the Notes, the Deed of Covenant or this Deed of Guarantee shall not have been finally adjudicated, settled or discharged.

(B) The Guarantor hereby acknowledges the right of every Holder to the production of this Deed of Guarantee.

18.23 (7) (A) The Guarantor hereby acknowledges and covenants that the obligations binding upon it contained in this Deed of Guarantee are owed to, and shall be for the benefit of, each and every Holder.

(B) Each Holder shall be entitled severally to enforce the said obligations against the Guarantor.

(8) The Guarantor may not assign or transfer all or part of its rights or obligations hereunder.

(9) (A) Any amount received or recovered by any Holder in respect of any sum expressed to be due to it from the Guarantor under this Deed of Guarantee in a currency other than the currency in which the same was due (the "due currency") whether as a result of, or of the enforcement of, a judgment or order of a court or tribunal of any jurisdiction, in the dissolution of the Guarantor or otherwise, shall only constitute a discharge to the Guarantor to the extent of the amount in the due currency which such Holder is able to purchase with the amount so received or recovered in such other currency on the date of that receipt or recovery (or, if it is not practicable to make such purchase on that date, on the first date on which it is practicable to do so).

(B) If that amount in the due currency is less than the amount in the due currency due to such Holder under this Deed of Guarantee the Guarantor shall indemnify it against any loss sustained by it as a result. In such event, the Guarantor shall indemnify such Holder against the cost of making any such purchase.

(C) These indemnities constitute a separate and independent obligation from the other obligations in this Deed of Guarantee, shall give rise to a separate and independent cause of action, shall apply irrespective of any indulgence granted by any Holder and shall continue in full force and effect despite any judgment, order, claim or proof for a liquidated amount in respect of any sum due under this Deed of Guarantee or any other judgment or order. No proof or evidence of any actual loss may be required.

(10) The illegality, invalidity or unenforceability of any provision of this Deed of Guarantee under the law of any jurisdiction shall not affect its legality, validity or enforceability under the law of any other jurisdiction nor the legality, validity or enforceability of any other provision.

(11)   (A) This Deed of Guarantee shall be governed by and construed in **18.24** accordance with the laws of England. The Guarantor irrevocably submits to the jurisdiction of the Courts of England for the purposes of any legal action or proceedings arising out of or in connection with this Deed ("Proceedings") and waives any objection to Proceedings in such courts whether on the grounds that the Proceedings have been brought in an inconvenient forum or otherwise.

(B) The foregoing submission is made for the benefit of each Holder from time to time and shall not affect the right of any Holder to take Proceedings in any other jurisdiction nor shall the taking of Proceedings in any jurisdiction preclude any party from taking Proceedings in any other jurisdiction.

(C) The Guarantor irrevocably appoints [............] (now of [............]) to receive, for it and on its behalf, service of process in any Proceedings in England. Such service shall be deemed completed on delivery to such agent whether or not it is forwarded to and received by the Guarantor.

(D) Nothing herein shall affect the right to serve process in any other manner permitted by law.

IN WITNESS whereof [GUARANTOR] has caused this Deed of Guarantee to be duly executed as its act and deed the day and year first above written.

[THE COMMON SEAL of
[GUARANTOR] was hereunto
affixed in accordance with its
Articles of Association and in the
presence of:—]

OR

[SIGNED, SEALED AND
DELIVERED on behalf of, and as
the act and deed of, [the
Guarantor] by [.............] in the
presence of:—]

SCHEDULE 5

Deed of Covenant

[Issuer]

Deed of Covenant

18.25 THIS DEED OF COVENANT is made on [...............] by [...............] (the "Issuer") in favour of the account holders of Centrale de Livraison de Valeurs Mobilières S.A. ("CEDEL") and Morgan Guaranty Trust Company of New York, Brussels Office, as operator of the Euro-clear System (the "Euro-clear Operator") specified below.

WHEREAS:—

(A) The Issuer has entered into a Euro-Commercial Paper Programme Agreement (the "Programme Agreement") dated [......................] with [..............] (the "Guarantor") and [...........................] and [.......... ......] as Issue Agent under which the Issuer proposes, from time to time, to issue bearer promissory notes in global and definitive form with the benefit of the guarantee of the Guarantor pursuant to a deed of guarantee (the "Deed of Guarantee") dated [...............].

(B) Rights to receive a portion of the proceeds payable upon the maturity of any such global bearer notes ("Global Notes") may be purchased by one or more of the Dealers and each Global Note will be delivered at the direction of such Dealer or Dealers to or to a depositary for CEDEL and/or the Euro-clear Operator. Any of such Dealers may then, from time to time, instruct CEDEL or the Euro-clear Operator, as the case may be, to debit such Dealer's securities account with CEDEL or the Euro-clear Operator respectively with those rights in respect of Global Notes and credit securities accounts of other account holders with CEDEL or the Euro-clear Operator, as the case may be, with corresponding rights in respect of Global Notes in accordance with the terms and conditions and operating procedures or management regulations of CEDEL or the Euro-clear Operator, as the case may be (the "Operating Regulations").

(C) Account holders with CEDEL or the Euro-clear Operator which have rights in respect of Global Notes credited to their securities accounts from time to time will be entitled to transfer such rights in respect of Global Notes and (subject to payment being received from or on behalf of the Issuer or the Guarantor) will be entitled to receive a proportion of the proceeds payable upon the maturity of any Global Note from CEDEL or the Euro-clear Operator, as the case may be, in respect of such rights in respect of Global Notes in accordance with the Operating Regulations.

(D) In certain circumstances, specified in each Global Note, it will become void. In such circumstances the Issuer will, subject to and in accordance with the terms of this Deed, pay to the account holders (other than the Euro-clear Operator and CEDEL) with CEDEL or the Euro-clear Operator, as the case may be, which, at the time such Global Note becomes void, have credited to their securities account with CEDEL or the Euro-clear Operator respectively rights in respect of such Global Notes (the "Relevant Account Holders") in respect of each such right, the amount which would be due to such person in respect of such right were such Global Note to have been paid in full (such amount being hereinafter referred to as the "principal amount" of such right in respect of such Global Note).

NOW THIS DEED WITNESSETH AS FOLLOWS:—

(1) (A) As used herein, "Termination Date" means the date on which: **18.26**

(i) complete performance of the obligations contained in this Deed of Covenant and in all Notes (as defined in the Programme Agreement) outstanding from time to time occurs; and

(ii) complete performance of the obligations contained in the Deed of Guarantee occurs; and

(iii) termination of the Programme Agreement in respect of all Dealers occurs,

whichever shall be later.

(B) Terms defined in the Programme Agreement shall have the same meaning when used herein.

(2) If any Global Note becomes void in accordance with the terms thereof the Issuer hereby undertakes to pay on demand to each of the Relevant Account Holders in respect of such Global Note the principal amount of the rights in respect of such Global Note which such Relevant Account Holder has, at the time at which such Global Note becomes void, credited to its securities account with CEDEL and/or the Euro-clear Operator, as the case may be.

(3) The records of CEDEL and/or the Euro-clear Operator, as the case may be, shall in the absence of manifest error be conclusive evidence of the identity of the Relevant Account Holders and the principal amount of rights in respect of Global Notes credited to the securities account of each Relevant Account Holder at any time.

(4) Any statement issued by CEDEL or, as the case may be, the Euro-clear Operator to any Relevant Account Holder relating to a specified Global Note or Global Notes and stating the principal amount of rights in respect of Global Notes which are credited to the securities account of such Relevant Account Holder shall in the absence of manifest error be conclusive evidence of the records of CEDEL or, as the case may be, the Euro-clear Operator for the purposes of Clause 3 (but without prejudice to any other means of producing such records in evidence). Each Global Note will bear the clearance system number allocated to such Global Note by CEDEL and/ or the Euro-clear Operator, as the case may be. It shall be conclusive evi-

dence that any entry in any securities account relates to any particular Global Note if the clearance system number allocated to such Global Note and the number identifying such entry are identical.

18.27 (5) All payments by the Issuer under this Deed shall be made without set-off or counterclaim and free and clear of, and without deduction for, any taxes, levies, duties, charges, deductions or withholdings, of any nature now or hereafter imposed, levied, collected, withheld or assessed in any jurisdiction unless such withholding or deduction is required by law. In that event the Issuer shall pay such additional amounts as would be necessary in order that the net amounts received by the Relevant Account Holder after such withholding or deduction shall equal the amount which would have been receivable hereunder in the absence of such withholding or deduction, except that no such additional amount shall be payable:—

(a) to, or to a third party on behalf of, a Relevant Account Holder who is subject to such taxes, levies, duties, deductions or withholdings in respect of its rights in the relevant Global Note by reason of his being connected with [...........] otherwise than merely by holding its rights in the relevant Global Note; or

(b) in respect of any demand made more than 30 days after the date upon which demand may first be made hereunder, except to the extent that the Relevant Account Holder would have been entitled to such additional amount on making such demand on the thirtieth such day.

(6) The Issuer hereby covenants to and agrees with the Relevant Account Holders that:—

(A) its payment obligations under this Deed rank and will at all times rank *pari passu* as to priority of payment with all its other unsecured and unsubordinated obligations, present and future, subject only to laws affecting creditors' rights generally;

(B) it will pay promptly, and in any event before any penalty becomes payable, any stamp, documentary, registration or similar duty or tax payable in [...........] or the United Kingdom in connection with the entry into, performance, enforcement or admissibility in evidence of this Deed and/or any amendment of or waiver in respect thereof, and shall indemnify each of the Relevant Account Holders against any liability with respect to or resulting from any delay in paying or omission to pay any such tax.

(7) (A) This Deed shall be deposited with and held by the Paying Agent (as defined in the Global Notes) until the Termination Date and for so long thereafter as any claim made against the Issuer or the Guarantor by any Relevant Account Holder in relation to the Global Notes or this Deed of Covenant or the Deed of Guarantee shall not have been finally adjudicated, settled or discharged.

(B) The Issuer hereby acknowledges the right of every Relevant Account Holder to the production of this Deed.

(8) (A) The Issuer hereby acknowledges and covenants that the benefit of the obligations binding upon it contained in this Deed shall be for the benefit of each and every Relevant Account Holder.

(B) Each Relevant Account Holder shall be entitled severally to enforce the said obligations against the Issuer.

(9) The Issuer may not assign or transfer all or part of its rights or obligations hereunder.   **18.28**

(10)   (A) Any amount received or recovered by any Relevant Account Holder in respect of any sum expressed to be due to it from the Issuer under this Deed in a currency other than the currency in which the same was due (the "due currency") whether as a result of, or of the enforcement of, a judgment or order of a court or tribunal of any jurisdiction, in the dissolution of the Issuer or otherwise, shall only constitute a discharge to the Issuer to the extent of the amount in the due currency which such Relevant Account Holder is able to purchase with the amount so received or recovered in such other currency on the date of that receipt or recovery (or, if it is not practicable to make that purchase on that date, on the first date on which it is practicable to do so).

(B) If that amount in the due currency is less than the amount in the due currency due to such Relevant Account Holder under this Deed the Issuer shall indemnify it against any loss sustained by it as a result. In such event, the Issuer shall indemnify such Relevant Account Holder against the cost of making any such purchase.

(C) These indemnities constitute a separate and independent obligation from the other obligations in this Deed, shall give rise to a separate and independent cause of action, shall apply irrespective of any indulgence granted by any Relevant Account Holder and shall continue in full force and effect despite any judgment, order, claim or proof for a liquidated amount in respect of any sum due under this Deed or any other judgment or order. No proof or evidence of any actual loss may be required.

(11) The illegality, invalidity or unenforceability of any provision of this   **18.29**
Deed under the law of any jurisdiction shall not affect its legality, validity or enforceability under the law of any other jurisdiction nor the legality, validity or enforceability of any other provision.

(12)   (A) This Deed is governed by, and shall be construed in accordance with, the laws of England. The Issuer irrevocably submits to the jurisdiction of the Courts of England for the purposes of any legal action or proceedings arising out of or in connection with this Deed ("Proceedings") and waives any objection to Proceedings in such courts whether on the grounds that the Proceedings have been brought in an inconvenient forum or otherwise.

(B) The foregoing submission is made for the benefit of each Relevant Account Holder from time to time and shall not affect the right of any Relevant Account Holder to take Proceedings in any other jurisdiction nor shall the taking of Proceedings in any jurisdiction preclude any party from taking Proceedings in any other jurisdiction.

(C) The Issuer irrevocably appoints [............] (now of [............])

to receive, for it and on its behalf, service of process in any Proceedings in England. Such service shall be deemed completed on delivery to such agent whether or not it is forwarded to and received by the Issuer.

(D) Nothing herein shall affect the right to serve process in any other manner permitted by law.

IN WITNESS whereof [ISSUER] has caused this Deed to be duly executed as its act and deed the day and year first above mentioned.

[SIGNED, SEALED AND
DELIVERED on behalf of, and as
the act and deed of, [the ISSUER]
by
in the presence of:—]

OR

[THE COMMON SEAL of [the
ISSUER] was hereunto affixed in
accordance with its Articles of
Association and in the presence
of:—]

Index